OpenGL®

SuperBible

Seventh Edition

OpenGL®

SuperBible

Seventh Edition

Comprehensive Tutorial and Reference

Graham Sellers
Richard S. Wright, Jr.
Nicholas Haemel

♦▼Addison-Wesley

New York • Boston • Indianapolis • San Francisco
Toronto • Montreal • London • Munich • Paris • Madrid
Capetown • Sydney • Tokyo • Singapore • Mexico City

For information about buying this title in bulk quantities, or for special sales opportunities (which may include electronic versions; custom cover designs; and content particular to your business, training goals, marketing focus, or branding interests), please contact our corporate sales department at corpsales@pearsoned.com or (800) 382-3419.

For government sales inquiries, please contact governmentsales@pearsoned.com.

For questions about sales outside the United States, please contact international@pearsoned.com.

Visit us on the Web: informit.com/aw

Library of Congress Cataloging-in-Publication Data
Wright, Richard S., Jr., 1965- author.
    OpenGL superBible : comprehensive tutorial and reference.—
Seventh edition / Graham Sellers, Richard S. Wright, Jr., Nicholas Haemel.
        pages   cm
    Includes bibliographical references and index.
    ISBN 978-0-672-33747-5 (pbk. : alk. paper)—ISBN 0-672-33747-9
(pbk. : alk. paper)
    1. Computer graphics. 2. OpenGL.   I. Sellers, Graham, author. II.
Haemel, Nicholas, author. III. Title.
    T385.W728 2016
    006.6'8—dc23
                                                    2015014278

ISBN-13: 978-0-672-33747-5
ISBN-10: 0-672-33747-9
Text printed in the United States on recycled paper at RR Donnelley in Crawfordsville, Indiana.
First printing, July 2015

Editor-in-Chief
Mark L. Taub

Executive Editor
Laura Lewin

Managing Editor
John Fuller

Full-Service Production Manager
Julie B. Nahil

Copy Editor
Jill Hobbs

Indexer
Larry D. Sweazy

Proofreader
Anna Popick

Technical Reviewer
Matías Goldberg

Editorial Assistant
Olivia Basegio

Compositor
diacriTech

For you, the reader.
—Graham Sellers

Contents

Figures

Tables

Listings

Foreword

When OpenGL was young, the highest-end SGI systems like the Reality Engine 2 cost $80,000 and could render 200,000 textured triangles per second, or 3,333 triangles per frame at 60 Hz. The CPUs of that era were slower than today, to be sure, but at around 100 MHz, that's still 500 CPU cycles for each triangle. It was pretty easy to be graphics limited back then, and the API reflected that—the only way to specify geometry was immediate mode! Well, there were also display lists for static geometry, which made being graphics-limited even easier.

OpenGL is not young anymore, the highest-end GPUs that it can run on cost around $1000, and they don't even list triangles per second in their basic product description anymore, but the number is north of 6 billion. Today these GPUs are in the middle of the single digit teraflops and several hundred gigabytes per second of bandwidth. CPUs have gotten faster, too: With 4 cores and around 3 GHz, they are shy of 200 gigaflops and have around 20 gigabytes per second of memory bandwidth. So where we had 500 CPU cycles for a triangle in the early days, we now have 0.5 cycles. Even if we could perfectly exploit all 4 cores, that would give us a paltry 2 CPU cycles for each triangle!

All that is to say that the growth in hardware graphics performance has outstripped conventional CPU performance growth by several orders of magnitude, and the consequences are pretty obvious today. Not only is the CPU frequently the limiting factor in graphics performance, we have an API that was designed against a different set of assumptions.

The good news with OpenGL is that it has evolved too. First it added vertex arrays so that a single draw command with fairly low CPU overhead gets amplified into a lot of GPU work. This helped for a while, but it wasn't enough. We added instancing to further increase the amount of work, but this was a somewhat limited form of work amplification, as we don't always want many instances of the same object in an organic, believable rendering.

Recognizing that these emerging limitations in the API had to be circumvented somehow, OpenGL designers began extending the interface to remove as much CPU-side overhead from the interface as possible. The "bindless" family of extensions allows the GPU to reference buffers and textures directly rather than going through expensive binding calls in the driver. Persistent maps allow the application to scribble on memory at the same time the GPU is referencing it. This sounds dangerous—and it can be!—but allowing the application to manage memory hazards relieves a tremendous burden from the driver and allows for far simpler, less general mechanisms to be employed. Sparse texture arrays allow applications to manage texture memory as well with similar, very low-overhead benefits. And finally multi-draw and multi-draw indirect added means the GPU can generate the very buffers that it sources for drawing, leaving the CPU a lot more available for other work.

All of these advances in OpenGL have been loosely lumped under the *AZDO* (Approaching Zero Driver Overhead) umbrella, and most of them have been incorporated into the core API. There are still significant areas for improvement as we try to get to an API that allows developers to render as much as they want, the way they want, without worrying that the CPU or driver overhead will get in the way. These features require a bit more work to make use of, but the results can be truly amazing! This edition of the *OpenGL*® *SuperBible* includes many new examples that make use of AZDO features and provide good guidance on how to get the CPU out of the way. In particular, you'll learn good ways to make use of zero copy, proper fencing, and bindless.

Cass Everitt
Oculus

Preface

This book is designed both for people who are learning computer graphics through OpenGL and for people who may already know about graphics but want to learn about OpenGL. The intended audience is students of computer science, computer graphics, or game design; professional software engineers; or simply just hobbyists and people who are interested in learning something new. We begin by assuming that the reader knows nothing about either computer graphics or OpenGL. The reader should be familiar with computer programming in C++, however.

One of our goals with this book was to ensure that there were as few forward references as possible and to require little or no assumed knowledge. The book is accessible and readable, and if you start from the beginning and read all the way through, you should come away with a good comprehension of how OpenGL works and how to use it effectively in your applications. After reading and understanding the content of this book, you will be well positioned to read and learn from more advanced computer graphics research articles and confident that you can take the principles that they cover and implement them in OpenGL.

It is *not* a goal of this book to cover every last feature of OpenGL—that is, to mention every function in the specification or every value that can be passed to a command. Rather, we intend to provide a solid understanding of OpenGL, introduce the fundamentals, and explore some of its more advanced features. After reading this book, readers should be comfortable looking up finer details in the OpenGL specification, experimenting with

OpenGL on their own machines, and using extensions (bonus features that add capabilities to OpenGL not required by the main specification).

The Architecture of the Book

This book is subdivided into three parts. In Part I, "Foundations," we explain what OpenGL is and how it connects to the graphics pipeline, and we give minimal working examples that are sufficient to demonstrate each section of it without requiring much, if any, knowledge of any other part of the whole system. We lay a foundation for the math behind three-dimensional computer graphics, and describe how OpenGL manages the large amounts of data that are required to provide a compelling experience to the users of such applications. We also describe the programming model for *shaders*, which form a core part of any OpenGL application.

In Part II, "In Depth," we introduce features of OpenGL that require some knowledge of multiple parts of the graphics pipeline and may refer to concepts mentioned in Part I. This allows us to cover more complex topics without glossing over details or telling you to skip forward in the book to find out how something really works. By taking a second pass over the OpenGL system, we are able to delve into where data goes as it leaves each part of OpenGL, as you'll already have been (at least briefly) introduced to its destination.

Finally, in Part III, "In Practice," we dive deeper into the graphics pipeline, cover some more advanced topics, and give a number of examples that use multiple features of OpenGL. We provide a number of worked examples that implement various rendering techniques, give a series of suggestions and advice on OpenGL best practices and performance considerations, and end up with a practical overview of OpenGL on several popular platforms, including mobile devices.

In Part I, we start gently and then blast through OpenGL to give you a taste of what's to come. Then, we lay the groundwork of knowledge that will be essential to you as you progress through the rest of the book. In this part, you will find the following chapters:

- Chapter 1, "Introduction," provides a brief introduction to OpenGL, including its origins, history, and current state.

- Chapter 2, "Our First OpenGL Program," jumps right into OpenGL and shows you how to create a simple OpenGL application using the source code provided with this book.

- Chapter 3, "Following the Pipeline," takes a more careful look at OpenGL and its various components, introducing each in a little more detail and adding to the simple example presented in the previous chapter.

- Chapter 4, "Math for 3D Graphics," introduces the foundations of math that is essential for effective use of OpenGL and the creation of interesting 3D graphics applications.

- Chapter 5, "Data," provides you with the tools necessary to manage data that will be consumed and produced by OpenGL.

- Chapter 6, "Shaders and Programs," takes a deeper look at *shaders*, which are fundamental to the operation of modern graphics applications.

In Part II, we take a more detailed look at several of the topics introduced in the first chapters. We dig deeper into each of the major parts of OpenGL and our example applications start to become a little more complex and interesting. In this part, you will find these six chapters:

- Chapter 7, "Vertex Processing and Drawing Commands," covers the inputs to OpenGL and the mechanisms by which semantics are applied to the raw data you provide.

- Chapter 8, "Primitive Processing," covers some higher-level concepts in OpenGL, including connectivity information, higher-order surfaces, and tessellation.

- Chapter 9, "Fragment Processing and the Framebuffer," looks at how high-level 3D graphics information is transformed by OpenGL into 2D images, and how your applications can determine the appearance of objects on the screen.

- Chapter 10, "Compute Shaders," illustrates how your applications can harness OpenGL for more than just graphics and make use of the incredible computing power locked up in a modern graphics card.

- Chapter 11, "Advanced Data Management," discusses topics related to managing large data sets, loading data efficiently, and arbitrating access to that data once loaded.

- Chapter 12, "Controlling and Monitoring the Pipeline," shows you how to get a glimpse into how OpenGL executes the commands you give it—including how long they take to execute, and how much data they produce.

In Part III, we build on the knowledge that you will have gained in reading the first two parts of the book and use it to construct example applications that touch on multiple aspects of OpenGL. We also get into the practicalities of building larger OpenGL applications and deploying them across multiple platforms. In this part, you will find three chapters:

- Chapter 13, "Rendering Techniques," covers several applications of OpenGL for graphics rendering, including simulation of light, artistic methods and even some nontraditional techniques.

- Chapter 14, "High-Performance OpenGL," digs into some topics related to getting the highest possible performance from OpenGL.

- Chapter 15, "Debugging and Stability," provides advice and tips on how to get your applications running without errors and how to debug problems with your programs.

Finally, several appendices are provided that describe the tools and file formats used in this book, discuss which versions of OpenGL support which features and list which extensions introduced those features, and give pointers to more useful OpenGL resources.

What's New in This Edition

In this book, we have expanded on the sixth edition to cover new features and topics introduced in OpenGL in versions 4.4 and 4.5 of the API. In the previous edition, we did not cover extensions—features that are entirely optional and not a mandatory part of the OpenGL core—and so left out a number of interesting topics. Since the release of the sixth edition of this book, some of these extensions have become fairly ubiquitous; in turn, we have decided to cover the ARB and KHR extensions. Thus extensions that have been ratified by Khronos (the OpenGL governing body) are part of this book.

We have built on the previous edition by expanding the book's application framework and adding new chapters and appendices that provide further insight and cover new topics. One important set of features enabled by the extensions that are now part of the book are the AZDO (Approaching Zero Driver Overhead) features, which are a way of using OpenGL that produces very low software overhead and correspondingly high performance. These features include *persistent maps* and *bindless textures*.

To make room for the new content, we decided to remove the chapter on platform specifics, which covered per-platform window system bindings. Also gone is official support for the Apple Mac platform. Almost all of the new content in this edition requires features introduced with OpenGL 4.4 or 4.5, or recent OpenGL extensions—none of which were supported by OS X at the time of writing. There is no expectation that Apple will further invest in its OpenGL implementation, so we encourage our readers to move away from the platform. To support multiple platforms, we recommend the use of cross-platform toolkits such as the excellent SDL (https://www.libsdl.org/) or glfw (http://www.glfw.org/) libraries. In fact, this book's framework is built on glfw, and it works well for us.

This book includes several new example applications, including demonstrations of new features, a texture compressor, text drawing, font rendering using distance fields, high-quality texture filtering, and multi-threaded programs using OpenMP. We also tried to address all of the errata and feedback we've received from our readers since the publication of the previous edition. We believe this to be the best update yet to the OpenGL$^®$ SuperBible yet.

We hope you enjoy it.

How to Build the Examples

Retrieve the sample code from the book's companion Web site, http://www.openglsuperbible.com, unpack the archive to a directory on your computer, and follow the instructions in the included HOWTOBUILD.TXT file for your platform of choice. The book's source code has been built and tested on Microsoft Windows (Windows 7 or later is required) and Linux (several major distributions). It is recommended that you install any available operating system updates and obtain the most recent graphics drivers from your graphics card manufacturer.

You may notice some minor discrepancies between the source code printed in this book and that in the source files. There are a number of reasons for this:

- This book is about OpenGL 4.5—the most recent version at the time of writing. The examples printed in the book are written assuming that OpenGL 4.5 is available on the target platform. However, we understand that in practice, operating systems, graphics drivers, and platforms may not have the *latest and greatest* available.

Consequently, where possible, we've made minor modifications to the example applications to allow them to run on earlier versions of OpenGL.

- Several months passed between when this book's text was finalized for printing and when the sample applications were packaged and posted to the Web. In that time, we discovered opportunities for improvement, whether that was uncovering new bugs, platform dependencies, or optimizations. The latest version of the source code on the Web will have those fixes and tweaks applied and will therefore deviate from the necessarily static copy printed in the book.

- There is not necessarily a one-to-one mapping of listings in the book's text and example applications in the Web package. Some example applications demonstrate more than one concept, some aren't mentioned in the book at all, and some listings in the book don't have an equivalent example application. Where possible, we've mentioned which of the example applications correspond to the listings in the book. We recommend that the reader take a close look at the example application package, as it includes some nuggets that may not be mentioned in the book.

Errata

We made a bunch of mistakes—we're certain of it. It's incredibly frustrating as an author to spot an error that you made and know that it has been printed, in books that your readers paid for, thousands and thousands of times. We have to accept that this will happen, though, and do our best to correct issues as we are able. If you think you see something that doesn't quite gel, check the book's Web site for errata:

http://www.openglsuperbible.com

Note from the Publisher

Some of the figures in the print edition of the book are dark due to the nature of the images themselves. To assist readers, color PDFs of figures are freely available at http://www.openglsuperbible.com and http://informit.com/title/9780672337475. In addition, PowerPoint slides of the figures for professors' classroom use are available at www.pearsonhighered.com/educator/product/OpenGL-Superbible-Comprehensive-Tutorial-and-Reference/9780672337475.page.

Acknowledgments

First, thanks to you—the reader. The best part of what I do is knowing that someone I've never met might benefit from all this. It's the biggest thrill, and the reason why people like me do this. I appreciate that you're reading this now and hope you get as much out of this book as I put into it.

I'd like to thank my wonderful wife, Chris, who's put up with me disappearing into my office for three editions of this book now. She's worked around my deadlines and cheered me on as I made (sometimes slow and painful) progress. I couldn't have done this without her. Thanks, too, to my kids, Jeremy and Emily. The answer to "What are you doing, dad?" is almost always "Working"—and you've always taken it in stride.

Thanks to my coauthors, Richard and Nick. You've let me run alone on this edition, but your names are on the cover because of your contributions—your fingerprints are etched into this book. Many thanks to Matías Goldberg, who performed a thorough technical review of the book on short notice.

Thanks again to Laura Lewin and Olivia Basegio and the Pearson team for letting me be me and just dropping random files and documents off whenever I felt like it. I don't work well with a plan, but seem to relish pressure and am really excellent at procrastination. I'm glad you guys put up with me.

Graham Sellers

About the Author

Graham Sellers is a classic geek. His family got their first computer (a BBC Model B) right before his sixth birthday. After his mum and dad stayed up all night programming it to play "Happy Birthday," he was hooked and determined to figure out how it worked. Next came basic programming and then assembly language. His first real exposure to graphics was via "demos" in the early 1990s, and then through Glide, and finally OpenGL in the late 1990s. Graham holds a master's in engineering from the University of Southampton, England.

Currently, Graham is a software architect at AMD. He represents AMD at the OpenGL ARB and has contributed to many extensions and to the core OpenGL Specification. Prior to that, he was a team lead at Epson, implementing OpenGL-ES and OpenVG drivers for embedded products. Graham holds several patents in the fields of computer graphics and image processing. When he's not working on OpenGL, he likes to disassemble and reverse-engineer old video game consoles (just to see how they work and what he can make them do). Originally from England, Graham now lives in Orlando, Florida, with his wife and two children.

Part I

Foundations

Chapter 1

Introduction

WHAT YOU'LL LEARN IN THIS CHAPTER

- What the graphics pipeline is and how OpenGL relates to it.

- The origins of OpenGL and how it came to be the way that it is today.

- Some of the fundamental concepts that we'll be building on throughout the book.

This book is about OpenGL. OpenGL is an interface that your application can use to access and control the graphics subsystem of the device on which it runs. This could be anything from a high-end graphics workstation, to a commodity desktop computer, to a video game console, to a mobile phone. Standardizing the interface to a subsystem increases portability and allows software developers to concentrate on creating quality products, producing interesting content, and ensuring the overall performance of their applications, rather than worrying about the specifics of the platforms they want them to run on. These standard interfaces are called application programming interfaces (APIs), of which OpenGL is one. This chapter introduces OpenGL, describes how it relates to the underlying graphics subsystem, and provides some history on the origin and evolution of OpenGL.

OpenGL and the Graphics Pipeline

Generating a product at high efficiency and volume generally requires two things: scalability and parallelism. In factories, this is achieved by using production lines. While one worker installs the engine in a car, another can be installing the doors, and yet another can be installing the wheels. By overlapping the phases of production of the product, with each phase being executed by a skilled technician who concentrates his or her energy on that single task, each phase becomes more efficient and overall productivity goes up. Also, by making many cars at the same time, a factory can have multiple workers installing multiple engines or wheels or doors and many cars can be on the production line at the same time, each at a different stage of completion.

The same is true in computer graphics. The commands from your program are taken by OpenGL and sent to the underlying graphics hardware, which works on them in an efficient manner to produce the desired result as quickly and efficiently as possible. There could be many commands lined up to execute on the hardware (a status referred to as *in flight*), and some may even be partially completed. This allows their execution to be overlapped such that a later stage of one command might run concurrently with an earlier stage of another command. Futhermore, computer graphics generally consists of many repitions of very similar tasks (such as figuring out what color a pixel should be), and these tasks are usually indpendent of one another—that is, the result of coloring one pixel doesn't depend on any other. Just as a car plant can build multiple cars simultaneously, so OpenGL can break up the work you give it and work on its fundamental elements *in parallel*. Through a combination of *pipelining* and *parallelism*, incredible performance of modern graphics processors is realized.

The goal of OpenGL is to provide an *abstraction layer* between your application and the underlying graphics subsystem, which is often a hardware accelerator made up of one or more custom, high-performance processors with dedicated memory, display outputs, and so on. This abstraction layer allows your application to not need to know who made the graphics processor (or graphics processing unit [GPU]), how it works, or how well it performs. Certainly it is possible to determine this information, but the point is that applications don't need to.

As a design principle, OpenGL must strike a balance between too high and too low an abstraction level. On the one hand, it must hide differences between various manufacturers' products (or between the various products of a single manufacturer) and system-specific traits such as screen resolution, processor architecture, installed operating system, and so on. On the other hand, the level of abstraction must be low enough that programmers can gain access to the underlying hardware and make best use of it. If OpenGL presented too high of an abstraction level, then it would be easy to create programs that fit the model, but very hard to use advanced features of the graphics hardware that weren't included. This is the type of model followed by software such as game engines—new features of the graphics hardware generally require relatively large changes in the engine for games built on top of it to gain access to them. If the abstraction level is too low, applications need to start worrying about architectural peculiarities of the system they're running on. Low levels of abstraction are common in video game consoles, for example, but don't fit well into a graphics library that must support devices ranging from mobile phones to gaming PCs to high-powered professional graphics workstations.

As technology advances, more and more research is being conducted in computer graphics, best practices are being developed, and bottlenecks and requirements are moving—and so OpenGL must also move to keep up.

The current state of the art in graphics processing units, on which most OpenGL implementations are based, is capable of many teraflops of computing power, has gigabytes of memory that can be accessed at hundreds of gigabytes per second, and can drive multiple, multi-megapixel displays at high refresh rates. GPUs are also extremely flexible, and are able to work on tasks that might not be considered graphics at all, such as physical simulations, artificial intelligence, and even audio processing.

Current GPUs consist of large numbers of small programmable processors called *shader cores* that run mini-programs called *shaders*. Each core has a relatively low throughput, processing a single instruction of the shader in one or more clock cycles and normally lacking advanced features such as out-of-order execution, branch prediction, super-scalar issues, and so on. However, each GPU might contain anywhere from a few tens to a few thousands of these cores, and together they can perform an immense amount of work. The graphics system is broken into a number of *stages*, each represented either by a shader or by a fixed-function, possibly configurable processing block. Figure 1.1 shows a simplified schematic of the graphics pipeline.

In Figure 1.1, the boxes with rounded corners are considered *fixed-function* stages, whereas the boxes with square corners are programmable, which means that they execute shaders that you supply. In practice, some or all of the fixed-function stages may really be implemented in shader code, too—it's just that you don't supply that code, but rather the GPU

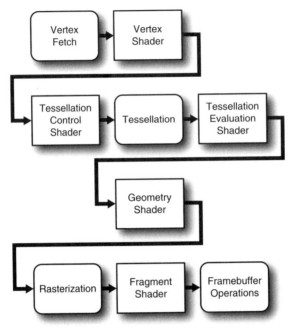

Figure 1.1: Simplified graphics pipeline

manufacturer generally supplies it as part of a driver, firmware, or other system software.

The Origins and Evolution of OpenGL

OpenGL has its origins at Silicon Graphics Inc. (SGI) and its IRIS GL. GL stood for (and still stands for) "graphics library," and in much of the modern OpenGL documentation you will see the term "the GL," meaning "the graphics library," originating from this era. Silicon Graphics was a manufacturer of high-end graphics workstations.[1] These were extremely expensive, and using a proprietary API for graphics wasn't helping. Other manufacturers were producing much more inexpensive solutions running on competing APIs that were often compatible with each other. In the early 1990s, SGI realized that portability was important and so decided to clean up IRIS GL, remove system-specific parts of the API, and release it as an open standard that could be implemented, royalty free, by anyone. The

---

1. Silicon Graphics, or more accurately SGI, still exists today, but went bankrupt in 2009. Its assets and brands were acquired by Rackable Systems, which assumed the moniker SGI but does not operate in the high-end graphics market.

very first version of OpenGL was released in June 1992 and was marked as OpenGL 1.0.

That year, SGI was also instrumental in establishing the OpenGL Architectural Review Board (ARB), the original members of which included companies such as Compaq, DEC, IBM, Intel, and Microsoft. Soon, other companies such as Hewlett-Packard, Sun Microsystems, Evans & Sutherland, and Intergraph joined the group. The OpenGL ARB is the standards body that designs, governs, and produces the OpenGL specification and is now a part of Khronos Group, which is a larger consortium of companies that oversees the development of many open standards. Some of these original members either no longer exist (perhaps having gone out of business or having been acquired by or merged with other companies) or are no longer members of the ARB, having left the graphics business or otherwise gone their own way. However, some still exist, either under new names or as the entity that was involved in the development of that very first version of OpenGL more than 20 years ago.

At time of writing, there have been 19 editions of the OpenGL specification. Their version numbers and time of publication are shown in Table 1.1. This book covers version 4.5 of the OpenGL specification, and most of the samples in it require up-to-date drivers and hardware to run.

Table 1.1: OpenGL Versions and Publication Dates

Version	Publication Date
OpenGL 1.0	January 1992
OpenGL 1.1	January 1997
OpenGL 1.2	March 1998
OpenGL 1.2.1	October 1998
OpenGL 1.3	August 2001
OpenGL 1.4	July 2002
OpenGL 1.5	July 2003
OpenGL 2.0	September 2004
OpenGL 2.1	July 2006
OpenGL 3.0	August 2008
OpenGL 3.1	March 2009
OpenGL 3.2	August 2009
OpenGL 3.3	March 2010

continued

Version	Publication Date
OpenGL 4.0	March 2010[2]
OpenGL 4.1	July 2010
OpenGL 4.2	August 2011
OpenGL 4.3	August 2012
OpenGL 4.4	July 2013
OpenGL 4.5	August 2014

Core Profile OpenGL

Twenty years is a long time in the development of cutting-edge technology. In 1992, the top-of-the-line Intel CPU was the 80486, math coprocessors were still optional, and the Pentium had not yet been invented (or at least released). Apple computers were still using Motorola 68K-derived processors and the PowerPC processors to which they would later switch would be made available during the second half of 1992. High-performance graphics acceleration was simply not something that was common in commodity home computers. If you didn't have access to a high-performance graphics workstation, you probably would have no hope of using OpenGL for anything. Software rendering ruled the world and the Future Crew's "Unreal" demo won the Assembly '92 demo party. The best you could hope for in a home computer was some basic filled polygons or sprite rendering capabilities. The state of the art in 1992 home computer 3D graphics is shown in Figure 1.2.

Over time, the price of graphics hardware came down, performance went up, and—partly due to low-cost acceleration add-in boards for PCs, and partly due to the increased performance of video game consoles—new features and capabilities showed up in affordable graphics processors and were added to OpenGL. Most of these features originated in *extensions* proposed by members of the OpenGL ARB. Some interacted well with each other and with existing features in OpenGL, and some did not. Also, as newer, better ways of squeezing performance out of graphics systems were invented, they were simply added to OpenGL, resulting in it having multiple ways of doing the same thing.

For many years, the ARB held a strong position on backward compatibility, as it still does today. However, this backward compatibility comes at a

---

2. Yes, two versions at the same time!

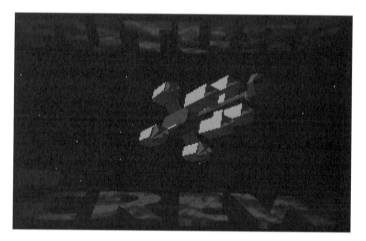

Figure 1.2: Future Crew's 1992 demo—Unreal

significant cost. Best practices have changed—what may have worked well or was not really a significant bottleneck on mid-1990s graphics hardware doesn't always fit modern graphics processor architecture well. Specifying how new features interact with the older legacy features isn't easy and, in many cases, can make it almost impossible to cleanly introduce a new feature to OpenGL. As for implementing OpenGL, this has become such a difficult task that drivers tend to have more bugs than they really should and graphics vendors need to spend considerable amounts of energy maintaining support for all kinds of legacy features that don't contribute to the advancement of or innovation in graphics.

For these reasons, in 2008, the ARB decided it would "fork" the OpenGL specification into two *profiles*. The first is the modern, *core* profile, which removes a number of legacy features, leaving only those that are truly accelerated by current graphics hardware. This specification is several hundred pages shorter[3] than the other version of the specification, the *compatibility* profile. The compatibility profile maintains backward compatibility with all revisions of OpenGL back to version 1.0. As a consequence, software written in 1992 should compile and run on a modern graphics card with a thousand times greater performance today than when that program was first produced.

The compatibility profile really exists to allow software developers to maintain legacy applications and to add features to them without having

---

3. The core profile specification is still pretty hefty at more than 800 pages long.

to tear out years of work to shift to a new API. However, the core profile is strongly recommended by most OpenGL experts as the profile that should be used for new application development. In particular, on some platforms, newer features are available only if you are using the core profile of OpenGL; on others, an application written using the core profile of OpenGL will run *faster* than that same application unmodified, except to request the compatibility profile, even if it uses only features that are available in core profile OpenGL. Finally, if a feature is in the compatibility profile but has been removed from the core profile of OpenGL, there's probably a good reason for that—and it's a reasonable indication that you shouldn't be using it. This book covers only the core profile of OpenGL; this is the last time we will mention the compatibility profile.

Primitives, Pipelines, and Pixels

As discussed, the model followed by OpenGL is that of a production line, or pipeline. Data flow within this model is generally one way, with data formed from commands called by your programs entering the front of the pipeline and flowing from stage to stage until it reaches the end of the pipeline. Along the way, shaders or other fixed-function blocks within the pipeline may pick up more data from *buffers* or *textures*, which are structures designed to store information that will be used during rendering. Some stages in the pipeline may even save data into these buffers or textures, allowing the application to read or save the data, or even permitting feedback to occur.

The fundamental unit of rendering in OpenGL is known as the *primitive*. OpenGL supports many types of primitives, but the three basic renderable primitive types are points, lines, and triangles. Everything you see rendered on the screen is a collection of (perhaps cleverly colored) points, lines, and triangles. Applications will normally break complex surfaces into a very large number of triangles and send them to OpenGL, where they are rendered using a hardware accelerator called a *rasterizer*. Triangles are, relatively speaking, pretty easy to draw. As polygons, triangles are always *convex*, so filling rules are easy to devise and follow. Concave polygons can always be broken down into two or more triangles, so hardware natively supports rendering triangles directly and relies on other subsystems[4] to break complex geometry into triangles. The rasterizer is

---

4. Sometimes these subsystems are more hardware modules, and sometimes they are functions of drivers implemented in software.

dedicated hardware that converts the three-dimensional representation of a triangle into a series of pixels that need to be drawn onto the screen.

Points, lines, and triangles are formed from collections of one, two, or three vertices, respectively. A *vertex* is simply a point within a coordinate space. In our case, we primarily consider a three-dimensional coordinate system. The graphics pipeline is broken down into two major parts. The first part, often known as the *front end*, processes vertices and primitives, eventually forming them into the points, lines, and triangles that will be handed off to the rasterizer. This is known as primitive assembly. After going through the rasterizer, the geometry has been converted from what is essentially a vector representation into a large number of independent pixels. These are handed off to the *back end*, which includes depth and stencil testing, fragment shading, blending, and updating of the output image.

As you progress through this book, you will see how to tell OpenGL to start working for you. We'll go over how to create buffers and textures and hook them up to your programs. We'll also see how to write shaders to process your data and how to configure the fixed-function blocks of OpenGL to do what you want. OpenGL is really a large collection of fairly simple concepts, built upon each other. Having a good foundation and a *big-picture* view of the system is essential, and over the next few chapters, we hope to provide that to you.

Summary

In this chapter you've been introduced to OpenGL and have read a little about its origins, history, status, and direction. You have seen the OpenGL pipeline and have been told how this book will progress. We have mentioned some of the terminology that we'll be using throughout the book. Over the next few chapters, you'll create your first OpenGL program, dig a little deeper into the various stages of the OpenGL pipeline, and then lay some foundations with some of the math that's useful in the world of computer graphics.

Chapter 2

Our First OpenGL Program

WHAT YOU'LL LEARN IN THIS CHAPTER

- How to create and compile shader code.

- How to draw with OpenGL.

- How to use the book's application framework to initialize your programs and clean up after yourself.

In this chapter, we introduce the simple application framework that is used for almost all of the samples in this book. This shows you how to create the main window with the book's application framework and how to render simple graphics into it. You'll also see what a very simple GLSL shader looks like, how to compile it, and how to use it to render simple points. The chapter concludes with your very first OpenGL triangle.

Creating a Simple Application

To introduce the application framework that'll be used in the remainder of this book, we'll start with an extremely simple example application. Of course, to write a large-scale OpenGL program you don't have to use our framework—in fact, we wouldn't recommend it, as it's quite simple. However, it does simplify things a little and allows you to get to writing OpenGL code sooner.

The application framework is brought into your application by including sb7.h in your source code. This is a C++ header file that defines a namespace called sb7 that includes the declaration of an application class, sb7::application, from which we can derive our examples. The framework also includes a number of utility functions and a simple math library called vmath to help you with some of the number crunching involved in OpenGL.

To create an application, we simply include sb7.h, derive a class from sb7::application, and, in exactly one of our source files, include an instance of the DECLARE_MAIN macro. This defines the main entry point of our application, which creates an instance of our class (the type of which is passed as a parameter to the macro) and calls its run() method, which implements the application's main loop.

In turn, this performs some initialization by first calling the startup() method and then calling the render() method in a loop. In the default implementation, both methods are defined as virtual functions with empty bodies. We override the render() method in our derived class and write our drawing code inside it. The application framework takes care of creating a window, handling input, and displaying the rendered results to the user. The complete source code for our first example is given in Listing 2.1 and its output is shown in Figure 2.1.

```
// Include the "sb7.h" header file
#include "sb7.h"

// Derive my_application from sb7::application
class my_application : public sb7::application
{
public:
    // Our rendering function
    void render(double currentTime)
    {
        // Simply clear the window with red
        static const GLfloat red[] = { 1.0f, 0.0f, 0.0f, 1.0f };
```

```
            glClearBufferfv(GL_COLOR, 0, red);
    }
};

// Our one and only instance of DECLARE_MAIN
DECLARE_MAIN(my_application);
```

Listing 2.1: Our first OpenGL application

The example shown in Listing 2.1 simply clears the whole screen to red.
This introduces our first OpenGL function, **glClearBufferfv()**. The
prototype of **glClearBufferfv()** is

```
void glClearBufferfv(GLenum buffer,
                     GLint drawBuffer,
                     const GLfloat * value);
```

All OpenGL functions start with gl and follow a number of naming
conventions, such as encoding some of their parameter types as suffixes on
the end of the function names. This allows a limited form of *overloading*
even in languages that don't directly support this ability. In this case, the
suffix fv means that the function consumes a vector (v) of floating-point
(f) values, where arrays (generally referenced by pointers in languages
like C) and vectors are used interchangeably by OpenGL.

The **glClearBufferfv()** function tells OpenGL to clear the buffer specified
by the first parameter (in this case GL_COLOR) to the value specified in its
third parameter. The second parameter, drawBuffer, is used when there
are multiple output buffers that could be cleared. Because we're using only
one here and drawBuffer is a zero-based index, we'll just set it to 0 in this
example. Here, that color is stored in the array red, which contains four
floating-point values—one each for red, green, blue, and alpha, in that
order.

The red, green, and blue terms should be self-explanatory. Alpha is a
fourth component that is associated with a color and is often used to
encode the *opacity* of a fragment. When used this way, setting alpha to 0
will make the fragment completely transparent, and setting it to 1
will make it completely opaque. The alpha value can also be stored in
the output image and used in some parts of OpenGL's calculations,
even though you can't see it. You can see that we set both the red and
alpha values to 1 and the others to 0. This specifies an opaque red
color. The result of running this application is shown in Figure 2.1.

Figure 2.1: The output of our first OpenGL application

This initial application isn't particularly interesting,[1] as all it does is fill the window with a solid red color. You will notice that our render() function takes a single parameter—currentTime. This contains the number of seconds since the application was started, and we can use it to create a simple animation. In this case, we can use it to change the color that we use to clear the window. Our modified render() function[2] is shown in Listing 2.2.

```
// Our rendering function
void render(double currentTime)
{
    const GLfloat color[] = { (float)sin(currentTime) * 0.5f + 0.5f,
                              (float)cos(currentTime) * 0.5f + 0.5f,
                              0.0f, 1.0f };
    glClearBufferfv(GL_COLOR, 0, color);
}
```

Listing 2.2: Animating color over time

Now our window fades from red through yellow, orange, green, and back to red again. Still not that exciting, but at least it does *something*.

---

1. This sample is especially uninteresting if you are reading this book in black and white!

2. If you're copying this code into your own example, you'll need to include <math.h> to get the declarations of sin() and cos().

Using Shaders

As we mentioned in the introduction to the graphics pipeline in Chapter 1, OpenGL works by connecting a number of mini-programs called shaders together with fixed-function glue. When you draw, the graphics processor executes your shaders and pipes their inputs and outputs along the pipeline until pixels[3] come out the end. To draw anything at all, you'll need to write at least a couple of shaders.

OpenGL shaders are written in a language called the OpenGL Shading Language, or GLSL. This language has its origins in C, but has been modified over time to make it better suited to running on graphics processors. If you are familiar with C, then it shouldn't be hard to pick up GLSL. The compiler for this language is built into OpenGL. The source code for your shader is placed into a *shader object* and compiled, and then multiple shader objects can be linked together to form a *program object*. Each program object can contain shaders for one or more shader stages. The shader stages of OpenGL are vertex shaders, tessellation control and evaluation shaders, geometry shaders, fragment shaders, and compute shaders. The minimal useful pipeline configuration consists of only a vertex shader[4] (or just a compute shader), but if you wish to see any pixels on the screen, you will also need a fragment shader.

Listing 2.3 shows our first vertex shader, which is about as simple as it gets. In the first line, we have the "`#version 450 core`" declaration, which tells the shader compiler that we intend to use version 4.5 of the shading language. Notice that we include the keyword `core` to indicate that we intend to use only features from the core profile of OpenGL.

Next, we have the declaration of our `main` function, which is where the shader starts executing. This is exactly the same as in a normal C program, except that the `main` function of a GLSL shader has no parameters. Inside our `main` function, we assign a value to `gl_Position`, which is part of the plumbing that connects the shader to the rest of OpenGL. All variables that start with `gl_` are part of OpenGL and connect shaders to each other or to the various parts of fixed functionality in OpenGL. In the vertex shader, `gl_Position` represents the output position of the vertex. The

---

3. Actually, there are a number of use cases of OpenGL that create no pixels at all. We will cover those in a while. For now, let's just draw some pictures.

4. If you try to draw anything when your pipeline does not contain a vertex shader, the results will be undefined and almost certainly not what you were hoping for.

value we assign (vec4(0.0, 0.0, 0.5, 1.0)) places the vertex right in the middle of OpenGL's *clip space*, which is the coordinate system expected by the next stage of the OpenGL pipeline.

```
#version 450 core

void main(void)
{
    gl_Position = vec4(0.0, 0.0, 0.5, 1.0);
}
```

Listing 2.3: Our first vertex shader

Our fragment shader is given in Listing 2.4. Again, this is an extremely simple example. It, too, starts with a #version 450 core declaration. Next, it declares color as an output variable using the out keyword. In fragment shaders, the value of output variables will be sent to the window or screen. In the main function, it assigns a constant to this output. By default, that value goes directly onto the screen and is vector of four floating-point values, one each for red, green, blue, and alpha, just like in the parameter to glClearBufferfv(). In this shader, the value we've used is vec4(0.0, 0.8, 1.0, 1.0), which is a cyan color.

```
#version 450 core

out vec4 color;

void main(void)
{
    color = vec4(0.0, 0.8, 1.0, 1.0);
}
```

Listing 2.4: Our first fragment shader

Now that we have both a vertex and a fragment shader, it's time to compile them and link them together into a program that can be run by OpenGL. This is similar to the way that programs written in C++ or other similar languages are compiled and linked to produce executables. The code to link our shaders together into a program object is shown in Listing 2.5.

```
GLuint compile_shaders(void)
{
    GLuint vertex_shader;
    GLuint fragment_shader;
    GLuint program;

    // Source code for vertex shader
```

```
static const GLchar * vertex_shader_source[] =
{
    "#version 450 core                              \n"
    "                                               \n"
    "void main(void)                                \n"
    "{                                              \n"
    "    gl_Position = vec4(0.0, 0.0, 0.5, 1.0);    \n"
    "}                                              \n"
};

// Source code for fragment shader
static const GLchar * fragment_shader_source[] =
{
    "#version 450 core                              \n"
    "                                               \n"
    "out vec4 color;                                \n"
    "                                               \n"
    "void main(void)                                \n"
    "{                                              \n"
    "    color = vec4(0.0, 0.8, 1.0, 1.0);          \n"
    "}                                              \n"
};

// Create and compile vertex shader
vertex_shader = glCreateShader(GL_VERTEX_SHADER);
glShaderSource(vertex_shader, 1, vertex_shader_source, NULL);
glCompileShader(vertex_shader);

// Create and compile fragment shader
fragment_shader = glCreateShader(GL_FRAGMENT_SHADER);
glShaderSource(fragment_shader, 1, fragment_shader_source, NULL);
glCompileShader(fragment_shader);

// Create program, attach shaders to it, and link it
program = glCreateProgram();
glAttachShader(program, vertex_shader);
glAttachShader(program, fragment_shader);
glLinkProgram(program);

// Delete the shaders as the program has them now
glDeleteShader(vertex_shader);
glDeleteShader(fragment_shader);

    return program;
}
```

Listing 2.5: Compiling a simple shader

In Listing 2.5, we introduce a handful of new functions:

- **glCreateShader()** creates an empty shader object, ready to accept source code and be compiled.

- **glShaderSource()** hands shader source code to the shader object so that it can keep a copy of it.

- **glCompileShader()** compiles whatever source code is contained in the shader object.

- **glCreateProgram()** creates a program object to which you can attach shader objects.

- **glAttachShader()** attaches a shader object to a program object.

- **glLinkProgram()** links all of the shader objects attached to a program object together.

- **glDeleteShader()** deletes a shader object. Once a shader has been linked into a program object, the program contains the binary code and the shader is no longer needed.

The shader source code from Listing 2.3 and Listing 2.4 is included in our program as constant strings that are passed to the **glShaderSource()** function, which copies them into the shader objects that we created with **glCreateShader()**. The shader object stores a copy of our source code; then, when we call **glCompileShader()**, it compiles the GLSL shader source code into an intermediate binary representation that is also stored in the shader object. The program object represents the linked executable that we will use for rendering. We attach our shaders to the program object using **glAttachShader()** and then call **glLinkProgram()**, which links the objects together into code that can be run on the graphics processor. Attaching a shader object to a program object creates a reference to the shader; we can then delete it, knowing that the program object will hold onto the shader's contents as long as it needs it. The compile_shaders function in Listing 2.5 returns the newly created program object.

When we call this function, we need to keep the returned program object somewhere so that we can use it to draw things. Also, we really don't want to recompile the whole program every time we want to use it. So, we need a function that is called once when the program starts up. The sb7 application framework provides just such a function: application::startup(), which we can override in our sample application and use to perform any one-time setup work.

One final thing that we need to do before we can draw anything is to create a *vertex array object* (VAO), which is an object that represents the vertex fetch stage of the OpenGL pipeline and is used to supply input to the vertex shader. As our vertex shader doesn't have any inputs right now, we don't need to do much with the VAO. Nevertheless, we still need to create the VAO so that OpenGL will let us draw. To create the VAO, we call the OpenGL function **glCreateVertexArrays()**; to attach it to our context, we call **glBindVertexArray()**. Their prototypes are shown here:

```
void glCreateVertexArrays(GLsizei n,
                          GLuint * arrays);

void glBindVertexArray(GLuint array);
```

The vertex array object maintains all of the state related to the input to the OpenGL pipeline. We will add calls to **glCreateVertexArrays()** and **glBindVertexArray()** to our startup() function. This pattern will become familiar to you as you learn more about OpenGL. Most things in OpenGL are represented by objects (like vertex array objects). We create them using a creation function (like **glCreateVertexArrays()**), and let OpenGL know that we want to use them by binding them to the context using a binding function (like **glBindVertexArray()**).

In Listing 2.6, we have overridden the startup() member function of the sb7::application class and put our own initialization code in it. Again, as with render(), the startup() function is defined as an empty virtual function in sb7::application and is called automatically by the run() function. From startup(), we call compile_shaders and store the resulting program object in the rendering_program member variable in our class. When our application is done running, we should also clean up after ourselves. Thus we have also overridden the shutdown() function; in it, we delete the program object that we created at start-up. Just as when we were done with our shader objects we called **glDeleteShader()**, so when we are done with our program objects we call **glDeleteProgram()**. In our shutdown() function, we also delete the vertex array object we created in our startup() function by calling the **glDeleteVertexArrays()** function.

```
class my_application : public sb7::application
{
public:
    // <snip>

    void startup()
    {
        rendering_program = compile_shaders();
        glCreateVertexArrays(1, &vertex_array_object);
        glBindVertexArray(vertex_array_object);
    }

    void shutdown()
    {
        glDeleteVertexArrays(1, &vertex_array_object);
        glDeleteProgram(rendering_program);
        glDeleteVertexArrays(1, &vertex_array_object);
    }
```

```
private:
    GLuint  rendering_program;
    GLuint  vertex_array_object;
};
```

Listing 2.6: Creating the program member variable

Now that we have a program, we need to execute the shaders in it and actually start drawing something on the screen. We modify our render() function to call **glUseProgram()** to tell OpenGL to use our program object for rendering and then call our first drawing command, **glDrawArrays()**. The updated listing is shown in Listing 2.7.

```
// Our rendering function
void render(double currentTime)
{
    const GLfloat color[] = { (float)sin(currentTime) * 0.5f + 0.5f,
                              (float)cos(currentTime) * 0.5f + 0.5f,
                              0.0f, 1.0f };
    glClearBufferfv(GL_COLOR, 0, color);

    // Use the program object we created earlier for rendering
    glUseProgram(rendering_program);

    // Draw one point
    glDrawArrays(GL_POINTS, 0, 1);
}
```

Listing 2.7: Rendering a single point

The **glDrawArrays()** function sends vertices into the OpenGL pipeline. Its prototype is

```
void glDrawArrays(GLenum mode,
                  GLint first,
                  GLsizei count);
```

For each vertex, the vertex shader (the one in Listing 2.3) is executed. The first parameter to **glDrawArrays()** is the mode parameter, which tells OpenGL what type of graphics primitive we want to render. In this case, we specified GL_POINTS because we want to draw a single point. The second parameter (first) is not relevant in this example, so we've set it to zero. Finally, the last parameter is the number of vertices to render. Each point is represented by a single vertex, so we tell OpenGL to render only one vertex, resulting in just one point being rendered. The result of running this program is shown in Figure 2.2.

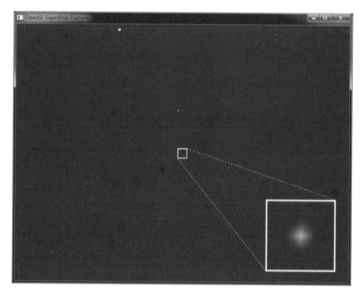

Figure 2.2: Rendering our first point

As you can see, there is a tiny point in the middle of the window. For your viewing pleasure, we've zoomed in on the point and shown it in the inset at the bottom right of the image. Congratulations! You've made your very first OpenGL rendering. Although it's not terribly impressive, it lays the groundwork for more interesting drawing and proves that our application framework and our first, extremely simple shaders are working.

To make our point a little more visible, we can ask OpenGL to draw it a little larger than a single pixel. To do this, we'll call the **glPointSize()** function, whose prototype is

```
void glPointSize(GLfloat size);
```

This function sets the diameter of the point in pixels to the value you specify in `size`. The maximum value that you can use for points is implementation defined. We will get deeper into the subject and go beyond stock OpenGL functionality, but for the time being, we will rely on the fact that OpenGL guarantees that the maximum supported point size is at least 64 pixels. By adding the line

```
glPointSize(40.0f);
```

Figure 2.3: Making our first point bigger

to our rendering function in Listing 2.7, we set the diameter of points to 40 pixels. The output is shown in Figure 2.3.

Drawing Our First Triangle

Drawing a single point is not really that impressive (even if it is really big!)—we already mentioned that OpenGL supports many different primitive types, and that the most important are points, lines, and triangles. In our toy example, we draw a single point by passing the token GL_POINTS to the **glDrawArrays()** function. What we really want to do is draw lines or triangles. As you may have guessed, we could have passed GL_LINES or GL_TRIANGLES to **glDrawArrays()** but there's one hitch: The vertex shader in Listing 2.3 places every vertex in the same place, right in the middle of clip space. For points, that's fine: OpenGL assigns area to points for you. But for lines and triangles, having two or more vertices in the exact same place produces a *degenerate primitive*, which is a line with zero length or a triangle with zero area. If we try to draw anything but points with this shader, we won't get any output at all because all of the primitives will be degenerate. To fix this, we need to modify our vertex shader to assign a different position to each vertex.

Fortunately, GLSL includes a special input to the vertex shader called gl_VertexID, which is the index of the vertex that is being processed at the time. The gl_VertexID input starts counting from the value given by the first parameter of **glDrawArrays()** and counts upward one vertex at a time for count vertices (the third parameter of **glDrawArrays()**). This input is one of the many *built-in variables* provided by GLSL, which represent data that is generated by OpenGL or that you should generate in your shader and give to OpenGL. (gl_Position, which we just covered, is another example of a built-in variable.) We can use this index to assign a different position to each vertex (see Listing 2.8, which does exactly this).

```
#version 450 core

void main(void)
{
    // Declare a hard-coded array of positions
    const vec4 vertices[3] = vec4[3](vec4( 0.25, -0.25, 0.5, 1.0),
                                     vec4(-0.25, -0.25, 0.5, 1.0),
                                     vec4( 0.25,  0.25, 0.5, 1.0));

    // Index into our array using gl_VertexID
    gl_Position = vertices[gl_VertexID];
}
```

Listing 2.8: Producing multiple vertices in a vertex shader

By using the shader of Listing 2.8, we can assign a different position to each of the vertices based on its value of gl_VertexID. The points in the array vertices form a triangle, and if we modify our rendering function to pass GL_TRIANGLES to **glDrawArrays()** instead of GL_POINTS, as shown in Listing 2.9, then we obtain the image shown in Figure 2.4.

```
// Our rendering function
void render(double currentTime)
{
    const GLfloat color[] = { 0.0f, 0.2f, 0.0f, 1.0f };
    glClearBufferfv(GL_COLOR, 0, color);

    // Use the program object we created earlier for rendering
    glUseProgram(rendering_program);

    // Draw one triangle
    glDrawArrays(GL_TRIANGLES, 0, 3);
}
```

Listing 2.9: Rendering a single triangle

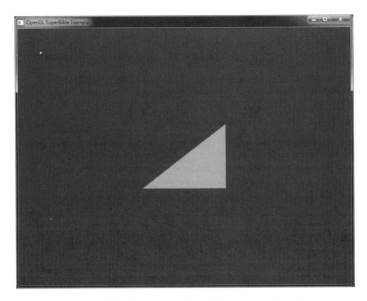

Figure 2.4: Our very first OpenGL triangle

Summary

This concludes the construction of our first OpenGL program. We will soon cover how to get data into your shaders from your application, how to pass your own inputs to the vertex shader, how to pass data from shader stage to shader stage, and more.

In this chapter, you have been briefly introduced to the sb7 application framework, compiled a shader, cleared the window, and drawn points and triangles. You have seen how to change the size of points using the **glPointSize()** function and have seen your first drawing command—**glDrawArrays()**.

Chapter 3

Following the Pipeline

WHAT YOU'LL LEARN IN THIS CHAPTER

- What each of the stages in the OpenGL pipeline does.

- How to connect your shaders to the fixed-function pipeline stages.

- How to create a program that uses every stage of the graphics pipeline simultaneously.

In this chapter, we will walk all the way along the OpenGL pipeline from start to finish, providing insight into each of the stages, which include fixed-function blocks and programmable shader blocks. You have already read a whirlwind introduction to the vertex and fragment shader stages. However, the application that you constructed simply drew a single triangle at a fixed position. If we want to render anything interesting with OpenGL, we're going to have to learn a lot more about the pipeline and all of the things you can do with it. This chapter introduces every part of the pipeline, hooks them up to one another, and provides an example shader for each stage.

Passing Data to the Vertex Shader

The vertex shader is the first *programmable* stage in the OpenGL pipeline and has the distinction of being the only mandatory stage in the graphics pipeline. However, before the vertex shader runs, a fixed-function stage known as *vertex fetching*, or sometimes *vertex pulling*, is run. This automatically provides inputs to the vertex shader.

Vertex Attributes

In GLSL, the mechanism for getting data in and out of shaders is to declare global variables with the `in` and `out` storage qualifiers. You were briefly introduced to the `out` qualifier in Chapter 2, "Our First OpenGL Program," when Listing 2.4 used it to output a color from the fragment shader. At the start of the OpenGL pipeline, we use the `in` keyword to bring inputs into the vertex shader. Between stages, `in` and `out` can be used to form conduits from shader to shader and pass data between them. We'll get to that shortly. For now, consider the input to the vertex shader and what happens if you declare a variable with an `in` storage qualifier. This marks the variable as an input to the vertex shader, which means that it is essentially an input to the OpenGL graphics pipeline. It is automatically filled in by the fixed-function vertex fetch stage. The variable becomes known as a *vertex attribute*.

Vertex attributes are how vertex data is introduced into the OpenGL pipeline. To declare a vertex attribute, you declare a variable in the vertex shader using the `in` storage qualifier. An example of this is shown in Listing 3.1, where we declare the variable `offset` as an input attribute.

```
#version 450 core

// 'offset' is an input vertex attribute
layout (location = 0) in vec4 offset;

void main(void)
{
    const vec4 vertices[3] = vec4[3](vec4( 0.25, -0.25, 0.5, 1.0),
                                     vec4(-0.25, -0.25, 0.5, 1.0),
                                     vec4( 0.25,  0.25, 0.5, 1.0));

    // Add 'offset' to our hard-coded vertex position
    gl_Position = vertices[gl_VertexID] + offset;
}
```

Listing 3.1: Declaration of a vertex attribute

In Listing 3.1, we have added the variable `offset` as an input to the vertex shader. As it is an input to the first shader in the pipeline, it will be filled automatically by the vertex fetch stage. We can tell this stage what to fill the variable with by using one of the many variants of the vertex attribute functions, **glVertexAttrib*()**. The prototype for **glVertexAttrib4fv()**, which we use in this example, is

```
void glVertexAttrib4fv(GLuint index,
                       const GLfloat * v);
```

Here, the parameter `index` is used to reference the attribute and `v` is a pointer to the new data to put into the attribute. You may have noticed the `layout` (`location = 0`) code in the declaration of the `offset` attribute. This is a *layout qualifier*, which we have used to set the *location* of the vertex attribute to zero. This location is the value we'll pass in `index` to refer to the attribute.

Each time we call one of the **glVertexAttrib*()** functions (of which there are many), it will update the value of the vertex attribute that is passed to the vertex shader. We can use this approach to animate our one triangle. Listing 3.2 shows an updated version of our rendering function that updates the value of `offset` in each frame.

```
// Our rendering function
virtual void render(double currentTime)
{
    const GLfloat color[] = { (float)sin(currentTime) * 0.5f + 0.5f,
                              (float)cos(currentTime) * 0.5f + 0.5f,
                              0.0f, 1.0f };
    glClearBufferfv(GL_COLOR, 0, color);

    // Use the program object we created earlier for rendering
    glUseProgram(rendering_program);

    GLfloat attrib[] = { (float)sin(currentTime) * 0.5f,
                         (float)cos(currentTime) * 0.6f,
                         0.0f, 0.0f };

    // Update the value of input attribute 0
    glVertexAttrib4fv(0, attrib);

    // Draw one triangle
    glDrawArrays(GL_TRIANGLES, 0, 3);
}
```

Listing 3.2: Updating a vertex attribute

When we run the program with the rendering function of Listing 3.2, the triangle will move in a smooth oval shape around the window.

Passing Data from Stage to Stage

So far, you have seen how to pass data into a vertex shader by creating a vertex attribute using the in keyword, how to communicate with fixed-function blocks by reading and writing built-in variables such as gl_VertexID and gl_Position, and how to output data from the fragment shader using the out keyword. However, it's also possible to send your own data from shader stage to shader stage using the same in and out keywords. Just as you used the out keyword in the fragment shader to create the output variable to which it writes its color values, so you can also create an output variable in the vertex shader by using the out keyword. Anything you write to an output variable in one shader is sent to a similarly named variable declared with the in keyword in the subsequent stage. For example, if your vertex shader declares a variable called vs_color using the out keyword, it would match up with a variable named vs_color declared with the in keyword in the fragment shader stage (assuming no other stages were active in between).

If we modify our simple vertex shader as shown in Listing 3.3 to include vs_color as an output variable, and correspondingly modify our simple fragment shader to include vs_color as an input variable as shown in Listing 3.4, we can pass a value from the vertex shader to the fragment shader. Then, rather than outputting a hard-coded value, the fragment can simply output the color passed to it from the vertex shader.

```
#version 450 core

// 'offset' and 'color' are input vertex attributes
layout (location = 0) in vec4 offset;
layout (location = 1) in vec4 color;

// 'vs_color' is an output that will be sent to the next shader stage
out vec4 vs_color;

void main(void)
{
    const vec4 vertices[3] = vec4[3](vec4( 0.25, -0.25, 0.5, 1.0),
                                     vec4(-0.25, -0.25, 0.5, 1.0),
                                     vec4( 0.25,  0.25, 0.5, 1.0));

    // Add 'offset' to our hard-coded vertex position
    gl_Position = vertices[gl_VertexID] + offset;

    // Output a fixed value for vs_color
    vs_color = color;
}
```

Listing 3.3: Vertex shader with an output

As you can see in Listing 3.3, we declare a second input to our vertex shader, color (this time at location 1), and write its value to the vs_output output. This is picked up by the fragment shader of Listing 3.4 and written to the framebuffer. This allows us to pass a color all the way from a vertex attribute that we can set with **glVertexAttrib*()** through the vertex shader, into the fragment shader, and out to the framebuffer. As a consequence, we can draw different-colored triangles!

```
#version 450 core

// Input from the vertex shader
in vec4 vs_color;

// Output to the framebuffer
out vec4 color;

void main(void)
{
    // Simply assign the color we were given by the vertex shader to our output
    color = vs_color;
}
```

Listing 3.4: Fragment shader with an input

Interface Blocks

Declaring interface variables one at a time is possibly the simplest way to communicate data between shader stages. However, in most nontrivial applications, you will likely want to communicate a number of different pieces of data between stages; these may include arrays, structures, and other complex arrangements of variables. To achieve this, we can group together a number of variables into an *interface block*. The declaration of an interface block looks a lot like a structure declaration, except that it is declared using the in or out keyword depending on whether it is an input to or output from the shader. An example interface block definition is shown in Listing 3.5.

```
#version 450 core

// 'offset' is an input vertex attribute
layout (location = 0) in vec4 offset;
layout (location = 1) in vec4 color;

// Declare VS_OUT as an output interface block
out VS_OUT
{
    vec4 color;      // Send color to the next stage
} vs_out;
```

```
void main(void)
{
    const vec4 vertices[3] = vec4[3](vec4( 0.25, -0.25, 0.5, 1.0),
                                     vec4(-0.25, -0.25, 0.5, 1.0),
                                     vec4( 0.25,  0.25, 0.5, 1.0));

    // Add 'offset' to our hard-coded vertex position
    gl_Position = vertices[gl_VertexID] + offset;

    // Output a fixed value for vs_color
    vs_out.color = color;
}
```

Listing 3.5: Vertex shader with an output interface block

Note that the interface block in Listing 3.5 has both a block name (VS_OUT, uppercase) and an instance name (vs_out, lowercase). Interface blocks are matched between stages using the block name (VS_OUT in this case), but are referenced in shaders using the instance name. Thus, modifying our fragment shader to use an interface block gives the code shown in Listing 3.6.

```
#version 450 core

// Declare VS_OUT as an input interface block
in VS_OUT
{
    vec4 color;     // Send color to the next stage
} fs_in;

// Output to the framebuffer
out vec4 color;

void main(void)
{
    // Simply assign the color we were given by the vertex shader to our output
    color = fs_in.color;
}
```

Listing 3.6: Fragment shader with an input interface block

Matching interface blocks by block name but allowing block instances to have different names in each shader stage serves two important purposes. First, it allows the name by which you refer to the block to be different in each stage, thereby avoiding confusing things such as having to use vs_out in a fragment shader. Second, it allows interfaces to go from being single items to arrays when crossing between certain shader stages, such as the vertex and tessellation or geometry shader stages, as we will see in a short while. Note that interface blocks are only for moving data from shader stage to shader stage—you can't use them to group together inputs to the vertex shader or outputs from the fragment shader.

Tessellation

Tessellation is the process of breaking a high-order primitive (which is known as a *patch* in OpenGL) into many smaller, simpler primitives such as triangles for rendering. OpenGL includes a fixed-function, configurable tessellation engine that is able to break up quadrilaterals, triangles, and lines into a potentially large number of smaller points, lines, or triangles that can be directly consumed by the normal rasterization hardware further down the pipeline. Logically, the tessellation phase sits directly after the vertex shading stage in the OpenGL pipeline and is made up of three parts: the tessellation control shader, the fixed-function tessellation engine, and the tessellation evaluation shader.

Tessellation Control Shaders

The first of the three tessellation phases is the tessellation control shader (TCS; sometimes known as simply the control shader). This shader takes its input from the vertex shader and is primarily responsible for two things: the determination of the level of tessellation that will be sent to the tessellation engine, and the generation of data that will be sent to the tessellation evaluation shader that is run after tessellation has occurred.

Tessellation in OpenGL works by breaking down high-order surfaces known as *patches* into points, lines, or triangles. Each patch is formed from a number of *control points*. The number of control points per patch is configurable and set by calling **glPatchParameteri()** with pname set to GL_PATCH_VERTICES and value set to the number of control points that will be used to construct each patch. The prototype of **glPatchParameteri()** is

```
void glPatchParameteri(GLenum pname,
                       GLint value);
```

By default, the number of control points per patch is three. Thus, if this is what you want (as in our example application), you don't need to call it at all. The maximum number of control points that can be used to form a single patch is implementation defined, but is guaranteed to be at least 32.

When tessellation is active, the vertex shader runs once per control point, while the tessellation control shader runs in batches on groups of control points where the size of each batch is the same as the number of vertices per patch. That is, vertices are used as control points and the result of the vertex shader is passed in batches to the tessellation control shader as its input. The number of control points per patch can be changed such that the number of control points that is output by the tessellation control shader can differ from the number of control points that it consumes. The number of control points produced by the control shader is set using an output layout qualifier in the control shader's source code. Such a layout qualifier looks like this:

```
layout (vertices = N) out;
```

Here, N is the number of control points per patch. The control shader is responsible for calculating the values of the output control points and for setting the tessellation factors for the resulting patch that will be sent to the fixed-function tessellation engine. The output tessellation factors are written to the gl_TessLevelInner and gl_TessLevelOuter built-in output variables, whereas any other data that is passed down the pipeline is written to user-defined output variables (those declared using the out keyword, or the special built-in gl_out array) as normal.

Listing 3.7 shows a simple tessellation control shader. It sets the number of output control points to three (the same as the default number of input control points) using the layout (vertices = 3) out; layout qualifier, copies its input to its output (using the built-in variables gl_in and gl_out), and sets the inner and outer tessellation level to 5. Higher numbers would produce a more densely tessellated output, and lower numbers would yield a more coarsely tessellated output. Setting the tessellation factor to 0 will cause the whole patch to be thrown away.

The built-in input variable gl_InvocationID is used as an index into the gl_in and gl_out arrays. This variable contains the zero-based index of the control point within the patch being processed by the current invocation of the tessellation control shader.

```
#version 450 core

layout (vertices = 3) out;

void main(void)
{
    // Only if I am invocation 0 ...
    if (gl_InvocationID == 0)
```

```
{
    gl_TessLevelInner[0] = 5.0;
    gl_TessLevelOuter[0] = 5.0;
    gl_TessLevelOuter[1] = 5.0;
    gl_TessLevelOuter[2] = 5.0;
}
// Everybody copies their input to their output
gl_out[gl_InvocationID].gl_Position =
    gl_in[gl_InvocationID].gl_Position;
}
```

Listing 3.7: Our first tessellation control shader

The Tessellation Engine

The tessellation engine is a fixed-function part of the OpenGL pipeline that takes high-order surfaces represented as patches and breaks them down into simpler primitives such as points, lines, or triangles. Before the tessellation engine receives a patch, the tessellation control shader processes the incoming control points and sets tessellation factors that are used to break down the patch. After the tessellation engine produces the output primitives, the vertices representing them are picked up by the tessellation evaluation shader. The tessellation engine is responsible for producing the parameters that are fed to the invocations of the tessellation evaluation shader, which it then uses to transform the resulting primitives and get them ready for rasterization.

Tessellation Evaluation Shaders

Once the fixed-function tessellation engine has run, it produces a number of output vertices representing the primitives it has generated. These are passed to the tessellation evaluation shader. The tessellation evaluation shader (TES; also called simply the evaluation shader) runs an invocation for each vertex produced by the tessellator. When the tessellation levels are high, the tessellation evaluation shader could run an extremely large number of times. For this reason, you should be careful with complex evaluation shaders and high tessellation levels.

Listing 3.8 shows a tessellation evaluation shader that accepts input vertices produced by the tessellator as a result of running the control shader shown in Listing 3.7. At the beginning of the shader is a layout qualifier that sets the tessellation mode. In this case, we selected the mode to be triangles. Other qualifiers, equal_spacing and cw, indicate that new vertices should be generated equally spaced along the tessellated polygon edges and that a clockwise vertex winding order should be used for the generated triangles. We will cover the other possible choices in the "Tessellation" section in Chapter 8.

The remainder of the shader assigns a value to gl_Position just like a vertex shader does. It calculates this using the contents of two more built-in variables. The first is gl_TessCoord, which is the *barycentric coordinate* of the vertex generated by the tessellator. The second is the gl_Position member of the gl_in[] array of structures. This matches the gl_out structure written to in the tessellation control shader given in Listing 3.7. This shader essentially implements pass-through tessellation. That is, the tessellated output patch is exactly the same shape as the original, incoming triangular patch.

```
#version 450 core

layout (triangles, equal_spacing, cw) in;

void main(void)
{
    gl_Position = (gl_TessCoord.x * gl_in[0].gl_Position +
                   gl_TessCoord.y * gl_in[1].gl_Position +
                   gl_TessCoord.z * gl_in[2].gl_Position);
}
```

Listing 3.8: Our first tessellation evaluation shader

To see the results of the tessellator, we need to tell OpenGL to draw only the outlines of the resulting triangles. To do this, we call **glPolygonMode()**, whose prototype is

```
void glPolygonMode(GLenum face,
                   GLenum mode);
```

The face parameter specifies which type of polygons we want to affect. Because we want to affect everything, we set it to GL_FRONT_AND_BACK. The other modes will be explained shortly. mode says how we want our polygons to be rendered. As we want to render in wireframe mode (i.e., lines), we set this to GL_LINE. The result of rendering our one triangle

Figure 3.1: Our first tessellated triangle

example with tessellation enabled and the two shaders of Listing 3.7 and Listing 3.8 is shown in Figure 3.1.

Geometry Shaders

The geometry shader is logically the last shader stage in the front end, sitting after the vertex and tessellation stages and before the rasterizer. The geometry shader runs once per primitive and has access to all of the input vertex data for all of the vertices that make up the primitive being processed. The geometry shader is also unique among the shader stages in that it is able to increase or reduce the amount of data flowing through the pipeline in a programmatic way. Tessellation shaders can also increase or decrease the amount of work in the pipeline, but only implicitly by setting the tessellation level for the patch. Geometry shaders, in contrast, include two functions—EmitVertex() and EndPrimitive()—that explicitly produce vertices that are sent to primitive assembly and rasterization.

Another unique feature of geometry shaders is that they can change the primitive mode mid-pipeline. For example, they can take triangles as input and produce a bunch of points or lines as output, or even create triangles from independent points. An example geometry shader is shown in Listing 3.9.

```
#version 450 core

layout (triangles) in;
layout (points, max_vertices = 3) out;

void main(void)
{
    int i;

    for (i = 0; i < gl_in.length(); i++)
    {
        gl_Position = gl_in[i].gl_Position;
        EmitVertex();
    }
}
```

Listing 3.9: Our first geometry shader

The shader shown in Listing 3.9 acts as another simple pass-through shader that converts triangles into points so that we can see their vertices. The first layout qualifier indicates that the geometry shader is expecting to see triangles as its input. The second layout qualifier tells OpenGL that the geometry shader will produce points and that the maximum number of points that each shader will produce will be three. In the main function, a loop runs through all of the members of the gl_in array, which is determined by calling its .length() function.

We actually know that the length of the array will be three because we are processing triangles and every triangle has three vertices. The outputs of the geometry shader are again similar to those of a vertex shader. In particular, we write to gl_Position to set the position of the resulting vertex. Next, we call EmitVertex(), which produces a vertex at the output of the geometry shader. Geometry shaders automatically call EndPrimitive() at the end of your shader, so calling this function explicitly is not necessary in this example. As a result of running this shader, three vertices will be produced and rendered as points.

By inserting this geometry shader into our simple one tessellated triangle example, we obtain the output shown in Figure 3.2. To create this image, we set the point size to 5.0 by calling **glPointSize()**. This makes the points large and highly visible.

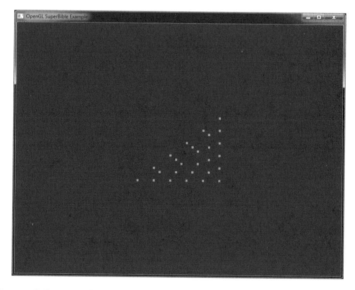

Figure 3.2: Tessellated triangle after adding a geometry shader

Primitive Assembly, Clipping, and Rasterization

After the front end of the pipeline has run (which includes vertex shading, tessellation, and geometry shading), a fixed-function part of the pipeline performs a series of tasks that take the vertex representation of our scene and convert it into a series of pixels, which in turn need to be colored and written to the screen. The first step in this process is primitive assembly, which is the grouping of vertices into lines and triangles. Primitive assembly still occurs for points, but it is trivial in that case.

Once primitives have been constructed from their individual vertices, they are *clipped* against the displayable region, which usually means the window or screen, but can also be a smaller area known as the *viewport*. Finally, the parts of the primitive that are determined to be potentially visible are sent to a fixed-function subsystem called the rasterizer. This block determines which pixels are covered by the primitive (point, line, or triangle) and sends the list of pixels on to the next stage—that is, fragment shading.

Clipping

As vertices exit the front end of the pipeline, their position is said to be in *clip space*. This is one of the many coordinate systems that can be used to represent positions. You may have noticed that the gl_Position variable that we have written to in our vertex, tessellation, and geometry shaders has a `vec4` type, and that the positions we have produced by writing to it are all four-component vectors. This is what is known as a *homogeneous* coordinate. The homogeneous coordinate system is used in projective geometry because much of the math ends up being simpler in homogeneous coordinate space than it does in regular Cartesian space. Homogeneous coordinates have one more component than their equivalent Cartesian coordinate, which is why our three-dimensional position vector is represented as a four-component variable.

Although the output of the front end is a four-component homogeneous coordinate, clipping occurs in Cartesian space. Thus, to convert from homogeneous coordinates to Cartesian coordinates, OpenGL performs a *perspective division*, which involves dividing all four components of the position by the last, w component. This has the effect of projecting the vertex from the homogeneous space to the Cartesian space, leaving w as 1.0. In all of the examples so far, we have set the w component of `gl_Position` as 1.0, so this division has not had any effect. When we explore projective geometry in a short while, we will discuss the effect of setting w to values other than 1.0.

After the projective division, the resulting position is in *normalized device space*. In OpenGL, the visible region of normalized device space is the volume that extends from -1.0 to 1.0 in the x and y dimensions and from 0.0 to 1.0 in the z dimension. Any geometry that is contained in this region may become visible to the user and anything outside of it should be discarded. The six sides of this volume are formed by planes in three-dimensional space. As a plane divides a coordinate space in two, the volumes on each side of the plane are called *half-spaces*.

Before passing primitives on to the next stage, OpenGL performs clipping by determining which side of each of these planes the vertices of each primitive lie on. Each plane effectively has an "outside" and an "inside." If a primitive's vertices all lie on the "outside" of any one plane, then the whole thing is thrown away. If all of primitive's vertices are on the "inside" of all the planes (and therefore inside the view volume), then it is passed through unaltered. Primitives that are partially visible (which means that they cross one of the planes) must be handled specially. More details about how this works is given in the "Clipping" section in Chapter 7.

Viewport Transformation

After clipping, all of the vertices of the geometry have coordinates that lie between -1.0 and 1.0 in the x and y dimensions. Along with a z coordinate that lies between 0.0 and 1.0, these are known as normalized device coordinates. However, the window that you're drawing to has coordinates that usually[1] start from $(0, 0)$ at the bottom left and range to $(w - 1, h - 1)$, where w and h are the width and height of the window in pixels, respectively. To place your geometry into the window, OpenGL applies the *viewport transform*, which applies a scale and offset to the vertices' normalized device coordinates to move them into *window coordinates*. The scale and bias to apply are determined by the viewport bounds, which you can set by calling **glViewport()** and **glDepthRange()**. Their prototypes are

```
void glViewport(GLint x, GLint y, GLsizei width, GLsizei height);
```

and

```
void glDepthRange(GLdouble nearVal, GLdouble farVal);
```

This transform takes the following form:

$$
\begin{pmatrix} x_w \\ y_w \\ z_w \end{pmatrix} = \begin{pmatrix} \frac{p_x}{2} x_d + o_x \\ \frac{p_y}{2} y_d + o_y \\ \frac{f-n}{2} z_d + \frac{n+f}{2} \end{pmatrix}
$$

Here, x_w, y_w, and z_w are the resulting coordinates of the vertex in window space, and x_d, y_d, and z_d are the incoming coordinates of the vertex in normalized device space. p_x and p_y are the width and height of the viewport in pixels, and n and f are the near and far plane distances in the z coordinate, respectively. Finally, o_x, o_y, and o_z are the origins of the viewport.

Culling

Before a triangle is processed further, it may be optionally passed through a stage called *culling*, which determines whether the triangle faces toward or away from the viewer and can decide whether to actually go ahead and draw it based on the result of this computation. If the triangle faces toward the viewer, then it is considered to be *front-facing*; otherwise, it is said to be *back-facing*. It is very common to discard triangles that are back-facing because when an object is closed, any back-facing triangle will be hidden by another front-facing triangle.

---

1. It's possible to change the coordinate convention such that the $(0, 0)$ origin is at the upper-left corner of the window, which matches the convention used in some other graphics systems.

To determine whether a triangle is front- or back-facing, OpenGL will determine its *signed* area in window space. One way to determine the area of a triangle is to take the cross product of two of its edges. The equation for this is

$$a = \frac{1}{2} \sum_{i=0}^{n-1} x_w^i y_w^{i \oplus 1} - x_w^{i \oplus 1} y_w^i$$

Here, x_w^i and y_w^i are the coordinates of the ith vertex of the triangle in window space and $i \oplus 1$ is $(i + 1)$ mod 3. If the area is positive, then the triangle is considered to be front-facing; if it is negative, then it is considered to be back-facing. The sense of this computation can be reversed by calling **glFrontFace()** with **dir** set to either GL_CW or GL_CCW (where CW and CCW stand for clockwise and counterclockwise, respectively). This is known as the *winding order* of the triangle, and the clockwise or counterclockwise terms refer to the order in which the vertices appear in window space. By default, this state is set to GL_CCW, indicating that triangles whose vertices are in counterclockwise order are considered to be front-facing and those whose vertices are in clockwise order are considered to be back-facing. If the state is GL_CW, then a is simply negated before being used in the culling process. Figure 3.3 shows this pictorially for the purpose of illustration.

Once the direction that the triangle is facing has been determined, OpenGL is capable of discarding either front-facing, back-facing, or even both types of triangles. By default, OpenGL will render all triangles, regardless of which way they face. To turn on culling, call **glEnable()** with **cap** set to GL_CULL_FACE. When you enable culling, OpenGL will cull back-facing triangles by default. To change which types of triangles are

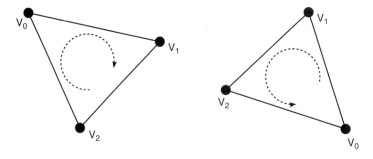

Figure 3.3: Clockwise (left) and counterclockwise (right) winding order

culled, call **glCullFace()** with face set to GL_FRONT, GL_BACK, or GL_FRONT_AND_BACK.

As points and lines don't have any geometric area,[2] this facing calculation doesn't apply to them and they can't be culled at this stage.

Rasterization

Rasterization is the process of determining which fragments might be covered by a primitive such as a line or a triangle. There are myriad algorithms for doing this, but most OpenGL systems will settle on a half-space–based method for triangles, as it lends itself well to parallel implementation. Essentially, OpenGL will determine a bounding box for the triangle in window coordinates and test every fragment inside it to determine whether it is inside or outside the triangle. To do this, it treats each of the triangle's three edges as a half-space that divides the window in two.

Fragments that lie on the interior of all three edges are considered to be inside the triangle and fragments that lie on the exterior of any of the three edges are considered to be outside the triangle. Because the algorithm to determine which side of a line a point lies on is relatively simple and is independent of anything besides the position of the line's endpoints and of the point being tested, many tests can be performed concurrently, providing the opportunity for massive parallelism.

Fragment Shaders

The fragment[3] shader is the last programmable stage in OpenGL's graphics pipeline. This stage is responsible for determining the color of each fragment before it is sent to the framebuffer for possible composition into the window. After the rasterizer processes a primitive, it produces a list of fragments that need to be colored and passes this list to the fragment

---

2. Obviously, once they are rendered to the screen, points and lines have area; otherwise, we wouldn't be able to see them. However, this area is artificial and can't be calculated directly from their vertices.

3. The term *fragment* is used to describe an element that may ultimately contribute to the final color of a pixel. The pixel may not end up being the color produced by any particular invocation of the fragment shader due to a number of other effects such as depth or stencil tests, blending, and multi-sampling, all of which will be covered later in the book.

shader. Here, an explosion in the amount of work in the pipeline occurs, as each triangle could produce hundreds, thousands, or even millions of fragments.

Listing 2.4 in Chapter 2 contains the source code of our first fragment shader. It's an extremely simple shader that declares a single output and then assigns a fixed value to it. In a real-world application, the fragment shader would normally be substantially more complex and be responsible for performing calculations related to lighting, applying materials, and even determining the depth of the fragment. Available as input to the fragment shader are several built-in variables such as gl_FragCoord, which contains the position of the fragment within the window. It is possible to use these variables to produce a unique color for each fragment.

Listing 3.10 provides a shader that derives its output color from gl_FragCoord. Figure 3.4 shows the output of running our original single-triangle program with this shader installed.

```
#version 450 core

out vec4 color;

void main(void)
{
    color = vec4(sin(gl_FragCoord.x * 0.25) * 0.5 + 0.5,
                 cos(gl_FragCoord.y * 0.25) * 0.5 + 0.5,
                 sin(gl_FragCoord.x * 0.15) * cos(gl_FragCoord.y * 0.15),
                 1.0);
}
```

Listing 3.10: Deriving a fragment's color from its position

As you can see, the color of each pixel in Figure 3.4 is now a function of its position and a simple screen-aligned pattern has been produced. The shader of Listing 3.10 created the checkered patterns in the output.

The gl_FragCoord variable is one of the built-in variables available to the fragment shader. However, just as with other shader stages, we can define our own inputs to the fragment shader, which will be filled in based on the outputs of whichever stage is last before rasterization. For example, if we have a simple program with only a vertex shader and fragment shader in it, we can pass data from the fragment shader to the vertex shader.

The inputs to the fragment shader are somewhat unlike inputs to other shader stages, in that OpenGL *interpolates* their values across the primitive

Figure 3.4: Result of Listing 3.10

that's being rendered. To demonstrate, we take the vertex shader of
Listing 3.3 and modify it to assign a different, fixed color for each vertex,
as shown in Listing 3.11.

```
#version 450 core

// 'vs_color' is an output that will be sent to the next shader stage
out vec4 vs_color;

void main(void)
{
    const vec4 vertices[3] = vec4[3](vec4( 0.25, -0.25, 0.5, 1.0),
                                     vec4(-0.25, -0.25, 0.5, 1.0),
                                     vec4( 0.25,  0.25, 0.5, 1.0));
    const vec4 colors[] = vec4[3](vec4( 1.0, 0.0, 0.0, 1.0),
                                  vec4( 0.0, 1.0, 0.0, 1.0),
                                  vec4( 0.0, 0.0, 1.0, 1.0));

    // Add 'offset' to our hard-coded vertex position
    gl_Position = vertices[gl_VertexID] + offset;

    // Output a fixed value for vs_color
    vs_color = color[gl_VertexID];
}
```

Listing 3.11: Vertex shader with an output

As you can see, in Listing 3.11 we added a second constant array that contains colors and index into it using gl_VertexID, writing its content to the vs_color output. In Listing 3.12 we modify our simple fragment shader to include the corresponding input and write its value to the output.

```
#version 450 core

// 'vs_color' is the color produced by the vertex shader
in vec4 vs_color;

out vec4 color;

void main(void)
{
    color = vs_color;
}
```

Listing 3.12: Deriving a fragment's color from its position

The result of using this new pair of shaders is shown in Figure 3.5. As you can see, the color changes smoothly across the triangle.

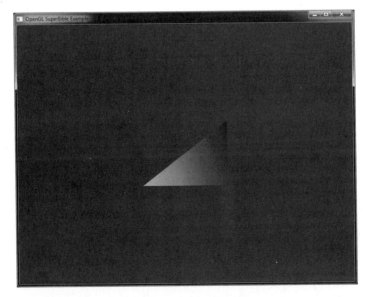

Figure 3.5: Result of Listing 3.12

Framebuffer Operations

The framebuffer is the last stage of the OpenGL graphics pipeline. It can represent the visible content of the screen and a number of additional regions of memory that are used to store per-pixel values other than color. On most platforms, this means the window you see on your desktop (or possibly the whole screen if your application covers it), which is owned by the operating system (or windowing system to be more precise). The framebuffer provided by the windowing system is known as the default framebuffer, but it is possible to provide your own if you wish to do things like render into off-screen areas. The state held by the framebuffer includes information such as where the data produced by your fragment shader should be written, what the format of that data should be, and so on. This state is stored in a *framebuffer object*. Also considered part of the framebuffer, but not stored per framebuffer object, is the pixel operation state.

Pixel Operations

After the fragment shader has produced an output, several things may happen to the fragment before it is written to the window, such as a determination of whether it even belongs in the window. Each of these things may be turned on or off by your application. The first thing that could happen is the *scissor test*, which tests your fragment against a rectangle that you can define. If it's inside the rectangle, then it will be processed further; if it's outside, it will be thrown away.

Next comes the *stencil test*. This compares a reference value provided by your application with the contents of the stencil buffer, which stores a single[4] value per pixel. The content of the stencil buffer has no particular semantic meaning and can be used for any purpose.

After the stencil test has been performed, the *depth test* is performed. The depth test is an operation that compares the fragment's z coordinate against the contents of the *depth buffer*. The depth buffer is a region of memory that, like the stencil buffer, is part of the framebuffer with enough space for a single value for each pixel; it contains the depth (which is related to distance from the viewer) of each pixel.

---

4. It's possible for a framebuffer to store multiple depth, stencil, or color values per pixel when a technique called *multi-sampling* is employed. We'll dig into this later in the book.

Normally, the values in the depth buffer range from 0 to 1, with 0 being the closest possible point in the depth buffer and 1 being the furthest possible point in the depth buffer. To determine whether a fragment is closer than other fragments that have already been rendered in the same place, OpenGL can compare the z component of the fragment's window-space coordinate against the value already in the depth buffer. If this value is less than what's already there, then the fragment is visible. The sense of this test can also be changed. For example, you can ask OpenGL to let fragments through that have a z coordinate that is greater than, equal to, or not equal to the content of the depth buffer. The result of the depth test also affects what OpenGL does to the stencil buffer.

Next, the fragment's color is sent to either the blending or logical operation stage, depending on whether the framebuffer is considered to store floating-point, normalized, or integer values. If the content of the framebuffer is either floating-point or normalized integer values, then blending is applied. Blending is a highly configurable stage in OpenGL and will be covered in detail in its own section.

In short, OpenGL is capable of using a wide range of functions that take components of the output of your fragment shader and of the current content of the framebuffer and calculate new values that are written back to the framebuffer. If the framebuffer contains unnormalized integer values, then logical operations such as logical AND, OR, and XOR can be applied to the output of your shader and the value currently in the framebuffer to produce a new value that will be written back into the framebuffer.

Compute Shaders

The first sections of this chapter describe the *graphics pipeline* in OpenGL. However, OpenGL also includes the *compute shader* stage, which can almost be thought of as a separate pipeline that runs indepdendently of the other graphics-oriented stages.

Compute shaders are a way of getting at the computational power possessed by the graphics processor in the system. Unlike the graphics-centric vertex, tessellation, geometry, and fragment shaders, compute shaders could be considered as a special, single-stage pipeline all on their own. Each compute shader operates on a single unit of work known as a *work item*; these items are, in turn, collected together into small groups called *local workgroups*. Collections of these workgroups can be sent into OpenGL's compute pipeline to be processed. The compute shader doesn't have any fixed inputs or outputs besides a handful of built-in variables to tell the shader which item it is working on. All processing performed by a compute shader is explicitly written to memory by the shader itself, rather than being consumed by a subsequent pipeline stage. A very basic compute shader is shown in Listing 3.13.

```
#version 450 core

layout (local_size_x = 32, local_size_y = 32) in;

void main(void)
{
    // Do nothing
}
```

Listing 3.13: Simple do-nothing compute shader

Compute shaders are otherwise just like any other shader stage in OpenGL. To compile one, you create a shader object with the type GL_COMPUTE_SHADER, attach your GLSL source code to it with **glShaderSource()**, compile it with **glCompileShader()**, and then link it into a program with **glAttachShader()** and **glLinkProgram()**. The result is a program object with a compiled compute shader in it that can be launched to do work for you.

The shader in Listing 3.13 tells OpenGL that the size of the local workgroup will be 32 by 32 work items, but then proceeds to do nothing. To create a compute shader that actually does something useful, you need to know a bit more about OpenGL—so we'll revisit this topic later in the book.

Using Extensions in OpenGL

All of the examples shown in this book so far have relied on the core functionality of OpenGL. However, one of OpenGL's greatest strengths is that it can be extended and enhanced by hardware manufacturers, operating system vendors, and even publishers of tools and debuggers. Extensions can have many different effects on OpenGL functionality.

An extension is any addition to a core version of OpenGL. Extensions are listed in the OpenGL extension registry[5] on the OpenGL Web site. These

---

5. Find the OpenGL extension registry at http://www.opengl.org/registry/.

extensions are written as a list of differences from a particular version of the OpenGL specification, and note what that version of OpenGL is. That means the text of the extensions describes how the core OpenGL specification must be changed if the extension is supported. However, popular and generally useful extensions are normally "promoted" into the core versions of OpenGL; thus, if you are running the latest and greatest version of OpenGL, there might not be that many extensions that are interesting but not part of the core profile. A complete list of the extensions that were promoted to each version of OpenGL and a brief synopsis of what they do is included in Appendix C, "OpenGL Features and Versions."

There are three major classifications of extensions: vendor, EXT, and ARB. Vendor extensions are written and implemented on one vendor's hardware. Initials representing the specific vendor are usually part of the extension name—"AMD" for Advanced Micro Devices or "NV" for NVIDIA, for example. It is possible that more than one vendor might support a specific vendor extension, especially if it becomes widely accepted. EXT extensions are written together by two or more vendors. They often start their lives as vendor-specific extensions, but if another vendor is interested in implementing the extension, perhaps with minor changes, it may collaborate with the original authors to produce an EXT version. ARB extensions are an official part of OpenGL because they are approved by the OpenGL governing body, the Architecture Review Board (ARB). These extensions are often supported by most or all major hardware vendors and may also have started out as vendor or EXT extensions.

This extension process may sound confusing at first. Hundreds of extensions currently are available! But new versions of OpenGL are often constructed from extensions programmers have found useful. In this way each extension gets its time in the sun. The ones that shine can be promoted to core; the ones that are less useful are not considered. This "natural selection" process helps to ensure only the most useful and important new features make it into a core version of OpenGL.

A useful tool to determine which extensions are supported in your computer's OpenGL implementation is Realtech VR's OpenGL Extensions Viewer. It is freely available from the Realtech VR Web site (see Figure 3.6).

Enhancing OpenGL with Extensions

Before using any extensions, you *must* make sure that they're supported by the OpenGL implementation that your application is running on. To find

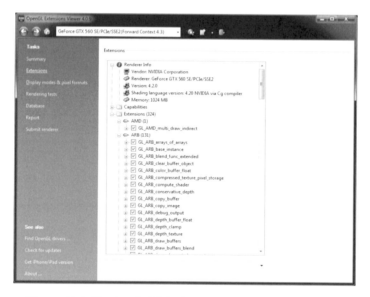

Figure 3.6: Realtech VR's OpenGL Extensions Viewer

out which extensions OpenGL supports, there are two functions that you can use. First, to determine the *number* of supported extensions, you can call **glGetIntegerv()** with the GL_NUM_EXTENSIONS parameter. Next, you can find out the name of each of the supported extensions by calling

```
const GLubyte* glGetStringi(GLenum name,
                            GLuint index);
```

You should pass GL_EXTENSIONS as the name parameter, and a value between 0 and 1 less than the number of supported extensions in index. The function returns the name of the extension as a string. To see if a specific extension is supported, you can simply query the number of extensions, and then loop through each supported extension and compare its name to the one you're looking for. The book's source code comes with a simple function that does this for you. **sb7IsExtensionSupported()** has the prototype

```
int sb7IsExtensionSupported(const char * extname);
```

This function is declared in the <sb7ext.h> header, takes the name of an extension, and returns non-zero if it is supported by the current OpenGL context and zero if it is not. Your application should always check for support for extensions you wish to use before using them.

Extensions generally add to OpenGL in some combination of four different ways:

- They can make things legal that weren't before, by simply removing restrictions from the OpenGL specification.

- They can add tokens or extend the range of values that can be passed as parameters to existing functions.

- They can extend GLSL to add functionality, built-in functions, variables, or data types.

- They can add entirely new functions to OpenGL itself.

In the first case, where things that once were considered errors no longer are, your application doesn't need to do anything besides start using the newly allowed behavior (once you have determined that the extension is supported, of course). Likewise, for the second case, you can just start using the new token values in the relevant functions, presuming that you have their values. The values of the tokens are in the extension specifications, so you can look them up there if they are not included in your system's header files.

To enable use of extensions in GLSL, you must first include a line at the beginning of shaders that use them to tell the compiler that you're going to need their features. For example, to enable the hypothetical GL_ABC_foobar_feature extension in GLSL, include the following in the beginning of your shader:

```
#extension GL_ABC_foobar_feature : enable
```

This tells the compiler that you intend to use the extension in your shader. If the compiler knows about the extension, it will let you compile the shader, even if the underlying hardware doesn't support the feature. If this is the case, the compiler should issue a warning if it sees that the extension is actually being used. Typically, extensions to GLSL will add preprocessor tokens to indicate their presence. For example, GL_ABC_foobar_feature will implicitly include

```
#define GL_ABC_foobar_feature 1
```

This means that you could write code such as

```
#if GL_ABC_foobar_feature
    // Use functions from the foobar extension
#else
```

```
    // Emulate or otherwise work around the missing functionality
#endif
```

This allows you to conditionally compile or execute functionality that is part of an extension that may or may not be supported by the underlying OpenGL implementation. If your shader absolutely requires support for an extension and will not work at all without it, you can instead include this more assertive code:

```
#extension GL_ABC_foobar_feature : require
```

If the OpenGL implementation does not support the GL_ABC_foobar_feature extension, then it will fail to compile the shader and report an error on the line including the #extension directive. In effect, GLSL extensions are opt-in features, and applications must[6] tell compilers up front which extensions they intend to use.

Next we come to extensions that introduce new functions to OpenGL. On most platforms, you don't have direct access to the OpenGL driver and extension functions don't just magically appear as available to your applications to call. Rather, you must ask the OpenGL driver for a *function pointer* that represents the function you want to call. Function pointers are generally declared in two parts; the first is the definition of the function pointer type, and the second is the function pointer variable itself. Consider this code as an example:

```
typedef void
(APIENTRYP PFNGLDRAWTRANSFORMFEEDBACKPROC) (GLenum mode,
                                            GLuint id);
PFNGLDRAWTRANSFORMFEEDBACKPROC glDrawTransformFeedback = NULL;
```

This declares the PFNGLDRAWTRANSFORMFEEDBACKPROC type as a pointer to a function taking GLenum and GLuint parameters. Next, it declares the glDrawTransformFeedback variable as an instance of this type. In fact, on many platforms, the declaration of the **glDrawTransformFeedback()** function is actually just like this. This seems pretty complicated, but fortunately the following header files include declarations of all of the

---

6. In practice, many implementations enable functionality included in some extensions by default and don't require that your shaders include these directives. However, if you rely on this behavior, your application is likely to not work on other OpenGL drivers. Because of this risk, you should always explicitly enable the extensions that you plan to use.

function prototypes, function pointer types, and token values introduced by all registered OpenGL extensions:

```
#include <glext.h>
#include <glxext.h>
#include <wglext.h>
```

These files can be found at the OpenGL extension registry Web site. The glext.h header contains both standard OpenGL extensions and many vendor-specific OpenGL extensions, the wglext.h header contains a number of extensions that are Windows specific, and the glxext.h header contains definitions that are X specific (X is the windowing system used on Linux and many other UNIX derivatives and implementations).

The method for querying the address of extension functions is actually platform specific. The book's application framework wraps up these intricacies into a handy function that is declared in the <sb7ext.h> header file. The function **sb7GetProcAddress()** has this prototype:

```
void * sb7GetProcAddress(const char * funcname);
```

Here, funcname is the name of the extension function that you wish to use. The return value is the address of the function, if it's supported, and NULL otherwise. Even if OpenGL returns a valid function pointer for a function that's part of the extension you want to use, that doesn't mean the extension is present. Sometimes the same function is part of more than one extension, and sometimes vendors ship drivers with partial implementations of extensions present. Always check for support for extensions using the official mechanisms or the **sb7IsExtensionSupported()** function.

Summary

In this chapter, you have taken a whirlwind trip down OpenGL's graphics pipeline. You have been (very) briefly introduced to each major stage and have created a program that uses each one of them, if only to do nothing impressive. We've glossed over or even neglected to mention several useful features of OpenGL with the intention of getting you from zero to rendering in as few pages as possible. You've also seen how OpenGL's pipeline and functionality can be enhanced by using extensions, which some of the examples later in the book will rely on. Over the next few chapters, you'll learn more fundamentals of computer graphics and of OpenGL, and then we'll take a second trip down the pipeline, dig deeper into the topics from this chapter, and get into some of the things we skipped in this preview of what OpenGL can do.

Chapter 4

Math for 3D Graphics

WHAT YOU'LL LEARN IN THIS CHAPTER

- What a vector is, and why you should care about them.

- What a matrix is, and why you should care more about them.

- How we use matrices and vectors to move geometry around.

- What the OpenGL conventions and coordinate spaces are.

So far, you have learned to draw points, lines, and triangles and have written simple shaders that pass your hard-coded vertex data through unmodified. We haven't really been rendering in 3D—which is odd for a book on 3D graphics! Well, to turn a collection of shapes into a coherent scene, you must arrange them in relation to one another and to the viewer. In this chapter, you start moving shapes and objects around in your coordinate system. The ability to place and orient your objects in a scene is a crucial tool for any 3D graphics programmer. As you will see, it is actually convenient to describe your objects' dimensions around the origin and then transform the objects into the desired positions.

Is This the Dreaded Math Chapter?

In most books on 3D graphics programming, yes, this would be the dreaded math chapter. However, you can relax; we take a more moderate approach to these principles than some texts.

One of the fundamental mathematical operations that will be performed by your shaders is the coordinate transform, which boils down to multiplying matrices with vectors and with each other. The keys to object and coordinate transformations are two matrix conventions used by OpenGL programmers. To familiarize you with these matrices, this chapter strikes a compromise between two extremes in computer graphics philosophy. On the one hand, we could warn you, "Please review a textbook on linear algebra before reading this chapter." On the other hand, we could perpetuate the deceptive reassurance that you can "learn to do 3D graphics without all those complex mathematical formulas." But we don't agree with either camp.

In reality, you can get along just fine without understanding the finer mathematics of 3D graphics, just as you can drive your car every day without having to know anything at all about automotive mechanics and the internal combustion engine. But you had better know enough about your car to realize that you need an oil change every so often, that you have to fill the tank with gas regularly, and that you must change the tires when they get bald. This knowledge makes you a responsible (and safe!) automobile owner. If you want to be a responsible and capable OpenGL programmer, the same standards apply. You need to understand at least the basics so you know what can be done and which tools best suit the job. If you are a beginner you will find that, with some practice, matrix math and vectors will gradually make more sense, and you will develop a more intuitive (and powerful) ability to make full use of the concepts we introduce in this chapter.

So even if you don't already have the ability to multiply two matrices in your head, you need to know what matrices are and how they serve as the means to OpenGL's 3D magic. But before you go dusting off that old linear algebra textbook (doesn't everyone have one?), have no fear: The sb7 library has a component called vmath that contains a number of useful classes and functions that can be used to represent and manipulate vectors and matrices. They can be used directly with OpenGL and are very similar in syntax and appearance to GLSL—the language you'll be writing your shaders in. So, you don't have to do all your matrix and vector manipulation yourself, but it's still a good idea to know what they are and how to apply them. See—you can eat your cake and have it, too!

A Crash Course in 3D Graphics Math

First, we do not pretend here that we will cover everything that is important for you to know. In fact, we will not even try to cover everything you should know. In this chapter, we are just going to cover what you *really* need to know. If you're already a math whiz, you should skip immediately to the section ahead on the standard 3D transformations. Not only do you already know what we are about to cover, but most math fans will be somewhat offended that we did not give sufficient space to their favorite feature of homogeneous coordinate spaces. Imagine one of those reality TV shows where you must escape a virtual swamp filled with crocodiles. How much 3D math do you really need to know to survive? That's what the next two sections are going to be about—3D math survival skills. The crocodiles do not care if you really know what a homogeneous coordinate space is.

Vectors, or Which Way Is Which?

The main input to OpenGL is the vertex, which has a number of attributes that normally include a position. Basically, this is a position in *xyz* coordinate space, and a given position in space is defined by exactly one and only one unique *xyz* triplet. An *xyz* triplet, however, can be represented by a vector (in fact, for the mathematically pure of heart, a position is actually a vector too—there, we threw you a bone). A vector is perhaps the single most important foundational concept to understand when it comes to manipulating 3D geometry. Those three values (*x*, *y*, and *z*) combined represent two important values: a direction and a magnitude.

Figure 4.1 shows a point in space (picked arbitrarily) and an arrow drawn from the origin of the coordinate system to that point in space. The point can be thought of as a vertex when you are stitching together triangles, but the arrow can be thought of as a vector. A vector is first, and most simply, a direction from the origin toward a point in space. We use vectors all the time in OpenGL to represent directional quantities. For example, the *x* axis is the vector (1, 0, 0). This says to go positive one unit in the *x* direction, and zero in the *y* and *z* directions. A vector is also how we point to where we are going—for example, which way is the camera pointing, or in which direction do we want to move to get away from that crocodile?

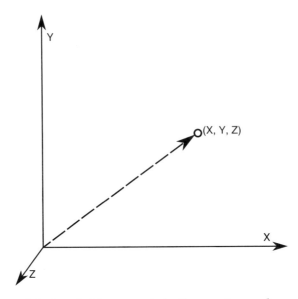

Figure 4.1: A point in space is both a vertex and a vector

The vector is so fundamental to the operation of OpenGL that vectors of various sizes are first-class types in GLSL and are given names such as `vec3` and `vec4` (representing three- and four-element vectors, respectively).

The second quantity a vector can represent is the magnitude. The magnitude of a vector is the length of the vector. For our *x*-axis vector (1, 0, 0), the length of the vector is 1. A vector with a length of 1 we call a *unit vector*. If a vector is not a unit vector and we want to scale it to make it one, we call that *normalization*. Normalizing a vector scales it such that its length becomes 1 and the vector is then said to be *normalized*. Unit vectors are important when we want to represent only a direction and not a magnitude. Also, if vector lengths appear in the equations we'll be using, they get a whole lot simpler when those lengths are 1! A magnitude can be important as well; for example, it can tell us how far we need to move in a given direction—how far away we need to get from that crocodile.

Vectors (and matrices) are such important concepts in 3D graphics that they are first-class citizens in GLSL—the language in which you write your shaders. However, this is not so in languages like C++. To allow you to use them in your C++ programs, the vmath library, which is provided with this book's source code, contains classes that can represent vectors and matrices that are named similarly to their GLSL counterparts. For instance, `vmath::vec3` can represent a three-component floating-point vector (*x, y, z*), vmath::vec4 can represent a four-component floating-point vector (*x, y, z, w*), and so on. The *w* coordinate is added to make the vector *homogeneous* but is typically set to 1.0. The *x, y,* and *z* values might later be divided by *w*, which, when it is 1.0, essentially leaves the *xyz* values alone. The classes in vmath are actually templated classes with type definitions to represent common types such as single- and double-precision floating-point values, and signed- and unsigned-integer variables. vmath::vec3 and vmath::vec4 are defined simply as follows:

```
typedef Tvec3<float> vec3;
typedef Tvec4<float> vec4;
```

Declaring a three-component vector is as simple as

```
vmath::vec3 vVector;
```

If you include using namespace vmath; in your source code, you can even write

```
vec3 vVector;
```

However, in these examples, we'll always qualify our use of the vmath library by explicitly using the vmath:: namespace. All of the vmath classes define a number of constructors and copy operators, which means you can declare and initialize vectors as follows:

```
vec3 vmath::vVertex1(0.0f, 0.0f, 1.0f);
vec4 vmath::vVertex2 = vec4(1.0f, 0.0f, 1.0f, 1.0f);
vec4 vmath::vVertex3(vVertex1, 1.0f);
```

Now, an array of three-component vertices, such as for a triangle, can be declared as

```
vec3 vmath::vVerts[] = { vmath::vec3(-0.5f, 0.0f, 0.0f),
                         vmath::vec3( 0.5f, 0.0f, 0.0f),
                         vmath::vec3( 0.0f, 0.5f, 0.0f) } ;
```

This should look similar to the code that we introduced in the "Drawing Our First Triangle" section in Chapter 2. The vmath library also includes lots of math-related functions and overrides most operators on its class to allow vectors and matrices to be added, subtracted, multiplied, transposed, and so on.

We need to be careful here not to gloss over that fourth *w* component too much. Most of the time when you specify geometry with vertex positions, a three-component vertex is all you want to store and send to OpenGL. For many directional vectors, such as a surface normal (a vector pointing perpendicular to a surface that is used for lighting calculations), a three-component vector suffices. However, we will soon delve into the world of matrices, and to transform a 3D vertex, you must multiply it by a 4×4 transformation matrix. The rules are you must multiply a four-component vector by a 4×4 matrix; if you try and use a three-component vector with a 4×4 matrix, the crocodiles will eat you! More on what all this means soon. Essentially, if you are going to do your own matrix operations on vectors, then you will probably want four-component vectors in many cases.

Common Vector Operators

Vectors behave as you would expect for operations such as addition, subtraction, unary negation, and so on. These operators perform a per-component calculation and result in a vector of the same size as their inputs. The vmath vector classes override the addition, subtraction, and unary negation operators, along with several others, to provide such functionality. This allows you to use code such as

```
vmath::vec3 a(1.0f, 2.0f, 3.0f);
vmath::vec3 b(4.0f, 5.0f, 6.0f);
vmath::vec3 c;

c = a + b;
c = a - b;
c += b;
c = -c;
```

However, there are many more operations on vectors that are explained from a mathematical perspective in the following subsections. They also have implementations in the vmath library, which will be outlined here.

Dot Product

Vectors can be added, subtracted, and scaled by simply adding, subtracting, or scaling their individual *xyz* components. An interesting and useful operation that can be applied only to two vectors, however, is called the *dot product*, which is also sometimes known as the *inner product*. The dot product between two (three-component) vectors returns a scalar (just one value) that is the cosine of the angle between the two vectors scaled by the product of their lengths. If the two vectors are of unit length, the value returned falls between −1.0 and 1.0 and is equal to the cosine of the angle between them. Of course, to get the actual angle between the vectors, you'd need to take the inverse cosine (or arccosine) of this value. The dot product is used extensively during lighting calculations and is

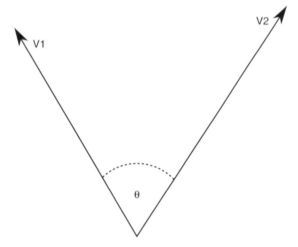

Figure 4.2: The dot product: cosine of the angle between two vectors

taken between a surface normal vector and a vector pointing toward a light source in diffuse lighting calculations. We will delve deeper into this type of shader code in the "Lighting Models" section in Chapter 13. Figure 4.2 shows two vectors, V1 and V2, and how the angle between them is represented by θ.

Mathematically, the dot product of two vectors V1 and V2 is calculated as

$$V1 \times V2 = V1.x \times V2.x + V1.y \times V2.y + V1.z \times V2.z$$

The vmath library has some useful functions that use the dot product operation. For starters, you can actually get the dot product itself between two vectors with the function vmath::dot, or with the dot member function of the vector classes.

```
vmath::vec3 a(...);
vmath::vec3 b(...);

float c = a.dot(b);
float d = dot(a, b);
```

As we mentioned, the dot product between a pair of unit vectors is a value (between -1.0 and $+1.0$) that represents the cosine of the angle between them. A slightly higher-level function, vmath::angle, actually returns this angle in radians.

```
float angle(const vmath::vec3& u, const vmath::vec3& v);
```

Cross Product

Another useful mathematical operation between two vectors is the *cross product*, which is also sometimes known as the *vector product*. The cross product between two vectors is a third vector that is perpendicular to the plane in which the first two vectors lie. The cross product of two vectors V1 and V2 is defined as

$$V1 \times V2 = \|V1\| \, \|V2\| \, sin(\theta)n$$

where n is the unit vector that is perpendicular to both V1 and V2. This means that if you normalize the result of a cross product, you get the normal to the plane. If V1 and V2 are both unit length, and are known to be perpendicular to each other, then you don't even need to normalize the result, as it will also be unit length. Figure 4.3 shows two vectors, V1 and V2, and their cross product V3.

The cross product of two three-dimensional vectors V1 and V2 can be calculated as

$$\begin{bmatrix} V3.x \\ V3.y \\ V3.z \end{bmatrix} = \begin{bmatrix} V1.y \cdot V2.z - V1.z \cdot V2.y \\ V1.z \cdot V2.x - V1.x \cdot V2.z \\ V1.x \cdot V2.y - V1.y \cdot V2.x \end{bmatrix}$$

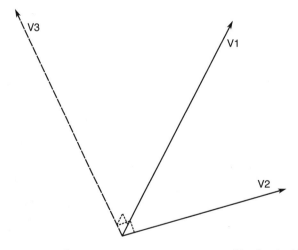

Figure 4.3: A cross product returns a vector perpendicular to its parameters

Again, the vmath library has functions that take the cross product of two vectors and return the resulting vector: one member function of the three-component vector classes and one global function.

```
vec3 a(...);
vec3 b(...);

vec3 c = a.cross(b);
vec3 d = cross(a, b);
```

Unlike in the dot product, the order of the vectors in the cross product is important. In Figure 4.3, V3 is the result of V2 cross V1. If you were to reverse the order of V1 and V2, the resulting vector V3 would point in the opposite direction. Applications of the cross product are numerous, from finding surface normals of triangles to constructing transformation matrices.

Length of a Vector

As we have already discussed, vectors have a direction and a magnitude. The magnitude of a vector is also known as its length. The magnitude of a three-dimensional vector can be found by using the following equation:

$$length(v) = \sqrt{v.x^2 + v.y^2 + v.z^2}$$

This can be generalized as the square root of the sum of the squares of the components of the vector.[1] In only two dimensions, this is simply Pythagoras's theorem: The square of the hypotenuse is equal to the sum of the squares of the other two sides. This extends to any number of dimensions, and the vmath library includes functions to calculate this for you.

```
template <typename T, int len>
static inline T length(const vecN<T,len>& v) { ... }
```

Reflection and Refraction

Common operations in computer graphics are calculating reflection and refraction vectors. Given an incoming vector R_{in} and a normal to a surface N, we wish to know the direction in which R_{in} will be reflected ($R_{reflect}$),

---

1. The sum of the squares of the components of a vector is also the dot product of a vector with itself.

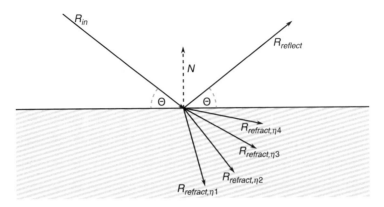

Figure 4.4: Reflection and refraction

and given a particular index of refraction η, the direction in which R_{in} will be refracted. We show this in Figure 4.4, with the refracted vectors for various values of η shown as $R_{refract,\eta1}$ through $R_{refract,\eta4}$.

Although Figure 4.4 shows the system in only two dimensions, we are interested in computing this in three dimensions (this is a 3D graphics book, after all). The math for calculating $R_{reflect}$ is

$$R_{reflect} = R_{in} - (2N \cdot R_{in})N$$

The math for calculating $R_{refract}$ for a given value of η is

$$k = 1 - \eta^2(1 - (N \cdot R)^2)$$

$$R_{refract} = \begin{cases} 0.0 & \text{if } k < 0.0 \\ \eta R - (\eta(N \cdot R) + \sqrt{k})N & \text{if } k \geq 0.0 \end{cases}$$

To get the desired result, both R and N must be unit-length vectors (i.e., they should be normalized before use). The two vmath functions, reflect() and refract(), implement these equations.

Matrices

The matrix is not just a Hollywood movie trilogy, but an exceptionally powerful mathematical tool that greatly simplifies the process of solving one or more equations with variables that have complex relationships with one another. One common example of this, near and dear to the hearts of graphics programmers, is coordinate transformations. For example, if you have a point in space represented by x, y, and z coordinates, and you need to know where that point is if you rotate it some number of degrees around some arbitrary point and orientation, you use a matrix. Why? Because the new x coordinate depends not only on the old x coordinate and the other rotation parameters, but also on what the y and z coordinates were. This kind of dependency between the variables and solution is just the sort of problem at which matrices excel. For fans of the *Matrix* movies who have a mathematical inclination, the term "matrix" is indeed an appropriate title.

Mathematically, a matrix is nothing more than a set of numbers arranged in uniform rows and columns—in programming terms, a two-dimensional array. A matrix doesn't have to be square, but all of the rows must have the same number of elements and all of the columns must have the same number of elements. The following are a selection of matrices. They don't represent anything in particular but serve only to demonstrate matrix structure. Note that it is also valid for a matrix to have a single column or row. A single row or column of numbers would more simply be called a vector, as discussed previously. In fact, as you will soon see, we can think of some matrices as a table of column vectors.

$$\begin{bmatrix} 1 & 4 & 7 \\ 2 & 5 & 8 \\ 3 & 6 & 9 \end{bmatrix} \begin{bmatrix} 0 & 42 \\ 1.5 & 0.877 \\ 2 & 14 \end{bmatrix} \begin{bmatrix} 1 \\ 2 \\ 3 \\ 4 \end{bmatrix}$$

"Matrix" and "vector" are two important terms that you see often in 3D graphics programming literature. When dealing with these quantities, you also see the term "scalar." A scalar is just an ordinary single number used to represent a magnitude or a specific quantity (you know—a regular old, plain, simple number... like before you cared or had all this jargon added to your vocabulary). Matrices can be multiplied and added together, but they can also be multiplied by vectors and scalar values. Multiplying a point (represented by a vector) by a matrix (representing a transformation) yields a new transformed point (another vector). Matrix transformations are actually not too difficult to understand but can be intimidating at first. Because an understanding of matrix transformations is fundamental to many 3D tasks, you should still make an attempt to become familiar with them. Fortunately, only a little understanding is enough to get you going and doing some pretty incredible things with OpenGL. Over time, and with a little more practice and study, you will master this mathematical tool yourself.

In the meantime, as previously for vectors, you will find a number of useful matrix functions and features available in the vmath library. The source code to this library is also available in the file vmath.h in the book's source code folder. This 3D math library greatly simplifies many tasks in this chapter and the ones to come. One *useful* feature of this library is that it lacks incredibly clever and highly optimized code! This makes the library highly portable and easy to understand. You'll also find it has a very GLSL-like syntax.

In your 3D programming tasks with OpenGL, you will use three sizes of matrices extensively: 2×2, 3×3, and 4×4. The vmath library has matrix data types that match those, defined by GLSL, such as

```
vmath::mat2 m1;
vmath::mat3 m2;
vmath::mat4 m3;
```

As in GLSL, the matrix classes in vmath define common operators such as addition, subtraction, unary negation, multiplication, and division, along with constructors and relational operators. Again, the matrix classes in vmath are built using templates and include type definitions for single- and double-precision floating-point, and signed- and unsigned-integer matrix types.

Matrix Construction and Operators

OpenGL represents a 4×4 matrix not as a two-dimensional array of floating values, but rather as a single array of 16 floating-point values. By default, OpenGL uses a *column-major* or *column-primary* layout for matrices. That is, for a 4×4 matrix, the first four elements represent the first column of the matrix, the next four elements represent the second column, and so on. This approach is different from many math libraries, which do take the two-dimensional array approach. For example, OpenGL prefers the first of these two examples:

```
GLfloat matrix[16];    // Nice OpenGL-friendly matrix

GLfloat matrix[4][4]; // Not as convenient for OpenGL programmers
```

OpenGL can use the second variation, but the first is a more efficient representation. The reason for this will become clear in a moment. These 16 elements represent the 4×4 matrix, as shown below. When the array elements traverse down the matrix columns one by one, we call this *column-major* matrix ordering. In memory, the 4×4 approach of the two-dimensional array (the second option in the preceding code) is laid out in a *row-major* order. In math terms, the two orientations are the transpose of each other.

$$\begin{bmatrix} A_{00} & A_{10} & A_{20} & A_{30} \\ A_{01} & A_{11} & A_{21} & A_{31} \\ A_{02} & A_{12} & A_{22} & A_{32} \\ A_{03} & A_{13} & A_{23} & A_{33} \end{bmatrix}$$

Representing the above matrix in colum-major order in memory produces an array as follows:

```
static const float A[] =
{
    A00, A01, A02, A03, A10, A11, A12, A13,
    A20, A21, A22, A23, A30, A31, A32, A33
};
```

In contrast, representing it in row-major order would require a layout such as this:

```
static const float A[] =
{
    A00, A10, A20, A30, A01, A11, A21, A31,
    A20, A21, A22, A23, A30, A31, A32, A33,
};
```

The real magic lies in the fact that these 16 values can represent a particular position in space and an orientation of the three axes with respect to the viewer. Interpreting these numbers is not hard at all. The four columns each represent a four-element vector.[2] To keep things simple for this book, we focus our attention on just the first three elements of the vectors in the first three columns. The fourth column vector contains the x, y, and z values of the transformed coordinate system's origin.

The first three elements of the first three columns are just directional vectors that represent the orientation (vectors here are used to represent a direction) of the x, y, and z axes in space. For most purposes, these three vectors are always at 90° angles from each other and are usually each of unit length (unless you are also applying a scale or shear). The mathematical term for this (in case you want to impress your friends) is *orthonormal* when the vectors are unit length, and *orthogonal* when they are not. Figure 4.5 shows the 4×4 transformation matrix with its components highlighted. Notice that the last row of the matrix is all 0s with the exception of the very last element, which is 1.

2. In fact, the vmath library internally represents matrices as arrays of its own vector classes, with each vector holding a column of the matrix.

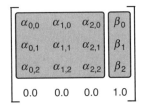

Figure 4.5: A 4 × 4 matrix representing rotation and translation

The upper-left 3×3 sub-matrix of the matrix shown in Figure 4.5 represents a rotation or orientation. The last column of the matrix represents a translation or position.

The most amazing thing is that if you have a 4×4 matrix that contains the position and orientation of a coordinate system, and you multiply a vertex expressed in the identity coordinate system (written as a column matrix or vector) by this matrix, the result is a new vertex that has been transformed to the new coordinate system. As a result, any position in space and any desired orientation can be uniquely defined by a 4×4 matrix, and if you multiply all of an object's vertices by this matrix, you transform the entire object to the given location and orientation in space!

In addition, if you transform an object's vertices from one space to another using one matrix, you can then transform *those* vertices by yet another matrix, transforming them again into another coordinate space. Given matrices A and B and vector v, we know that

$$A \cdot (B \cdot v)$$

is equivalent to

$$(A \cdot B) \cdot v$$

This relationship arises because matrix multiplication is *associative*. Herein lies the magic: It is possible to stack a whole bunch of transforms together by multiplying the matrices that represent those transforms and using the resulting matrix as a single term in the final product.

The final appearance of your scene or object can depend greatly on the order in which the modeling transformations are applied. This is particularly true of translation and rotation. We can see this as a

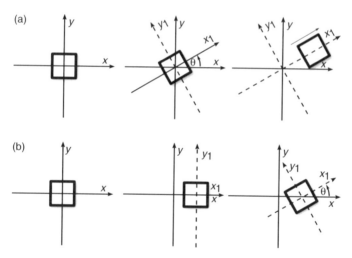

Figure 4.6: Modeling transformations: (a) rotation, then translation and (b) translation, then rotation

consequence of the associativity and commutativity rules for matrix multiplication. We can group together sequences of transformations in any way we like because matrix multiplication is associative, but the order in which the matrices appear in the multiplication matters because matrix multiplication is *not* commutative.

Figure 4.6(a) illustrates a progression of a square rotated first about the z axis and then translated down the newly transformed x axis, and Figure 4.6(b) illustrates first translating the same square along the x axis and then rotating it around around the z axis. The difference in the final dispositions of the square occurs because each transformation is performed with respect to the last transformation performed. In Figure 4.6(a), the square is rotated with respect to the origin first. In Figure 4.6(b), after the square is translated, the rotation is performed around the newly translated origin.

Understanding Transformations

If you think about it, most 3D graphics aren't really 3D. We use 3D concepts and terminology to describe what something looks like; then this 3D data is "squished" onto a 2D computer screen. We call the process of squishing 3D data down into 2D data *projection*. We refer to the projection whenever we want to describe the type of transformation (orthographic or perspective) that occurs during vertex processing, but projection is only one of the types of transformations that occur in OpenGL. Transformations also allow you to rotate objects around; move them about; and even stretch, shrink, and warp them.

Coordinate Spaces in OpenGL

A series of one or more transforms can be represented as a matrix, and multiplication by that matrix effectively moves a vector from one coordinate space to another. Several coordinate spaces are commonly used in OpenGL programming. Any number of geometric transformations can occur between the time you specify your vertices and the time they appear on the screen, but the most common are modeling, viewing, and projection. In this section, we examine each of the coordinate spaces commonly used in 3D computer graphics (and summarized in Table 4.1), and the transforms used to move vectors between them.

A matrix that moves coordinates from one space to another is normally named for those spaces. For example, a matrix that transforms an object's vertices from model space into view space is commonly referred to as a model–view matrix.

Table 4.1: Common Coordinate Spaces Used in 3D Graphics

Coordinate Space	What It Represents
Model space	Positions relative to a local origin. Also sometimes known as *object space*.
World space	Positions relative to a global origin (i.e., their location within the world).
View space	Positions relative to the viewer. Also sometimes called *camera* or *eye space*.
Clip space	Positions of vertices after projection into a nonlinear homogeneous coordinate.
Normalized device coordinate (NDC) space	Vertex coordinates are said to be in NDC after their clip space coordinates have been divided by their own w component.
Window space	Positions of vertices in pixels, relative to the origin of the window.

Object Coordinates

Most of your vertex data will typically begin life in *object space*, which is also commonly known as *model space*. In object space, positions of vertices are interpreted relative to a local origin. Consider a spaceship model. The origin of the model is probably going to be somewhere logical, such as the tip of the craft's nose, at its center of gravity, or where the pilot might sit. In a 3D modeling program, returning to the origin and zooming out sufficiently should show you the whole spaceship. The origin of a model is often the point about which you might rotate it to place it into a new orientation. It wouldn't make sense to place the origin far outside the model, because rotating the object about that point would apply significant translation as well as rotation.

World Coordinates

The next common coordinate space is world space. This is where coordinates are stored relative to a fixed, global origin. To continue the spaceship analogy, this could be the center of a play-field or other fixed body such as a nearby planet. Once in world space, all objects exist in a common frame. Often, this is the space in which lighting and physics calculations are performed.

View Coordinates

An important concept throughout this chapter is that of view coordinates, also often referred to as *camera* or *eye* coordinates. View coordinates are relative to the position of the observer (hence the terms "camera" and "eye") regardless of any transformations that may occur; you can think of them as "absolute" coordinates. Thus, eye coordinates represent a virtual fixed coordinate system that is used as a common frame of reference.

Figure 4.7 shows the view coordinate system from two viewpoints. On the left, the view coordinates are represented as seen by the observer of the scene (that is, perpendicular to the monitor). On the right, the view coordinate system is rotated slightly so you can better see the relation of the z axis. Positive x and y are pointed right and up, respectively, from the viewer's perspective. Positive z travels away from the origin toward the user, and negative z values travel farther away from the viewpoint into the screen. The screen lies at the z coordinate 0.

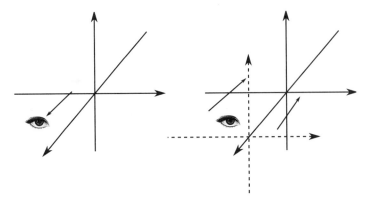

Figure 4.7: Two perspectives of view coordinates

When you draw in 3D with OpenGL, you use the Cartesian coordinate system. In the absence of any transformations, the system in use is identical to the eye coordinate system just described.

Clip and Normalized Device Space

Clip space is the coordinate space in which OpenGL performs clipping. When your vertex shader writes to gl_Position, this coordinate is considered to be in clip space. This is always a four-dimensional homogenous coordinate. Upon exiting clip space, all four of the vertex's components are divided through by the w component. Obviously, after this, w becomes equal to 1.0. If w is not 1.0 before this division, the x, y, and z components are effectively scaled by the inverse of w. This allows for effects such as perspective foreshortening and projection. The result of the division is considered to be in normalized device coordinate space (NDC space). Clearly, if the resulting w component of a clip space coordinate is 1.0, then clip space and NDC space become identical.

Coordinate Transformations

As noted, coordinates may be moved from space to space by multiplying their vector representations by *transformation matrices*. Transformations are used to manipulate your model and the particular objects within it. These transformations move objects into place, rotate them, and scale them. Figure 4.8 illustrates three of the most common modeling transformations that you will apply to your objects. Figure 4.8(a) shows translation, in

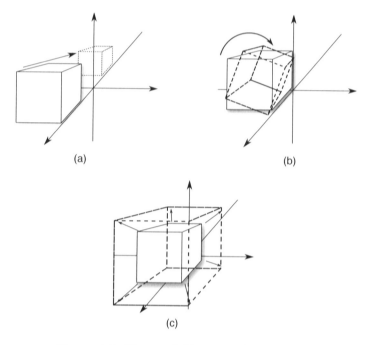

(a)

(b)

(c)

Figure 4.8: The modeling transformations

which an object is moved along a given axis. Figure 4.8(b) shows a rotation, in which an object is rotated about one of the axes. Finally, Figure 4.8(c) shows the effects of scaling, where the dimensions of the object are increased or decreased by a specified amount. Scaling can occur non-uniformly (the various dimensions can be scaled by different amounts), so you can use scaling to stretch and shrink objects.

Each of these standard transforms can be represented as a matrix by which you can multiply your vertex coordinates to calculate their positions after the transformation. The following subsections discuss the construction of those matrices, both mathematically and using the functions provided in the vmath library.

The Identity Matrix

There are a number of important types of transformation matrices you need to be familiar with before we start trying to use them. The first is the identity matrix. As shown below, the identity matrix contains all zeros except a series of ones that traverse the matrix diagonally. The 4×4 identity matrix looks like this:

$$\begin{bmatrix} 1.0 & 0.0 & 0.0 & 0.0 \\ 0.0 & 1.0 & 0.0 & 0.0 \\ 0.0 & 0.0 & 1.0 & 0.0 \\ 0.0 & 0.0 & 0.0 & 1.0 \end{bmatrix}$$

Multiplying a vertex by the identity matrix is equivalent to multiplying it by 1; it does nothing to it.

$$\begin{bmatrix} 1.0 & 0.0 & 0.0 & 0.0 \\ 0.0 & 1.0 & 0.0 & 0.0 \\ 0.0 & 0.0 & 1.0 & 0.0 \\ 0.0 & 0.0 & 0.0 & 1.0 \end{bmatrix} \begin{bmatrix} v.x \\ v.y \\ v.z \\ v.w \end{bmatrix} = \begin{bmatrix} 1 \cdot v.x + 0 \cdot v.y + 0 \cdot v.z + 0 \cdot v.w \\ 0 \cdot v.x + 1 \cdot v.y + 0 \cdot v.z + 0 \cdot v.w \\ 0 \cdot v.x + 0 \cdot v.y + 1 \cdot v.z + 0 \cdot v.w \\ 0 \cdot v.x + 0 \cdot v.y + 0 \cdot v.z + 1 \cdot v.w \end{bmatrix} = \begin{bmatrix} v.x \\ v.y \\ v.z \\ v.w \end{bmatrix}$$

Objects drawn using the identity matrix are untransformed; they are at the origin (last column), and the x, y, and z axes are defined to be the same as those in eye coordinates.

Obviously, identity matrices for 2×2 matrices, 3×3 matrices, and matrices of other dimensions exist and simply have ones in their diagonal. All identity matrices are square. There are no non-square identity matrices. Any identity matrix is its own transpose. You can make an identity matrix for OpenGL in C++ code like this:

```
// Using a raw array:
GLfloat m1[] = { 1.0f, 0.0f, 0.0f, 0.0f,    // X Column
                 0.0f, 1.0f, 0.0f, 0.0f,    // Y Column
                 0.0f, 0.0f, 1.0f, 0.0f,    // Z Column
                 0.0f, 0.0f, 0.0f, 1.0f };  // W Column

// Or using the vmath::mat4 constructor:
vmath::mat4 m2{ vmath::vec4(1.0f, 0.0f, 0.0f, 0.0f),    // X Column
                vmath::vec4(0.0f, 1.0f, 0.0f, 0.0f),    // Y Column
                vmath::vec4(0.0f, 0.0f, 1.0f, 0.0f),    // Z Column
                vmath::vec4(0.0f, 0.0f, 0.0f, 1.0f) };  // W Column
```

There are also shortcut functions in the vmath library that construct identity matrices for you. Each matrix class has a static member function that produces an identity matrix of the appropriate dimensions:

```
vmath::mat2 m2 = vmath::mat2::identity();
vmath::mat3 m3 = vmath::mat3::identity();
vmath::mat4 m4 = vmath::mat4::identity();
```

If you recall, the very first vertex shader we used in Chapter 2, "Our First OpenGL Program," was a pass-through shader. It did not transform the vertices at all, but simply passed the hard-coded data on untouched in the default coordinate system with no matrix applied to the vertices at all. We could have multiplied all of the vertices by the identity matrix, but that would have been a wasteful and pointless operation.

The Translation Matrix

A translation matrix simply moves the vertices along one or more of the three axes. Figure 4.9 shows, for example, translating a cube up the y axis by ten units.

The formulation of a 4×4 translation matrix is as follows:

$$\begin{bmatrix} 1.0 & 0.0 & 0.0 & t_x \\ 0.0 & 1.0 & 0.0 & t_y \\ 0.0 & 0.0 & 1.0 & t_z \\ 0.0 & 0.0 & 0.0 & 1.0 \end{bmatrix}$$

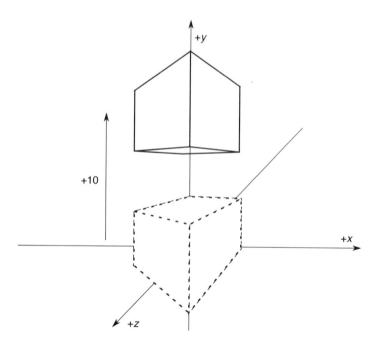

Figure 4.9: A cube translated ten units in the positive y direction

Here, t_x, t_y, and t_z represent the translation in the x, y, and z axes, respectively. Examining the structure of the translation matrix reveals one of the reasons why we need to use four-dimensional homogeneous coordinates to represent positions in 3D graphics. Consider the position vector v, whose w component is 1.0. Multiplying by a translation matrix of the form above yields

$$\begin{bmatrix} 1.0 & 0.0 & 0.0 & t_x \\ 0.0 & 1.0 & 0.0 & t_y \\ 0.0 & 0.0 & 1.0 & t_z \\ 0.0 & 0.0 & 0.0 & 1.0 \end{bmatrix} \begin{bmatrix} v_x \\ v_y \\ v_z \\ 1.0 \end{bmatrix} \begin{bmatrix} v_x + t_x \\ v_y + t_y \\ v_z + t_z \\ 1.0 \end{bmatrix}$$

As you can see, t_x, t_y, and t_z have been added to the components of v, producing translation. Had the w component of v not been 1.0, then using this matrix for translation would have resulted in t_x, t_y, and t_z being scaled by that value, affecting the output of the transformation. In practice, position vectors are almost always encoded using four components with w (the last) being 1.0, whereas direction vectors are encoded either simply using three components, or as four components with w being zero. Thus, multiplying a four-component direction vector by a translation matrix doesn't change it at all. The vmath library contains two functions that will construct a 4×4 translation matrix for you using either three separate components or a 3D vector:

```
template <typename T>
static inline Tmat4<T> translate(T x, T y, T z) { ... }

template <typename T>
static inline Tmat4<T> translate(const vecN<T,3>& v) { ... }
```

The Rotation Matrix

To rotate an object about one of the three coordinate axes, or indeed any arbitrary vector, you have to devise a rotation matrix. The form of a rotation matrix depends on the axis about which we wish to rotate. To rotate about the x axis, we use

$$R_x(\theta) = \begin{bmatrix} 1.0 & 0.0 & 0.0 & 0.0 \\ 0.0 & \cos\theta & \sin\theta & 0.0 \\ 0.0 & -\sin\theta & \cos\theta & 0.0 \\ 0.0 & 0.0 & 0.0 & 1.0 \end{bmatrix}$$

Here, $R_x(\theta)$ represents a rotation around the x axis by an angle of θ. Likewise, to rotate around the y or z axes, we can use

$$R_y(\theta) = \begin{bmatrix} \cos\theta & 0.0 & -\sin\theta & 0.0 \\ 0.0 & 1.0 & 0.0 & 0.0 \\ \sin\theta & 0.0 & \cos\theta & 0.0 \\ 0.0 & 0.0 & 0.0 & 1.0 \end{bmatrix} \quad R_z(\theta) = \begin{bmatrix} \cos\theta & -\sin\theta & 0.0 & 0.0 \\ \sin\theta & \cos\theta & 0.0 & 0.0 \\ 0.0 & 0.0 & 1.0 & 0.0 \\ 0.0 & 0.0 & 0.0 & 1.0 \end{bmatrix}$$

It is possible to multiply these three matrices together to produce a composite transform matrix and then rotate by a given amount around each of the three axes in a single matrix–vector multiplication operation. The matrix to do this is

$$R_z(\psi)\,R_y(\theta)\,R_x(\phi) = \begin{bmatrix} c_\theta c_\psi & c_\phi s_\psi + s_\phi s_\theta c_\psi & s_\phi s_\psi - c_\phi s_\theta c_\psi & 0.0 \\ -c_\theta s_\psi & c_\phi c_\psi - s_\phi s_\theta s_\psi & s_\phi c_\psi + c_\phi s_\theta s_\psi & 0.0 \\ s_\theta & -s_\phi c_\theta & c_\phi c_\theta & 0.0 \\ 0.0 & 0.0 & 0.0 & 1.0 \end{bmatrix}$$

Here, s_ψ, s_θ, and s_ϕ indicate the sine of ψ, θ, and ϕ, respectively, and c_ψ, c_θ, and c_ϕ indicate the cosine of ψ, θ, and ϕ, respectively. If this seems like a huge chunk of math, don't worry—again, a couple of vmath functions come to the rescue:

```
template <typename T>
static inline Tmat4<T> rotate(T angle_x, T angle_y, T_angle_z);
```

You can also perform a rotation around an arbitrary axis by specifying x, y, and z values for that vector. To see the axis of rotation, you can just draw a line from the origin to the point represented by (x,y,z). The vmath library also includes code to produce this matrix from an angle-axis representation:

```
template <typename T>
static inline Tmat4<T> rotate(T angle, T x, T y, T z);

template <typename T>
static inline Tmat4<T> rotate(T angle, const vecN<T,3>& axis);
```

These two overloads of the vmath::rotate function produce a rotation matrix representing a rotation of angle degrees round the axis specified by x, y, and z for the first variant, or by the vector v for the second. Here, we perform a rotation around the vector specified by the x, y, and z arguments. The angle of rotation is in the counterclockwise direction measured in degrees and specified by the argument angle. In the simplest of cases, the rotation is around only one of the coordinate system's cardinal axes (x, y, or z).

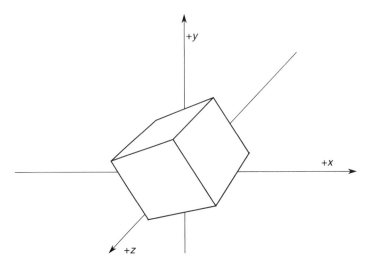

Figure 4.10: A cube rotated about an arbitrary axis

The following code, for example, creates a rotation matrix that rotates vertices 45° around an arbitrary axis specified by (1,1,1), as illustrated in Figure 4.10.

```
vmath::mat4 rotation_matrix = vmath::rotate(45.0, 1.0, 1.0, 1.0);
```

Notice in this example the use of degrees. This function internally converts degrees to radians because, unlike computers, many programmers prefer to think in terms of degrees.

Euler Angles

Euler angles are a set of three angles[3] that represent orientation in space. Each angle represents a rotation around one of three orthogonal vectors that define our frame (for example, the x, y, and z axes). As you have read, the order in which matrix transformations are performed is important, as performing some transformations (such as rotations) in different orders will produce different results. This is due to the non-commutative nature of matrix multiplication. Thus, given a set of Euler angles, should you rotate first around the x axis, then around y, and then z, or should you perform the rotations in the opposite order, or even do y first? Well, so long as you're consistent, it doesn't really matter.

3. In a three-dimensional frame.

Representation of orientations as a set of three angles has some advantages. For example, this type of representation is fairly intuitive, which is important if you plan to hook the angles up to a user interface. Another benefit is that it's pretty straightforward to interpolate angles, construct a rotation matrix at each point, and see smooth, consistent motion in your final animation. However, Euler angles also come with a serious pitfall—*gimbal lock*.

Gimbal lock occurs when a rotation by one angle reorients one of the axes to be aligned with another of the axes. Any further rotation around either of the two now-colinear axes will result in the same transformation of the model, removing a degree of freedom from the system. Thus, Euler angles are not suitable for concatenating transforms or accumulating rotations.

To avoid this, our vmath::rotate functions are able to take an angle by which to rotate and an axis about which to rotate. Of course, stacking three rotations together—one in each of the x, y, and z axes—allows you to use Euler angles if you must, but it is much preferable to use angle-axis representation for rotations, or to use *quaternions* to represent transformations and convert them to matrices as needed.

The Scaling Matrix

Our final "standard" transformation matrix is a scaling matrix. A scaling transform changes the size of an object by expanding or contracting all the vertices along the three axes by the factors specified. A scaling matrix has the following form:

$$\begin{bmatrix} s_x & 0.0 & 0.0 & 0.0 \\ 0.0 & s_y & 0.0 & 0.0 \\ 0.0 & 0.0 & s_z & 0.0 \\ 0.0 & 0.0 & 0.0 & 1.0 \end{bmatrix}$$

Here, s_x, s_y, and s_z represent the scaling factor in the x, y, and z dimensions, respectively. Creating a scaling matrix with the vmath library is similar to the method for creating a translation or rotation matrix. Three functions exist to construct this matrix for you:

```
template <typename T>
static inline Tmat4<T> scale(T x, T y, T z) { ... }

template <typename T>
static inline Tmat4<T> scale(const Tvec3<T>& v) { ... }

template <typename T>
static inline Tmat4<T> scale(T x) { ... }
```

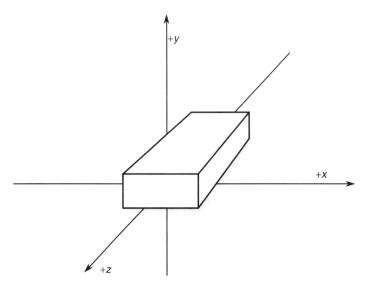

Figure 4.11: A non-uniform scaling of a cube

The first of these scales independently in the x, y, and z axes by the values given in the *x*, *y*, and *z* parameters. The second performs the same function but uses a three-component vector rather than three separate parameters to represent the scale factors. The final function scales by the same amount, *x*, in all three dimensions. Scaling does not have to be uniform, and you can use it to both stretch and squeeze objects along different directions. For example, a $10 \times 10 \times 10$ cube could be scaled by two in the *x* and *z* directions as shown in Figure 4.11.

Concatenating Transformations

As you have learned, coordinate transforms can be represented by matrices, and transformation of a vector from one space to another involves a simple matrix–vector multiplication operation. Multiplying by a sequence of matrices can apply a sequence of transformations. It is not necessary to store the intermediate vectors after each matrix–vector multiplication. Rather, it is possible and generally preferable to first multiply together all of the matrices making up a single set of related transformations to produce a single matrix representing the entire transformation sequence. This matrix can then be used to transform vectors directly from the source to the destination coordinate spaces.

Remember, order is important. When writing code with vmath or in GLSL, you should always multiply a matrix by a vector and read the sequence of transformations in reverse order. For example, consider the following code sequence:

```
vmath::mat4 translation_matrix = vmath::translate(4.0f, 10.0f, -20.0f);
vmath::mat4 rotation_matrix = vmath::rotate(45.0f,
                                     vmath::vec3(0.0f, 1.0f, 0.0f));
vmath::vec4 input_vertex = vmath::vec4(...);

vmath::vec4 transformed_vertex = translation_matrix *
                                 rotation_matrix *
                                 input_vertex;
```

This code first rotates a model 45° around the y axis (due to rotation_matrix) and then translates it by 4 units in the x axis, 10 units in the y axis, and negative 20 units in the z axis (due to translation_matrix). This places the model in a particular orientation and then moves it into position. Reading the sequence of transformations backward gives the order of operations (rotation, then translation). We could rewrite this code as follows:

```
vmath::mat4 translation_matrix = vmath::translate(4.0f, 10.0f, -20.0f);
vmath::mat4 rotation_matrix = vmath::rotate(45.0f,
                                     vmath::vec3(0.0f, 1.0f, 0.0f));
vmath::mat4 composite_matrix = translation_matrix * rotation_matrix;
vmath::vec4 input_vertex = vmath::vec4(...);

vmath::vec4 transformed_vertex = composite_matrix *
                                 input_vertex;
```

Here, composite_matrix is formed by multiplying the translation matrix by the rotation matrix, forming a composite that represents the rotation followed by the translation. This matrix can then be used to transform any number of vertices or other vectors. If you have a lot of vertices to transform, this can greatly speed up your calculation. Each vertex now takes only one matrix–vector multiplication operation rather than two.

Care must be taken here. It's too easy to read (or write) the sequence of transformations left-to-right as you would code. If we were to multiply our translation and rotation matrices together in that order, then in the first transform we would move the origin of the model; the rotation operation would then take place around that new origin, potentially sending our model flying off into space!

Quaternions

A quaternion is a four-dimensional quantity that is similar in some ways to a complex number. It has a real part and *three* imaginary parts (as compared to a complex number's one imaginary part). Just as a complex number has an imaginary part i, a quaternion has three imaginary parts, i, j, and k. Mathematically, a quaternion q is represented as

$$q = (x + yi + zj + wk)$$

The imaginary parts of the quaternion have properties similar to the imaginary part of a complex number. In particular:

$$i^2 = j^2 = k^2 = ikj = -1$$

Also, the product of any two of i, j, and k gives whichever one was not part of that product. Thus:

$$i = jk$$
$$j = ik$$
$$k = ji$$

Given this, we can see that it is possible to multiply two quaternions together as follows:

$$q_1 = (x_1 + y_1 i + z_1 j + w_1 k)$$
$$q_2 = (x_2 + y_2 i + z_2 j + w_2 k)$$
$$q_1 q_2 = x_1 x_2 - y_1 y_2 - z_1 z_2 - w_1 w_2$$
$$+ (x_1 y_2 + y_1 x_2 + z_1 w_2 - w_1 z_2)i$$
$$+ (x_1 z_2 - y_1 w_2 + z_1 x_2 + w_1 y_2)j$$
$$+ (x_1 w_2 + y_1 z_2 - z_1 y_2 + w_1 x_2)k$$

As with complex numbers, multiplication of quaternions is non-commutative. Addition and subtraction for quaternions is defined as simple vector addition and subtraction, with the terms being added or subtracted on a component-by-component basis. Other functions such as unary negation and magnitude also behave as expected for a four-component vector. Although a quaternion is a four-component entity, it is common practice to represent a quaternion as a real scalar part and a three-component imaginary vector part. Such representation is often written

$$q = (r, \vec{v})$$

Okay, great—but this isn't the dreaded math chapter, right? This is about computer graphics, OpenGL, and all that fun stuff. Well, here's where quaternions get really useful. Recall that our rotation functions take an angle and an axis to rotate around. Well, we can represent those two quantities as a quaternion by stuffing the angle in the real part and the axis in the vector part, yielding a quaternion that represents a rotation around any axis.

A sequence of rotations can be represented by a series of quaternions multiplied together, producing a single resulting quaternion that encodes the whole lot in one go. While it's possible to make a bunch of matrices that represent rotation around the various Cartesian axes and then multiply them all together, that method is susceptible to gimbal lock. If you do the same thing with a sequence of quaternions, gimbal lock cannot occur. For your coding pleasure, vmath includes the vmath::quaternion class that implements most of the functionality described here.

The Model–View Transform

In a simple OpenGL application, one of the most common transformations is to take a model from model space to view space so as to render it. In effect, we move the model first into world space (i.e., place it relative to the world's origin) and then from there into view space (placing it relative to the viewer). This process establishes the vantage point of the scene. By default, the point of observation in a perspective projection is at the origin (0,0,0) looking down the negative z axis (*into* the monitor or screen). This point of observation is moved relative to the eye coordinate system to provide a specific vantage point. When the point of observation is located at the origin, as in a perspective projection, objects drawn with positive z values are behind the observer. In an orthographic projection, however, the viewer is assumed to be infinitely far away on the positive z axis and can see everything within the viewing volume.

Because this transform takes vertices from model space (which is also sometimes known as object space) directly into view space and effectively bypasses world space, it is often referred to as the model–view transform and the matrix that encodes this transformation is known as the model–view matrix.

The model transform essentially places objects into world space. Each object is likely to have its own model transform, which will generally consist of a sequence of scale, rotation, and translation operations. The result of multiplying the positions of vertices in model space by the model transform is a set of positions in world space. This transformation is sometimes called the model–world transform.

The view transformation allows you to place the point of observation anywhere you want and look in any direction. Determining the viewing transformation is like placing and pointing a camera at the scene. In the grand scheme of things, you must apply the viewing transformation before any other modeling transformations. The reason is that it appears to move the current working coordinate system with respect to the eye coordinate system. All subsequent transformations then occur based on the newly modified coordinate system. The transform that moves coordinates from world space to view space is sometimes called the world–view transform.

Concatenating the model–world and world–view transform matrices by multiplying them together yields the model–view matrix (i.e., the matrix that takes coordinates from model to view space). There are some advantages to doing this. First, there are likely to be many models in your scene and many vertices in each model. Using a single composite transform to move the model into view space is more efficient than moving it first into world space and then into view space as explained earlier. The second advantage has more to do with the numerical accuracy of single-precision floating-point numbers: The world could be huge and computation performed in world space will have different precision depending on how far the vertices are from the world origin. However, if you perform the same calculations in view space, then precision is dependent on how far vertices are *from the viewer*, which is probably what you want—a great deal of precision is applied to objects that are close to the viewer at the expense of precision very far from the viewer.

The Lookat Matrix

If you have a vantage point at a known location and a thing you want to look at, you will wish to place your your virtual camera at that location and then point it in the right direction. To orient the camera correctly, you also need to know which way is up; otherwise, the camera could spin around its forward axis and, even though it would still be technically be pointing in the right direction, this is almost certainly not what you want. So, given an origin, a point of interest, and a direction that we consider to be up, we want to construct a sequence of transforms, ideally baked together into a single matrix, that will represent a rotation that will point a camera in the correct direction and a translation that will move the origin to the center of the camera. This matrix is known as a *lookat matrix* and can be constructed using only the math covered in this chapter so far.

First, we know that subtracting two positions gives us a vector which would move a point from the first position to the second and that normalizing that vector result gives us its directional. So, if we take the coordinates of a point of interest, subtract from that the position of our camera, and then normalize the resulting vector, we have a new vector that represents the direction of view from the camera to the point of interest. We call this the *forward* vector.

Next, we know that if we take the cross product of two vectors, we will receive a third vector that is orthogonal (at a right angle) to both input vectors. Well, we have two vectors—the forward vector we just calculated, and the *up* vector, which represents the direction we consider to be upward. Taking the cross product of those two vectors results in a third vector that is orthogonal to each of them and points sideways with respect to our camera. We call this the *sideways* vector. However, the up and forward vectors are not necessarily orthogonal to each other and we need a third orthogonal vector to construct a rotation matrix. To obtain this vector, we can simply apply the same process again—taking the cross product of the forward vector and our sideways vector to produce a third that is orthogonal to both and that represents *up* with respect to the camera.

These three vectors are of unit length and are all orthogonal to one another, so they form a set of orthonormal basis vectors and represent our view frame. Given these three vectors, we can construct a rotation matrix that will take a point in the standard Cartesian basis and move it into the basis of our camera. In the following math, e is the eye (or camera) position, p is the point of interest, and u is the up vector. Here we go.

First, construct our forward vector, f:

$$f = \frac{p - e}{\|p - e\|}$$

Next, take the cross product of f and u to construct a side vector s:

$$s = f \times u$$

Now, construct a new up vector u' in our camera's reference:

$$u' = s \times f$$

Finally, construct a rotation matrix representing a reorientation into our newly constructed orthonormal basis:

$$R = \begin{bmatrix} s.x & u'.x & f.x & 0.0 \\ s.y & u'.y & f.y & 0.0 \\ s.z & u'.z & f.z & 0.0 \\ 0.0 & 0.0 & 0.0 & 1.0 \end{bmatrix}$$

Right, we're not quite finished. To transform objects into the camera's frame, not only do we need to orient everything correctly, but we also need to move the origin to the position of the camera. We do this by simply translating the resulting vectors by the negative of the camera's position. Remember how a translation matrix is constructed simply by placing the offset into that rightmost column of the matrix? Well, we can do that here, too:

$$T = \begin{bmatrix} s.x & u'.x & f.x & -e.x \\ s.y & u'.y & f.y & -e.y \\ s.z & u'.z & y.z & -e.z \\ 0.0 & 0.0 & 0.0 & 1.0 \end{bmatrix}$$

Finally, we have our lookat matrix, T.

If this seems like a lot of steps to you, you're in luck. There's a function in the vmath library that will construct the matrix for you:

```
template <typename T>
static inline Tmat4<T> lookat(const vecN<T,3>& eye,
                              const vecN<T,3>& center,
                              const vecN<T,3>& up) { ... }
```

The matrix produced by the vmath::lookat function can be used as the basis for your camera matrix—the matrix that represents the position and orientation of your camera. In other words, this can be your view matrix.

Projection Transformations

The projection transformation is applied to your vertices after the model–view transformation. This projection actually defines the viewing volume and establishes clipping planes. The clipping planes are plane equations in 3D space that OpenGL uses to determine whether geometry can be seen by the viewer. More specifically, the projection transformation specifies how a finished scene (after all the modeling is done) is projected to the final image on the screen. You learn more about two types of projections—orthographic and perspective.

In an orthographic, or parallel, projection, all the polygons are drawn on screen with exactly the relative dimensions specified. Lines and polygons are mapped directly to the 2D screen using parallel lines, which means no matter how far away something is, it is still drawn the same size, just flattened against the screen. This type of projection is typically used for rendering two-dimensional images such as the front, top, and side elevations in blueprints or two-dimensional graphics such as text or on-screen menus.

A perspective projection shows scenes more as they appear in real life instead of as a blueprint. The hallmark of perspective projections is foreshortening, which makes distant objects appear smaller than nearby objects of the same size. Lines in 3D space that might be parallel do not always appear parallel to the viewer. With a railroad track, for instance, the rails are parallel, but using perspective projection, they appear to converge at some distant point. The benefit of perspective projection is that you don't have to figure out where lines converge or how much smaller distant objects are. All you need to do is specify the scene using the model–view transformations and then apply the perspective projection matrix. Linear algebra works all the magic for you.

Figure 4.12 compares orthographic and perspective projections on two different scenes. As you can see in the orthographic projection shown on the left, the cubes do not appear to change in size as they move farther from the viewer. However, in the perspective projection shown on the right, the cubes get smaller and smaller as they get farther from the viewer.

Orthographic projections are used most often for 2D drawing purposes where you want an exact correspondence between pixels and drawing units. You might use them for a schematic layout, text, or perhaps a 2D graphing application. You also can use an orthographic projection for 3D renderings when the depth of the rendering has a very small depth in comparison to the distance from the viewpoint. Perspective projections are used for rendering scenes that contain wide-open spaces or objects that need to have foreshortening applied. For the most part, perspective projections are typical for 3D graphics. In fact, looking at a 3D object with an orthographic projection can be somewhat unsettling.

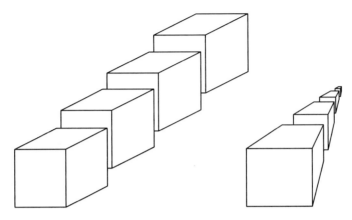

Figure 4.12: A side-by-side example of an orthographic versus perspective projection

Perspective Matrices

Once your vertices are in view space, we need to get them into clip space, which we do by applying our projection matrix, which may represent a perspective or orthographic projection (or some other projection). A commonly used perspective matrix is a *frustum matrix*. A frustum matrix is a projection matrix that produces a perspective projection such that clip space takes the shape of a rectangular frustum, which is a truncated rectangular pyramid. Its parameters are the distance to the near and far planes and the world-space coordinate of the left, right, top, and bottom clipping planes. A frustrum matrix takes the following form:

$$\begin{bmatrix} \frac{2 \cdot near}{right-left} & 0.0 & \frac{right+left}{right-left} & 0.0 \\ 0.0 & \frac{2 \cdot near}{top-bottom} & \frac{top+bottom}{top-bottom} & 0.0 \\ 0.0 & 0.0 & \frac{near+far}{near-far} & \frac{2 \cdot near \cdot far}{near-far} \\ 0.0 & 0.0 & -1.0 & 0.0 \end{bmatrix}$$

The vmath function to do this is vmath::frustum:

```
static inline mat4 frustum(float left,
                           float right,
                           float bottom,
                           float top,
                           float n,
                           float f) { ... }
```

Another common method for constructing a perspective matrix is to directly specify a field of view as an angle (in degrees, perhaps), an aspect ratio (generally derived by dividing the window's width by its height), and the view-space positions of the near and far planes. This is somewhat simpler to specify, and produces only symmetric frustra. However, this is almost always what you'll want. The vmath function to do this is vmath::perspective:

```
static inline mat4 perspective(float fovy /* in degrees */,
                               float aspect,
                               float n,
                               float f) { ... }
```

Orthographic Matrices

If you wish to use an orthographic projection for your scene, then you can construct a (somewhat simpler) orthographic projection matrix. An orthographic projection matrix is simply a scaling matrix that linearly maps view-space coordinates into clip-space coordinates. The parameters to construct the orthographic projection matrix are the left, right, top, and bottom coordinates in view space of the bounds of the scene, and the position of the near and far planes. The form of the matrix is

$$
\begin{bmatrix}
\frac{2}{right-left} & 0.0 & 0.0 & \frac{left+right}{left-right} \\
0.0 & \frac{2}{top-bottom} & 0.0 & \frac{bottom+top}{bottom-top} \\
0.0 & 0.0 & \frac{2}{near-far} & \frac{near+far}{far-near} \\
0.0 & 0.0 & 0.0 & 1.0
\end{bmatrix}
$$

Again, there's a vmath function to construct this matrix for you, vmath::ortho:

```
static inline mat4 ortho(float left,
                         float right,
                         float bottom,
                         float top,
                         float near,
                         float far) { ... }
```

Interpolation, Lines, Curves, and Splines

Interpolation is a term used to describe the process of finding values that lie between a set of known points. Consider the equation of the line passing through points A and B:

$$
P = A + t\vec{D}
$$

where P is any point on the line and $\vec{D}$ is the vector from A to B:

$$\vec{D} = (B - A)$$

We can therefore write this equation as

$$P = A + t\,(B - A) \quad \text{or}$$
$$P = (1 - t)\,A + tB$$

It is easy to see that when t is 0, P is equal to A; and when t is 1, P is equal to $A + B - A$, which is simply B. Such a line is shown in Figure 4.13.

If t lies between 0.0 and 1.0, then P will end up somewhere between A and B. Values of t outside this range will push P off the ends of the line. You should be able to see that by smoothly varying t, we can move point P from A to B and back. This is known as *linear interpolation*. The values of A and B (and therefore P) can have any number of dimensions. For example, they could be scalar values; two-dimensional values such as points on a graph; three-dimensional values such as coordinates in 3D space, colors, and so on; or even higher-dimension quantities such as matrices, arrays, or even whole images. In many cases, linear interpolation doesn't make much sense (for example, linearly interpolating between two matrices generally doesn't produce a meaningful result), but angles, positions, and other coordinates can normally be interpolated safely.

Linear interpolation is such a common operation in graphics that GLSL includes a built-in function specifically for this purpose, `mix`:

```
vec4 mix(vec4 A, vec4 B, float t);
```

The `mix` function comes in several versions taking different dimensionalities of vectors or scalars as the A and B inputs and taking scalars or matching vectors for t.

Figure 4.13: Finding a point on a line

Curves

If moving everything along a straight line between two points is all we wanted to do, then this would be enough. However, in the real world, objects move in smooth curves and accelerate and decelerate smoothly. A curve can be represented by three or more *control points*. For most curves, there are more than three control points, two of which form the endpoints; the others define the shape of the curve. Consider the simple curve shown in Figure 4.14.

The curve shown in Figure 4.14 has three control points, A, B, and C. A and C are the endpoints of the curve and B defines the shape of the curve. If we join points A and B with one line and points B and C together with another line, then we can interpolate along the two lines using a simple linear interpolation to find a new pair of points, D and E. Now, given these two points, we can join them with yet another line and interpolate along it to find a new point, P. As we vary our interpolation parameter, t,

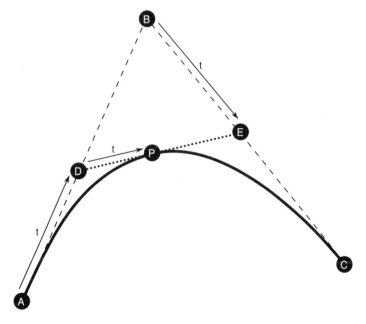

Figure 4.14: A simple Bézier curve

point P will move in a smooth curved path from A to D. Expressed mathematically, this is

$$D = A + t(B - A)$$
$$E = B + t(C - B)$$

$$P = D + t(E - D)$$

Substituting for D and E and doing a little crunching, we come up with the following:

$$P = A + t(B - A) + t((B + (t(C - B))) - (A + t(B - A))))$$
$$P = A + t(B - A) + tB + t^2(C - B) - tA - t^2(B - A)$$
$$P = A + t(B - A + B - A) + t^2(C - B - B + A)$$
$$P = A + 2t(B - A) + t^2(C - 2B + A)$$

You should recognize this as a *quadratic* equation in t. The curve that it describes is known as a *quadratic Bézier curve*. We can actually implement this very easily in GLSL using the `mix` function, as all we're doing is linearly interpolating (mixing) the results of two previous interpolations.

```
vec4 quadratic_bezier(vec4 A, vec4 B, vec4 C, float t)
{
    vec4 D = mix(A, B, t);      // D = A + t(B - A)
    vec4 E = mix(B, C, t);      // E = B + t(C - B)

    vec4 P = mix(D, E, t);      // P = D + t(E - D)

    return P;
}
```

By adding a fourth control point as shown in Figure 4.15, we can increase the order by 1 and produce a *cubic* Bézier curve.

We now have four control points, A, B, C, and D. The process for constructing the curve is similar to that for the quadratic Bézier curve. We form a first line from A to B, a second line from B to C, and a third line from C to D. Interpolating along each of the three lines gives rise to three new points, E, F, and G. Using these three points, we form two more lines, one from E to F and another from F to G, interpolating along which gives rise to points H and I, between which we can interpolate to find our final point, P. Therefore, we have

$$E = A + t(B - A)$$
$$F = B + t(C - B)$$
$$G = C + t(D - C)$$

$$H = E + t(F - E)$$
$$I = F + t(G - F)$$
$$P = H + t(I - H)$$

If you think these equations look familiar, you're right: Our points E, F, and G form a quadratic Bézier curve that we use to interpolate to our final point P. If we were to substitute the equations for E, F, and G into the equations for H and I, then substitute *those* into the equation for P, and crunch through the expansions, we would be left with a cubic equation with terms in t^3—hence the name *cubic Bézier curve*. Again, we can implement this simply and efficiently in terms of linear interpolations in GLSL using the mix function:

```
vec4 cubic_bezier(vec4 A, vec4 B, vec4 C, vec4 D, float t)
{
    vec4 E = mix(A, B, t);      // E = A + t(B - A)
    vec4 F = mix(B, C, t);      // F = B + t(C - B)
    vec4 G = mix(C, D, t);      // G = C + t(D - C)

    vec4 H = mix(E, F, t);      // H = E + t(F - E)
    vec4 I = mix(F, G, t);      // I = F + t(G - F)

    vec4 P = mix(H, I, t);      // P = H + t(I - H)

    return P;
}
```

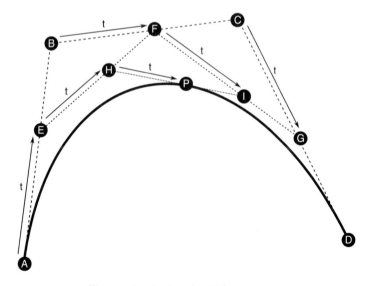

Figure 4.15: A cubic Bézier curve

Just as the structure of the equations for a cubic Bézier curve "includes" the equations for a quadratic curve, so, too, does the code to implement them. In fact, we can layer these curves on top of each other, using the code for one to build the next.

```
vec4 cubic_bezier(vec4 A, vec4 B, vec4 C, vec4 D, float t)
{
    vec4 E = mix(A, B, t);      // E = A + t(B - A)
    vec4 F = mix(B, C, t);      // F = B + t(C - B)
    vec4 G = mix(C, D, t);      // G = C + t(D - C)

    return quadratic_bezier(E, F, G, t);
}
```

Now that we see this pattern, we can take it further and produce even higher-order curves. For example, a *quintic* Bézier curve (one with five control points) can be implemented as

```
vec4 quintic_bezier(vec4 A, vec4 B, vec4 C, vec4 D, vec4 E, float t)
{
    vec4 F = mix(A, B, t);      // F = A + t(B - A)
    vec4 G = mix(B, C, t);      // G = B + t(C - B)
    vec4 H = mix(C, D, t);      // H = C + t(D - C)
    vec4 I = mix(D, E, t);      // I = D + t(E - D)

    return cubic_bezier(F, G, H, I, t);
}
```

This layering could theoretically be applied over and over for any number of control points. However, in practice, curves with more than four control points are not commonly used. Rather, we use *splines*.

Splines

A spline is effectively a long curve made up of several smaller curves (such as Béziers) that locally define their shape. At least the control points representing the ends of the curves are shared between segments,[4] and often one or more of the interior control points are either shared or linked in some way between adjacent segments. Any number of curves can be joined together in this way, allowing arbitrarily long paths to be formed. Take a look at the curve shown in Figure 4.16.

---

4. This is what sticks the curves together to form a spline. These control points are known as *welds* and the control points in between are referred to as *knots*.

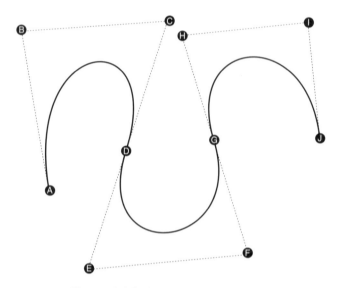

Figure 4.16: A cubic Bézier spline

In Figure 4.16, the curve is defined by ten control points, A through J, which form three cubic Bézier curves. The first is defined by A, B, C, and D, the second shares D and further uses E, F, and G, and the third shares G and adds H, I, and J. This type of spline is known as a *cubic Bézier spline* because it is constructed from a sequence of cubic Bézier curves. This is also known as a *cubic B-spline*—a term that may be familiar to anyone who has read much about graphics in the past.

To interpolate point P along the spline, we simply divide it into three regions, allowing t to range from 0.0 to 3.0. Between 0.0 and 1.0, we interpolate along the first curve, moving from A to D. Between 1.0 and 2.0, we interpolate along the second curve, moving from D to G. When t is between 2.0 and 3.0, we interpolate along the final curve between G and J. Thus, the integer part of t determines the curve segment along which we are interpolating and the fractional part of t is used to interpolate along that segment. Of course, we can scale t as we wish. For example, if we take a value between 0.0 and 1.0 and multiply it by the number of segments in the curve, we can continue to use our original range of values for t regardless of the number of control points in a curve.

The following code will interpolate a vector along a cubic Bézier spline with ten control points (and thus three segments):

```
vec4 cubic_bspline_10(vec4 CP[10], float t)
{
    float f = t * 3.0;
    int i = int(floor(f));
    float s = fract(t);

    if (t <= 0.0)
        return CP[0];

    if (t >= 1.0)
        return CP[9];

    vec4 A = CP[i * 3];
    vec4 B = CP[i * 3 + 1];
    vec4 C = CP[i * 3 + 2];
    vec4 D = CP[i * 3 + 3];

    return cubic_bezier(A, B, C, D, s);
}
```

If we use a spline to determine the position or orientation of an object, we will find that we must be very careful about our choice of control point locations to keep motion smooth and fluid. The rate of change in the value of our interpolated point P (i.e., its velocity) is the differential of the equation of the curve with respect to t. If this function is discontinuous, then P will suddenly change direction and our objects will appear to jump around. Furthermore, the rate of change of P's velocity (its acceleration) is the second-order derivative of the spline equation with respect to t. If the acceleration is not smooth, then P will appear to suddenly speed up or slow down.

A function that has a continuous first derivative is known as C^1 continuous; similarly, a curve that has a continuous second derivative is known as C^2 continuous. Bézier curve segments are both C^1 and C^2 continuous, but to ensure that we maintain continuity over the welds of a spline, we need to ensure that each segment starts off where the previous ended in terms of position, direction of movement, and rate of change. A rate of travel in a particular direction is simply a velocity. Thus, rather than assigning arbitrary control points to our spline, we can assign a velocity at each weld. If the same velocity of the curve at each weld is used in the computation of the curve segments on either side of that weld, then we will have a spline function that is both C^1 and C^2 continuous.

This should make sense if you take another look at Figure 4.16—there are no kinks and the curve is nice and smooth through the welds (points D and G). Now look at the control points on either side of the welds. For example, take points C and E, which surround D. C and E form a straight line and D lies right in the middle of it. In fact, we can call the line segment from D to E the velocity at D, or $\vec{V_D}$. Given the position of point D (the weld) and the velocity of the curve $\vec{V_D}$ at D, then C and E can be calculated as

$$C = D - \vec{V_D}$$
$$E = D + \vec{V_D}$$

Likewise, if $\vec{V_A}$ represents the velocity at A, B can be calculated as

$$B = A + \vec{V_A}$$

Thus, you should be able to see that given the positions and velocities at the welds of a cubic B-spline, we can dispense with all of the other control points and compute them on the fly as we evaluate each of the control points. A cubic B-spline represented this way (as a set of weld positions and velocities) is known as a *cubic Hermite spline*, or sometimes simply a cspline. The cspline is an extremely useful tool for producing smooth and natural animations.

Summary

In this chapter, you learned some mathematical concepts crucial to using OpenGL for the creation of 3D scenes. Even if you can't juggle matrices in your head, you now know what matrices are and how they are used to perform the various transformations. You also learned how to construct and manipulate the matrices that represent the viewer and viewport properties. You should now understand how to place your objects in the scene and determine how they are viewed on screen. This chapter also introduced the powerful concept of a frame of reference, and you saw how easy it is to manipulate frames and convert them into transformations.

Finally, we introduced the use of the vmath library that accompanies this book. This library is written entirely in portable C++ and provides a handy toolkit of miscellaneous math and helper routines that can be used along with OpenGL.

Surprisingly, we did not cover a single new OpenGL function call in this entire chapter. Yes, this was the math chapter, and you might not have even noticed if you think math is just about formulas and calculations. Vectors and matrices, and the application thereof, are absolutely crucial to being able to use OpenGL to render 3D objects and worlds. However, it's important to note that OpenGL doesn't impose any particular math convention upon you and does not itself provide any math functionality. If you use a different 3D math library, or even roll your own, you will still find yourself following the patterns laid out in this chapter for manipulating your geometry and 3D worlds. Now, go ahead and start making some!

Chapter 5

Data

- How to create buffers and textures that you can use to store data that your program can access.

- How to get OpenGL to supply the values of your vertex attributes automatically.

- How to access textures and buffers from your shaders.

In the examples you've seen so far, either we have used hard-coded data directly in our shaders, or we have passed values to shaders one at a time. While sufficient to demonstrate the configuration of the OpenGL pipeline, this is hardly representative of modern graphics programming. Recent graphics processors are designed as streaming processors that consume and produce huge amounts of data. Passing a few values to OpenGL at a time is extremely inefficient. To allow data to be stored and accessed by OpenGL, we include two main forms of data storage—buffers and textures. In this chapter, we first introduce buffers, which are linear blocks of untyped data and can be seen as generic memory allocations. Next, we introduce textures, which are normally used to store multidimensional data, such as images or other data types.

Buffers

In OpenGL, buffers are linear allocations of memory that can be used for a number of purposes. They are represented by *names*, which are essentially opaque handles that OpenGL uses to identify them. Before you can start using buffers, you have to ask OpenGL to reserve some names for you and then use them to allocate memory and put data into that memory. The memory allocated for a buffer object is called its *data store*. The data store of the buffer is where OpenGL stores its data. You can put data into the buffer using OpenGL commands, or you can *map* the buffer object, which means that you can get a pointer that your application can use to write directly into (or read directly out of) the buffer.

Once you have the name of a buffer, you can attach it to the OpenGL context by *binding* it to a buffer binding point. Binding points are sometimes referred to as *targets*; these terms may be used interchangeably.[1] There are a large number of buffer binding points in OpenGL and each has a different use, although the buffers you bind to them are the same. For example, you can use the contents of a buffer to automatically supply the inputs of a vertex shader, to store the values of variables that will be used by your shaders, or as a place for shaders to store the data they produce. You can even use the same buffer for multiple purposes at the same time.

Creating Buffers and Allocating Memory

Before you can ask OpenGL to allocate memory, you need to create a buffer object to represent that allocation. Like most objects in OpenGL, buffer objects are represented by a GLuint variable, which is generally called its *name*. One or more buffer objects can be created using the **glCreateBuffers()** function, whose prototype is

```
void glCreateBuffers(GLsizei n, GLuint* buffers);
```

The first parameter to **glCreateBuffers()**, n, is the number of buffer objects to create. The second parameter, buffers, is the address of the variable or variables that will be used to store the names of the buffer objects. If you need to create only one buffer object, set n to 1 and set buffers to the address of a single GLuint variable. If you need to create more than one buffer at a time, simply set n to that number and point

---

1. It's not technically correct to conflate *target* and *binding point*, because a single target may have multiple binding points. However, for most use cases, it is well understood what is meant.

buffers to the beginning of an array of at least n GLuint variables. OpenGL will just trust that the array is big enough and will write that many buffer names to the pointer that you specify.

Each of the names you get back from **glCreateBuffers()** represents a single buffer object. You can bind the buffer objects to the current OpenGL context by calling **glBindBuffer()**, the prototype of which is

```
void glBindBuffer(GLenum target, GLuint buffer);
```

Before you can actually use the buffer objects, you need to allocate their *data stores*, which is another term for the memory represented by the buffer object. The functions that are used to allocate memory using a buffer object are **glBufferStorage()** and **glNamedBufferStorage()**. Their prototypes are

```
void glBufferStorage(GLenum target,
                     GLsizeiptr size,
                     const void* data,
                     GLbitfield flags);
void glNamedBufferStorage(GLuint buffer,
                          GLsizeiptr size,
                          const void* data,
                          GLbtifield flags);
```

The first function affects the buffer object bound to the binding point specified by target; the second function directly affects the buffer specified by buffer. The remainder of the parameters serve the same purpose in both functions. The size parameter specifies how big the storage region is to be, in bytes. The data parameter is used to pass a pointer to any data that you want to initialize the buffer with. If this is NULL, then the storage associated with the buffer object will at first be uninitialized. The final parameter, flags, is used to tell OpenGL how you're planning to use the buffer object.

Once storage has been allocated for a buffer object using either **glBufferStorage()** or **glNamedBufferStorage()**, it cannot be reallocated or respecified, but is considered *immutable*. To be clear, the contents of the buffer object's data store can be changed, but its size or usage flags may not. If you need to resize a buffer, you need to delete it, create a new one, and set up new storage for that.

The most interesting parameter to these two functions is the flags parameter. This should give OpenGL enough information to allocate memory suitable for your intended purpose and allow it to make an informed decision about the storage requirements of the buffer. flags is a

Table 5.1: Buffer Storage Flags

Flag	Description
GL_DYNAMIC_STORAGE_BIT	Buffer contents can be updated directly.
GL_MAP_READ_BIT	Buffer data store will be mapped for reading.
GL_MAP_WRITE_BIT	Buffer data store will be mapped for writing.
GL_MAP_PERSISTENT_BIT	Buffer data store can be mapped persistently.
GL_MAP_COHERENT_BIT	Buffer maps are to be coherent.
GL_CLIENT_STORAGE_BIT	If all other conditions can be met, prefer storage local to the client (CPU) rather than to the server (GPU).

GLbitfield type, which means that it's a combination of one or more bits. The flags that you can set are shown in Table 5.1.

The flags listed in Table 5.1 may seem a little terse and probably deserve more explanation. In particular, the absence of certain flags can mean something to OpenGL, some flags may be used only in combination with others, and the specification of these flags can have an effect on what you're allowed to do with the buffer later. We'll provide a brief explanation of each of these flags here and then dive deeper into some of their meanings as we cover further functionality.

First, the GL_DYNAMIC_STORAGE_BIT flag is used to tell OpenGL that you mean to update the contents of the buffer directly—perhaps once for every time that you use the data. If this flag is not set, OpenGL will assume that you're not likely to need to change the contents of the buffer and might put the data somewhere that is less accessible. If you don't set this bit, you won't be able to use commands like **glBufferSubData()** to update the buffer content, although you will be able to write into it directly from the GPU using other OpenGL commands.

The mapping flags GL_MAP_READ_BIT, GL_MAP_WRITE_BIT, GL_MAP_PERSISTENT_BIT, and GL_MAP_COHERENT_BIT tell OpenGL if and how you're planning to map the buffer's data store. Mapping is the process of getting a pointer that you can use from your application that represents the underlying data store of the buffer. For example, you may map the buffer for read or write access only if you specify the GL_MAP_READ_BIT or GL_MAP_WRITE_BIT flags, respectively. Of course, you can specify both if you wish to map the buffer for both reading and writing.

If you specify GL_MAP_PERSISTENT_BIT, then this flag tells OpenGL that you wish to map the buffer and then *leave it mapped* while you call other drawing comands. If you don't set this bit, then OpenGL requires that you don't have the buffers mapped while you're using it from drawing commands. Supporting *persistent maps* might come at the expense of some performance, so it's best not to set this bit unless you really need to. The final bit, GL_MAP_COHERENT_BIT, goes further and tells OpenGL that you want to be able to share data quite tightly with the GPU. If you don't set this bit, you need to tell OpenGL when you've written data into the buffer, even if you don't unmap it.

```
// The type used for names in OpenGL is GLuint
GLuint buffer;

// Create a buffer
glCreateBuffers(1, &buffer);

// Specify the data store parameters for the buffer
glNamedBufferStorage(
                buffer,              // Name of the buffer
                1024 * 1024,         // 1 MiB of space
                NULL,                // No initial data
                GL_MAP_WRITE_BIT);   // Allow map for writing

// Now bind it to the context using the GL_ARRAY_BUFFER binding point
glBindBuffer(GL_ARRAY_BUFFER, buffer);
```

Listing 5.1: Creating and initializing a buffer

After the code in Listing 5.1 has executed, buffer contains the name of a buffer object that has been initialized to represent one megabyte of storage for whatever data we choose. Using the GL_ARRAY_BUFFER target to refer to the buffer object suggests to OpenGL that we're planning to use this buffer to store vertex data, but we'll still be able to take that buffer and bind it to some other target later. There are a handful of ways to get data into the buffer object. You may have noticed the NULL pointer that we pass as the third argument to **glNamedBufferStorage()** in Listing 5.1. Had we instead supplied a pointer to some data, that data would have been used to initialize the buffer object. Using this pointer, however, allows us to set only the initial data to be stored in the buffer.

Another way get data into a buffer is to give the buffer to OpenGL and tell it to copy data there. This allows you to dynamically update the content of a buffer after it has already been initialized. To do this, we call either

glBufferSubData() or **glNamedBufferSubData()**, passing the size of the data
we want to put into the buffer, the offset in the buffer where we want it to
go, and a pointer to the data in memory that should be put into the buffer.
glBufferSubData() and **glNamedBufferSubData()** are declared as follows:

```
void glBufferSubData(GLenum target,
                     GLintptr offset,
                     GLsizeiptr size,
                     const GLvoid * data);
void glNamedBufferSubData(GLuint buffer,
                          GLintptr offset,
                          GLsizeiptr size,
                          const void * data);
```

To update a buffer object using **glBufferSubData()**, you must have told
OpenGL that you want to put data into it that way. To do this, include
GL_DYNAMIC_STORAGE_BIT in the flags parameter to **glBufferStorage()** or
glNamedBufferStorage(). Like **glBufferStorage()** and
glNamedBufferStorage(), **glBufferSubData()** affects the buffer bound to
the binding point specified by target, and **glNamedBufferSubData()** affects
the buffer object specified by buffer. Listing 5.2 shows how we can put
the data originally used in Listing 3.1 into a buffer object, which is the first
step in automatically feeding a vertex shader with data.

```
// This is the data that we will place into the buffer object
static const float data[] =
{
     0.25, -0.25, 0.5, 1.0,
    -0.25, -0.25, 0.5, 1.0,
     0.25,  0.25, 0.5, 1.0
};

// Put the data into the buffer at offset zero
glBufferSubData(GL_ARRAY_BUFFER, 0, sizeof(data), data);
```

Listing 5.2: Updating the content of a buffer with **glBufferSubData()**

Another method for getting data into a buffer object is to ask OpenGL for
a pointer to the memory that the buffer object represents and then copy
the data there yourself. This is known as *mapping* the buffer. Listing 5.3
shows how to do this using the **glMapNamedBuffer()** function.

```
// This is the data that we will place into the buffer object
static const float data[] =
{
     0.25, -0.25, 0.5, 1.0,
    -0.25, -0.25, 0.5, 1.0,
     0.25,  0.25, 0.5, 1.0
};
```

```
// Get a pointer to the buffer's data store
void * ptr = glMapNamedBuffer(buffer, GL_WRITE_ONLY);

// Copy our data into it...
memcpy(ptr, data, sizeof(data));

// Tell OpenGL that we're done with the pointer
glUnmapNamedBuffer(GL_ARRAY_BUFFER);
```

Listing 5.3: Mapping a buffer's data store with **glMapNamedBuffer()**

As with many other buffer functions in OpenGL, there are two versions—one that affects the buffer bound to one of the targets of the current context, and one that operates directly on a buffer whose name you specify. Their prototypes are

```
void *glMapBuffer(GLenum target,
                  GLenum usage);
void *glMapNamedBuffer(GLuint buffer,
                       GLenum usage);
```

To unmap the buffer, we call either **glUnmapBuffer()** or **glUnmapNamedBuffer()**, as shown in Listing 5.3. Their prototypes are

```
void glUnmapBuffer(GLenum target);
void glUnmapNamedBuffer(GLuint buffer);
```

Mapping a buffer is useful if you don't have all the data handy when you call the function. For example, you might be about to generate the data, or to read it from a file. If you wanted to use **glBufferSubData()** (or the initial pointer passed to **glBufferData()**), you'd have to generate or read the data into temporary memory and then get OpenGL to make another copy of the data into the buffer object. If you map a buffer, you can simply read the contents of the file directly into the mapped buffer. When you unmap it, if OpenGL can avoid making a copy of the data, it will. Regardless of whether we used **glBufferSubData()** or **glMapBuffer()** and an explicit copy to get data into our buffer object, it now contains a copy of data[] and we can use it as a source of data to feed our vertex shader.

The **glMapBuffer()** and **glMapNamedBuffer()** functions can sometimes be a little heavy handed. They map the entire buffer, and do not provide any information about the type of mapping operation to be performed besides the usage parameter. Even that serves only as a hint. A more surgical

approach can be taken by calling either **glMapBufferRange()** or
glMapNamedBufferRange(), whose prototypes are

```
void *glMapBufferRange(GLenum target,
                       GLintptr offset,
                       GLsizeiptr length,
                       GLbitfield access);

void *glMapNamedBufferRange(GLuint buffer,
                            GLintptr offset,
                            GLsizeiptr length,
                            GLbitfield access);
```

As with the **glMapBuffer()** and **glMapNamedBuffer()** functions, there are
two versions of these functions—one that affects a currently bound buffer
and one that affects a directly specified buffer object. These functions,
rather than mapping the entire buffer object, map only a specific range of
the buffer object. This range is given using the offset and length
parameters. The parameter contains flags that tell OpenGL how the
mapping should be performed. These flags can be a combination of any of
the bits listed in Table 5.2.

Table 5.2: Buffer-Mapping Flags

Flag	Description
GL_MAP_READ_BIT	Buffer data store will be mapped for reading.
GL_MAP_WRITE_BIT	Buffer data store will be mapped for writing.
GL_MAP_PERSISTENT_BIT	Buffer data store can be mapped persistently.
GL_MAP_COHERENT_BIT	Buffer maps are to be coherent.
GL_MAP_INVALIDATE_RANGE_BIT	Tells OpenGL that you no longer care about the data in the specified range.
GL_MAP_INVALIDATE_BUFFER_BIT	Tells OpenGL that you no longer care about any of the data in the whole buffer.
GL_MAP_FLUSH_EXPLICIT_BIT	You promise to tell OpenGL about any data you modify inside the mapped range.
GL_MAP_UNSYNCHRONIZED_BIT	Tells OpenGL that you will perform any synchronization yourself.

As with the bits that you can pass to **glBufferStorage()**, these bits can control some advanced functionality of OpenGL and, in some cases, their correct usage depends on other OpenGL functionality. However, these bits are *not* hints and OpenGL will enforce their correct usage. You should set GL_MAP_READ_BIT if you plan to read from the buffer and GL_MAP_WRITE_BIT if you plan to write to it. Reading or writing into the mapped range without setting the appropriate bits is an error. The GL_MAP_PERSISTENT_BIT and GL_MAP_COHERENT_BIT flags have similar meanings to their identically named counterparts in **glBufferStorage()**. All four of these bits are required to match between when you specify storage and when you request a mapping. That is, if you want to map a buffer for reading using the GL_MAP_READ_BIT flag, then you must also specify the GL_MAP_READ_BIT flag when you call **glBufferStorage()**.

We'll dig deeper into the remaining flags when we cover synchronization primitives a little later in the book. However, because of the additional control and stronger contract provided by **glMapBufferRange()** and **glMapNamedBufferRange()**, it is generally preferred to call these functions rather than **glMapNamedBuffer()** (or **glMapBuffer()**). You should get into the habit of using these functions even if you're not using any of their more advanced features.

Filling and Copying Data in Buffers

After allocating storage space for your buffer object using **glBufferStorage()**, one possible next step is to fill the buffer with known data. Whether you use the initial data parameter of **glBufferStorage()**, use **glBufferSubData()** to put the initial data in the buffer, or use **glMapBufferRange()** to obtain a pointer to the buffer's data store and fill it with your application, you will need to get the buffer into a known state before you can use it productively. If the data you want to put into a buffer is a constant value, it is probably much more efficient to call **glClearBufferSubData()** or **glClearNamedBufferSubData()**, whose prototypes are

```
void glClearBufferSubData(GLenum target,
                          GLenum internalformat,
                          GLintptr offset,
                          GLsizeiptr size,
                          GLenum format,
                          GLenum type,
                          const void * data);
```

```
void glClearNamedBuffeSubData(GLuint buffer,
                              GLenum internalformat,
                              GLintptr offset,
                              GLsizeiptr size,
                              GLenum format,
                              GLenum type,
                              const void * data);
```

These functions take a pointer to a variable containing the values that you
want to clear the buffer object to and, after converting it to the format
specified in internalformat, replicate the data across the range of the
buffer's data store specified by offset and size, both of which are
measured in bytes. format and type tell OpenGL about the data pointed
to by data. The format can be one of GL_RED, GL_RG, GL_RGB, or GL_RGBA to
specify one-, two-, three-, or four-channel data, for example. Meanwhile,
type should represent the data type of the components. For instance, it
could be GL_UNSIGNED_BYTE or GL_FLOAT to specify unsigned bytes or
floating-point data, respectively. The most common types supported by
OpenGL and their corresponding C data types are listed in Table 5.3.

Once your data has been sent to the GPU, it's entirely possible you may
want to share that data between buffers or copy the results from one buffer
into another. OpenGL provides an easy-to-use way of doing that.
glCopyBufferSubData() and **glCopyNamedBufferSubData()** let you specify
which buffers are involved as well as the size and offsets to use.

```
void glCopyBufferSubData(GLenum readtarget,
                         GLenum writetarget,
                         GLintptr readoffset,
                         GLintptr writeoffset,
                         GLsizeiptr size);
```

Table 5.3: Basic OpenGL Type Tokens and Their Corresponding C Types

Type Token	C Type
GL_BYTE	GLchar
GL_UNSIGNED_BYTE	GLuchar
GL_SHORT	GLshort
GL_UNSIGNED_SHORT	GLushort
GL_INT	GLint
GL_UNSIGNED_INT	GLuint
GL_FLOAT	GLfloat
GL_DOUBLE	GLdouble

```
void glCopyNamedBufferSubData(GLuint readBuffer,
                              GLuint writeBuffer,
                              GLintptr readOffset,
                              GLintptr writeOffset,
                              GLsizeiptr size);
```

For **glCopyBufferSubData()**, the readtarget and writetarget are the targets where the two buffers you want to copy data between are bound. They can be buffers bound to any of the available buffer binding points. However, since buffer binding points can have only one buffer bound at a time, you couldn't copy between two buffers that are both bound to the GL_ARRAY_BUFFER target, for example. Thus, when you perform the copy, you need to pick two targets to bind the buffers to, which will disturb the OpenGL state.

To resolve this, OpenGL provides the GL_COPY_READ_BUFFER and GL_COPY_WRITE_BUFFER targets. These targets were added specifically to allow you to copy data from one buffer to another without any unintended side effects. Because they are not used for anything else in OpenGL, you can bind your read and write buffers to these binding points without affecting any other buffer target.

Alternatively, you can use the **glCopyNamedBufferSubData()** form, which takes the names of the two buffers directly. Of course, you can specify the same buffer for both readBuffer and writeBuffer to copy a region of data between two offsets in the same buffer object. Be careful that the regions to be copied don't overlap, though, as in this case the results of the copy are undefined. You can consider **glCopyNamedBufferSubData()** as a form of the C function memcpy for buffer objects.

The readoffset and writeoffset parameters tell OpenGL where in the source and destination buffers to read or write the data, and the size parameter tells it how big the copy should be. Be sure that the ranges you are reading from and writing to remain within the bounds of the buffers; otherwise, your copy will fail.

You may notice the types of readoffset, writeoffset, and size, which are GLintptr and GLsizeiptr. These types are special definitions of integer types that are at least wide enough to hold a pointer variable.

Feeding Vertex Shaders from Buffers

In Chapter 2, "Our First OpenGL Program," you were briefly introduced to the vertex array object (VAO). During that discussion, we explained how the VAO represented the inputs to the vertex shader—though at the time, we didn't use any real inputs to our vertex shaders and opted instead for hard-coded arrays of data. Then, in Chapter 3 we introduced the concept of *vertex attributes*, but we discussed only how to change their static values. Although the vertex array object stores these static attribute values for you, it can do a lot more. Before we can proceed, we need to create a vertex array object to store our vertex array state and bind it to our context so that we can use it:

```
GLuint vao;
glCreateVertexArrays(1, &vao);
glBindVertexArray(vao);
```

Now that we have our VAO created and bound, we can start filling in its state. Rather than using hard-coded data in the vertex shader, we can instead rely entirely on the value of a vertex attribute and ask OpenGL to fill it automatically using the data stored in a buffer object that we supply. Each vertex attribute gets to fetch data from a buffer bound to one of several *vertex buffer bindings*. To set the binding that a vertex attribute uses to reference a buffer, call the **glVertexArrayAttribBinding()** function:

```
void glVertexArrayAttribBinding(GLuint vaobj,
                                GLuint attribindex,
                                GLuint bindingindex);
```

The **glVertexArrayAttribBinding()** function tells OpenGL that when the vertex array object named vaobj is bound, the vertex attribute at the index specified in attribindex should source its data from the buffer bound at bindingindex.

To tell OpenGL which buffer object our data is in and where in that buffer object the data resides, we use the **glVertexArrayVertexBuffer()** function to bind a buffer to one of the vertex buffer bindings. We use the **glVertexArrayAttribFormat()** function to describe the layout and format of the data, and finally we enable automatic filling of the attribute by calling **glEnableVertexAttribArray()**. The prototype of **glVertexArrayVertexBuffer()** is

```
void glVertexArrayVertexBuffer(GLuint vaobj,
                               GLuint bindingindex,
                               GLuint buffer,
                               GLintptr offset,
                               GLsizei stride);
```

Here, the first parameter is the vertex array object whose state you're modifying. The second parameter, bindingindex, is the index of the vertex buffer, which matches the parameter sent to **glVertexArrayAttribBinding()**. The buffer parameter specifies the name of the buffer object that we're binding. The last two parameters, `offset` and `stride`, tell OpenGL where in the buffer object the attribute data lies. `offset` says where the first vertex's data starts and `stride` says how far apart each vertex is. Both are measured in bytes.

Next, we have **`glVertexArrayAttribFormat()`**, whose prototype is

```
void glVertexArrayAttribFormat(GLuint vaobj,
                               GLuint attribindex,
                               GLint size,
                               GLenum type,
                               GLboolean normalized,
                               GLuint relativeoffset);
```

For **`glVertexArrayAttribFormat()`**, the first parameter is again the vertex array whose state we're modifying. `attribindex` is the index of the vertex attribute. You can define a large number of attributes as input to a vertex shader and then refer to them by their index, as explained in the "Vertex Attributes" section in Chapter 3. `size` is the number of components that are stored in the buffer for each vertex and `type` is the type of the data, which would normally be one of the types in Table 5.3.

The `normalized` parameter tells OpenGL whether the data in the buffer should be normalized (scaled between 0.0 and 1.0) before being passed to the vertex shader or if it should be left alone and passed as is. This parameter is ignored for floating-point data, but for integer data types, such as GL_UNSIGNED_BYTE or GL_INT, it is important. For example, if GL_UNSIGNED_BYTE data is normalized, it is divided by 255 (the maximum value representable by an unsigned byte) before being passed to a floating-point input to the vertex shader. The shader will therefore see values of the input attribute between 0.0 and 1.0. However, if the data is not normalized, it is simply cast to floating-point values and the shader will receive numbers between 0.0 and 255.0, even though the input to the vertex shader consists of floating-point data.

The `stride` parameter tells OpenGL how many bytes are between the start of one vertex's data and the start of the next, but you can set this parameter to 0 to let OpenGL calculate it for you based on the values of `size` and `type`. Finally, `relativeoffset` is the offset from the vertex's data where the specific attribute's data starts. This all seems pretty complex, but the pseudocode to compute the location in a buffer object is fairly simple:

```
location = binding[attrib.binding].memory + // Start of data store in memory
           binding[attrib.binding].offset + // Offset of vertex attribute in buffer
           binding[attrib.binding].stride * vertex.index + // Start of *this* vertex
           vertex.relative_offset;           // Start of attribute relative to vertex
```

Finally, **glEnableVertexAttribArray()** and the converse
glDisableVertexAttribArray() have the prototypes:

```
void glEnableVertexAttribArray(GLuint index);
```

When a vertex attribute is enabled, OpenGL will feed data to the vertex
shader based on the format and location information you've provided
with **glVertexArrayVertexBuffer()** and **glVertexArrayAttribFormat()**.
When the attribute is disabled, the vertex shader will be provided
with the static information you provide with a call to **glVertexAttrib*()**.

Listing 5.4 shows how to use **glVertexArrayVertexBuffer()** and
glVertexArrayAttribFormat() to configure a vertex attribute. Notice that
we also call **glEnableVertexArrayAttrib()** after setting up the offset, stride,
and format information. This tells OpenGL to use the data in the buffer to
fill the vertex attribute rather than using data we provide through one of
the **glVertexAttrib*()** functions.

```
// First, bind a vertex buffer to the VAO
glVertexArrayVertexBuffer(vao,                    // Vertex array object
                          0,                      // First vertex buffer binding
                          buffer,                 // Buffer object
                          0,                      // Start from the beginning
                          sizeof(vmath::vec4));   // Each vertex is one vec4

// Now, describe the data to OpenGL, tell it where it is, and turn on automatic
// vertex fetching for the specified attribute
glVertexArrayAttribFormat(vao,                    // Vertex array object
                          0,                      // First attribute
                          4,                      // Four components
                          GL_FLOAT,               // Floating-point data
                          GL_FALSE,               // Normalized - ignored for floats
                          0);                     // First element of the vertex

glEnableVertexArrayAttrib(vao, 0);
```

Listing 5.4: Setting up a vertex attribute

After Listing 5.4 has been executed, OpenGL will automatically fill the first
attribute in the vertex shader with data it has read from the buffer that was
bound to the VAO by **glVertexArrayVertexBuffer()**.

We can modify our vertex shader to use only its input vertex attribute
rather than a hard-coded array. This updated shader is shown in
Listing 5.5.

```
#version 450 core

layout (location = 0) in vec4 position;

void main(void)
{
    gl_Position = position;
}
```

Listing 5.5: Using an attribute in a vertex shader

As you can see, the shader of Listing 5.5 is greatly simplified over the original shader shown in Chapter 2. Gone is the hard-coded array of data. As an added bonus, this shader can be used with an arbitrary number of vertices. You can literally put millions of vertices' worth of data into your buffer object and draw them all with a single command such as a call to **glDrawArrays()**.

If you are done using data from a buffer object to fill a vertex attribute, you can disable that attribute again with a call to **glDisableVertexAttribArray()**, whose prototype is

```
void glDisableAttribArray(GLuint index);
```

Once you have disabled the vertex attribute, it goes back to being static and passing the value you specify with **glVertexAttrib*()** to the shader.

Using Multiple Vertex Shader Inputs

As you have learned, you can get OpenGL to feed data into your vertex shaders and use data you've placed in buffer objects. You can also declare multiple inputs to your vertex shaders, and assign each one a unique location that can be used to refer to it. Combining these things together means that you can get OpenGL to provide data to multiple vertex shader inputs simultaneously. Consider the input declarations to a vertex shader shown in Listing 5.6.

```
layout (location = 0) in vec3 position;
layout (location = 1) in vec3 color;
```

Listing 5.6: Declaring two inputs to a vertex shader

If you have a linked program object whose vertex shader has multiple inputs, you can determine the locations of those inputs by calling

```
GLint glGetAttribLocation(GLuint program,
                          const GLchar * name);
```

Here, `program` is the name of the program object containing the vertex shader and `name` is the name of the vertex attribute. In our example declarations of Listing 5.6, passing `"position"` to **glGetAttribLocation()** will cause it to return 0, and passing `"color"` will cause it to return 1. Passing something that is not the name of a vertex shader input will cause **glGetAttribLocation()** to return −1. Of course, if you always specify locations for your vertex attributes in your shader code, then **glGetAttribLocation()** should return whatever you specified. If you don't specify locations in shader code, OpenGL will assign locations for you, and those locations will be returned by **glGetAttribLocation()**.

There are two ways to connect vertex shader inputs to your application's data, referred to as *separate attributes* and *interleaved attributes*. When attributes are separate, they are located either in different buffers or at least at different locations in the same buffer. For example, if you want to feed data into two vertex attributes, you could create two buffer objects, bind each to a different vertex buffer binding with a call to **glVertexArrayVertexBuffer()**, and then specify the two indices of the two vertex buffer binding points that you used when you call **glVertexArrayAttribBinding()** for each. Alternatively, you could place the data at different offsets within the same buffer, bind it to a single vertex buffer binding with one call to **glVertexArrayVertexBuffer()**, and then call **glVertexArrayAttribBinding()** for both attributes, passing the same binding index to each. Listing 5.7 shows this approach.

```
GLuint buffer[2];
GLuint vao;

static const GLfloat positions[] = { ... };
static const GLfloat colors[] = { ... };

// Create the vertex array object
glCreateVertexArrays(1, &vao)

// Get create two buffers
glCreateBuffers(2, &buffer[0]);

// Initialize the first buffer
glNamedBufferStorage(buffer[0], sizeof(positions), positions, 0);

// Bind it to the vertex array - offset zero, stride = sizeof(vec3)
glVertexArrayVertexBuffer(vao, 0, buffer[0], 0, sizeof(vmath::vec3));

// Tell OpenGL what the format of the attribute is
glVertexArrayAttribFormat(vao, 0, 3, GL_FLOAT, GL_FALSE, 0);
```

```
// Tell OpenGL which vertex buffer binding to use for this attribute
glVertexArrayAttribBinding(vao, 0, 0);

// Enable the attribute
glEnableVertexArrayAttrib(vao, 0);

// Perform similar initialization for the second buffer
glNamedBufferStorage(buffer[1], sizeof(colors), colors, 0);
glVertexArrayVertexBuffer(vao, 1, buffer[1], 0, sizeof(vmath::vec3));
glVertexArrayAttribFormat(vao, 1, 3, GL_FLOAT, GL_FALSE, 0);
glVertexArrayAttribBinding(vao, 1, 1);
glEnableVertexAttribArray(1);
```

Listing 5.7: Multiple separate vertex attributes

In both cases of separate attributes, we have used *tightly packed* arrays of data to feed both attributes. This is effectively structure-of-arrays (SoA) data. We have a set of tightly packed, independent arrays of data. However, it's also possible to use an array-of-structures (AoS) form of data. Consider how the following structure might represent a single vertex:

```
struct vertex
{
    // Position
    float x;
    float y;
    float z;

    // Color
    float r;
    float g;
    float b;
};
```

Now we have two inputs to our vertex shader (position and color) interleaved together in a single structure. Clearly, if we make an array of these structures, we have an AoS layout for our data. To represent this with calls to **glVertexArrayVertexBuffer()**, we have to use its stride parameter. The stride parameter tells OpenGL how far apart *in bytes* the beginning of each vertex's data is. If we leave it as 0, OpenGL will use the same data for every vertex. However, to use the vertex structure declared above, we can simply use sizeof(vertex) for the stride parameter and everything will work out. Listing 5.8 shows the code to do this.

```
GLuint vao;
GLuint buffer;

static const vertex vertices[] = { ... };

// Create the vertex array object
glCreateVertexArrays(1, &vao);
```

```
// Allocate and initialize a buffer object
glCreateBuffers(1, &buffer);
glNamedBufferStorage(buffer, sizeof(vertices), vertices, 0);

// Set up two vertex attributes - first positions
glVertexArrayAttribBinding(vao, 0, 0);
glVertexArrayAttribFormat(vao, 0, 3, GL_FLOAT, GL_FALSE, offsetof(vertex, x));
glEnableVertexArrayAttrib(0);

// Now colors
glVertexArrayAttribBinding(vao, 1, 0);
glVertexArrayAttribFormat(vao, 1, 3, GL_FLOAT, GL_FALSE, offsetof(vertex, r));
glEnableVertexArrayAttrib(1);

// Finally, bind our one and only buffer to the vertex array object
glVertexArrayVertexBuffer(vao, 0, buffer);
```

Listing 5.8: Multiple interleaved vertex attributes

After executing the code in Listing 5.8, you can bind the vertex array object and start pulling data from the buffers bound to it.

After the vertex format information has been set up with calls to **glVertexArrayAttribFormat()**, you can change the vertex buffers that are bound with further calls to **glVertexArrayAttribBinding()**. If you want to render a lot of geometry stored in different buffers but with similar vertex formats, simply call **glVertexArrayAttribBinding()** to switch buffers and start drawing from them.

Loading Objects from Files

As you can see, you could potentially use a large number of vertex attributes in a single vertex shader. As we progress through various techniques, you will see that we'll regularly use four or five vertex attributes, and possibly more. Filling buffers with data to feed all of these attributes and then setting up the vertex array object and all of the vertex attribute pointers can be a chore. Further, encoding all of your geometry data directly in your application isn't practical for anything but the simplest models. Therefore, it makes sense to store model data in files and load it into your application. There are plenty of model file formats out there, and most modeling programs support several of the more common formats.

For the purpose of this book, we have devised a simple object file definition called an .SBM file, which stores the information we need without being either too simple or too overly engineered. Complete documentation for the format is found in Appendix B, "The SBM File Format." The sb7 framework also includes a loader for this model format, called `sb7::object`. To load an object file, create an instance of `sb7::object` and call its load function as follows:

```
sb7::object my_object;

my_object.load("filename.sbm");
```

If this operation is successful, the model will be loaded into the instance of `sb7::object` and you will be able to render it. During loading, the class will create and set up the object's vertex array object and then configure all of the vertex attributes contained in the model file. The class also includes a render function that binds the object's vertex array object and calls the appropriate drawing command. For example, calling

```
my_object.render();
```

will render a single copy of the object with the current shaders. In many of the examples in the remainder of this book, we'll simply use our object loader to load object files (several of which are included with the book's source code) and render them.

Uniforms

Although not really a form of storage, uniforms are an important way to get data into shaders and to hook them up to your application. You have already seen how to pass data to a vertex shader using vertex attributes, and you have seen how to pass data from stage to stage using interface blocks. Uniforms allow you to pass data directly from your application into any shader stage. There are two flavors of uniforms, which differ based on how they are declared. The first are uniforms declared in the default block and the second are uniform blocks, whose values are stored in buffer objects. We will discuss both now.

Default Block Uniforms

While attributes are needed for per-vertex positions, surface normals, texture coordinates, and so on, a uniform is how we pass data into a shader that stays the same—is uniform—for an entire primitive batch or longer. Probably the single most common uniform for a vertex shader is the transformation matrix. We use transformation matrices in our vertex shaders to manipulate vertex positions and other vectors. Any shader variable can be specified as a uniform, and uniforms can be in any of the shader stages (even though we discuss only vertex and fragment shaders in

this chapter). Making a uniform is as simple as placing the keyword
uniform at the beginning of the variable declaration:

```
uniform float fTime;
uniform int iIndex;
uniform vec4 vColorValue;
uniform mat4 mvpMatrix;
```

Uniforms are always considered to be; and they cannot be assigned values
by your shader code. However, you can initialize their default values at
declaration time in a manner such as this:

```
uniform int answer = 42;
```

If you declare the same uniform in multiple shader stages, each of those
stages will "see" the same value of that uniform.

Arranging Your Uniforms

After a shader has been compiled and linked into a program object, you
can use one of the many functions defined by OpenGL to set the shader's
values (assuming you don't want the defaults defined by the shader). Just
as with vertex attributes, these functions refer to uniforms by their *location*
within their program object. It is possible to specify the locations of
uniforms in your shader code by using a location *layout qualifier*. When
you do this, OpenGL will try to assign the locations that you specify to the
uniforms in your shaders. The location layout qualifier looks like this:

```
layout (location = 17) uniform vec4 myUniform;
```

Notice the similarity between the location layout qualifer for uniforms and
the one we've used for vertex shader inputs. In this case, myUniform will be
allocated to location 17. If you don't specify a location for your uniforms
in your shader code, OpenGL will automatically assign locations to them
for you. You can figure out which locations were assigned by calling the
glGetUniformLocation() function, whose prototype is

```
GLint glGetUniformLocation(GLuint program,
                           const GLchar* name);
```

This function returns a signed integer that represents the location of the
variable named by name in the program specified by program. For example,
to get the location of a uniform variable named vColorValue, we would do
something like this:

```
GLint iLocation = glGetUniformLocation(myProgram, "vColorValue");
```

In the previous example, passing "myUniform" to **glGetUniformLocation()** would result in the value 17 being returned. If you know a priori where your uniforms are because you assigned locations to them in your shaders, then you don't need to find them and you can avoid the calls to **glGetUniformLocation()**. This is the recommended way of doing things.

If the return value of **glGetUniformLocation()** is −1, it means the uniform name could not be located in the program. You should bear in mind that even if a shader compiles correctly, a uniform name may still "disappear" from the program if it is not used directly in at least one of the attached shaders—even if you assign it a location explicitly in your shader source code. You do not need to worry about uniform variables being optimized away, but if you declare a uniform and then do not use it, the compiler will toss it out. Also, know that shader variable names are case sensitive, so you must get the case right when you query their locations.

Setting Uniforms

OpenGL supports a large number of data types both in the shading language and in the API. To to allow you to pass all this data around, it includes a huge number of functions just for setting the value of uniforms. A single scalar or vector data type can be set with any of the following variations on the **glUniform*()** function.

For example, consider the following four variables declared in a shader:

```
layout (location = 0) uniform float fTime;
layout (location = 1) uniform int iIndex;
layout (location = 2) uniform vec4 vColorValue;
layout (location = 3) uniform bool bSomeFlag;
```

To find and set these values in the shader, your C/C++ code might look something like this:

```
glUseProgram(myShader);
glUniform1f(0, 45.2f);
glUniform1i(1, 42);
glUniform4f(2, 1.0f, 0.0f, 0.0f, 1.0f);
glUniform1i(3, GL_FALSE);
```

Note that we used an integer version of **glUniform*()** to pass in a `bool` value. Booleans can also be passed in as floats, with 0.0 representing `false` and any non-zero value representing `true`.

The **glUniform*()** function also comes in flavors that take a pointer, potentially to an array of values. These forms end in the letter v, indicating that they consume a vector, and take a `count` value that represents how many elements are in each array of *x* number of components, where *x* is the number at the end of the function name. For example, suppose you had this uniform with four components:

```
uniform vec4 vColor;
```

In C/C++, you could represent this as an array of floats:

```
GLfloat vColor[4] = {  1.0f, 1.0f, 1.0f, 1.0f };
```

But this is a single array of four values, so passing it into the shader would look like this:

```
glUniform4fv(iColorLocation, 1, vColor);
```

Now suppose you had an array of color values in your shader:

```
uniform vec4 vColors[2];
```

Then in C++, you could represent the data and pass it in like this:

```
GLfloat vColors[4][2] = { {  1.0f, 1.0f, 1.0f, 1.0f } ,
                          {  1.0f, 0.0f, 0.0f, 1.0f } };
...
glUniform4fv(iColorLocation, 2, vColors);
```

At its simplest, you can set a single floating-point uniform like this:

```
GLfloat fValue = 45.2f;
glUniform1fv(iLocation, 1, &fValue);
```

Finally, we see how to set a matrix uniform. Shader matrix data types only come in the single- and double-precision floating-point variety, so we have far less variation. To set the values in uniform matrices, we call the **glUniformMatrix*()** * commands.

In all of these functions, the variable `count` represents the number of matrices stored at the pointer parameter `m` (yes, you can have arrays of matrices!). The Boolean flag `transpose` is set to GL_FALSE if the matrix is already stored in column-major ordering (the way OpenGL prefers). Setting this value to GL_TRUE causes the matrix to be transposed when it is copied into the shader. This might be useful if you are using a matrix library that uses a row-major matrix layout instead (for example, some other graphics APIs use row-major ordering and you might want to use a library designed for one of them).

Uniform Blocks

Eventually, the shaders you'll be writing will become very complex. Some of them will require a lot of constant data, and passing all this to the shader using uniforms can become quite inefficient. If you have a lot of shaders in an application, you'll need to set up the uniforms for every one of those shaders, which means a lot of calls to the various `glUniform*()` functions. You'll also need to keep track of which uniforms change. Some change for every object and some change once per frame, while others may require initializing only once for the whole application. This means that you either need to update different sets of uniforms in different places in your application (making it more complex to maintain) or update all the uniforms all the time (costing performance).

To alleviate the cost of all the `glUniform*()` calls, to make updating a large set of uniforms simpler, and to be able to easily share a set of uniforms between different programs, OpenGL allows you to combine a group of uniforms into a *uniform block* and store the whole block in a buffer object. The buffer object is just like any other that has been described earlier. You can quickly set the whole group of uniforms by either changing your buffer binding or overwriting the content of a bound buffer. You can also leave the buffer bound while you change programs, and the new program will see the current set of uniform values. This functionality is called the uniform buffer object (UBO). In fact, the uniforms you've used up until now live in the default block. Any uniform declared at the global scope in a shader ends up in the default uniform block. You can't keep the default block in a uniform buffer object; you need to create one or more named uniform blocks.

To declare a set of uniforms to be stored in a buffer object, you need to use a named uniform block in your shader. This looks a lot like the interface blocks described in the "Interface Blocks" section in Chapter 3, but it uses the `uniform` keyword instead of `in` or `out`. Listing 5.9 shows what the code looks like in a shader.

```
uniform TransformBlock
{
    float scale;            // Global scale to apply to everything
    vec3  translation;      // Translation in X, Y, and Z
    float rotation[3];      // Rotation around X, Y, and Z axes
    mat4 projection_matrix; // A generalized projection matrix to apply
                            // after scale and rotate
} transform;
```

Listing 5.9: Example uniform block declaration

This code declares a uniform block whose name is `TransformBlock`. It also declares a single instance of the block called `transform`. Inside the shader, you can refer to the members of the block using its instance name, `transform` (for example, `transform.scale` or `transform.projection_matrix`). However, to set up the data in the buffer object that you'll use to back the block, you need to know the location of a member of the block; for that, you need the block name, `TransformBlock`. If you wanted to have multiple instances of the block, each with its own buffer, you could make `transform` an array. The members of the block will have the same locations within each block, but there will now be several instances of the block that you can refer to in the shader. Querying the locations of members within a block is important when you want to fill the block with data, which is explained in the following section.

Building Uniform Blocks

Data accessed in the shader via named uniform blocks can be stored in buffer objects. In general, it is the application's job to fill the buffer objects with data using functions like **glBufferData()** and **glMapBuffer()**. The question is, then, what is the data in the buffer supposed to look like? There are actually two possibilities here, and whichever one you choose is a trade-off.

The first method is to use a standard, agreed-upon layout for the data. This means that your application can just copy data into the buffers and assume specific locations for members within the block—you can even store the data on disk ahead of time and simply read it straight into a buffer that's been mapped using **glMapBuffer()**. The standard layout may leave some empty space between the various members of the block, making the buffer larger than it needs to be, and you might trade some performance for this convenience. Even so, using the standard layout is probably safe in almost all situations.

Another alternative is to let OpenGL decide where it would like the data. This can produce the most efficient shaders, but it means that your application needs to figure out where to put the data so that OpenGL can read it. Under this scheme, the data stored in uniform buffers is arranged in a *shared* layout. This is the default layout and is what you get if you don't explicitly ask OpenGL for something else. With the shared layout, the data in the buffer is laid out however OpenGL decides is best for runtime performance and access from the shader. This can sometimes allow for greater performance to be achieved by the shaders, but it requires more work from the application. The reason this is called the shared layout is that while OpenGL has arranged the data within the buffer, that arrangement will be the same between multiple programs and shaders sharing the same declaration of the uniform block. This allows you to use the same buffer object with any program. To use the shared layout, the application must determine the locations within the buffer object of the members of the uniform block.

First, we'll describe the *standard* layout, which is what we recommend that you use for your shaders (even though it's not the default). To tell OpenGL that you want to use the standard layout, you need to declare the uniform block with a layout qualifier. A declaration of a `TransformBlock` uniform block, with the standard layout qualifier, `std140`, is shown in Listing 5.10.

```
layout(std140) uniform TransformBlock
{
    float scale;              // Global scale to apply to everything
    vec3  translation;        // Translation in X, Y, and Z
    float rotation[3];        // Rotation around X, Y, and Z axes
    mat4 projection_matrix;   // A generalized projection matrix to
                              // apply after scale and rotate
} transform;
```

Listing 5.10: Declaring a uniform block with the `std140` layout

Once a uniform block has been declared to use the standard, or `std140`, layout, each member of the block consumes a predefined amount of space in the buffer and begins at an offset that is predictable by following a set of rules. A summary of the rules follows.

Any type consuming N bytes in a buffer begins on an N-byte boundary within that buffer. That means that standard GLSL types such as `int`, `float`, and `bool` (which are all defined to be 32-bit or 4-byte quantities) begin on multiples of 4 bytes. A vector of these types of length 2 always begins on a $2N$-byte boundary. For example, a `vec2`, which is 8 bytes long in memory, always starts on an 8-byte boundary. Three- and four-element vectors always start on a $4N$-byte boundary; `vec3` and `vec4` types start on 16-byte boundaries, for instance. Each member of an array of scalar or vector types (arrays of `int` or `vec3`, for example) always starts on a boundary defined by these same rules, but rounded up to the alignment of a `vec4`. In particular, this means that arrays of anything but `vec4` (and $N \times 4$ matrices) won't be tightly packed, but instead will have a gap between each of the elements. Matrices are essentially treated like short arrays of vectors, and arrays of matrices are treated like very long arrays of vectors. Finally, structures and arrays of structures have additional packing requirements; the whole structure starts on the boundary required by its largest member, rounded up to the size of a `vec4`.

Particular attention must be paid to the difference between the `std140` layout and the packing rules that are often followed by your C++ (or other application language) compiler of choice. In particular, an array in a uniform block is not necessarily tightly packed. This means that you can't create, for example, an array of `float` in a uniform block and simply copy data from a C array into it, because the data from the C array will be packed and the data in the uniform block won't be.

This all sounds complex, but it is logical and well defined, and allows a large range of graphics hardware to implement uniform buffer objects efficiently. Returning to our `TransformBlock` example, we can figure out the offsets of the members of the block within the buffer using these rules. Listing 5.11 shows an example of a uniform block declaration along with the offsets of its members.

```
layout(std140) uniform TransformBlock
{
//   Member                       base alignment   offset      aligned offset
     float scale;          // 4                    0           0
     vec3  translation;    // 16                   4           16
     float rotation[3];    // 16                   28          32 (rotation[0])
                           //                                  48 (rotation[1])
                           //                                  64 (rotation[2])
     mat4 projection_matrix; // 16                 80          80 (column 0)
                           //                                  96 (column 1)
                           //                                  112 (column 2)
                           //                                  128 (column 3)
} transform;
```

Listing 5.11: Example uniform block with offsets

There is a complete example of the alignments of various types in the original `ARB_uniform_buffer_object` extension specification.

As an alternative to using the `std140` layout, it's possible to directly specify the offsets of members of uniform blocks in your shader code. You still have to follow the alignment rules as required by `std140`, but you can do things like leave gaps between members and declare members out of order. To specify the offsets of members in a uniform block, use the `offset` layout qualifier. For an example, see Listing 5.12.

```
layout(std140) uniform ManuallyLaidOutBlock
{
    layout (offset = 32) vec4    foo;    // At offset 32 bytes
    layout (offset = 8) vec2     bar;    // At offset 8 bytes
    layout (offset = 48) vec3    baz;    // At offset 48 bytes
} myBlock;
```

Listing 5.12: Uniform block with user-specified offsets

In Listing 5.12 you will notice that the first member in the block, foo, is declared as starting at offset 32 in the block. This is fine because 32 is a multiple of 16 (the size of a vec4) and meets the alignment requirements for the type of foo. bar starts at offset 8—again, this satisfies the alignment requirements for a variable of type vec2. However, it's *before* foo in memory—we have decared the members out of order. Next, we declare baz at offset 48. Although baz is a vec3 variable, it must be aligned on a 16-byte boundary.

It's also possible to explicitly align types on boundaries that are multiples of their native alignment. To do this, we use the align layout qualifier. This is used similarly to the offset layout qualifier, but simply pushes the member to the next multiple of the specified alignment, so long as it meets the alignment requirements of the member. The align qualifier can be used on a whole block to force all of its members to be aligned to the specified size. You can use align and offset together to push members to the next offset that is greater than or equal to its specified value *and* is a multiple of of the block alignment.

In Listing 5.13, we have redeclared our ManuallyLaidOutBlock uniform block with an alignment of 16. This satisfies the requirements of vec4 and vec3 types, so the offsets of foo and baz are not affected. However, the natural alignment of bar is only 8 bytes, which is not a multiple of 16. Therefore, baz will be aligned on the next 16-byte boundary after the specified alignment (which is 16).

```
layout (std140, align = 16) uniform ManuallyLaidOutBlock
{
    layout (offset = 32) vec4    foo;    // At offset 32 bytes
    layout (offset = 8) vec2     bar;    // At offset 16 bytes
    layout (offset = 48) vec3    baz;    // At offset 48 bytes
} myBlock;
```

Listing 5.13: Uniform block with user-specified alignments

You can, of course, choose to leave everything in the hands of OpenGL by using the shared layout, and it *might* produce a slightly more efficient layout than `std140`, but it's probably not worth the additional effort. If you really want to use the shared layout, you can determine the offsets that OpenGL assigned to your block members. Each member of a uniform block has an index that is used to refer to it to find its size and location within the block. To get the index of a member of a uniform block, call

```
void glGetUniformIndices(GLuint program,
                         GLsizei uniformCount,
                         const GLchar ** uniformNames,
                         GLuint * uniformIndices);
```

This function allows you to get the indices of a large set of uniforms—perhaps even all of the uniforms in a program—with a single call to OpenGL, even if they're members of different blocks. It takes a count of the number of uniforms you'd like the indices for (`uniformCount`) and an array of uniform names (`uniformNames`) and puts their indices in an array for you (`uniformIndices`). Listing 5.14 contains an example of how you would retrieve the indices of the members of `TransformBlock`, which we declared earlier.

```
static const GLchar * uniformNames[4] =
{
    "TransformBlock.scale",
    "TransformBlock.translation",
    "TransformBlock.rotation",
    "TransformBlock.projection_matrix"
};
GLuint uniformIndices[4];

glGetUniformIndices(program, 4, uniformNames, uniformIndices);
```

Listing 5.14: Retrieving the indices of uniform block members

After this code has run, you have the indices of the four members of the uniform block in the `uniformIndices` array. Now that you have the indices, you can use them to find the locations of the block members within the buffer. To do this, call

```
void glGetActiveUniformsiv(GLuint program,
                           GLsizei uniformCount,
                           const GLuint * uniformIndices,
                           GLenum pname,
                           GLint * params);
```

This function can give you a lot of information about specific uniform block members. The information that we're interested in is the offset of the member within the buffer, the array stride (for `TransformBlock.rotation`), and the matrix stride (for `TransformBlock.projection_matrix`). These values tell us where to put data within the buffer so that it can be seen in the shader. We can retrieve these from OpenGL by setting pname to GL_UNIFORM_OFFSET, GL_UNIFORM_ARRAY_STRIDE, and GL_UNIFORM_MATRIX_STRIDE, respectively. Listing 5.15 shows what the code looks like.

```
GLint uniformOffsets[4];
GLint arrayStrides[4];
GLint matrixStrides[4];
glGetActiveUniformsiv(program, 4, uniformIndices,
                      GL_UNIFORM_OFFSET, uniformOffsets);
glGetActiveUniformsiv(program, 4, uniformIndices,
                      GL_UNIFORM_ARRAY_STRIDE, arrayStrides);
glGetActiveUniformsiv(program, 4, uniformIndices,
                      GL_UNIFORM_MATRIX_STRIDE, matrixStrides);
```

Listing 5.15: Retrieving the information about uniform block members

Once the code in Listing 5.15 has run, uniformOffsets contains the offsets of the members of the TransformBlock block, arrayStrides contains the strides of the array members (only rotation, for now), and matrixStrides contains the strides of the matrix members (only projection_matrix).

The other information that you can find out about uniform block members includes the data type of the uniform, the size in bytes that it consumes in memory, and layout information related to arrays and matrices within the block. You need some of that information to initialize a buffer object with more complex types, although the size and types of the members should be known to you already if you wrote the shaders. The other accepted values for pname and what you get back are listed in Table 5.4.

Table 5.4: Uniform Parameter Queries via **glGetActiveUniformsiv()**

Value of pname	What You Get Back
GL_UNIFORM_TYPE	The data type of the uniform as a GLenum.
GL_UNIFORM_SIZE	The size of arrays, in units of whatever GL_UNIFORM_TYPE gives you. If the uniform is not an array, this will always be 1.
GL_UNIFORM_NAME_LENGTH	The length, in characters, of the names of the uniforms.

continued

Table 5.4: *Continued*

Value of pname	What You Get Back
GL_UNIFORM_BLOCK_INDEX	The index of the block that the uniform is a member of.
GL_UNIFORM_OFFSET	The offset of the uniform within the block.
GL_UNIFORM_ARRAY_STRIDE	The number of bytes between consecutive elements of an array. If the uniform is not an array, this will be 0.
GL_UNIFORM_MATRIX_STRIDE	The number of bytes between the first element of each column of a column-major matrix or each row of a row-major matrix. If the uniform is not a matrix, this will be 0.
GL_UNIFORM_IS_ROW_MAJOR	Each element of the output array will either be 1 if the uniform is a row-major matrix, or 0 if it is a column-major matrix or not a matrix at all.

If the type of the uniform you're interested in is a simple type such as `int`, `float`, `bool`, or even vectors of these types (`vec4` and so on), all you need is its offset. Once you know the location of the uniform within the buffer, you can either pass the offset to `glBufferSubData()` to load the data at the appropriate location, or use the offset directly in your code to assemble the buffer in memory. We demonstrate the latter option here because it reinforces the idea that the uniforms are stored in memory, just like vertex information can be stored in buffers. It also means fewer calls are made to OpenGL, which can sometimes lead to higher performance. For these examples, we assemble the data in the application's memory and then load it into a buffer using `glBufferSubData()`. Alternatively, you could use `glMapBufferRange()` to get a pointer to the buffer's memory and assemble the data directly into that.

Let's start by setting the simplest uniform in the `TransformBlock` block, `scale`. This uniform is a single float whose location is stored in the first element of our `uniformIndices` array. Listing 5.16 shows how to set the value of the single float.

```
// Allocate some memory for our buffer (don't forget to free it later)
unsigned char * buffer = (unsigned char *)malloc(4096);

// We know that TransformBlock.scale is at uniformOffsets[0] bytes
// into the block, so we can offset our buffer pointer by that and
// store the scale there.
*((float *)(buffer + uniformOffsets[0])) = 3.0f;
```

Listing 5.16: Setting a single float in a uniform block

Next, we can initialize data for `TransformBlock.translation`. This is a
`vec3`, which means it consists of three floating-point values packed tightly
together in memory. To update this, all we need to do is find the location
of the first element of the vector and store three consecutive floats in
memory starting there. This is shown in Listing 5.17.

```
// Put three consecutive GLfloat values in memory to update a vec3
((float *)(buffer + uniformOffsets[1]))[0] = 1.0f;
((float *)(buffer + uniformOffsets[1]))[1] = 2.0f;
((float *)(buffer + uniformOffsets[1]))[2] = 3.0f;
```

Listing 5.17: Retrieving the indices of uniform block members

Now, we tackle the array `rotation`. We could have also used a `vec3` here,
but for the purposes of this example, we use a three-element array to
demonstrate the use of the `GL_UNIFORM_ARRAY_STRIDE` parameter. When
the `shared` layout is used, arrays are defined as a sequence of elements
separated by an implementation-defined stride in bytes. This means that
we have to place the data at locations in the buffer defined both by
`GL_UNIFORM_OFFSET` and `GL_UNIFORM_ARRAY_STRIDE`, as in the code snippet
of Listing 5.18.

```
// TransformBlock.rotations[0] is at uniformOffsets[2] bytes into
// the buffer. Each element of the array is at a multiple of
// arrayStrides[2] bytes past that.
const GLfloat rotations[] = {  30.0f, 40.0f, 60.0f };
unsigned int offset = uniformOffsets[2];

for (int n = 0; n < 3; n++)
{
    *((float *)(buffer + offset)) = rotations[n];
    offset += arrayStrides[2];
}
```

Listing 5.18: Specifying the data for an array in a uniform block

Finally, we set up the data for `TransformBlock.projection_matrix`.
Matrices in uniform blocks behave much like arrays of vectors. For

column-major matrices (which is the default), each column of the matrix is treated like a vector, the length of which is the height of the matrix. Likewise, a row-major matrix is treated like an array of vectors where each row is an element in that array. Just like normal arrays, the starting offset for each column (or row) in the matrix is determined by an implementation-defined quantity. This can be queried by passing the GL_UNIFORM_MATRIX_STRIDE parameter to **glGetActiveUniformsiv()**. Each column of the matrix can be initialized using code similar to that used to initialize the vec3 TransformBlock.translation. This setup code is given in Listing 5.19.

```
// The first column of TransformBlock.projection_matrix is at
// uniformOffsets[3] bytes into the buffer. The columns are
// spaced matrixStride[3] bytes apart and are essentially vec4s.
// This is the source matrix - remember, it's column major.
const GLfloat matrix[] =
{
    1.0f, 2.0f, 3.0f, 4.0f,
    9.0f, 8.0f, 7.0f, 6.0f,
    2.0f, 4.0f, 6.0f, 8.0f,
    1.0f, 3.0f, 5.0f, 7.0f
};

for (int i = 0; i < 4; i++)
{
    GLuint offset = uniformOffsets[3] + matrixStride[3] * i;
    for (j = 0; j < 4; j++)
    {
        *((float *)(buffer + offset)) = matrix[i * 4 + j];
        offset += sizeof(GLfloat);
    }
}
```

Listing 5.19: Setting up a matrix in a uniform block

This method of querying offsets and strides works for any of the layouts. With the shared layout, it is the only option. However, it's somewhat inconvenient, and as you can see, you need quite a lot of code to lay out your data in the buffer in the correct way. This is why we recommend that you use the *standard* layout. This allows you to determine where in the buffer data should be placed based on a set of rules that specify the sizes and alignments for the various data types supported by OpenGL. These rules are common across all OpenGL implementations, so you don't need to query anything to use them (although, should you query offsets and strides, the results will be correct). There is some chance that you'll trade a small amount of shader performance for its use, but the savings in code complexity and application performance are well worth it.

Regardless of which packing mode you choose, you can bind your buffer full of data to a uniform block in your program. Before you can do this, you need to retrieve the index of the uniform block. Each uniform block in a program has a compiler-assigned index. There is a fixed maximum number of uniform blocks that can be used by a single program, as well as a maximum number that can be used in any given shader stage. You can find these limits by calling **glGetIntegerv()** with the GL_MAX_UNIFORM_BUFFERS parameter (for the total per program) and either GL_MAX_VERTEX_UNIFORM_BUFFERS, GL_MAX_GEOMETRY_UNIFORM_BUFFERS, GL_MAX_TESS_CONTROL_UNIFORM_BUFFERS, GL_MAX_TESS_EVALUATION_UNIFORM_BUFFERS, or GL_MAX_FRAGMENT_UNIFORM_BUFFERS for the vertex, geometry, tessellation control, tessellation evaluation, and fragment shader limits, respectively. To find the index of a uniform block in a program, call

```
GLuint glGetUniformBlockIndex(GLuint program,
                    const GLchar * uniformBlockName);
```

This returns the index of the named uniform block. In our example uniform block declaration here, uniformBlockName would be "TransformBlock". There is a set of buffer binding points to which you can bind a buffer to provide data for the uniform blocks. It is essentially a two-step process to bind a buffer to a uniform block. Uniform blocks are assigned binding points, and then buffers can be bound to those binding points, matching buffers with uniform blocks. This way, different programs can be switched in and out without changing buffer bindings, and the fixed set of uniforms will automatically be seen by the new program. Contrast this to the values of the uniforms in the default block, which are per program state. Even if two programs contain uniforms with the same names, their values must be set for each program and will change when the active program is changed.

To assign a binding point to a uniform block, call

```
void glUniformBlockBinding(GLuint program,
                    GLuint uniformBlockIndex,
                    GLuint uniformBlockBinding);
```

Here, program is the program where the uniform block you're changing lives. uniformBlockIndex is the index of the uniform block to which you're assigning a binding point; you just retrieved that by calling **glGetUniformBlockIndex()**. uniformBlockBinding is the index of the uniform block binding point. An implementation of OpenGL supports a fixed maximum number of binding points, and you can determine that limit by calling `glGetIntegerv()` with the GL_MAX_UNIFORM_BUFFER_BINDINGS parameter.

Alternatively, you can specify the binding index of your uniform blocks directly in your shader code. To do this, we again use the layout qualifier, this time with the `binding` keyword. For example, to assign our TransformBlock block to binding 2, we could declare it as

```
layout(std140, binding = 2) uniform TransformBlock
{
    ...
}   transform;
```

Notice that the `binding` layout qualifier can be specified at the same time as the `std140` (or any other) qualifier. Assigning bindings in your shader source code avoids the need to call `glUniformBlockBinding()`, or even to determine the block's index from your application; consequently, it is usually the best method of assigning block location.

Once you've assigned binding points to the uniform blocks in your program, whether through the `glUniformBlockBinding()` function or through a layout qualifier, you can bind buffers to those same binding points to make the data in the buffers appear in the uniform blocks. To do this, call

```
glBindBufferBase(GL_UNIFORM_BUFFER, index, buffer);
```

Here, GL_UNIFORM_BUFFER tells OpenGL that we're binding a buffer to one of the uniform buffer binding points; index is the index of the binding point and should match what you specified either in your shader or in uniformBlockBinding in your call to `glUniformBlockBinding()`; and buffer is the name of the buffer object that you want to attach. It's important to note that index is not the index of the uniform block (uniformBlockIndex in `glUniformBlockBinding()`), but rather the index of the uniform buffer binding point. This is a common mistake to make and is easy to miss.

This mixing and matching of binding points with uniform block indices is illustrated in Figure 5.1.

In Figure 5.1, there is a program with three uniform blocks (Harry, Bob, and Susan) and three buffer objects (A, B, and C). Harry is assigned to

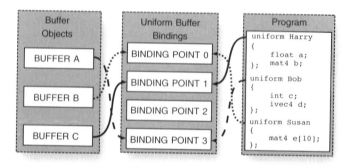

Figure 5.1: Binding buffers and uniform blocks to binding points

binding point 1, and buffer C is bound to binding point 1, so Harry's data comes from buffer C. Likewise, Bob is assigned to binding point 3, to which buffer A is bound, so Bob's data comes from buffer A. Finally, Susan is assigned to binding point 0 and buffer B is bound to binding point 0, so Susan's data comes from buffer B. Notice that binding point 2 is not used. That doesn't matter. There could be a buffer bound there, but the program doesn't use it.

The code to set this up is simple and is given in Listing 5.20.

```
// Get the indices of the uniform blocks using glGetUniformBlockIndex
GLuint harry_index = glGetUniformBlockIndex(program, "Harry");
GLuint bob_index   = glGetUniformBlockIndex(program, "Bob");
GLuint susan_index = glGetUniformBlockIndex(program, "Susan");

// Assign buffer bindings to uniform blocks, using their indices
glUniformBlockBinding(program, harry_index, 1);
glUniformBlockBinding(program, bob_index, 3);
glUniformBlockBinding(program, susan_index, 0);

// Bind buffers to the binding points
// Binding 0, buffer B, Susan's data
glBindBufferBase(GL_UNIFORM_BUFFER, 0, buffer_b);
// Binding 1, buffer C, Harry's data
glBindBufferBase(GL_UNIFORM_BUFFER, 1, buffer_c);
// Note that we skipped binding 2
// Binding 3, buffer A, Bob's data
glBindBufferBase(GL_UNIFORM_BUFFER, 3, buffer_a);
```

Listing 5.20: Specifying bindings for uniform blocks

If we had set the bindings for our uniform blocks in our shader code by using the `binding` layout qualifier, we could have avoided the calls to `glUniformBlockBinding()` in Listing 5.20. This approach is shown in Listing 5.21.

```
layout (binding = 1) uniform Harry
{
    // ...
};

layout (binding = 3) uniform Bob
{
    // ...
};

layout (binding = 0) uniform Susan
{
    // ...
};
```

Listing 5.21: Uniform blocks binding layout qualifiers

After a shader containing the declarations shown in Listing 5.21 is compiled and linked into a program object, the bindings for the Harry, Bob, and Susan uniform blocks will be set to the same things as they would be after executing Listing 5.20. Setting the uniform block binding in the shader can be useful for a number of reasons. First, it reduces the number of calls to OpenGL that your application must make. Second, it allows the shader to associate a uniform block with a particular binding point without the application needing to know its name. This can be helpful if you have some data in a buffer with a standard layout, but want to refer to it with different names in different shaders.

A common use for uniform blocks is to separate steady state from transient state. By setting up the bindings for all your programs using a standard convention, you can leave buffers bound when you change the program. For example, if you have some relatively fixed state—say the projection matrix, the size of the viewport, and a few other things that change once per frame or less often—you can leave that information in a buffer bound to binding point 0. Then, if you set the binding for the fixed state to 0 for all programs, whenever you switch program objects using `glUseProgram()`, the uniforms will be sitting there in the buffer, ready to use.

Suppose you have a fragment shader that simulates some material (cloth or metal, for example); you could put the parameters for the material into another buffer. In your program that shades each material, bind the uniform block containing the material parameters to binding point 1. Each object would maintain a buffer object containing the parameters of its surface. As you render each object, it uses the common material shader and simply binds its parameter buffer to buffer binding point 1.

A final significant advantage of uniform blocks is that they can be quite large. The maximum size of a uniform block can be determined by calling **glGetIntegerv()** and passing the GL_MAX_UNIFORM_BLOCK_SIZE parameter. Also, the number of uniform blocks that you can access from a single program can be retrieved by calling **glGetIntegerv()** and passing the GL_MAX_UNIFORM_BLOCK_BINDINGS parameter. OpenGL guarantees that uniform blocks may be at least 64K in size, and that you can have at least 14 of them referenced by a single program. Taking the example of the previous paragraph a little further, you could pack all of the properties for all of the materials used by your application into a single, large uniform block containing a big array of structures. As you render the objects in your scene, you need simply communicate the index within the array of the material you wish to use. You can achieve that with a static vertex attribute or traditional uniform, for example. This could be substantially faster than replacing the contents of a buffer object or changing uniform buffer bindings between each object. If you're really clever, you could even render objects made up of multiple surfaces with different materials using a single drawing command.

Using Uniforms to Transform Geometry

In Chapter 4, "Math for 3D Graphics," you learned how to construct matrices that represent several common transformations including scale, translation, and rotation, and how to use the sb7::vmath library to do the heavy lifting for you. You also saw how to multiply matrices to produce a composite matrix that represents the whole transformation sequence. Given a point of interest and the camera's location and orientation, you can build a matrix that will transform objects into the coordinate space of the viewer. Also, you can build matrices that represent perspective and orthographic projections onto the screen.

Furthermore, in this chapter you have seen how to feed a vertex shader with data from buffer objects, and how to pass data into your shaders through uniforms (whether in the default uniform block or in a uniform buffer). Now it's time to put all this information together and build a program that does a little more than pass vertices through untransformed.

Our example program will be the classic spinning cube. We'll create geometry representing a unit cube located at the origin and store it in buffer objects. Then, we will use a vertex shader to apply a sequence of transforms to it to move it into world space. We will construct a basic view matrix, multiply our model and view matrices together to produce a model–view matrix, and create a perspective transformation matrix representing some of the properties of our camera. Finally, we will pass these into a simple vertex shader using uniforms and draw the cube on the screen.

First, let's set up the cube geometry using a vertex array object. The code to do this is shown in Listing 5.22.

```
// First create and bind a vertex array object
glGenVertexArrays(1, &vao);
glBindVertexArray(vao);

static const GLfloat vertex_positions[] =
{
    -0.25f,  0.25f, -0.25f,
    -0.25f, -0.25f, -0.25f,
     0.25f, -0.25f, -0.25f,

     0.25f, -0.25f, -0.25f,
     0.25f,  0.25f, -0.25f,
    -0.25f,  0.25f, -0.25f,

    /* MORE DATA HERE */

    -0.25f,  0.25f, -0.25f,
     0.25f,  0.25f, -0.25f,
     0.25f,  0.25f,  0.25f,

     0.25f,  0.25f,  0.25f,
    -0.25f,  0.25f,  0.25f,
    -0.25f,  0.25f, -0.25f
};

// Now generate some data and put it in a buffer object
glGenBuffers(1, &buffer);
glBindBuffer(GL_ARRAY_BUFFER, buffer);
glBufferData(GL_ARRAY_BUFFER,
             sizeof(vertex_positions),
             vertex_positions,
             GL_STATIC_DRAW);
// Set up our vertex attribute
glVertexAttribPointer(0, 3, GL_FLOAT, GL_FALSE, 0, NULL);
glEnableVertexAttribArray(0);
```

Listing 5.22: Setting up cube geometry

Next, on each frame, we need to calculate the position and orientation of our cube and calculate the matrix that represents them. We can also build the camera matrix by simply translating in the z direction. Once we have built these matrices, we can multiply them together and pass them as uniforms into our vertex shader. The code to do this is shown in Listing 5.23.

```
float f = (float)currentTime * (float)M_PI * 0.1f;
vmath::mat4 mv_matrix =
    vmath::translate(0.0f, 0.0f, -4.0f) *
    vmath::translate(sinf(2.1f * f) * 0.5f,
                     cosf(1.7f * f) * 0.5f,
                     sinf(1.3f * f) * cosf(1.5f * f) * 2.0f) *
    vmath::rotate((float)currentTime * 45.0f, 0.0f, 1.0f, 0.0f) *
    vmath::rotate((float)currentTime * 81.0f, 1.0f, 0.0f, 0.0f);
```

Listing 5.23: Building the model–view matrix for a spinning cube

The projection matrix can be rebuilt whenever the window size changes.
The sb7::application framework provides a function called onResize
that handles resize events. If we override this function, then when the
window size changes, it will be called and we can create a projection
matrix. We can load that into a uniform as well in our rendering loop. If
the window size changes, we'll also need to update our viewport with a
call to **glViewport()**. Once we have put all our matrices into our uniforms,
we can draw the cube geometry with the **glDrawArrays()** function. The
code to update the projection matrix is shown in Listing 5.24 and the
remainder of the rendering loop is shown in Listing 5.25.

```
void onResize(int w, int h)
{
    sb7::application::onResize(w, h);
    aspect = (float)info.windowWidth / (float)info.windowHeight;
    proj_matrix = vmath::perspective(50.0f,
                                     aspect,
                                     0.1f,
                                     1000.0f);
}
```

Listing 5.24: Updating the projection matrix for the spinning cube

```
// Clear the framebuffer with dark green
glClearBufferfv(GL_COLOR, 0, sb7::color::Green);

// Activate our program
glUseProgram(program);

// Set the model-view and projection matrices
glUniformMatrix4fv(mv_location, 1, GL_FALSE, mv_matrix);
glUniformMatrix4fv(proj_location, 1, GL_FALSE, proj_matrix);

// Draw 6 faces of 2 triangles of 3 vertices each = 36 vertices
glDrawArrays(GL_TRIANGLES, 0, 36);
```

Listing 5.25: Rendering loop for the spinning cube

Before we can actually render anything, we'll need to write a simple vertex
shader to transform the vertex positions using the matrices we've been

given and to pass along the color information so that the cube isn't just a flat blob. The vertex shader is shown in Listing 5.26 and the fragment shader is shown in Listing 5.27.

```
#version 450 core

in vec4 position;

out VS_OUT
{
    vec4 color;
} vs_out;

uniform mat4 mv_matrix;
uniform mat4 proj_matrix;

void main(void)
{
    gl_Position = proj_matrix * mv_matrix * position;
    vs_out.color = position * 2.0 + vec4(0.5, 0.5, 0.5, 0.0);
}
```

Listing 5.26: Spinning cube vertex shader

```
#version 450 core

out vec4 color;

in VS_OUT
{
    vec4 color;
} fs_in;

void main(void)
{
    color = fs_in.color;
}
```

Listing 5.27: Spinning cube fragment shader

A few frames of the resulting application are shown in Figure 5.2.

Of course, now that we have our cube geometry in a buffer object and a model–view matrix in a uniform, there's nothing to stop us from updating the uniform and drawing many copies of the cube in a single frame. In Listing 5.28 we've modified the rendering function to calculate a new model–view matrix many times and repeatedly draw our cube. Also, because we're going to render many cubes in this example, we'll need to clear the depth buffer before rendering the frame. Although not shown here, we also modified our startup function to enable depth testing and set the depth test function to GL_LEQUAL. The result of rendering with our modified program is shown in Figure 5.3.

Figure 5.2: A few frames from the spinning cube application

```
// Clear the framebuffer with dark green and clear
// the depth buffer to 1.0
glClearBufferfv(GL_COLOR, 0, sb7::color::Green);
glClearBufferfi(GL_DEPTH_STENCIL, 0, 1.0f, 0);

// Activate our program
glUseProgram(program);

// Set the model-view and projection matrices
glUniformMatrix4fv(proj_location, 1, GL_FALSE, proj_matrix);

// Draw 24 cubes...
for (i = 0; i < 24; i++)
{
    // Calculate a new model-view matrix for each one
    float f = (float)i + (float)currentTime * 0.3f;
    vmath::mat4 mv_matrix =
        vmath::translate(0.0f, 0.0f, -20.0f) *
        vmath::rotate((float)currentTime * 45.0f, 0.0f, 1.0f, 0.0f) *
        vmath::rotate((float)currentTime * 21.0f, 1.0f, 0.0f, 0.0f) *
        vmath::translate(sinf(2.1f * f) * 2.0f,
                         cosf(1.7f * f) * 2.0f,
                         sinf(1.3f * f) * cosf(1.5f * f) * 2.0f);
    // Update the uniform
    glUniformMatrix4fv(mv_location, 1, GL_FALSE, mv_matrix);

    // Draw - notice that we haven't updated the projection matrix
    glDrawArrays(GL_TRIANGLES, 0, 36);
}
```

Listing 5.28: Rendering loop for the spinning cube

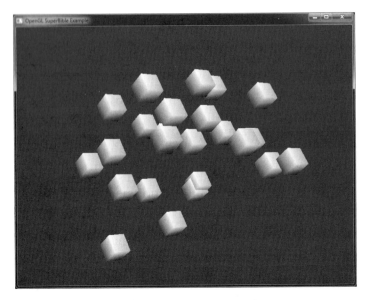

Figure 5.3: Many cubes!

Shader Storage Blocks

In addition to the read-only access to buffer objects that is provided by uniform blocks, buffer objects can be used for general storage from shaders using *shader storage blocks*. These are declared in a similar manner to uniform blocks and backed in the same way by binding a range of a buffer object to one of the indexed GL_SHADER_STORAGE_BUFFER targets. However, the biggest difference between a uniform block and a shader storage block is that your shader can *write* into the shader storage block; furthermore, it can even perform *atomic operations* on members of a shader storage block. Shader storage blocks also have a much higher upper size limit.

To declare a shader storage block, simply declare a block in the shader just like you would a uniform block; however, rather than use the `uniform` keyword, use the `buffer` qualifier. Like uniform blocks, shader storage blocks support the `std140` packing layout qualifier, but they also support the `std430`[2] packing layout qualifier, which allows arrays of integers and

---

2. The `std140` and `std430` packing layouts are named for the version of the shading language with which they were introduced—`std140` with GLSL 1.40, which was part of OpenGL 3.1, and `std430` with GLSL 4.30, which was the version released with OpenGL 4.3.

floating-point variables (and structures containing them) to be tightly packed (something that is sorely lacking in the std140 layout). This allows for better efficiency of memory use and tighter cohesion with structure layouts generated by compilers for languages such as C++. An example shader storage block declaration is shown in Listing 5.29.

```
#version 450 core

struct my_structure
{
    int         pea;
    int         carrot;
    vec4        potato;
};

layout (binding = 0, std430) buffer my_storage_block
{
    vec4            foo;
    vec3            bar;
    int             baz[24];
    my_structure    veggies;
};
```

Listing 5.29: Example shader storage block declaration

The members of a shader storage block can be referred to just as any other variable. To read from them, you could, for example, use them as a parameter to a function; to write into them, you simply assign to them. When the variable is used in an expression, the source of data will be the buffer object; when the variable is assigned to, the data will be written into the buffer object. You can place data into the buffer using functions like **glBufferData()** just as you would with a uniform block. Because the buffer is writable by the shader, if you call **glMapBufferRange()** with GL_MAP_READ_BIT (or GL_MAP_WRITE_BIT) as the access mode, you will be able to read the data produced by your shader.

Shader storage blocks and their backing buffer objects provide additional advantages over uniform blocks. For example, their size is not really limited. Of course, if you go overboard, OpenGL may fail to allocate memory for you, but there really isn't a hard-wired practical upper limit to the size of a shader storage block. Also, the newer packing rules for std430 allow an application's data to be more efficiently packed and directly accessed than would be possible with a uniform block. It is worth noting, though, that due to the stricter alignment requirements of uniform blocks and smaller minimum size, some hardware may handle uniform blocks differently than shader storage blocks and execute more efficiently when reading from them. Listing 5.30 shows how you might use a shader storage block in place of regular inputs in a vertex shader.

```
#version 450 core

struct vertex
{
    vec4            position;
    vec3            color;
};

layout (binding = 0, std430) buffer my_vertices
{
    vertex          vertices[];
};

uniform mat4 transform_matrix;

out VS_OUT
{
    vec3            color;
} vs_out;

void main(void)
{
    gl_Position = transform_matrix * vertices[gl_VertexID].position;
    vs_out.color = vertices[gl_VertexID].color;
}
```

Listing 5.30: Using a shader storage block in place of vertex attributes

Although it may seem that shader storage blocks offer so many advantages that they almost make uniform blocks and vertex attributes redundant, you should be aware that their additional flexibility makes it difficult for OpenGL to truly optimize access to storage blocks. For example, some OpenGL implementations may be able to provide faster access to uniform blocks given the knowledge that their content will always be constant. Also, reading the input data for vertex attributes may happen long before your vertex shader runs, letting OpenGL's memory subsystem keep up. Reading vertex data right in the middle of your shader might slow it down quite a bit.

Atomic Memory Operations

In addition to simple reading and writing of memory, shader storage blocks allow you to perform *atomic operations* on memory. An atomic operation is a sequence of a read from memory potentially followed by a write to memory that must be uninterrupted for the result to be correct. Consider a case where two shader invocations perform the operation m = m + 1; using the same memory location represented by m. Each invocation will load the current value stored in the memory location represented by m, add 1 to it, and then write it back to memory at the same location.

If each invocation operates in lockstep, then we will end up with the wrong value in memory unless the operation can be made atomic. This is because the first invocation will load the value from memory, then the second invocation will read the *same* value from memory. Both invocations will increment their copy of the value, the first invocation will write its incremented value back to memory, and finally the second invocation will overwrite that value with the same, incremented value that it calculated. This problem only gets worse when there are many more than two invocations running at a time.

To get around this problem, atomic operations cause the complete read–modify–write cycle to complete for one invocation before any other invocation gets a chance to even read from memory. In theory, if multiple shader invocations perform atomic operations on different memory locations, then everything should run nice and fast and work just as if you had written the naïve m = m + 1; code in your shader. If two invocations access the same memory locations (a condition known as *contention*), then they will be *serialized* and only one will get to go at one time. To execute an atomic operation on a member of a shader storage block, you call one of the atomic memory functions listed in Table 5.5.

Table 5.5: Atomic Operations on Shader Storage Blocks

Atomic Function	Behavior
atomicAdd(mem, data)	Reads from mem, adds it to data, writes the result back to mem, and then returns the value originally stored in mem.
atomicAnd(mem, data)	Reads from mem, logically ANDs it with data, writes the result back to mem, and then returns the value originally stored in mem.
atomicOr(mem, data)	Reads from mem, logically ORs it with data, writes the result back to mem, and then returns the value originally stored in mem.

continued

Atomic Function	Behavior
`atomicXor(mem, data)`	Reads from mem, logically exclusive ORs it with data, writes the result back to mem, and then returns the value originally stored in mem.
`atomicMin(mem, data)`	Reads from mem, determines the minimum of the retrieved value and data, writes the result back to mem, and then returns the value originally stored in mem.
`atomicMax(mem, data)`	Reads from mem, determines the maximum of the retrieved value and data, writes the result back to mem, and then returns the value originally stored in mem.
`atomicExchange(mem, data)`	Reads from mem, writes the value of data into mem, and then returns the value originally stored in mem.
`atomicCompSwap(mem, comp, data)`	Reads from mem, compares the retrieved value with comp, and, if they are equal, writes data into mem, but always returns the value originally stored in mem.

In Table 5.5, all of the functions have an integer (`int`) and unsigned integer (`uint`) version. For the integer versions, mem is declared as `inout int` mem; data and comp (for `atomicCompSwap`) are declared as `int` data; and `int` comp and the return values of all functions are `int`. Likewise, for the unsigned integer versions, all parameters are declared using `uint` and the return type of the function is `uint`. Notice that there are no atomic operations on floating-point variables, vectors or matrices, or integer values that are not 32 bits wide. All of the atomic memory access functions shown in Table 5.5 return the value that was in memory *prior* to the atomic operation taking place. When an atomic operation is attempted by multiple invocations of your shader to the same location at the same time, they are *serialized*, which means that they take turns. This means that you're not guaranteed to receive any particular return value from an atomic memory operation.

Synchronizing Access to Memory

When you are only reading from a buffer, data is *almost* always going to be available when you think it should be and you don't need to worry about the order in which your shaders read from it. However, when your shader starts writing data into buffer objects, either through writes to variables in shader storage blocks or through explicit calls to the atomic operation functions that might write to memory, there are cases where you need to avoid *hazards*.

Memory hazards fall roughly into three categories:

- A read-after-write (RAW) hazard can occur when your program attempts to read from a memory location right after it has written to it. Depending on the system architecture, the read and write may be reordered such that the read actually ends up being executed *before* the write is complete, resulting in the old data being returned to the application.

- A write-after-write (WAW) hazard can occur when a program performs a write to the same memory location twice in a row. You might expect that whatever data was written last would overwrite the data written first and be the value that ends up staying in memory. Again, on some architectures this is not guaranteed; in some circumstances the *first* data written by the program might actually be the data that ends up in memory.

- A write-after-read (WAR) hazard normally occurs only in parallel processing systems (such as graphics processors) and may happen when one thread of execution (such as a shader invocation) performs a write to memory after another thread believes that it has read from memory. If these operations are reordered, the thread that performed the read may end up getting the data that was written by the second thread without expecting it.

Because of the deeply pipelined and highly parallel nature of the systems that OpenGL is expected to be running on, it includes a number of mechanisms to alleviate and control memory hazards. Without these features, OpenGL implementations would need to be far more conservative about reordering your shaders and running them in parallel. The main apparatus for dealing with memory hazards is the *memory barrier*.

A memory barrier essentially acts as a marker that tells OpenGL, "Hey, if you're going to start reordering things, that's fine—just don't let anything

I say after this point actually happen before anything I say before it." You can insert barriers both in your application code—with calls to OpenGL—and in your shaders.

Using Barriers in Your Application

The function to insert a barrier is **glMemoryBarrier()** and its prototype is

```
void glMemoryBarrier(GLbitfield barriers);
```

The **glMemoryBarrier()** function takes a GLbitfield parameter, barriers, which allows you to specify which of OpenGL's memory subsystems should obey the barrier and which are free to ignore it and continue as they would have. The barrier affects ordering of memory operations in the categories specified in barriers. If you want to bash OpenGL with a big hammer and just synchronize everything, you can set barriers to GL_ALL_BARRIER_BITS. However, there are quite a number of bits defined that you can add together to be more precise about what you want to synchronize. A few examples are listed here:

- Including GL_SHADER_STORAGE_BARRIER_BIT tells OpenGL that you want it to let any accesses (writes in particular) performed by shaders that are run before the barrier complete before letting any shaders access the data after the barrier. Thus, if you write into a shader storage buffer from a shader and then call **glMemoryBarrier()** with GL_SHADER_STORAGE_BARRIER_BIT included in barriers, shaders you run after the barrier will "see" that data. Without such a barrier, this is not guaranteed.

- Including GL_UNIFORM_BARRIER_BIT in barriers tells OpenGL that you might have written something into memory that might be used as a uniform buffer after the barrier, and it should wait to make sure that shaders that write into the buffer have completed before letting shaders that use it as a uniform buffer run. You would set this, for example, if you wrote into a buffer using a shader storage block in a shader and then wanted to use that buffer as a uniform buffer later.

- Including GL_VERTEX_ATTRIB_ARRAY_BARRIER_BIT ensures that OpenGL will wait for shaders that write to buffers to complete before using any of those buffers as the source of vertex data through a vertex attribute. For example, you would set this if you write into a buffer through a shader storage block and then want to use that buffer as part of a vertex array to feed data into the vertex shader of a subsequent drawing command.

There are plenty more of these bits that control the ordering of shaders with respect to OpenGL's other subsystems; we will introduce them as we talk more in depth about those subsystems. The key points about `glMemoryBarrier()` are that the items included in barriers are the *destination* subsystems and that the mechanism by which you updated the data is assumed to be writing it to memory with a shader.

Using Barriers in Your Shaders

Just as you can insert memory barriers in your application's code to control the ordering of memory accesses performed by your shaders relative to your application, so you can also insert barriers into your shaders to stop OpenGL from reading or writing memory in some order other than what your shader code says. The basic memory barrier function in GLSL is

```
void memoryBarrier();
```

If you call `memoryBarrier()` from your shader code, any memory reads or writes that you might have performed will complete before the function returns. This means that it's safe to read data back that you might have just written. Without a barrier, it's even possible that when you read from a memory location that you just wrote to, OpenGL will return the *old* data instead of the new!

To provide finer control over which types of memory accesses are ordered, there are some more specialized versions of the `memoryBarrier()` function. For example, `memoryBarrierBuffer()` orders transactions on reads and writes to buffers, but to nothing else. We'll introduce the other barrier functions as we talk about the types of data that they protect.

Atomic Counters

Atomic counters are a special type of variable that represents storage that is shared across multiple shader invocations. This storage is backed by a buffer object, and functions are provided in GLSL to increment and decrement the values stored in the buffer. What is special about these operations is that they are *atomic*: Just like with the equivalent functions for members of shader storage blocks (shown in Table 5.5), they return the original value of the counter before it was modified. Just like the other atomic operations, if two shader invocations increment the same counter at the same time, OpenGL will make them take turns. One shader invocation will receive the original value of the counter, the other will receive the original value plus 1, and the final value of the counter will be that of the original value plus 2. Also, just as with shader storage block atomics, there is no guarantee of the order in which these operations will occur, so you can't rely on receiving any specific value.

To declare an atomic counter in a shader, do this:

```
layout (binding = 0) uniform atomic_uint my_variable;
```

OpenGL provides a number of binding points to which you can bind the buffers where it will store the values of atomic counters. Additionally, each atomic counter is stored at a specific offset within the buffer object. The buffer binding index and the offset within the buffer bound to that binding can be specified using the `binding` and `offset` layout qualifiers, which can be applied to an atomic counter uniform declaration. For example, if we wish to place my_variable at offset 8 within the buffer bound to atomic counter binding point 3, then we could write:

```
layout (binding = 3, offset = 8) uniform atomic_uint my_variable;
```

To provide storage for the atomic counter, we can now bind a buffer object to the GL_ATOMIC_COUNTER_BUFFER indexed binding point. Listing 5.31 shows how to do this.

```
// Generate a buffer name
GLuint buf;
glGenBuffers(1, &buf);
// Bind it to the generic GL_ATOMIC_COUNTER_BUFFER target and
// initialize its storage
glBindBuffer(GL_ATOMIC_COUNTER_BUFFER, buf);
glBufferData(GL_ATOMIC_COUNTER_BUFFER, 16 * sizeof(GLuint),
             NULL, GL_DYNAMIC_COPY);
// Now bind it to the fourth indexed atomic counter buffer target
glBindBufferBase(GL_ATOMIC_COUNTER_BUFFER, 3, buf);
```

Listing 5.31: Setting up an atomic counter buffer

Before using the atomic counter in your shader, it's a good idea to reset it first. To do this, you can either call **glBufferSubData()** and pass the address of a variable holding the value you want to reset the counter(s) to; map the buffer using **glMapBufferRange()** and write the values directly into it; or use **glClearBufferSubData()**. Listing 5.32 shows an example of all three methods.

```
// Bind our buffer to the generic atomic counter buffer
// binding point
glBindBuffer(GL_ATOMIC_COUNTER_BUFFER, buf);
```

```
// Method 1 - use glBufferSubData to reset an atomic counter
const GLuint zero = 0;
glBufferSubData(GL_ATOMIC_COUNTER_BUFFER, 2 * sizeof(GLuint),
                sizeof(GLuint), &zero);

// Method 2 - Map the buffer and write the value directly into it
GLuint * data =
    (GLuint *)glMapBufferRange(GL_ATOMIC_COUNTER_BUFFER,
                              0, 16 * sizeof(GLuint),
                              GL_MAP_WRITE_BIT |
                              GL_MAP_INVALIDATE_RANGE_BIT);
data[2] = 0;
glUnmapBuffer(GL_ATOMIC_COUNTER_BUFFER);

// Method 3 - use glClearBufferSubData
glClearBufferSubData(GL_ATOMIC_COUNTER_BUFFER,
                     GL_R32UI,
                     2 * sizeof(GLuint),
                     sizeof(GLuint),
                     GL_RED_INTEGER, GL_UNSIGNED_INT,
                     &zero);
```

Listing 5.32: Setting up an atomic counter buffer

Now that you have created a buffer and bound it to an atomic counter buffer target, and you have declared an atomic counter uniform in your shader, you are ready to start counting things. First, to increment an atomic counter, call

```
uint atomicCounterIncrement(atomic_uint c);
```

This function reads the current value of the atomic counter, adds 1 to it, writes the new value back to the atomic counter, and returns the original value it read—and it does it all atomically. Because the order of execution between different invocations of your shader is not defined, calling atomicCounterIncrement twice in a row won't necessarily give you two consecutive values.

Next, to decrement an atomic counter, call

```
uint atomicCounterDecrement(atomic_uint c);
```

This function reads the current value of the atomic counter, subtracts 1 from it, writes the value back into the atomic counter, and returns the *new* value of the counter to you. Notice that this is the opposite of atomicCounterIncrement. If only one invocation of a shader is executing, and it calls atomicCounterIncrement followed by atomicCounterDecrement, it should receive the same value from both functions. However, in most cases, many invocations of the shader will be executing in parallel; in practice, it is unlikely that you will receive the same value from a pair of calls to these functions.

If you simply want to know the value of an atomic counter, you can call

```
uint atomicCounter(atomic_uint c);
```

This function simply returns the current value stored in the atomic counter c.

As an example of using atomic counters, Listing 5.33 shows a simple fragment shader that increments an atomic counter each time it executes. This has the effect of producing the screen space area of the objects rendered with this shader in the atomic counter.

```
#version 450 core

layout (binding = 0, offset = 0) uniform atomic_uint area;

void main(void)
{
    atomicCounterIncrement(area);
}
```

Listing 5.33: Counting area using an atomic counter

One thing you might notice about the shader in Listing 5.33 is that it doesn't have any regular outputs (variables declared with the out storage qualifier) and won't write any data into the framebuffer. In fact, we'll disable writing to the framebuffer while we run this shader. To turn off writing to the framebuffer, we can call

```
glColorMask(GL_FALSE, GL_FALSE, GL_FALSE, GL_FALSE);
```

To turn framebuffer writes back on again, we can call

```
glColorMask(GL_TRUE, GL_TRUE, GL_TRUE, GL_TRUE);
```

Because atomic counters are stored in buffers, it's possible now to bind our atomic counter to another buffer target, such as one of the GL_UNIFORM_BUFFER targets, and retrieve its value in a shader. This allows us to use the value of an atomic counter to control the execution of shaders that your program runs later. Listing 5.34 shows an example shader that reads the result of our atomic counter through a uniform block and uses it as part of the calculation of its output color.

```
#version 450 core

layout (binding = 0) uniform area_block
{
    uint     counter_value;
};

out vec4 color;

uniform float max_area;

void main(void)
{
    float brightness = clamp(float(counter_value) / max_area,
                             0.0, 1.0);

    color = vec4(brightness, brightness, brightness, 1.0);
}
```

Listing 5.34: Using the result of an atomic counter in a uniform block

When we execute the shader in Listing 5.33, it simply counts the area of the geometry that's being rendered. That area then shows up in Listing 5.34 as the first and only member of the area_block uniform buffer block. We divide it by the maximum expected area and then use that result as the brightness of further geometry. Consider what happens when we render with these two shaders. If an object is close to the viewer, it will appear larger and cover more screen area—the ultimate value of the atomic counter will be greater. When the object is far from the viewer, it will be smaller and the atomic counter won't reach such a high value. The value of the atomic counter will be reflected in the uniform block in the second shader, affecting the brightness of the geometry it renders.

Synchronizing Access to Atomic Counters

Atomic counters represent locations in buffer objects. While shaders are executing, their values may well reside in special memory inside the graphics processor (which is what makes them faster than simple atomic memory operations on members of shader storage blocks, for example). However, when your shader is done executing, the values of the atomic counters will be written back into memory. As such, incrementing and decrementing atomic counters is considered a form of memory operation and so can be susceptible to the hazards described earlier in this chapter. In fact, the **glMemoryBarrier()** function supports a bit specifically for synchronizing access to atomic counters with other parts of the OpenGL pipeline. Calling

```
glMemoryBarrier(GL_ATOMIC_COUNTER_BARRIER_BIT);
```

will ensure that any access to an atomic counter in a buffer object will reflect updates to that buffer by a shader. You should call glMemoryBarrier() with the GL_ATOMIC_COUNTER_BARRIER_BIT set when something has *written* to a buffer that you want to see reflected in the values of your atomic counters. If you update the values in a buffer by using an atomic counter and then use that buffer for something else, the bit you include in the barriers parameter to glMemoryBarrier() should correspond to what you want that buffer to be used for, which will not necessarily include GL_ATOMIC_COUNTER_BARRIER_BIT.

Similarly, there is a version of the GLSL memoryBarrier() function, called memoryBarrierAtomicCounter(), that ensures operations on atomic counters are completed before it returns.

Textures

Textures are a structured form of storage that can be made accessible to shaders both for reading and for writing. They are most often used to store image data and come in many forms and arrangements. Perhaps the most common texture layout is two-dimensional, but textures can also be created in one-dimensional or three-dimensional layouts, array forms (with multiple textures stacked together to form one logical object), cubes, and so on. Textures are represented as objects that can be generated, bound to *texture units*, and manipulated. To use textures, we first need to ask OpenGL to create some for us by calling glCreateTextures(). At this point, the name we get back represents a just-created texture object ready to be filled with data and used by binding it to a context.

Creating and Initialzing Textures

The full creation of a texture involves specifying the type of texture you want to create, and then telling OpenGL the size of the image you want to store in it. Listing 5.35 shows how to create a new texture object with glCreateTextures(), use glBindTexture() to bind it to the GL_TEXTURE_2D target (which is one of several available texture targets), and then use the glTexStorage2D() function to allocate storage for the texture.

```
// The type used for names in OpenGL is GLuint
GLuint texture;

// Create a new 2D texture object
glCreateTextures(GL_TEXTURE_2D, 1, &texture);
```

```
// Specify the amount of storage we want to use for the texture
glTextureStorage2D(texture,           // Texture object
                   1,                 // 1 mipmap level
                   GL_RGBA32F,        // 32-bit floating-point RGBA data
                   256, 256);         // 256 x 256 texels

// Now bind it to the context using the GL_TEXTURE_2D binding point
glBindTexture(GL_TEXTURE_2D, texture);
```

Listing 5.35: Generating, initializing, and binding a texture

Compare Listing 5.1 and Listing 5.35, noting how similar they are. In both cases, you create a new object, define the storage for the data it contains, and then bind it to a target ready for use by your OpenGL program. For textures, the function we've used to do this is **glTextureStorage2D()**. It takes as parameters the name of the texture we want to allocate storage for; the number of *levels* that are used in *mipmapping*, which we are not using here (but will explain shortly); the *internal format* of the texture (we chose GL_RGBA32F here, which is a four-channel floating-point format); and the width and height of the texture. When we call this function, OpenGL will allocate enough memory to store a texture with those dimensions for us. After defining storage for the texture, we can bind it to the context to use it. Next, we need to specify some data for the texture. To do this, we use **glTexSubImage2D()** as shown in Listing 5.36.

```
// Define some data to upload into the texture
float * data = new float[256 * 256 * 4];

// generate_texture() is a function that fills memory with image data
generate_texture(data, 256, 256);

// Assume that "texture" is a 2D texture that we created earlier
glTextureSubImage2D(texture,          // Texture object
                    0,                // Level 0
                    0, 0,             // Offset 0, 0
                    256, 256,         // 256 x 256 texels, replace entire image
                    GL_RGBA,          // Four-channel data
                    GL_FLOAT,         // Floating-point data
                    data);            // Pointer to data

// Free the memory we allocated before - OpenGL now has our data
delete [] data;
```

Listing 5.36: Updating texture data with **glTexSubImage2D()**

After the code in Listing 5.36 has run, OpenGL keeps a copy of the original texture data that we gave it and we're free to release the application's memory to the operating system.

If all you want to do is initialize a texture to a fixed value, then you can use **glClearTexSubImage()**, whose prototype is

```
void glClearTexSubImage(GLuint texture,
                        GLint level,
                        GLint xoffset,
                        GLint yoffset,
                        GLint zoffset,
                        GLsizei width,
                        GLsizei height,
                        GLsizei depth,
                        GLenum format,
                        GLenum type,
                        const void * data);
```

For **glClearTexSubImage()**, any texture type can be passed in texture—the dimensionality of the texture is deduced from the object you pass. level specifies the mipmap level you want to clear; xoffset, yoffset, and zoffset provide the starting offset of the region to be cleared; and width, height, and depth specify the dimensions of the region. The format and type parameters are interpreted exactly as they are for **glTexSubImage2D()**, but data is assumed to be a single texel's worth of data, which is then replicated across the whole texture. This command is not particularly useful if you're about to fill the texture with known data or bind the texture to a framebuffer to draw into it, but it can be very useful when you are going to write directly to the texture as an image variable in a shader, which will be discussed shortly.

Texture Targets and Types

The example in Listing 5.36 demonstrates how to create a 2D texture by binding a new name to the 2D texture target specified with GL_TEXTURE_2D. This is just one of several targets that are available to bind textures to, and a new texture object takes on the type determined by the target to which it is first bound. Thus, texture targets and types are often used interchangably. Table 5.6 lists the available targets and describes the type of texture that will be created when a new name is bound to that target.

The GL_TEXTURE_2D texture target is probably the one you will deal with the most. This is our standard, two-dimensional image that you imagine would represent a picture. The GL_TEXTURE_1D and GL_TEXTURE_3D types allow you to create one-dimensional and three-dimensional textures, respectively. A 1D texture behaves just like a 2D texture with a height of 1,

Table 5.6: Texture Targets and Description

Texture Target (GL_TEXTURE_*)	Description
1D	One-dimensional texture
2D	Two-dimensional texture
3D	Three-dimensional texture
RECTANGLE	Rectangle texture
1D_ARRAY	One-dimensional array texture
2D_ARRAY	Two-dimensional array texture
CUBE_MAP	Cube map texture
CUBE_MAP_ARRAY	Cube map array texture
BUFFER	Buffer texture
2D_MULTISAMPLE	Two-dimensional multisample texture
2D_MULTISAMPLE_ARRAY	Two-dimensional array multisample texture

for the most part. A 3D texture, however, can be used to represent a *volume* and actually has a three-dimensional texture coordinate. Rectangle textures[3] are a special case of 2D textures that have subtle differences in how they are read in shaders and which parameters they support.

The GL_TEXTURE_1D_ARRAY and GL_TEXTURE_2D_ARRAY types represent arrays of texture images aggregated into single objects. They are covered in more detail later in this chapter. Likewise, cube map textures (created by binding a texture name to the GL_TEXTURE_CUBE_MAP target) represent a collection of six square images that form a cube, which can be used to simulate lighting environments, for example. Just as the GL_TEXTURE_1D_ARRAY and GL_TEXTURE_2D_ARRAY targets represent 1D and 2D textures that are arrays of 1D or 2D images, so the GL_TEXTURE_CUBE_MAP_ARRAY target represents a texture that is an array of cube maps.

Buffer textures, represented by the GL_TEXTURE_BUFFER target, are a special type of texture that are much like a 1D texture, except that their storage is actually represented by a buffer object. In addition, they differ from a 1D texture in that their maximum size can be much larger than a 1D texture.

---

3. Rectangle textures were introduced into OpenGL when not all hardware could support textures whose dimensions were not integer powers of 2. Modern graphics hardware supports this almost universally, so rectangle textures have essentially become a subset of the 2D texture, and there isn't much need to use one in preference to a 2D texture.

The minimum requirement from the OpenGL specification is 65,536 texels, but in practice most implementations will allow you to create much larger buffers—usually in the range of several hundred megabytes. Buffer textures also lack a few of the features supported by the 1D texture type, such as filtering and mipmaps.

Finally, the multisample texture types GL_TEXTURE_2D_MULTISAMPLE and GL_TEXTURE_2D_MULTISAMPLE_ARRAY are used for *multisample antialiasing*, which is a technique for improving image quality, especially at the edges of lines and polygons.

Reading from Textures in Shaders

Once you've created a texture object and placed some data in it, you can read that data in your shaders and use it to color fragments, for example. Textures are represented in shaders as *sampler variables* and are hooked up to the outside world by declaring uniforms with sampler types. Just as there can be textures with various dimensionalities that can be created and used through the various texture targets, so there are corresponding sampler variable types that can be used in GLSL to represent them. The sampler type that represents two-dimensional textures is sampler2D. To access our texture in a shader, we can create a uniform variable with the sampler2D type, and then use the texelFetch built-in function with that uniform and a set of texture coordinates at which to read from the texture. Listing 5.37 shows an example of how to read from a texture in GLSL.

```
#version 450 core

uniform sampler2D s;

out vec4 color;

void main(void)
{
    color = texelFetch(s, ivec2(gl_FragCoord.xy), 0);
}
```

Listing 5.37: Reading from a texture in GLSL

The shader of Listing 5.37 simply reads from the uniform sampler s using a texture coordinate derived from the built-in variable gl_FragCoord. This variable is an input to the fragment shader that holds the floating-point coordinate of the fragment being processed in window coordinates. However, the texelFetch function accepts integer-point coordinates that range from $(0, 0)$ to the width and height of the texture. Therefore, we

Figure 5.4: A simple textured triangle

construct a two-component integer vector (`ivec2`) from the x and y components of `gl_FragCoord`. The third parameter to `texelFetch` is the mipmap level of the texture. Because the texture in this example has only one level, we set it to zero. The result of using this shader with our single-triangle example is shown in Figure 5.4.

Sampler Types

Each dimensionality of texture has a target to which texture objects are bound, as introduced in the previous section, and each target has a corresponding sampler type that is used in the shader to access them. Table 5.7 lists the basic texture types and the sampler that should be used in shaders to access them.

Table 5.7: Basic Texture Targets and Sampler Types

Texture Target	Sampler Type
GL_TEXTURE_1D	sampler1D
GL_TEXTURE_2D	sampler2D
GL_TEXTURE_3D	sampler3D

continued

Texture Target	Sampler Type
GL_TEXTURE_RECTANGLE	sampler2DRect
GL_TEXTURE_1D_ARRAY	sampler1DArray
GL_TEXTURE_2D_ARRAY	sampler2DArray
GL_TEXTURE_CUBE_MAP	samplerCube
GL_TEXTURE_CUBE_MAP_ARRAY	samplerCubeArray
GL_TEXTURE_BUFFER	samplerBuffer
GL_TEXTURE_2D_MULTISAMPLE	sampler2DMS
GL_TEXTURE_2D_MULTISAMPLE_ARRAY	sampler2DMSArray

As shown in Table 5.7, to create a 1D texture and then use it in your shader, you would bind a new texture name to the GL_TEXTURE_1D target and then use a sampler1D variable in your shader to read from it. Likewise, for 2D textures, you'd use GL_TEXTURE_2D and sampler2D; for 3D textures, you'd use GL_TEXTURE_3D and sampler3D; and so on.

The GLSL sampler types sampler1D, sampler2D, and so on represent floating-point data. It is also possible to store signed and unsigned integer data in textures and retrieve it in your shader. To represent a texture containing signed integer data, we prefix the equivalent floating-point sampler type with the letter i. Similarly, to represent a texture containing unsigned integer data, we prefix the equivalent floating-point sampler type with the letter u. For example, a 2D texture containing signed integer data would be represented by a variable of type isampler2D, and a 2D texture containing unsigned integer data would be represented by a variable of type usampler2D.

As shown in our introductory example of Listing 5.37, we read from textures in shaders using the texelFetch built-in function. There are actually many variations of this function, because it is *overloaded*. This means that there are several versions of the function, each of which has a different set of function parameters. Each function takes a sampler variable as the first parameter, with the main differentiator between the functions being the type of that sampler. The remaining parameters to the function depend on the type of sampler being used. In particular, the number of components in the texture coordinate depends on the dimensionality of the sampler, and the return type of the function depends on the type of the sampler (floating point, signed, or unsigned integer). For example, the following are all declarations of the texelFetch function:

```
vec4 texelFetch(sampler1D s, int P, int lod);
vec4 texelFetch(sampler2D s, ivec2 P, int lod);
ivec4 texelFetch(isampler2D s, ivec2 P, int lod);
uvec4 texelFetch(usampler3D s, ivec3 P, int lod);
```

Notice how the version of texelFetch that takes a sampler1D sampler type expects a one-dimensional texture coordinate, int P, but the version that takes a sampler2D expects a two-dimensional coordinate, ivec2 P. You can also see that the return type of the texelFetch function is influenced by the type of sampler that it takes. The version of texelFetch that takes a sampler2D produces a floating-point vector, whereas the version that takes an isampler2D sampler returns an integer vector. This type of overloading is similar to that supported by languages such as C++. That is, functions can be overloaded by parameter types, but not by return type, unless that return type is determined by one of the parameters.

All of the texture functions return a four-component vector, regardless of whether that vector is floating-point or integer, and independently from the format of the texture object bound to the texture unit referenced by the sampler variable. If you read from a texture that contains fewer than four channels, the default value of 0 will be filled in for the green and blue channels and 1 will be filled in for the alpha channel. If one or more channels of the returned data never get used by your shader, that's fine: It's likely that the shader compiler will optimize away any code that becomes redundant as a result.

You can get more information about the samplers in your shader by using a few other functions provided by GLSL. First, the textureSize function returns the size of the texture. It, too, is overloaded and returns a different-dimension result that depends on the argument you specify. A few examples follow:

```
int textureSize(sampler1D sampler, int lod);
ivec2 textureSize(sampler2D sampler, int lod);
ivec3 textureSize(gsampler3D sampler, int lod);
```

Like the texelFetch function, textureSize takes an lod parameter, which specifies which of the texture's mipmap levels you'd like to know the size of. If you're working with multisample textures (a special kind of texture that has multiple colors, or *samples* for each texel), you can find out how many samples it contains by calling

```
int textureSamples(sampler2DMS sampler);
```

The textureSamples function returns the number of samples in the texture as a single integer. Again, several overloaded versions of this function exist for the various sampler types, but they all return a single integer.

Loading Textures from Files

In our simple example, we generated the texture data directly in our application. However, this clearly isn't practical in a real-world application where you most likely have images stored on disk or on the other end of a network connection. Your options are either to convert your textures into hard-coded arrays (yes, there are utilities that will do this for you) or to load them from files within your application.

There are lots of image file formats that store pictures with or without compression, some of which are more suited to photographs and some of which are more suited to line drawings or text. However, very few image formats exist that can properly store all of the formats supported by OpenGL or represent advanced features such as mipmaps, cube maps, and so on. One such format is .KTX, or the *Khronos TeXture format*, which was specifically designed for the storage of pretty much anything that can be represented as an OpenGL texture. In fact, the .KTX file format includes most of the parameters you need to pass to texturing functions such as **glTextureStorage2D()** and **glTextureSubImage2D()** to load the texture directly in the file.

The structure of a .KTX file header is shown in Listing 5.38.

```
struct header
{
    unsigned char       identifier[12];
    unsigned int        endianness;
    unsigned int        gltype;
    unsigned int        gltypesize;
    unsigned int        glformat;
    unsigned int        glinternalformat;
    unsigned int        glbaseinternalformat;
    unsigned int        pixelwidth;
    unsigned int        pixelheight;
    unsigned int        pixeldepth;
    unsigned int        arrayelements;
    unsigned int        faces;
    unsigned int        miplevels;
    unsigned int        keypairbytes;
};
```

Listing 5.38: The header of a .KTX file

In this header, identifier contains a series of bytes that allow the application to verify that this is a legal .KTX file and endianness contains a known value that will be different depending on whether a little-endian or big-endian machine created the file. The gltype, glformat, glinternalformat, and glbaseinternalformat fields are actually the raw values of the GLenum types that will be used to load the texture. The gltypesize field stores the size, in bytes, of one element of data in the gltype type, and is used in case the endianness of the file does not match the native endianness of the machine loading the file, in which case each element of the texture must be byte swapped as it is loaded. The remaining fields—pixelwidth, pixelheight, pixeldepth, arrayelements, faces, and miplevels—store information about the dimensions of the texture. Finally, the keypairbytes field is used to allow applications to store additional information after the header and before the texture data. After this information, the raw texture data begins.

Because the .KTX file format was designed specifically for use in OpenGL-based applications, writing the code to load a .KTX file is actually pretty straightforward. Even so, a basic loader for .KTX files is included in this book's source code. To use the loader, you can simply reserve a new name for a texture using **glGenTextures()**, and then pass it, along with the name of the .KTX file, to the loader. If you wish, you can even omit the OpenGL name for the texture (or pass 0) and the loader will call **glCreateTextures()** for you. If the .KTX file is recognized, the loader will bind the texture to the appropriate target and load it with the data from the .KTX file. An example is shown in Listing 5.39.

```
// Generate a name for the texture
glGenTextures(1, &texture);

// Load texture from file
sb7::ktx::file::load("media/textures/icemoon.ktx", texture);
```

Listing 5.39: Loading a .KTX file

If you think that Listing 5.39 looks simple, you're right! The .KTX loader takes care of almost all the details for you. If the loader is successful in loading and allocating the texture, it will return the name of the texture you passed in (or the one it generated for you); if it fails for some reason, it will return 0. If you want to use the texture, you'll need to bind it to one of the texture units. Don't forget to delete the texture when you're done with it by calling **glDeleteTextures()** on the name returned by the .KTX loader. Applying the texture loaded in Listing 5.39 to the whole viewport produces the image shown in Figure 5.5.

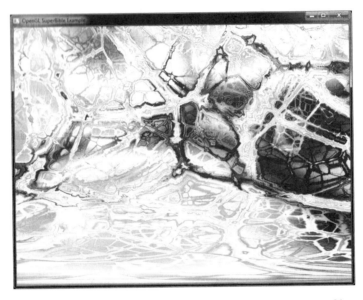

Figure 5.5: A full-screen texture loaded from a .KTX file

Texture Coordinates

In the simple example shown earlier in this chapter, we used the current fragment's window-space coordinate as the position at which to read from the texture. You can actually use any values you want, though in a fragment shader, they will usually be derived from one of the inputs that are smoothly interpolated from across each primitive by OpenGL. It is then the vertex (or geometry or tessellation evaluation) shader's responsibility to produce the values of these coordinates. The vertex shader will generally pull the texture coordinates from a per-vertex input and pass them through unmodified. When you use multiple textures in your fragment shader, there is nothing to stop you from using a unique set of texture coordinates for each texture, but for many applications a single set of texture coordinates will be used for every texture.

A simple vertex shader that accepts a single texture coordinate and passes it through to the fragment shader is shown in Listing 5.40; the corresponding fragment shader is shown in Listing 5.41.

```
#version 450 core

uniform mat4 mv_matrix;
uniform mat4 proj_matrix;

layout (location = 0) in vec4 position;
layout (location = 4) in vec2 tc;
```

```
out VS_OUT
{
    vec2 tc;
} vs_out;

void main(void)
{
    // Calculate the position of each vertex
    vec4 pos_vs = mv_matrix * position;

    // Pass the texture coordinate through unmodified
    vs_out.tc = tc;

    gl_Position = proj_matrix * pos_vs;
}
```

Listing 5.40: Vertex shader with a single texture coordinate

The shader shown in Listing 5.41 not only takes as input the texture coordinate produced by the vertex shader, but also scales it non-uniformly. The texture's wrapping mode is set to GL_REPEAT, which means that the texture will be repeated several times across the object.

```
#version 450 core

layout (binding = 0) uniform sampler2D tex_object;

// Input from vertex shader
in VS_OUT
{
    vec2 tc;
} fs_in;

// Output to framebuffer
out vec4 color;

void main(void)
{
    // Simply read from the texture at the (scaled) coordinates and
    // assign the result to the shader's output.
    color = texture(tex_object, fs_in.tc * vec2(3.0, 1.0));
}
```

Listing 5.41: Fragment shader with a single texture coordinate

By passing a texture coordinate with each vertex, we can *wrap* a texture around an object. Texture coordinates can then be generated offline procedurally or assigned by hand by an artist using a modeling program and stored in an object file. If we load a simple checkerboard pattern into a texture and apply it to an object, we can see how the texture is wrapped around it. Such an example is shown in Figure 5.6. On the left is the object with a checkerboard pattern wrapped around it. On the right is the same object using a texture loaded from a file.

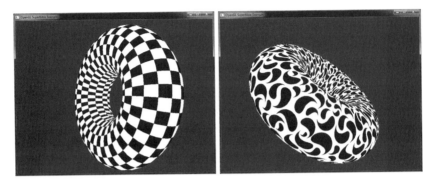

Figure 5.6: An object wrapped in simple textures

Controlling How Texture Data Is Read

OpenGL provides a lot of flexibility in how it reads data from textures and returns it to your shader. Usually, texture coordinates are normalized—that is, they range between 0.0 and 1.0. OpenGL lets you control what happens when the texture coordinates you supply fall outside this range. This is called the *wrapping mode* of the sampler. Also, you get to decide how values *between* the real samples are calculated. This is called the *filtering mode* of a sampler. The parameters controlling the wrapping and filtering modes of a sampler are stored in a *sampler object.*

To create one or more sampler objects, call

```
void glCreateSamplers(GLsizei n, GLuint * samplers);
```

Here, n is the number of sampler objects you want to create and `samplers` is the address of at least n unsigned integer variables that will be used to store the names of the newly created sampler objects.

Sampler objects are manipulated in the same way as other objects in OpenGL. The two main functions you will use to set the parameters of a sampler object are

```
void glSamplerParameteri(GLuint sampler,
                         GLenum pname,
                         GLint param);
```

and

```
void glSamplerParameterf(GLuint sampler,
                         GLenum pname,
                         GLfloat param);
```

Notice that **glSamplerParameteri()** and **glSamplerParameterf()** both take the sampler object name as the first parameter. You will need to bind a sampler object to use it, but in this case you bind it to a texture unit just as you would a texture. The function used to bind a sampler object to one of the texture units is **glBindSampler()**, whose prototype is

```
void glBindSampler(GLuint unit, GLuint sampler);
```

Rather than taking a texture target, **glBindSampler()** takes the index of the texture unit to which it should bind the sampler object. Together, the sampler object and the texture object bound to a given texture unit form a complete set of data and parameters required for constructing texels as demanded by your shaders. By separating the parameters of the texture sampler from the texture data, three important behaviors become possible:

- You can use the same set of sampling parameters for a large number of textures without specifying those parameters for each of the textures.

- You can change the texture bound to a texture unit without updating the sampler parameters.

- You can read from the same texture with multiple sets of sampler parameters at the same time.

Although nontrivial applications will likely opt to use their own sampler objects, each texture effectively contains an embedded sampler object that includes the sampling parameters to be used for that texture when no sampler object is bound to the corresponding texture unit. You can think of this as the default sampling parameters for a texture. To access the sampler object stored inside the texture object, call

```
void glTextureParameterf(GLuint texture,
                         GLenum pname,
                         GLfloat param);
```

or

```
void glTextureParameteri(GLuint texture,
                         GLenum pname,
                         GLint param);
```

In these cases, the `texture` parameter specifies the texture whose embedded sampler object you want to access and pname and `parameter` have the same meanings as for **glSamplerParameteri()** and **glSamplerParameterf()**.

Using Multiple Textures

If you want to use multiple textures in a single shader, you'll need to create multiple sampler uniforms and set them up to reference different texture units. You'll also need to bind multiple textures to your context at the same time. To allow this, OpenGL supports multiple texture units. The number of units supported can be queried by calling **glGetIntegerv()** with the GL_MAX_COMBINED_TEXTURE_IMAGE_UNITS parameter, as in

```
GLint units;
glGetIntegerv(GL_MAX_COMBINED_TEXTURE_IMAGE_UNITS, &units);
```

This will tell you the maximum number of texture units that might be accessible to all shader stages at any one time. To bind a texture to a specific texture unit, rather than calling **glBindTexture()** as you have been doing so far, you need to instead call **glBindTextureUnit()**, whose prototype is

```
void glBindTextureUnit(GLuint unit,
                       GLuint texture);
```

Here, unit is the zero-based index of the unit to which you want to bind the texture and texture is the name of the texture object you're going to bind. As an example, we can bind multiple textures by performing the following:

```
GLuint textures[3];

// Create three 2D textures
glCreateTextures(3, GL_TEXTURE_2D, &textures);

// Bind the three textures to the first three texture units
glBindTextureUnit(0, textures[0]);
glBindTextureUnit(1, textures[1]);
glBindTextureUnit(2, textures[2]);
```

Once you have bound multiple textures to your context, you need to make the sampler uniforms in your shaders refer to the different units. Samplers (which represent a texture and a set of sampling parameters) are represented by uniform variables in your shaders. If you don't initialize them, they will, by default, refer to unit 0. This might be fine for a simple application that uses a single texture (you'll notice that we've settled for that default in our examples so far), but the uniforms will need to be initialized to refer to the correct texture units in more complex applications. To do this, you can initialize its value at shader compilation time by using the binding layout qualifier in your shader code. To create three sampler uniforms referring to texture units 0, 1, and 2, we can write

```
layout (binding = 0) uniform sampler2D foo;
layout (binding = 1) uniform sampler2D bar;
layout (binding = 2) uniform sampler2D baz;
```

After compiling this code and linking it into a program object, the sampler foo will reference texture unit 0, bar will reference unit 1, and baz will reference unit 2. Setting the unit to which a sampler refers directly in the shader code is convenient and explicit and does not require changes to the application's source code. This is the method we will use in the majority of the samples in the remainder of the book.

Texture Filtering

There is almost never a one-to-one correspondence between texels in the texture map and pixels on the screen. A careful programmer could achieve this result, but only by texturing geometry[4] that was carefully planned to appear on screen such that the texels and pixels lined up. (This is actually often done when OpenGL is used for image processing applications.) Consequently, texture images are always either stretched or shrunk as they are applied to geometric surfaces. Due to the orientation of the geometry, a given texture could even be stretched in one dimension and shrunk in another dimension at the same time across the surface of some object.

In the samples presented so far, we have been using the texelFetch() function, which fetches a single texel from the selected texture at specific integer texture coordinates. Clearly, if we want to achieve a fragment-to-texel ratio that is not an integer, this function isn't going to cut it. Here, we need a more flexible function, and that function is simply called texture(). Like texelFetch(), it has several overloaded prototypes:

```
vec4 texture(sampler1D s, float P);
vec4 texture(sampler2D s, vec2 P);
ivec4 texture(isampler2D s, vec2 P);
uvec4 texture(usampler3D s, vec3 P);
```

As you might have noticed, unlike the texelFetch() function, the texture() function accepts *floating-point* texture coordinates. The range 0.0 to 1.0 in each dimension maps exactly once onto the texture. Obviously, not every possible value between 0.0 and 1.0 is going to map directly to a single texture—sometimes the coordinate will fall *between* texels. Further, the texture coordinates can even stray far outside the range 0.0 to 1.0. The next few sections describe how OpenGL takes these floating-point numbers and uses them to produce texel values for your shaders.

---

4. Such geometry is common in 2D graphics rendering such as user-interface elements, text, and so on.

The process of calculating color fragments from a stretched or shrunken texture map is called *texture filtering*. Stretching a texture is also known as *magnification* and shrinking a texture is also known as *minification*. Using the sampler parameter functions, OpenGL allows you to set the method of constructing the values of texels under both magnification and minification. These conditions are known as *filters*. The parameter names for these two filters are GL_TEXTURE_MAG_FILTER and GL_TEXTURE_MIN_FILTER for the magnification and minification filters, respectively. For now, you can select from two basic texture filters for them, GL_NEAREST and GL_LINEAR, which correspond to nearest neighbor and linear filtering, respectively. Make sure you always choose one of these two filters for the GL_TEXTURE_MIN_FILTER—the default filter setting does not work without mipmaps (see the "Mipmaps" section, up next).

Nearest neighbor filtering is the simplest and fastest filtering method you can choose. With this approach, texture coordinates are evaluated and plotted against a texture's texels, and whichever texel the coordinate falls in, that color is used for the fragment texture color. In signal processing terms, this is known as *point sampling*. Nearest neighbor filtering is characterized by large blocky pixels when the texture is stretched over an especially large area. An example is shown on the left of Figure 5.7. You can set the texture filter for both the minification and the magnification filters by using these two function calls:

```
glSamplerParameteri(sampler, GL_TEXTURE_MIN_FILTER, GL_NEAREST);
glSamplerParameteri(sampler, GL_TEXTURE_MAG_FILTER, GL_NEAREST);
```

Linear filtering requires more work than nearest neighbor filtering but often is worth the extra overhead. On today's commodity hardware, the extra cost of linear filtering is approximately zero. Linear filtering works not by taking the nearest texel to the texture coordinate, but rather by applying the weighted average of the texels surrounding the texture coordinate (a linear interpolation). For this interpolated fragment to match the texel color exactly, the texture coordinate needs to fall directly in the center of the texel. Linear filtering is characterized by "fuzzy" graphics when a texture is stretched. This fuzziness, however, often lends a more realistic and less artificial look than the jagged blocks of the nearest neighbor filtering mode. A contrasting example is shown on the right of Figure 5.7. You can set linear filtering simply enough by using the following lines:

```
glSamplerParameteri(sampler, GL_TEXTURE_MIN_FILTER, GL_LINEAR);
glSamplerParameteri(sampler, GL_TEXTURE_MAG_FILTER, GL_LINEAR);
```

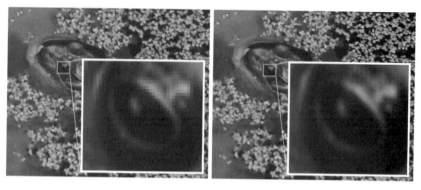

Figure 5.7: Texture filtering—nearest neighbor (left) and linear (right)

As you can see in Figure 5.7, the image on the left (which has nearest neighbor filtering applied) is blocky and jagged, especially around areas of high contrast. The image on the right of Figure 5.7, however, is smooth (if a little blurry).

Mipmaps

Mipmapping is a powerful texturing technique that can improve both the rendering performance and the visual quality of a scene. It does this by addressing two common problems with standard texture mapping.

The first is an effect called scintillation (aliasing artifacts) that appears on the surface of objects rendered very small on screen compared to the relative size of the texture applied. Scintillation can be seen as a sort of sparkling that occurs as the sampling area on a texture map moves disproportionately to its size on the screen. The negative effects of scintillation are most noticeable when the camera or the objects are in motion.

The second issue is more performance related but is due to the same scenario that leads to scintillation. That is, a large amount of texture memory is used to store the texture, but it is accessed very sparsely as adjacent fragments on the screen access texels that are disconnected in texture space. This causes texturing performance to suffer greatly as the size of the texture increases and the sparsity of access becomes greater.

The solution to both of these problems is to simply use a smaller texture map. However, this solution then creates a new problem: When near the same object, it must be rendered larger, and a small texture map will then be stretched to the point of creating a hopelessly blurry or blocky textured object. The solution to both of these issues is mipmapping. Mipmapping gets its name from the Latin phrase *multum in parvo,* which means "many things in a small place." In essence, you load not just a single image into the texture object, but a whole series of images from largest to smallest into a single "mipmapped" texture. OpenGL then uses a new set of filter modes to choose the best-fitting texture or textures for the given geometry. At the cost of some extra memory (and possibly considerably more processing work), you can eliminate scintillation and the texture memory processing overhead for distant objects simultaneously, while maintaining higher-resolution versions of the texture available when needed.

A mipmapped texture consists of a series of texture images, each one-half the size on each axis or one-fourth the total number of pixels of the previous image. This scenario is shown in Figure 5.8. Mipmap levels do not have to be square, but the halving of the dimensions continues until the last image is 1×1 texel. When one of the dimensions reaches 1, further divisions occur on the other dimension only. For 2D textures, using a square set of mipmaps requires about one-third more memory than not using mipmaps at all.

Mipmap levels are loaded with **glTextureSubImage2D()** (for 2D textures). Now the level parameter comes into play, because it specifies which mip level the image data is for. The first level is 0, then 1, 2, and so on. If mipmapping is not being used, you would typically use only level 0. When you allocate your texture with **glTextureStorage2D()** (or the appropriate function for the type of texture you're allocating), you can set the number of levels to include in the texture in the levels parameter. Then, you can use mipmapping with those levels present in the texture. You can further constrain the number of mipmap levels that will be used during rendering by setting the base and maximum levels to be used with the GL_TEXTURE_BASE_LEVEL and GL_TEXTURE_MAX_LEVEL texture parameters. For example, if you want to specify that only mip levels 0 through 4 should be accessed, you call glTextureParameteri twice as shown here:

```
glTextureParameteri(texture, GL_TEXTURE_BASE_LEVEL, 0);
glTextureParameteri(texture, GL_TEXTURE_MAX_LEVEL, 4);
```

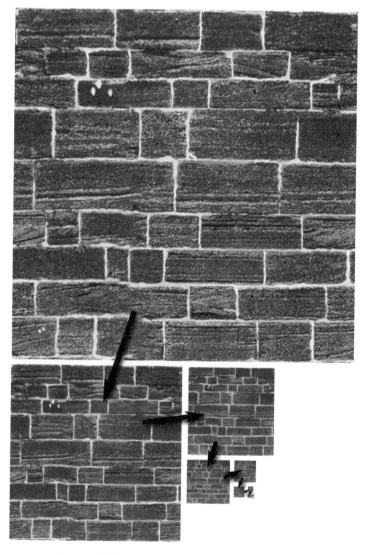

Figure 5.8: A series of mipmapped images

Mipmap Filtering

Mipmapping adds a new twist to the two basic texture filtering modes
GL_NEAREST and GL_LINEAR by giving four permutations for mipmapped
filtering modes. They are listed in Table 5.8.

Constant	Description
GL_NEAREST	Perform nearest neighbor filtering using only the base mip level.
GL_LINEAR	Perform linear filtering using only the base mip level.
GL_NEAREST_MIPMAP_NEAREST	Select the nearest mip level and perform nearest neighbor filtering.
GL_NEAREST_MIPMAP_LINEAR	Perform a linear interpolation between mip levels and perform nearest neighbor filtering within each.
GL_LINEAR_MIPMAP_NEAREST	Select the nearest mip level and perform linear filtering within it.
GL_LINEAR_MIPMAP_LINEAR	Perform a linear interpolation between mip levels and perform linear filtering; also called *trilinear* filtering.

Just loading the mip levels with **glTextureSubImage2D()** does not by itself enable mipmapping. If the minification filter mode in the texture or associated sampler object is set to GL_LINEAR or GL_NEAREST, only the base texture level is used, and any mip levels loaded are ignored. You must specify one of the mipmapped filters listed for the loaded mip levels to be used. The constants have the form GL_<FILTER>_MIPMAP_<SELECTOR>, where <FILTER> specifies the texture filter to be used on the mip level selected, and <SELECTOR> specifies how the mip level is selected. For example, NEAREST selects the nearest matching mip level. Using LINEAR for the selector creates a linear interpolation between the two nearest mip levels, which is again filtered by the chosen texture filter.

Which filter you select varies depending on the application and the performance requirements at hand. GL_NEAREST_MIPMAP_NEAREST, for example, gives very good performance and low aliasing (scintillation) artifacts, but nearest neighbor filtering is often not visually pleasing. GL_LINEAR_MIPMAP_NEAREST is often used to speed up applications because a higher-quality linear filter is used, but a fast selection (nearest) is made between the different-sized mip levels available. Note that you can use the GL_<*>_MIPMAP_<*> filter modes only for the GL_TEXTURE_MIN_FILTER setting—the GL_TEXTURE_MAG_FILTER setting must always be either GL_NEAREST or GL_NEAREST.

Using NEAREST as the mipmap selector (as in both examples in the preceding paragraph), however, can also leave an undesirable visual artifact. For oblique views, you can often see the transition from one mip level to another across a surface. It can be seen as a distortion line or a sharp transition from one level of detail to another. The GL_LINEAR_MIPMAP_LINEAR and GL_NEAREST_MIPMAP_LINEAR filters perform an additional interpolation between mip levels to eliminate this transition zone, but at the extra cost of substantially more processing overhead. The GL_LINEAR_MIPMAP_LINEAR filter is often referred to as trilinear mipmapping and, although there are more advanced techniques for image filtering, produces very good results. In practice, there is very little performance difference between GL_LINEAR_MIPMAP_NEAREST and GL_LINEAR_MIPMAP_LINEAR; thus, given that the latter provides superior visual quality, it's a good idea to just use that mode unless you have a particular reason not to.

Generating Mip Levels

As mentioned previously, mipmapping for 2D textures requires approximately one-third more texture memory than just loading the base texture image. It also requires that all the smaller versions of the base texture image be available for loading. Sometimes this can be inconvenient because the lower-resolution images may not necessarily be available to either the programmer or the end user of your software. While having precomputed mip levels for your textures yields the very best results, it is convenient and somewhat common to have OpenGL generate the textures for you. You can generate all the mip levels for a texture once you've loaded level 0 with the function **glGenerateTextureMipmap()**.

```
void glGenerateTextureMipmap(GLenum target);
```

The texture parameter can refer to a texture of type GL_TEXTURE_1D, GL_TEXTURE_2D, GL_TEXTURE_3D, GL_TEXTURE_CUBE_MAP, GL_TEXTURE_1D_ARRAY, or GL_TEXTURE_2D_ARRAY (more on these last three later). The quality of the filter used to create the smaller textures may vary widely from implementation to implementation. In addition, generating mipmaps on the fly may not be any faster than actually loading prebuilt mipmaps. This is something to think about in performance-critical applications. For the very best visual quality (as well as for consistency), you should load your own pregenerated mipmaps. This book's .KTX file loader supports loading mipmaps from .KTX files on disk.

Figure 5.9: A tunnel rendered with three textures and mipmapping

Mipmaps in Action

The example program `tunnel` shows off mipmapping as described in this chapter and demonstrates visually the different filtering and mipmap modes. This sample program loads three textures at start-up and then switches between them to render a tunnel. The prefiltered images that make up the textures are stored in the .KTX files containing the texture data. The tunnel has a brick wall pattern with different materials on the floor and ceiling. The output from `tunnel` is shown in Figure 5.9 with the texture minification mode set to `GL_LINEAR_MIPMAP_LINEAR`. As you can see, the texture becomes blurrier as you get farther down the tunnel.

Texture Wrap

Normally, you specify texture coordinates between 0.0 and 1.0 to map out the texels in a texture map. If texture coordinates fall outside this range, OpenGL handles them according to the current texture wrapping mode specified in the sampler object. You can set the wrap mode for each component of the texture coordinate individually by calling `glSamplerParameteri()` with `GL_TEXTURE_WRAP_S`, `GL_TEXTURE_WRAP_T`, or `GL_TEXTURE_WRAP_R` as the parameter name. The wrap mode can then be set to one of the following values: `GL_REPEAT`, `GL_MIRRORED_REPEAT`, `GL_CLAMP_TO_EDGE`, or `GL_CLAMP_TO_BORDER`. The value of

GL_TEXTURE_WRAP_S affects 1D, 2D, and 3D textures; GL_TEXTURE_WRAP_T affects only 2D and 3D textures; and GL_TEXTURE_WRAP_R affects only 3D textures.

The GL_REPEAT wrap mode simply causes the texture to repeat in the direction in which the texture coordinate has exceeded 1.0. The texture repeats again for every integer texture coordinate. This mode is useful for applying a small tiled texture to large geometric surfaces. Well-done seamless textures can lend the appearance of a seemingly much larger texture, but at the cost of a much smaller texture image. The GL_MIRRORED_REPEAT mode is similar, but as each component of the texture passes 1.0, it starts moving back toward the origin of the texture until it reaches 2.0, at which point the pattern repeats. it is The other modes do not repeat, but are "clamped"—thus their name.

If the only implication of the wrap mode is whether the texture repeats, you would need just two wrap modes: repeat and clamp. However, the texture wrap mode also has a great deal of influence on how texture filtering is done at the edges of the texture maps. For GL_NEAREST filtering, there are no consequences to the wrap mode because the texture coordinates are always snapped to some particular texel within the texture map. However, the GL_LINEAR filter takes an average of the pixels surrounding the evaluated texture coordinate, which creates a problem for texels that lie along the edges of the texture map. This problem is resolved quite neatly when the wrap mode is GL_REPEAT. The texel samples are simply taken from the next row or column, which in repeat mode wraps back around to the other side of the texture. This mode works perfectly for textures that wrap around an object and meet on the other side (such as spheres).

The clamped texture wrap mode offers a couple of options for the way texture edges are handled. For GL_CLAMP_TO_BORDER, the needed texels are taken from the texture border color (which can be set by passing GL_TEXTURE_BORDER_COLOR to **glSamplerParameterfv()**). The GL_CLAMP_TO_EDGE wrap mode forces texture coordinates out of range to be sampled along the last row or column of valid texels.

Figure 5.10 shows a simple example of the various texture wrapping modes. The same mode is used for both the S and T components of the texture coordinates. The four squares in the image have the same texture applied to them, but with different texture wrapping modes used. The texture is a simple square with nine arrows pointing up and to the right, with a bright band around the top and right edges. For the top left square,

Figure 5.10: Example of texture coordinate wrapping modes

the GL_CLAMP_TO_BORDER mode is used. The border color has been set to a dark color; it is clear that when OpenGL ran out of texture data, it used the dark color instead. However, in the lower-left square, the GL_CLAMP_TO_EDGE mode is used. In this case, the bright band is continued to the top and right of the texture data.

The lower-right square is drawn using the GL_REPEAT mode, which wraps the texture over and over. As you can see, there are several copies of our arrow texture, and all the arrows are pointing in the same direction. Compare this to the square on the upper-right of Figure 5.10. It is using the GL_MIRRORED_REPEAT mode and, as you can see, the texture has been repeated across the square. However, the first copy of the image is the right way around, then the next copy is flipped, the next copy is the right way around again, and so on.

One final texture repeat mode is GL_MIRROR_CLAMP_TO_EDGE, which is a hybrid of the GL_MIRRORED_REPEAT and GL_CLAMP_TO_EDGE modes. In GL_MIRROR_CLAMP_TO_EDGE, the texture coordinate is handled normally between 0.0 and 1.0; between 1.0 and 2.0 (and between 0.0 and −1.0), it is handled as if the mode were GL_MIRRORED_REPEAT (the texture is

Figure 5.11: GL_MIRROR_CLAMP_TO_EDGE in action

repeated mirrored); and then outside that range, it is clamped to the edge of the texture. This mode is useful when you have a texture that is symmetrical around some point and you wish to mirror it once and once only. Figure 5.11 shows an example of this mode in action.

In Figure 5.11, the lens flare texture is symmetrical around its center, so only a single quarter of the image need be stored in the texture. This texture is mirrored in both the x and y dimensions to create the complete image. The picture on the left of Figure 5.11 uses the GL_CLAMP_TO_BORDER mode to make the area outside the texture appear black. The image on the right of Figure 5.11 uses the GL_MIRROR_CLAMP_TO_EDGE mode to mirror the image horizontally and vertically to show the complete flare.

Array Textures

Previously we discussed the idea that multiple textures could be accessed at once via different texture units. This is extremely powerful and useful as your shader can gain access to several texture objects at the same time by declaring multiple sampler uniforms. We can actually take this a bit further by using a feature called *array textures*. With an array texture, you can load up several 1D, 2D, or cube map images into a single texture object. The concept of having more than one image in a single texture is not new. It happens with mipmapping, as each mip level is a distinct image, and with cube mapping, where each face of the cube map has its own image and even its own set of mip levels. With texture arrays, however, you can have a whole array of texture images bound to a single texture object and then index through them in the shader, thus greatly increasing the amount of texture data available to your application at any one time.

Most texture types have an array equivalent. You can create 1D and 2D array textures, and even cube map array textures. However, you can't create a 3D array texture, as this is not supported by OpenGL. As with cube maps, array textures can have mipmaps. Another interesting thing to note is that if you were to create an array of sampler uniforms in your shader, the value you use to index into that array must be uniform. However, with a texture array, each lookup into the texture map can come from a different element of the array. In part to distinguish between elements of an array of textures and a single element of an array texture, the elements are usually referred to as *layers*.

You may be wondering what the difference between a 2D array texture and a 3D texture is (or a 1D array texture and a 2D texture, for that matter). The biggest difference is probably that no filtering is applied between the layers of an array texture. Also, the maximum number of array texture layers supported by an implementation may be greater than the maximum 3D texture size, for example.

Loading a 2D Array Texture

To create a 2D array, simply create a new texture object bound to the GL_TEXTURE_2D_ARRAY target, allocate storage for it using **glTexStorage3D()**, and then load the images into it using one or more calls to **glTexSubImage3D()**. Notice the use of the 3D versions of the texture storage and data functions. These are required because the depth and z coordinates passed to them are interpreted as the array element, or *layer*. Simple code to load a 2D array texture is shown in Listing 5.42.

```
GLuint tex;

glCreateTextures(GL_TEXTURE_2D_ARRAY1, &tex);

glTextureStorage3D(tex,
                   8,
                   GL_RGBA8,
                   256,
                   256,
                   100);

for (int i = 0; i < 100; i++)
{
    glTextureSubImage3D(tex,
                        0,
                        0, 0,
```

```
                              i,
                              256, 256,
                              1,
                              GL_RGBA,
                              GL_UNSIGNED_BYTE,
                              image_data[i]);
         }
```

Listing 5.42: Initializing an array texture

Conveniently, the .KTX file format supports array textures, so the book's
loader code can load them directly from disk. Simply use
sb7::ktx::file::load to load an array texture from a file.

To demonstrate texture arrays, we create a program that renders a large
number of cartoon aliens raining on the screen. The sample uses an array
texture where each slice of the texture holds one of 64 separate images of
an alien. The array texture is packed into a single .KTX file called
alienarray.ktx, which we load into a single texture object. To render the
alien rain, we draw hundreds of instances of a four-vertex triangle strip,
each of which forms a quad. Using the instance number as the index into
the texture array gives each quad a different texture, even though all of the
quads are drawn with the same command. Additionally, we use a uniform
buffer to store a per-instance orientation, x offset, and y offset that are set
up by the application.

In this case, our vertex shader uses no vertex attributes and is shown in its
entirety in Listing 5.43.

```
#version 450 core

layout (location = 0) in int alien_index;

out VS_OUT
{
    flat int alien;
    vec2 tc;
} vs_out;

struct droplet_t
{
    float x_offset;
    float y_offset;
    float orientation;
    float unused;
};

layout (std140) uniform droplets
{
    droplet_t droplet[256];
};
```

```
void main(void)
{
    const vec2[4] position = vec2[4](vec2(-0.5, -0.5),
                                      vec2( 0.5, -0.5),
                                      vec2(-0.5,  0.5),
                                      vec2( 0.5,  0.5));
    vs_out.tc = position[gl_VertexID].xy + vec2(0.5);
    float co = cos(droplet[alien_index].orientation);
    float so = sin(droplet[alien_index].orientation);
    mat2 rot = mat2(vec2(co, so),
                    vec2(-so, co));
    vec2 pos = 0.25 * rot * position[gl_VertexID];
    gl_Position = vec4(pos.x + droplet[alien_index].x_offset,
                       pos.y + droplet[alien_index].y_offset,
                       0.5, 1.0);
}
```

Listing 5.43: Vertex shader for the alien rain sample

In our vertex shader, the position of the vertex and its texture coordinate
are taken from a hard-coded array. We calculate a per-instance rotation
matrix, rot, allowing our aliens to spin. Along with the texture
coordinate, vs_out.tc, we pass the value of gl_InstanceID (modulo 64) to
the fragment shader via vs_out.alien. In the fragment shader, we simply
use the incoming values to sample from the texture and write to our
output. The fragment shader is shown in Listing 5.44.

```
#version 450 core

layout (location = 0) out vec4 color;

in VS_OUT
{
    flat int alien;
    vec2 tc;
} fs_in;

layout (binding = 0) uniform sampler2DArray tex_aliens;

void main(void)
{
    color = texture(tex_aliens, vec3(fs_in.tc, float(fs_in.alien)));
}
```

Listing 5.44: Fragment shader for the alien rain sample

Notice how in Listing 5.44 we sample from our array texture using a vec3
texture coordinate. This coordinate is constructed from the 2D texture
coordinate interpolated from our vertex shader's output as well as from the
integer[5] alien index.

---

5. Yes, it's odd that GLSL expects a floating-point value for the index into an array texture, but
that's just the way it is.

Accessing Texture Arrays

In the fragment shader (shown in Listing 5.44), we declare our sampler for the 2D array texture, sampler2DArray. To sample this texture we use the texture function as normal, but pass in a three-component texture coordinate. The first two components of this texture coordinate, the s and t components, are used as typical two-dimensional texture coordinates. The third component, the p element, is actually an integer index into the texture array. Recall that we set this index in the vertex shader, and it is going to vary from 0 to 63, with a different value for each alien.

The complete rendering loop for the alien rain sample is shown in Listing 5.45.

```
void render(double currentTime)
{
    static const GLfloat black[] = { 0.0f, 0.0f, 0.0f, 0.0f };
    float t = (float)currentTime;

    glViewport(0, 0, info.windowWidth, info.windowHeight);
    glClearBufferfv(GL_COLOR, 0, black);

    glUseProgram(render_prog);

    glBindBufferBase(GL_UNIFORM_BUFFER, 0, rain_buffer);
    vmath::vec4 * droplet =
        (vmath::vec4 *)glMapBufferRange(
                        GL_UNIFORM_BUFFER,
                        0,
                        256 * sizeof(vmath::vec4),
                        GL_MAP_WRITE_BIT |
                        GL_MAP_INVALIDATE_BUFFER_BIT);

    for (int i = 0; i < 256; i++)
    {
        droplet[i][0] = droplet_x_offset[i];
        droplet[i][1] = 2.0f - fmodf((t + float(i)) *
                                droplet_fall_speed[i], 4.31f);
        droplet[i][2] = t * droplet_rot_speed[i];
        droplet[i][3] = 0.0f;
    }
    glUnmapBuffer(GL_UNIFORM_BUFFER);

    int alien_index;
    for (alien_index = 0; alien_index < 256; alien_index++)
    {
        glVertexAttribI1i(0, alien_index);
        glDrawArrays(GL_TRIANGLE_STRIP, 0, 4);
    }
}
```

Listing 5.45: Rendering loop for the alien rain sample

As you can see, there is only a simple loop around one drawing command in our rendering function. On each frame, we update the values of the data in the rain_buffer buffer object that we use to store our per-droplet

Figure 5.12: Output of the alien rain sample

values. Then, we execute a loop of 256 calls to **glDrawArrays()**, which will draw 256 individual aliens. On each iteration of the loop, we update the alien_index input to the vertex shader. Note that we use the **glVertexAttribI*()** variant of **glVertexAttrib*()**, as we are using an integer input to our vertex shader. The final output of the alien rain sample program is shown in Figure 5.12.

Writing to Textures in Shaders

A texture object is a collection of images that, when the mipmap chain is included, supports filtering, texture coordinate wrapping, and so on. Not only does OpenGL allow you to read from textures with all of those features, it also allows you to *write to* textures directly in your shaders. Just as you use a sampler variable in shaders to represent an entire texture and the associated sampler parameters (whether from a sampler object or from the texture object itself), so you can use an *image* variable to represent a single image from a texture.

Image variables are declared just like sampler uniforms. There are several types of image variables that represent different data types and image dimensionalities. Table 5.9 shows the image types available to OpenGL.

Table 5.9: Image Types

Image Type	Description
image1D	1D image
image2D	2D image
image3D	3D image
imageCube	Cube map image
imageCubeArray	Cube map array image
imageRect	Rectangle image
image1DArray	1D array image
image2DArray	2D array image
imageBuffer	Buffer image
image2DMS	2D multisample image
image2DMSArray	2D multisample array image

First, you need to declare an image variable as a uniform so that you can associate it with an *image unit*. Such a declaration generally looks like this:

```
uniform image2D my_image;
```

Once you have an image variable, you can read from it using the imageLoad function and write into it using the imageStore function. Both of these functions are *overloaded*, which means that there are multiple versions of each for various parameter types. The versions for the image2D type are

```
vec4 imageLoad(readonly image2D image, ivec2 P);
void imageStore(image2D image, ivec2 P, vec4 data);
```

The imageLoad() function will read the data from image at the coordinates specified in P and return it to your shader. Similarly, the imageStore() function will take the values you provide in data and store them into image at P. Notice that the type of P is an *integer* type (an integer vector in the case of 2D images). This is just like the texelFetch() function—no filtering is performed for loads and filtering really doesn't make sense for stores. The dimension of P and the return type of the function depend on the type of the image parameter.

Just as with sampler types, image variables can represent floating-point data stored in images. However, it's also possible to store signed and unsigned integer data in images, in which case the image type is prefixed with i or u, respectively (as in `iimage2D` and `uimage2D`). When an integer image variable is used, the return type of the `imageLoad` function and the data type of the `data` parameter to `imageStore` change appropriately. For example, we have

```
ivec4 imageLoad(readonly iimage2D image, ivec2 P);
void  imageStore(iimage2D image, ivec2 P, ivec4 data);
uvec4 imageLoad(readonly uimage2D image, ivec2 P);
void  imageStore(uimage2D image, ivec2 P, uvec4 data);
```

To bind a texture for load and store operations, you need to bind it to an *image unit* using the **glBindImageTexture()** function, whose prototype is

```
void glBindImageTexture(GLuint unit,
                        GLuint texture,
                        GLint level,
                        GLboolean layered,
                        GLint layer,
                        GLenum access,
                        GLenum format);
```

The function looks like it has a lot of parameters, but they're all fairly self-explanatory. First, the `unit` parameter is a zero-based index of the image unit to which you want to bind the image. Next, the `texture` parameter is the name of a texture object that you've created using **glCreateTextures()** and allocated storage for with **glTextureStorage2D()** (or the appropriate function for the type of texture you're using). `level` specifies which mipmap level you want to access in your shader, starting with zero for the base level and progressing to the number of mipmap levels in the image.

The `layered` parameter should be set to GL_FALSE if you want to bind a single layer of an array texture as a regular 1D or 2D image, in which case the `layer` parameter specifies the index of that layer. Otherwise, `layered` should be set to GL_TRUE and a whole level of an arrray texture will be bound to the image unit (with `layer` being ignored).

Finally, the `access` and `format` parameters describe how you will use the data in the image. `access` should be one of GL_READ_ONLY, GL_WRITE_ONLY, or GL_READ_WRITE to say that you plan to only read, only write, or do both to the image, respectively. The `format` parameter specifies the format in which the data in the image should be interpreted. There is a lot of flexibility here, with the only real requirement being that the image's internal format (the one you specified in **glTextureStorage2D()**) is in the same *class* as the one specified in the `format` parameter. Table 5.10 lists the acceptable image formats and their classes.

Table 5.10: Image Data Format Classes

Format	Class
GL_RGBA32F	4×32
GL_RGBA32I	4×32
GL_RGBA32UI	4×32
GL_RGBA16F	4×16
GL_RGBA16UI	4×16
GL_RGBA16I	4×16
GL_RGBA16_SNORM	4×16
GL_RGBA16	4×16
GL_RGBA8UI	4×8
GL_RGBA8I	4×8
GL_RGBA8_SNORM	4×8
GL_RGBA8	4×8
GL_R11F_G11F_B10F	(a)
GL_RGB10_A2UI	(b)
GL_RGB10_A2	(b)
GL_RG32F	2×32
GL_RG32UI	2×32
GL_RG32I	2×32
GL_RG16F	2×16
GL_RG16UI	2×16
GL_RG16I	2×16
GL_RG16_SNORM	2×16
GL_RG16	2×16
GL_RG8UI	2×8
GL_RG8I	2×8
GL_RG8	2×8
GL_RG8_SNORM	2×8
GL_R32F	1×32
GL_R32UI	1×32
GL_R32I	1×32
GL_R16F	1×16
GL_R16UI	1×16
GL_R16I	1×16
GL_R16_SNORM	1×16

continued

Table 5.10: *Continued*

Format	Class
GL_R16	1×16
GL_R8UI	1×8
GL_R8I	1×8
GL_R8	1×8
GL_R8_SNORM	1×8

Referring to Table 5.10, you can see that the GL_RGBA32F, GL_RGBA32I, and GL_RGBA32UI formats are in the same format class (4×32), which means that you can take a texture that has a GL_RGBA32F internal format and bind one of its levels to an image unit using the GL_RGBA32I or GL_RGBA32UI image format. When you store into an image, the appropriate number of bits from your source data are chopped off and written to the image as is. However, if you want to read from an image, you must also supply a matching image format using a *format layout qualifier* in your shader code.

The GL_R11F_G11F_B10F format, which has the marker (a) for its format class, and GL_RGB10_A2UI and GL_RGB10_A2, which have the marker (b) for their format class, have their own special classes. GL_R11F_G11F_B10F is not compatible with anything else, and GL_RGB10_A2UI and GL_RGB10_A2 are compatible only with each other.

The appropriate format layout qualifiers for each of the various image formats are shown in Table 5.11.

Table 5.11: Image Data Format Classes

Format	Format Qualifier
GL_RGBA32F	rgba32f
GL_RGBA32I	rgba32i
GL_RGBA32UI	rgba32ui
GL_RGBA16F	rgba16f
GL_RGBA16UI	rgba16ui
GL_RGBA16I	rgba16i

continued

Format	Format Qualifier
GL_RGBA16_SNORM	rgba16_snorm
GL_RGBA16	rgba16
GL_RGB10_A2UI	rgb10_a2ui
GL_RGB10_A2	rgb10_a2
GL_RGBA8UI	rgba8ui
GL_RGBA8I	rgba8i
GL_RGBA8_SNORM	rgba8_snorm
GL_RGBA8	rgba8
GL_R11F_G11F_B10F	r11f_g11f_b10f
GL_RG32F	rg32f
GL_RG32UI	rg32ui
GL_RG32I	rg32i
GL_RG16F	rg16f
GL_RG16UI	rg16ui
GL_RG16I	rg16i
GL_RG16_SNORM	rg16_snorm
GL_RG16	rg16
GL_RG8UI	rg8ui
GL_RG8I	rg8i
GL_RG8_SNORM	rg8_snorm
GL_RG8	rg8
GL_R32F	r32f
GL_R32UI	r32ui
GL_R32I	r32i
GL_R16F	r16f
GL_R16UI	r16ui
GL_R16I	r16i
GL_R16_SNORM	r16_snorm
GL_R16	r16
GL_R8UI	r8ui
GL_R8I	r8i
GL_R8_SNORM	r8_snorm
GL_R8	r8

Listing 5.46 shows an example fragment shader that copies data from one image to another using image loads and stores, logically inverting that data along the way.

```
#version 450 core

// Uniform image variables:
// Input image - note use of format qualifier because of loads
layout (binding = 0, rgba32ui) readonly uniform uimage2D image_in;
// Output image
layout (binding = 1) uniform writeonly uimage2D image_out;

void main(void)
{
    // Use fragment coordinate as image coordinate
    ivec2 P = ivec2(gl_FragCoord.xy);

    // Read from input image
    uvec4 data = imageLoad(image_in, P);

    // Write inverted data to output image
    imageStore(image_out, P, ~data);
}
```

Listing 5.46: Fragment shader performing image loads and stores

Obviously, the shader shown in Listing 5.46 is quite trivial. However, the power of image loads and stores is that you can include any number of them in a single shader and their coordinates can be anything. This means that a fragment shader is not limited to writing out to a fixed location in the framebuffer, but can write anywhere in an image, and can write to multiple images by using multiple image uniforms. Furthermore, any shader stage can write data into images, not just fragment shaders. Be aware, though, that with this power comes a lot of responsibility. It's perfectly easy for your shader to trash its own data—if multiple shader invocations write to the same location in an image, it's not well defined what will happen unless you use *atomics*, which are described in the context of images in the next section.

Atomic Operations on Images

Just as with the shader storage blocks described earlier in this chapter, you can perform *atomic operations* on data stored in images. Again, an atomic operation is a sequence of a read, a modification, and a write that must be indivisible to achieve the desired result. Also, like atomic operations on members of a shader storage block, atomic operations on images are performed using a number of built-in functions in GLSL. These functions are listed in Table 5.12.

Table 5.12: Atomic Operations on Images

Atomic Function	Behavior
imageAtomicAdd	Reads from image at P, adds it to data, writes the result back to image at P, and then returns the value originally stored in image at P.
imageAtomicAnd	Reads from image at P, logically ANDs it with data, writes the result back to image at P, and then returns the value originally stored in image at P.
imageAtomicOr	Reads from image at P, logically ORs it with data, writes the result back to image at P, and then returns the value originally stored in image at P.
imageAtomicXor	Reads from image at P, logically exclusive ORs it with data, writes the result back to image at P, and then returns the value originally stored in image at P.
imageAtomicMin	Reads from image at P, determines the minimum of the retrieved value and data, writes the result back to image at P, and returns the value originally stored in image at P.
imageAtomicMax	Reads from image at P, determines the maximum of the retrieved value and data, writes the result back to image at P, and returns the value originally stored in image at P.
imageAtomicExchange	Reads from image at P, writes the value of data into mem, and then returns the value originally stored in image at P.
imageAtomicCompSwap	Reads from image at P, compares the retrieved value with comp and, if they are equal, writes data into image at P, and returns the value originally stored in image at P.

For all of the functions listed in Table 5.12 except for imageAtomicCompSwap, the parameters are an image variable, a coordinate, and a piece of data. The dimension of the coordinate depends on the type of image variable. 1D images use a single integer coordinate, 2D images and 1D array images take a 2D integer vector (i.e., `ivec2`), and 3D images and 2D array images take a 3D integer vector (i.e., `ivec3`). For example, we have

```
uint imageAtomicAdd(uimage1D image, int P, uint data);
uint imageAtomicAdd(uimage2D image, ivec2 P, uint data);
uint imageAtomicAdd(uimage3D image, ivec3 P, uint data);
```

and so on. The `imageAtomicCompSwap` is unique in that it takes an additional parameter, `comp`, which it compares with the existing content in memory. If the value of `comp` is equal to the value already in memory, then it is replaced with the value of `data`. The prototypes of `imageAtomicCompSwap` include

```
uint imageAtomicCompSwap(uimage1D image, int P, uint comp, uint data);
uint imageAtomicCompSwap(uimage2D image, ivec2 P, uint comp, uint data);
uint imageAtomicCompSwap(uimage3D image, ivec3 P, uint comp, uint data);
```

All of the atomic functions return the data that was originally in memory before the operation was performed. This is useful if you wish to append data to a list, for example. To do this, you would simply determine how many items you want to append to the list, call `imageAtomicAdd` with the number of elements, and then start writing your new data into memory at the location that it returns. Although you can't add an arbitrary number to an atomic counter (and the number of atomic counters supported in a single shader is usually not great), you can do similar things with shader storage buffers.

The memory you write to could be a shader storage buffer or another image variable. If the image containing the "filled count" variables is pre-initialized to 0, then the first shader invocation to attempt to append to the list will receive 0 as the location and write there, the next invocation will receive whatever the first added, the next will receive whatever the third added, and so on.

Another application for atomics is constructing data structures such as linked lists in memory. To build a linked list from a shader, you need three pieces of storage—the first is somewhere to store the list items, the second is somewhere to store the item count, and the third is the "head pointer," which is the index of the last item in the list. Again, you can use a shader storage buffer to store items for the linked list, an atomic counter to store the current item count, and an image to store the head pointer for the list(s). To append an item to the list, you would follow three steps:

1. Increment the atomic counter and retrieve its previous value, which is returned by `atomicCounterIncrement`.

2. Use `imageAtomicExchange` to exchange the updated counter value with the current head pointer.

3. Store your data into the data store. The structure for each element includes a *next* index, which you fill with the previous value of the head pointer retrieved in step 2.

If the "head pointer" image is a 2D image the size of the framebuffer, then you can use this method to create a per-pixel list of fragments. You can later walk this list and perform whatever operations you like. The shader shown in Listing 5.47 demonstrates how to append fragments to a linked list stored in a shader storage buffer by using a 2D image to store the head pointers and an atomic counter to keep the fill count.

```glsl
#version 450 core

// Atomic counter for filled size
layout (binding = 0, offset = 0) uniform atomic_uint fill_counter;

// 2D image to store head pointers
layout (binding = 0) uniform uimage2D head_pointer;

// Shader storage buffer containing appended fragments
struct list_item
{
    vec4        color;
    float       depth;
    int         facing;
    uint        next;
};

layout (binding = 0, std430) buffer list_item_block
{
    list_item    item[];
};

// Input from vertex shader
in VS_OUT
{
    vec4 in;
} fs_in;
```

```
void main(void)
{
    ivec2 P = ivec2(gl_FragCoord.xy);

    uint index = atomicCounterIncrement(fill_counter);

    uint old_head = imageAtomicExchange(head_pointer, P, index);

    item[index].color = fs_in.color;
    item[index].depth = gl_FragCoord.z;
    item[index].facing = gl_FrontFacing ? 1 : 0;
    item[index].next = old_head;
}
```

Listing 5.47: Filling a linked list in a fragment shader

You might notice the use of the gl_FrontFacing built-in variable. This is a Boolean input to the fragment shader whose value is generated by the back-face culling stage described in the "Primitive Assembly, Clipping, and Rasterization" section in Chapter 3. Even if back-face culling is disabled, this variable will still contain true if the polygon is considered front-facing and false otherwise.

Before executing this shader, the head pointer image is cleared to a known value that can't possibly be the index of an item in the list (such as the maximum value of an unsigned integer) and the atomic counter is reset to 0. The first item appended will be item 0, that value will be written to the head pointer, and its "next" index will contain the reset value of the head pointer image. The next value appended to the list will be at index 1, which is written to the head pointer, the old value of which (0) is written to the "next" index and so on. The result is that the head pointer image contains the index of the last item appended to the list and each item contains the index of the previous one appended. Eventually, the "next" index of an item will be the value originally used to clear the head image, which indicates that the end of the list has been reached.

To traverse the list, we load the index of the first item in it from the head pointer image and read it from the shader storage buffer. For each item, we simply follow the "next" index until we reach the end of the list, or until the maximum number of fragments has been traversed (which protects us from accidentally running off the end of the list). The shader shown in Listing 5.48 shows an example. The shader walks the linked list, keeping a running total of the depth of the fragments stored for each pixel. The depth value of front-facing primitives is added to the running total and the depth value of back-facing primitives is subtracted from the total. The result is the total filled depth of the interior of convex objects, which can be used to render volumes and other filled spaces.

```glsl
#version 450 core

// 2D image to store head pointers
layout (binding = 0, r32ui) coherent uniform uimage2D head_pointer;

// Shader storage buffer containing appended fragments
struct list_item
{
    vec4        color;
    float       depth;
    int         facing;
    uint        next;
};

layout (binding = 0, std430) buffer list_item_block
{
    list_item   item[];
};

layout (location = 0) out vec4 color;

const uint max_fragments = 10;

void main(void)
{
    uint frag_count = 0;
    float depth_accum = 0.0;
    ivec2 P = ivec2(gl_FragCoord.xy);

    uint index = imageLoad(head_pointer, P).x;

    while (index != 0xFFFFFFFF && frag_count < max_fragments)
    {
        list_item this_item = item[index];

        if (this_item.facing != 0)
        {
            depth_accum -= this_item.depth;
        }
        else
        {
            depth_accum += this_item.depth;
        }

        index = this_item.next;
        frag_count++;
    }

    depth_accum *= 3000.0;

    color = vec4(depth_accum, depth_accum, depth_accum, 1.0);
}
```

Listing 5.48: Traversing a linked list in a fragment shader

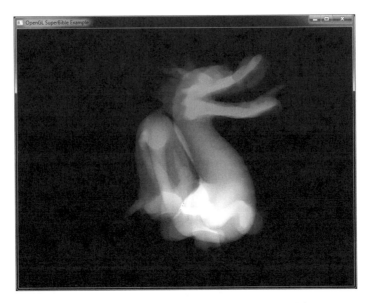

Figure 5.13: Resolved per-fragment linked lists

The result of rendering with the shaders of Listings 5.47 and 5.48 is shown in Figure 5.13.

Synchronizing Access to Images

As images represent large regions of memory and we have just explained how to write directly into images from your shaders, you may have guessed that we'll now explain the memory barrier types that you can use to synchronize access to that memory. Just as with buffers and atomic counters, you can call

```
glMemoryBarrier(GL_SHADER_IMAGE_ACCESS_BIT);
```

You should call **glMemoryBarrier()** with the GL_SHADER_IMAGE_ACCESS_BIT set when something has *written* to an image that you want read from images later—including other shaders.

Similarly, a version of the GLSL memoryBarrier() function, memoryBarrierImage(), ensures that operations on images from inside your shader are completed before it returns.

Texture Compression

Textures can take up an incredible amount of space. Modern games can easily use a gigabyte or more of texture data in a single level. That's a lot of data! Where do you put it all? Textures are an important part of making rich, realistic, and impressive scenes, but if you can't load all of the data onto the GPU, your rendering will be slow, if not impossible. One way to deal with storing and using a large amount of texture data is to compress the data. Compressed textures have two major benefits. First, they reduce the amount of storage space required for image data. Although the texture formats supported by OpenGL are generally not compressed as aggressively as in formats such as JPEG, they do provide substantial space benefits. The second (and possibly more important) benefit is that, because the graphics processor needs to read less data when fetching from a compressed texture, less *memory bandwidth* is required when compressed textures are used.

OpenGL supports a number of compressed texture formats. All OpenGL implementations support at least the compression schemes listed in Table 5.13.

Table 5.13: Native OpenGL Texture Compression Formats

Formats (GL_COMPRESSED_*)	Type
RED	Generic
RG	Generic
RGB	Generic
RGBA	Generic
SRGB	Generic
SRGB_ALPHA	Generic
RED_RGTC1	RGTC
SIGNED_RED_RGTC1	RGTC
RG_RGTC2	RGTC
SIGNED_RG_RGTC2	RGTC
RGBA_BPTC_UNORM	BPTC
SRGB_ALPHA_BPTC_UNORM	BPTC
RGB_BPTC_SIGNED_FLOAT	BPTC
RGB_BPTC_UNSIGNED_FLOAT	BPTC
RGB8_ETC2	ETC2

continued

Table 5.13: *Continued*

Formats (GL_COMPRESSED_*)	Type
SRGB8_ETC2	ETC2
RGB8_PUNCHTHROUGH_ALPHA1_ETC2	ETC2
SRGB8_PUNCHTHROUGH_ALPHA1_ETC2	ETC2
RGBA8_ETC2_EAC	ETC2
SRGB8_ALPHA8_ETC2_EAC	ETC2
R11_EAC	EAC
SIGNED_R11_EAC	EAC
RG11_EAC	EAC
SIGNED_RG11_EAC	EAC

The first six formats listed in Table 5.13 are generic and allow the OpenGL driver to decide which compression mechanism to use. As a result, your driver can use the format that best suits the current conditions. The catch is that the choice is implementation specific; although your code will work on many platforms, the result of rendering with them might not be the same.

The RGTC (Red–Green Texture Compression) format breaks a texture image into 4×4 texel blocks, compressing the individual channels within each block using a series of codes. This compression mode works only for one- and two-channel signed and unsigned textures, and only for certain texel formats. You don't need to worry about the exact compression scheme unless you are planning on writing a compressor. Just note that the space savings from using RGTC is 50%.

The BPTC (Block Partitioned Texture Compression) format also breaks textures up into blocks of 4×4 texels, each represented as 128 bits (16 bytes) of data in memory. The blocks are encoded using a rather complex scheme that essentially comprises a pair of endpoints and a representation of the position on a line between those two endpoints. It allows the endpoints to be manipulated to generate a variety of values as output for each texel. The BPTC formats are capable of compressing 8-bit per-channel normalized data and 32-bit per-channel floating-point data. The compression ratio for BPTC formats ranges from 25% for RGBA floating-point data to 33% for RGB 8-bit data.

Ericsson Texture Compression (ETC2) and Ericsson Alpha Compression (EAC)[6] are low-bandwidth formats that are also[7] available in OpenGL ES 3.0. They are designed for extremely low bit-per-pixel applications such as those found in mobile devices, which have substantially less memory bandwidth than the high-performance GPUs found in desktop and workstation computers.

Your implementation may also support other compressed formats, such as S3TC[8] and ETC1. You should check for the availability of formats not required by OpenGL before attempting to use them. The best way to do so is to check for support of the related extension. For example, if your implementation of OpenGL supports the S3TC format, it will advertise the `GL_EXT_texture_compression_s3tc` extension string.

Using Compression

You can ask OpenGL to compress a texture in some formats when you load it, although it's strongly recommended to compress textures yourself and store the compressed texture in a file. If OpenGL does support compression for your selected format, all you have to do is request that the internal format be one of the compressed formats; OpenGL will then take your uncompressed data and compress it as the texture image is loaded. There is no real difference in how you use compressed textures and uncompressed textures. The GPU handles the conversion when it samples from the texture. Many imaging tools used for creating textures and other images allow you to save your data directly in a compressed format.

The `.KTX` file format allows compressed data to be stored in it and the book's texture loader will load compressed images transparently to your application. You can check whether a texture is compressed by calling **glGetTexLevelParameteriv()** with one of two parameters. First, you can check the `GL_TEXTURE_INTERNAL_FORMAT` parameter of the texture and explicitly test whether it's one of the compressed formats. To do this, either keep a lookup table of recognized formats in your application or call

---

6. Although this is the official acronym, it's a bit of a misnomer: EAC can be used for more than just alpha compression.

7. The EAC and ETC2 formats were added to OpenGL 4.3 in an effort to drive convergence between desktop and mobile versions of the API. At the time of writing, few if any desktop GPUs actually supported them natively, with most OpenGL implementations decompressing the data you give them. Use them with caution.

8. S3TC is also known as the earlier version of the DXT format.

`glGetInternalFormativ()` with the parameter GL_TEXTURE_COMPRESSED. Alternatively, simply pass the GL_TEXTURE_COMPRESSED parameter directly to `glGetTexLevelParameteriv()`, which will return GL_TRUE if the texture has compressed data in it and GL_FALSE otherwise.

Once you have loaded a texture using a nongeneric compressed internal format, you can get the compressed image back by calling `glGetCompressedTexImage()`. Just pick the texture target and mipmap level you are interested in. Because you may not know how the image is compressed or which format is used, you should check the image size to make sure you have enough room for the whole surface. You can do this by calling `glGetTexParameteriv()` and passing the GL_TEXTURE_COMPRESSED_IMAGE_SIZE token.

```
Glint imageSize = 0;
glGetTextureParameteriv(GL_TEXTURE_2D,
                        GL_TEXTURE_COMPRESSED_IMAGE_SIZE,
                        &imageSize);
void *data = malloc(imageSize);
glGetCompressedTextureImage(GL_TEXTURE_2D, 0, data);
```

If you want to load compressed texture images yourself rather than using the book's .KTX loader, you can call **glTextureStorage2D()** or **glTextureStorage3D()** with the desired compressed internal format to allocate storage for the texture, and then call **glCompressedTextureSubImage()** 2D or **glCompressedTextureSubImage()** 3D to upload data into it. When you do this, you need to ensure that xoffset, yoffset, and other parameters obey the texture format's specific rules. In particular, most texture compression formats compress blocks of texels. These blocks are usually sizes such as 4×4 texels. The regions that you update with **glCompressedTexSubImage2D()** need to line up on block boundaries for these formats to work.

Shared Exponents

Although shared exponent textures are not technically a compressed format in the truest sense, they do allow you to use floating-point texture data while saving storage space. Instead of storing an exponent for each of the R, G, and B values, shared exponent formats use the same exponent value for the whole texel. The fractional and exponential parts of each value are stored as integers and then assembled when the texture is sampled. For the format GL_RGB9_E5, 9 bits are used to store each color and 5 bits are the common exponent for all channels. This format packs three floating-point values into 32 bits; that's a savings of 67%! To make use of shared exponents, you can get the texture data directly in this format from a content creation tool or write a converter that compresses your float RGB values into a shared exponent format.

Texture Views

In most cases when you're using textures, you'll know ahead of time which format your textures are in and what you're going to use them for, and your shaders will match the data they're fetching. For instance, a shader that expects to read from a 2D array texture might declare a sampler uniform as a `sampler2DArray`. Likewise, a shader that expects to read from an integer format texture might declare a corrseponding sampler as `isampler2D`. However, there may be times when the textures you create and load might not match what your shaders expect. In this case, you can use *texture views* to reuse the texture data in one texture object with another. This has two main use cases (although there are certainly many more):

- A texture view can be used to "pretend" that a texture of one type is actually a texture of a different type. For example, you can take a 2D texture and create a view of it that treats it as a 2D array texture with only one layer.

- A texture view can be used to pretend that the data in the texture object is actually a different format than what is really stored in memory. For example, you might take a texture with an internal format of GL_RGBA32F (i.e., four 32-bit floating-point components per texel) and create a view of it that sees them as GL_RGBA32UI (four 32-bit unsigned integers per texel) so that you can get at the individual bits of the texels.

Of course, you can do both of these things at the same time—that is, take a texture and create a view of it with both a different format and a different type.

Creating Texture Views

To create a view of a texture, we use the **glTextureView()** function, whose prototype is

```
void glTextureView(GLuint texture,
                   GLenum target,
                   GLuint origtexture,
                   GLenum internalformat,
```

```
                    GLuint minlevel,
                    GLuint numlevels,
                    GLuint minlayer,
                    GLuint numlayers);
```

The first parameter, texture, is the name of the texture object you'd like to make into a view. You should get this name from a call to **glGenTextures()**. Next, target specifies which *type* of texture you'd like to create. This can be pretty much any of the texture targets (GL_TEXTURE_1D, GL_TEXTURE_CUBE_MAP, or GL_TEXTURE_2D_ARRAY, for example), but it must be *compatible* with the type of the original texture, whose name is given in origtexture. The compatibility between various targets is indicated in Table 5.14.

As you can see, for most texture targets you can at least create a view of the texture with the same target. The exception is buffer textures, which are essentially already views of a buffer object—you can simply attach the same buffer object to another buffer texture to get another view of its data.

The internalformat parameter specifies the internal format for the new texture view. This must be compatible with the internal format of the

Table 5.14: Texture View Target Compatibility

If origtexture is... (GL_TEXTURE_*)	You can create a view of it as... (GL_TEXTURE_*)
1D	1D or 1D_ARRAY
2D	2D or 2D_ARRAY
3D	3D
CUBE_MAP	CUBE_MAP, 2D, 2D_ARRAY, or CUBE_MAP_ARRAY
RECTANGLE	RECTANGLE
BUFFER	*none*
1D_ARRAY	1D or 1D_ARRAY
2D_ARRAY	2D or 2D_ARRAY
CUBE_MAP_ARRAY	CUBE_MAP, 2D, 2D_ARRAY, or CUBE_MAP_ARRAY
2D_MULTISAMPLE	2D_MULTISAMPLE or 2D_MULTISAMPLE_ARRAY
2D_MULTISAMPLE_ARRAY	2D_MULTISAMPLE or 2D_MULTISAMPLE_ARRAY

original texture. This point can be tricky to understand, so we'll explain it in a moment.

The last four parameters allow you to make a view of a *subset* of the original texture's data. The minlevel and numlevels parameters specify the first mipmap level and the number of mipmap levels, respectively, to include in the view. This allows you to create a texture view that represents part of an entire mipmap pyramid of another texture. For example, to create a texture that represents just the base level (level 0) of another texture, you can set minlevel to 0 and numlevels to 1. To create a view that represents the four lowest-resolution mipmaps of a ten-level texture, you would set minlevel to 6 and numlevels to 4.

Similarly, minlayer and numlayers can be used to create a view of a subset of the layers of an array texture. For instance, if you want to create an array texture view that represents the middle four layers of a 20-layer array texture, you can set minlayer to 8 and numlayers to 4. Whatever you choose for the minlevel, numlevels, minlayer, and numlayers parameters, they must be consistent with the source and destination textures. For example, if you want to create a non-array texture view representing a single layer of an array texture, you must set minlayer to a layer that actually exists in the source texture and numlayers to 1 because the destination doesn't have any layers (rather, it effectively has one layer).

We mentioned that the internal format of the source texture and the new texture view (specified in the internalformat parameter) must be compatible with each other. To be compatible, two formats must be in the same *class*. Several format classes are available; they are listed, along with the internal formats that are members of that class, in Table 5.15.

Table 5.15: Texture View Format Compatibility

Format Class	Members of the Class
128-bit	GL_RGBA32F, GL_RGBA32UI, GL_RGBA32I
96-bit	GL_RGB32F, GL_RGB32UI, GL_RGB32I
64-bit	GL_RGBA16F, GL_RG32F, GL_RGBA16UI, GL_RG32UI, GL_RGBA16I, GL_RG32I, GL_RGBA16, GL_RGBA16_SNORM
48-bit	GL_RGB16, GL_RGB16_SNORM, GL_RGB16F, GL_RGB16UI, GL_RGB16I

continued

Format Class	Members of the Class
32-bit	GL_RG16F, GL_R11F_G11F_B10F, GL_R32F, GL_RGB10_A2UI, GL_RGBA8UI, GL_RG16UI, GL_R32UI, GL_RGBA8I, GL_RG16I, GL_R32I, GL_RGB10_A2, GL_RGBA8, GL_RG16, GL_RGBA8_SNORM, GL_RG16_SNORM, GL_SRGB8_ALPHA8, GL_RGB9_E5
24-bit	GL_RGB8, GL_RGB8_SNORM, GL_SRGB8, GL_RGB8UI, GL_RGB8I
16-bit	GL_R16F, GL_RG8UI, GL_R16UI, GL_RG8I, GL_R16I, GL_RG8, GL_R16, GL_RG8_SNORM, GL_R16_SNORM
8-bit	GL_R8UI, GL_R8I, GL_R8, GL_R8_SNORM
RGTC1_RED	GL_COMPRESSED_RED_RGTC1, GL_COMPRESSED_SIGNED_RED_RGTC1
RGTC2_RG	GL_COMPRESSED_RG_RGTC2, GL_COMPRESSED_SIGNED_RG_RGTC2
BPTC_UNORM	GL_COMPRESSED_RGBA_BPTC_UNORM, GL_COMPRESSED_SRGB_ALPHA_BPTC_UNORM
BPTC_FLOAT	GL_COMPRESSED_RGB_BPTC_SIGNED_FLOAT, GL_COMPRESSED_RGB_BPTC_UNSIGNED_FLOAT

In addition to formats that match each other's classes, you can always create a view of a texture with the same format as the original—even for formats that are not listed in Table 5.15.

Once you have created a view of a texture, you can use it like any other texture of the new type. For instance, if you have a 2D array texture, and you create a 2D non-array texture view of one of its layers, you can call **glTexSubImage2D()** to put data into the view, and the same data will end up in the corresponding layer of the array texture. As another example, you can create a 2D non-array texture view of a single layer of a 2D array texture and access it from a sampler2D uniform in a shader. Likewise, you can create a single-layer 2D array texture view of a 2D non-array texture and access that from a sampler2DArray uniform in a shader.

Summary

In this chapter you have learned about how OpenGL deals with the vast amounts of data required for graphics rendering. At the start of the pipeline, you saw how to automatically feed your vertex shaders with data using buffer objects. We also discussed methods of getting constant values, known as uniforms, into your shaders—first using buffers and then using the *default uniform block*. This block is also where the uniforms that represent textures, images, and storage buffers live; we used them to show you how to directly read and write images from and to textures and buffers using your shader code. You saw how to take a texture and pretend that part of it is actually a different type of texture, possibly with a different data format. You also learned about atomic operations, which touched on the massively parallel nature of modern graphics processors.

Chapter 6

Shaders and Programs

WHAT YOU'LL LEARN IN THIS CHAPTER

- The fundamentals of the OpenGL shading language.

- How to find out if your shaders compiled, and what went wrong if they didn't.

- How to retrieve and cache binaries of your compiled shaders and use them later for rendering.

So far in this book, you have read about the OpenGL pipeline, written some simple OpenGL programs, and seen some rendering. We have covered basic computer graphics fundamentals, some 3D math, and more. Modern graphics applications spend most of their time executing shaders, and graphics programmers spend a lot of their time writing shaders. Before you can write really compelling programs, you'll need to understand shaders, the OpenGL programming model, and the types of operations that a graphics processor does well (and those that it does poorly). In this chapter, we'll take a deeper dive into the OpenGL Shading Language, also known as GLSL. We'll discuss a number of its features and subtleties and provide you with a strong foundation from which you can put your ideas into practice.

Language Overview

GLSL is in the class of languages that can be considered "C-like." That is, its syntax and model are much like those of C, albeit with a number of differences that make GLSL more suitable for graphics and parallel execution in general. One of the major differences between C and GLSL is that matrix and vector types are first-class citizens in GLSL. That means that they are built into the language. Another major difference between GLSL and C is that GLSL is designed to run on massively parallel implementations—most graphics processors will run thousands of copies (or *invocations*) of your shaders at the same time. GLSL also has several limitations to make allowances for these types of implementations. For example, recursion is not allowed in GLSL, and precision requirements for floating-point numbers are not as strict as the IEEE standards that govern most C implementations.

Data Types

GLSL supports both scalar and vector data types, arrays and structures, and a number of opaque data types that represent textures and other data structures.

Scalar Types

The scalar data types supported in GLSL are 32- and 64-bit floating-point numbers, 32-bit signed and unsigned integers, and Boolean values. No support is provided for other commonly used types available in C, such as `short`, `char`, or strings. Also, GLSL doesn't support pointers or integer types larger than 32 bits. The scalar types supported in GLSL are shown in Table 6.1.

Table 6.1: Scalar Types in GLSL

Type	Definition
`bool`	A Boolean value that can either be `true` or `false`
`float`	IEEE-754 formatted 32-bit floating-point quantity
`double`	IEEE-754 formatted 64-bit floating-point quantity
`int`	32-bit two's-complement signed integer
`unsigned int`	32-bit unsigned integer

Signed and unsigned integers behave as would be expected in a C program. That is, signed integers are stored as two's-complement numbers and have a range from $-2{,}147{,}483{,}648$ to $2{,}147{,}483{,}647$; unsigned integers have a range from 0 to $4{,}294{,}967{,}295$. If you add numbers together such that they overflow their ranges, they will wrap around.

Floating-point numbers are effectively defined as they are in the IEEE-754 standard. That is, 32-bit floating-point numbers have a sign bit, 8 exponent bits, and 23 mantissa bits. The sign bit is set if the number is negative and clear if it is positive. The 8 exponent bits represent a number between -127 and $+127$, which is biased into the range 0 to 254 by adding 127 to its value. The mantissa represents the significant digits of the number; there are 23 of them, plus an implied binary 1 digit in the 24th position. Given the sign bit s, exponent e, and mantissa m, the actual value of a 32-bit floating-point number is given by

$$n = (-1)^s (1 + \sum_{i=1}^{23} b_{-i} 2^{-i}) \times 2^{(e-127)}$$

Similarly, double-precision numbers follow the IEEE-754 standard with a sign bit, 11 exponent bits, and 52 mantissa bits. The sign bit is defined as in 32-bit floating point, the exponent represents a value between -1022 and 1023, and the 52-bit mantissa represents the significant digits of the number, with an additional implied 1 in the 53rd position. The actual value of the 64-bit double-precision floating-point number is

$$n = (-1)^s (1 + \sum_{i=1}^{52} b_{-i} 2^{-i}) \times 2^{(e-1023)}$$

GLSL is not required to adhere strictly to the IEEE-754 standard for everything. For most operations the precision will be good enough and behavior is well defined. However, in some operations, such as propagation of NaN (not a number) values, and with behavior of infinities and denormals, some deviation is allowed for. In general, though, writing code that relies on exact behavior of NaNs and infinities is not a good idea, as many processors perform poorly on these types of values. For built-in functions such as trigonometric functions, even more leeway is given by GLSL. Finally, GLSL has no support for exceptions. Thus, if you do something unreasonable such as dividing a number by zero, you won't know that something is wrong until you see unexpected results come out of your shader.

Vectors and Matrices

Vectors of all supported scalar types and matrices of single- and double-precision floating-point types are supported by GLSL. Vector and matrix type names are decorated with their underlying scalar type's name; the exceptions are floating-point vectors and matrices, which have no decoration. Table 6.2 shows all of the vector and matrix types in GLSL.

Vectors may be constructed from other vectors, from a single scalar, from sequences of scalars, or from any combination of scalars and vectors of the appropriate type, so long as there are enough fields in total to fill the destination. Thus, the following are all legal constructors:

```
vec3 foo = vec3(1.0);
vec3 bar = vec3(foo);
vec4 baz = vec4(1.0, 2.0, 3.0, 4.0);
vec4 bat = vec4(1.0, foo);
```

The components of a vector may be accessed as if the vector were an array. That is, the four components of

```
vec4 foo;
```

Table 6.2: Vector and Matrix Types in GLSL

Dimension	Scalar Type				
Scalar	bool	float	double	int	unsigned int
2-Element Vector	bvec2	vec2	dvec2	ivec2	uvec2
3-Element Vector	bvec3	vec3	dvec3	ivec3	uvec3
4-Element Vector	bvec4	vec4	dvec4	ivec4	uvec4
2 × 2 Matrix	—	mat2	dmat2	—	—
2 × 3 Matrix	—	mat2x3	dmat2x3	—	—
2 × 4 Matrix	—	mat2x4	dmat2x4	—	—
3 × 2 Matrix	—	mat3x2	dmat3x2	—	—
3 × 3 Matrix	—	mat3	dmat3	—	—
3 × 4 Matrix	—	mat3x4	dmat3x4	—	—
4 × 2 Matrix	—	mat4x2	dmat4x2	—	—
4 × 3 Matrix	—	mat4x3	dmat4x3	—	—
4 × 4 Matrix	—	mat4	dmat4	—	—

may be accessed as follows:

```
float x = foo[0];
float y = foo[1];
float z = foo[2];
float w = foo[3];
```

Alternatively, vectors may be accessed as if they were structures with fields representing their components. The first component can be accessed through the .x, .s, or .r field. The second component is accessed through the .y, .t, or .g field. The third is accessed through the .z, .p, or .b field. Finally, the fourth component can be accessed through the .w, .q, or .a field. This seems confusing, but x, y, z, and w are often used to denote positions or directions; r, g, b, and a are often used to represent colors; and s, t, p,[1] and q[2] are used to denote texture coordinates. If you were to write the vector's structure in C, it would look something like this:

```
typedef union vec4_t
{
  struct
  {
    float x;
    float y;
    float z;
    float w;
  };
  struct
  {
    float s;
    float t;
    float p;
    float q;
  };
  struct
  {
    float r;
    float g;
    float b;
    float a;
  };
} vec4;
```

However, this isn't the end of the story—vectors also support *swizzling*, or the stacking of fields into vectors of their own. For example, the first three components of foo (which is a vec4) could be extracted by writing foo.xyz (or foo.rgb or foo.stp). The powerful thing is that you can also specify these fields in any order you wish, and you can repeat them. So, foo.zyx would produce a three-element vector with the x and z fields of

---

1. p is used as the third component of a texture coordinate because r is already taken for color.

2. q is used for the fourth component of a texture coordinate because it comes after p.

foo swapped, and `foo.rrrr` would produce a four-element vector with the r component of `foo` in every field. Note that you can't mix and match the conceptually separate x, y, z, and w fields with the s, t, p, and q or r, g, b, and a fields. For example, you can't write `foo.xyba`.

Matrices are also first-class types in GLSL. In GLSL, matrices appear as if they are arrays of vectors, and each element of that array (which is a vector) represents a column of the matrix. Because each of those vectors can also be treated like an array, a column of a matrix behaves as an array, effectively allowing matrices to be treated like two-dimensional arrays. For example, if we declare bar as a `mat4` type, then `bar[0]` is a `vec4` representing its first column, and `bar[0][0]` is the first component of that vector (as is `bar[0].x`), `bar[0][1]` is the second component of the vector (which is equivalent to `bar[0].y`), and so on. Continuing, `bar[1]` is the second column, `bar[2]` is the third column, and so on. Again, if you were to write this in C, it would look something like this:

```
typedef vec4 mat4[4];
```

Standard operators, such as + and -, are defined for vectors and matrices. The multiplication operator (∗) is defined between two vectors to be component-wise, and between two matrices or a matrix and a vector as a matrix–matrix or matrix–vector multiplication operation. Division of vectors and matrices by scalars behaves as expected. Division of vectors and matrices by other vectors and matrices is executed component-wise, so it requires the two operands to be of the same dimension.

Arrays and Structures

You can build aggregate types both as arrays and as structures, including arrays of structures and structures of arrays. Structure types are declared much as they would be in C++. In particular, there is no `typedef` keyword in GLSL; rather, structure definitions in GLSL implicitly declare a new type as they do in C++. Structure types may be forward declared by simply writing `struct my_structure;`, where `my_structure` is the name of the new structure type being declared.

There are two ways to declare an array in GLSL. The first is similar to the syntax used in C or C++, where the array size is appended to the variable name. The following are examples of this type of declaration:

```
float foo[5];
ivec2 bar[13];
dmat3 baz[29];
```

The second syntax is to implicitly declare the type of the whole array by appending the size to the *element type* rather than the variable name. Thus the above declaration could equivalently be written as follows:

```
float[5] foo;
ivec2[13] bar;
dmat3[29] baz;
```

To a C programmer, this may seem odd. However, it's actually a very powerful feature because it allows types to be implicitly defined without the `typedef` keyword, which GLSL lacks. One example use of this is to declare a function that returns an array:

```
vec4[4] functionThatReturnsArray()
{
    vec4[4] foo = ...

    return foo;
}
```

Declaring array types in this form also implicitly defines the constructor for the array. This means that you can write:

```
float[6] var = float[6](1.0, 2.0, 3.0, 4.0, 5.0, 6.0);
```

However, in this case, recent versions[3] of GLSL also allow the traditional, C-style array initializer syntax to be used:

```
float var[6] = { 1.0, 2.0, 3.0, 4.0, 5.0, 6.0 };
```

Arrays may be included in structures, and you can build arrays of structure types (which may themselves include structures). So, for example, the following structure and array definitions are legal in GLSL:

```
struct foo
{
    int a;
    vec2 b;
    mat4 c;
};

struct bar
{
    vec3 a;
    foo[7] b;
};

bar[29] baz;
```

---

3. Curly brace {...} style initializer lists were introduced in GLSL 4.20 along with OpenGL 4.2. If you are writing shaders that might need to run in an earlier version of GLSL, you may want to stick to the implicit array type initialization by construction.

In this code, baz is an array of 29 instances of bar, which contains 1 vec3 and 7 instances of foo, which contains an int, a vec2, and a mat4.

Arrays also include a special *method*[4] called .length(), which returns the number of elements in the array. This allows, for example, loops to be constructed that iterate over all the elements in array. It's interesting to note that because there is a duality between vectors and arrays in GLSL, the .length() function works on vectors (giving their size, naturally). Also, because matrices are essentially arrays of vectors, .length(), when applied to a matrix, gives the number of columns it has. The following are a few examples of applications of the .length() function:

```
float a[10];                   // Declare an array of 10 elements
float b[a.length()];           // Declare an array of the same size
mat4 c;
float d = float(c.length());   // d is now 4
int e = c[0].length();         // e is the height of c (4)

int i;

// This loop iterates 10 times
for (i = 0; i < a.length(); i++)
{
  b[i] = a[i];
}
```

Although GLSL doesn't officially support multidimensional arrays, it does support arrays of arrays. This means that you can put array types into arrays—when you index into the first array, you get back an array, into which you can index, and so on. So, consider the following:

```
float a[10];         // 'a' is an array of 10 floats.
float b[10][2];      // 'b' is an array of 2 arrays of 10 floats.
float c[10][2][5];   // 'c' is an array of 5 arrays of 2 arrays of 10 floats.
```

Here, a is a regular, one-dimensional array. b may look like a two-dimensional array, but it's actually a one-dimensional array of arrays, each of which has 10 elements. There is a subtle difference here. In particular, if you were to write b[1].length(), you would get 10. Following on then, c is a one-dimensional array of 5 one-dimensional arrays of 2 elements, each of which is a one-dimensional array of 10 elements. c[3].length() produces 2 and c[3][1].length() produces 10.

---

4. GLSL doesn't support member functions in the traditional C++ sense, but an exception is made in this case.

Built-In Functions

There are literally hundreds of built-in functions in GLSL. Many of them are used to work with textures and memory and will be covered in detail in those contexts in this book. In this section, we'll look at functions that deal strictly with data—basic math, matrix, vector, and data packing and unpacking funtions will be covered here.

Terminology

Given the very large number of types in GLSL, the language includes support for function *overloading*, which means that functions can have multiple definitions, each with a different set of parameters. Rather than enumerate all of the types supported for each of the functions, some standard terminology is used in the GLSL specification to group classes of data types together such that families of functions can be referred to more concisely. We will sometimes use those terms here to refer to groups of types also. The following are terms that are used both in the GLSL specification and in this book:

- genType means any single-precision floating-point scalar or vector, or one of `float`, `vec2`, `vec3`, or `vec4`.

- genUType means any unsigned integer scalar or vector, or one of `uint`, `uvec2`, `uvec3`, or `uvec4`.

- genIType means any signed integer scalar or vector, or one of `int`, `ivec2`, `ivec3`, or `ivec4`.

- genDType means any double-precision floating-point scalar or vector, or one of `double`, `dvec2`, `dvec3`, or `dvec4`.

- mat means any single-precision floating-point matrix—for example, `mat2`, `mat3`, `mat4`, or any of the non-square matrix forms.

- dmat means any double-precision floating-point matrix—for example, `dmat2`, `dmat3`, `dmat4`, or any of the non-square matrix forms.

Built–In Matrix and Vector Functions

As has been discussed in some detail, vectors and matrices are first-class citizens in GLSL, and where it makes sense, built-in operators such as +, -, *, and / work directly on vector and matrix types. However, a number of functions are provided to deal specifically with vectors and matrices.

The matrixCompMult() function performs a component-wise multiplication of two matrices. Remember, the * operator for two matrices is defined to perform a traditional matrix multiplication in GLSL. Clearly, the two matrix parameters to matrixCompMult() must be the same size.

Matrices may be transposed using the built-in transpose() function. If you transpose a non-square matrix, its dimensions are simply swapped.

To find the inverse of a matrix, GLSL provides the inverse() built-in function for the mat2, mat3, and mat4 types as well as their double-precision equivalents, dmat2, dmat3, and dmat4. Be aware, though, that finding the inverse of a matrix is fairly expensive. Thus, if the matrix is likely to be constant, you should calculate the inverse in your application and load it into your shader as a uniform. Non-square matrices do not have inverses and so are not supported by the inverse() function. Similarly, the determinant() function calculates the determinant of any square matrix. For ill-conditioned matrices, the determinant and the inverse do not exist, so calling inverse() or determinant() on such a matrix will produce an undefined result.

The outerProduct() function performs an outer product of two vectors. Effectively, this takes two vectors as inputs, treats the first as a $1 \times N$ matrix and the second as an $N \times 1$ matrix, and then multiplies them together. The resulting $N \times N$ matrix is returned.

If you need to compare two vectors to each other, a number of built-in functions will do this for you in a component-by-component manner: lessThan(), lessThanEqual(), greaterThan(), greaterThanEqual(), equal(), and notEqual(). Each of these functions takes two vectors of the same type and size, applies the operation that its name suggests, and returns a Boolean vector of the same size of the function's parameters (that is, a bvec2, bvec3, or bvec4). Each component of this Boolean vector contains the result of the comparison for the corresponding components in the source parameters.

Given a Boolean vector, you can test it to see if any of its components are true using the any() function; you can determine whether *all* of its components are true with the all() function. You can also invert the value of a Boolean vector using the not() function.

GLSL provides a large number of built-in functions for dealing with vectors. These include length(), which returns the length of a vector, and distance(), which returns the distance between two points (which is the same as the length of the vector produced by subtracting one point from the other). The `normalize()` function divides a vector by its own length, producing a vector that has a length of 1, but points in the same direction as the source. The `dot()` and `cross()` functions can be used to find the dot and cross products of two vectors, respectively.

The `reflect()` and `refract()` functions take an input vector and a normal to a plane and calculate the reflected or refracted vector that results. `refract()` takes the index of refraction, *eta*, as a parameter in addition to the incoming and normal vectors. The math behind this is explained in the "Reflection and Refraction" section in Chapter 4. Likewise, the `faceforward()` function takes an input vector and two surface normals. If the dot product of the input vector and the second normal vector is negative, then it returns the first normal vector; otherwise, it returns the negative of the first normal vector. As you might have guessed from its name, this function can be used to determine whether a plane is front- or back-facing with respect to a particular view direction. Facingness was covered in Chapter 3, "Following the Pipeline."

Built–In Math Functions

GLSL supports many built-in functions to perform mathematical operations and to manipulate data in variables. The common math functions include `abs()`, `sign()`, `ceil()`, `floor()`, `trunc()`, `round()`, `roundEven()`, `fract()`, `mod()`, `modf()`, `min()`, and `max()`. For the most part, these functions operate on vectors as well as scalars, but otherwise behave like their counterparts in the C standard libraries. The `roundEven()` function doesn't have a direct equivalent in C—this function rounds its argument to the nearest integer, but breaks ties when there is a fractional part of 0.5 by rounding to the nearest *even* number. That is, 7.5 and 8.5 will both round to 8, 42.5 will round to 42 and 43.5 will round to 44.

Two implicit declarations of the `clamp()` function are

```
vec4 clamp(vec4 x, float minVal, float maxVal);
vec4 clamp(vec4 x, vec4 minVal, vec4 maxVal);
```

This function clamps the incoming vector x to the range specified by minVal and maxVal (which may be scalars or vectors). For example, specifying minVal to be 0.0 and maxVal to be 1.0 constrains x to be in the range 0.0 to 1.0. This is such a common range to which to clamp numbers that graphics hardware often has a special case for this range, and some shading languages even include a built-in function specifically to clamp inputs to this range.

A few more special functions are mix(), step(), and smoothstep(). mix() performs a linear interpolation between two of its inputs using the third as a weighting factor. It can effectively be implemented as

```
vec4 mix(vec4 x, vec4 y, float a)
{
    return x + a * (y - x);
}
```

Again, this is such a common operation in graphics that it is a built-in function in the shading language and graphics hardware may have special functionality to implement this directly.

The step() function generates a step function (a function that has a value of either 0.0 or 1.0) based on its two inputs. It is defined as

```
vec4 step(vec4 edge, vec4 x);
```

It returns 0.0 if x < edge and 1.0 if x >= edge.

The smoothstep() function is not as aggressive and produces a smooth fade between two of its inputs based on where the value of its third lies between the first two. It is defined as

```
vec4 smoothstep(vec4 edge0, vec4 edge1, vec4 x);
```

smoothstep() can effectively be implemented as

```
vec4 smoothstep(vec4 edge0, vec4 edge1, vec4 x)
{
    vec4 t = clamp((x - edge0) / (edge1 - edge0), 0.0, 1.0);
    return t * t * (vec4(3.0) - 2.0 * t);
}
```

The shape produced by smoothstep() is known as a Hermite curve and the operation it performs is *Hermite interpolation*. The general shape of the curve is shown in Figure 6.1.

The fma() function performs a fused multiply–add operation. That is, it multiplies the first two of its parameters together and then adds the third. The intermediate result of the operation is generally kept at a higher precision than the source operands, producing a more accurate result than if you were to write those two operations directly in your code. In some

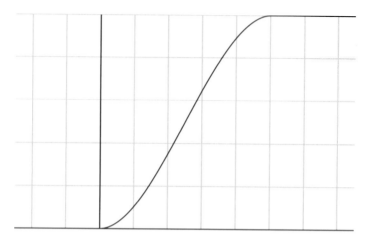

Figure 6.1: Shape of a Hermite curve

graphics processors, the fused multiply–add function may be more efficient than a sequence of a multiplication followed by a separate addition operation.

Most of the math functions in GLSL presume that you are using floating-point numbers in the majority of your shader code. However, there are a few cases where you might be using integers, and GLSL includes a handful of functions that are designed to help you perform arithmetic on very large integer (or fixed-point) numbers. In particular, uaddCarry() and usubBorrow() allow you to perform add with carry and subtract with borrow operations, and imulExtended() and umulExtended() allow you to multiply a pair of 32-bit signed- or unsigned-integer values together, respectively, producing a 64-bit result as a further pair of 32-bit values.

In addition to all this low-level arithmetic functionality, GLSL includes support for all of the expected trigonometry functions, such as sin(), cos(), and tan(); their inverses, asin(), acos(), and atan(); and the hyperbolic forms of those functions, sinh(), cosh(), tanh(), asinh(), acosh(), and atanh(). Exponentional functions are also included: pow(), exp(), log(), exp2(), log2(), sqrt(), and inversesqrt(). Because most of the GLSL functions dealing with angles work in *radians*, even though sometimes it might be convenient to work in degrees, GLSL also includes the radians() function (which takes an angle in degrees and converts it to radians) and the degrees() function (which takes an angle in radians and converts it into degrees).

Built-In Data Manipulation Functions

In addition to all of the functions that do real processing work, GLSL includes a lot of built-in functions that allow you to get at the innards of your data. For example, frexp() allows you to break apart a floating-point number into its mantissa and exponent parts, and ldexp() allows you to build a new floating-point number from a mantissa and exponent that you supply. This allows some direct manipulation of the values of floating-point numbers.

If you need even more control over floating-point numbers, intBitsToFloat() and uintBitsToFloat() allow you to take a signed- or unsigned-integer number, resepectively, and reinterpret its raw bits as a 32-bit floating-point number. To go the opposite way, floatBitsToInt() and floatBitsToUint() take a floating-point number and hand it back to you as either a signed- or unsigned-integer value, respectively. These four functions let you literally tear a floating-point number apart, mess with its bits, and put it back together again. You need to be careful when doing this, however, as not all bit combinations form valid floating-point numbers, and it's quite possible to generate NaNs (not a number values), denormals, or infinities. To test whether a floating-point number represents a NaN or an infinity, you can call isnan() or isinf().

In addition to enabling you to tear apart floating-point numbers and then put them back together again, GLSL includes a number of functions to take floating-point vectors, scale them to various bit depths (such as 8- or 16-bit values), and pack them together into a single 32-bit quantity. For example, the packUnorm4x8() and packSnorm4x8() functions pack a vec4 value into four unsigned or signed 8-bit integer values, respectively, and then pack those four 8-bit values together into a single uint. The unpackUnorm4x8() and unpackSnorm4x8() functions go the other way. The packUnorm2x16(), packSnorm2x16(), unpackUnormx16(), and unpackSnorm16() functions are the equivalents that handle vec2 variables, packing and unpacking them as 16-bit quantities into a uint.

The term norm in these functions refers to *normalized*. In this context, normalization essentially means scaling a value to map it onto a new range. Here, floating-point values are either in the range 0.0 to 1.0 for unsigned normalized data, or in the range −1.0 to 1.0 for signed normalized data. The ends of the input range are mapped to the lower and upper bounds of the output range. For example, for unsigned normalized 8-bit data, an unsigned byte with a value of 0 corresponds to 0.0 in floating point, and an unsigned byte with a value of 255 (the maximum value representable by an unsigned 8-bit number) maps to 1.0.

The packDouble2x32() and unpackDouble2x32() functions perform similar operations on double variables, and the packHalf2x16() functions perform these operations on 16-bit floating-point quantities. It should be noted that GLSL does not include direct support for 16-bit floating-point variables, although data can be stored in memory in that format. Instead, GLSL includes functionality to unpack such data into usable data types in the shading language.

If you just want to get at a subsection of the bits in a signed or unsigned integer, you can use the bitfieldExtract() function to pull a specified chunk of bits out of an unsigned integer (or a vector of unsigned integers). If the input value to the function is a signed integer, then the result is sign extended; otherwise, it is zero extended. Once you have manipulated the bits, you can put them back into the integer using the bitfieldInsert() function.

Other bitfield operations supported by GLSL include the bitfieldReverse(), bitCount(), findLSB(), and findMSB() functions, which reverse the order of a subset of bits in an integer, count the number of set bits in an integer, and find the index of the least significant or most significant bit that is set in an integer, respectively.

Compiling, Linking, and Examining Programs

Each OpenGL implementation has a compiler and linker built in that will take your shader code, compile it to an internal binary form, and link it together so that it can be run on a graphics processor. This process may fail for various reasons, so it is important to be able to figure out why. The compilation or link stage may have failed, for example. Even if they succeed, perhaps some other factor has changed the way that your program behaves.

Getting Information from the Compiler

To this point in the book, all of the shaders we've presented have been perfect, tested, and bug free. We've done very little, if any, error checking and have just blasted ahead assuming that everything will work fine. However, in the real world, at least during development, your shaders will likely have bugs, typos, or errors in them. The shader compiler can help you find problems and squash them. The first step is to determine whether a shader compiled. Once you have set the shader's source code and called

glCompileShader(), you can get the compilation status back from OpenGL by calling **glGetShaderiv()**. Its prototype is

```
void glGetShaderiv(GLuint shader,
                   GLenum pname,
                   GLint * params);
```

Here, shader is the name of the shader object you'd like to know about, pname is the parameter you want to get from the shader object, and params is the address of a variable where OpenGL should put the result. To find out if a shader compiled successfully, you can set pname to GL_COMPILE_STATUS. The variable pointed to by params will be set to 0 if the shader failed to compile and to 1 if it compiled successfully. Incidentally, 1 and 0 are the numerical values of GL_TRUE and GL_FALSE, respectively, so you can test against those definitions if you wish.

Other values for pname that can be passed to **glGetShaderiv()** include the following:

- GL_SHADER_TYPE, which returns the type of shader that the object is (e.g., GL_VERTEX_SHADER or GL_FRAGMENT_SHADER)

- GL_DELETE_STATUS, which returns GL_TRUE or GL_FALSE to indicate whether **glDeleteShader()** has been called on the shader object

- GL_SHADER_SOURCE_LENGTH, which returns the total length of the source code associated with the shader object

- GL_INFO_LOG_LENGTH, which returns the length of the information log contained in the shader object

The last token, GL_INFO_LOG_LENGTH, tells you the length of the information log that the shader object contains. This log is generated when the shader is compiled. Initially, it's empty, but as the shader compiler parses and compiles the shader, it generates a log that contains output similar to what you might be familiar with in the regular compiler world. You can then retrieve the log from the shader object by calling **glGetShaderInfoLog()**, whose prototype is

```
void glGetShaderInfoLog(GLuint shader,
                        GLsizei bufSize,
                        GLsizei * length,
                        GLchar * infoLog);
```

Again, shader is the name of the shader object whose log you want to get. infoLog should be pointed at a buffer that will have the log written into it by OpenGL. The buffer should be big enough to hold the entire log—you can get its size through the **glGetShaderiv()** function. If you care about only the first few lines of the log, you can use a fixed-size buffer for infoLog. In any case, the size of the buffer you're using should be in bufSize. The actual amount of data written into infoLog will be written into the variable pointed to by length in OpenGL. Listing 6.1 shows an example of how to retrieve the log from a shader object.

```
// Create, attach source to, and compile a shader...
GLuint fs = glCreateShader(GL_FRAGMENT_SHADER);
glShaderSource(fs, 1, &source, NULL);
glCompileShader(fs);

// Now, get the info log length...
GLint log_length;
glGetShaderiv(fs, GL_INFO_LOG_LENGTH, &log_length);

// Allocate a string for it...
std::string str;

str.reserve(log_length);

// Get the log...
glGetShaderInfoLog(fs, log_length, NULL, str.c_str());
```

Listing 6.1: Retrieving the compiler log from a shader

If your shader contains errors or suspect code that might generate compiler warnings, then OpenGL's shader compiler will tell you about it in the log. Consider the following shader, which contains deliberate errors:

```
#version 450 core

layout (location = 0) out vec4 color;

uniform scale;
uniform vec3 bias;

void main(void)
{
    color = vec4(1.0, 0.5, 0.2, 1.0) * scale + bias;
}
```

Compiling this shader produces the following log on the author's machine. You will likely see something similar on your own:

```
ERROR: 0:5: error(#12) Unexpected qualifier
ERROR: 0:10: error(#143) Undeclared identifier: scale
WARNING: 0:10: warning(#402) Implicit truncation of vector from
size: 4 to size: 3
ERROR: 0:10: error(#162) Wrong operand types: no operation "+" exists
that takes a left-hand operand of type "4-component vector of vec4" and
a right operand of type "uniform 3-component vector of vec3" (or there
is no acceptable conversion)
ERROR: error(#273) 3 compilation errors.  No code generated
```

As you can see, several errors and a warning have been generated and recorded in the shader's information log. For this particular compiler, the format of the error messages is ERROR or WARNING followed by the string index (remember, `glShaderSource()` allows you to attach multiple source strings to a single shader object), followed by the line number. Let's look at the errors one by one:

```
ERROR: 0:5: error(#12) Unexpected qualifier
```

Line 5 of our shader is this:

```
uniform scale;
```

It seems that we have forgotten the type of the `scale` uniform. We can fix that by giving `scale` a type (it's supposed to be `vec4`). The next three issues are on the same line:

```
ERROR: 0:10: error(#143) Undeclared identifier: scale
WARNING: 0:10: warning(#402) Implicit truncation of vector from
size: 4 to size: 3
ERROR: 0:10: error(#162) Wrong operand types: no operation "+" exists
that takes a left-hand operand of type "4-component vector of vec4" and
a right operand of type "uniform 3-component vector of vec3" (or there
is no acceptable conversion)
```

The first one says that `scale` is an undefined identifier—that is, the compiler doesn't know what `scale` is. This is because of that first error on line 5: We haven't actually defined `scale` yet. Next is a warning that we are attempting to truncate a vector from a four-component type to a three-component type. This might not be a serious issue, given that the compiler might be confused as a result of another error on the very same line. This warning is saying that there is no version of the + operator that can add a `vec3` and a `vec4`. It appears because, even once we've given `scale` its `vec4` type, bias has been declared as a `vec3` and therefore can't be added to a `vec4` variable. A potential fix is to change the type of bias to `vec4`.

If we apply our now known fixes to the shader (shown in Listing 6.1), we have

```
#version 450 core

layout (location = 0) out vec4 color;

uniform vec4 scale;
uniform vec4 bias;

void main(void)
{
    color = vec4(1.0, 0.5, 0.2, 1.0) * scale + bias;
}
```

Once we compile this updated shader, we should have success: Calling **glGetShaderiv()** with pname set to GL_COMPILE_STATUS should return GL_TRUE, and the new info log should either be empty or simply indicate success.

Getting Information from the Linker

Just as compilation may fail, so linking of programs may also fail or not go exactly the way you planned. While the compiler will produce an info log when you call **glCompileShader()**, when you call **glLinkProgram()**, the linker can also produce a log that you can query to figure out what happened. Also, a program object has several properties, including its link status, resource usage, and so on, that you can retrieve. In fact, a linked program has quite a bit more status than a compiled shader. You can retrieve all of this information by using **glGetProgramiv()**, whose prototype is

```
void glGetProgramiv(GLuint program,
                    GLenum  pname,
                    GLint * params);
```

Notice that **glGetProgramiv()** is very similar to **glGetShaderiv()**. The first parameter, program, is the name of the program object whose information you want to retrieve. The last parameter, params, is the address of a variable where you would like OpenGL to write that information. Just like **glGetShaderiv()**, **glGetProgramiv()** takes a parameter called pname that indicates what you would like to know about the program object. There are many more valid values for pname for program objects as well, including these:

- GL_DELETE_STATUS, like the same property of shaders, indicates whether **glDeleteProgram()** has been called for the program object.

- GL_LINK_STATUS, similarly to the GL_COMPILE_STATUS property of a shader, indicates the success of linking the program.

- GL_INFO_LOG_LENGTH returns the info log length for the program.

- GL_ATTACHED_SHADERS returns the number of shaders that are attached to the program.

- GL_ACTIVE_ATTRIBUTES returns the number of attributes that the vertex shader in the program actually[5] uses.

---

5. More precisely, that the compiler thinks the vertex shader uses.

- GL_ACTIVE_UNIFORMS returns the number of uniforms used by the program.

- GL_ACTIVE_UNIFORM_BLOCKS returns the number of uniform blocks used by the program.

You can tell whether a program has been successfully linked by calling **glGetProgramiv()** with pname set to GL_LINK_STATUS. If it returns GL_TRUE in params, then linking worked. You can also get the information log from a program just as you can from a shader. To do this, you can call **glGetProgramInfoLog()**, whose prototype is

```
void glGetProgramInfoLog(GLuint program,
                         GLsizei bufSize,
                         GLsizei * length,
                         GLchar * infoLog);
```

The parameters to **glGetProgramInfoLog()** work just the same as they do for **glGetShaderInfoLog()**, except that instead of shader, we have program (the name of the program object whose log you want to read). Now, consider the shader shown in Listing 6.2.

```
#version 450 core

layout (location = 0) out vec4 color;

vec3 myFunction();

void main(void)
{
    color = vec4(myFunction(), 1.0);
}
```

Listing 6.2: Fragment shader with external function declaration

Listing 6.2 includes a declaration of an external function. This works similarly to C programs, where the actual definition of the function is contained in a separate source file. OpenGL expects that the function body for myFunction will be defined in one of the fragment shaders attached to the program object (remember, you can attach multiple shaders of the same type to the same program object and have them link together). When you call **glLinkProgram()**, OpenGL will look in all the fragment shaders for a function called myFunction; if it doesn't find this function, it will generate a link error. Trying to link just this fragment shader into a program object generates the following error message:

```
Vertex shader(s) failed to link, fragment shader(s) failed to link.
ERROR: error(#401) Function: myFunction() is not implemented
```

To resolve this error, we can either include the body of myFunction in the shader of Listing 6.2, or attach a second fragment shader to the same program object that includes the function body.

Separate Programs

So far, all of the programs you have used have been considered *monolithic* program objects. That is, they contain a shader for each stage that is active. You have attached a vertex shader, a fragment shader, and possibly tessellation or geometry shaders to a single program object and then called glLinkProgram() to link the program object into a single representation of the entire pipeline. This type of linking might allow a compiler to perform inter-stage optimizations such as eliminating code in a vertex shader that contributes to an output that is never used by the subsequent fragment shader. However, this scheme comes at a potential cost of flexibility and possibly performance to the application. For every combination of vertex, fragment, and possibly other shaders, you need to have a unique program object, and linking all those programs doesn't come cheap.

For example, consider the case where you want to change only a fragment shader. With a monolithic program, you would need to link the same vertex shader to two or more different fragment shaders, creating a new program object for each combination. If you have multiple fragment shaders and multiple vertex shaders, you now need a program object for each combination of shaders. This problem gets worse as you add more shaders and shader stages to the mix. Eventually, you may end up with a combinatorial explosion of shader combinations that can quickly balloon into thousands of permutations, or more.

To alleviate this problem, OpenGL supports linking program objects in *separable* mode. A program linked this way can contain shaders for only a single stage in the pipeline or for just a few of the stages. Multiple program objects, each representing a section of the OpenGL pipeline, can then be attached to a *program pipeline object* and matched together at runtime rather than at link time. Shaders attached to a single program object can still benefit from inter-stage optimizations, but the program objects attached to a program pipeline object can be switched around at will with relatively little cost in performance.

To use a program object in separable mode, you need to tell OpenGL what you plan to do *before* you link it by calling **glProgramParameteri()** with pname set to GL_PROGRAM_SEPARABLE and value set to GL_TRUE. This tells

OpenGL not to eliminate any outputs from a shader that it thinks aren't being used. It will also arrange any internal data layout such that the last shader in the program object can communicate with the first shader in another program object with the same input layout. Next, you should create a program pipeline object with **glGenProgramPipelines()**, and then attach programs to it representing the sections of the pipeline you wish to use. To do so, call **glUseProgramStages()**, passing in the name of the program pipeline object, a bitfield indicating which stages to use, and the name of a program object that contains those stages.

Listing 6.3 shows an example in which we set up a program pipeline object with two programs, one containing only a vertex shader and one containing only a fragment shader.

```
// Create a vertex shader
GLuint vs = glCreateShader(GL_VERTEX_SHADER);

// Attach source and compile
glShaderSource(vs, 1, vs_source, NULL);
glCompileShader(vs);

// Create a program for our vertex stage and attach the vertex shader to it
GLuint vs_program = glCreateProgram();
glAttachShader(vs_program, vs);

// Important part - set the GL_PROGRAM_SEPARABLE flag to GL_TRUE *then* link
glProgramParameteri(vs_program, GL_PROGRAM_SEPARABLE, GL_TRUE);
glLinkProgram(vs_program);

// Now do the same with a fragment shader
GLuint fs = glCreateShader(GL_FRAGMENT_SHADER);
glShaderSource(fs, 1, fs_source, NULL);
glCompileShader(fs);
GLuint fs_program = glCreateProgram();
glAttachShader(fs_program, vs);
glProgramParameteri(fs_program, GL_PROGRAM_SEPARABLE, GL_TRUE);
glLinkProgram(fs_program);

// The program pipeline represents the collection of programs in use:
// Generate the name for it here.
GLuint program_pipeline;
glGenProgramPipelines(1, &program_pipeline);

// Now use the vertex shader from the first program and the fragment shader
// from the second program.
glUseProgramStages(program_pipeline, GL_VERTEX_SHADER_BIT, vs_program);
glUseProgramStages(program_pipeline, GL_FRAGMENT_SHADER_BIT, fs_program);
```

Listing 6.3: Configuring a separable program pipeline

Although this simple example includes only two program objects, each with just a single shader in it, it's possible to have more complex arrangements where more than two program objects are used, or where one or more of the program objects contain more than one shader. For example, tessellation control and tessellation evaluation shaders are often tightly coupled, such that one does not make much sense without the other. Also, very often when tessellation is used, it is possible to use a pass-through vertex shader and do all of the real vertex shader work either in the tessellation control shader or in the tessellation evaluation shader. In those cases, it may make sense to couple a vertex shader and both tessellation shaders in one program object, but still use separable programs to be able to switch the fragment shader on the fly.

If you really do want to create a simple program object with exactly one shader object in it, you can take a shortcut and call

```
GLuint glCreateShaderProgramv(GLenum type,
                              GLsizei count,
                              const char ** strings);
```

The **glCreateShaderProgramv()** function takes the type of shader you want to compile (e.g., GL_VERTEX_SHADER or GL_FRAGMENT_SHADER), the number of source strings, and a pointer to array of strings (just like **glShaderSource()**), and compiles those strings into a new shader object. Then, it internally attaches that shader object to a new program object, sets its separable hint to TRUE, links it, deletes the shader object, and returns the program object to you. You can then use this program object in your program pipeline objects.

Once you have a program pipeline object with a bunch of shader stages compiled into program objects and attached to it, you can make it the current pipeline by calling **glBindProgramPipeline()**:

```
void glBindProgramPipeline(GLuint pipeline);
```

Here, `pipeline` is the name of the program pipeline object that you wish to use. Once the program pipeline object is bound, its programs will be used for rendering or compute operations.

Interface Matching

GLSL provides a specific set of rules for how the outputs from one shader stage are matched up with the corresponding inputs in the next stage. When you link a set of shaders together into a single program object, OpenGL's linker will tell you if you didn't match things up correctly. However, when you use separate program objects for each stage, the matching occurs when you switch program objects—and not lining things up correctly can cause effects ranging from subtle failures of your program to things not working at all. It is therefore very important to follow these rules to avoid these kinds of issues, especially when you are using separate program objects.

In general, the output variables of one shader stage end up connected to the inputs of the subsequent stage if they match exactly in name and type. The variables must also match in qualification. For interface blocks, the two blocks on either side of the interface must have the same members, with the same names, declared in the same order. The same applies for structures (used as either inputs and outputs, or as members of interface blocks). If the interface variable is an array, both sides of the interface should declare the same number of elements in that array. The only exception is for the inputs and outputs for tessellation and geometry shaders, which change from single elements to arrays along the way.

If you link shaders for multiple stages together in a single program object, OpenGL may realize that an interface member isn't required and that it can eliminate it from the shader(s). As an example, if the vertex shader writes a constant to a particular output and the fragment shader then consumes that data as an input, OpenGL might remove the code to produce that constant from the vertex shader and instead use the constant directly in the fragment shader. When separate programs are used, OpenGL can't do this and must consider every part of the interface to be active and used.

It can be a pain to remember to name all of your input and output variables the same way in every shader in your application, especially as the number of shaders grows or as more developers start contributing shaders. However, it is possible to use a `layout` qualifier to assign a location to each input and output in a set of shaders. Where possible, OpenGL will use the locations of each input and output to match them together. In that case, the names of the variables don't matter, and they need match only in type and qualification.

It is possible to query the input and output interfaces of a program object by calling **glGetProgramInterfaceiv()** and **glGetProgramResourceiv()**, whose prototypes are

```
void glGetProgramInterfaceiv(GLuint program,
                             GLenum programInterface,
                             GLenum pname,
                             GLint * params);
```

and

```
void glGetProgramResourceiv(GLuint program,
                            GLenum programInterface,
                            GLuint index,
                            GLsizei propCount,
                            const Glenum * props,
                            GLsizei bufSize,
                            GLsizei * length,
                            GLint * params);
```

Here, program is the name of the program object whose interface properties you want to discover, and programInterface should be GL_PROGRAM_INPUT or GL_PROGRAM_OUTPUT to specify that you want to know about the inputs or outputs of the program, respectively.

For **glGetProgramInterfaceiv()**, pname should be GL_ACTIVE_RESOURCES, and the number of separate inputs or outputs of program will be written into the variable pointed to by params. You can then read from this list of inputs or outputs by passing the index of the resource in the index parameter of **glGetProgramResourceiv()**. **glGetProgramResourceiv()** returns multiple properties in a single function call, and the number of properties to return is given in propCount. props is an array of tokens specifying which properties you'd like to retrieve. Those properties will be written to the array whose address is given in params and whose size (in elements) is given in bufSize. If length is not NULL, then the actual number of properties will be written into the variable that it points at.

The values in the props array can be any of the following:

- GL_TYPE returns the type of the interface member in the corresponding element of params.

- GL_ARRAY_SIZE returns the length of the interface array if it is an array, or zero if it is not.

- GL_REFERENCED_BY_VERTEX_SHADER,
  GL_REFERENCED_BY_TESS_CONTROL_SHADER,
  GL_REFERENCED_BY_TESS_EVALUATION_SHADER,
  GL_REFERENCED_BY_GEOMETRY_SHADER,
  GL_REFERENCED_BY_FRAGMENT_SHADER, and
  GL_REFERENCED_BY_COMPUTE_SHADER return zero or non-zero depending on whether the input or output is referenced by the vertex, tessellation control, evaluation, geometry, fragment, or compute shader stages, respectively.

- GL_LOCATION returns the shader-specified or OpenGL-generated location for the input or output in the corresponding element of params.

- GL_LOCATION_INDEX can be used only when programInterface specifies GL_PROGRAM_OUTPUT; it returns the index of the output of a fragment shader.

- GL_IS_PER_PATCH lets you know if an output of a tessellation control shader or an input to a tessellation evaluation shader is declared as a per-patch interface.

You can determine the name of an input or output by calling **glGetProgramResourceName()**:

```
void glGetProgramResourceName(GLuint program,
                              GLenum programInterface,
                              GLuint index,
                              GLsizei bufSize,
                              GLsizei * length,
                              char * name);
```

Again, program, programInterface, and index have the same meaning as they do for **glGetProgramResourceiv()**. bufSize is the size of the buffer pointed to by name. If it is not NULL, length points to a variable that will have the actual length of the name written into it. As an example, Listing 6.4 shows a simple program that will print information about the active outputs of the program object.

```
// Get the number of outputs
GLint outputs;
glGetProgramInterfaceiv(program, GL_PROGRAM_OUTPUT,
                        GL_ACTIVE_RESOURCES, &outputs);

// A list of tokens describing the properties we wish to query
static const GLenum props[] = { GL_TYPE, GL_LOCATION };

// Various local variables
GLint i;
GLint params[2];
GLchar name[64];
const char * type_name;

for (i = 0; i < outputs; i++)
{
    // Get the name of the output
    glGetProgramResourceName(program, GL_PROGRAM_OUTPUT, i,
                             sizeof(name), NULL, name);

    // Get other properties of the output
    glGetProgramResourceiv(program, GL_PROGRAM_OUTPUT, i,
                           2, props, 2, NULL, params);
```

```
    // type_to_name() is a function that returns the GLSL name of
    // type given its enumerant value
    type_name = type_to_name(params[0]);

    // Print the result
    printf("Index %d: %s %s @ location %d.\n",
            i, type_name, name, params[1]);
}
```

Listing 6.4: Printing interface information

Look at the output declarations in the following snippet of a fragment shader:

```
out vec4 color;
layout (location = 2) out ivec2 data;
out float extra;
```

Given these declarations, the code shown in Listing 6.4 prints the following:

```
Index 0: vec4 color @ location 0.
Index 1: ivec2 data @ location 2.
Index 2: float extra @ location 1.
```

Notice that the listing of the active outputs appears in the order that they were declared in. However, since we explicitly specified output location 2 for data, the GLSL compiler went back and used location 1 for extra. We are also able to correctly determine the types of the outputs using this code. Although in your applications you will likely know the types and names of all of your outputs, this kind of functionality is very useful for development tools and debuggers that may not know the origins of the shaders that they are working with.

Shader Subroutines

Even when your programs are linked in separable mode, switching between program objects can be fairly expensive from a performance perspective. As an alternative, it may be possible to use *subroutine uniforms*. This special type of uniform behaves something like a function pointer in C. To use a subroutine uniform, we declare a subroutine type, declare one or more compatible subroutines (which are essentially just functions with a special declaration format), and then "point" our subroutine uniforms at these functions. A simple example is shown in Listing 6.5.

```
#version 450 core

// First, declare the subroutine type
subroutine vec4 sub_mySubroutine(vec4 param1);
```

```
// Next, declare a couple of functions that can be used as subroutines...
subroutine (sub_mySubroutine)
vec4 myFunction1(vec4 param1)
{
    return param1 * vec4(1.0, 0.25, 0.25, 1.0);
}

subroutine (sub_mySubroutine)
vec4 myFunction2(vec4 param1)
{
    return param1 * vec4(0.25, 0.25, 1.0, 1.0);
}

// Finally, declare a subroutine uniform that can be "pointed"
// at subroutine functions matching its signature
subroutine uniform sub_mySubroutine mySubroutineUniform;

// Output color
out vec4 color;
void main(void)
{
    // Call subroutine through uniform
    color = mySubroutineUniform(vec4(1.0));
}
```

Listing 6.5: Example subroutine uniform declaration

When you link a program that includes subroutines, each subroutine in each stage is assigned an index. If you are using version 430 of GLSL or newer (this is the version shipped with OpenGL 4.3), you can assign the indices yourself in shader code using the index layout qualifier. So, we could declare the subroutines from Listing 6.5 as follows:

```
layout (index = 2)
subroutine (sub_mySubroutine)
vec4 myFunction1(vec4 param1)
{
    return param1 * vec4(1.0, 0.25, 0.25, 1.0);
}

layout (index = 1);
subroutine (sub_mySubroutine)
vec4 myFunction2(vec4 param1)
{
    return param1 * vec4(0.25, 0.25, 1.0, 1.0);
}
```

If you are using a version of GLSL earlier than 430, then OpenGL will assign indices for you and you have no say in the matter. Either way, you can find out what those indices are by calling **glGetProgramResourceIndex()**:

```
GLuint glGetProgramResourceIndex(GLuint program,
                                 GLenum programInterface,
                                 const char * name);
```

Here, program is the name of the linked program containing the subroutine; programInterface is one of GL_VERTEX_SUBROUTINE, GL_TESS_CONTROL_SUBROUTINE, GL_TESS_EVALUATION_SUBROUTINE, GL_GEOMETRY_SUBROUTINE, GL_FRAGMENT_SUBROUTINE, or GL_COMPUTE_SUBROUTINE to indicate which shader stage you're asking about; and name is the name of the subroutine. If a subroutine with the name name is not found in the appropriate stage of the program, then this function returns GL_INVALID_VALUE.

Going the other way, given the indices of subroutines in a program, you can get their names by calling **glGetProgramResourceName()**:

```
void glGetProgramResourceName(GLuint program,
                              GLenum programInterface,
                              GLuint index,
                              GLsizei bufSize,
                              GLsizei * length,
                              char *  name);
```

Here, program is the name of the program object containing the subroutines, programInterface is one of the same tokens accepted by **glGetProgramResourceIndex()**, index is the index of the subroutine within the program, bufsize is the size of the buffer whose address is in name, and length is the address of a variable that will be filled with the actual number of characters written into name.

The number of active subroutines in a particular stage of a program can be determined by calling **glGetProgramStageiv()**:

```
void glGetProgramStageiv(GLuint program,
                         GLenum shadertype,
                         GLenum pname,
                         GLint *values);
```

Again, program is the name of the program object containing the shader and shadertype indicates which stage of the program you're asking about. To get the number of active subroutines in the relevant stage of the program, pname should be set to GL_ACTIVE_SUBROUTINES. The result is written into the variable whose address you place in values. When you call **glGetActiveSubroutineName()**, index should be between 0 and 1 less than this value.

Once you know the names of the subroutines in a program object (either because you wrote the shader or because you queried the names), you can set their values by calling **glUniformSubroutinesuiv()**:

```
void glUniformSubroutinesuiv(GLenum shadertype,
                             GLsizei count,
                             const GLunit *indices);
```

This function sets count subroutine uniforms in the shader stage given by shadertype in the active program to point at the subroutines whose indices are given in the first count elements of the array pointed to by indices. Subroutine uniforms are a little different than other uniforms in several ways:

- The state for a subroutine uniform is stored in the current OpenGL context rather than in the program object. This allows subroutine uniforms to have different values within the same program object when that object is used in different contexts.

- The values of subroutine uniforms are lost when the current program object is changed using **glUseProgram()**, when you call **glUseProgramStages()** or **glBindProgramPipeline()**, or if you relink the current program object. This means that you need to reset those values every time you use a new program or new program stages.

- It is not possible to change the value of a subset of the subroutine uniforms in a stage of a program object. **glUniformSubroutinesuiv()** sets the value of count uniforms, starting from 0. Any uniforms beyond count will be left with their previous value. Remember, though, that the default value of subroutine uniforms is not defined, so not setting them at all and then calling them could cause bad things to happen.

In our simple example, after linking our program object, we can run the following code to determine the indices of our subroutine functions because we haven't assigned explicit locations to them in our shader code:

```
subroutines[0] = glGetProgramResourceIndex(render_program,
                                GL_FRAGMENT_SHADER_SUBROUTINE,
                                "myFunction1");
subroutines[1] = glGetProgramResourceIndex(render_program,
                                GL_FRAGMENT_SHADER_SUBROUTINE,
                                "myFunction2");
```

Our rendering loop is shown in Listing 6.6.

```
void subroutines_app::render(double currentTime)
{
    int i = (int)currentTime;
```

```
    glUseProgram(render_program);

    glUniformSubroutinesuiv(GL_FRAGMENT_SHADER, 1, &subroutines[i & 1]);

    glDrawArrays(GL_TRIANGLE_STRIP, 0, 4);
}
```

Listing 6.6: Setting values of subroutine uniforms

This function draws a quad using a simple vertex shader that was also linked into our program object. After setting the current program with a call to **glUseProgram()**, it resets the values of the only subroutine uniform in the program. Remember, the values of all of the subroutine uniforms "go away" when you change the current program. The subroutine at which we point the uniform changes every second. Using the fragment shader shown in Listing 6.5, the window will be rendered red for one second, then blue for one second, then red again, and so on.

In general, you can expect setting the value of a single subroutine uniform to take less time than changing a program object. Therefore, if you have several similar shaders, it may be worthwhile to combine them into one and then use a subroutine uniform to choose which path to take in a particular context. You can even declare multiple versions of your main() function (with different names), create a subroutine uniform that can point at any of them, and then call it from your real main() function.

Program Binaries

Once you have compiled and linked a program, it is possible to ask OpenGL to provide a binary object that represents its internal version of the program. At some point in the future, your application can hand that binary back to OpenGL and bypass the compiler and linker. If you wish to use this feature, you should call **glProgramParameteri()** with pname set to GL_PROGRAM_BINARY_RETRIEVABLE_HINT set to GL_TRUE before calling **glLinkProgram()**. This tells OpenGL that you plan to get the binary data back from it and that it should hang on to that binary and have it ready to pass to you.

Before you can retrieve the binary for a program object, you need to figure out how long it will be and allocate sufficient memory to store it. To do this, you can call **glGetProgramiv()** and set pname to GL_PROGRAM_BINARY_LENGTH. The resulting value written into params is the number of bytes you will need to set aside for the program binary.

Next, you can call **glGetProgramBinary()** to actually retrieve the binary representation of the program object. The prototype of **glGetProgramBinary()** is

```
void glGetProgramBinary(GLuint program,
                        GLsizei bufsize,
                        GLsizei * length,
                        GLenum * binaryFormat,
                        void * binary);
```

Given the name of a program object in `program`, this function will write the binary representation of the program into the memory pointed to by `binary`, and write a token representing the format of that program binary into `binaryFormat`. The size of this region of memory is passed in `bufsize` and must be large enough to store the entire program binary, which is why it is necessary to query the binary size with **glGetProgramiv()** first. The actual number of bytes written is stored in the variable whose address is passed in `length`. The format of the binary is likely to be proprietary and specific to the vendor that created your OpenGL drivers. However, it's important to hold onto the value written to `binaryFormat`, because you'll need to pass it back to OpenGL later, along with the contents of the binary, to load it again. Listing 6.7 shows a simple example that retrieves a program binary from OpenGL.

```
// Create a simple program containing only a vertex shader
static const GLchar source[] = { ... };

// First create and compile the shader
GLuint shader;
shader = glCreateShader(GL_VERTEX_SHADER);
glShaderSource(shader, 1, suorce, NULL);
glCompileShader(shader);

// Create the program and attach the shader to it
GLuint program;
program = glCreateProgram();
glAttachShader(program, shader);

// Set the binary retrievable hint and link the program
glProgramParameteri(program, GL_PROGRAM_BINARY_RETRIEVABLE_HINT, GL_TRUE);
glLinkProgram(program);

// Get the expected size of the program binary
GLint binary_size = 0;
glGetProgramiv(program, GL_PROGRAM_BINARY_SIZE, &binary_size);

// Allocate some memory to store the program binary
unsigned char * program_binary = new unsigned char [binary_size];

// Now retrieve the binary from the program object
GLenum binary_format = GL_NONE;
glGetProgramBinary(program, binary_size, NULL, &binary_format, program_binary);
```

Listing 6.7: Retrieving a program binary

Once you have the program binary, you can save it to disk (possibly compressed) and use it next time your program starts. This can save you the time necessary to compile shaders and link programs before you can start rendering. The program binary format will probably[6] be specific to your graphics card vendor and likely will not be portable from machine to machine, or even from driver to driver on the same machine. This feature is not currently designed as a distribution mechanism, but rather as more of a caching mechanism.

This may seem like a fairly large limitation, such that program binaries are not of much use—and have only relatively simple programs like those outlined in this book. However, consider a very large application such as a video game. It may include hundreds or thousands of shaders, and may compile multiple variants of those shaders. The start-up time on many video games is very long, and using program binaries to cache compiled shaders from run to run of a game can save a lot of time. However, another issue that plagues complex applications is runtime recompilation of shaders.

Most features of OpenGL are supported directly by modern graphics processors. However, some of them require some level of work in a shader. When your application compiles shaders, the OpenGL implementation will assume the most common case for most states and compile the shader assuming that is the way it will be used. If it is used in a way that is not handled by this default compilation of the shaders, the OpenGL implementation may need to at least partially recompile parts of the shader to deal with the changes. That can cause a noticeable stutter in the execution of the application.

For this reason, it's strongly recommended that you compile your shaders and then link your program with GL_PROGRAM_BINARY_RETRIEVABLE_HINT set to GL_TRUE, but wait until you've used the shaders a few times for real rendering before retrieving the binaries. This will give the OpenGL implementation a chance to recompile any shaders that need it, and store a number of versions of each program in a single binary. The next time you load the binary and the OpenGL implementation realizes that it needs a particular variant of the program, it will find it already compiled in the binary blob you just handed it.

---

6. It is conceivable that one or more OpenGL vendors could get together and define a standard binary format in an extension that is understood by multiple parties. At the time of this book's writing, that has not happened.

Once you're ready to give the program binary back to OpenGL, call **glProgramBinary()** on a fresh program object, with binaryFormat and length set to the values you got back from **glGetProgramBinary()** and with the data loaded into the buffer that you pass in binary. This will reload the program object with the data it contained when you queried the binary on the last run of your application. If the OpenGL driver doesn't recognize the binary you give it or can't load it for some reason, the **glProgramBinary()** call will fail. In this case, you'll need to supply the original GLSL source for the shaders and recompile them.

Summary

This chapter discussed shaders and how they work, the GLSL programming language, how OpenGL uses shaders, and where they fit within the graphics pipeline. At this point, you should have a good understanding of the basic concepts involved in writing the shaders you'll need for your programs. You also learned how to retrieve binary shaders from OpenGL so that your applications can cache them and store them away for later. When your shaders don't work (which is inevitable during the development of any application), you should be able to get information from OpenGL that will help you figure out why. With a little practice, and with your knowledge of the topics covered earlier in this book, you should be ready to write some interesting OpenGL programs.

Part II

In Depth

Chapter 7

Vertex Processing and Drawing Commands

WHAT YOU'LL LEARN IN THIS CHAPTER

- How to get data from your application into the front of the graphics pipeline.

- What the various OpenGL drawing commands are and what their parameters do.

- How your transformed geometry gets into your application's window.

In Chapter 3, "Following the Pipeline," we followed the OpenGL pipeline from start to finish, producing a simple application that exercised every shader stage with a minimal example that was just enough to make it do something. We even showed you a simple compute shader that did nothing at all! However, the result of all this was a single tessellated triangle broken into points. Since then, you have learned some of the math involved in 3D computer graphics, have seen how to set up the pipeline to do more than draw a single triangle, and have received a deeper introduction to GLSL, the OpenGL Shading Language. In this chapter, we dig deeper into the first couple of stages of the OpenGL pipeline—vertex assembly and vertex shading. We'll see how drawing commands are structured and how they can be used to send work into the OpenGL pipeline, and how that ends up in primitives being produced ready for rasterization.

Vertex Processing

The first programmable stage in the OpenGL pipeline (i.e., one that you can write a shader for) is the vertex shader. Before the shader runs, OpenGL will fetch the inputs to the vertex shader in the *vertex fetch* stage, which we will describe first. Your vertex shader's resposibility is to set the position[1] of the vertex that will be fed to the next stage in the pipeline. It can also set a number of other user-defined and built-in outputs that further describe the vertex to OpenGL.

Vertex Shader Inputs

The first step in any OpenGL graphics pipeline is actually the vertex fetch stage, unless the configuration does not require any vertex attributes, as was the case in some of our earliest examples. This stage runs before your vertex shader and is responsible for forming its inputs. You have already been introduced to the **glVertexAttribPointer()** function and we have explained how it hooks data in buffers up to vertex shader inputs. Now we'll take a closer look at vertex attributes.

In the example programs presented thus far, we've used only a single vertex attribute and have filled it with four-component floating-point data, which matches the data types we have used for our uniforms, uniform blocks, and hard-coded constants. However, OpenGL supports a large number of vertex attributes, and each can have its own format, data type, number of components, and so on. Also, OpenGL can read the data for each attribute from a different buffer object. **glVertexAttribPointer()** is a handy way to set up virtually everything about a vertex attribute. However, it can actually be considered more of a helper function that sits on top of a few lower-level functions: **glVertexAttribFormat()** **glVertexAttribBinding()**, and **glBindVertexBuffer()**. Their prototypes are

```
void glVertexAttribFormat(GLuint attribindex, GLint size,
                          GLenum type, GLboolean normalized,
                          GLuint relativeoffset);

void glVertexAttribBinding(GLuint attribindex,
                           GLuint bindingindex);

void glBindVertexBuffer(GLuint bindingindex,
                        GLuint buffer,
                        GLintptr offset,
                        GLintptr stride);
```

---

1. Under certain circumstances, you may even omit this.

To understand how these functions work, first let's consider a simple vertex shader fragment that declares a number of inputs. In Listing 7.1, notice the use of the location layout qualifier to set the locations of the inputs explicitly in the shader code.

```
#version 450 core

// Declare a number of vertex attributes
layout (location = 0) in vec4 position;
layout (location = 1) in vec3 normal;
layout (location = 2) in vec2 tex_coord;
// Note that we intentionally skip location 3 here
layout (location = 4) in vec4 color;
layout (location = 5) in int material_id;
```

Listing 7.1: Declaration of multiple vertex attributes

The shader fragment in Listing 7.1 declares five inputs: position, normal, tex_coord, color, and material_id. Now, consider that we are using a data structure to represent our vertices, which is defined in C as follows:

```
typedef struct VERTEX_t
{
    vmath::vec4     position;
    vmath::vec3     normal;
    vmath::vec2     tex_coord;
    GLubyte         color[3];
    int             material_id;
} VERTEX;
```

Notice that our vertex structure in C mixes use of vmath types and plain-old data (for color).

The first attribute is pretty standard and should be familiar to you—it's the position of the vertex, specified as a four-component floating-point vector. To describe this input using the **glVertexAttribFormat()** function, we would set size to 4 and type to GL_FLOAT. The second attribute, the normal of the geometry at the vertex, is in normal and would be passed to **glVertexAttribFormat()** with size set to 3 and type set to GL_FLOAT. Likewise, tex_coord can be used as a two-dimensional texture coordinate and might be specified by setting size to 2 and type to GL_FLOAT.

The color input to the vertex shader is declared as a **vec4**, but the color member of our VERTEX structure is actually an array of 3 bytes. Both the size (number of elements) and the data type are different. OpenGL can convert the data for you as it reads it into the vertex shader. To hook our 3-byte color member up to our four-component vertex shader input, we call **glVertexAttribFormat()** with size set to 3 and type set to GL_UNSIGNED_BYTE. This is where the normalized parameter comes in. As you probably know, the range of values representable by an unsigned byte is 0 to 255. However, that's not what we want in our vertex shader. There, we want to represent colors as values between 0.0 and 1.0. If you set normalized to GL_TRUE, then OpenGL will automatically divide each component of the input by the maximum possible representable positive value, *normalizing* it.

Because two's-complement numbers are able to represent a greater-magnitude negative number than positive number, this can place one value below −1.0 (−128 for GLbyte, −32,768 for GLshort, and −2,147,483,648 for GLint). Those most negative numbers are treated specially and are clamped to the floating-point value −1.0 during normalization. If normalized is GL_FALSE, then the value will be converted directly to floating point and presented to the vertex shader. In the case of unsigned byte data (like color), this means that the values will be between 0.0 and 255.0.

Table 7.1 shows the tokens that can be used for the type parameter, their corresponding OpenGL types, and the range of values that they can represent.

In Table 7.1, the floating-point types (GLhalf, GLfloat, and GLdouble) don't have ranges because they can't be normalized. The GLfixed type is a special case. It represents *fixed-point* data that is made up of 32 bits with the binary point at position 16 (halfway through the number); as

Table 7.1: Vertex Attribute Types

Type	OpenGL Type	Range
GL_BYTE	GLbyte	−128 to 127
GL_SHORT	Glshort	−32,768 to 32,767
GL_INT	GLint	−2,147,483,648 to 2,147,483,647
GL_FIXED	GLfixed	−32,768 to 32,767
GL_UNSIGNED_BYTE	GLubyte	0 to 255
GL_UNSIGNED_SHORT	GLushort	0 to 65,535
GL_UNSIGNED_INT	GLuint	4,294,967,295
GL_HALF_FLOAT	GLhalf	—
GL_FLOAT	GLfloat	—
GL_DOUBLE	GLdouble	—

such, it is treated as one of the floating-point types and cannot be normalized.

In addition to the scalar types shown in Table 7.1, `glVertexAttribFormat()` supports several *packed* data formats that use a single integer to store multiple components. The two packed data formats supported by OpenGL are GL_UNSIGNED_INT_2_10_10_10_REV and GL_INT_2_10_10_10_REV, which both represent four components packed into a single 32-bit word.

The GL_UNSIGNED_INT_2_10_10_10_REV format provides 10 bits for each of the x, y, and z components of the vector and only 2 bits for the w component, which are all treated as unsigned quantities. This gives a range of 0 to 1023 for each of x, y, and z, and 0 to 3 for w. Likewise, the GL_INT_2_10_10_10_REV format provides 10 bits for x, y, and z, and 2 bits for w, but in this case each component is treated as a signed quantity. That means that while x, y, and z have a range of -512 to 511, w may range from -2 to 1. While this may not seem terribly useful, there are a number of use cases for three component vectors with more than 8 bits of precision (24 bits in total) but that do not require 16 bits of precision (48 bits in total). Even though those last 2 bits might be wasted, 10 bits of precision per component provides what is needed.

When one of the packed data types (GL_UNSIGNED_INT_2_10_10_10_REV or GL_INT_2_10_10_10_REV) is specified, then `size` must be set either to 4 or the special value GL_BGRA. The latter applies an automatic swizzle to the incoming data to reverse the order of the r, g, and b components (which are equivalent to the x, y, and z components) of the incoming vectors. This provides compatibility with data stored in that order[2] without needing to modify your shaders.

Finally, returning to our example vertex declaration, we have the `material_id` field, which is an integer. In this case, because we want to pass an integer value as is to the vertex shader, we'll use a variation on the `glVertexAttribFormat()`, `glVertexAttribIFormat()`, whose prototype is

```
void glVertexAttribIFormat(GLuint attribindex,
                           GLint size,
                           GLenum type,
                           GLuint relativeoffset);
```

Again, the `attribindex`, `size`, `type`, and `relativeoffset` parameters specify the attribute index, number of components, type of those

---

2. The BGRA ordering is quite common in some image formats and is the default ordering used by some graphics APIs.

components, and offset from the start of the vertex of the attribute that's being set up, respectively. However, you'll notice that the `normalized` parameter is missing. That's because this version of `glVertexAttribFormat()` is *only* for integer types—type must be one of the integer types (GL_BYTE, GL_SHORT, or GL_INT; one of their unsigned counterparts; or one of the packed data formats) and integer inputs to a vertex shader are never normalized. Thus, the complete code to describe our vertex format is

```
// position
glVertexAttribFormat(0, 4, GL_FLOAT, GL_FALSE, offsetof(VERTEX, position));

// normal
glVertexAttribFormat(1, 3, GL_FLOAT, GL_FALSE, offsetof(VERTEX, normal));

// tex_coord
glVertexAttribFormat(2, 2, GL_FLOAT, GL_FALSE, offsetof(VERTEX, texcoord));

// color[3]
glVertexAttribFormat(4, 3, GL_UNSIGNED_BYTE, GL_TRUE, offsetof(VERTEX, color));

// material_id
glVertexAttribIFormat(5, 1, GL_INT, offsetof(VERTEX, material_id));
```

Now that you've set up the vertex attribute format, you need to tell OpenGL which buffers to read the data from. If you recall our discussion of uniform blocks and how they map to buffers, you can apply similar logic to vertex attributes. Each verex shader can have any number of input attributes (up to an implementation-defined limit), and OpenGL can provide data for them by reading from any number of buffers (again, up to a limit). Some vertex attributes can share space in a buffer; others may reside in different buffer objects. Rather than individually specifying which buffer objects are used for each vertex shader input, we can instead group inputs together and associate groups of them with a set of buffer binding points. Then, when you change the buffer bound to one of these binding points, it will change the buffer used to supply data for all of the attributes that are mapped to that binding point.

To establish the mapping between vertex shader inputs and buffer binding points, you can call **glVertexAttribBinding()**. The first to parameter **glVertexAttribBinding()**, `attribindex`, is the index of the vertex attribute; the second parameter, `bindingindex`, is the buffer binding point index. In our example, we're going to store all of the vertex attributes in a single buffer. To set this up, we simply call **glVertexAttribBinding()** once for each attribute and specify zero for the bindingindex parameter each time:

```
glVertexAttribBinding(0, 0);    // position
glVertexAttribBinding(1, 0);    // normal
```

```
glVertexAttribBinding(2, 0);    // tex_coord
glVertexAttribBinding(4, 0);    // color
glVertexAttribBinding(5, 0);    // material_id
```

However, we could establish a more complex binding scheme. Suppose, for example, that we wanted to store position, normal, and tex_coord in one buffer, color in a second buffer, and material_id in a third buffer. We could set this up as follows:

```
glVertexAttribBinding(0, 0);    // position
glVertexAttribBinding(1, 0);    // normal
glVertexAttribBinding(2, 0);    // tex_coord
glVertexAttribBinding(4, 1);    // color
glVertexAttribBinding(5, 2);    // material_id
```

Finally, we need to bind a buffer object to each of the binding points that is used by our mapping. To do this, we call **glBindVertexBuffer()**. This function takes four parameters: bindingindex, buffer, offset, and stride. The first is the index of the buffer binding point where you want to bind the buffer, and the second is the name of the buffer object that you're going to bind. offset is an offset into the buffer object where the vertex data starts, and stride is the distance, in bytes, between the start of each vertex's data in the buffer. If your data is tightly packed (that is, there are no gaps between the vertices), you can just set this to the total size of your vertex data (which would be sizeof(VERTEX) in our example); otherwise, you'll need to add the size of the gaps to the size of the vertex data.

Vertex Shader Outputs

After your vertex shader has decided what to do with the vertex data, it must send the data to its outputs. We have already discussed the gl_Position built-in output variable, and have shown how you can create your own outputs from shaders that can be used to pass data into the following stages. Along with gl_Position, OpenGL defines a few more output variables—gl_PointSize, gl_ClipDistance[], and gl_CullDistance[]—and wraps them up into an interface block called gl_PerVertex. Its declaration is

```
out gl_PerVertex
{
    vec4  gl_Position;
    float gl_PointSize;
    float gl_ClipDistance[];
    float gl_CullDistance[];
};
```

Again, you should be familiar with gl_Position. gl_ClipDistance[] and gl_CullDistance[] are used for clipping and culling, which will be described in some detail later in this chapter. The other output, gl_PointSize, is used for controlling the size of points that might be rendered.

Variable Point Sizes

By default, OpenGL will draw points with a size of a single fragment. However, as you saw in Chapter 2, "Our First OpenGL Program", you can change the size of points that OpenGL draws by calling **glPointSize()**. The maximum size that OpenGL will draw your points is implementation defined, but it will be least 64 pixels. You determine the actual upper limit by calling **glGetIntegerv()** to find the value of GL_POINT_SIZE_RANGE. This function writes *two* integers to the output variable, so make sure you point it at an array of two integers. The first element of the array will be filled with the minimum point size (which will be at most 1), and the second element will be filled with the maximum point size.

Of course, setting all of your points to be big blobs isn't going to produce particularly appealing images. To deal with this issue, you can set the point size programmatically in the vertex shader (or whatever stage is last in the front end). To do this, write the desired value of the point diameter to the built-in variable gl_PointSize. Once you have a shader that does this, you need to tell OpenGL that you wish to use the size written to the point size variable. To do this, call

```
glEnable(GL_PROGRAM_POINT_SIZE);
```

A common use for this function is to determine the size of a point based on its distance from the viewer. When you use the **glPointSize()** function to set the size of points, every point will have the same size no matter what their positions are. By choosing a value for gl_PointSize, you can implement any function you wish and each point produced by a single draw command can have a different size. This includes points generated in the geometry shader or by the tessellation engine when the tessellation evaluation shader specifies point_mode.

The following formula is often used to implement distance-based point size attenuation, where d is the distance of the point from the eye and a, b, and c are configurable parameters of a quadratic equation. You can store those in uniforms and update them with your application, or if you have a particular set of parameters in mind, you might want to make them constants in your vertex shader. For example, if you want a constant size, set a to a non-zero value and b and c to zero. If a and c are zero and b is non-zero, then point size will fall off linearly with distance. Likewise, if a and b are zero but c is non-zero, then point size will fall off quadratically with distance.

$$\text{size} = \text{clamp}\left(\sqrt{\frac{1.0}{a + b \times d + c \times d^2}}\right)$$

Drawing Commands

Until now, we have written every example using only a single drawing command—**glDrawArrays()**. OpenGL includes many drawing commands, however. While some could be considered supersets of others, they can be generally categorized as either indexed or non-indexed and as direct or indirect. All of these possibilities are covered in the next few sections.

Indexed Drawing Commands

The **glDrawArrays()** command is a non-indexed drawing command. That is, the vertices are issued in order, and any vertex data stored in buffers and associated with vertex attributes is simply fed to the vertex shader in the order that it appears in the buffer. An indexed draw, in contrast, includes an indirection step that treats the data in each of those buffers as an array; rather than index into that array sequentially, the command reads from another array of indices. After reading the index, OpenGL uses its value to index into the array. To make an indexed drawing command work, you need to bind a buffer to the GL_ELEMENT_ARRAY_BUFFER target. This buffer will contain the indices of the vertices that you want to draw. Next, you call one of the indexed drawing commands, all of which contain the word Elements in their names. For example, **glDrawElements()** is the simplest of these functions; its prototype is

```
void glDrawElements(GLenum mode,
                    GLsizei count,
                    GLenum type,
                    const GLvoid * indices);
```

When you call **glDrawElements()**, mode and type have the same meaning as they do for **glDrawArrays()**. type specifies the type of data used to store

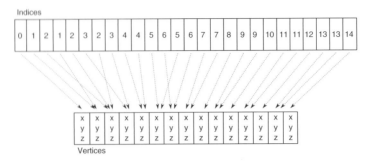

Figure 7.1: Indices used in an indexed draw

each index and may be GL_UNSIGNED_BYTE to indicate 1 byte per index, GL_UNSIGNED_SHORT to indicate 16 bits per index, or GL_UNSIGNED_INT to indicate 32 bits per index. Although indices is defined as a pointer, it is actually interpreted as the offset into the buffer currently bound to the GL_ELEMENT_ARRAY_BUFFER binding where the first index is stored. Figure 7.1 shows how the indices specified by a call to **glDrawElements()** are used by OpenGL.

The **glDrawArrays()** and **glDrawElements()** commands are actually subsets of the complete functionality supported by the direct drawing commands of OpenGL. The set of the most generalized OpenGL drawing commands is given in Table 7.2; all other OpenGL drawing commands can be expressed in terms of these functions.

Recall the spinning cube example in Chapter 5, "Data," and in particular the geometry setup performed in Listing 5.22. To draw a cube, we drew 12 triangles (two for each face of the cube), and each one consumed 36 vertices. However, a cube really has only 8 corners, so it should need only 8 vertices of information, right? We can use an indexed draw to greatly reduce the amount of vertex data, especially for geometry that has a lot of vertices. We can rewrite the setup code of Listing 5.22 to define just the

Table 7.2: Draw Type Matrix

Draw Type	Command
Direct, Non-Indexed	glDrawArraysInstancedBaseInstance()
Direct, Indexed	glDrawElementsInstancedBaseVertexBaseInstance()
Indirect, Non-Indexed	glMultiDrawArraysIndirect()
Indirect, Indexed	glMultiDrawElementsIndirect()

8 corners of the cube, but also define a set of 36 indices that tell OpenGL which corner to use for each vertex of each triangle. The new setup code looks like Listing 7.2.

```
static const GLfloat vertex_positions[] =
{
    -0.25f, -0.25f, -0.25f,
    -0.25f,  0.25f, -0.25f,
     0.25f, -0.25f, -0.25f,
     0.25f,  0.25f, -0.25f,
     0.25f, -0.25f,  0.25f,
     0.25f,  0.25f,  0.25f,
    -0.25f, -0.25f,  0.25f,
    -0.25f,  0.25f,  0.25f,
};

static const GLushort vertex_indices[] =
{
    0, 1, 2,
    2, 1, 3,
    2, 3, 4,
    4, 3, 5,
    4, 5, 6,
    6, 5, 7,
    6, 7, 0,
    0, 7, 1,
    6, 0, 2,
    2, 4, 6,
    7, 5, 3,
    7, 3, 1
};

glGenBuffers(1, &position_buffer);
glBindBuffer(GL_ARRAY_BUFFER, position_buffer);
glBufferData(GL_ARRAY_BUFFER,
             sizeof(vertex_positions),
             vertex_positions,
             GL_STATIC_DRAW);
glVertexAttribPointer(0, 3, GL_FLOAT, GL_FALSE, 0, NULL);
glEnableVertexAttribArray(0);

glGenBuffers(1, &index_buffer);
glBindBuffer(GL_ELEMENT_ARRAY_BUFFER, index_buffer);
glBufferData(GL_ELEMENT_ARRAY_BUFFER,
             sizeof(vertex_indices),
             vertex_indices,
             GL_STATIC_DRAW);
```

Listing 7.2: Setting up indexed cube geometry

As you can see from Listing 7.2, the total amount of data required to represent our cube is greatly reduced—it went from 108 floating-point values (36 triangles times 3 components each, which is 432 bytes) down to 24 floating-point values (just the 8 corners at 3 components each, which is 72 bytes) and 36 16-bit integers (another 72 bytes), for a total of 144 bytes, representing a reduction of two thirds. To use the index data in vertex_indices, we need to bind a buffer to the

GL_ELEMENT_ARRAY_BUFFER and put the indices in it just as we did with the vertex data. In Listing 7.2, we do that immediately after we set up the buffer containing the vertex positions.

Once you have a set of vertices and their indices in memory, you'll need to change your rendering code to use **glDrawElements()** (or one of the more advanced versions of it) instead of **glDrawArrays()**. Our new rendering loop for the spinning cube example is shown in Listing 7.3.

```
// Clear the framebuffer with dark green
static const GLfloat green[] = { 0.0f, 0.25f, 0.0f, 1.0f };
glClearBufferfv(GL_COLOR, 0, green);

// Activate our program
glUseProgram(program);

// Set the model-view and projection matrices
glUniformMatrix4fv(mv_location, 1, GL_FALSE, mv_matrix);
glUniformMatrix4fv(proj_location, 1, GL_FALSE, proj_matrix);

// Draw 6 faces of 2 triangles of 3 vertices each = 36 vertices
glDrawElements(GL_TRIANGLES, 36, GL_UNSIGNED_SHORT, 0);
```

Listing 7.3: Drawing indexed cube geometry

Notice that we're still drawing 36 vertices, but now 36 *indices* will be used to index into an array of only 8 unique vertices. The result of rendering with the vertex index and position data in our two buffers and a call to **glDrawElements()** is identical to that shown in Figure 5.2.

The Base Vertex

The first advanced version of **glDrawElements()** that takes an extra parameter is **glDrawElementsBaseVertex()**, whose prototype is

```
void glDrawElementsBaseVertex(GLenum mode,
                              GLsizei count,
                              GLenum type,
                              GLvoid * indices,
                              GLint  basevertex);
```

When you call **glDrawElementsBaseVertex()**, OpenGL will fetch the vertex index from the buffer bound to the GL_ELEMENT_ARRAY_BUFFER and then add basevertex to it before it is used to index into the array of vertices. This allows you to store a number of different pieces of geometry in the same buffer and then offset into it using basevertex. Figure 7.2 shows how base vertex is added to vertices in an indexed drawing command.

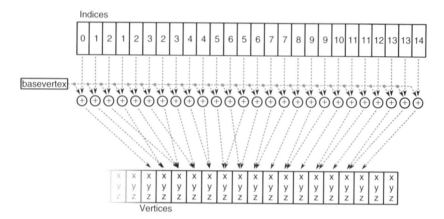

Figure 7.2: Base vertex used in an indexed draw

As you can see from Figure 7.2, each vertex index is essentially fed into an addition operation, which adds the base vertex to it before OpenGL fetches the underlying vertex data. Clearly, if basevertex is zero, then **glDrawElementsBaseVertex()** is equivalent to **glDrawElements()**. In fact, we consider calling **glDrawElements()** to be equivalent to calling **glDrawElementsBaseVertex()** with basevertex set to zero.

Combining Geometry Using Primitive Restart

Many tools are available that "stripify" geometry. The idea underlying these tools is that by taking "triangle soup," meaning a large collection of unconnected triangles, and attempting to merge it into a set of triangle strips, performance can be improved. This works because each individual triangle is represented by three vertices, but a triangle strip reduces this to a single vertex per triangle (not counting the first triangle in the strip). By converting the geometry from triangle soup to triangle strips, there is less geometry data to process, and the system should run faster. If the tool does a good job and produces a small number of long strips containing many triangles each, this generally works well. There has been a lot of research into this type of algorithm, and a new method's success is measured by passing some well-known models through the new "stripifier" and comparing the number and average length of the strips generated by the new tool to those produced by current state-of-the-art stripifiers.

Despite all of this research, the reality is that a soup can be rendered with a single call to **glDrawArrays()** or **glDrawElements()**, but unless we use the functionality that is about to be introduced, a set of strips needs to be rendered with separate calls to OpenGL. As a consequence, there are likely to be a lot more function calls in a program that uses stripified geometry. Moreover, if the stripping application hasn't done a decent job or if the model just doesn't lend itself well to stripification, this can eat up any performance gains achieved by using strips in the first place.

A feature that can help here is *primitive restart*. Primitive restart applies to the GL_TRIANGLE_STRIP, GL_TRIANGLE_FAN, GL_LINE_STRIP, and GL_LINE_LOOP geometry types. It is a method of informing OpenGL when one strip (or fan or loop) has ended and another should be started. To indicate the position in the geometry where one strip ends and the next begins, a special marker is placed as a reserved value in the element array. As OpenGL fetches vertex indices from the element array, it checks for this special index value; whenever it comes across it, OpenGL ends the current strip and starts a new one with the next vertex. This mode is disabled by default but can be enabled by calling

```
glEnable(GL_PRIMITIVE_RESTART);
```

and disabled again by calling

```
glDisable(GL_PRIMITIVE_RESTART);
```

When primitive restart mode is enabled, OpenGL watches for the special index value as it fetches values from the element array buffer. When it comes across this value, it stops the current strip and starts a new one. To set the index that OpenGL should watch for, call

```
glPrimitiveRestartIndex(index);
```

OpenGL watches for the value specified by index and uses that as the primitive restart marker. Because the marker is a vertex index, primitive restart is best used with indexed drawing functions such as **glDrawElements()**. If you draw with a non-indexed drawing command such as **glDrawArrays()**, the primitive restart index is simply ignored.

The default value of the primitive restart index is zero. Because that's almost certainly the index of a real vertex that will be contained in the model, it's a good idea to set the restart index to a new value whenever you're using primitive restart mode. A good value to use is the maximum value representable by the index type you're using (0xFFFFFFFF for GL_UNSIGNED_INT, 0xFFFF for GL_UNSIGNED_SHORT, and 0xFF for GL_UNSIGNED_BYTE) because you can be almost certain that it will not be

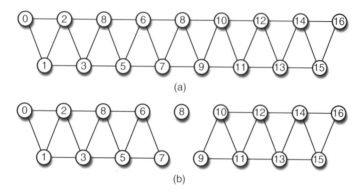

Figure 7.3: Triangle strips (a) without primitive restart and (b) with primitive restart

used as a valid index of a vertex. Many stripping tools have an option to create either separate strips or a single strip with the restart index in it. The stripping tool may use a predefined index or output the index it used when creating the stripped version of the model (for example, one greater than the number of vertices in the model). You need to know which option is used and use the **glPrimitiveRestartIndex()** function to set it to use the output of the tool in your application. The primitive restart feature is illustrated in Figure 7.3.

In Figure 7.3, a triangle strip is pictured with the vertices marked with their indices. In Figure 7.3(a), the strip is made up of 17 vertices, which produces a total of 15 triangles in a single, connected strip. By enabling primitive restart mode and setting the primitive restart index to 8, as in Figure 7.3(b), the eighth index (whose value is also 8) is recognized by OpenGL as the special restart marker, and the triangle strip is terminated at vertex 7. The actual position of vertex 8 is ignored because it is not seen by OpenGL as the index of a real vertex. The next vertex processed (vertex 9) becomes the start of a new triangle strip. Thus, while 17 vertices are still sent to OpenGL, the result is that two separate triangle strips of 8 vertices and 6 triangles each are drawn.

Instancing

There will probably be times when you want to draw the same object many times. Imagine a fleet of starships or a field of grass. There could be thousands of copies of what are essentially identical sets of geometry, modified only slightly from instance to instance. A simple application might just loop over all of the individual blades of grass in a field and render them separately, calling **glDrawArrays()** once for each blade and perhaps updating a set of shader uniforms on each iteration. If each blade of grass was made up of a strip of four triangles, the code might look something like Listing 7.4.

```
glBindVertexArray(grass_vao);
for (int n = 0; n < number_of_blades_of_grass; n++)
{
    SetupGrassBladeParameters();
    glDrawArrays(GL_TRIANGLE_STRIP, 0, 6);
}
```

Listing 7.4: Drawing the same geometry many times

How many blades of grass are there in a field? What is the value of number_of_blades_of_grass? It could be thousands, maybe millions. Each blade of grass is likely to take up a very small area on the screen, and the number of vertices representing the blade is also very small. Your graphics card doesn't really have a lot of work to do to render a single blade of grass, and the system is likely to spend most of its time sending commands to OpenGL rather than actually drawing anything. OpenGL addresses this through instanced rendering, which is a way to ask it to draw many copies of the same geometry.

Instanced rendering is a method provided by OpenGL to specify that you want to draw many copies of the same geometry with a single function call. This functionality is accessed through instanced rendering functions, such as

```
void glDrawArraysInstanced(GLenum mode,
                           GLint first,
                           GLsizei count,
                           GLsizei instancecount);
```

and

```
void glDrawElementsInstanced(GLenum mode,
                             GLsizei count,
                             GLenum type,
                             const void * indices,
                             GLsizei instancecount);
```

These two functions behave much like **glDrawArrays()** and **glDrawElements()**, except that they tell OpenGL to render instancecount copies of the geometry. The first parameters of each (mode, first, and count for **glDrawArraysInstanced()**, and mode, count, type, and indices for **glDrawElementsInstanced()**) have the same meaning as in the regular, non-instanced versions of the functions. When you call one of these functions, OpenGL makes any preparations it needs to draw your geometry (such as copying vertex data to the graphics card's memory) only once and then renders the same vertices many times.

If you set **instancecount** to 1, then **glDrawArraysInstanced()** and **glDrawElementsInstanced()** will draw a single instance of your geometry. Obviously, this is equivalent to calling **glDrawArrays()** or **glDrawElements()**, but we normally state this equivalency the other way around—that is, we say that calling **glDrawArrays()** is equivalent to calling **glDrawArraysInstanced()** with **instancecount** set to 1 and that calling **glDrawElements()** is equivalent to calling **glDrawElementsInstanced()** with **instancecount** set to 1. As we discussed earlier, though, calling **glDrawElements()** is also equivalent to calling **glDrawElementsBaseVertex()** with **basevertex** set to 0. In fact, there is another drawing command that combines both **basevertex** and **instancecount**: **glDrawElementsInstancedBaseVertex()**. Its prototype is

```
void glDrawElementsInstancedBaseVertex(GLenum mode,
                                       GLsizei count,
                                       GLenum type,
                                       GLvoid * indices,
                                       GLsizei instancecount,
                                       GLint  basevertex);
```

So, in fact, calling **glDrawElements()** is equivalent to calling **glDrawElementsInstancedBaseVertex()** with **instancecount** set to 1 and **basevertex** set to 0. Likewise, calling **glDrawElementsInstanced()** is equivalent to calling **glDrawElementsInstancedBaseVertex()** with **basevertex** set to 0.

Finally, just as we can pass **basevertex** to **glDrawElementsBaseVertex()** and **glDrawElementsInstancedBaseVertex()**, so we can pass a **baseinstance** parameter to versions of the instanced drawing commands. These functions are **glDrawArraysInstancedBaseInstance()**, **glDrawElementsInstancedBaseInstance()**, and the exceedingly long **glDrawElementsInstancedBaseVertexBaseInstance()**, which takes both a **basevertex** and a **baseinstance** parameter. Now that we have introduced all of the direct drawing commands, it should be clear that they are all subsets of **glDrawArraysInstancedBaseInstance()** and **glDrawElementsInstancedBaseVertexBaseInstance()**, and that where they are missing, **basevertex** and **baseinstance** are assumed to be 0 and **instancecount** is assumed to be 1.

If all that these functions did was send many copies of the same vertices to OpenGL as if `glDrawArrays()` or `glDrawElements()` had been called in a tight loop, they wouldn't be very useful. In fact, one thing that makes instanced rendering usable and very powerful is a special, built-in variable in GLSL named gl_InstanceID. The gl_InstanceID variable appears in the vertex as if it were a static integer vertex attribute. When the first copy of the vertices is sent to OpenGL, gl_InstanceID will be 0. It will then be incremented once for each copy of the geometry and will eventually reach instancecount -1.

The `glDrawArraysInstanced()` function essentially operates as if the pseudocode in Listing 7.5 were executed. To reiterate, this is pseudocode—gl_InstanceID is not a real vertex attribute and you can't set it as shown in the listing.

```
// Loop over all of the instances (i.e. instancecount)
for (int n = 0; n < instancecount; n++)
{
    // Set the gl_InstanceID attribute - here gl_InstanceID is a C variable
    // holding the location of the "virtual" gl_InstanceID input.
    glVertexAttrib1i(gl_InstanceID, n);

    // Now, when we call glDrawArrays, the gl_InstanceID variable in the
    // shader will contain the index of the instance that's being rendered.
    glDrawArrays(mode, first, count);
}
```

Listing 7.5: Pseudocode for **glDrawArraysInstanced()**

Likewise, the `glDrawElementsInstanced()` function operates similarly to the pseudocode in Listing 7.6. Again, this is pseudocode and won't compile as written.

```
for (int n = 0; n < instancecount; n++)
{
    // Set the value of gl_InstanceID
    glVertexAttrib1i(gl_InstanceID, n);

    // Make a normal call to glDrawElements
    glDrawElements(mode, count, type, indices);
}
```

Listing 7.6: Pseudocode for **glDrawElementsInstanced()**

Of course, gl_InstanceID is not a real vertex attribute, and you can't get a location for it by calling **glGetAttribLocation()**. The value of gl_InstanceID is managed by OpenGL and is very likely generated in hardware, meaning that it's essentially free to use in terms of performance. The power of instanced rendering comes from imaginative use of this variable, along with instanced arrays, which are explained in a moment.

The value of gl_InstanceID can be used directly as a parameter to a shader function or to index into data such as textures or uniform arrays. To return to our example of the field of grass, let's figure out what we're going to do with gl_InstanceID to make our field not just be thousands of identical blades of grass growing out of a single point. Each of our grass blades is made out of a little triangle strip with four triangles in it, for a total of just six vertices. It could be tricky to get them to all look different. However, with some shader magic, we can make each blade of grass look sufficiently different so as to produce an interesting output. We won't go over the shader code here, but we will walk through a few ideas of how you can use gl_InstanceID to add variation to your scenes.

First, we need each blade of grass to have a different position; otherwise, they'll all be drawn on top of each other. Let's arrange the blades of grass more or less evenly. If the number of blades of grass we're going to render is a power of 2, we can use half of the bits of gl_InstanceID to represent the x coordinate of the blade, and the other half to represent the z coordinate (our ground lies in the x–z plane, with y being altitude). For this example, we render 2^{20}, or a little over 1 million blades of grass (actually 1,048,576 blades, but who's counting?). By using the ten least significant bits (bits 9 through 0) as the x coordinate and the ten most significant bits (19 through 10) as the z coordinate, we have a uniform grid of grass blades. Let's take a look at Figure 7.4 to see what we have so far.

Our uniform grid of grass probably looks a little plain, as if a particularly attentive groundskeeper hand-planted each blade. What we really need to do is displace each blade of grass by some random amount within its grid square. That'll make the field look a little less uniform. A simple way of generating random numbers is to multiply a seed value by a large number and take a subset of the bits of the resulting product and use it as the input to a function. We're not aiming for a perfect distribution here, so this simple generator should do. Usually, with this type of algorithm, you'd reuse the seed value as input to the next iteration of the random number generator. In this case, though, we can just use gl_InstanceID directly because we're really generating the next few numbers after gl_InstanceID in a pseudo-random sequence. By iterating over our pseudo-random function only a couple of times, we can get a reasonably random distribution. Because we need to displace in both the x and z directions, we generate two successive random numbers from gl_InstanceID and use

Figure 7.4: First attempt at an instanced field of grass

them to displace the blade of grass within the plane. Look at Figure 7.5 to see what we get now.

Figure 7.5: Slightly perturbed blades of grass

At this point, our field of grass is distributed evenly, with random perturbations in position for each blade of grass. All the grass blades look the same, though. (Actually, we used the same random number generator to assign a slightly different color to each blade of grass just so that they'd show up in the figures.) We can apply some variation over the field to make each blade look slightly different. This is something that we'd probably want to have control over, so we use a texture to hold information about blades of grass.

You have x and z coordinates for each blade of grass that were calculated by generating a grid coordinate directly from gl_InstanceID and then generating a random number and displacing the blade within the x–z plane. That coordinate pair can be used to look up a texel within a 2D texture, and you can put whatever you want in it. Let's control the length of the grass using the texture. We can put a length parameter in the texture (let's use the red channel) and multiply the y coordinate of each vertex of the grass geometry by that to make longer or shorter grass. A value of 0 in the texture would produce very short (or nonexistent) grass, and a value of 1 would produce grass of some maximum length. Now you can design a texture where each texel represents the length of the grass in a region of your field. Why not draw a few crop circles?

At this point, the grass is evenly distributed over the field, and you have control of the length of the grass in different areas. However, the grass blades are still just scaled copies of each other. Perhaps we can introduce some more variation. We decide to rotate each blade of grass around its axis according to another parameter from the texture. We use the green channel of the texture to store the angle through which the grass blade should be rotated around the y axis, with 0 representing no rotation and 1 representing a full 360 degrees. We've still performed only one texture fetch in our vertex shader, and the only input to the shader is still gl_InstanceID. Things are starting to come together. Take a look at Figure 7.6.

Our field is still looking a little bland. The grass just sticks straight up and doesn't move. Real grass sways in the wind and gets flattened when things roll over it. We need the grass to bend, and we'd like to have control over that behavior. Why not use another channel from the parameter texture (the blue channel) to control a bend factor? We can use that as another angle and rotate the grass around the x axis before we apply the rotation in the green channel. This allows us to make the grass bend over based on the parameter in the texture. Use 0 to represent no bending (the grass

Figure 7.6: Control over the length and orientation of our grass

stands straight up) and 1 to represent fully flattened grass. Normally, the grass will sway gently, so the parameter will have a low value. When the grass gets flattened, the value can be much higher.

Finally, we can control the color of the grass. It seems logical to just store the color of the grass in a large texture. This might be a good idea if you want to draw a sports field with lines, markings, or advertising on it, for example, but it's fairly wasteful if the grass is all varying shades of green. Instead, let's make a palette for our grass in a 1D texture and use the final channel within our parameter texture (the alpha channel) to store the index into that palette. The palette can start with an anemic-looking dead-grass yellow at one end and a lush, deep green at the other end. Now we read the alpha channel from the parameter texture along with all the other parameters and use it to index into the 1D texture—a dependent texture fetch. Our final field is shown in Figure 7.7.

Our final field has approximately 1 million blades of grass, evenly distributed, with application control over length, "flatness," direction of bend or sway, and color. Remember, the only input to the shader that differentiates one blade of grass from another is gl_InstanceID, the total amount of geometry sent to OpenGL is six vertices, and the total amount of code required to draw all the grass in the field is a single call to glDrawArraysInstanced().

Figure 7.7: The final field of grass

The parameter texture can be read using linear texturing to provide smooth transitions between regions of grass and can be a fairly low resolution. If you want to make your grass wave in the wind or get trampled as hoards of armies march across it, you can animate the texture by updating it every frame or two and uploading a new version of it before you render the grass. Also, because gl_InstanceID is used to generate random numbers, adding an offset to this variable before passing it to the random number generator allows a different but predetermined chunk of "random" grass to be generated with the same shader.

Getting Your Data Automatically

When you call one of the instanced drawing commands such as glDrawArraysInstanced() or glDrawElementsInstanced(), the built-in variable gl_InstanceID will be available in your shaders to tell you which instance you're working on, and it will be incremented by 1 for each new instance of the geometry that you're rendering. It's actually available even when you're not using one of the instanced drawing functions—it'll just be zero in those cases. This means that you can use the same shaders for instanced and non-instanced rendering.

You can use gl_InstanceID to index into arrays that are the same length as the number of instances that you're rendering. For example, you can use it to look up texels in a texture or to index into a uniform array. Really, what you're actually doing is treating the array as if it were an "instanced attribute." That is, a new value of the attribute is read for each instance you're rendering. OpenGL can feed this data to your shader automatically using a feature called instanced arrays. To use instanced arrays, declare an input to your shader in the usual way. The input attribute will have an index that you would use in calls to functions like **glVertexAttribPointer()**. Normally, the vertex attributes would be read per vertex and a new value would be fed to the shader. However, to make OpenGL read attributes from the arrays once per instance, you can call

```
void glVertexAttribDivisor(GLuint index,
                           GLuint divisor);
```

Pass the index of the attribute to the function in `index` and set `divisor` to the number of instances you'd like to pass between each new value being read from the array. If `divisor` is zero, then the array becomes a regular vertex attribute array with a new value read per vertex. If `divisor` is non-zero, however, new data is read from the array once every `divisor` instance. For example, if you set `divisor` to 1, you'll get a new value from the array for each instance. If you set `divisor` to 2, you'll get a new value for every second instance, and so on. You can mix and match the divisors, setting different values for each attribute. An example of when you might want to use this functionality would be when you want to draw a set of objects with different colors. Consider the simple vertex shader in Listing 7.7.

```
#version 450 core

in vec4 position;
in vec4 color;

out Fragment
{
    vec4 color;
} fragment;

uniform mat4 mvp;

void main(void)
{
    gl_Position = mvp * position;
    fragment.color = color;
}
```

Listing 7.7: Simple vertex shader with per-vertex color

Normally, the attribute color would be read once per vertex, so every vertex would end up having a different color. The application would have to supply an array of colors with as many elements as there were vertices in the model. Also, it wouldn't be possible for every instance of the object to have a different color because the shader doesn't know anything about instancing. We can make color an instanced array if we call

```
glVertexAttribDivisor(index_of_color, 1);
```

where index_of_color is the index of the slot to which the color attribute has been bound. Now, a new value of color will be fetched from the vertex array once per instance. Every vertex within any particular instance will receive the same value for color, and the result will be that each instance of the object will be rendered in a different color. The size of the vertex array holding the data for color needs to be only as long as the number of indices we want to render. If we increase the value of the divisor, new data will be read from the array with less and less frequency. If the divisor is 2, a new value of color will be presented every second instance; if the divisor is 3, color will be updated every third instance; and so on.

If we render geometry using this simple shader, each instance will be drawn on top of the others. We need to modify the position of each instance so that we can see each one. We can use another instanced array for this. Listing 7.8 shows a simple modification to the vertex shader in Listing 7.7.

```
#version 450 core

in vec4 position;
in vec4 instance_color;
in vec4 instance_position;

out Fragment
{
    vec4 color;
}   fragment;

uniform mat4 mvp;

void main(void)
{
    gl_Position = mvp * (position + instance_position);
    fragment.color = instance_color;
}
```

Listing 7.8: Simple instanced vertex shader

Now, we have a per-instance position as well as a per-vertex position. We can add these together in the vertex shader before multiplying with the model–view-projection matrix. We can set the instance_position input attribute to an instanced array by calling

```
glVertexAttribDivisor(index_of_instance_position, 1);
```

Again, index_of_instance_position is the index of the location to which the instance_position attribute has been bound. Any type of input attribute can be made instanced using **glVertexAttribDivisor()**. This example is simple and uses only a translation (the value held in instance_position). A more advanced application could use matrix vertex attributes or pack some transformation matrices into uniforms and pass matrix weights in instanced arrays. For example, the application can use this approach to render an army of soldiers, each with a different pose, or a fleet of spaceships, all flying in different directions.

Now let's hook this simple shader up to a real program. First, we load our shaders in the usual way before linking the program. The vertex shader is shown in Listing 7.8, the fragment shader simply passes the color input to its output, and the application code to hook all this up is shown in Listing 7.9. In the code, we declare some data and load it into a buffer and attach it to a vertex array object. Some of the data is used as per-vertex positions, but the rest is used as per-instance colors and positions.

```
static const GLfloat square_vertices[] =
{
    -1.0f, -1.0f, 0.0f, 1.0f,
     1.0f, -1.0f, 0.0f, 1.0f,
     1.0f,  1.0f, 0.0f, 1.0f,
    -1.0f,  1.0f, 0.0f, 1.0f
};

static const GLfloat instance_colors[] =
{
    1.0f, 0.0f, 0.0f, 1.0f,
    0.0f, 1.0f, 0.0f, 1.0f,
    0.0f, 0.0f, 1.0f, 1.0f,
    1.0f, 1.0f, 0.0f, 1.0f
};

static const GLfloat instance_positions[] =
{
    -2.0f, -2.0f, 0.0f, 0.0f,
     2.0f, -2.0f, 0.0f, 0.0f,
     2.0f,  2.0f, 0.0f, 0.0f,
    -2.0f,  2.0f, 0.0f, 0.0f
};

GLuint offset = 0;
```

```
glGenVertexArrays(1, &square_vao);
glGenBuffers(1, &square_vbo);
glBindVertexArray(square_vao);
glBindBuffer(GL_ARRAY_BUFFER, square_vbo);
glBufferData(GL_ARRAY_BUFFER,
             sizeof(square_vertices) +
             sizeof(instance_colors) +
             sizeof(instance_positions), NULL, GL_STATIC_DRAW);
glBufferSubData(GL_ARRAY_BUFFER, offset,
                sizeof(square_vertices),
                square_vertices);
offset += sizeof(square_vertices);
glBufferSubData(GL_ARRAY_BUFFER, offset,
                sizeof(instance_colors), instance_colors);
offset += sizeof(instance_colors);
glBufferSubData(GL_ARRAY_BUFFER, offset,
                sizeof(instance_positions), instance_positions);
offset += sizeof(instance_positions);

glVertexAttribPointer(0, 4, GL_FLOAT, GL_FALSE, 0, 0);
glVertexAttribPointer(1, 4, GL_FLOAT, GL_FALSE, 0,
                      (GLvoid *)sizeof(square_vertices));
glVertexAttribPointer(2, 4, GL_FLOAT, GL_FALSE, 0,
                      (GLvoid *)(sizeof(square_vertices) +
                                 sizeof(instance_colors)));

glEnableVertexAttribArray(0);
glEnableVertexAttribArray(1);
glEnableVertexAttribArray(2);
```

Listing 7.9: Getting ready for instanced rendering

Now all that remains is to set the vertex attribute divisors for the
instance_color and instance_position attribute arrays

```
glVertexAttribDivisor(1, 1);
glVertexAttribDivisor(2, 1);
```

We draw four instances of the geometry we put into our vertex buffer.
Each instance consists of four vertices, each with its own position, which
means that the same vertex in each instance has the same position.
However, all of the vertices in a single instance see the same value of
instance_color and instance_position, and a new value of each is
presented to each instance. Our rendering loop looks like this:

```
static const GLfloat black[] = { 0.0f, 0.0f, 0.0f, 0.0f };
glClearBufferfv(GL_COLOR, 0, black);

glUseProgram(instancingProg);
glBindVertexArray(square_vao);
glDrawArraysInstanced(GL_TRIANGLE_FAN, 0, 4, 4);
```

Figure 7.8: Result of instanced rendering

What we get is shown in Figure 7.8. In the figure, you can see that four rectangles have been rendered. Each is at a different position, and each has a different color. This technique can be extended to thousands or even millions of instances, and modern graphics hardware should be able to handle this without any issue.

When you have instanced vertex attributes, you can use the baseInstance parameter to drawing commands such as **glDrawArraysInstancedBaseInstance()** to *offset* where in their respective buffers the data is read from. If you set this to zero (or call one of the functions that lacks this parameter), the data for the first instance comes from the start of the array. However, if you set it to a non-zero value, the index within the instanced array from which the data comes is offset by that value. This is very similar to the baseVertex parameter described earlier.

The actual formula for calculating the index from which attributes are fetched is

$$\left\lfloor \frac{instance}{divisor} \right\rfloor + baseInstance$$

We will use the `baseInstance` parameter in some of the following examples to provide offsets into instanced vertex arrays.

Indirect Draws

So far, we have covered only direct drawing commands. In these commands, we pass the parameters of the drawing command, such as the number of vertices or instances, directly to the function. However, there is a family of drawing commands that allow the parameters of each drawing command to be stored in a buffer object. As a consequence, at the time that your application calls the drawing command, it doesn't actually need to know those parameters—only the location in the buffer where the parameters are stored. This opens a few interesting possibilities:

- Your application can generate the parameters for a drawing command ahead of time, possibly even offline, and then load them into a buffer and send them to OpenGL when it's ready to draw.

- You can get OpenGL to generate the parameters at runtime by executing a shader that stores those parameters in a buffer object, effectively causing the GPU to generate its own work.

- You can use many threads on the CPU to generate the parameters for drawing commands. Because the commands are not sent directly to OpenGL but rather are stored in a buffer for later processing, there is no issue with using many threads for this operation.

There are four indirect drawing commands in OpenGL. The first two have direct equivalents: **glDrawArraysInstancedBaseInstance()** is similar to **glDrawArraysIndirect()** and **glDrawElementsInstancedBaseVertexBaseInstance()** is similar to **glDrawElementsIndirect()**. The prototypes of these indirect functions are

```
void glDrawArraysIndirect(GLenum mode,
                          const void * indirect);
```

and

```
void glDrawElementsIndirect(GLenum mode,
                            GLenum type,
                            const void * indirect);
```

For both functions, mode is one of the primitive modes, such as
GL_TRIANGLES or GL_PATCHES. For **glDrawElementsIndirect()**, type is the
type of the indices to be used (just like the type parameter to
glDrawElements()) and should be set to GL_UNSIGNED_BYTE,
GL_UNSIGNED_SHORT, or GL_UNSIGNED_INT. For both functions, indirect is
interpreted as an offset into the buffer object bound to the
GL_DRAW_INDIRECT_BUFFER target, but the contents of the buffer at this
address differ depending on which function is being used. When
expressed as a C-style structure definition, for **glDrawArraysIndirect()**, the
form of the data in the buffer is

```
typedef struct {
    GLuint vertexCount;
    GLuint instanceCount;
    GLuint firstVertex;
    GLuint baseInstance;
} DrawArraysIndirectCommand;
```

For **glDrawElementsIndirect()**, the form of the data in the buffer is

```
typedef struct {
    GLuint vertexCount;
    GLuint instanceCount;
    GLuint firstIndex;
    GLint  baseVertex;
    GLuint baseInstance;
} DrawElementsIndirectCommand;
```

Calling **glDrawArraysIndirect()** will cause OpenGL to behave as if you
had called **glDrawArraysInstancedBaseInstance()** with the mode you
passed to **glDrawArraysIndirect()** but with the count, first,
instancecount, and baseinstance parameters taken from the
vertexCount, firstVertex, instanceCount, and baseInstance fields of
the DrawArraysIndirectCommand structure stored in the buffer object at
the offset given in the indirect parameter.

Likewise, calling **glDrawElementsIndirect()** will cause OpenGL to behave
as if you had called **glDrawElementsInstancedBaseVertexBaseInstance()**
with the mode and type parameters passed directly through, and with the
count, instancecount, basevertex, and baseinstance parameters taken
from the vertexCount, instanceCount, baseVertex, and baseInstance
fields of the DrawElementsIndirectCommand structure in the buffer.
However, one difference here is that the firstIndex parameter is in units
of indices rather than bytes, so it is multiplied by the size of the index type
to form the offset that would have been passed in the indices parameter
to **glDrawElements()**.

As handy as it may seem to be able to do this, what makes this feature particularly powerful is the *multi* versions of these two functions:

```
void glMultiDrawArraysIndirect(GLenum mode,
                               const void * indirect,
                               GLsizei drawcount,
                               GLsizei stride);
```

and

```
void glMultiDrawElementsIndirect(GLenum mode,
                                 GLenum type,
                                 const void * indirect,
                                 GLsizei  drawcount,
                                 GLsizei  stride);
```

These two functions behave very similarly to **glDrawArraysIndirect()** and **glDrawElementsIndirect()**. However, you have probably noticed two additional parameters to each of the functions. Both functions essentially perform the same operation as their non-multi variants in a loop on an array of DrawArraysIndirectCommand or DrawElementsIndirectCommand structures. drawcount specifies the number of structures in the array, and stride specifies the number of bytes between the start of each of the structures in the buffer object. If stride is zero, then the arrays are considered to be tightly packed. Otherwise, you can have structures with additional data in between them, and OpenGL will skip over that data as it traverses the array.

The practical upper limit on the number of drawing commands you can batch together using these functions depends only on the amount of memory available to store them. The drawcount parameter can literally range to the billions, but with each command taking 16 or 20 bytes, 1 billion draw commands would consume 20 gigabytes of memory and probably take several seconds or even minutes to execute. However, it's perfectly reasonable to batch together tens of thousands of draw commands into a single buffer. Given this, you can either preload a buffer object with the parameters for many draw commands or generate a very large number of commands on the GPU. When you generate the parameters for your drawing commands using the GPU directly into the buffer object, you don't need to wait for those parameters to be ready before calling the indirect draw command that will consume them, and the parameters never make a round trip from the GPU to your application and back.

Listing 7.10 shows a simple example of how **glMultiDrawArraysIndirect()** might be used.

```
typedef struct {
    GLuint vertexCount;
    GLuint instanceCount;
    GLuint firstVertex;
    GLuint baseInstance;
} DrawArraysIndirectCommand;

DrawArraysIndirectCommand draws[] =
{
    {
        42,      // Vertex count
        1,       // Instance count
        0,       // First vertex
        0        // Base instance
    },
    {
        192,
        1,
        327,
        0,
    },
    {
        99,
        1,
        901,
        0
    }
};

// Put 'draws[]' into a buffer object
GLuint buffer;

glGenBuffers(1, &buffer);
glBindBuffer(GL_DRAW_INDIRECT_BUFFER, buffer);
glBufferData(GL_DRAW_INDIRECT_BUFFER, sizeof(draws),
             draws, GL_STATIC_DRAW);

// This will produce 3 draws (the number of elements in draws[]), each
// drawing disjoint pieces of the bound vertex arrays
glMultiDrawArraysIndirect(GL_TRIANGLES,
                          NULL,
                          sizeof(draws) / sizeof(draws[0]),
                          0);
```

Listing 7.10: Example use of an indirect draw command

Simply batching together three drawing commands isn't really that interesting, though. To show the real power of the indirect draw command, we'll draw an asteroid field. This field will consist of 30,000 individual asteroids. First, we will take advantage of the sb7::object class's ability to store multiple meshes within a single file. When such a file is loaded from disk, all of the vertex data is loaded into a single buffer object and associated with a single vertex array object. Each of the sub-objects has a starting vertex and a count of the number of vertices used to describe it. We can retrieve these from the object loader by calling `sb7::object::get_sub_object_info()`. The total number of sub-objects in the `.sbm` file is made available through the `sb7::object::get_sub_object_count()` function. Therefore, we can construct an indirect draw buffer for our asteroid field using the code shown in Listing 7.11.

```
object.load("media/objects/asteroids.sbm");

glGenBuffers(1, &indirect_draw_buffer);
glBindBuffer(GL_DRAW_INDIRECT_BUFFER, indirect_draw_buffer);
glBufferData(GL_DRAW_INDIRECT_BUFFER,
             NUM_DRAWS * sizeof(DrawArraysIndirectCommand),
             NULL,
             GL_STATIC_DRAW);

DrawArraysIndirectCommand * cmd = (DrawArraysIndirectCommand *)
    glMapBufferRange(GL_DRAW_INDIRECT_BUFFER,
                     0,
                     NUM_DRAWS * sizeof(DrawArraysIndirectCommand),
                     GL_MAP_WRITE_BIT | GL_MAP_INVALIDATE_BUFFER_BIT);

for (i = 0; i < NUM_DRAWS; i++)
{
    object.get_sub_object_info(i % object.get_sub_object_count(),
                               cmd[i].first,
                               cmd[i].count);
    cmd[i].primCount = 1;
    cmd[i].baseInstance = i;
}

glUnmapBuffer(GL_DRAW_INDIRECT_BUFFER);
```

Listing 7.11: Setting up the indirect draw buffer for asteroids

Next, we need a way to communicate which asteroid we're drawing to the vertex shader. There is no direct way to get this information from the indirect draw command into the shader. However, we can take advantage of the fact that all drawing commands are actually instanced drawing commands—commands that draw just a single copy of the object can be considered to draw a single instance. Therefore, we can set up an instanced vertex attribute, set the baseInstance field of the indirect drawing command structure to the index within that attribute's array of the data that we wish to pass to the vertex shader, and then use that data for whatever we wish. In Listing 7.11, notice that we set the baseInstance field of each structure to the loop counter.

Next, we need to set up a corresponding input to our vertex shader. The input declaration for our asteroid field renderer is shown in Listing 7.12.

```
#version 450 core

layout (location = 0) in vec4 position;
layout (location = 1) in vec3 normal;

layout (location = 10) in uint draw_id;
```

Listing 7.12: Vertex shader inputs for asteroids

As usual, we have a position and normal input. However, we've also used an attribute at location 10, draw_id, to store our draw index. This attribute will be instanced and associated with a buffer that simply contains an identity mapping. We'll use the sb7::object loader's functions to access and modify its vertex array object to inject our extra vertex attribute. The code to do this is shown in Listing 7.13.

```
glBindVertexArray(object.get_vao());

glGenBuffers(1, &draw_index_buffer);
glBindBuffer(GL_ARRAY_BUFFER, draw_index_buffer);
glBufferData(GL_ARRAY_BUFFER,
             NUM_DRAWS * sizeof(GLuint),
             NULL,
             GL_STATIC_DRAW);

GLuint * draw_index =
    (GLuint *)glMapBufferRange(GL_ARRAY_BUFFER,
                               0,
                               NUM_DRAWS * sizeof(GLuint),
                               GL_MAP_WRITE_BIT |
                               GL_MAP_INVALIDATE_BUFFER_BIT);

for (i = 0; i < NUM_DRAWS; i++)
{
    draw_index[i] = i;
}

glUnmapBuffer(GL_ARRAY_BUFFER);

glVertexAttribIPointer(10, 1, GL_UNSIGNED_INT, 0, NULL);
glVertexAttribDivisor(10, 1);
glEnableVertexAttribArray(10);
```

Listing 7.13: Per-indirect draw attribute setup

Once we've set up our draw_id vertex shader input, we can use it to make each mesh unique. Without this step, each asteroid would be a simple rock placed at the origin. In this example, we will directly create an orientation and translation matrix in the vertex shader from draw_id. The complete vertex shader is shown in Listing 7.14.

```
#version 450 core

layout (location = 0) in vec4 position;
layout (location = 1) in vec3 normal;

layout (location = 10) in uint draw_id;

out VS_OUT
{
    vec3 normal;
    vec4 color;
} vs_out;

uniform float time = 0.0;

uniform mat4 view_matrix;
uniform mat4 proj_matrix;
uniform mat4 viewproj_matrix;

const vec4 color0 = vec4(0.29, 0.21, 0.18, 1.0);
const vec4 color1 = vec4(0.58, 0.55, 0.51, 1.0);

void main(void)
{
    mat4 m1;
    mat4 m2;
    mat4 m;
    float t = time * 0.1;
    float f = float(draw_id) / 30.0;

    float st = sin(t * 0.5 + f * 5.0);
    float ct = cos(t * 0.5 + f * 5.0);

    float j = fract(f);
    float d = cos(j * 3.14159);

    // Rotate around Y
    m[0] = vec4(ct, 0.0, st, 0.0);
    m[1] = vec4(0.0, 1.0, 0.0, 0.0);
    m[2] = vec4(-st, 0.0, ct, 0.0);
    m[3] = vec4(0.0, 0.0, 0.0, 1.0);

    // Translate in the XZ plane
    m1[0] = vec4(1.0, 0.0, 0.0, 0.0);
    m1[1] = vec4(0.0, 1.0, 0.0, 0.0);
    m1[2] = vec4(0.0, 0.0, 1.0, 0.0);
    m1[3] = vec4(260.0 + 30.0 * d, 5.0 * sin(f * 123.123), 0.0, 1.0);

    m = m * m1;

    // Rotate around X
    st = sin(t * 2.1 * (600.0 + f) * 0.01);
    ct = cos(t * 2.1 * (600.0 + f) * 0.01);

    m1[0] = vec4(ct, st, 0.0, 0.0);
    m1[1] = vec4(-st, ct, 0.0, 0.0);
    m1[2] = vec4(0.0, 0.0, 1.0, 0.0);
    m1[3] = vec4(0.0, 0.0, 0.0, 1.0);

    m = m * m1;

    // Rotate around Z
    st = sin(t * 1.7 * (700.0 + f) * 0.01);
```

```
ct = cos(t * 1.7 * (700.0 + f) * 0.01);

m1[0] = vec4(1.0, 0.0, 0.0, 0.0);
m1[1] = vec4(0.0, ct, st, 0.0);
m1[2] = vec4(0.0, -st, ct, 0.0);
m1[3] = vec4(0.0, 0.0, 0.0, 1.0);

m = m * m1;

// Non-uniform scale
float f1 = 0.65 + cos(f * 1.1) * 0.2;
float f2 = 0.65 + cos(f * 1.1) * 0.2;
float f3 = 0.65 + cos(f * 1.3) * 0.2;

m1[0] = vec4(f1, 0.0, 0.0, 0.0);
m1[1] = vec4(0.0, f2, 0.0, 0.0);
m1[2] = vec4(0.0, 0.0, f3, 0.0);
m1[3] = vec4(0.0, 0.0, 0.0, 1.0);

m = m * m1;

gl_Position = viewproj_matrix * m * position;
vs_out.normal = mat3(view_matrix * m) * normal;
vs_out.color = mix(color0, color1, fract(j * 313.431));
}
```

Listing 7.14: Asteroid field vertex shader

In the vertex shader shown in Listing 7.14, we calculate the orientation, position, and color of the asteroid directly from draw_id. First, we convert draw_id to floating point and scale it. Next, we calculate a number of translation, scaling, and rotation matrices based on its value and the value of the time uniform. These matrices are concatenated to form a model matrix, m. The position is transformed first by the model matrix and then by the view-projection matrix. The vertex's normal is also transformed by the model and view matrices. Finally, an output color is computed for the vertex by interpolating between two colors (one is a chocolate brown, the other a sandy gray) to give the asteroid its final color. A simple lighting scheme is used in the fragment shader to give the asteroids a sense of depth.

The rendering loop for this application is extremely simple. First, we set up our view and projection matrices, and then we render all of the models with a single call to **glMultiDrawArraysIndirect()**. The drawing code is shown in Listing 7.15.

```
glBindVertexArray(object.get_vao());

if (mode == MODE_MULTIDRAW)
{
    glMultiDrawArraysIndirect(GL_TRIANGLES, NULL, NUM_DRAWS, 0);
}
```

```
else if (mode == MODE_SEPARATE_DRAWS)
{
    for (j = 0; j < NUM_DRAWS; j++)
    {
        GLuint first, count;
        object.get_sub_object_info(j % object.get_sub_object_count(),
                                   first, count);
        glDrawArraysInstancedBaseInstance(GL_TRIANGLES,
                                          first,
                                          count,
                                          1, j);
    }
}
```

Listing 7.15: Drawing asteroids

As you can see from Listing 7.15, we first bind the object's vertex array object by calling `object.get_vao()` and passing the result to **glBindVertexArray()**. When mode is MODE_MULTIDRAW, the entire scene is drawn with a single call to **glMultiDrawArraysIndirect()**. However, if mode is MODE_SEPARATE_DRAWS, we loop over all of the loaded sub-objects and draw each separately by passing the same parameters that are loaded into the indirect draw buffer directly to a call to **glDrawArraysInstancedBaseInstance()**. Depending on your OpenGL implementation, the separate draw mode could be substantially slower. The resulting output is shown in Figure 7.9.

Figure 7.9: Result of asteroid rendering program

In our example, using a typical consumer graphics card, we can achieve 60 frames per second with 30,000 unique[3] models, which is equivalent to 1.8 million drawing commands every second. Each mesh has approximately 500 vertices, which means that we're rendering almost 1 billion vertices per second, and our bottlneck is almost certainly not the rate at which we are submitting drawing commands.

With clever use of the `draw_id` input (or other instanced vertex attributes), more interesting geometry with more complex variation could be rendered. For example, we could use texture mapping to apply surface detail, storing a number of different surfaces in an array texture and selecting a layer using `draw_id`. Although in this example we compute the transformation matrices directly in our vertex shader using `draw_id`, it's also possible to put large arrays of matrices in a uniform block or shader storage buffer and use `draw_id` to index into it, giving better control over the placement of objects by the application. There's also no reason why the content of the indirect draw buffer needs to be static. In fact, we can generate its content directly in the graphics process by using various techniques to achieve truly dynamic rendering without application intervention.

Storing Transformed Vertices

In OpenGL, it is possible to save the results of the vertex, tessellation evaluation, or geometry shader into one or more buffer objects. This feature, which is known as *transform feedback*, is effectively the last stage in the front end. It is a nonprogrammable, fixed-function stage in the OpenGL pipeline that is nonetheless highly configurable. When transform feedback is used, a specified set of attributes output from the last stage in the current shader pipeline (whether that be a vertex, tessellation evaluation, or geometry shader) is written into a set of buffers.

When no geometry shader is present, vertices processed by the vertex shader and perhaps the tessellation evaluation shader are recorded. When a geometry shader is present, the vertices generated by the `EmitVertex()` function are stored, allowing a variable amount of data to be recorded depending on what the shader does. The buffers used for capturing the

---

3. The asteroids in this example are not truely unique—they are selected from a large batch of unique rock models, and then a different scale and color are applied to each one. The chance of finding two rocks of the same shape, at the same scale, and with the same color is vanishingly small.

output of vertex and geometry shaders are known as transform feedback buffers. Once data has been placed into a buffer using transform feedback, it can be read back by using a function like **glGetBufferSubData()** or by mapping it into the application's address space using **glMapBuffer()** and then reading from it directly. It can also be used as the source of data for subsequent drawing commands. For the remainder of this section, we will refer to the last stage in the front end as the vertex shader. However, be aware that if a geometry or tessellation evaluation shader is present, the last stage is the one whose outputs are saved by transform feedback.

Using Transform Feedback

To set up transform feedback, we must tell OpenGL which of the outputs from the front end we want to record. The outputs from the last stage of the front end are sometimes referred to as *varyings*. The function to tell OpenGL which ones to record is **glTransformFeedbackVaryings()**, and its prototype is

```
void glTransformFeedbackVaryings(GLuint program,
                                 GLsizei count,
                                 const GLchar * const * varying,
                                 GLenum bufferMode);
```

The first parameter to **glTransformFeedbackVaryings()** is the name of a program object. The transform feedback varying state is actually maintained as part of a program object. This means that different programs can record different sets of vertex attributes, even if the same vertex or geometry shaders are used in them. The second parameter is the number of outputs (or varyings) to record and is also the length of the array whose address is given in the third parameter, varying. This third parameter is simply an array of C-style strings giving the names of the varyings to record. These are the names of the output variables in the vertex shader. Finally, the last parameter (bufferMode) specifies the mode in which the varyings are to be recorded. This must be either GL_SEPARATE_ATTRIBS or GL_INTERLEAVED_ATTRIBS. If bufferMode is GL_INTERLEAVED_ATTRIBS, the varyings are recorded into a single buffer, one after another. If bufferMode is GL_SEPARATE_ATTRIBS, each of the varyings is recorded into its own buffer. Consider the following piece of vertex shader code, which declares the output varyings:

```
out vec4 vs_position_out;
out vec4 vs_color_out;
out vec3 vs_normal_out;
```

```
out vec3 vs_binormal_out;
out vec3 vs_tangent_out;
```

To specify that the varyings `vs_position_out`, `vs_color_out`, and so on should be written into a single interleaved transform feedback buffer, the following C code could be used in your application:

```
static const char * varying_names[] =
{
    "vs_position_out",
    "vs_color_out",
    "vs_normal_out",
    "vs_binormal_out",
    "vs_tangent_out"
};

const int num_varyings = sizeof(varying_names) /
                         sizeof(varying_names[0]);

glTransformFeedbackVaryings(program,
                            num_varyings,
                            varying_names,
                            GL_INTERLEAVED_ATTRIBS);
```

Not all of the outputs from your vertex (or geometry) shader need to be stored into the transform feedback buffer. It is possible to save a subset of the vertex shader outputs to the transform feedback buffer and send more to the fragment shader for interpolation. Likewise, it is possible to save some outputs from the vertex shader that are not used by the fragment shader into a transform feedback buffer. Because of this, outputs from the vertex shader that may have been considered inactive (because they're not used by the fragment shader) may become active due to their being stored in a transform feedback buffer. Therefore, after specifying a new set of transform feedback varyings by calling **glTransformFeedbackVaryings()**, it is necessary to link the program object using

```
glLinkProgram(program);
```

If you change the set of varyings captured by transform feedback, you need to link the program object again; otherwise, your changes won't have any affect. Once the transform feedback varyings have been specified and the program has been linked, it may be used in the usual way. Before actually capturing anything, however, you need to create a buffer and bind it to an indexed transform feedback buffer binding point. Of course, before any data can be written to a buffer, space must be allocated in the buffer for it. To allocate space without specifying data, call

```
GLuint buffer;
glGenBuffers(1, &buffer);
glBindBuffer(GL_TARNSFORM_FEEDBACK_BUFFER, buffer);
glBufferData(GL_TRANSFORM_FEEDBACK_BUFFER, size, NULL, GL_DYNAMIC_COPY);
```

When you allocate storage for a buffer, there are many possible values for the usage parameter, but GL_DYNAMIC_COPY is probably a good choice for a transform feedback buffer. The DYNAMIC part tells OpenGL that the data is likely to change often but will probably be used a few times between each update. The COPY part says that you plan to update the data in the buffer through OpenGL functionality (such as transform feedback) and then hand that data back to OpenGL for use in another operation (such as drawing).

When you have specified the transform feedback mode as GL_INTERLEAVED_ATTRIBS, all of the stored vertex attributes are written one after another into a single buffer. To specify which buffer the transform feedback data will be written to, you need to bind a buffer to one of the indexed transform feedback binding points. There are actually multiple GL_TRANSFORM_FEEDBACK_BUFFER binding points for this purpose, which are conceptually separate but related to the general binding GL_TRANSFORM_FEEDBACK_BUFFER binding point. A schematic of this is shown in Figure 7.10.

To bind a buffer to any of the indexed binding points, call

```
glBindBufferBase(GL_TRANSFORM_FEEDBACK_BUFFER, index, buffer);
```

As before, GL_TRANSFORM_FEEDBACK_BUFFER tells OpenGL that we're binding a buffer object to store the results of transform feedback. The last parameter, buffer, is the name of the buffer object we want to bind. The extra parameter, index, is the index of the GL_TRANSFORM_FEEDBACK_BUFFER binding point. Note that there is no way to directly address any of the extra binding points provided by **glBindBufferBase()** through a function like **glBufferData()** or **glCopyBufferSubData()**. However, when you call **glBindBufferBase()**, it actually binds the buffer to the indexed binding point and to the generic binding point. Therefore, you can use the extra binding points to allocate

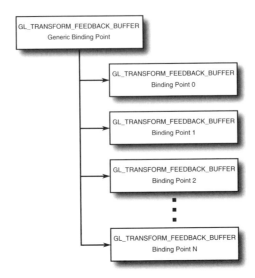

Figure 7.10: Relationship of transform feedback binding points

space in the buffer if you access the general binding point right after calling **glBindBufferBase()**.

A slightly more advanced version of **glBindBufferBase()** is **glBindBufferRange()**, whose prototype is

```
void glBindBufferRange(GLenum target,
                       GLuint index,
                       GLuint buffer,
                       GLintptr offset,
                       GLsizeiptr size);
```

The **glBindBufferRange()** function allows you to bind a section of a buffer to an indexed binding point, whereas **glBindBuffer()** and **glBindBufferBase()** can only bind the whole buffer at once. The first three parameters (target, index, and buffer) have the same meanings as in **glBindBufferBase()**. The offset and size parameters are used to specify the beginning and length of the section of the buffer that you'd like to bind, respectively. You can even bind different sections of the same buffer to several different indexed binding points simultaneously. This enables you to use transform feedback in GL_SEPARATE_ATTRIBS mode to write each attribute of the output vertices into separate sections of a single buffer. If your application packs all attributes into a single vertex buffer and uses **glVertexAttribPointer()** to specify non-zero offsets into the buffer, then you can make the output of transform feedback match the input of your vertex shader.

If you specified that all of the attributes should be recorded into a single transform feedback buffer by using the GL_INTERLEAVED_ATTRIBS parameter to **glTransformFeedbackVaryings()**, the data will be tightly packed and written into the buffer bound to the first GL_TRANSFORM_FEEDBACK_BUFFER binding point (that with index 0). However, if you specified that the mode for transform feedback is GL_SEPARATE_ATTRIBS, each output from the vertex shader will be recorded into its own separate buffer (or section of a buffer, if you used **glBindBufferRange()**). In this case, you need to bind multiple buffers or buffer sections as transform feedback buffers. The index parameter must be between 0 and 1 less than the maximum number of varyings that can be recorded into separate buffers using transform feedback mode. This limit depends on your graphics hardware and drivers and can be found by calling **glGetIntegerv()** with the GL_MAX_TRANSFORM_FEEDBACK_SEPARATE_ATTRIBS parameter. This limit is also applied to the count parameter to **glTransformFeedbackVaryings()**.

There is no fixed limit on the number of separate varyings that can be written to transform feedback buffers in GL_INTERLEAVED_ATTRIBS mode, but there is a maximum number of components that can be written into a buffer. For example, it is possible to write more vec3 varyings than vec4 varyings into a buffer using transform feedback. Again, this limit depends on your graphics hardware and can be found using **glGetIntegerv()** with the GL_MAX_TRANSFORM_FEEDBACK_INTERLEAVED_COMPONENTS parameter.

If you need to, you can leave gaps in the output structures stored in the transform feedback buffer. When you do this, OpenGL will write a few elements, then skip some space in the output buffer, then write a few more components, and so on, leaving the unused space in the buffer unmodified. To achieve this outcome, you can include one of the "virtual" varying names—gl_SkipComponents1, gl_SkipComponents2, gl_SkipComponents3, or gl_SkipComponents4—to skip one, two, three, or four components' worth of storage space in the output buffer, respectively.

Finally, it is possible to write one set of output varyings interleaved into one buffer while writing another set of attributes into another buffer. To do this, we use another special "virtual" varying name, gl_NextBuffer, which tells **glTransformFeedbackVaryings()** to move on to the next buffer binding index. When you use gl_NextBuffer, the bufferMode parameter must be GL_INTERLEAVED_ATTRIBS. As an example, consider this code:

```
static const char * varying_names[] =
{
    "carrots",
    "peas",
    "gl_NextBuffer",
    "beans",
    "potatoes"
};

const int num_varyings = sizeof(varying_names) / sizeof(varying_names[0]);

glTransformFeedbackVaryings(program,
                            num_varyings,
                            varying_names,
                            GL_INTERLEAVED_ATTRIBS);
```

After running this code and then calling **glLinkProgram()**, the transform feedback stage will be configured to write carrots and peas into the first of the transform feedback buffers and beans and potatoes into the second buffer. You could even skip the first buffer binding altogether by setting the first varying name to gl_NextBuffer.

Starting, Pausing, and Stopping Transform Feedback

Once the buffers that are to receive the results of the transform feedback have been bound, transform feedback mode is activated by calling

```
void glBeginTransformFeedback(GLenum primitiveMode);
```

Now whenever vertices pass through OpenGL's front end, output varyings from the last shader will be written to the transform feedback buffers. The parameter to the function, primitiveMode, tells OpenGL which types of geometry to expect. The acceptable parameters are GL_POINTS, GL_LINES, and GL_TRIANGLES. When you call **glDrawArrays()** or another OpenGL drawing function, the basic geometric type must match what you have specified as the transform feedback primitive mode, or you must have a geometry shader that outputs the appropriate primitive type. For example, if primitiveMode is GL_TRIANGLES, then the last stage of the front end must produce triangles. Thus, if you have a geometry shader, it must output **triangle_strip** primitives; if you have a tessellation evaluation shader (and no geometry shader), its output mode must be triangles; and if you have neither, you must call **glDrawArrays()** with GL_TRIANGLES,

Table 7.3: Values for `primitiveMode`

Value of primitiveMode	Allowed Draw Types
GL_POINTS	GL_POINTS
GL_LINES	GL_LINES, GL_LINE_STRIP, GL_LINE_LOOP
GL_TRIANGLES	GL_TRIANGLES, GL_TRIANGLE_STRIP, GL_TRIANGLE_FAN

GL_TRIANGLE_STRIP, or GL_TRIANGLE_FAN. The mapping of transform feedback primitive mode to draw types is shown in Table 7.3.

In addition to the modes listed in Table 7.3, GL_PATCHES can be used for the drawing command's mode parameter, so long as either the tessellation evaluation shader or the geometry shader (if present) is configured to output the right type of primitives. Once transform feedback mode is activated, OpenGL will record your selected outputs from the front end into transform feedback buffers. You can temporarily suspend this recording by calling

```
void glPauseTransformFeedback();
```

When transform feedback mode is paused, it can be restarted again by calling

```
void glResumeTransformFeedback();
```

At this point, OpenGL will continue to record the output of the front end from wherever it left off in the transform feedback buffers. So long as transform feedback is not paused, vertices are recorded into the transform feedback buffers until transform feedback mode is exited or until the space allocated for the transform feedback buffers is exhausted. To exit transform feedback mode, call

```
glEndTransformFeedback();
```

All rendering that occurs between the calls to **glBeginTransformFeedback()** and **glEndTransformFeedback()** results in data being written into the currently bound transform feedback buffers. Each time **glBeginTransformFeedback()** is called, OpenGL starts writing data at the beginning of the buffers bound for transform feedback, overwriting what might be there already. Some care should be taken while transform feedback is active, as changing transform feedback state between calls to `glBeginTransformFeedback()` and `glEndTransformFeedback()` is not allowed. For example, it's not possible to change the transform feedback buffer bindings or to resize or reallocate any of the transform feedback buffers while transform feedback mode is active. This includes cases where transform feedback is paused, even though it's not recording during those times.

Ending the Pipeline with Transform Feedback

In many applications of transform feedback, it may well be that you simply want to store the vertices that the transform feedback stage produces, but you don't actually want to *draw* anything. As transform feedback logically sits right before rasterization in the OpenGL pipeline, we can ask OpenGL to turn off rasterization (and therefore anything after it) by calling

```
glEnable(GL_RASTERIZER_DISCARD);
```

This stops OpenGL from processing primitives any further after transform feedback has been executed. The result is that our vertices are recorded into the output transform feedback buffers, but nothing is actually rasterized. To turn rasterization back on, we call

```
glDisable(GL_RASTERIZER_DISCARD);
```

This disables the rasterizer discard operation, enabling rasterization.

Transform Feedback Example: Physical Simulation

In the `springmass` example, we build a physical simulation of a mesh of springs and masses. Each vertex represents a weight, which is connected to up to four neighbors by elastic tethers. The example iterates over the vertices, processing each one with a vertex shader. A number of advanced features are used in this example. We use a texture buffer object (TBO) to hold vertex position data in addition to a regular attribute array. The same buffer is bound to both the TBO and the vertex attribute associated with the position input to the vertex shader. This allows us to arbitrarily access the current position of other vertices in the system. We also use an integer vertex attribute to hold indices of neighboring vertices. Furthermore, we use transform feedback to store the positions and velocities of each of the masses between each iteration of the algorithm.

For each vertex, we need a position, velocity, and mass. We can pack the positions and masses into one vertex array and pack the velocities into another. Each element of the position array is actually a `vec4`, with the x, y, and z components containing the three-dimensional coordinate of the vertex, and the w component containing the weight of the vertex. The velocity array can simply be an array of `vec3`s. Additionally, we use an array of `ivec4`s to store information about the springs connecting the weights together. There is one `ivec4` for each vertex, and each of the four components of the vector contains the index of the vertex that is connected to the other end of the spring. We call this the connection vector. It allows us to connect each mass to up to four other masses. To record that there is no connection, we point the store at −1 in the component of the connection vector (see Figure 7.11).

Consider vertex 12. It has associated with it an `ivec4` connection vector containing <7, 13, 17, 11>—the indices of the vertices to which it is connected. Likewise, the connection vector for vertex 13 contains <8, 14, 18, 12>. There is a bidirectional connection between vertices 12 and 13. The vertices at the edges of the mesh don't have all of their springs attached, so vertex 14 has a connection vector containing <9, −1, 19, 13>.

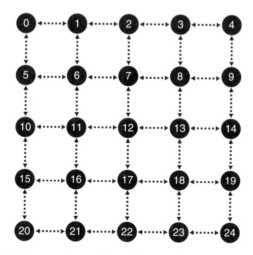

Figure 7.11: Connections of vertices in the spring mass system

Notice that the y component of the vector contains −1, indicating that
there is no spring there.

As each of the connection vectors, we store either the index of the vertex
to which we are connected or −1 to indicate that no connection is present.
We know that by storing −1 in each of the connection vector
components, we can fix that vertex in place. No matter what the forces
acting on it, the vector's position won't be updated. This allows us to fix
the position of some of the vertices and hold the structure in place. If all
components of the connection vector are −1, then the calculations for
updating the position and velocity of the vertex will be skipped by simply
setting the force associated with that vertex to zero. The code to set up the
initial positions and velocities of each node and the connection vectors for
our spring mass system is shown in Listing 7.16.

```
vmath::vec4 * initial_positions = new vmath::vec4 [POINTS_TOTAL];
vmath::vec3 * initial_velocities = new vmath::vec3 [POINTS_TOTAL];
vmath::ivec4 * connection_vectors = new vmath::ivec4 [POINTS_TOTAL];

int n = 0;

for (j = 0; j < POINTS_Y; j++)
{
    float fj = (float)j / (float)POINTS_Y;
    for (i = 0; i < POINTS_X; i++)
    {
        float fi = (float)i / (float)POINTS_X;

        initial_positions[n] = vmath::vec4((fi - 0.5f) * (float)POINTS_X,
                                           (fj - 0.5f) * (float)POINTS_Y,
                                           0.6f * sinf(fi) * cosf(fj),
                                           1.0f);
        initial_velocities[n] = vmath::vec3(0.0f);

        connection_vectors[n] = vmath::ivec4(-1);

        if (j != (POINTS_Y - 1))
        {
            if (i != 0)
                connection_vectors[n][0] = n - 1;

            if (j != 0)
                connection_vectors[n][1] = n - POINTS_X;

            if (i != (POINTS_X - 1))
                connection_vectors[n][2] = n + 1;

            if (j != (POINTS_Y - 1))
                connection_vectors[n][3] = n + POINTS_X;
        }
        n++;
    }
}

glGenVertexArrays(2, m_vao);
```

```
glGenBuffers(5, m_vbo);

for (i = 0; i < 2; i++)
{
    glBindVertexArray(m_vao[i]);

    glBindBuffer(GL_ARRAY_BUFFER, m_vbo[POSITION_A + i]);
    glBufferData(GL_ARRAY_BUFFER,
                 POINTS_TOTAL * sizeof(vmath::vec4),
                 initial_positions, GL_DYNAMIC_COPY);
    glVertexAttribPointer(0, 4, GL_FLOAT, GL_FALSE, 0, NULL);
    glEnableVertexAttribArray(0);

    glBindBuffer(GL_ARRAY_BUFFER, m_vbo[VELOCITY_A + i]);
    glBufferData(GL_ARRAY_BUFFER,
                 POINTS_TOTAL * sizeof(vmath::vec3),
                 initial_velocities, GL_DYNAMIC_COPY);
    glVertexAttribPointer(1, 3, GL_FLOAT, GL_FALSE, 0, NULL);
    glEnableVertexAttribArray(1);

    glBindBuffer(GL_ARRAY_BUFFER, m_vbo[CONNECTION]);
    glBufferData(GL_ARRAY_BUFFER,
                 POINTS_TOTAL * sizeof(vmath::ivec4),
                 connection_vectors, GL_STATIC_DRAW);
    glVertexAttribIPointer(2, 4, GL_INT, 0, NULL);
    glEnableVertexAttribArray(2);
}

delete [] connection_vectors;
delete [] initial_velocities;
delete [] initial_positions;

// Attach the buffers to a pair of TBOs
glGenTextures(2, m_pos_tbo);
glBindTexture(GL_TEXTURE_BUFFER, m_pos_tbo[0]);
glTexBuffer(GL_TEXTURE_BUFFER, GL_RGBA32F, m_vbo[POSITION_A]);
glBindTexture(GL_TEXTURE_BUFFER, m_pos_tbo[1]);
glTexBuffer(GL_TEXTURE_BUFFER, GL_RGBA32F, m_vbo[POSITION_B]);
```

Listing 7.16: Spring mass system vertex setup

To update the system, we run a vertex shader that obtains its own position
and connection vector using regular vertex attributes. It then looks up the
current positions of the vertices it's connected to by indexing into the TBO
using the elements of the connection vector (which is also a regular vertex
attribute). The code for initializing the TBOs is shown at the end of
Listing 7.16.

For each connected vertex, the shader can calculate the distance to it and,
therefore, the extension of the virtual spring between them. From this, it
can calculate the force exerted upon it by the spring, calculate the
acceleration this produces given the mass of the vertex, and produce a new
position and velocity vector to use in the next iteration. It sounds
complex, but it's not—it's just Newtonian physics and Hooke's law.

Hooke's law is

$$F = -kx$$

where F is the force exerted by the spring, k is the spring constant (how stiff the spring is), and x is the extension of the spring. The spring's extension is relative to its resting length. For our system, we keep the rest lengths of the springs the same and store this length in a uniform. Any stretching of the spring produces a positive value of x, and any compression of the spring produces a negative value of x. The instantaneous length of the spring is simply the length of the vector from one of its ends to the other—exactly what we'll calculate in the vertex shader.

We give the force a direction by multiplying the linear force F by the direction along the spring. We introduce the variable d, which is simply the normalized direction along the spring:

$$\vec{F} = \vec{d}F$$

This gives us the force applied to the mass due to the extension or compression of the spring. If we were to simply apply this force to the mass, the system would oscillate and, due to numerical imprecision, would eventually become unstable. All real spring systems have some loss due to friction, which can be modeled by including damping into the force equation. The force due to damping is determined by the equation

$$\vec{F}_d = -c\vec{v}$$

where c represents the damping coefficient. Ideally, we would calculate the damping force for each spring, but for this simple system, a single force based on the mass's velocity will do. Also, we use the initial velocity at each time-step to approximate the continuous differential that would be required by this equation. In our shader, we initialize F by calculating the damping force and then accumulate the force exerted by each spring on the mass. Finally, we apply gravity to the system by treating it as simply one more force acting on each mass. Gravity is a constant force that generally acts in a downward direction. We can just add that to the initial force acting on the mass:

$$F_{total} = G - \vec{dk}x - c\vec{v}$$

Once we have the total force, we can simply apply Newton's laws. Newton's second law allows us to calculate the acceleration of the mass:

$$F = m\vec{a}$$

$$\vec{a} = \frac{\vec{F}}{m}$$

Here, F is the force we just calculated using gravity, the damping coefficient, and Hooke's law; m is the mass of the vertex (stored in the w component of the position attribute); and a is the resulting acceleration. We can plug the initial velocity (which we get from our other attribute array) into the following equations of motion to find out what our final velocity will be and how far we moved in a fixed time:

$$\vec{v} = \vec{u} + \vec{a}t$$

$$\vec{s} = \vec{u} + \frac{\vec{a}t^2}{2}$$

where u is the initial velocity (read from our velocity attribute array), v is the final velocity, t is our time-step (supplied by the application), and s is the distance we've traveled. Don't forget that a, u, v, and s are all vectors. All that's left to do is write the shaders and hook them up to an application. Listing 7.17 shows what the vertex shader looks like.

```
#version 450 core

// This input vector contains the vertex position in xyz, and the
// mass of the vertex in w
layout (location = 0) in vec4 position_mass;
// This is the current velocity of the vertex
layout (location = 1) in vec3 velocity;
// This is our connection vector
layout (location = 2) in ivec4 connection;

// This is a TBO that will be bound to the same buffer as the
// position_mass input attribute
layout (binding = 0) uniform samplerBuffer tex_position;

// The outputs of the vertex shader are the same as the inputs
out vec4 tf_position_mass;
out vec3 tf_velocity;
```

```
// A uniform to hold the time-step. The application can update this.
uniform float t = 0.07;

// The global spring constant
uniform float k = 7.1;

// Gravity
const vec3 gravity = vec3(0.0, -0.08, 0.0);

// Global damping constant
uniform float c = 2.8;

// Spring resting length
uniform float rest_length = 0.88;

void main(void)
{
    vec3 p = position_mass.xyz;      // p can be our position
    float m = position_mass.w;       // m is the mass of our vertex
    vec3 u = velocity;               // u is the initial velocity
    vec3 F = gravity * m - c * u;    // F is the force on the mass
    bool fixed_node = true;          // Becomes false when force is applied

    for (int i = 0; i < 4; i++)
    {
        if (connection[i] != -1)
        {
            // q is the position of the other vertex
            vec3 q = texelFetch(tex_position, connection[i]).xyz;
            vec3 d = q - p;
            float x = length(d);
            F += -k * (rest_length - x) * normalize(d);
            fixed_node = false;
        }
    }

    // If this is a fixed node, reset force to zero
    if (fixed_node)
    {
        F = vec3(0.0);
    }

    // Acceleration due to force
    vec3 a = F / m;

    // Displacement
    vec3 s = u * t + 0.5 * a * t * t;

    // Final velocity
    vec3 v = u + a * t;

    // Constrain the absolute value of the displacement per step
    s = clamp(s, vec3(-25.0), vec3(25.0));

    // Write the outputs
    tf_position_mass = vec4(p + s, m);
    tf_velocity = v;
}
```

Listing 7.17: Spring mass system vertex shader

That wasn't so hard, was it? To execute the shader, we iterate over the set of vertices that we placed in buffers earlier. We need to double-buffer the position and velocity information, which means that we read from one set of buffers and write to the other set on one pass, and then swap the buffers around so that the data moves back and forth from one buffer to the other. The connection information remains the same on each pass, so it's going to be constant. To do this, we use the two VAOs that we set up earlier. The first VAO has one set of position and velocity attributes attached to it, along with the common connection information. The other VAO has the other set of position and velocity attributes attached and the same common connection information.

In addition to the VBOs, we need two TBOs. We use each buffer simultaneously as both a position VBO and a TBO. This seems strange, but is perfectly legal in OpenGL—after all, we're just reading from the same buffer via two different methods. To set this up, we generate two textures, bind them to the GL_TEXTURE_BUFFER binding point, and attach the buffers to them using `glTexBuffer()`. When we bind VAO A, we also bind texture A. When we bind VAO B, we bind texture B. That way, the same data appears in both the position vertex attribute and the tex_position `samplerBuffer` buffer texture.

The code to set this up isn't particularly complex, but it is repetitive. A complete implementation can be found on this book's Web site. The example application includes the code to create and initialize the buffers, perform double-buffering, and visualize the results. The application fixes a few of the vertices in place so that the whole system doesn't just fall off the bottom of the screen. Once we have all of the buffers hooked up, we can simulate a time-step in the system with a single call to `glDrawArrays()`. Each node in the system is represented by a single GL_POINTS primitive. If we initialize the system and let it run, we see a result that looks like Figure 7.12.

On each frame we run the physical simulation several times, and on each iteration we swap the VAOs and TBOs. This iterative loop is shown in Listing 7.18. Each iteration of the loop updates the positions and velocities of all the nodes once. Iterating the simulation several times rather than just using a larger time-step in the simulation leads to greater stability and less oscillation of nodes, which produces a better visual result.

```
int i;
glUseProgram(m_update_program);

glEnable(GL_RASTERIZER_DISCARD);
```

```
for (i = iterations_per_frame; i != 0; --i)
{
    glBindVertexArray(m_vao[m_iteration_index & 1]);
    glBindTexture(GL_TEXTURE_BUFFER, m_pos_tbo[m_iteration_index & 1]);
    m_iteration_index++;
    glBindBufferBase(GL_TRANSFORM_FEEDBACK_BUFFER, 0,
                     m_vbo[POSITION_A + (m_iteration_index & 1)]);
    glBindBufferBase(GL_TRANSFORM_FEEDBACK_BUFFER, 1,
                     m_vbo[VELOCITY_A + (m_iteration_index & 1)]);
    glBeginTransformFeedback(GL_POINTS);
    glDrawArrays(GL_POINTS, 0, POINTS_TOTAL);
    glEndTransformFeedback();
}

glDisable(GL_RASTERIZER_DISCARD);
```

Listing 7.18: Spring mass system iteration loop

During iteration, we enable *rasterizer discard*, which stops data from
passing further down the pipeline beyond the transform feedback stage.
We then disable rasterizer discard once we are finished with the iteration
so that we can render the resulting system to the screen. After enough
iterations have been performed, we can render the points in the system in
whatever way we wish. Using a simple program for rendering, we draw the
nodes of the system as points and the connections between them as lines.
Our code is shown in Listing 7.19 and the resulting image is shown in
Figure 7.12.

```
static const GLfloat black[] = { 0.0f, 0.0f, 0.0f, 0.0f };

glViewport(0, 0, info.windowWidth, info.windowHeight);
glClearBufferfv(GL_COLOR, 0, black);

glUseProgram(m_render_program);

if (draw_points)
{
    glPointSize(4.0f);
    glDrawArrays(GL_POINTS, 0, POINTS_TOTAL);
}

if (draw_lines)
{
    glBindBuffer(GL_ELEMENT_ARRAY_BUFFER, m_index_buffer);
    glDrawElements(GL_LINES, CONNECTIONS_TOTAL * 2,
                   GL_UNSIGNED_INT, NULL);
}
```

Listing 7.19: Spring mass system rendering loop

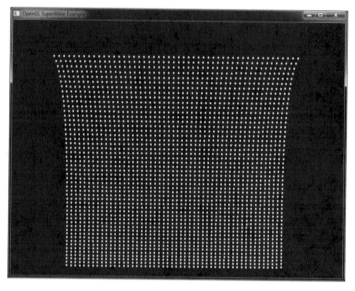

Figure 7.12: Simulation of points connected by springs

The image in Figure 7.12 is not particularly interesting, but it does demonstrate that our simulation is running correctly. To make the visual result more appealing, we can set the point size to a larger value, and we can also issue a second, indexed draw using `glDrawElements()` and `GL_LINES` primitives to visualize the connections between nodes. Note that the same vertex positions can be used as input to this second pass, but we need to construct another buffer to use with the `GL_ELEMENT_ARRAY` binding that contains the indices of the vertices at the end of each spring. This additional step is also performed by the example program. Figure 7.13 shows the final result.

Of course, the physical simulation (and the vertex data produced by it) can be used for anything. This particular system would provide a reasonable approximation to cloth, although it is elementary. It does not, for instance, handle self-interaction, which would be important for a realistic cloth simulation. However, many systems in which particles interact in a deterministic way can be modeled and simulated using only a vertex shader and transform feedback.

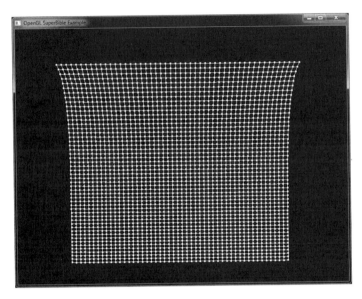

Figure 7.13: Visualizing springs in the spring mass system

Clipping

As explained in Chapter 3, clipping is the process of determining which primitives may be fully or partially visible and constructing a set of primitives from them that will lie entirely inside the viewport.

For points, clipping is trivial: If the coordinate of the point is inside the region then it should be processed further, whereas if it is outside the region it should be discarded. Clipping lines is a little more complex. If both ends of the line lie on the outside of the same plane of the clipping volume (for example, if the x component of both ends of the line is less than -1.0), then the line is trivially discarded. If both ends of the line lie inside the clipping volume, then it is trivially accepted. If one end of the line is inside the clipping volume or if the endpoints of the line lie such that it may cut through the clipping volume, then the line must be clippped against the volume to create a shorter line that lies within it. Figure 7.14 demonstrates trivially accepted, trivially discarded, and nontrivially clipped lines shown in two dimensions for clarity.

In Figure 7.14, the line marked A is trivially accepted because both of its endpoints are entirely within the viewport (represented as a dotted

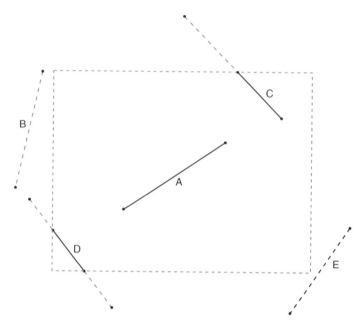

Figure 7.14: Clipping lines

rectangle). The line marked B is trivially rejected because both of its endpoints are outside the left edge of the viewport. Line C is clipped against the top edge of the viewport and line D is clipped against the left *and* bottom edges of the viewport. This is nontrivial clipping and results in vertices being moved along the line to make it fit into the viewport. Line E is a special case—the first endpoint is on the outside of the right edge of the viewport but the second is inside the right edge. However, the second endpoint of E is outside the bottom edge of the viewport, whereas the first is inside that edge. OpenGL will still discard this line, but internally it may temporarily clip the line against one or the other of the viewport edges before determining that there is nothing to be drawn.

The clipping of triangles poses a problem that appears to be more complex but is actually solved in a similar manner. As with lines, triangles may be trivially discarded if all three of their vertices lie outside the same clipping plane and may be trivially accepted if all of their vertices lie inside the clipping volume. If the triangle lies partially inside and partially outside the clipping volume, then it must be clipped by cutting it into a number of smaller triangles that fit within the volume. Figure 7.15 demonstrates

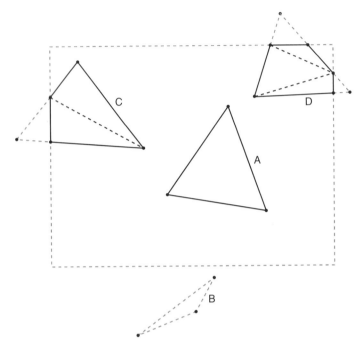

Figure 7.15: Clipping triangles

the process in two dimensions, although of course this really happens in three dimensions in OpenGL.

As you can see, the triangle marked A in Figure 7.15 is trivially accepted because all three of its vertices lie inside the viewport. Triangle B is trivially discarded because all three of its vertices lie outside of the same edge of the viewport. Triangle C crosses the left edge of the viewport and must be clipped. An additional vertex is generated by OpenGL and the original triangle is split into two parts. Triangle D is clipped against the right and top edges of the viewport. An additional vertex is produced for each clipped edge and new triangles are created to fill the polygonal shape that is produced. In fact, this is generally true—for each edge that a triangle clips, one extra vertex and one extra triangle are produced.

The Guard Band

As you can see in Figure 7.15, triangles that are partially visible but clip against one or more of the viewport edges can, depending on the

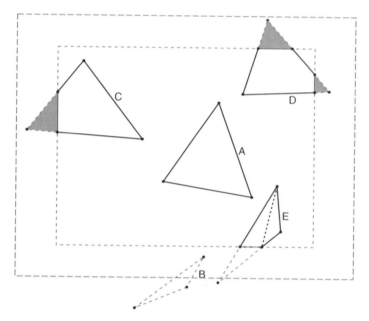

Figure 7.16: Clipping triangles using a guard band

implementation, be broken into multiple smaller triangles. This can cause a performance problem for GPUs that process triangles at a fixed rate. In some cases, it may be faster to allow such triangles to pass through the clipping phase unmodified and instead have the rasterizer throw away parts that will not be visible. To implement this, some GPUs include a *guard band*, which is a region outside clip space in which triangles are allowed to pass through even though they will not be visible. The guard band is illustrated in Figure 7.16.

The presence of a guard band does not affect trivially accepted or trivially rejected triangles—those are either passed through or thrown away as they were before. However, triangles that clip against one or more edges of the viewport but otherwise fall inside the guard band are also considered to be trivially accepted and are not broken up. Only triangles that clip against one or more edges of the guard band *and* protude into the viewport are broken into multiple triangles. Referring to Figure 7.16, we see that triangle A is trivially accepted as before and triangle B is trivially rejected as before. However, triangles C and D are no longer broken up. Rather, they are passed through the clipper unmodified and the shaded areas are later discarded during rasterization. Only the newly introduced triangle E is broken into sub-triangles for rasterization, because it clips against both the viewport (the inner dotted rectangle) and the guard band (the outer dotted rectangle).

In practice, the width of the guard band (the gap between the inner and outer dotted rectangles) is quite large—usually at least as big as the viewport itself, and you'd have to draw some pretty huge triangles to hit both. While none of these issues will have any visible effect on the output of your program, they may affect its performance, and so this is useful information.

User-Defined Clipping

One way to determine which side of a plane a point lies on is to calculate the signed distance from that point to the plane. When you know the signed distance from a point to a plane, its absolute value determines how far the point is to the plane, and its sign determines which side of the plane the point is on. Therefore, you can use the sign of this distance to determine whether you are inside or outside a plane. OpenGL may or may not use that method to perform view volume clipping, but you can use it to implement your own clipping algorithms.

In addition to the six distances to the six standard clip planes making up the view frustum, a set of additional distances is available to the application that can be written inside the vertex or geometry shaders. The clip distances are available for writing in the vertex shader through the built-in variable gl_ClipDistance[], which is an array of floating-point values. As you learned earlier in this chapter, gl_ClipDistance[] is a member of the gl_PerVertex block and can be written from the vertex shader, tessellation evaluation, or geometry shader—whichever comes last. The number of clip distances supported depends on your implementation of OpenGL. These distances are interpreted exactly the same way as the built-in clip distances. If a shader writer wants to use user-defined clip distances, they should be enabled by the application by calling

```
glEnable(GL_CLIP_DISTANCE0 + n);
```

Here, n is the index of the clip distance to enable. The tokens GL_CLIP_DISTANCE1, GL_CLIP_DISTANCE2, and so on up to GL_CLIP_DISTANCE5 are usually defined in standard OpenGL header files.

However, the maximum value of n is implementation defined and can be found by calling **glGetIntegerv()** with the token GL_MAX_CLIP_DISTANCES. You can disable the user-defined clip distance by calling **glDisable()** with the same token. If the user-defined clip distance at a particular index is not enabled, the value written to gl_ClipDistance[] at that index is ignored.

As with the built-in clipping planes, the sign of the distance written into the gl_ClipDistance[] array is used to determine whether a vertex is inside or outside the user-defined clipping volume. If the signs of all the distances for every vertex of a single triangle are negative, the triangle is clipped. If it is determined that the triangle may be partially visible, then the clip distances are linearly interpolated across the triangle and the visibility determination is made at each pixel. Thus, the rendered result will be a linear approximation to the per-vertex distance function evaluated by the vertex shader. This allows a vertex shader to clip geometry against an arbitrary set of planes (the distance of a point to a plane can be found with a simple dot product).

The gl_ClipDistance[] array is also available as an input to the fragment shader. Fragments that would have a negative value in any element of gl_ClipDistance[] are clipped away and never reach the fragment shader. However, any fragment that has only positive values in gl_ClipDistance[] passes through the fragment shader, and this value can then be read and used by the shader for any purpose. For example, this functionality may be used to fade the fragment by reducing its alpha value as its clip distance approaches zero. This allows a large primitive clipped against a plane by the vertex shader to fade smoothly or be antialiased by the fragment shader, rather than generating a hard clipped edge.

If all of the vertices making up a single primitive (point, line, or triangle) are clipped against the same plane, then the whole primitive is eliminated. This functionality seems to make sense and behaves as expected for regular polygon meshes. However, when using points and lines, you need to be careful. With points, you can render a point with a single vertex that covers multiple pixels by setting the gl_PointSize parameter to a value greater than 1.0. When gl_PointSize is large, a big point is rendered around the vertex. Thus, if you have a large point that is moving slowly toward and eventually off the edge of the screen, it will suddenly disappear when the center of the point exits the view volume and the vertex representing that point is clipped. Likewise, OpenGL can render wide lines. If a line is drawn whose vertices are both outside one of the clipping planes but would otherwise be visible, nothing will be drawn. This can produce strange popping artifacts if you're not careful.

Listing 7.20 illustrates how a vertex shader might write to two clip distances. For the first clip distance, we determine the distance of the object–space vertex to a plane defined by the four-component vector, clip_plane. For the second distance, we consider the distance from each vertex to a sphere. To do this, we take the length of the vector from the view–space vertex to the center of the sphere and subtract the sphere's radius (which is stored in the w component of clip_sphere).

```
#version 450 core

// More uniforms here

// Clip plane
uniform vec4 clip_plane = vec4(1.0, 1.0, 0.0, 0.85);
uniform vec4 clip_sphere = vec4(0.0, 0.0, 0.0, 4.0);

void main(void)
{
    // Lighting code goes here

    // Write clip distances
    gl_ClipDistance[0] = dot(position, clip_plane);
    gl_ClipDistance[1] = length(position.xyz / position.w -
                                clip_sphere.xyz) - clip_sphere.w;

    // Calculate the clip-space position of each vertex
    gl_Position = proj_matrix * P;
}
```

Listing 7.20: Clipping an object against a plane and a sphere

The result of rendering with the shader shown in Listing 7.20 appears in Figure 7.17.

As you can see in Figure 7.17, the dragon has been clipped not only against the flat plane, but also around the curved surface of the sphere. When the clip distance is linearly interpolated against a curved surface such as a sphere, then the resulting clipped geometry will be a linear approximation to that curve. For good results, then, the original geometry must be reasonably detailed.

In addition to clipping as controlled by gl_ClipDistance[], OpenGL supports culling based on these distances. To enable culling, rather than writing to gl_ClipDistance[], your shader should write to gl_CullDistance[] instead. The difference between gl_ClipDistance[] and gl_CullDistance[] is that when vertices have a negative value for gl_ClipDistance[], the resulting primitive is clipped against the inferred plane. If some of the vertices of a primitive have positive values and some have negative values for gl_ClipDistance[], then the primitive will be partially visible. In contrast, if *any* vertex of a primitive has a negative

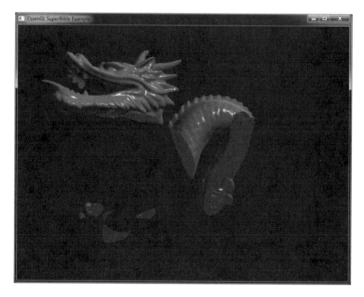

Figure 7.17: Rendering with user clip distances

value for gl_CullDistance[], then the whole primitive will be discarded (or culled).

Summary

This chapter covered in some detail the mechanisms by which OpenGL reads vertex data from the buffers that you provide and the means by which you map the inputs to your vertex shader to those inputs. We also discussed the responsibilities of the vertex shader and the built-in output variables that it can write. You have seen how the vertex shader can set not only the resulting positions of the vertices that it produces, but also the sizes of any points that might be rendered, and even how it can control the clipping process to allow you to clip objects against arbitrary shapes.

This chapter also introduced transform feedback—a powerful stage in OpenGL that allows the vertex shader to store arbitrary data into buffers. We looked at how OpenGL clips the primitives it generates against the visible region of the window and how primitives are moved from clip space into not just a single viewport, but many viewports. In the next chapter, we'll take another look at the front-end stages of tessellation and geometry shaders, which operate somewhat similarly to vertex shaders and will leverage the knowledge you've gained in this chapter.

Chapter 8

Primitive Processing

WHAT YOU'LL LEARN IN THIS CHAPTER

- How to use tessellation to add geometric detail to your scenes.

- How to use geometry shaders to process whole primitives and create geometry on the fly.

In the previous chapters, you read about the OpenGL pipeline and were at least briefly introduced to the functions of each of its stages. We've covered the vertex shader stage in some detail, including how its inputs are formed and where its outputs go. A vertex shader runs once on each of the vertices you send OpenGL and produces one set of outputs for each. The next few stages of the pipeline seem similar to vertex shaders at first, but can actually be considered *primitive processing* stages. First, the two tessellation shader stages and the fixed-function tessellator that they flank together process *patches*. Next, the geometry shader processes entire primitives (points, lines, and triangles) and runs once for each. In this chapter, we'll cover both tessellation and geometry shading, and investigate some of the OpenGL features that they unlock.

Tessellation

As explained in the "Tessellation" section in Chapter 3, tessellation is the process of breaking a large primitive referred to as a *patch* into many smaller primitives before rendering them. There are many uses for tessellation, but the most common application is to add geometric detail to otherwise lower-fidelity meshes. In OpenGL, tessellation is produced using three distinct stages of the pipeline—the tessellation control shader (TCS), the fixed-function tessellation engine, and the tessellation evaluation shader (TES). Logically, these three stages fit between the vertex shader and the geometry shader stages. When tessellation is active, incoming vertex data is first processed in the usual way by the vertex shader and then passed, in groups, to the tessellation control shader.

The tessellation control shader operates on groups of up to 32 vertices[1] at a time, where the group is collectively known as a patch. In the context of tessellation, the input vertices are often referred to as *control points*. The tessellation control shader is responsible for generating three things:

- The per-patch inner and outer tessellation factors

- The position and other attributes for each output control point

- Per-patch user-defined varyings

The tessellation factors are sent on to the fixed-function tessellation engine, which uses them to determine the way that it will break up the patch into smaller primitives. Besides the tessellation factors, the output of a tessellation control shader is a new patch (i.e., a new collection of vertices) that is passed to the tessellation evaluation shader after the patch has been tessellated by the tessellation engine. If some of the data is common to all output vertices (such as the color of the patch), then that data may be marked as *per patch*. When the fixed-function tessellator runs, it generates a new set of vertices spaced across the patch as determined by the tessellation factors and the tessellation mode, which is set using a layout declaration in the tessellation evaluation shader. The only input to the tessellation evaluation shader generated by OpenGL is a set of coordinates indicating where in the patch the vertex lies. When the tessellator is generating triangles, those coordinates are *barycentric*

---

1. The minimum number of vertices per patch required to be supported by the OpenGL specification is 32. However, the upper limit is not fixed and may be determined by retrieving the value of GL_MAX_PATCH_VERTICES.

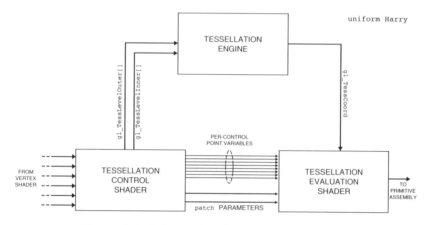

Figure 8.1: Schematic of OpenGL tessellation

coordinates. When the tessellation engine is generating lines or triangles, those coordinates are simply a pair of normalized values indicating the relative position of the vertex. This data is stored in the gl_TessCoord input variable. The schematic in Figure 8.1 shows the setup.

Tessellation Primitive Modes

The tessellation mode is used to determine how OpenGL breaks up patches into primitives before passing them on to rasterization. This mode is set using an input layout qualifier in the tessellation evaluation shader and may be one of quads, triangles, or isolines. This primitive mode controls not only the form of the primitives produced by the tessellator, but also the interpretation of the gl_TessCoord input variable in the tessellation evaluation shader.

Tessellation Using Quads

When the chosen tessellation mode is set to quads, the tessellation engine will generate a quadrilateral (or quad) and break it up into a set of triangles. The two elements of the gl_TessLevelInner[] array should be written by the tessellation control shader and control the level of tessellation applied to the innermost region within the quad. The first element sets the tessellation applied in the horizontal (*u*) direction and the second element sets the tessellation level applied in the vertical (*v*) direction. Also, all four elements of the gl_TessLevelOuter[] array should be written by the tessellation control shader and are used to determine the

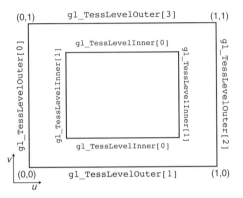

Figure 8.2: Tessellation factors for quad tessellation

level of tessellation applied to the outer edges of the quad. This is shown in Figure 8.2.

When the quad is tessellated, the tessellation engine generates vertices across a two-dimensional domain normalized within the quad. The value stored in the gl_TessCoord input variable sent to the tessellation evaluation shader is then a two-dimensional vector (that is, only the x and y components of gl_TessCoord are valid) containing the normalized coordinates of the vertex within the quad. The tessellation evaluation shader can use these coordinates to generate its outputs from the inputs passed by the tessellation control shader. An example of quad tessellation produced by the tessmodes sample application is shown in Figure 8.3.

In Figure 8.3, the inner tessellation factors in the u and v directions were set to 9.0 and 7.0, respectively. The outer tessellation factors were set to 3.0 and 5.0, respectively, in the u and v directions. This was accomplished using the very simple tessellation control shader shown in Listing 8.1.

```
#version 450 core

layout (vertices = 4) out;

void main(void)
{
    if (gl_InvocationID == 0)
    {
        gl_TessLevelInner[0] = 9.0;
        gl_TessLevelInner[1] = 7.0;
        gl_TessLevelOuter[0] = 3.0;
        gl_TessLevelOuter[1] = 5.0;
```

```
            gl_TessLevelOuter[2] = 3.0;
            gl_TessLevelOuter[3] = 5.0;
        }

    gl_out[gl_InvocationID].gl_Position =
        gl_in[gl_InvocationID].gl_Position;
}
```

Listing 8.1: Simple quad tessellation control shader example

The result of setting the tessellation factors in this way is visible in
Figure 8.3. If you look closely, you will see that along the horizontal outer
edges there are five divisions and along the vertical ones there are three
divisions. On the interior, you can see that there are nine divisions along
the horizontal axis and seven divisions along the vertical axis.

The tessellation evaluation shader that generated Figure 8.3 is shown in
Listing 8.2. Notice that the tessellation mode is set using the quads input
layout qualifier near the front of the tessellation evaluation shader. The
shader then uses the x and y components of gl_TessCoordinate to
perform its own interpolation of the vertex position. In this case, the
gl_in[] array is four elements long (as specified in the control shader
shown in Listing 8.1).

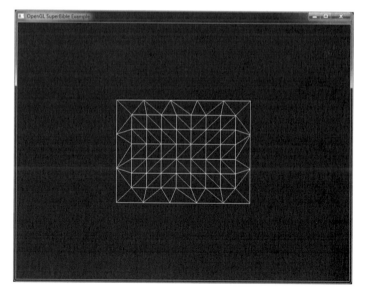

Figure 8.3: Quad tessellation example

```
#version 450 core

layout (quads) in;

void main(void)
{
    // Interpolate along bottom edge using x component of the
    // tessellation coordinate
    vec4 p1 = mix(gl_in[0].gl_Position,
                  gl_in[1].gl_Position,
                  gl_TessCoord.x);
    // Interpolate along top edge using x component of the
    // tessellation coordinate
    vec4 p2 = mix(gl_in[2].gl_Position,
                  gl_in[3].gl_Position,
                  gl_TessCoord.x);
    // Now interpolate those two results using the y component
    // of tessellation coordinate
    gl_Position = mix(p1, p2, gl_TessCoord.y);
}
```

Listing 8.2: Simple quad tessellation evaluation shader example

Tessellation Using Triangles

When the tessellation mode is set to `triangles` (again, using
an input layout qualifier in the tessellation control shader), the tessellation
engine produces a triangle that is then broken into many smaller triangles.
Only the first element of the `gl_TessLevelInner[]` array is used, and this
level is applied to the entirety of the inner area of the tessellated triangle.
The first three elements of the `gl_TessLevelOuter[]` array are used to set
the tessellation factors for the three edges of the triangle. This is shown in
Figure 8.4.

As the tessellation engine generates the vertices corresponding to the
tessellated triangles, each vertex is assigned a three-dimensional coordinate

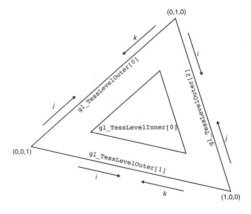

Figure 8.4: Tessellation factors for triangle tessellation

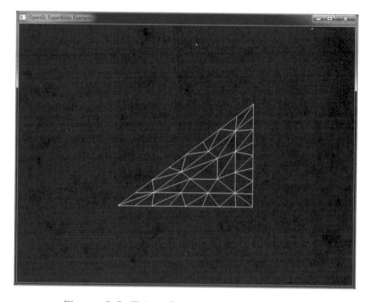

Figure 8.5: Triangle tessellation example

called a *barycentric coordinate*. The three components of a barycentric coordinate can be used to form a weighted sum of three inputs representing the corners of a triangle and to arrive at a value that is linearly interpolated across that triangle. An example of triangle tessellation is shown in Figure 8.5.

The tessellation control shader used to generate Figure 8.5 is shown in Listing 8.3. Notice how similar it is to Listing 8.1, in that all it does is write constants into the inner and outer tessellation levels and pass through the control point positions unmodified.

```glsl
#version 450 core

layout (vertices = 3) out;

void main(void)
{
    if (gl_InvocationID == 0)
    {
        gl_TessLevelInner[0] = 5.0;
        gl_TessLevelOuter[0] = 8.0;
        gl_TessLevelOuter[1] = 8.0;
        gl_TessLevelOuter[2] = 8.0;
    }

    gl_out[gl_InvocationID].gl_Position =
        gl_in[gl_InvocationID].gl_Position;
}
```

Listing 8.3: Simple triangle tessellation control shader example

Listing 8.3 sets the inner tessellation level to 5.0 and all three outer tessellation levels to 8.0. Again, looking closely at Figure 8.5, you can see that each of the outer edges of the tessellated triangle has eight divisions and each of the inner edges has five divisions. The tessellation evaluation shader that produced Figure 8.5 is shown in Listing 8.4.

```
#version 450 core

layout (triangles) in;

void main(void)
{
    gl_Position = (gl_TessCoord.x * gl_in[0].gl_Position) +
                  (gl_TessCoord.y * gl_in[1].gl_Position) +
                  (gl_TessCoord.z * gl_in[2].gl_Position);
}
```

Listing 8.4: Simple triangle tessellation evaluation shader example

Again, to produce a position for each vertex generated by the tessellation engine, we simply calculate a weighted sum of the input vertices. This time, all three components of gl_TessCoord are used and represent the relative weights of the three vertices making up the outermost tessellated triangle. Of course, we're free to do anything we wish with the barycentric coordinates, the inputs from the tessellation control shader, and any other data we have access to in the evaluation shader.

Tessellation Using Isolines

Isoline tessellation is a mode of the tessellation engine in which, rather than producing triangles, it produces real line primitives running along lines of equal v coordinates in the tessellation domain. Each line is broken up into segments along the u direction. The two outer tessellation factors stored in the first two components of gl_TessLevelOuter[] are used to specify the number of lines and the number of segments per line, respectively, and the inner tessellation factors (gl_TessLevelInner[]) are not used at all. This is shown in Figure 8.6.

The tessellation control shader shown in Listing 8.5 simply sets both the outer tessellation levels to 5.0 and doesn't write to the inner tessellation levels. The corresponding tessellation evaluation shader is shown in Listing 8.6.

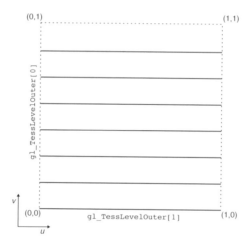

Figure 8.6: Tessellation factors for isoline tessellation

```glsl
#version 450 core

layout (vertices = 4) out;

void main(void)
{
    if (gl_InvocationID == 0)
    {
        gl_TessLevelOuter[0] = 5.0;
        gl_TessLevelOuter[1] = 5.0;
    }

    gl_out[gl_InvocationID].gl_Position =
        gl_in[gl_InvocationID].gl_Position;
}
```

Listing 8.5: Simple isoline tessellation control shader example

Notice that Listing 8.6 is virtually identical to Listing 8.2 except that the input primitive mode is set to `isolines`.

```glsl
#version 450 core

layout (isolines) in;

void main(void)
{
    // Interpolate along bottom edge using the x component of the
    // tessellation coordinate
    vec4 p1 = mix(gl_in[0].gl_Position,
                  gl_in[1].gl_Position,
                  gl_TessCoord.x);
```

```
// Interpolate along top edge using the x component of the
// tessellation coordinate
vec4 p2 = mix(gl_in[2].gl_Position,
              gl_in[3].gl_Position,
              gl_TessCoord.x);
// Now interpolate those two results using the y component
// of the tessellation coordinate
gl_Position = mix(p1, p2, gl_TessCoord.y);
}
```

Listing 8.6: Simple isoline tessellation evaluation shader example

The result of our extremely simple isoline tessellation example is shown in Figure 8.7.

Figure 8.7 doesn't really seem all that interesting. It's also difficult to see that each of the horizontal lines is actually made up of several segments. If, however, we change the tessellation evaluation shader to that shown in Listing 8.7, we can generate the image shown in Figure 8.8.

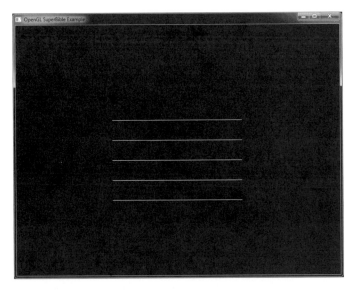

Figure 8.7: Isoline tessellation example

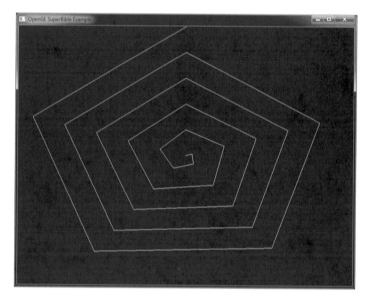

Figure 8.8: Tessellated isoline spirals example

```
#version 450 core

layout (isolines) in;

void main(void)
{
    float r = (gl_TessCoord.y + gl_TessCoord.x / gl_TessLevelOuter[0]);
    float t = gl_TessCoord.x * 2.0 * 3.14159;
    gl_Position = vec4(sin(t) * r, cos(t) * r, 0.5, 1.0);
}
```

Listing 8.7: Isoline spirals tessellation evaluation shader

The shader in Listing 8.7 converts the incoming tessellation coordinates into polar form, with the radius r calculated as smoothly extending from 0 to 1, and with the angle t as a scaled version of the x component of the tessellation coordinate that produces a single revolution on each isoline. This creates the spiral pattern shown in Figure 8.8, where the segments of the lines are clearly visible.

Tessellation Point Mode

In addition to rendering tessellated patches using triangles or lines, it's possible to render the generated vertices as individual points. This so-called *point mode* is enabled using the point_mode input layout qualifier in the tessellation evaluation shader just like any other tessellation mode.

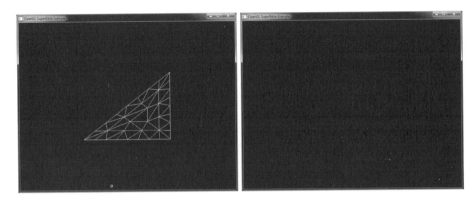

Figure 8.9: Triangle tessellated using point mode

When you specify that point mode should be used, the resulting primitives are points. However, this approach is somewhat orthogonal to the use of the quads, triangles, or isolines layout qualifiers. That is, you should specify point_mode *in addition* to one of the other layout qualifiers. The quads, triangles, and isolines still control the generation of gl_TessCoord and the interpretation of the inner and outer tessellation levels. For example, if the tessellation mode is quads, then gl_TessCoord is a two-dimensional vector, whereas if the tessellation mode is triangles then it is a three-dimensional barycentric coordinate. Likewise, if the tessellation mode is isolines, only the outer tessellation levels are used; if it is triangles or quads, the inner tessellation levels are used as well.

Figure 8.9 shows a version of Figure 8.5 rendered using point mode next to the original image. To produce the figure on the right, we simply change the input layout qualifier of Listing 8.4 to read

```
layout (triangles, point_mode) in;
```

As you can see, the layout of the vertices is identical on both sides of Figure 8.9. On the right, however, each vertex has been rendered as a single point.

Tessellation Subdivision Modes

The tessellation engine works by generating a triangle or quad primitive and then subdividing its edges into a number of segments determined by the inner and outer tessellation factors produced by the tessellation control shader. Next, it groups the generated vertices into points, lines, or triangles and sends them on for further processing. In addition to specifying the type of primitives generated by the tessellation engine, you have quite a bit of control over how the engine subdivides the edges of the generated primitives.

By default, the tessellation engine will subdivide each edge into a number of equal-sized parts where the number of parts is set by the corresponding tessellation factor. This is known as equal_spacing mode. Although it is the default, it can be made explicit by including the following layout qualifier in your tessellation evaluation shader:

```
layout (equal_spacing) in;
```

Equal spacing mode is perhaps the easiest mode to comprehend: Simply set the tessellation factor to the number of segments you wish to subdivide your patch primitive into along each edge, and the tessellation engine takes care of the rest. Although it may seem simple, the equal_spacing mode comes with a significant disadvantage: When you alter the tessellation factor, it is always rounded to up to the next nearest integer, producing a visible jump from one level to the next as the tessellation factor changes. The two other modes, fractional_even_spacing and fractional_odd_spacing, alleviate this problem by allowing the segments to be non-equal in length. These modes are fractional_even_spacing and fractional_odd_spacing and again, you can set these modes by using input layout qualifiers as follows:

```
layout (fractional_even_spacing) in;
// or
layout (fractional_odd_spacing) in;
```

With fractional even spacing, the tessellation factor is rounded to the next-lower even integer and the edge is subdivided as if that were the tessellation factor. With fractional odd spacing, the tessellation factor is rounded down to the next-lower odd number and the edge is subdivided as if that were the tessellation factor. Of course, with either scheme, there is a small remaining segment that doesn't have the same length as the other segments. That last segment is cut in half, with each half having the same length as the other and therefore being a *fractional* segment.

Figure 8.10 shows the same triangle tessellated with equal_spacing mode on the left, fractional_even_spacing mode in the center, and fractional_odd_spacing mode on the right. In all three images shown in Figure 8.10, the inner and outer tessellation factors have been set to 5.3.

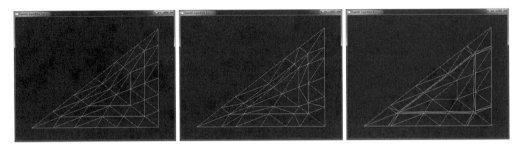

Figure 8.10: Tessellation using different subdivision modes

In the leftmost image showing `equal_spacing` mode, you should be able to see that the number of segments along each of the outer edges of the triangle is 6—the next integer after 5.3. In the center image, which shows `fractional_even_spacing` mode, there are 4 equal-sized segments (4 is the next lower even integer to 5.3) and then two additional smaller segments. Finally, in the rightmost image, which demonstrates `fractional_odd_spacing` mode, there are 5 equal-sized segments (5 is the next lower odd integer to 5.3) and two very skinny segments that make up the rest.

If the tessellation level is animated, either by being explicitly turned up and down using a uniform or by being calculated in the tessellation control shader, the lengths of the equal-sized segments and the two filler segments will change smoothly and dynamically. Whether you choose `fractional_even_spacing` or `fractional_odd_spacing` really depends on which looks better in your application—there is generally no real advantage to either. However, unless you need a guarantee that tessellated edges will have equal-sized segments, and if you can live with popping when the tessellation level changes, `fractional_even_spacing` or `fractional_odd_spacing` will generally look better in any dynamic application than `equal_spacing`.

Controlling the Winding Order

In Chapter 3, "Following the Pipeline," we introduced culling and explained how the *winding order* of a primitive affects how OpenGL decides whether to render it. Normally, the winding order of a primitive is determined by the order in which your application presents vertices to OpenGL. However, when tessellation is active, OpenGL generates all the vertices and connectivity information for you. To allow you to control the winding order of the resulting primitives, you can specify whether you want the vertices to be generated in clockwise or counterclockwise order. Again, this is set using an input layout qualifier in the tessellation evaluation shader. To indicate that you want clockwise winding order, use the following layout qualifier:

```
layout (cw) in;
```

To specify that the winding order of the primitives generated by the tessellation engine be counterclockwise, include this qualifier:

```
layout (ccw) in;
```

The `cw` and `ccw` layout qualifiers can be combined with the other input layout qualifiers specified in the tessellation control shader. By default, the winding order is counterclockwise, so you can omit this layout qualifier if that is what you need. Also, it should be self-evident that winding order applies only to triangles. If your application generates isolines or points, then the winding order is ignored—your shader can still include the winding order layout qualifier, but it won't be used.

Passing Data between Tessellation Shaders

In this section, we have looked at how to set the inner and outer tessellation levels for the quad, triangle, and point primitive modes. However, the images in Figures 8.3 through 8.8 aren't particularly exciting, in part because we haven't done anything except compute the positions of the resulting vertices and shade the resulting primitives solid white. In fact, we have rendered all of these images using lines by setting the polygon mode to GL_LINE with the **glPolygonMode()** function. To produce something a little more interesting, we need to pass more data along the pipeline.

Before a tessellation control shader is run, each vertex represents a control point; the vertex shader runs once for each input control point and produces its output as normal. The vertices (or control points) are then grouped together and passed together to the tessellation control shader. The tessellation control shader processes this group of control points and produces a new group of control points that may or may not have the same number of elements in it as the original group. The tessellation control shader actually runs once for each control point in the *output* group, but each invocation of the tessellation control shader has access to all of the input control points. For this reason, both the inputs to and outputs from a tessellation control shader are represented as arrays. The input arrays are sized by the number of control points in each patch, which is set by calling

```
glPatchParameteri(GL_PATCH_VERTICES, n);
```

Here, n is the number of vertices per patch. By default, the number of vertices per patch is 3. The size of the input arrays in the tessellation control shader is set by this parameter and their contents come from the vertex shader. The built-in variable gl_in[] is always available and is declared as an array of the gl_PerVertex structure. This structure is where the built-in outputs go after you write to them in your vertex shader. All other outputs from the vertex shader become arrays in the tessellation control shader as well. In particular, if you use an output block in your vertex shader, the instance of that block becomes an array of instances in the tessellation control shader. So, for example,

```
out VS_OUT
{
    vec4        foo;
    vec3        bar;
    int         baz
} vs_out;
```

becomes

```
in VS_OUT
{
    vec4        foo;
    vec3        bar;
    int         baz;
} tcs_in[];
```

in the tessellation evaluation shader.

The output of the tessellation control shader is also an array, but its size is set by the vertices output layout qualifier at the front of the shader. It is quite common to set the input and output vertex count to the same value (as was the case in the examples earlier in this section) and then pass the input directly to the output from the tessellation control shader. However, there's no requirement to use this approach, and the size of the output arrays in the tessellation control shader is limited by the value of the GL_MAX_PATCH_VERTICES constant.

The outputs of the tessellation control shader are arrays, so the inputs to the tessellation evaluation shader are also similarly sized arrays. The tessellation evaluation shader runs once per generated vertex and, like the tessellation control shader, has access to all of the data for all of the vertices in the patch.

In addition to the per-vertex data passed from the tessellation control shader to the tessellation evaluation shader in arrays, you can pass data directly between the stages that is constant across an entire patch. To do this, simply declare the output variable in the tessellation control shader and the corresponding input in the tessellation evaluation shader using the patch keyword. In this case the variable does not have to be declared as an array (although you are welcome to use arrays as patch qualified variables) because there is only one instance per patch.

Rendering without a Tessellation Control Shader

The purpose of the tessellation control shader is to perform tasks such as computing the value of per-patch inputs to the tessellation evaluation shader and to calculate the values of the inner and outer tessellation levels that will be used by the fixed-function tessellator. However, in some simple applications, there are no per-patch inputs to the tessellation evaluation shader and the tessellation control shader simply writes constants to the tessellation levels. In this case, it's possible to set up a program with a tessellation evaluation shader, but without a tessellation control shader.

When no tessellation control shader is present, the default value for all inner and outer tessellation levels is 1.0. You can change this by calling **glPatchParameterfv()**, whose prototype is

```
void glPatchParameterfv(GLenum pname,
                        const GLfloat * values);
```

If pname is GL_PATCH_DEFAULT_INNER_LEVEL, then values should point to an array of two floating-point values that will be used as the new default inner tessellation levels in the absence of a tessellation control shader. Likewise, if pname is GL_PATCH_DEFAULT_OUTER_LEVEL, then values should point to an array of four floating-point values that will be used as the new default outer tessellation levels.

If no tessellation control shader is part of the current pipeline, then the number of control points that is presented to the tessellation evaluation shader is the same as the number of control points per patch set by **glPatchParameteri()** when the pname parameter is set to GL_PATCH_VERTICES. In this case, the input to the tessellation evaluation shader comes directly from the vertex shader. That is, the input to the tessellation evaluation shader is an array formed from the outputs of the vertex shader invocations that generated the patch.

Communication between Shader Invocations

While the primary purpose of output variables in tessellation control shaders is to pass data to the tessellation evaluation shader, they also have a secondary purpose—namely, to communicate data between control shader invocations. As you have read, the tessellation control shader runs a single invocation for each *output* control point in a patch. Each output variable in the tessellation control shader is therefore an array, the length of which is the number of control points in the output patch. Normally, each tessellation control shader invocation will take responsibility for writing to one element of this array.

What might not be obious is that tessellation control shaders can actually *read* from their output variables—including those that might be written by other invocations! The tessellation control shader is designed in such a way that the invocations can run in parallel. However, there is no ordering guarantee that governs how those shaders actually execute your code. Thus, when you read from another invocation's output variable, you cannot tell whether that invocation has actually written data there.

To deal with this lack of visibility, GLSL includes the `barrier()` function. It is known as a flow-control barrier, because it dictates the relative order of execution of multiple shader invocations. The `barrier()` function really shines when used in compute shaders—we'll get to that later. However, it's available in a limited form in tessellation control shaders, as well, albeit with a number of restrictions. In particular, in a tessellation control shader, `barrier()` may only be called directly from within your `main()` function and can't be inside any control flow structures (such as `if`, `else`, `while`, or `switch`).

When you call `barrier()`, the tessellation control shader invocation stops and waits for all the other invocations in the same patch to catch up. Its execution doesn't resume until all the other invocations have reached the same point. As a consequence, if you write to an output variable in a tessellation control shader and then call `barrier()`, you can be sure that all the other invocations have done the same thing by the time `barrier()` returns, meaning it's safe to read from the other invocations' output variables.

Tessellation Example: Terrain Rendering

To demonstrate a potential use for tessellation, we will cover a simple terrain rendering system based on quadrilateral patches and *displacement mapping*. The code for this example is part of the `dispmap` sample.
A displacement map is a texture that contains the displacement from a surface at each location. Each patch represents a small region of a landscape that is tessellated depending on its likely screen-space area. Each tessellated vertex is moved along the tangent to the surface by the value stored in the displacement map. This adds geometric detail to the surface without needing to explicitly store the position of each tessellated vertex. Rather, only the displacements from an otherwise flat landscape are stored in the displacement map and are applied at runtime in the tessellation evaluation shader. The displacement map (which is also known as a height map) used in the example is shown in Figure 8.11.

Our first step is to set up a simple vertex shader. As each patch is effectively a simple quad, we can use a constant in the shader to represent the four vertices rather than setting up vertex arrays for it. The complete shader is shown in Listing 8.8. The shader uses the instance number (stored in `gl_InstanceID`) to calculate an offset for the patch, which is a one-unit square in the x–z plane, centered on the origin. In this application, we will render a grid of 64×64 patches, so the x and y offsets for the patch are calculated by taking `gl_InstanceID` modulo 64 and

Figure 8.11: Displacement map used in terrain example

`gl_InstanceID` divided by 64. The vertex shader also calculates the texture coordinates for the patch, which are passed to the tessellation control shader in `vs_out.tc`.

```
#version 450 core

out VS_OUT
{
    vec2 tc;
} vs_out;

void main(void)
{
    const vec4 vertices[] = vec4[](vec4(-0.5, 0.0, -0.5, 1.0),
                                   vec4( 0.5, 0.0, -0.5, 1.0),
                                   vec4(-0.5, 0.0,  0.5, 1.0),
                                   vec4( 0.5, 0.0,  0.5, 1.0));

    int x = gl_InstanceID & 63;
    int y = gl_InstanceID >> 6;
    vec2 offs = vec2(x, y);

    vs_out.tc = (vertices[gl_VertexID].xz + offs + vec2(0.5)) / 64.0;
    gl_Position = vertices[gl_VertexID] + vec4(float(x - 32), 0.0,
                                               float(y - 32), 0.0);
}
```

Listing 8.8: Vertex shader for terrain rendering

Next, we come to the tessellation control shader. Again, the complete shader is shown in Listing 8.9. In this example, the bulk of the rendering algorithm is implemented in the tessellation control shader, and the majority of the code is executed only by the first invocation. Once we have determined that we are the first invocation by checking that `gl_InvocationID` is zero, we calculate the tessellation levels for the whole patch.

First, we project the corners of the patch into normalized device coordinates by multiplying the incoming coordinates by the model–view-projection matrix and then dividing each of the four points by its own homogeneous .w component.

Next, we calculate the length of each of the four edges of the patch in normalized device space after projecting them onto the x–y plane by ignoring their z components. Then, the shader calculates the tessellation level of each edge of the patch as a function of its length using a simple scale and bias. Finally, the inner tessellation factors are simply set to the minimum of the outer tessellation factors calculated from the edge lengths in the horizontal or vertical directions.

You may have noticed a piece of code in Listing 8.9 that checks whether all of the z coordinates of the projected control points are less than zero and then sets the outer tessellation levels to zero in such a case. This optimization culls entire patches that are behind[2] the viewer.

```
#version 450 core

layout (vertices = 4) out;

in VS_OUT
{
    vec2 tc;
} tcs_in[];

out TCS_OUT
{
    vec2 tc;
} tcs_out[];

uniform mat4 mvp;

void main(void)
{
    if (gl_InvocationID == 0)
    {
        vec4 p0 = mvp * gl_in[0].gl_Position;
        vec4 p1 = mvp * gl_in[1].gl_Position;
        vec4 p2 = mvp * gl_in[2].gl_Position;
        vec4 p3 = mvp * gl_in[3].gl_Position;
        p0 /= p0.w;
        p1 /= p1.w;
        p2 /= p2.w;
        p3 /= p3.w;
        if (p0.z <= 0.0 ||
            p1.z <= 0.0 ||
            p2.z <= 0.0 ||
            p3.z <= 0.0)
        {
            gl_TessLevelOuter[0] = 0.0;
            gl_TessLevelOuter[1] = 0.0;
            gl_TessLevelOuter[2] = 0.0;
            gl_TessLevelOuter[3] = 0.0;
        }
        else
        {
            float l0 = length(p2.xy - p0.xy) * 16.0 + 1.0;
            float l1 = length(p3.xy - p2.xy) * 16.0 + 1.0;
            float l2 = length(p3.xy - p1.xy) * 16.0 + 1.0;
            float l3 = length(p1.xy - p0.xy) * 16.0 + 1.0;
            gl_TessLevelOuter[0] = l0;
            gl_TessLevelOuter[1] = l1;
            gl_TessLevelOuter[2] = l2;
            gl_TessLevelOuter[3] = l3;
```

---

2. This optimization is not fool-proof. If the viewer was at the bottom of a very steep cliff and was looking directly upwards, all four corners of the base patch might be behind the viewer, whereas the cliff cutting through the patch would extend into the viewer's field of view.

```
                    gl_TessLevelInner[0] = min(l1, l3);
                    gl_TessLevelInner[1] = min(l0, l2);
            }
    }

    gl_out[gl_InvocationID].gl_Position = gl_in[gl_InvocationID].gl_Position;
    tcs_out[gl_InvocationID].tc = tcs_in[gl_InvocationID].tc;
}
```

Listing 8.9: Tessellation control shader for terrain rendering

Once the tessellation control shader has calculated the tessellation levels
for the patch, it simply copies its input to its output. It does this per
instance and passes the resulting data to the tessellation evaluation shader,
which is shown in Listing 8.10.

```
#version 450 core

layout (quads, fractional_odd_spacing) in;

uniform sampler2D tex_displacement;

uniform mat4 mvp;
uniform float dmap_depth;

in TCS_OUT
{
    vec2 tc;
} tes_in[];

out TES_OUT
{
    vec2 tc;
} tes_out;

void main(void)
{
    vec2 tc1 = mix(tes_in[0].tc, tes_in[1].tc, gl_TessCoord.x);
    vec2 tc2 = mix(tes_in[2].tc, tes_in[3].tc, gl_TessCoord.x);
    vec2 tc = mix(tc2, tc1, gl_TessCoord.y);

    vec4 p1 = mix(gl_in[0].gl_Position,
                  gl_in[1].gl_Position,
                  gl_TessCoord.x);
    vec4 p2 = mix(gl_in[2].gl_Position,
                  gl_in[3].gl_Position,
                  gl_TessCoord.x);
    vec4 p = mix(p2, p1, gl_TessCoord.y);

    p.y += texture(tex_displacement, tc).r * dmap_depth;

    gl_Position = mvp * p;
    tes_out.tc = tc;
}
```

Listing 8.10: Tessellation evaluation shader for terrain rendering

The tessellation evaluation shader shown in Listing 8.10 first calculates the texture coordinate of the generated vertex by linearly interpolating the texture coordinates passed from the tessellation control shader of Listing 8.9 (which were in turn generated by the vertex shader of Listing 8.8). Next, it applies a similar interpolation to the incoming control point positions to produce the position of the outgoing vertex. However, it then uses the texture coordinate that it calculated to offset the vertex in the y direction before multiplying that result by the model–view-projection matrix (the same one that was used in the tessellation control shader). It also passes the computed texture coordinate to the fragment shader in tes_out.tc. That fragment shader is shown in Listing 8.11.

```
#version 450 core

out vec4 color;

layout (binding = 1) uniform sampler2D tex_color;

in TES_OUT
{
    vec2 tc;
} fs_in;

void main(void)
{
    color = texture(tex_color, fs_in.tc);
}
```

Listing 8.11: Fragment shader for terrain rendering

The fragment shader shown in Listing 8.11 is really quite simple. All it does is use the texture coordinate that the tessellation evaluation shader gave it to look up a color for the fragment. The result of rendering with this set of shaders is shown in Figure 8.12.

If we've done our job correctly, you shouldn't be able to tell that the underlying geometry is tessellated. However, if you look at the wireframe version of the image shown in Figure 8.13, you can clearly see the underlying triangular mesh of the landscape. The goals of the program are that all of the triangles rendered on the screen have roughly similar screen-space area and that sharp transitions in the level of tessellation are not visible in the rendered image.

Figure 8.12: Terrain rendered using tessellation

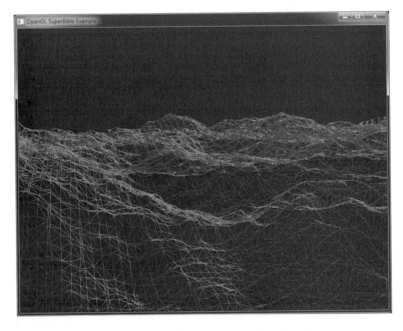

Figure 8.13: Tessellated terrain in wireframe

Tessellation Example: Cubic Bézier Patches

In the displacement mapping example, all we did was use a (very large) texture to drive displacement from a flat surface and then use tessellation to increase the number of polygons in the scene. This is a type of brute-force, data-driven approach to geometric complexity. In the cubicbezier example described here, we will use math to drive geometry—we're going to render a *cubic Bézier patch*. If you revisit Chapter 4, "Math for 3D Graphics", you'll see that we've covered all the number crunching we'll need here.

A cubic Bézier patch is a type of *higher-order surface* and is defined by *control points*[3] that provide input to the interpolation functions that define the surface's shape. A Bézier patch has 16 control points, laid out in a 4 × 4 grid. Very often (including in this example), those control points are equally spaced in two dimensions, varying only in distance from a shared plane. However, they don't have to be. Free-form Bézier patches are an extremely powerful modeling tool being used natively by many pieces of modeling and design software. With OpenGL tessellation, it's possible to render them directly.

The simplest method of rendering a Bézier patch is to treat the four control points in each row of the patch as the control points for a single cubic Bézier curve, just as was described in Chapter 4. Given our 4 × 4 grid of control points, we have four curves; if we interpolate along each of them using the same value of t, we will end up with four new points. We use these four points as the control points for a second cubic Bézier curve. Interpolating along this second curve using a new value for t gives us a second point that lies on the patch. The two values of t (let's call them t_0 and t_1) are the *domain* of the patch and are handed to us by the tessellation evaluation shader in gl_TessCoord.xy.

In this example, we'll perform tessellation in view space. That is, in our vertex shader, we'll transform our patch's control points into view space by multiplying their coordinates by the model–view matrix. This simple vertex shader is shown in Listing 8.12.

```
#version 450 core

in vec4 position;

uniform mat4 mv_matrix;
```

---

3. It should now be evident why the tessellation control shader is so named.

```
void main(void)
{
    gl_Position = mv_matrix * position;
}
```

Listing 8.12: Cubic Bézier patch vertex shader

Once our control points are in view space, they are passed to our tessellation control shader. In a more advanced[4] algorithm, we could project the control points into screen space, determine the length of the curve, and set the tessellation factors appropriately. However, in this example, we'll settle for a simple fixed tessellation factor. As in previous examples, we set the tessellation factor only when gl_InvocationID is zero, but pass all of the other data through once per invocation. The tessellation control shader is shown in Listing 8.13.

```
#version 450 core

layout (vertices = 16) out;

void main(void)
{
    if (gl_InvocationID == 0)
    {
        gl_TessLevelInner[0] = 16.0;
        gl_TessLevelInner[1] = 16.0;
        gl_TessLevelOuter[0] = 16.0;
        gl_TessLevelOuter[1] = 16.0;
        gl_TessLevelOuter[2] = 16.0;
        gl_TessLevelOuter[3] = 16.0;
    }

    gl_out[gl_InvocationID].gl_Position =
        gl_in[gl_InvocationID].gl_Position;
}
```

Listing 8.13: Cubic Bézier patch tessellation control shader

Next, we come to the tessellation evaluation shader, which is where the meat of the algorithm is found. The shader in its entirety is shown in Listing 8.14. You should recognize the cubic_bezier and quadratic_bezier functions from Chapter 4. The evaluate_patch function is responsible for evaluating[5] the vertex's coordinate given the input patch coordinates and the vertex's position within the patch.

---

4. To do this right, we'd need to evaluate the length of the Bézier curve, which involves calculating an integral over a non-closed form... which is hard.

5. You should also now see why the tessellation evaluation shader is so named.

```
#version 450 core

layout (quads, equal_spacing, cw) in;

uniform mat4 mv_matrix;
uniform mat4 proj_matrix;

out TES_OUT
{
    vec3 N;
} tes_out;

vec4 quadratic_bezier(vec4 A, vec4 B, vec4 C, float t)
{
    vec4 D = mix(A, B, t);
    vec4 E = mix(B, C, t);

    return mix(D, E, t);
}

vec4 cubic_bezier(vec4 A, vec4 B, vec4 C, vec4 D, float t)
{
    vec4 E = mix(A, B, t);
    vec4 F = mix(B, C, t);
    vec4 G = mix(C, D, t);

    return quadratic_bezier(E, F, G, t);
}

vec4 evaluate_patch(vec2 at)
{
    vec4 P[4];
    int i;

    for (i = 0; i < 4; i++)
    {
        P[i] = cubic_bezier(gl_in[i + 0].gl_Position,
                            gl_in[i + 4].gl_Position,
                            gl_in[i + 8].gl_Position,
                            gl_in[i + 12].gl_Position,
                            at.y);
    }

    return cubic_bezier(P[0], P[1], P[2], P[3], at.x);
}

const float epsilon = 0.001;

void main(void)
{
    vec4 p1 = evaluate_patch(gl_TessCoord.xy);
    vec4 p2 = evaluate_patch(gl_TessCoord.xy + vec2(0.0, epsilon));
    vec4 p3 = evaluate_patch(gl_TessCoord.xy + vec2(epsilon, 0.0));

    vec3 v1 = normalize(p2.xyz - p1.xyz);
    vec3 v2 = normalize(p3.xyz - p1.xyz);

    tes_out.N = cross(v1, v2);

    gl_Position = proj_matrix * p1;
}
```

Listing 8.14: Cubic Bézier patch tessellation evaluation shader

In our tessellation evaluation shader, we calculate the surface normal to the patch by evaluating the patch position at two points very close to the point under consideration, using the additional points to calculate two vectors that lie on the patch and then taking their cross product. This result is passed to the fragment shader shown in Listing 8.15.

```
#version 450 core

out vec4 color;

in TES_OUT
{
    vec3 N;
} fs_in;

void main(void)
{
    vec3 N = normalize(fs_in.N);

    vec4 c = vec4(1.0, -1.0, 0.0, 0.0) * N.z +
             vec4(0.0, 0.0, 0.0, 1.0);

    color = clamp(c, vec4(0.0), vec4(1.0));
}
```

Listing 8.15: Cubic Bézier patch fragment shader

This fragment shader performs a very simple lighting calculation using the z component of the surface normal. The result of rendering with this shader is shown in Figure 8.14.

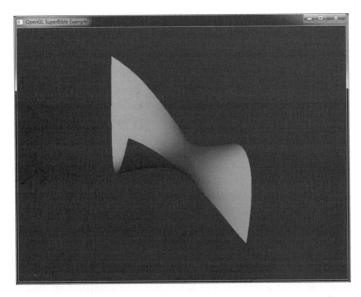

Figure 8.14: Final rendering of a cubic Bézier patch

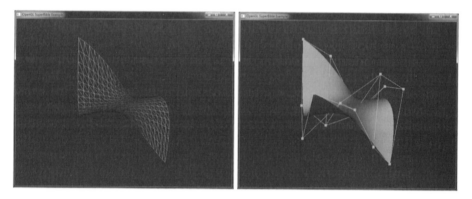

Figure 8.15: A Bézier patch and its control cage

Because the rendered patch shown in Figure 8.14 is smooth, it is difficult to see the tessellation that has been applied to the shape. The left side of Figure 8.15 shows a wireframe representation of the tessellated patch, and the right side of Figure 8.15 shows the patch's control points and the control cage, which is formed by creating a grid of lines between the control points.

Geometry Shaders

The geometry shader is unique in contrast to the other shader types in that it processes a whole primitive (triangle, line, or point) at once and can actually change the amount of data in the OpenGL pipeline programmatically. A vertex shader processes one vertex at a time; it cannot access any other vertex's information and is strictly one-in, one-out. That is, it cannot generate new vertices, and it cannot stop the vertex from being processed further by OpenGL. The tessellation shaders operate on patches and can set tessellation factors, but have little further control over how patches are tessellated, and cannot produce disjoint primitives. Likewise, the fragment shader processes a single fragment at a time, cannot access any data owned by another fragment, cannot create new fragments, and can destroy fragments only by discarding them. A geometry shader, in contrast, has access to all of the vertices in a primitive (up to six with the primitive modes GL_TRIANGLES_ADJACENCY and GL_TRIANGLE_STRIP_ADJACENCY), can change the type of a primitive, and can even create and destroy primitives.

Geometry shaders are an optional part of the OpenGL pipeline. When no geometry shader is present, the outputs from the vertex or tessellation evaluation shader are interpolated across the primitive being rendered and are fed directly to the fragment shader. When a geometry shader is present, however, the outputs of the vertex or tessellation evaluation shader become the inputs to the geometry shader, and the outputs of the geometry shader are interpolated and fed to the fragment shader. The geometry shader can further process the output of the vertex or tessellation evaluation shader and, if it is generating new primitives (a process called amplification), can apply different transformations to each primitive as it creates them.

The Pass-Through Geometry Shader

As explained in Chapter 3, the simplest geometry shader that allows you to render anything is the *pass-through* shader, which is shown in Listing 8.16.

```
#version 450 core

layout (triangles) in;
layout (triangle_strip) out;
layout (max_vertices = 3) out;

void main(void)
{
    int i;

    for (i = 0; i < gl_in.length(); i++)
    {
        gl_Position = gl_in[i].gl_Position;
        EmitVertex();
    }
    EndPrimitive();
}
```

Listing 8.16: Source code for a simple geometry shader

This simple pass-through geometry shader sends its input to its output without modifying it. It looks similar to a vertex shader, but there are a few extra differences to cover. Going over the shader a few lines at a time makes everything clear. The first few lines simply set the version number (450) of the shader, just like in any other shader. The next few lines are the first geometry shader–specific parts. They are shown again in Listing 8.17.

```
#version 450 core

layout (triangles) in;
layout (triangle_strip) out;
layout (max_vertices = 3) out;
```

Listing 8.17: Geometry shader layout qualifiers

These lines set the input and output primitive modes using a layout qualifier. In this particular shader we're using `triangles` for the input and `triangle_strip` for the output. Other primitive types, along with the layout qualifier, are covered later. For the geometry shader's output, we specify not only the primitive type, but also the maximum number of vertices expected to be generated by the shader (through the `max_vertices` qualifier). This shader produces individual triangles (generated as very short triangle strips), so we specified 3 here.

Next is our `main()` function, which is again similar to what might be seen in a vertex or fragment shader. The shader contains a loop, and the loop runs a number of times as determined by the length of the built-in array, `gl_in`. This is another geometry shader–specific variable. Because the geometry shader has access to all of the vertices of the input primitive, the input has to be declared as an array. All of the built-in variables that are written by the vertex shader (such as `gl_Position`) are placed into a structure, and an array of these structures is presented to the geometry shader in the variable called `gl_in`.

The length of the `gl_in[]` array is determined by the input primitive mode. In this particular shader, triangles are the input primitive mode, so the size of `gl_in[]` is 3. The inner loop is given again in Listing 8.18.

```
for (i = 0; i < gl_in.length(); i++)
{
    gl_Position = gl_in[i].gl_Position;
    EmitVertex();
}
```

Listing 8.18: Iterating over the elements of `gl_in[]`

Inside our loop, we generate vertices by simply copying the elements of `gl_in[]` to the geometry shader's output. A geometry shader's outputs are similar to a vertex shader's outputs. Here, we're writing to `gl_Position`, just as we would in a vertex shader. When we're done setting up all of the new vertex's attributes, we call `EmitVertex()`. This built-in function, which is specific to geometry shaders, tells the shader that we're done with our work for this vertex and that it should store all that information away and prepare to set up the next vertex.

Finally, after the loop has finished executing, there's a call to another geometry shader–only function, `EndPrimitive()`. `EndPrimitive()` tells the shader that we're done producing vertices for the current primitive and that it should move on to the next one. We specified `triangle_strip` as the output for our shader, so if we call EmitVertex() more than three times, OpenGL continues adding triangles to the triangle strip. If we need our geometry shader to generate separate, individual triangles or multiple, unconnected triangle strips (remember, geometry shaders can create new geometry or amplify existing geometry), we could call EndPrimitive() between each one to mark their boundaries. If you don't call EndPrimitive() somewhere in your shader, the primitive is automatically ended when the shader ends.

Using Geometry Shaders in an Application

Geometry shaders, like the other shader types, are created by calling the **glCreateShader()** function and using GL_GEOMETRY_SHADER as the shader type:

```
glCreateShader(GL_GEOMETRY_SHADER);
```

Once the shader has been created, it is used like any other shader object. You give OpenGL your shader source code by calling the **glShaderSource()** function, compile the shader by calling the **glCompileShader()** function, and attach it to a program object by calling the **glAttachShader()** function. Then the program is linked as normal using the **glLinkProgram()** function. Now that you have a program object with a geometry shader linked into it, when you draw geometry using a function like **glDrawArrays()**, the vertex shader will run once per vertex, the geometry shader will run once per primitive (point, line, or triangle), and the fragment will run once per fragment. The primitives received by a geometry shader must match what it is expecting based on its own input primitive mode. When tessellation is not active, the primitive mode you use in your drawing commands must match the input primitive mode of the geometry shader. For example, if the geometry shader's input primitive mode is points, then you may use only GL_POINTS when you call **glDrawArrays()**. If the geometry shader's input primitive mode is triangles, then you may use GL_TRIANGLES, GL_TRIANGLE_STRIP, or GL_TRIANGLE_FAN in your **glDrawArrays()** call. A complete list of the geometry shader input primitive modes and the allowed geometrytypes is given in Table 8.1.

Table 8.1: Allowed Draw Modes for Geometry Shader Input Modes

Geometry Shader Input Mode	Allowed Draw Modes
points	GL_POINTS
lines	GL_LINES, GL_LINE_LOOP, GL_LINE_STRIP
triangles	GL_TRIANGLES, GL_TRIANGLE_FAN, GL_TRIANGLE_STRIP
lines_adjacency	GL_LINES_ADJACENCY, GL_LINE_STRIP_ADJACENCY
triangles_adjacency	GL_TRIANGLES_ADJACENCY, GL_TRIANGLE_STRIP_ADJACENCY

When tessellation is active, the mode you use in your drawing commands should always be GL_PATCHES. OpenGL will then convert the patches into points, lines, or triangles during the tessellation process. In this case, the input primitive mode of the geometry shader should match the tessellation primitive mode. The input primitive type is specified in the body of the geometry shader using a layout qualifier. The general form of the input layout qualifier is

```
layout (primitive_type) in;
```

This code specifies that primitive_type is the input primitive type that the geometry shader is expected to handle, and primitive_type must be one of the supported primitive modes: points, lines, triangles, lines_adjacency, or triangles_adjacency. The geometry shader runs once per primitive. In other words, it will run once per point for GL_POINTS; once per line for GL_LINES, GL_LINE_STRIP, and GL_LINE_LOOP; and once per triangle for GL_TRIANGLES, GL_TRIANGLE_STRIP, and GL_TRIANGLE_FAN. The inputs to the geometry shader are presented in arrays containing all of the vertices making up the input primitive. The predefined inputs are stored in a built-in array called gl_in[], which is an array of structures defined in Listing 8.19.

```
in gl_PerVertex
{
    vec4  gl_Position;
    float gl_PointSize;
    float gl_ClipDistance[];
} gl_in[];
```

Listing 8.19: Definition of `gl_in[]`

The members of this structure are the built-in variables that are written in the vertex shader: `gl_Position`, `gl_PointSize`, and `gl_ClipDistance[]`. You should recognize this structure from its declaration as an output block in the vertex shader described earlier in this chapter. These variables appear as global variables in the vertex shader because the block doesn't have an instance name there, but their values end up in the `gl_in[]` array of block instances when they appear in the geometry shader. Other variables written by the vertex shader also become arrays in the geometry shader. In the case of individual varyings, outputs in the vertex shader are declared as usual, and the inputs to the geometry shader have a similar declaration, except that they are arrays. Consider a vertex shader that defines outputs as follows:

```
out vec4 color;
out vec3 normal;
```

The corresponding input to the geometry shader would be

```
in vec4 color[];
in vec3 normal[];
```

Notice that both the `color` and `normal` varyings have become arrays in the geometry shader. If you have a large amount of data to pass from the vertex to the geometry shader, it can be convenient to wrap per-vertex information passed from the vertex shader to the geometry shader within an interface block. In this case, your vertex shader will have a definition like this:

```
out VertexData
{
    vec4 color;
    vec3 normal;
} vertex;
```

The corresponding input to the geometry shader would look like this:

```
in VertexData
{
    vec4 color;
    vec3 normal;
    // More per-vertex attributes can be inserted here
} vertex[];
```

With this declaration, you can access the per-vertex data in the geometry
shader using vertex[n].color and so on. The length of the input arrays
in the geometry shader depends on the type of primitives that it processes.
For example, points are formed from a single vertex, so the arrays will
contain only a single element; in contrast, triangles are formed from three
vertices, so the arrays will be three elements long. If you're writing a
geometry shader that's designed specifically to process a certain primitive
type, you can explicitly size your input arrays, which provides a small
amount of additional compile-time error checking. Otherwise, you can let
your arrays be automatically sized by the input primitive type layout
qualifier. A complete mapping of the input primitive modes and the
resulting size of the input arrays is shown in Table 8.2.

You also need to specify the primitive type that will be generated by the
geometry shader. Again, this is determined using a layout qualifier, like so:

```
layout (primitive_type) out;
```

This is similar to the input primitive type layout qualifier, with the only
difference being that you are declaring the output of the shader using the
out keyword. The allowable output primitive types from the geometry
shader are points, line_strip, and triangle_strip. Notice that
geometry shaders support only the output of the strip primitive types (not
counting points—obviously, there is no such thing as a point strip).

Table 8.2: Sizes of Input Arrays to Geometry Shaders

Input Primitive Type	Size of Input Arrays
points	1
lines	2
triangles	3
lines_adjacency	4
triangles_adjacency	6

There is one final layout qualifier that you must specify to configure the geometry shader. Because a geometry shader is capable of producing a variable amount of data per vertex, you must tell OpenGL how much space to allocate for all that data by specifying the maximum number of vertices that the geometry shader is expected to produce. To do so, use the following layout qualifier:

```
layout (max_vertices = n) out;
```

This sets the maximum number of vertices that the geometry shader may produce to n. Because OpenGL may allocate buffer space to store intermediate results for each vertex, this should be the smallest number possible that still allows your application to run correctly. For example, if you are planning to take points and produce one line at a time, then you can safely set this value to 2. This gives the shader hardware the best opportunity to run fast. If you plan to heavily tessellate the incoming geometry, you might want to set this value to a much higher number, although doing so may incur some performance costs. The upper limit on the number of vertices that a geometry shader can produce depends on your OpenGL implementation. It is guaranteed to be at least 256, but the absolute maximum can be found by calling **glGetIntegerv()** with the GL_MAX_GEOMETRY_OUTPUT_VERTICES parameter.

You can also declare more than one layout qualifier with a single statement by separating the qualifiers with a comma, like so:

```
layout (triangle_strip, max_vertices = n) out;
```

With these layout qualifiers, a boilerplate #version declaration, and an empty main() function, you should be able to produce a geometry shader that compiles and links but does absolutely nothing. In fact, it will discard any geometry you send it, and nothing will be drawn by your application. We now need to introduce two important functions: EmitVertex() and EndPrimitive(). If you don't call these functions, nothing will be drawn.

EmitVertex() tells the geometry shader that you've finished filling in all of the information for this vertex. Setting up the vertex works much like setting up the vertex shader. You need to write into the built-in variable gl_Position. This sets the clip space coordinates of the vertex that is produced by the geometry shader, just like in a vertex shader. Any other attributes that you want to pass from the geometry shader to the fragment shader can be declared in an interface block or as global variables in the geometry shader. Whenever you call EmitVertex(), the geometry shader stores the values currently in all of its output variables and uses them to generate a new vertex. You can call `EmitVertex()` as many times as you like in a geometry shader, until you reach the limit you specified in your `max_vertices` layout qualifier. Each time, you put new values into your output variables to generate a new vertex.

An important thing to note about `EmitVertex()` is that it makes the values of any of your output variables (such as `gl_Position`) undefined. So, for example, if you want to emit a triangle with a single color, you need to set that color with every one of your vertices; otherwise, you will end up with undefined results.

`EmitPrimitive()` indicates that you have finished appending vertices to the end of the primitive. Don't forget, geometry shaders support only the strip primitive types (`line_strip` and `triangle_strip`). If your output primitive type is `triangle_strip` and you call `EmitVertex()` more than three times, the geometry shader will produce multiple triangles in a strip. Likewise, if your output primitive type is `line_strip` and you call `EmitVertex()` more than twice, you'll get multiple lines. In the geometry shader, `EndPrimitive()` refers to the strip. If you want to draw individual lines or triangles, you have to call `EndPrimitive()` after every two or three vertices. You can also draw multiple strips by calling `EmitVertex()` many times between multiple calls to `EndPrimitive()`.

One final thing to note about calling `EmitVertex()` and `EndPrimitive()` in the geometry shader is that if you haven't produced enough vertices to produce a single primitive (for example, if you're generating `triangle_strip` outputs and you call `EndPrimitive()` after two vertices), nothing is produced for that primitive, and the vertices you've already produced are simply thrown away.

Discarding Geometry in the Geometry Shader

The geometry shader in your program runs once per primitive. What you do with that primitive is entirely up to you. The two functions `EmitVertex()` and `EndPrimitive()` allow you to programmatically append new vertices to your triangle or line strip and to start new strips. You can call them as many times as you want (until you reach the maximum defined by your implementation). You're also allowed to not call them at all. This allows you to clip geometry away and discard primitives. If your geometry shader runs and you never call `EmitVertex()` for that particular primitive, nothing will be drawn. To illustrate this behavior, we can implement a custom back-face culling routine that culls geometry as if it

were viewed from an arbitrary point in space. This is implemented in the
gsculling example.

First, we set up our shader version and declare our geometry shader to
accept triangles and produce triangle strips. Back-face culling doesn't really
make a lot of sense for lines or points. We also define a uniform that will
hold our custom viewpoint in world space. This is shown in Listing 8.20.

```
#version 330

// Input is triangles, output is triangle strip. Because we're going
// to do a 1-in, 1-out shader producing a single triangle output for
// each one input, max_vertices can be 3 here.
layout (triangles) in;
layout (triangle_strip, max_vertices=3) out;

// Uniform variables that will hold our custom viewpoint and
// model-view matrix
uniform vec3 viewpoint;
uniform mav4 mv_matrix;
```

Listing 8.20: Configuring the custom culling geometry shader

Inside our main() function, we need to find the face normal for the
triangle. This is simply the cross product of any two vectors in the plane of
the triangle—we can use the triangle edges for this. Listing 8.21 shows
how this is done.

```
// Calculate two vectors in the plane of the input triangle
vec3 ab = gl_in[1].gl_Position.xyz - gl_in[0].gl_Position.xyz;
vec3 ac = gl_in[2].gl_Position.xyz - gl_in[0].gl_Position.xyz;
vec3 normal = normalize(cross(ab, ac));
```

Listing 8.21: Finding a face normal in a geometry shader

Now that we have the normal, we can determine whether it faces toward
or away from our user-defined viewpoint. To do so, we need to transform
the normal into the same coordinate space as the viewpoint, which is
world space. Assuming we have the model–view matrix in a uniform,
simply multiply the normal by this matrix. To be more accurate, we should
multiply the vector by the inverse of the transpose of the upper-left 3×3
submatrix of the model–view matrix. This is known as the normal matrix,
and you're free to implement it and put it in its own uniform if you like.
However, if your model–view matrix contains only translation, uniform
scale (no shear), and rotation, you can use it directly. Don't forget, the
normal is a three-element vector, and the model–view matrix is a 4×4
matrix. We need to extend the normal to a four-element vector before we

can multiply the two. We can then take the dot product of the resulting vector with the vector from the viewpoint to any point on the triangle.

If the sign of the dot product is negative, that means the normal is facing away from the viewer and the triangle should be culled. If it is positive, the triangle's normal is pointing toward the viewer, and we should pass the triangle on. The code to transform the face normal, perform the dot product, and test the sign of the result is shown in Listing 8.22.

```
// Calculate the transformed face normal in view space
vec3 transformed_normal = (vec4(normal, 0.0) * mv_matrix).xyz;

// Extract the z component of the transformed normal
float d = normal.z;

// Emit a primitive only if the sign of the z component is positive
if (d > 0.0)
{
    for (int i = 0; i < 3; i++)
    {
        gl_Position = gl_in[i].gl_Position;
        EmitVertex();
    }
    EndPrimitive();
}
```

Listing 8.22: Conditionally emitting geometry in a geometry shader

In Listing 8.22, if the dot product is positive, we copy the input vertices to the output of the geometry shader and call EmitVertex() for each one. If the dot product is negative, we don't do anything at all. This results in the incoming triangle being discarded and nothing being drawn.

In this particular example, we are generating at most one triangle output for each triangle input to the geometry shader. Although the output of the geometry shader is a triangle strip, our strips contain only a single triangle. Therefore, we don't strictly need to make a call to EndPrimitive(). We just leave it there for completeness.

Figure 8.16 shows the result of this shader. In Figure 8.16, the virtual viewer has been moved to different positions. As you can see, different parts of the model have been culled away by the geometry shader. This example isn't particularly useful, but it does demonstrate the geometry shader's ability to perform geometry culling based on application-defined criteria.

Figure 8.16: Geometry culled from different viewpoints

Modifying Geometry in the Geometry Shader

The previous example either discarded geometry or passed it through unmodified. It is also possible to modify vertices as they pass through the geometry shader to create new, derived shapes. Even though your geometry shader is passing vertices on a one-to-one basis (that is, no amplification or culling is taking place), you can still do things that would not be possible with a vertex shader alone. If the input geometry is in the form of triangle strips or fans, for example, the resulting geometry will have shared vertices and shared edges. Using the vertex shader to move shared vertices will move all of the triangles that share that vertex. It is not possible, then, to separate two triangles that share an edge in the original geometry using the vertex shader alone. However, this is trivial using the geometry shader.

Consider a geometry shader that accepts triangles and produces `triangle_strip` as output. The input to a geometry shader that accepts triangles is individual triangles, regardless of whether they originated from a `glDrawArrays()` or a `glDrawElements()` function call, or whether the primitive type was GL_TRIANGLES, GL_TRIANGLE_STRIP, or GL_TRIANGLE_FAN. Unless the geometry shader outputs more than three vertices, the result is independent, unconnected triangles.

In the next example, we "explode" a model by pushing all of the triangles out along their face normals. It doesn't matter whether the original model is drawn with individual triangles or with triangle strips or fans. As in the previous example, the input is triangles, the output is `triangle_strip`, and the maximum number of vertices produced by the geometry shader is three because we're not amplifying or decimating geometry. The setup code for this example is shown in Listing 8.23.

```
#version 330

// Input is triangles, output is triangle strip. Because we're going to do a
// 1-in, 1-out shader producing a single triangle output for each one input,
```

```
// max_vertices can be 3 here.
layout (triangles) in;
layout (triangle_strip, max_vertices=3) out;
```

Listing 8.23: Setting up the "explode" geometry shader

To project the triangle outward, we need to calculate the face normal of each triangle. Again, to do this we can take the cross product of two vectors in the plane of the triangle—two edges of the triangle. For this task, we can reuse the code from Listing 8.21. Now that we have the triangle's face normal, we can project vertices along that normal by an application-controlled amount. That amount can be stored in a uniform (we call it explode_factor) and updated by the application. This simple code is shown in Listing 8.24.

```
for (int i = 0; i < 3; i++)
{
    gl_Position = gl_in[i].gl_Position +
                  vec4(explode_factor * normal, 0.0);
}
```

Listing 8.24: Pushing a face out along its normal

The result of running this geometry shader on a model is shown in Figure 8.17. The model has been deconstructed, and the individual triangles have become visible.

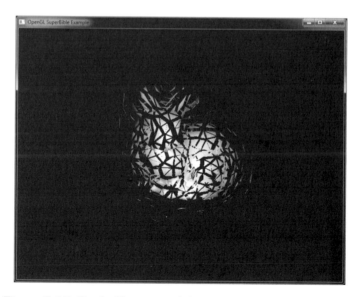

Figure 8.17: Exploding a model using the geometry shader

Generating Geometry in the Geometry Shader

Just as you are not required to call `EmitVertex()` or `EndPrimitive()` at all if you don't want to produce any output from the geometry shader, so it is possible to call `EmitVertex()` and `EndPrimitive()` as many times as you need to produce new geometry. That is, you can continue to call these functions until you reach the maximum number of output vertices that you declared at the beginning of your geometry shader. This functionality can be used for things like making multiple copies of the input or breaking the input into smaller pieces. This is the subject of the next example, which is the `gstessellate` example in the book's accompanying source code. The input to our shader is a tetrahedron centered on the origin. Each face of the tetrahedron is made from a single triangle. We tessellate incoming triangles by producing new vertices halfway along each edge and then moving all of the resulting vertices so that they are variable distances from the origin. This transforms our tetrahedron into a spiked shape.

Because the geometry shader operates in object space (remember, the tetrahedron's vertices are centered on the origin), we do not need to perform any coordinate transforms in the vertex shader. Instead, we do the transforms in the geometry shader after we've generated the new vertices. For this purpose, we need a simple, pass-through vertex shader, which is shown in Listing 8.25.

```
#version 330

in vec4 position;

void main(void)
{
    gl_Position = position;
}
```

Listing 8.25: Pass-through vertex shader

This shader passes just the vertex position to the geometry shader. If other attributes are associated with the vertices, such as texture coordinates or normals, you need to pass them through the vertex shader to the geometry shader as well.

As in the previous example, we accept triangles as input to the geometry shader and produce a triangle strip. We break the strip after every triangle so that we can produce separate, independent triangles. In this example, we produce four output triangles for every input triangle. We need to declare our maximum output vertex count as 12—four triangles times three vertices. We also need to declare a uniform matrix to store the model–view transformation matrix in the geometry shader because we do that transform after generating vertices. Listing 8.26 shows this code.

```
#version 450 core

layout (triangles) in;
layout (triangle_strip, max_vertices = 12) out;

// A uniform to store the model-view-projection matrix
uniform mat4 mvp;
```

Listing 8.26: Setting up the "tessellator" geometry shader

First, let's copy the incoming vertex coordinates into a local variable. Then, given the original, incoming vertices, we find the midpoint of each edge by taking their average. In this case, however, rather than simply dividing by 2, we multiply by a scale factor, which will allow us to alter the spikyness of the resulting object. Code to do this is shown in Listing 8.27.

```
// Copy the incoming vertex positions into some local variables
vec3 a = gl_in[0].gl_Position.xyz;
vec3 b = gl_in[1].gl_Position.xyz;
vec3 c = gl_in[2].gl_Position.xyz;

// Find a scaled version of their midpoints
vec3 d = (a + b) * stretch;
vec3 e = (b + c) * stretch;
vec3 f = (c + a) * stretch;

// Now, scale the original vertices by an inverse of the midpoint
// scale
a *= (2.0 - stretch);
b *= (2.0 - stretch);
c *= (2.0 - stretch);
```

Listing 8.27: Generating new vertices in a geometry shader

Because we plan to generate several triangles using almost identical code, we can put that code into a function (shown in Listing 8.28) and call it from our main tessellation function.

```
void make_face(vec3 a, vec3 b, vec3 c)
{
    vec3 face_normal = normalize(cross(c - a, c - b));
    vec4 face_color = vec4(1.0, 0.2, 0.4, 1.0) * (mat3(mvMatrix) * face_normal
    gl_Position = mvpMatrix * vec4(a, 1.0);
    color = face_color;
    EmitVertex();
```

```
    gl_Position = mvpMatrix * vec4(b, 1.0);
    color = face_color;
    EmitVertex();

    gl_Position = mvpMatrix * vec4(c, 1.0);
    color = face_color;
    EmitVertex();

    EndPrimitive();
}
```

Listing 8.28: Emitting a single triangle from a geometry shader

Notice that the make_face function calculates a face color based on the face's normal in addition to emitting the positions of its vertices. Now, we simply call make_face four times from our main function, which is shown in Listing 8.29.

```
make_face(a, d, f);
make_face(d, b, e);
make_face(e, c, f);
make_face(d, e, f);
```

Listing 8.29: Using a function to produce faces in a geometry shader

Figure 8.18 shows the result of our simple geometry shader–based tessellation program.

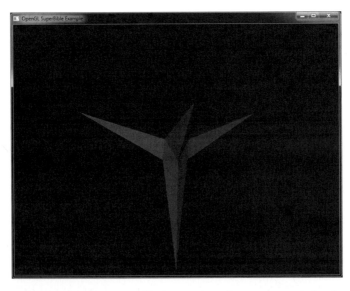

Figure 8.18: Basic tessellation using the geometry shader

Note that using the geometry shader for heavy tessellation may not produce the most optimal performance. If something more complex than the output shown in this example is desired, it's best to use the hardware tessellation functions of OpenGL. However, if simple amplification of between two and four output primitives for each input primitive is desired, the geometry shader is probably the way to go.

Changing the Primitive Type in the Geometry Shader

So far, all of the geometry shader examples we've examined have taken triangles as input and produced triangle strips as output. This doesn't change the geometry type. However, geometry shaders can input and output different types of geometry. For example, you can transform points into triangles or triangles into points. In the normalviewer example, which we'll describe next, we're going to change the geometry type from triangles to lines. For each vertex input to the shader, we take the vertex normal and represent it as a line. We also take the face normal and represent that as another line. This allows us to visualize the model's normals—both at each vertex and for each face. If you want to draw the normals over the top of the original model, however, you must draw everything twice—once with the geometry shader to visualize the normals and once without the geometry shader to show the model. You can't output a mix of two different primitives from a single geometry shader.

For our geometry shader, in addition to the members of the gl_in structure, we need the per-vertex normal, which must be passed through the vertex shader. An updated version of the pass-through vertex shader from Listing 8.25 is given in Listing 8.30.

```
#version 330

in vec4 position;
in vec3 normal;

out Vertex
{
    vec3 normal;
} vertex;

void main(void)
{
    gl_Position = position;
    vertex.normal = normal;
}
```

Listing 8.30: A pass-through vertex shader that includes normals

This code passes the position attribute straight through to the gl_Position built-in variable and places the normal into an output block.

The setup code for the geometry shader is shown in Listing 8.31. In this example we accept triangles and produce line strips, each consisting of a single line. Because we output a separate line for each normal we visualize, we produce two vertices for each vertex consumed, plus two more for the face normal. Therefore, the maximum number of vertices that we output per input triangle is eight. To match the vertex output block that we declared in the vertex shader, we also need to declare a corresponding input interface block in the geometry shader. As we're going to do the object space to world space transformation in the geometry shader, we declare a mat4 uniform called mvp to represent the model–view-projection matrix. This is necessary so that we can keep the vertex's position in the same coordinate system as its normal until we produce the new vertices representing the line.

```
#version 330

layout (triangles) in;
layout (line_strip) out;
layout (max_vertices = 8) out;

in Vertex
{
    vec3 normal;
}  vertex[];

// Uniform to hold the model-view-projection matrix
uniform mat4 mvp;

// Uniform to store the length of the visualized normals
uniform float normal_length;
```

Listing 8.31: Setting up the "normal visualizer" geometry shader

Each input vertex is transformed into its final position and emitted from the geometry shader, and then a second vertex is produced by displacing the input vertex along its normal and transforming that into its final position. This makes all of our normals have a length of 1, but allows any scaling encoded in our model–view-projection matrix to be applied to them along with the model. We multiply the normals by the application-supplied uniform normal_length, allowing them to be scaled to match the model. Our inner loop is shown in Listing 8.32.

```
gl_Position = mvp * gl_in[0].gl_Position;
gs_out.normal = gs_in[0].normal;
```

```
gs_out.color = gs_in[0].color;
EmitVertex();

gl_Position = mvp * (gl_in[0].gl_Position +
                     vec4(gs_in[0].normal * normal_length, 0.0));
gs_out.normal = gs_in[0].normal;
gs_out.color = gs_in[0].color;
EmitVertex();
EndPrimitive();
```

Listing 8.32: Producing lines from normals in the geometry shader

This generates a short line segment at each vertex pointing in the direction of the normal. Now, we need to produce the face normal. To do so, we need to pick a suitable place from which to draw the normal, and we need to calculate the face normal itself in the geometry shader along which to draw the line.

As in the earlier example given in Listing 8.33, we use a cross product of two of the triangle's edges to find the face normal. To pick a starting point for the line, we choose the centroid of the triangle, which is simply the average of the coordinates of the input vertices. Listing 8.33 shows the shader code.

```
vec3 ab = gl_in[1].gl_Position.xyz - gl_in[0].gl_Position.xyz;
vec3 ac = gl_in[2].gl_Position.xyz - gl_in[0].gl_Position.xyz;
vec3 face_normal = normalize(cross(ab, ac));

vec4 tri_centroid = (gl_in[0].gl_Position +
                     gl_in[1].gl_Position +
                     gl_in[2].gl_Position) / 3.0;

gl_Position = mvp * tri_centroid;
gs_out.normal = gs_in[0].normal;
gs_out.color = gs_in[0].color;
EmitVertex();

gl_Position = mvp * (tri_centroid +
                     vec4(face_normal * normal_length, 0.0));
gs_out.normal = gs_in[0].normal;
gs_out.color = gs_in[0].color;
EmitVertex();
EndPrimitive();
```

Listing 8.33: Drawing a face normal in the geometry shader

Now when we render a model, we get the image shown in Figure 8.19.

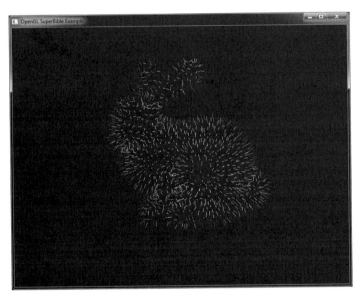

Figure 8.19: Displaying the normals of a model using a geometry shader

Multiple Streams of Storage

When only a vertex shader is present, there is a simple one-in, one-out relationship between the vertices coming into the shader and the vertices stored in the transform feedback buffer. When a geometry shader is present, each shader invocation may store zero, one, or more vertices into the bound transform feedback buffers. In fact, we can actually configure up to four output *streams* and use the geometry shader to send its output to whichever one it chooses. This approach can be used, for example, to sort geometry or to render some primitives while storing other geometry in transform feedback buffers. Nevertheless, several major limitations apply when multiple output streams are used in a geometry shader. First, the output primitive mode from the geometry shader for all streams must be set to `points`. Second, although it's possible to simultaneously render geometry and store data into transform feedback buffers, just the first stream may be rendered—the others are used for storage only. If your application fits within these constraints, however, this functionality can be a very powerful feature.

To set up multiple output streams from your geometry shader, use the `stream` layout qualifier to select one of four streams. Like most other output layout qualifiers, the `stream` qualfier may be applied directly to a single output or to an output block. It can also be applied directly to the `out` keyword without declaring an output variable, in which case it will affect all further output declarations until another `stream` layout qualifier is encountered. For example, consider the following output declarations in a geometry shader:

```
out vec4                    foo; // 'foo' is in stream 0 (the default).
layout (stream=2) out vec4  bar; // 'bar' is part of stream 2.
out vec4                    baz; // 'baz' is back in stream 0.
layout (stream=1) out;           // Everything from here on is in stream 1.
out int                     apple;  // 'apple' and 'orange' are part
out int                     orange; // of stream 1.
layout (stream=3) out MY_BLOCK   // All of 'MY_BLOCK' is in stream 3.
{
    vec3                    purple;
    vec3                    green;
};
```

In the geometry shader, when you call `EmitVertex()`, the vertex will be recorded into the first output stream (stream 0). Likewise, when you call `EndPrimitive()`, it will end the primitive being recorded to stream 0. However, you can call `EmitStreamVertex()` and `EndStreamPrimitive()`, both of which take an integer argument specifying the stream to which to send the output:

```
void EmitStreamVertex(int stream);

void EndStreamPrimitive(int stream);
```

The `stream` argument must be a compile-time constant. If rasterization is enabled, then any primitives sent to stream 0 will be rasterized.

New Primitive Types Introduced by the Geometry Shader

Four new primitive types were introduced with geometry shaders: GL_LINES_ADJACENCY, GL_LINE_STRIP_ADJACENCY, GL_TRIANGLES_ADJACENCY, and GL_TRIANGLE_STRIP_ADJACENCY. These primitive types are truly useful only when you're rendering with a geometry shader active. When the new adjacency primitive types are used, for each line or triangle passed into the geometry shader, the shader has access not only to the vertices defining that primitive, but also to the vertices of the primitive that is next to the one it's processing.

When you render using GL_LINES_ADJACENCY, each line segment consumes four vertices from the enabled attribute arrays. The two center vertices make up the line; the first and last vertices are considered the adjacent vertices. The inputs to the geometry shader are therefore four-element arrays. In fact, because the input and output types of the geometry shader do not have to be related, GL_LINES_ADJACENCY can be seen as a way of sending generalized four-vertex primitives to the geometry shader. The geometry shader is free to transform them into whatever it pleases. For example, your geometry shader could convert each set of four vertices into a triangle strip made up of two triangles. This allows you to render quads using the GL_LINES_ADJACENCY primitive. It should be noted, though, that if you draw using GL_LINES_ADJACENCY when no geometry shader is active, regular lines will be drawn using the two innermost vertices of each set of four vertices. The two outermost vertices will be discarded, and the vertex shader will not run on them at all.

Using GL_LINE_STRIP_ADJACENCY produces a similar effect. The difference is that the entire strip is considered to be a primitive, with one additional vertex on each end. If you send eight vertices to OpenGL using GL_LINES_ADJACENCY, the geometry shader will run twice, whereas if you send the same vertices using GL_LINE_STRIP_ADJACENCY, the geometry shader will run five times.

Figure 8.20 should make things clear. The eight vertices in the top row are sent to OpenGL with the GL_LINES_ADJACENCY primitive mode. The geometry shader runs twice on four vertices each time—ABCD and EFGH. In the second row, the same eight vertices are sent to OpenGL using the GL_LINE_STRIP_ADJACENCY primitive mode. This time, the geometry shader runs five times—ABCD, BCDE, and so on until EFGH. In each case, the solid arrows are the lines that would be rendered if no geometry shader were present.

The GL_TRIANGLES_ADJACENCY primitive mode works similarly to the GL_LINES_ADJACENCY mode. A triangle is sent to the geometry shader for each set of six vertices in the enabled attribute arrays. The first, third, and fifth vertices are considered to make up the real triangle, and the second, fourth, and sixth vertices are considered to be in between the triangle's vertices. In turn, the inputs to the geometry shader are six-element arrays.

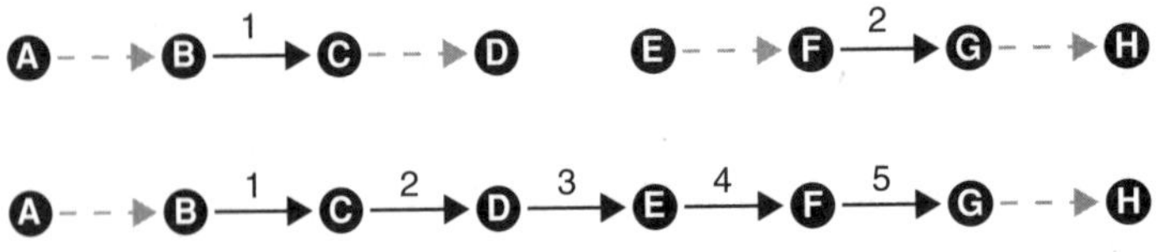

Figure 8.20: Lines produced using lines with adjacency primitives

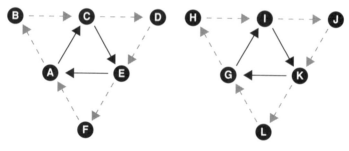

Figure 8.21: Triangles produced using GL_TRIANGLES_ADJACENCY

As before, because you can do anything you want to the vertices using the geometry shader, GL_TRIANGLES_ADJACENCY is a good way to get arbitrary six-vertex primitives into the geometry shader. Figure 8.21 shows this case.

The final, perhaps most complex (or, alternatively, most difficult to understand) of these primitive types is GL_TRIANGLE_STRIP_ADJACENCY. This primitive represents a triangle strip in which every other vertex (the first, third, fifth, seventh, ninth, and so on) forms the strip. The vertices in between are the adjacent vertices. Figure 8.22 demonstrates the principle. In the figure, the vertices A through P represent 16 vertices sent to OpenGL. A triangle strip is generated from every other vertex (A, C, E, G, I, and so on), and the vertices that come between them (B, D, F, H, J, and so on) are the adjacent vertices.

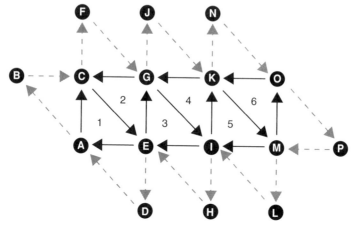

Figure 8.22: Triangles produced using GL_TRIANGLE_STRIP_ADJACENCY

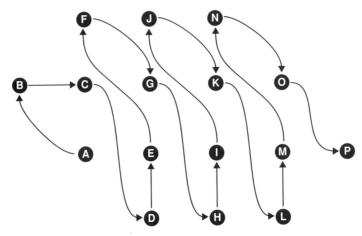

Figure 8.23: Ordering of vertices for GL_TRIANGLE_STRIP_ADJACENCY

There are special cases for the triangles that come at the beginning and end of the strip. Once the strip is started, however, the vertices fall into a regular pattern that is more clearly seen in Figure 8.23.

The rules for the ordering of GL_TRIANGLE_STRIP_ADJACENCY are spelled out clearly in the OpenGL specification—in particular, the special cases are noted there. You are encouraged to read that section of the specification if you want to work with this primitive type.

Rendering Quads Using a Geometry Shader

In computer graphics, the word *quad* is used to describe a quadrilateral—a shape with four sides. Modern graphics APIs do not support rendering quads directly, primarily because modern graphics hardware does not support quads. When a modeling program produces an object made from quads, it will often include the option to export the geometry data by converting each quad into a pair of triangles. These are then rendered by the graphics hardware directly. In some graphics hardware, quads are supported, but internally the hardware will do the conversion from quads to pairs of triangles for you.

In many cases, breaking a quad into a pair of triangles works out just fine and the visual image isn't much different than what would have been rendered had native support for quads been present. However, there is a large class of cases where breaking a quad into a pair of triangles *doesn't* produce the correct result. Take a look at Figure 8.24.

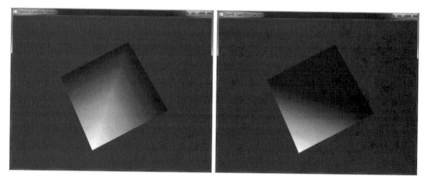

Figure 8.24: Rendering a quad using a pair of triangles

In Figure 8.24, we have rendered a quad as a pair of triangles. In both images, the vertices are wound in the same order. There are three black vertices and one white vertex. In the left image, the split between the triangles runs vertically through the quad. The topmost and two side vertices are black and the bottom-most vertex is white. The seam between the two triangles is clearly visible as a bright line. In the right image, the quad has been split horizontally. This has produced the topmost triangle, which contains only black vertices and is therefore entirely black, and the bottom-most triangle, which contains one white vertex and two black ones, therefore displaying a black to white gradient.

The reason for these differences is that during rasterization and interpolation of the per-vertex colors presented to the fragment shader, we're only rendering a triangle. There are only three vertices' worth of information available to us at any given time; as a consequence, we can't take into consideration the "other" vertex in the quad.

Clearly, neither image is correct, but neither is obviously better than the other. Also, the two images are radically different. If we rely on our export tools—or, even worse, a runtime library—to split quads for us, we do not have any control over which of these two images we'll get. What can we do about that problem? Well, the geometry shader is able to accept primitives with the GL_LINES_ADJACENCY type, and each of these primitives has four vertices—exactly enough to represent a quad. Thus, by using lines with adjacency, we can get four vertices' worth of information at least as far as the geometry shader.

Next, we need to deal with the rasterizer. Recall that the output of the geometry shader can be only points, lines, or triangles. Thus the best we can do is to break each quad (represented by a `lines_adjacency` primitive) into a pair of triangles. You might think this leaves us in the same spot as we were earlier. However, we now have the advantage that we can pass whatever information we like on to the fragment shader.

To correctly render a quad, we must consider the parameterization of the domain over which we want to interpolate our colors (or any other attribute). For triangles, we use barycentric coordinates, which are three-dimensional coordinates used to weight the three corners of the triangle. However, for a quad, we can use a two-dimensional parameterization. Consider the quad shown in Figure 8.25.

Domain parameterization of a quad is two-dimensional and can be represented as a two-dimensional vector. This can be smoothly interpolated over the quad to find the value of the vector at any point within it. For each of the quad's four vertices A, B, C, and D, the values of the vector will be $(0, 0)$, $(0, 1)$, $(1, 0)$, and $(1, 1)$, respectively. We can generate these values per vertex in our geometry shader and pass them to the fragment shader.

To use this vector to retrieve the interpolated values of our other per-fragment attributes, we make the following observation: The value of any interpolant will move smoothly between vertices A and B and between vertices C and D with the x component of the vector. Likewise, a

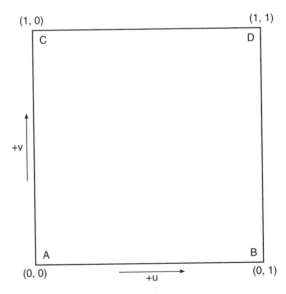

Figure 8.25: Parameterization of a quad

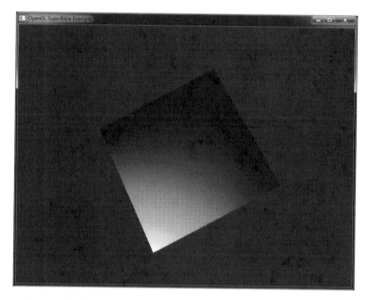

Figure 8.26: Quad rendered using a geometry shader

value along the edge AB will move smoothly to the corresponding value on the edge CD. Thus, given the values of the attributes at the vertices A through D, we can use the domain parameter to interpolate a value for each attribute at any point inside the quad.

Our geometry shader simply passes all four of the per-vertex attributes, unmodified, as flat outputs to the fragment shader, along with a smoothly varying domain parameter per vertex. The fragment shader then uses the domain parameter and *all four* per-vertex attributes to perform the interpolation directly.

The geometry shader is shown in Listing 8.34 and the fragment shader is shown in Listing 8.35; both are taken from the gsquads example. Finally, the result of rendering the same geometry as in Figure 8.24 is shown in Figure 8.26.

```
#version 450 core

layout (lines_adjacency) in;
layout (triangle_strip, max_vertices = 6) out;

in VS_OUT
{
    vec4 color;
} gs_in[4];
```

```
out GS_OUT
{
    flat vec4 color[4];
    vec2 uv;
} gs_out;

void main(void)
{
    gl_Position = gl_in[0].gl_Position;
    gs_out.uv = vec2(0.0, 0.0);
    EmitVertex();

    gl_Position = gl_in[1].gl_Position;
    gs_out.uv = vec2(1.0, 0.0);
    EmitVertex();

    gl_Position = gl_in[2].gl_Position;
    gs_out.uv = vec2(1.0, 1.0);

    // We're only writing the output color for the last
    // vertex here because it's a flat attribute,
    // and the last vertex is the provoking vertex by default
    gs_out.color[0] = gs_in[1].color;
    gs_out.color[1] = gs_in[0].color;
    gs_out.color[2] = gs_in[2].color;
    gs_out.color[3] = gs_in[3].color;
    EmitVertex();

    EndPrimitive();

    gl_Position = gl_in[0].gl_Position;
    gs_out.uv = vec2(0.0, 0.0);
    EmitVertex();

    gl_Position = gl_in[2].gl_Position;
    gs_out.uv = vec2(1.0, 1.0);
    EmitVertex();

    gl_Position = gl_in[3].gl_Position;
    gs_out.uv = vec2(0.0, 1.0);

    // Again, only write the output color for the last vertex
    gs_out.color[0] = gs_in[1].color;
    gs_out.color[1] = gs_in[0].color;
    gs_out.color[2] = gs_in[2].color;
    gs_out.color[3] = gs_in[3].color;
    EmitVertex();

    EndPrimitive();
}
```

Listing 8.34: Geometry shader for rendering quads

```
#version 450 core

in GS_OUT
{
    flat vec4 color[4];
    vec2 uv;
} fs_in;
```

```
out vec4 color;

void main(void)
{
    vec4 c1 = mix(fs_in.color[0], fs_in.color[1], fs_in.uv.x);
    vec4 c2 = mix(fs_in.color[2], fs_in.color[3], fs_in.uv.x);

    color = mix(c1, c2, fs_in.uv.y);
}
```

Listing 8.35: Fragment shader for rendering quads

Multiple Viewport Transformations

In the "Viewport Transformation" section in Chapter 3, you learned about the viewport transformation and discovered how you can specify the rectangle of the window you're rendering into by calling **glViewport()** and **glDepthRange()**. Normally, you would set the viewport dimensions to cover the entire window or screen, depending on whether your application is running on a desktop or taking over the whole display. However, it's possible to move the viewport around and draw into multiple virtual windows within a single larger framebuffer. Furthermore, OpenGL allows you to use multiple viewports *at the same time*—a feature known as viewport arrays.

To use a viewport array, we first need to specify the bounds of the viewports we want to use. To do so, we can call **glViewportIndexedf()** or **glViewportIndexedfv()**, whose prototypes are

```
void glViewportIndexedf(GLuint index,
                        GLfloat x,
                        GLfloat y,
                        GLfloat w,
                        GLfloat h);

void glViewportIndexedfv(GLuint index,
                         const GLfloat * v);
```

For both **glViewportIndexedf()** and **glViewportIndexedfv()**, index is the index of the viewport you wish to modify. Notice that the viewport parameters to the indexed viewport commands are floating-point values rather than the integers used for **glViewport()**. OpenGL supports a minimum[6] of 16 viewports, so index can range from 0 to 15. Likewise, each viewport has its own depth range, which can be specified by calling **glDepthRangeIndexed()**, whose prototype is

---

6. The actual number of viewports supported by OpenGL can be determined by querying the value of GL_MAX_VIEWPORTS.

```
void glDepthRangeIndexed(GLuint index,
                         GLdouble n,
                         GLdouble f);
```

Again, index may be between 0 and 15. In fact, **glViewport()** really sets
the extent of all of the viewports to the same range, and **glDepthRange()**
sets the depth range of all viewports to the same range. If you want to set
more than one or two of the viewports at a time, you might consider using
glViewportArrayv() and **glDepthRangeArrayv()**, whose prototypes are

```
void glViewportArrayv(GLuint first,
                      GLsizei count,
                      const GLfloat * v);

void glDepthRangeArrayv(GLuint first,
                        GLsizei count,
                        const GLdouble * v);
```

These functions set either the viewport extents or depth range for count
viewports starting with the viewport indexed by first to the parameters
specified in the array v. For **glViewportArrayv()**, the array contains a
sequence of x, y, width, height values, in that order. For
glDepthRangeArrayv(), the array contains a sequence of n, f pairs, in that
order.

Once you have specified your viewports, you need to direct geometry into
them. This is done by using a geometry shader. Writing to the built-in
variable gl_ViewportIndex selects the viewport to render into. Listing 8.36
shows what such a geometry shader might look like.

```
#version 450 core

layout (triangles, invocations = 4) in;
layout (triangle_strip, max_vertices = 3) out;

layout (std140, binding = 0) uniform transform_block
{
    mat4 mvp_matrix[4];
};

in VS_OUT
{
    vec4 color;
} gs_in[];

out GS_OUT
{
    vec4 color;
} gs_out;
```

```
void main(void)
{
    for (int i = 0; i < gl_in.length(); i++)
    {
        gs_out.color = gs_in[i].color;
        gl_Position = mvp_matrix[gl_InvocationID] *
                      gl_in[i].gl_Position;
        gl_ViewportIndex = gl_InvocationID;
        EmitVertex();
    }
    EndPrimitive();
}
```

Listing 8.36: Rendering to multiple viewports in a geometry shader

When the shader in Listing 8.36 executes, it produces four invocations of
the shader. On each invocation, it sets the value of gl_ViewportIndex to
the value of gl_InvocationID, directing the result of each of the geometry
shader instances to a separate viewport. Also, for each invocation, it uses a
separate model–view-projection matrix that it retrieves from the uniform
block, transform_block. Of course, a more complex shader could be
constructed, but this example is sufficient to demonstrate the direction of
transformed geometry into a number of different viewports. We have
implemented this code in the multipleviewport example, and the result
of running this shader on our simple spinning cube is shown in
Figure 8.27.

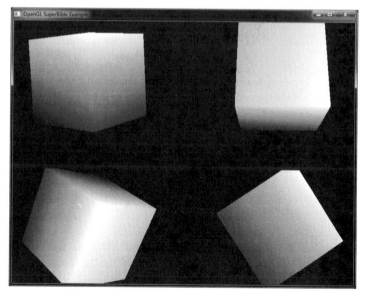

Figure 8.27: Result of rendering to multiple viewports

You can clearly see the four copies of the cube rendered by Listing 8.36 in Figure 8.27. Because each was rendered into its own viewport, it is clipped separately. Where the cubes extend past the edges of their respective viewports, their corners are cut off by OpenGL's clipping stage.

Summary

In this chapter, you have learned about the two tessellation shader stages, the fixed-function tessellation engine, and the way they interact. You have also explored geometry shaders and seen how both the tessellator and the geometry shader can be used to change the amount of data in the OpenGL pipeline. In addition, you have discovered some of the additional functionality in OpenGL that can be accessed using tessellation and geometry shaders. Conceptually, tessellation shaders and geometry shaders process vertices in groups. In the case of tessellation shaders, those groups form patches; in the case of geometry shaders, they form traditional primitives such as as lines and triangles. A variety of special adjacency primitive types are also accessible to geometry shaders. After the geometry shader ends, primitives are eventually sent to the rasterizer and then to per-fragment operations, which are the subject of the next chapter.

Chapter 9

Fragment Processing and the Framebuffer

WHAT YOU'LL LEARN IN THIS CHAPTER

- How data is passed into fragment shaders, how to control the way the data is sent there, and what to do with it once the data gets there.

- How to create your own framebuffers and control the format of the data that they store.

- How to produce more than one output from a single fragment shader.

- How to get data out of your framebuffer and into textures, buffers, and your application's memory.

This chapter is all about the *back end*—everything that happens after rasterization. Here we will take an in-depth look at some of the interesting things you can do with a fragment shader, and we consider what happens to your data once it leaves the fragment shader and how to get it back into your application. We will also look at ways to improve the quality of the images that your applications produce, from rendering in high dynamic range to antialiasing techniques (compensating for the pixelating effect of the display) and alternative color spaces that you can render into.

Fragment Shaders

You have already been introduced to the fragment shader stage. It is the stage in the pipeline where your shader code determines the color of each fragment before it is sent for composition into the framebuffer. The fragment shader runs once per fragment, where a fragment is a virtual element of processing that might end up contributing to the final color of a pixel. Its inputs are generated by the fixed-function interpolation phase that executes as part of rasterization. By default, all members of the input blocks to the fragment shader are smoothly interpolated across the primitive being rasterized, with the endpoints of that interpolation being fed by the last stage in the front end (which may be the vertex, tessellation evaluation, or geometry shader stages). However, you have quite a bit of control over how that interpolation is performed and even whether interpolation is performed at all.

Interpolation and Storage Qualifiers

In earlier chapters, you read about some of the storage qualifiers supported by GLSL. There are a few storage qualifiers that can be used to control interpolation that you can use for advanced rendering. They include `flat` and `noperspective`, which we quickly review here.

Disabling Interpolation

When you declare an input to your fragment shader, that input is generated, or interpolated across the primitive being rendered. However, whenever you pass an integer from the front end to the back end, interpolation must be disabled—something done automatically for you because OpenGL isn't capable of smoothly interpolating integers. It is also possible to explicitly disable interpolation for floating-point fragment shader inputs. Fragment shader inputs for which interpolation has been disabled are known as *flat* inputs (in contrast to *smooth* inputs, referring to the smooth interpolation normally performed by OpenGL). To create a flat input to the fragment shader for which interpolation is not performed, declare it using the `flat` storage[1] qualifier:

```
flat in vec4 foo;
flat in int  bar;
flat in mat3 baz;
```

---

1. It's legal to explicitly declare floating-point fragment shader inputs with the `smooth` storage qualifier, although doing so is normally redundant because it is the default.

You can apply interpolation qualifiers to input blocks, as well, which is where the `smooth` qualifier comes in handy. Interpolation qualifiers applied to blocks are inherited by its members—that is, they are applied automatically to all members of the block. However, it's possible to apply a different qualifier to individual members of the block. Consider this snippet:

```
flat in INPUT_BLOCK
{
    vec4       foo;
    int        bar;
    smooth mat3 baz;
};
```

Here, `foo` has interpolation disabled because it inherits the `flat` qualification from the parent block. `bar` is automatically flat because it is an integer. However, even though `baz` is a member of a block that has the `flat` interpolation qualifier, it is smoothly interpolated because it has the `smooth` interpolation qualifier applied at the member level.

While we are describing this functionality in terms of fragment shader inputs, don't forget that the storage and interpolation qualifiers used on the corresponding outputs in the front end must match those used at the input of the fragment shader. In other words, whatever the last stage in your front end, whether it's a vertex, tessellation evaluation, or geometry shader, you should also declare the matching output with the `flat` qualifier.

When flat inputs to a fragment are in use, their value comes from only one of the vertices in a primitive. When the primitives being rendered are single points, then there is only one choice as to where to get the data. However, when the primitives being rendered are lines or triangles, either the first or last vertex in the primitive is used. The vertex from which the values for flat fragment shader inputs are taken is known as the provoking vertex. You can decide whether it should be the first or last vertex by calling the following function:

```
void glProvokingVertex(GLenum provokeMode);
```

Here, `provokeMode` indicates which vertex should be used and valid values are `GL_FIRST_VERTEX_CONVENTION` and `GL_LAST_VERTEX_CONVENTION`. The default is `GL_LAST_VERTEX_CONVENTION`.

Interpolating without Perspective Correction

As you have learned, OpenGL interpolates the values of fragment shader inputs across the face of primitives such as triangles, and presents a new value to each invocation of the fragment shader. By default, the interpolation is performed smoothly in the space of the primitive being rendered. If you were to look at the triangle flat on, then, the steps that the shader inputs take across its surface would be equal. However, OpenGL performs interpolation in screen space as it steps from pixel to pixel. Very rarely is a triangle seen directly face on, so perspective foreshortening means that the step in each varying from pixel to pixel is not constant—that is, the steps are not linear in screen space. OpenGL corrects for this by using *perspective-correct interpolation*. To implement this feature, it interpolates values that *are* linear in screen space and uses the results to derive the actual values of the shader inputs at each pixel.

Consider a texture coordinate, uv, that is to be interpolated across a triangle. Neither u nor v is linear in screen space. However (due to some math that is beyond the scope of this section), $\frac{u}{w}$ and $\frac{v}{w}$ *are* linear in screen space, as is $\frac{1}{w}$ (the fourth component of the fragment's coordinate). So, what OpenGL actually interpolates is

$$\frac{u}{w}, \frac{v}{w}, \text{and } \frac{1}{w}$$

At each pixel, it reciprocates $\frac{1}{w}$ to find w and then multiplies $\frac{u}{w}$ and $\frac{v}{w}$ by w to find u and v. This provides perspective-correct values of the interpolants to each instance of the fragment shader.

Normally, this outcome is what you want. At other times, however, you don't want this result. If you actually want interpolation to be carried out in screen space regardless of the orientation of the primitive, you can use the `noperspective` storage qualifier

```
noperspective out vec2 texcoord;
```

in the vertex shader (or whatever shader is last in the front end of your pipeline), and

```
noperspective in vec2 texcoord;
```

in the fragment shader, for example. The results of using perspective-correct and screen-space linear (`noperspective`) rendering are shown in Figure 9.1.

The top set of images in Figure 9.1 shows perspective-correct interpolation applied to a pair of triangles as its angle to the viewer changes. Meanwhile,

Figure 9.1: Contrasting perspective-correct and linear interpolation

the bottom set of images in Figure 9.1 shows how the `noperspective` storage qualifier has affected the interpolation of texture coordinates. As the pair of triangles moves to a more and more oblique angle relative to the viewer, the texture becomes more and more skewed.

Per-Fragment Tests

Once the fragment shader has run, OpenGL needs to figure what do to with the fragments that are generated. Geometry has been clipped and transformed into normalized device space, so all of the fragments that are produced by rasterization are known to be on the screen (or inside the window). However, OpenGL then performs a number of other tests on the fragment to determine if and how it should be written to the framebuffer. These tests (in logical order) are the *scissor test*, the *stencil test*, and the *depth test*. They are covered in pipeline order in the following sections.

Scissor Testing

The scissor rectangle is an arbitrary rectangle that you can specify in screen coordinates which allows you to further clip rendering to a particular region. Unlike in the viewport, geometry is not clipped directly against the scissor rectangle, but rather individual fragments are tested against the rectangle as part of post-rasterization[2] processing. As with viewport rectangles, OpenGL supports an array of scissor rectangles. To set them up, you can call **glScissorIndexed()** or **glScissorIndexedv()**, whose prototypes are

```
void glScissorIndexed(GLuint index,
                      GLint left,
                      GLint bottom,
                      GLsizei width,
                      GLsizei height);

void glScissorIndexedv(GLuint index,
                       const GLint * v);
```

For both functions, the index parameter specifies which scissor rectangle you want to change. The left, bottom, width, and height parameters describe a region in window coordinates that defines the scissor rectangle. For **glScissorIndexedv()**, the left, bottom, width, and height parameters are stored (in that order) in an array whose address is passed in v.

As a convenience function, it is possible to set the rectangle for every scissor, regardless of the number supported by the OpenGL implementation, by calling

```
void glScissor(GLint x,
               GLint y,
               GLsizei width,
               GLsizei height);
```

If you wanted the scissor rectangle to be the same for all viewports except for one, you could call **glScissor()** to reset all of the scissor rectangles, and then call **glScissorIndexed()** to update the one that you want to be unique. You can also set a complete set of scissor rectangles in a single call to the following function:

```
void glScissorArrayv(GLuint first,
                     GLsizei count,
                     const GLint *v);
```

This function works just like **glViewportArrayv()** in that it updates the count scissor rectangles starting from first. The array v is organized as x, y, width, height in memory.

To select a scissor rectangle, the gl_ViewportIndex built-in output from the geometry shader is used (yes, the same output that selects the viewport).

---

2. Some OpenGL implementations may apply scissoring either at the end of the geometry stage or in an early part of rasterization. Here, we are describing only the logical OpenGL pipeline.

Given an array of viewports and an array of scissor rectangles, the
same index is used for both arrays. To enable scissor testing globally, call

```
glEnable(GL_SCISSOR_TEST);
```

To disable it, call

```
glDisable(GL_SCISSOR_TEST);
```

If you want to enable or disable scissor testing for only a single viewport
rectangle, call

```
glEnablei(GL_SCISSOR_TEST, index);
```

and

```
glDisablei(GL_SCISSOR_TEST, index);
```

glEnablei() and **glDisablei()** are the *indexed* forms of **glEnable()** and
glDisable(). Here, index is the index of the viewport rectangle for which
you wish to enable or disable scissor testing. As with **glScissorIndexed()**
and **glScissor()**, **glEnablei()** enables and **glDisablei()** disables scissoring
for a single viewport rectangle, and **glEnable()** and **glDisable()** control all
viewport rectangles.

The scissor test starts off disabled, so unless you need to use it, you don't
need to do anything. If we again use the shader of Listing 8.36 (which
employs an instanced geometry shader to write to gl_ViewportIndex),
enable the scissor test, and set some scissor rectangles, we can mask off
sections of rendering. Listing 9.1 shows part of the code from the
multiscissor that sets up our scissor rectangles and Figure 9.2 shows the
result of rendering with this code.

```
// Turn on scissor testing
glEnable(GL_SCISSOR_TEST);

// Each rectangle will be 7/16 of the screen
int scissor_width = (7 * info.windowWidth) / 16;
int scissor_height = (7 * info.windowHeight) / 16;

// Four rectangles - lower left first...
glScissorIndexed(0, 0, 0, scissor_width, scissor_height);

// Lower right...
glScissorIndexed(1,
                 info.windowWidth - scissor_width, 0,
                 info.windowWidth - scissor_width, scissor_height);
```

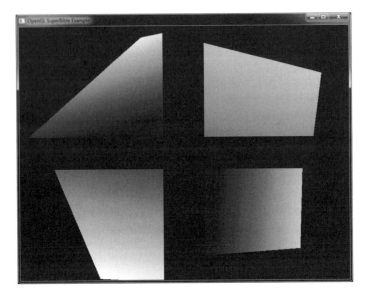

Figure 9.2: Rendering with four different scissor rectangles

```
// Upper left...
glScissorIndexed(2,
                0, info.windowHeight - scissor_height,
                scissor_width, scissor_height);

// Upper right...
glScissorIndexed(3,
                info.windowWidth - scissor_width,
                info.windowHeight - scissor_height,
                scissor_width, scissor_height);
```

Listing 9.1: Setting up scissor rectangle arrays

An important point to remember about the scissor test is that when you clear the framebuffer using **glClear()** or **glClearBufferfv()**, the first scissor rectangle is applied as well. As a consequence, you can clear an arbitrary rectangle of the framebuffer using the scissor rectangle, but errors might arise if you leave the scissor test enabled at the end of a frame and then try to clear the framebuffer ready for the next frame.

Stencil Testing

The next step in the fragment pipeline is the stencil test. You can think of the stencil test as cutting out a shape in cardboard and then using that cutout to spray-paint the shape on a mural. The spray paint hits the wall only in places where the cardboard is cut out (just like a real stencil). If the pixel format of the framebuffer includes a stencil buffer, you can similarly mask your draws to the framebuffer. You can enable stenciling by calling **glEnable()** and passing GL_STENCIL_TEST in the cap parameter. Most implementations support only stencil buffers that contain eight bits, but some configurations may support fewer bits (or more, although this is extremely uncommon).

Your drawing commands can have a direct effect on the stencil buffer, and the value of the stencil buffer can have a direct effect on the pixels you draw. To control interactions with the stencil buffer, OpenGL provides two commands: **glStencilFuncSeparate()** and **glStencilOpSeparate()**. OpenGL lets you set both of these separately for front- and back-facing geometry. The prototypes of **glStencilFuncSeparate()** and **glStencilOpSeparate()** are

```
void glStencilFuncSeparate(GLenum face,
                           GLenum func,
                           GLint ref,
                           GLuint mask);

void glStencilOpSeparate(GLenum face,
                         GLenum sfail,
                         GLenum dpfail,
                         GLenum dppass);
```

First let's look at **glStencilFuncSeparate()**, which controls the conditions under which the stencil test passes or fails. The test is applied separately for front-facing and back-facing primitives, each of which has its own state. You can pass GL_FRONT, GL_BACK, or GL_FRONT_AND_BACK for face, signifying which geometry will be affected. The value of func can be any of the values in Table 9.1; they specify under which conditions geometry will pass the stencil test.

Table 9.1: Stencil Functions

Function	Pass Condition
GL_NEVER	Never pass test.
GL_ALWAYS	Always pass test.
GL_LESS	Reference value is less than buffer value.
GL_LEQUAL	Reference value is less than or equal to buffer value.

Continued

Function	Pass Condition
GL_EQUAL	Reference value is equal to buffer value.
GL_GEQUAL	Reference value is greater than or equal to buffer value.
GL_GREATER	Reference value is greater than buffer value.
GL_NOTEQUAL	Reference value is not equal to buffer value.

The ref value is the reference used to compute the pass or fail result, and the mask parameter lets you control which bits of the reference and the buffer are compared. In pseudocode, the operation of the stencil test is effectively implemented as

```
GLuint current = GetCurrentStencilContent(x, y);
if (compare(current & mask,
            ref & mask,
            front_facing ? front_op : back_op))
{
    passed = true;
}
else
{
    passed = false;
}
```

The next step is to tell OpenGL what to do when the stencil test passes or fails by using **glStencilOpSeparate()**. This function takes four parameters, with the first specifying which faces will be affected. The next three parameters control what happens after the stencil test is performed and can be any of the values in Table 9.2. The second parameter, sfail, is the action taken if the stencil test fails. The dpfail parameter specifies the action taken if the depth buffer test fails, and the final parameter, dppass, specifies what happens if the depth buffer test passes. Because stencil testing comes before depth testing (which we'll discuss in a moment), should the stencil test fail, the fragment is killed right there and no further processing is performed—which explains why there are only three operations here rather than four.

So how does this actually work out? Let's look at a simple example of typical usage shown in Listing 9.2. The first step is to clear the stencil buffer to 0 by calling **glClearBufferiv()** with buffer set to GL_STENCIL, drawBuffer set to 0, and value pointing to a variable containing 0. Next a window border is drawn that may contain details such as a player's score

Table 9.2: Stencil Operations

Function	Result
GL_KEEP	Do not modify the stencil buffer.
GL_ZERO	Set stencil buffer value to 0.
GL_REPLACE	Replace stencil value with reference value.
GL_INCR	Increment stencil with saturation.
GL_DECR	Decrement stencil with saturation.
GL_INVERT	Bitwise invert stencil value.
GL_INCR_WRAP	Increment stencil without saturation.
GL_DECR_WRAP	Decrement stencil without saturation.

and statistics. To set the stencil test to always pass with the reference value of 1, you call **glStencilFuncSeparate()**. Next, tell OpenGL to replace the value in the stencil buffer only when the depth test passes by calling **glStencilOpSeparate()** followed by rendering the border geometry. This turns the border area pixels to 1 while the rest of the framebuffer remains at 0. Finally, set up the stencil state so that the stencil test will pass only if the stencil buffer value is 0 and then render the rest of the scene. This causes all pixels that would overwrite the border we just drew to fail the stencil test and not be drawn to the framebuffer. Listing 9.2 shows an example of how stencil testing can be used.

```
// Clear stencil buffer to 0
const GLint zero;
glClearBufferiv(GL_STENCIL, 0, &zero);

// Set up stencil state for border rendering
glStencilFuncSeparate(GL_FRONT, GL_ALWAYS, 1, 0xff);
glStencilOpSeparate(GL_FRONT, GL_KEEP, GL_ZERO, GL_REPLACE);

// Render border decorations
. . .

// Now, border decoration pixels have a stencil value of 1.
// All other pixels have a stencil value of 0.

// Set up stencil state for regular rendering;
// fail if pixel would overwrite border
glStencilFuncSeparate(GL_FRONT_AND_BACK, GL_LESS, 1, 0xff);
glStencilOpSeparate(GL_FRONT, GL_KEEP, GL_KEEP, GL_KEEP);

// Render the rest of the scene; will not render over stenciled
// border content
. . .
```

Listing 9.2: Example stencil buffer usage and stencil border decorations

There are also two other stencil functions: **glStencilFunc()** and **glStencilOp()**. They behave just as **glStencilFuncSeparate()** and **glStencilOpSeparate()** would if you were to set the face parameter to GL_FRONT_AND_BACK.

Controlling Updates to the Stencil Buffer

By clever manipulation of the stencil operation modes (setting them all to the same value, or judicious use of GL_KEEP, for example), you can perform some relatively flexible operations on the stencil buffer. However, beyond this, it's possible to control updates to individual bits of the stencil buffer. The **glStencilMaskSeparate()** function takes a bitfield indicating which bits in the stencil buffer should be updated and which should be left alone. Its prototype is

```
void glStencilMaskSeparate(GLenum face, GLuint mask);
```

As with the stencil test function there are two sets of state—one for front-facing primitives and one for back-facing primitives. Just as with **glStencilFuncSeparate()**, the face parameter specifies which types of primitives should be affected. The mask parameter is a bitfield that maps to the bits in the stencil buffer—if the stencil buffer has fewer than 32 bits (8 is the maximum supported by most current OpenGL implementations), only that many of the least-significant bits of mask are used. If a mask bit is set to 1, the corresponding bit in the stencil buffer can be updated. Conversely, if the mask bit is 0, the corresponding stencil bit will not be written to. For instance, consider the following code:

```
GLuint mask = 0x000F;
glStencilMaskSeparate(GL_FRONT, mask);
glStencilMaskSeparate(GL_BACK, ~mask);
```

In this example, the first call to **glStencilMaskSeparate()** affects front-facing primitives and enables the lower four bits of the stencil buffer for writing while leaving the rest disabled. The second call to **glStencilMaskSeparate()** sets the opposite mask for back-facing primitives. This essentially allows you to pack two stencil values together into an 8-bit stencil buffer—the lower four bits being used for front-facing primitives and the upper four bits being used for back-facing primitives.

Depth Testing

After stencil operations are complete and if depth testing is enabled, OpenGL tests the depth value of a fragment against the existing content of the depth buffer. If depth writes are also enabled and the fragment has passed the depth test, the depth buffer is updated with the depth value of the fragment. If the depth test fails, the fragment is discarded and does not pass to the following fragment operations.

The input to the primitive assembly stage is a set of vertex positions that make up primitives. Each has a z coordinate. This coordinate is scaled and biased such that the normal[3] visible range of values lies between 0 and 1. This is the value that's usually stored in the depth buffer. During depth testing, OpenGL reads the depth value of the fragment from the depth buffer at the current fragment's coordinate and compares it to the generated depth value for the fragment being processed.

You can choose which comparison operator is used to figure out if the fragment "passed" the depth test. To set the depth comparison operator (or *depth function*), call **glDepthFunc()**, whose prototype is

```
void glDepthFunc(GLenum func);
```

Here, func is one of the available depth comparison operators. The legal values for func and what they mean are shown in Table 9.3.

Table 9.3: Depth Comparison Functions

Function	Meaning
GL_ALWAYS	The depth test always passes—all fragments are considered to have passed the depth test.
GL_NEVER	The depth test never passes—all fragments are considered to have failed the depth test.
GL_LESS	The depth test passes if the new fragment's depth value is less than the old fragment's depth value.
GL_LEQUAL	The depth test passes if the new fragment's depth value is less than or equal to the old fragment's depth value.
GL_EQUAL	The depth test passes if the new fragment's depth value is equal to the old fragment's depth value.

Continued

---

3. It's possible to turn off this visibility check and consider all fragments to be visible, even if they lie outside the 0 to 1 range that is stored in the depth buffer.

Function	Meaning
GL_NOTEQUAL	The depth test passes if the new fragment's depth value is not equal the old fragment's depth value.
GL_GREATER	The depth test passes if the new fragment's depth value is greater than the old fragment's depth value.
GL_GEQUAL	The depth test passes if the new fragment's depth value is greater than or equal to the old fragment's depth value.

If the depth test is disabled, it is as if the depth test always passes (i.e., the depth function is set to GL_ALWAYS), with one exception: The depth buffer is updated only when the depth test is enabled. If you want your geometry to be written into the depth buffer unconditionally, you must enable the depth test and set the depth function to GL_ALWAYS. By default, the depth test is disabled. To turn it on, call

```
glEnable(GL_DEPTH_TEST);
```

To turn it off again, simply call **glDisable()** with the GL_DEPTH_TEST parameter. It is a very common mistake to disable the depth test and expect it to be updated. Again, the depth buffer is not updated unless the depth test is also enabled, so if you want to render into the depth buffer without testing, you need to *enable* depth testing and set the depth test mode to GL_ALWAYS.

Controlling Updates of the Depth Buffer

Writes to the depth buffer can be turned on and off, regardless of the result of the depth test. Remember, the depth buffer is updated only if the depth test is turned on (although the test function can be set to GL_ALWAYS if you don't actually need depth testing and just wish to update the depth buffer). The **glDepthMask()** function takes a Boolean flag that turns writes to the depth buffer on if it's GL_TRUE and off if it's GL_FALSE. For example,

```
glDepthMask(GL_FALSE);
```

will turn writes to the depth buffer off, regardless of the result of the depth test. You can use this, for example, to draw geometry that should be tested against the depth buffer, but that shouldn't update it. By default, the depth mask is set to GL_TRUE, which means you won't need to change it if you want depth testing and writing to behave in the usual way.

Depth Clamping

OpenGL represents the depth of each fragment as a finite number, scaled between 0 and 1. A fragment with a depth of 0 is intersecting the near plane (and would be jabbing you in the eye if it were real), and a fragment with a depth of 1 is at the farthest representable depth but not infinitely far away. To eliminate the far plane and draw things at any arbitrary distance, we would need to store arbitrarily large numbers in the depth buffer—something that's not really possible. To get around this, OpenGL has the option to turn off clipping against the near and far planes and instead clamp the generated depth values to the range 0 to 1. This means that any geometry that protrudes behind the near plane or beyond the far plane will essentially be projected onto that plane.

To enable depth clamping (and simultaneously turn off clipping against the near and far planes), call

```
glEnable(GL_DEPTH_CLAMP);
```

To disable depth clamping, call

```
glDisable(GL_DEPTH_CLAMP);
```

Figure 9.3 illustrates the effect of enabling depth clamping and drawing a primitive that intersects the near plane. It is simpler to demonstrate this in two dimensions, and so the left image in Figure 9.3 displays the view frustum as if we are looking straight down on it. The dark line represents the primitive that would have been clipped against the near plane, and the dotted line represents the portion of the primitive that was clipped away.

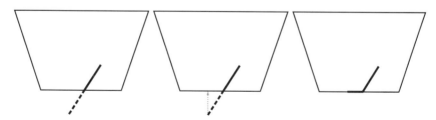

Figure 9.3: Effect of depth clamping at the near plane

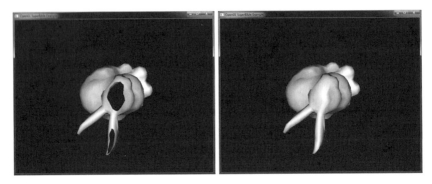

Figure 9.4: A clipped object with and without depth clamping

When depth clamping is enabled, rather than clipping the primitive, the depth values that would have been generated outside the range 0 to 1 are clamped into that range, effectively projecting the primitive onto the near plane (or the far plane, if the primitive would have clipped that). The center image in Figure 9.3 shows this projection. What actually gets rendered is shown in the right image in Figure 9.3. The dark line represents the values that eventually get written into the depth buffer. Figure 9.4 shows how this translates to a real application.

In the left image in Figure 9.4, the geometry has become so close to the viewer that it is partially clipped against the near plane. As a result, the portions of the polygons that would have been behind the near plane are simply not drawn; their absence leaves a large hole in the model. You can see right through to the other side of the object, and the image is quite visibly incorrect. In the right image in Figure 9.4, depth clamping has been enabled. As you can see, the geometry that was lost in the left image is back and fills the hole in the object. The values in the depth buffer aren't technically correct, but this hasn't translated into visual anomalies and the picture produced looks better than that in the left image.

Early Testing

Logically, the depth and stencil tests occur *after* the fragment has been shaded, but most graphics hardware is capable of performing the tests before your shader runs and avoiding the cost of executing that shader if the ownership test fails. However, if a shader has side effects (such as directly writing to a texture) or would otherwise affect the outcome of the test, OpenGL can't perform the tests first, and must always run your shader. If it did not, its behavior would not match the logical specification that defines the depth test as running *after* the shader. In addition, it must always wait for the shader to finish executing before it can perform depth testing or update the stencil buffer.

One particular example of something you can do in your shader that will stop OpenGL from performing the depth test before executing it is writing to the built-in gl_FragDepth output. The special built-in variable gl_FragDepth is available for you as a place to write an updated depth value. If the fragment shader doesn't write to this variable, the interpolated depth generated by OpenGL is used as the fragment's depth value. Your fragment shader can either calculate an entirely new value for gl_FragDepth or derive one from the value gl_FragCoord.z. This new value is subsequently used by OpenGL both as the reference for the depth test and as the value written to the depth buffer should the depth test pass. You can use this functionality, for example, to slightly perturb the values in the depth buffer and create physically bumpy surfaces. Of course, you'd need to shade such surfaces appropriately to make them appear bumpy, but when new objects are tested against the content of the depth buffer, the result will match the shading.

Because your shader changes the fragment's depth value when you write to gl_FragDepth, there's no way that OpenGL can perform the depth test before the shader runs because it doesn't know what you're going to put there. For this scenario, OpenGL provides some layout qualifiers that let you tell it what you plan to do with the depth value.

Recall that the range of values in the depth buffer are between 0.0 and 1.0, and that the depth test comparison operators include functions such as GL_LESS and GL_GREATER. Now, if you set the depth test function to GL_LESS (which would pass for any fragment that is *closer* to the viewer than what is currently in the framebuffer), for example, then if you set gl_FragDepth to a value that is less than it would have been otherwise, the fragment will pass the depth test regardless of what the shader does, and the original test result will remain valid. In this case, OpenGL now knows that it can perform the depth test before running your fragment shader, even though the logical pipeline has it running afterward.

The layout qualifier you use to tell OpenGL what you're going to do to the depth is applied to a *redeclaration* of gl_FragDepth. The redeclaration of gl_FragDepth can take any of the following forms:

```
layout (depth_any) out float gl_FragDepth;
layout (depth_less) out float gl_FragDepth;
layout (depth_greater) out float gl_FragDepth;
layout (depth_unchanged) out float gl_FragDepth;
```

If you use the depth_any layout qualifier, you're telling OpenGL that you might write *any* value to gl_FragDepth. This is effectively the default—if OpenGL sees that your shader writes to gl_FragDepth, it has no idea what you did to it and assumes that the result could be anything. If you specify depth_less, you're effectively saying that whatever you write to gl_FragDepth will result in the fragment's depth value being *less* than it would have been otherwise. In this case, results from the GL_LESS and GL_LEQUAL comparison functions remain valid. Similarly, using depth_greater indicates that your shader will only make the fragment's depth *greater* than it would have been and, therefore, the results of the GL_GREATER and GL_GEQUAL tests remain valid.

The final qualifier, depth_unchanged, is somewhat unique. It tells OpenGL that whatever you do to gl_FragDepth, it's free to assume you haven't written anything to this variable that would change the result of the depth test. In the case of depth_any, depth_less, and depth_greater, although OpenGL becomes free to perform depth testing before your shader executes under certain circumstances, there are still times when it must run your shader and wait for it to finish. With depth_unchanged, you are telling OpenGL that no matter what you do with the fragment's depth value, the original result of the test remains valid. You might choose to use this if you plan to perturb the fragment's depth slightly, but not in a way that would make it intersect any other geometry in the scene (or if you don't care if it does).

Regardless of which layout qualifier you apply to a redecalaration of gl_FragDepth and what OpenGL decides to do about it, the value you write into gl_FragDepth will be clamped into the range 0.0 to 1.0 and then written into the depth buffer.

Color Output

The color output stage is the last part of the OpenGL pipeline before fragments are written to the framebuffer. It determines what happens to your color data between when it leaves your fragment shader and when it is finally displayed to the user.

Blending

For fragments that pass the per-fragment tests, *blending* is performed. Blending allows you to combine the incoming source color with the color already in the color buffer or with other constants using one of the many supported blend equations. If the buffer you are drawing to is fixed-point, the incoming source colors will be clamped to 0.0 to 1.0 before any blending operations occur. Blending is enabled by calling

```
glEnable(GL_BLEND);
```

and disabled by calling

```
glDisable(GL_BLEND);
```

The blending functionality of OpenGL is powerful and highly configurable. It works by multiplying the source color (the value produced by your shader) by the *source factor*, then multiplying the color in the framebuffer by the *destination factor*, and then combining the results of these multiplications using an operation that you can choose called the *blend equation*.

Blend Functions

To choose the source and destination factors by which OpenGL will multiply the result of your shader and the value in the framebuffer, respectively, you can call **glBlendFunc()** or **glBlendFuncSeparate()**. **glBlendFunc()** lets you set the source and destination factors for all four channels of data (red, green, blue, and alpha). **glBlendFuncSeparate()** allows you to set one source and destination factor for the red, green, and blue channels and another source and destination factor for the alpha channel.

```
glBlendFuncSeparate(GLenum srcRGB, GLenum dstRGB,
                    GLenum srcAlpha, GLenum dstaAlpha);

glBlendFunc(GLenum src, GLenum dst);
```

The possible values for these calls are found in Table 9.4. There are four sources of data that might be used in a blending function: the first source color (R_{s0}, G_{s0}, B_{s0}, and A_{s0}), the second source color (R_{s1}, G_{s1}, B_{s1}, and A_{s1}), the destination color (R_d, G_d, B_d, and A_d), and the constant blending color (R_c, G_c, B_c, and A_c). The last value, the constant blending color, can be set by calling **glBlendColor()**:

```
glBlendColor(GLfloat red, GLfloat green,
             GLfloat blue, GLfloat alpha);
```

In addition to all of these sources, the constant values 0 and 1 can be used as any of the product terms.

Table 9.4: Blend Functions

Blend Function	RGB	Alpha
GL_ZERO	$(0, 0, 0)$	0
GL_ONE	$(1, 1, 1)$	1
GL_SRC_COLOR	(R_{s0}, G_{s0}, B_{s0})	A_{s0}
GL_ONE_MINUS_SRC_COLOR	$(1, 1, 1) - (R_{s0}, G_{s0}, B_{s0})$	$1 - A_{s0}$
GL_DST_COLOR	(R_d, G_d, B_d)	A_d
GL_ONE_MINUS_DST_COLOR	$(1, 1, 1) - (R_d, G_d, B_d)$	$1 - A_d$
GL_SRC_ALPHA	(A_{s0}, A_{s0}, A_{s0})	A_{s0}
GL_ONE_MINUS_SRC_ALPHA	$(1, 1, 1) - (A_{s0}, A_{s0}, A_{s0})$	$1 - A_{s0}$
GL_DST_ALPHA	(A_d, A_d, A_d)	A_d
GL_ONE_MINUS_DST_ALPHA	$(1, 1, 1) - (A_d, A_d, A_d)$	$1 - A_d$
GL_CONSTANT_COLOR	(R_c, G_c, B_c)	A_c
GL_ONE_MINUS_CONSTANT_COLOR	$(1, 1, 1) - (R_c, G_c, B_c)$	$1 - A_c$
GL_CONSTANT_ALPHA	(A_c, A_c, A_c)	A_c
GL_ONE_MINUS_CONSTANT_ALPHA	$(1, 1, 1) - (A_c, A_c, A_c)$	$1 - A_c$
GL_ALPHA_SATURATE	(f, f, f) $f = \min(A_{s0}, 1 - A_d)$	1
GL_SRC1_COLOR	(R_{s1}, G_{s1}, B_{s1})	A_{s1}
GL_ONE_MINUS_SRC1_COLOR	$(1, 1, 1) - (R_{s1}, G_{s1}, B_{s1})$	$1 - A_{s1}$
GL_SRC1_ALPHA	(A_{s1}, A_{s1}, A_{s1})	A_{s1}
GL_ONE_MINUS_SRC1_ALPHA	$(1, 1, 1) - (A_{s1}, A_{s1}, A_{s1})$	$1 - A_{s1}$

As a simple example, consider the code shown in Listing 9.3. This code clears the framebuffer to a mid-orange color, turns on blending, sets the blend color to a mid-blue color, and then draws a small cube with every possible combination of source and destination blending function.

```
static const GLfloat orange[] = { 0.6f, 0.4f, 0.1f, 1.0f };
glClearBufferfv(GL_COLOR, 0, orange);

static const GLenum blend_func[] =
{
    GL_ZERO,
    GL_ONE,
    GL_SRC_COLOR,
    GL_ONE_MINUS_SRC_COLOR,
    GL_DST_COLOR,
    GL_ONE_MINUS_DST_COLOR,
    GL_SRC_ALPHA,
    GL_ONE_MINUS_SRC_ALPHA,
    GL_DST_ALPHA,
    GL_ONE_MINUS_DST_ALPHA,
```

```
            GL_CONSTANT_COLOR,
            GL_ONE_MINUS_CONSTANT_COLOR,
            GL_CONSTANT_ALPHA,
            GL_ONE_MINUS_CONSTANT_ALPHA,
            GL_SRC_ALPHA_SATURATE,
            GL_SRC1_COLOR,
            GL_ONE_MINUS_SRC1_COLOR,
            GL_SRC1_ALPHA,
            GL_ONE_MINUS_SRC1_ALPHA
        };
        static const int num_blend_funcs = sizeof(blend_func) /
                                    sizeof(blend_func[0]);
        static const float x_scale = 20.0f / float(num_blend_funcs);
        static const float y_scale = 16.0f / float(num_blend_funcs);
        const float t = (float)currentTime;

        glEnable(GL_BLEND);
        glBlendColor(0.2f, 0.5f, 0.7f, 0.5f);
        for (j = 0; j < num_blend_funcs; j++)
        {
            for (i = 0; i < num_blend_funcs; i++)
            {
                vmath::mat4 mv_matrix =
                    vmath::translate(9.5f - x_scale * float(i),
                                     7.5f - y_scale * float(j),
                                     -50.0f) *
                        vmath::rotate(t * -45.0f, 0.0f, 1.0f, 0.0f) *
                        vmath::rotate(t * -21.0f, 1.0f, 0.0f, 0.0f);

                glUniformMatrix4fv(mv_location, 1, GL_FALSE, mv_matrix);

                glBlendFunc(blend_func[i], blend_func[j]);

                glDrawElements(GL_TRIANGLES, 36, GL_UNSIGNED_SHORT, 0);
            }
        }
```

Listing 9.3: Rendering with all blending functions

The result of rendering with the code in Listing 9.3 is shown in Figure 9.5. This image is also shown in Color Plate 1 and was generated by the blendmatrix sample application.

Dual-Source Blending

You may have noticed that some of the factors in Table 9.4 use source 0 colors (R_{s0}, G_{s0}, B_{s0}, and A_{s0}), and others use source 1 colors (R_{s1}, G_{s1}, B_{s1}, and A_{s1}). Your shaders can export more than one final color for a given color buffer by setting up the outputs used in your shader and assigning them indices using the index layout qualifier. An example is shown below:

```
layout (location = 0, index = 0) out vec4 color0;
layout (location = 0, index = 1) out vec4 color1;
```

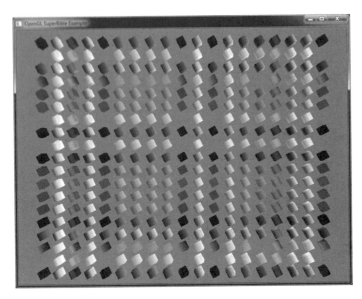

Figure 9.5: All possible combinations of blending functions

Here, color0_0 will be used for the GL_SRC_COLOR factor and color0_1 will be used for the GL_SRC1_COLOR. When you use dual-source blending functions, the number of separate color buffers that you can use might be limited. You can find out how many dual output buffers are supported by querying the value of GL_MAX_DUAL_SOURCE_DRAW_BUFFERS.

Blend Equation

Once the source and destination factors have been multiplied by the source and destination colors, the two products need to be combined together. This is done using an equation that you can set by calling **glBlendEquation()** or **glBlendEquationSeparate()**. As with the blend functions, you can choose one blend equation for the red, green, and blue channels and another for the alpha channel—use **glBlendEquationSeparate()** to do this. If you want both equations to be the same, you can call **glBlendEquation()**.

```
glBlendEquation(GLenum mode);

glBlendEquationSeparate(GLenum modeRGB,
                        GLenum modeAlpha);
```

For **glBlendEquation()**, the sole parameter, mode, selects the same mode for all of the red, green, blue, and alpha channels. For **glBlendEquationSeparate()**, an equation can be chosen for the red, green,

Equation	RGB	Alpha
GL_FUNC_ADD	$S_{rgb} * RGB_s +$ $D_{rgb} * RGB_d$	$S_a * A_s +$ $D_a * A_d$
GL_FUNC_SUBTRACT	$S_{rgb} * RGB_s -$ $D_{rgb} * RGB_d$	$S_a * A_s -$ $D_a * A_d$
GL_FUNC_REVERSE_ SUBTRACT	$D_{rgb} * RGB_d -$ $S_{rgb} * RGB_s$	$D_a * A_d -$ $S_a * A_s$
GL_MIN	$\min(RGB_s, RGB_d)$	$\min(A_s, A_d)$
GL_MAX	$\max(RGB_s, RGB_d)$	$\min(A_s, A_d)$

and blue channels (specified in modeRGB) and another for the alpha channel (specified in modeAlpha). The values you pass to the two functions are shown in Table 9.5.

In Table 9.5, RGB_s represents the source red, green, and blue values; RGB_d represents the destination red, green, and blue values; A_s and A_d represent the source and destination alpha values; S_{rgb} and D_{rgb} represent the source and destination blend factors; and S_a and D_a represent the source and destination alpha factors (chosen by **glBlendFunc()** or **glBlendFuncSeparate()**).

Logical Operations

Once the pixel color is in the same format and bit depth as the framebuffer, there are two more steps that can affect the final result. The first allows you to apply a logical operation to the pixel color before it is passed on. When logical operations are enabled, the effects of blending are ignored. Logic operations do not affect floating-point buffers. You can enable logic ops by calling

```
glEnable(GL_COLOR_LOGIC_OP);
```

and disable them by calling

```
glDisable(GL_COLOR_LOGIC_OP);
```

Table 9.6: Logic Operations

Operation	Result
GL_CLEAR	Set all values to 0
GL_AND	Source & Destination
GL_AND_REVERSE	Source & ~Destination
GL_COPY	Source
GL_AND_INVERTED	~Source & Destination
GL_NOOP	Destination
GL_XOR	Source ^Destination
GL_OR	Source | Destination
GL_NOR	~(Source | Destination)
GL_EQUIV	~(Source ^Destination)
GL_INVERT	~Destination
GL_OR_REVERSE	Source | ~Destination
GL_COPY_INVERTED	~Source
GL_OR_INVERTED	~Source | Destination
GL_NAND	~(Source & Destination)
GL_SET	Set all values to 1

Logic operations use the values of the incoming pixel and the existing framebuffer to compute a final value. You can pick the operation that computes the final value by calling **glLogicOp()**. The possible options are listed in Table 9.6. The prototype of **glLogicOp()** is

```
glLogicOp(GLenum op);
```

where op is one of the values from Table 9.6.

Logic operations are applied separately to each color channel, and operations that combine source and destination are performed bitwise on the color values. Logic ops are not commonly used in today's graphics applications but remain part of OpenGL because the functionality is still supported on common GPUs.

Color Masking

One of the last modifications that can be made to a fragment before it is written is *masking*. By now you should recognize that three different types of data can be written by a fragment shader: color, depth, and stencil data. Just as you can mask off updates to the stencil and depth buffers, so you can also apply a mask to the updates of the color buffer.

To mask color writes or prevent color writes from happening, you can use **glColorMask()** and **glColorMaski()**. We briefly introduced **glColorMask()** in Chapter 5, "Data," when we turned on and off writing to the framebuffer. However, you don't have to mask all color channels at once; for instance, you can choose to mask the red and green channels while permitting writes to the blue channel. Each function takes four Boolean parameters that control updates to each of the red, green, blue, and alpha channels of the color buffer. You can pass in GL_TRUE to one of these parameters to allow writes for the corresponding channel to occur, or GL_FALSE to mask these writes. The first function, **glColorMask()**, allows you to mask all buffers currently enabled for rendering; the second function, **glColorMaski()**, allows you to set the mask for a specific color buffer (there can be many if you're rendering off screen). The prototypes of these two functions are

```
glColorMask(GLboolean red,
            GLboolean green,
            GLboolean blue,
            GLboolean alpha);

glColorMaski(GLuint index,
            GLboolean red,
            GLboolean green,
            GLboolean blue,
            GLboolean alpha);
```

For both functions, red, green, blue, and alpha can be set to either GL_TRUE or GL_FALSE to indicate whether the red, green, blue, or alpha channels should be written to the framebuffer. For **glColorMaski()**, index is the index of the color attachment to which masking should apply. Each color attachment can have its own color mask settings. For example, you could write only the red channel to attachment 0, only the green channel to attachment 1, and so on.

Mask Usage

Write masks can be useful for many operations. For instance, if you want to fill a shadow volume with depth information, you can mask off all color writes because only the depth information is important. Or if you want to draw a decal directly to screen space, you can disable depth writes to prevent the depth data from being polluted. The key point about masks is that you can set them and immediately call your normal rendering paths, which may set up necessary buffer state and output all color, depth, and stencil data you would normally use without needing any knowledge of the mask state. You don't have to alter your shaders to not write some value, detach some set of buffers, or change the enabled draw buffers. The rest of your rendering paths can be completely oblivious and still generate the right results.

Off-Screen Rendering

Until now, all of the rendering your programs have performed has been directed into a window, or perhaps the computer's main display. The output of your fragment shader goes into the *back buffer*, which is normally owned by the operating system or window system that your application is running on, and is eventually displayed to the user. Its parameters are set when you choose a format for the rendering context. Because this is a platform-specific operation, you have little control over what the underlying storage format really is. Also, for the samples in this book to run on many platforms, the book's application framework takes care of setting this system up for you, hiding many of the details.

However, OpenGL includes features that allow you to set up your own framebuffer and use it to draw directly into textures. You can then use these textures later for further rendering or processing. You also have a lot of control over the format and layout of the framebuffer. For example, when you use the default framebuffer, it is implicitly sized to the size of the window or display, and rendering outside the display (if the window is obscured or dragged off the side of the screen, for example) is undefined because the corresponding pixels' fragment shaders might not run. However, with a user-supplied framebuffer, the maximum size of the textures you render to is limited only by the maximum supported by the implementation of OpenGL you're running on, and rendering to any location in it is always defined.

User-supplied framebuffers are represented by OpenGL as *framebuffer objects*. As with most objects in OpenGL, you can create one or more framebuffer objects by using the appropriate creation function, `glCreateFramebuffers()`:

```
void glCreateFramebuffers(GLsizei n, GLuint *framebuffers);
```

This function creates n new framebuffer objects and places their names in the array you pass to framebuffers. Of course, you can simply set n to 1 and pass the address of a single GLuint variable in framebuffers.

Alternatively, you can reserve a name for a framebuffer object and bind it to the context to initialize it. To generate names for framebuffer objects, call **glGenFramebuffers()**; to bind a framebuffer to the context, call **glBindFramebuffer()**. The prototypes of these functions are

```
void glGenFramebuffers(GLsizei n,
                       GLuint * framebuffers);

void glBindFramebuffer(GLenum target,
                       GLuint framebuffer);
```

Just like **glCreateFramebuffers()**, **glGenFramebuffers()** takes a count in n and hands back a list of names in framebuffers that you are able to use as framebuffer objects. The **glBindFramebuffer()** function makes your application-supplied framebuffer object the current framebuffer (instead of the default one). The framebuffer is one of the names that you got from a call to **glGenFramebuffers()** and the target parameter will normally be GL_FRAMEBUFFER. However, it's possible to bind two framebuffers at the same time—one for reading and one for writing.

To bind a framebuffer for reading only, set target to GL_READ_FRAMEBUFFER. Likewise, to bind a framebuffer just for rendering, set target to GL_DRAW_FRAMEBUFFER. The framebuffer bound for drawing will be the destination for all of your rendering (including stencil and depth values used during their respective tests and colors read during blending). The framebuffer bound for reading will be the source of data if you want to read back pixel data or copy data from the framebuffer into textures, as we'll explain shortly. Setting target to GL_FRAMEBUFFER actually binds the object to both the read and draw framebuffer targets, and this is normally what you want.

To get back to rendering to the default framebuffer (usually the one associated with the application's window), simply call **glBindFramebuffer()** and pass 0 for the framebuffer parameter.

Once you have created a framebuffer object, you can attach textures to it to serve as the storage for the rendering you're going to do. There are three types of attachment supported by the framebuffer—the depth, stencil, and color attachments, which serve as the depth, stencil, and color buffers, respectively. To attach a texture to a framebuffer, we can call either **glNamedFramebufferTexture()** or **glFramebufferTexture()**, whose prototypes are

```
void glNamedFramebufferTexture(GLuint framebuffer,
                               GLenum attachment,
                               GLuint texture,
                               GLint level);
```

```
void glFramebufferTexture(GLenum target,
                          GLenum attachment,
                          GLuint texture,
                          GLint level);
```

For **glNamedFramebufferTexture()**, framebuffer is the name of the framebuffer object you're going to attach the texture to, whereas for **glFramebufferTexture()**, target is the binding point where the framebuffer object you want to attach a texture to is bound. This should be GL_READ_FRAMEBUFFER, GL_DRAW_FRAMEBUFFER, or just GL_FRAMEBUFFER. In this case, GL_FRAMEBUFFER is considered to be equivalent to GL_DRAW_FRAMEBUFFER; thus, if you use this token, OpenGL will attach the texture to the framebuffer object bound to the GL_DRAW_FRAMEBUFFER target.

attachment tells OpenGL to which attachment you want to attach the texture. It can be GL_DEPTH_ATTACHMENT to attach the texture to the depth buffer attachment, or GL_STENCIL_ATTACHMENT to attach it to the stencil buffer attachment. Because several texture formats include depth and stencil values packed together, OpenGL also allows you to set attachment to GL_DEPTH_STENCIL_ATTACHMENT to indicate that you want to use the same texture for both the depth and stencil buffers.

To attach a texture as the color buffer, set attachment to GL_COLOR_ATTACHMENT0. In fact, you can set attachment to GL_COLOR_ATTACHMENT1, GL_COLOR_ATTACHMENT2, and so on to attach multiple textures for rendering to. We'll get to that possibility momentarily, but first we'll look at an example of how to set up a framebuffer object for rendering to.

Last, texture is the name of the texture you want to attach to the framebuffer, and level is the mipmap level of the texture you want to render into.

Before we can render to the framebuffer's attachments, we need to tell OpenGL that's where we want rendering to go. Usually, rendering goes to the back buffer, which is part of the default framebuffer. When we're rendering to a user-defined framebuffer like the one we just created, we need to tell OpenGL to render to our framebuffer instead of the default one. To do this, call one of the following:

```
void glDrawBuffer(GLenum mode);

void glNamedFramebufferDrawBuffer(GLuint framebuffer, GLenum mode);
```

Which buffer will be drawn to is a property of a framebuffer object (either yours or the default). The **glDrawBuffer()** function implicitly operates on the framebuffer currently bound to GL_DRAW_FRAMEBUFFER, whereas **glNamedFramebufferDrawBuffer()** operates on the framebuffer object you pass in the framebuffer parameter. For both functions, mode specifies where drawing will go. GL_BACK is generally used with the default framebuffer and GL_COLOR_ATTACHMENT0 is often used for off-screen rendering into a user-defined framebuffer. There are many more settings that can be used for rendering to more than one texture at once, rendering directly to the screen, or even rendering stereoscopic images. For now, setting mode to GL_COLOR_ATTACHMENT0 will do what we want. Listing 9.4 shows a complete example of setting up a framebuffer object with a depth buffer and a texture to render into.

```
// Create a framebuffer object and bind it
glCreateFramebuffers(1, &fbo);
glBindFramebuffer(GL_FRAMEBUFFER, fbo);

// Create a texture for our color buffer
glGenTextures(1, &color_texture);
glBindTexture(GL_TEXTURE_2D, color_texture);
glTexStorage2D(GL_TEXTURE_2D, 1, GL_RGBA8, 512, 512);

// We're going to read from this, but it won't have mipmaps,
// so turn off mipmaps for this texture
glTexParameteri(GL_TEXTURE_2D, GL_TEXTURE_MIN_FILTER, GL_LINEAR);
glTexParameteri(GL_TEXTURE_2D, GL_TEXTURE_MAG_FILTER, GL_LINEAR);

// Create a texture that will be our FBO's depth buffer
glGenTextures(1, &depth_texture);
glBindTexture(GL_TEXTURE_2D, depth_texture);
glTexStorage2D(GL_TEXTURE_2D, 1, GL_DEPTH_COMPONENT32F, 512, 512);

// Now, attach the color and depth textures to the FBO
glFramebufferTexture(GL_FRAMEBUFFER,
                     GL_COLOR_ATTACHMENT0,
                     color_texture, 0);
glFramebufferTexture(GL_FRAMEBUFFER,
                     GL_DEPTH_ATTACHMENT,
                     depth_texture, 0);

// Tell OpenGL that we want to draw into the framebuffer's first
// (and only) color attachment
static const GLenum draw_buffers[] = { GL_COLOR_ATTACHMENT0 };
glDrawBuffers(1, draw_buffers);
```

Listing 9.4: Setting up a simple framebuffer object

After this code has executed, all we need to do is call **glBindFramebuffer()** again and pass our newly created framebuffer object, and all rendering will be directed into the depth and color textures we specified. Once we're done rendering into our own framebuffer, we can use the resulting image as a regular texture and read from it in our shaders. Listing 9.5 shows an example of doing this.

```
// Bind our off-screen FBO
glBindFramebuffer(GL_FRAMEBUFFER, fbo);

// Set the viewport and clear the depth and color buffers
glViewport(0, 0, 512, 512);
glClearBufferfv(GL_COLOR, 0, green);
glClearBufferfv(GL_DEPTH, 0, &one);

// Activate our first, non-textured program
glUseProgram(program1);

// Set our uniforms and draw the cube
glUniformMatrix4fv(proj_location, 1, GL_FALSE, proj_matrix);
glUniformMatrix4fv(mv_location, 1, GL_FALSE, mv_matrix);
glDrawArrays(GL_TRIANGLES, 0, 36);

// Now return to the default framebuffer
glBindFramebuffer(GL_FRAMEBUFFER, 0);

// Reset our viewport to the window width and height, clear the
// depth and color buffers
glViewport(0, 0, info.windowWidth, info.windowHeight);
glClearBufferfv(GL_COLOR, 0, blue);
glClearBufferfv(GL_DEPTH, 0, &one);

// Bind the texture we just rendered to for reading
glBindTexture(GL_TEXTURE_2D, color_texture);

// Activate a program that will read from the texture
glUseProgram(program2);

// Set uniforms and draw
glUniformMatrix4fv(proj_location2, 1, GL_FALSE, proj_matrix);
glUniformMatrix4fv(mv_location2, 1, GL_FALSE, mv_matrix);
glDrawArrays(GL_TRIANGLES, 0, 36);

// Unbind the texture and we're done
glBindTexture(GL_TEXTURE_2D, 0);
```

Listing 9.5: Rendering to a texture

The code shown in Listing 9.5 is taken from the basicfbo sample and first binds our user-defined framebuffer, sets the viewport to the dimensions of the framebuffer, and clears the color buffer with a dark green color. It then proceeds to draw our simple cube model. This results in the cube being rendered into the texture we previously attached to the GL_COLOR_ATTACHMENT0 attachment point on the framebuffer. Next, we unbind our FBO, returning to the default framebuffer that represents our window. We render the cube again, this time with a shader that uses the texture we just rendered to. The result is that an image of the first cube we rendered is shown on each face of the second cube. Output of the program is shown in Figure 9.6.

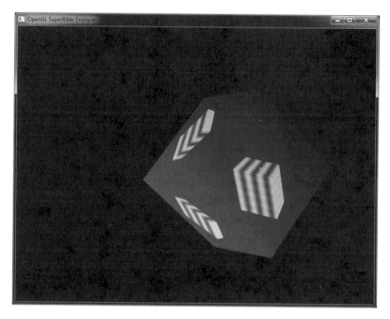

Figure 9.6: Result of rendering into a texture

Multiple Framebuffer Attachments

In the last section, we introduced the concept of user-defined framebuffers, which are also known as FBOs. An FBO allows you to render into textures that you create in your application. Because the textures are owned and allocated by OpenGL, they are decoupled from the operating or window system and so can be extremely flexible. The upper limit on their size depends only on OpenGL and not on the attached displays, for example. You also have full control over their format.

Another extremely useful feature of user-defined framebuffers is that they support multiple attachments. That is, you can attach multiple textures to a single framebuffer and render into them simultaneously with a single fragment shader. Recall that to attach your texture to your FBO, you called **glFramebufferTexture()** or **glNamedFramebufferTexture()** and passed GL_COLOR_ATTACHMENT0 as the attachment parameter, but we mentioned that you can also pass GL_COLOR_ATTACHMENT1, GL_COLOR_ATTACHMENT2, and so on. In fact, OpenGL supports attaching at least eight textures to a single FBO. Listing 9.6 shows an example of setting up an FBO with three color attachments.

```
static const GLenum draw_buffers[] =
{
    GL_COLOR_ATTACHMENT0,
    GL_COLOR_ATTACHMENT1,
    GL_COLOR_ATTACHMENT2
};

// First, generate and bind our framebuffer object
glGenFramebuffers(1, &fbo);
glBindFramebuffer(GL_FRAMEBUFFER, fbo);

// Generate three texture names
glGenTextures(3, &color_texture[0]);

// For each one...
for (int i = 0; i < 3; i++)
{
    // Bind and allocate storage for it
    glBindTexture(GL_TEXTURE_2D, color_texture[i]);
    glTexStorage2D(GL_TEXTURE_2D, 9, GL_RGBA8, 512, 512);

    // Set its default filter parameters
    glTexParameteri(GL_TEXTURE_2D,
                    GL_TEXTURE_MIN_FILTER, GL_LINEAR);
    glTexParameteri(GL_TEXTURE_2D,
                    GL_TEXTURE_MAG_FILTER, GL_LINEAR);

    // Attach it to our framebuffer object as color attachments
    glFramebufferTexture(GL_FRAMEBUFFER,
                         draw_buffers[i], color_texture[i], 0);
}

// Now create a depth texture
glGenTextures(1, &depth_texture);
glBindTexture(GL_TEXTURE_2D, depth_texture);
glTexStorage2D(GL_TEXTURE_2D, 9, GL_DEPTH_COMPONENT32F, 512, 512);

// Attach the depth texture to the framebuffer
glFramebufferTexture(GL_FRAMEBUFFER, GL_DEPTH_ATTACHMENT,
                     depth_texture, 0);

// Set the draw buffers for the FBO to point to the color attachments
glDrawBuffers(3, draw_buffers);
```

Listing 9.6: Setting up an FBO with multiple attachments

To render into multiple attachments from a single fragment shader, we must declare multiple outputs in the shader and associate them with the attachment points. To do this, we use a *layout qualifier* to specify each output's location; this term refers to the index of the attachment to which that output will be sent. Listing 9.7 shows an example.

```
layout (location = 0) out vec4 color0;
layout (location = 1) out vec4 color1;
layout (location = 2) out vec4 color2;
```

Listing 9.7: Declaring multiple outputs in a fragment shader

Once you have declared multiple outputs in your fragment shader, you can write different data into each of them and that data will be directed into the framebuffer color attachment indexed by the output's location. Remember, the fragment shader still executes only once for each fragment produced during rasterization, and the data written to each of the shader's outputs will be written at the same position within each of the corresponding framebuffer attachments.

In Listing 9.6, notice that we're using the **glDrawBuffers()** (plural) function rather than **glDrawBuffer()** (singular). This allows us to set the draw buffers corresponding to each of the locations declared in the shader. The output at location 0 will be written into the buffer specified in the first element of the array passed to **glDrawBuffers()**, the output at location 1 will be written into the second element of the array, and so on. There is no reason for the outputs to be tightly packed—you could use locations 2, 5, and 7 if you wished, so long as you set up the entries in the array passed to **glDrawBuffers()** appropriately. Note, though, that some implementations of OpenGL will not perform as well if you don't tightly pack shader outputs. Furthermore, it's possible to discard some of the outputs of a shader even if it writes to them by setting the corresponding element of the **glDrawBuffers()** array to GL_NONE.

Layered Rendering

In the "Array Textures" section in Chapter 5, we described a form of texture called the *array texture*, which represents a stack of 2D textures arranged as an array of *layers* that you can index into in a shader. It's also possible to render into array textures by attaching them to a framebuffer object and using a geometry shader to specify which layer you want the resulting primitives to be rendered into. Listing 9.8 is taken from the gslayered sample and illustrates how to set up a framebuffer object that uses a 2D array texture as a color attachment. Such a framebuffer is known as a *layered framebuffer*. In addition to creating an array texture to use as a color attachment, you can create an array texture with a depth or stencil format and attach it to the depth or stencil attachment points of the framebuffer object. That texture will then become your depth or stencil buffer, allowing you to perform depth and stencil testing in a layered framebuffer.

```
// Create a texture for our color attachment, bind it, and allocate
// storage for it. This will be 512 x 512 with 16 layers.
GLuint color_attachment;
glGenTextures(1, &color_attachment);

glBindTexture(GL_TEXTURE_2D_ARRAY, color_attachment);
glTexStorage3D(GL_TEXTURE_2D_ARRAY, 1, GL_RGBA8, 512, 512, 16);
```

```
// Do the same thing with a depth buffer attachment
GLuint depth_attachment;
glGenTextures(1, &depth_attachment);

glBindTexture(GL_TEXTURE_2D_ARRAY, depth_attachment);
glTexStorage3D(GL_TEXTURE_2D_ARRAY, 1, GL_DEPTH_COMPONENT, 512, 512, 16);

// Now create a framebuffer object and bind our textures to it
GLuint fbo;
glGenFramebuffers(1, &fbo);
glBindFramebuffer(GL_FRAMEBUFFER, fbo);

glFramebufferTexture(GL_FRAMEBUFFER, GL_COLOR_ATTACHMENT0,
                     color_attachment, 0);
glFramebufferTexture(GL_FRAMEBUFFER, GL_DEPTH_ATTACHMENT,
                     depth_attachment, 0);

// Finally, tell OpenGL that we plan to render to the color
// attachment
static const GLuint draw_buffers[] = { GL_COLOR_ATTACHMENT0 };

glDrawBuffers(1, draw_buffers);
```

Listing 9.8: Setting up a layered framebuffer

Once you have created an array texture and attached it to a framebuffer
object, you can then render into it as normal. If you don't use a geometry
shader, all rendering goes into the first layer of the array—the slice at
index 0. However, if you wish to render into a different layer, you will
need to write a geometry shader. In the geometry shader, the built-in
variable gl_Layer is available as an output. When you write a value into
gl_Layer, that value will be used to index into the layered framebuffer to
select the layer of the attachments to render into. Listing 9.9 shows a
simple geometry shader that renders 16 copies of the incoming geometry,
each with a different model–view matrix, into an array texture and passes
a per-invocation color along to the fragment shader.

```
#version 450 core

// 16 invocations of the geometry shader, triangles in
// and triangles out
layout (invocations = 16, triangles) in;
layout (triangle_strip, max_vertices = 3) out;

in VS_OUT
{
    vec4 color;
    vec3 normal;
} gs_in[];

out GS_OUT
{
    vec4 color;
    vec3 normal;
} gs_out;
```

```
// Declare a uniform block with one projection matrix and
// 16 model-view matrices
layout (binding = 0) uniform BLOCK
{
    mat4 proj_matrix;
    mat4 mv_matrix[16];
};

void main(void)
{
    int i;

    // 16 colors to render our geometry
    const vec4 colors[16] = vec4[16](
        vec4(0.0, 0.0, 1.0, 1.0), vec4(0.0, 1.0, 0.0, 1.0),
        vec4(0.0, 1.0, 1.0, 1.0), vec4(1.0, 0.0, 1.0, 1.0),
        vec4(1.0, 1.0, 0.0, 1.0), vec4(1.0, 1.0, 1.0, 1.0),
        vec4(0.0, 0.0, 0.5, 1.0), vec4(0.0, 0.5, 0.0, 1.0),
        vec4(0.0, 0.5, 0.5, 1.0), vec4(0.5, 0.0, 0.0, 1.0),
        vec4(0.5, 0.0, 0.5, 1.0), vec4(0.5, 0.5, 0.0, 1.0),
        vec4(0.5, 0.5, 0.5, 1.0), vec4(1.0, 0.5, 0.5, 1.0),
        vec4(0.5, 1.0, 0.5, 1.0), vec4(0.5, 0.5, 1.0, 1.0)
    );

    for (i = 0; i < gl_in.length(); i++)
    {
        // Pass through all the geometry
        gs_out.color = colors[gl_InvocationID];
        gs_out.normal = mat3(mv_matrix[gl_InvocationID]) * gs_in[i].normal;
        gl_Position = proj_matrix *
                        mv_matrix[gl_InvocationID] *
                        gl_in[i].gl_Position;
        // Assign gl_InvocationID to gl_Layer to direct rendering
        // to the appropriate layer
        gl_Layer = gl_InvocationID;
        EmitVertex();
    }

    EndPrimitive();
}
```

Listing 9.9: Layered rendering using a geometry shader

The result of running the geometry shader shown in Listing 9.9 is that we
have an array texture with a different view of a model in each slice.
Obviously, we can't directly display the contents of an array texture, so we
must now use our texture as the source of data in another shader. The
vertex shader in Listing 9.10 along with the corresponding fragment
shader in Listing 9.11 display the contents of an array texture.

```
#version 450 core

out VS_OUT
{
    vec3 tc;
} vs_out;
```

```
void main(void)
{
    int vid = gl_VertexID;
    int iid = gl_InstanceID;
    float inst_x = float(iid % 4) / 2.0;
    float inst_y = float(iid >> 2) / 2.0;

    const vec4 vertices[] = vec4[](vec4(-0.5, -0.5, 0.0, 1.0),
                                   vec4( 0.5, -0.5, 0.0, 1.0),
                                   vec4( 0.5,  0.5, 0.0, 1.0),
                                   vec4(-0.5,  0.5, 0.0, 1.0));

    vec4 offs = vec4(inst_x - 0.75, inst_y - 0.75, 0.0, 0.0);

    gl_Position = vertices[vid] *
                vec4(0.25, 0.25, 1.0, 1.0) + offs;
    vs_out.tc = vec3(vertices[vid].xy + vec2(0.5), float(iid));
}
```

Listing 9.10: Displaying an array texture—vertex shader

The vertex shader in Listing 9.10 simply produces a quad based on the
vertex index. In addition, it offsets the quad using a function of the
instance index such that rendering 16 instances will produce a 4×4 grid of
quads. Finally, it produces a texture coordinate using the x and y
components of the vertex along with the instance index as the third
component. Because we will use this coordinate to fetch from an array
texture, this third component will select the layer. The fragment shader in
Listing 9.11 simply reads from the array texture using the supplied texture
coordinates and sends the result to the color buffer.

```
#version 450 core

layout (binding = 0) uniform sampler2DArray tex_array;

layout (location = 0) out vec4 color;

in VS_OUT
{
    vec3 tc;
} fs_in;

void main(void)
{
    color = texture(tex_array, fs_in.tc);
}
```

Listing 9.11: Displaying an array texture—fragment shader

The result of the program is shown in Figure 9.7. As you can see, 16 copies
of the torus have been rendered, each with a different color and

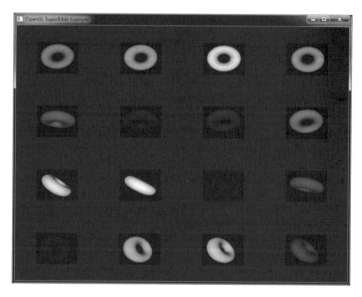

Figure 9.7: Result of the layered rendering example

orientation. Each of the 16 copies is then drawn into the window by reading from a separate layer of the array texture.

Rendering into a 3D texture works in almost exactly the same way. You simply attach the whole 3D texture to a framebuffer object as one of its color attachments and then set the gl_Layer output as normal. The value written to gl_Layer becomes the z coordinate of the slice within the 3D texture where data produced by the fragment shader will be written. It's even possible to render into multiple slices of the same texture (array or 3D) at the same time by binding a layer to each of the framebuffer attachments (remember, there will be at least eight attachments supported by any implementation of OpenGL). To do this, call **glFramebufferTextureLayer()**, whose prototype is

```
void glFramebufferTextureLayer(GLenum target,
                               GLenum attachment,
                               GLuint texture,
                               GLint level,
                               GLint layer);
```

The **glFramebufferTextureLayer()** function works just like **glFramebufferTexture()**, except that it takes one additional parameter, layer, which specifies the layer of the texture that you wish to attach to the framebuffer. For instance, the code in Listing 9.12 creates a 2D array texture with eight layers and attaches each of the layers to the corresponding color attachment of a framebuffer object.

```
GLuint tex;
glGenTextures(1, &tex);
glBindTexture(GL_TEXTURE_2D_ARRAY, tex);
glTexStorage3D(GL_TEXTURE_2D_ARRAY, 1, GL_RGBA8, 256, 256, 8);

GLuint fbo;
glGenFramebuffers(1, &fbo);
glBindFramebuffer(GL_FRAMEBUFFER, fbo);

int i;
for (i = 0; i < 8; i++)
{
    glFramebufferTextureLayer(GL_FRAMEBUFFER,
                              GL_COLOR_ATTACHMENT0 + i,
                              tex,
                              0,
                              i);
}

static const GLenum draw_buffers[] =
{
    GL_COLOR_ATTACHMENT0, GL_COLOR_ATTACHMENT1,
    GL_COLOR_ATTACHMENT2, GL_COLOR_ATTACHMENT3,
    GL_COLOR_ATTACHMENT4, GL_COLOR_ATTACHMENT5,
    GL_COLOR_ATTACHMENT6, GL_COLOR_ATTACHMENT7
};
glDrawBuffers(8, &draw_buffers[0]);
```

Listing 9.12: Attaching texture layers to a framebuffer

Now, when you render into the framebuffer created in Listing 9.12, your fragment shader can have up to eight outputs and each will be written to a different layer of the texture.

Rendering to Cubemaps

As far as OpenGL is concerned, a cubemap is really a special case of an array texture. A single cubemap is just an array of six slices, and a cubemap array texture is an array of an integer multiple of six slices. You attach a cubemap texture to a framebuffer object in exactly the same way as shown in Listing 9.8, except that rather than creating a 2D array texture, you create a cubemap texture. The cubemap has six faces that are known as positive and negative x, positive and negative y, and positive and negative z, and they appear in that order in the array texture. When you write 0 into gl_Layer in your geometry shader, rendering will go to the positive x face of the cubemap. Writing 1 into gl_Layer sends output to the negative x face, writing 2 sends output to the positive y face, and so on, until eventually writing 5 sends output to the negative z face.

If you create a cubemap array texture and attach it to a framebuffer object, writing to the first six layers will render into the first cube, writing to the next six layers will render into the second cube, and so on. So, if you set gl_Layer to 6, you will write to the positive x face of the second cube in the array. If you set gl_Layer to 1234, you will render into the positive z face of the the 205th face.

Just as with 2D array textures, it's possible to attach individual faces of a cubemap to the various attachment points of a single framebuffer object. In this case, we use the **glFramebufferTexture()** 2D function, whose prototype is

```
void glFramebufferTexture2D(GLenum target,
                            GLenum attachment,
                            GLenum textarget,
                            GLuint texture,
                            GLint level);
```

Again, this function works just like **glFramebufferTexture()**, except that it has one additional parameter, textarget. This can be set to specify which face of the cubemap you want to attach to the attachment. To attach the cubemap's positive x face, set this to GL_CUBE_MAP_POSITIVE_X; for the negative x face, set it to GL_CUBE_MAP_NEGATIVE_X. Similar tokens are available for the y and z faces. Using this approach, you could bind all of the faces of a single cubemap[4] to the attachment points on a single framebuffer and render into all of them at the same time.

Framebuffer Completeness

Before we can finish up with framebuffer objects, there is one last important topic. Just because you are happy with the way you set up your FBO doesn't mean your OpenGL implementation is ready to render. The only way to find out if your FBO is set up correctly and in such a way that the implementation can use it is to check for *framebuffer completeness*. Framebuffer completeness is similar in concept to texture completeness. If a texture doesn't have all required mipmap levels specified with the right sizes, formats, and so on, that texture is incomplete and can't be used. There are two categories of completeness: attachment completeness and whole framebuffer completeness.

---

4. While this is certainly possible, rendering the same thing to all faces of a cubemap has limited utility.

Attachment Completeness

Each attachment point of an FBO must meet certain criteria to be considered complete. If any attachment point is incomplete, the whole framebuffer will also be incomplete. Some of the cases that cause an attachment to be incomplete follow:

- No image is associated with the attached object.

- The attached image has a width or height of zero.

- A non–color-renderable format is attached to a color attachment.

- A non–depth-renderable format is attached to a depth attachment.

- A non–stencil-renderable format is attached to a stencil attachment.

To determine whether a color, depth, or stencil format is renderable, you can call `glGetInternalformativ()` with the parameter GL_COLOR_RENDERABLE (for color), GL_DEPTH_RENDERABLE (for depth), or GL_STENCIL_RENDERABLE (for stencil). The result, which is written to the params parameter of `glGetInternalformativ()`, will be GL_TRUE if the format is renderable and GL_FALSE otherwise. To get even more information about the renderable nature of a format, you can call `glGetInternalformativ()` with the parameter GL_FRAMEBUFFER_RENDERABLE, in which case params will be filled with GL_FULL_SUPPORT if there are no issues rendering to the format, GL_CAVEAT_SUPPORT if there is an issue such as limited performance or precision, or GL_NONE to indicate that the format cannot be rendered to at all.

Whole Framebuffer Completeness

Not only does each attachment point have to be valid and meet certain criteria, but the framebuffer object as a whole must also be complete. The default framebuffer, if one exists, will always be complete. Common cases for the whole framebuffer being incomplete follow:

- `glDrawBuffers()` has mapped an output to an FBO attachment where no image is attached.

- The combination of internal formats is not supported by the OpenGL driver.

Checking the Framebuffer

When you think you are finished setting up an FBO, you can check whether it is complete by calling

```
GLenum fboStatus = glCheckFramebufferStatus(GL_DRAW_FRAMEBUFFER);
```

or

```
GLenum fboStatus = glCheckNamedFramebufferStatus(framebuffer);
```

The **glCheckFramebufferStatus()** function tests the framebuffer bound to the target specified as its only parameter, whereas the **glCheckNamedFramebufferStatus()** function checks the framebuffer you give it explicitly. If either function returns GL_FRAMEBUFFER_COMPLETE, all is well, and you may use the FBO. The return values of **glCheckFramebufferStatus()** and **glCheckNamedFramebufferStatus()** provide clues as to what might be wrong if the framebuffer is not complete. Table 9.7 describes all possible return conditions and what they mean.

Table 9.7: Framebuffer Completeness Return Values

Return Value (GL_FRAMEBUFFER_*)	Description
COMPLETE	A user-defined FBO is bound and is complete. OK to render.
UNDEFINED	The current FBO binding is 0, but no default framebuffer exists.
INCOMPLETE_ATTACHMENT	One of the buffers enabled for rendering is incomplete.
INCOMPLETE_MISSING_ATTACHMENT	No buffers are attached to the FBO and it is not configured for rendering without attachments.
UNSUPPORTED	The combination of internal buffer formats is not supported.
INCOMPLETE_LAYER_TARGETS	Not all color attachments are layered textures or bound to the same target.

Many of these return values are helpful when debugging an application but are less useful after an application has shipped. Nonetheless, the first example application checks to make sure none of these conditions occurred. It's also possible to try out an advanced configuration, and if **glCheckFramebufferStatus()** says it's not supported, fall back to a more conservative approach. It pays to perform this check in applications that use FBOs, making sure your use case hasn't hit some implementation-dependent limitation. An example of how this might look is shown in Listing 9.13.

```
GLenum fboStatus = glCheckFramebufferStatus(GL_DRAW_FRAMEBUFFER);
if(fboStatus != GL_FRAMEBUFFER_COMPLETE)
{
    switch (fboStatus)
    {
    case GL_FRAMEBUFFER_UNDEFINED:
        // Oops, no window exists?
        break;
    case GL_FRAMEBUFFER_INCOMPLETE_ATTACHMENT:
        // Check the status of each attachment
        break;
    case GL_FRAMEBUFFER_INCOMPLETE_MISSING_ATTACHMENT:
        // Attach at least one buffer to the FBO
        break;
    case GL_FRAMEBUFFER_INCOMPLETE_DRAW_BUFFER:
        // Check that all attachments enabled via
        // glDrawBuffers exist in FBO
    case GL_FRAMEBUFFER_INCOMPLETE_READ_BUFFER:
        // Check that the buffer specified via
        // glReadBuffer exists in FBO
        break;
    case GL_FRAMEBUFFER_UNSUPPORTED:
        // Reconsider formats used for attached buffers
        break;
    case GL_FRAMEBUFFER_INCOMPLETE_MULTISAMPLE:
        // Make sure the number of samples for each
        // attachment is the same
        break;
    case GL_FRAMEBUFFER_INCOMPLETE_LAYER_TARGETS:
        // Make sure the number of layers for each
        // attachment is the same
        break;
    }
}
```

Listing 9.13: Checking completeness of a framebuffer object

If you attempt to perform any command that reads from or writes to the framebuffer while an incomplete FBO is bound, the command simply returns after throwing the error GL_INVALID_FRAMEBUFFER_OPERATION, which is retrievable by calling **glGetError()**.

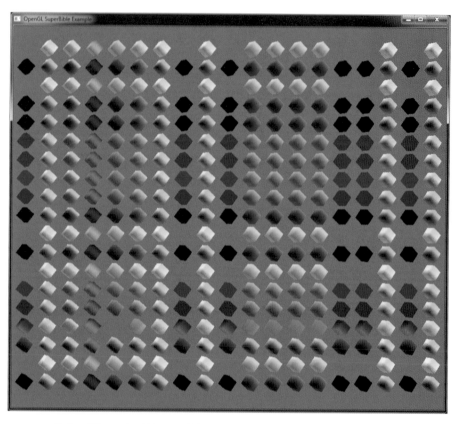

Color Plate 1: All possible combinations of blend function

Color Plate 2: Rendering to a stereo display

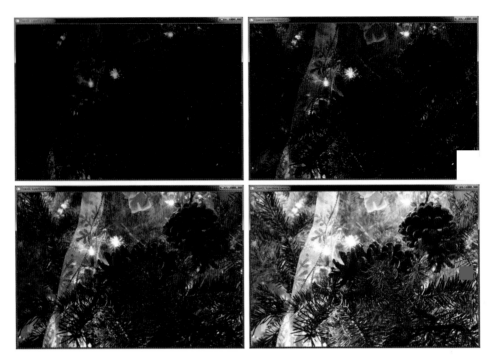

Color Plate 3: Different views of an HDR image

Color Plate 4: Adaptive tone mapping

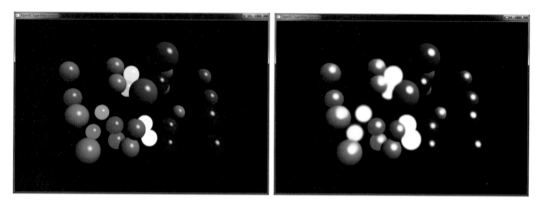

Color Plate 5: Bloom filtering: no bloom (left) and bloom (right)

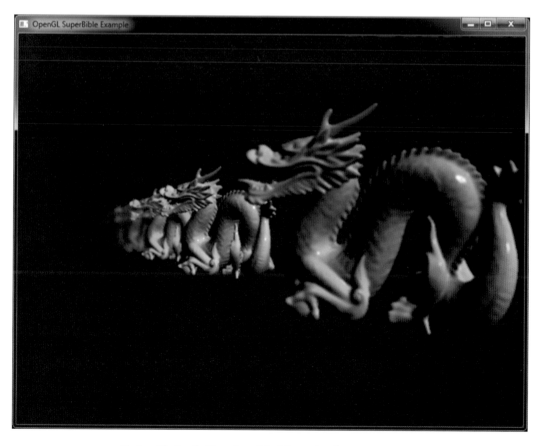

Color Plate 6: Depth of field applied to an image

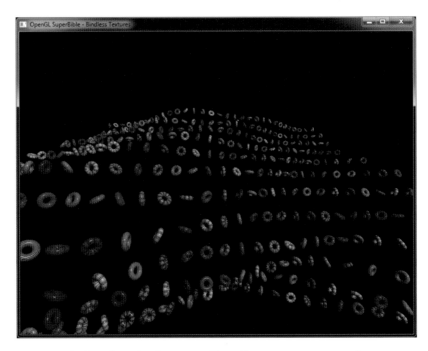

Color Plate 7: Output of bindless texture example

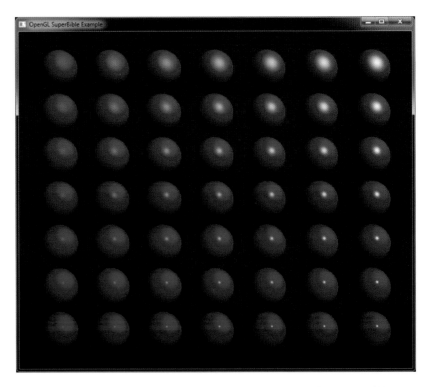

Color Plate 8: Varying specular parameters of a material

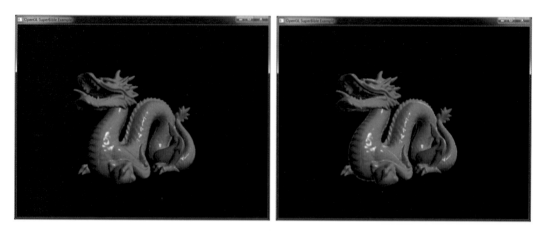

Color Plate 9: Result of rim lighting example

Color Plate 10: Normal mapping in action

Color Plate 11: Depth of field applied in a photograph

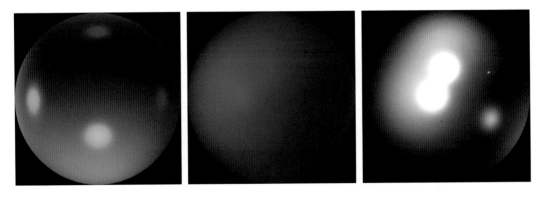

Color Plate 12: A selection of spherical environment maps

Color Plate 13: A golden environment-mapped dragon

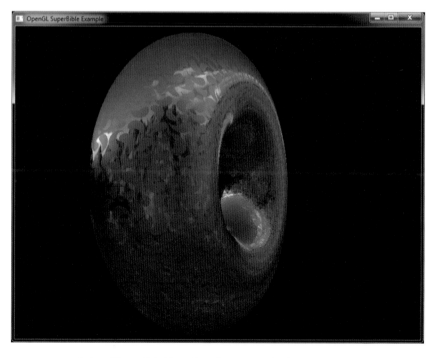

Color Plate 14: Result of per-pixel gloss example

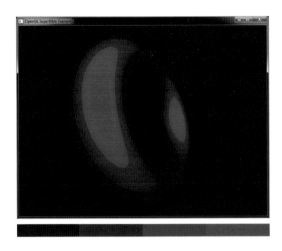

Color Plate 15: Toon shading output with color ramp

Color Plate 16: Real-time rendering of the Julia set

Color Plate 17: Ray tracing with four bounces

Read Framebuffers Need to Be Complete, Too!

In the previous examples, we tested the FBO attached to the draw buffer binding point, GL_DRAW_FRAMEBUFFER. But a framebuffer attached to GL_READ_FRAMEBUFFER also has to be attachment complete and whole-framebuffer complete for reads to work. Because only one read buffer can be enabled at a time, making sure an FBO is complete for reading is a little easier.

Rendering in Stereo

Most[5] human beings have two eyes. We use these two eyes to help us judge distance by providing parallax shift—a slight difference between the images our two eyes see. There are many depth queues, including depth from focus, from differences in lighting, and from the relative movement of objects as we move our point of view. OpenGL is able to produce pairs of images that, depending on the display device used, can be presented separately to your two eyes and increase the sense of depth of the image. There are plenty of display devices available, including binocular displays (devices with a separate physical display for each eye), shutter and polarized displays that require glasses to view, and autostereoscopic displays that don't require you to put anything on your face. OpenGL doesn't really care about how the image is displayed, only that you wish to render two views of the scene—one for the left eye and one for the right eye.

To display images in stereo requires some cooperation from the windowing or operating system and therefore the mechanism to create a stereo display is platform specific. The gory details of this are buried deep in platform-specific window system bindings and are best handled by framework code—whether you use ours or someone else's. For now, we can use the facilities provided by the sb7 application framework to create our stereo window for us. In your application, you can override sb7::application::init, call the base class function, and then set info.flags.stereo to 1 as shown in Listing 9.14. Because some OpenGL implementations may require your application to cover the whole display (which is known as full-screen rendering), you can also set the info.flags.fullscreen flag in your init function to make the application use a full-screen window.

---

5. Those readers with fewer than two eyes may wish to skip to the next section.

```
void my_application::init()
{
    info.flags.stereo = 1;
    info.flags.fullscreen = 1;   // Set this if your OpenGL
                                 // implementation requires
                                 // fullscreen for stereo rendering.

}
```

Listing 9.14: Creating a stereo window

Remember, not all displays support stereo output and not all OpenGL implementations will allow you to create a stereo window. However, if you have access to the necessary display and OpenGL implementation, you should have a window that runs in stereo. Now we need to render into it. The simplest way to render in stereo is to simply draw the entire scene twice. Before rendering into the left eye image, call

```
glDrawBuffer(GL_BACK_LEFT);
```

When you want to render into the right eye image, call

```
glDrawBuffer(GL_BACK_RIGHT);
```

To produce a pair of images with a compelling depth effect, you need to construct transformation matrices representing the views observed by the left and right eyes. Remember, our model matrix transforms our model into world space, and world space is global, applying the same way regardless of the viewer. However, the view matrix essentially transforms the world into the frame of the viewer. As the viewer is in a different location for each of the eyes, the view matrix must be different for each of the two eyes. Therefore, when we render to the left view, we use the left view matrix, and when we render to the right view, we use the right view matrix.

The simplest form of stereo view matrix pairs simply translates the left and right views away from each other on the horizontal axis. Optionally, you can also rotate the view matrices inward toward the center of view. Alternatively, you can use the vmath::lookat function to generate your view matrices for you. Simply place your eye at the left eye location (slightly left of the viewer position) and the center of the object of interest to create the left view matrix, and then do the same with the right eye position to create the right view matrix, as in Listing 9.15.

```
void my_application::render(double currentTime)
{
    static const vmath::vec3 origin(0.0f);
    static const vmath::vec3 up_vector(0.0f, 1.0f, 0.0f);
    static const vmath::vec3 eye_separation(0.01f, 0.0f, 0.0f);
```

```
        vmath::mat4 left_view_matrix =
            vmath::lookat(eye_location - eye_separation,
                          origin,
                          up_vector);

        vmath::mat4 right_view_matrix =
            vmath::lookat(eye_location + eye_separation,
                          origin,
                          up_vector);

        static const GLfloat black[] = { 0.0f, 0.0f ,0.0f, 0.0f };
        static const GLfloat one = 1.0f;

        // Setting the draw buffer to GL_BACK ends up drawing in
        // both the back left and back right buffers. Clear both.
        glDrawBuffer(GL_BACK);
        glClearBufferfv(GL_COLOR, 0, black);
        glClearBufferfv(GL_DEPTH, 0, &one);

        // Now, set the draw buffer to back left
        glDrawBuffer(GL_BACK_LEFT);

        // Set our left model-view matrix product
        glUniformMatrix4fv(model_view_loc, 1,
                           left_view_matrix * model_matrix);

        // Draw the scene
        draw_scene();

        // Set the draw buffer to back right
        glDrawBuffer(GL_BACK_RIGHT);

        // Set the right model-view matrix product
        glUniformMatrix4fv(model_view_loc, 1,
                           right_view_matrix * model_matrix);

        // Draw the scene... again.
        draw_scene();
    }
```

Listing 9.15: Drawing into a stereo window

Clearly, the code in Listing 9.15 renders the entire scene twice. Depending
on the complexity of your scene, that could be very, very expensive—
literally doubling the cost of rendering the scene. One possible tactic
is to switch between the GL_BACK_LEFT and GL_BACK_RIGHT draw buffers
between each and every object in your scene. This can mean that updates
to state (such as binding textures or changing the current program) can
be performed only once, but changing the draw buffer can be as expensive
as any other state-changing function. As we learned earlier in the chapter,
though, it's possible to render into more than one buffer at a time by
outputting two vectors from your fragment shader. In fact, consider what
would happen if you used a fragment shader with two outputs and then call

```
    static const GLenum buffers[] = { GL_BACK_LEFT, GL_BACK_RIGHT }
    glDrawBuffers(2, buffers);
```

After this, the first output of your fragment shader will be written to the left eye buffer, and the second output will be written to the right eye buffer. This is great! Now we can render to both eyes at the same time! Well, not so fast. Remember, even though the fragment shader can output to a number of different draw buffers, the location within each of those buffers will be the same. How do we draw a different image into each of the buffers?

What we can do is use a geometry shader to render into a layered framebuffer with two layers, one for the left eye and one for the right eye. We will use geometry shader instancing to run the geometry shader twice, and write the invocation index into the layer to direct the two copies of the data into the two layers of the framebuffer. In each invocation of the geometry shader, we can select one of two model–view matrices and essentially perform all of the work of the vertex shader in the geomtry shader. Once we're done rendering the whole scene, the framebuffer's two layers will contain the left and right eye images. All that is needed now is to render a full screen quad with a fragment shader that reads from the two layers of the array texture and writes the result into its two outputs, which are directed into the left and right eye views.

Listing 9.16 shows the simple geometry shader that we'll use in our application to render both views of our stereo scene in a single pass.

```
#version 450 core

layout (triangles, invocations = 2) in;
layout (triangle_strip, max_vertices = 3) out;

uniform matrices
{
    mat4 model_matrix;
    mat4 view_matrix[2];
    mat4 projection_matrix;
};

in VS_OUT
{
    vec4 color;
    vec3 normal;
    vec2 texture_coord;
} gs_in[];

out GS_OUT
{
    vec4 color;
    vec3 normal;
    vec2 texture_coord;
} gs_out;

void main(void)
```

```
{
    // Calculate a model-view matrix for the current eye
    mat4 model_view_matrix = view_matrix[gl_InvocationID] *
                             model_matrix;

    for (int i = 0; i < gl_in.length(); i++)
    {
        // Output layer is invocation ID
        gl_Layer = gl_InvocationID;
        // Multiply by the model matrix, the view matrix for the
        // appropriate eye, and then the projection matrix
        gl_Position = projection_matrix *
                      model_view_matrix *
                      gl_in[i].gl_Position;
        gs_out.color = gs_in[i].color;
        // Don't forget to transform the normals...
        gs_out.normal = mat3(model_view_matrix) * gs_in[i].normal;
        gs_out.texcoord = gs_in[i].texcoord;
        EmitVertex();
    }

    EndPrimitive();
}
```

Listing 9.16: Rendering to two layers with a geometry shader

Now that we've rendered our scene into our layered framebuffer, we can attach the underlying array texture and draw a full-screen quad to copy the result into the left and right back buffers with a single shader. Such a shader is shown in Listing 9.17.

```
#version 450 core

layout (location = 0) out vec4 color_left;
layout (location = 1) out vec4 color_right;

in vec2 tex_coord;

uniform sampler2DArray back_buffer;

void main(void)
{
    color_left = texture(back_buffer, vec3(tex_coord, 0.0));
    color_right = texture(back_buffer, vec3(tex_coord, 1.0));
}
```

Listing 9.17: Copying from an array texture to a stereo back buffer

Figure 9.8 shows this application running on a real stereo monitor. A photograph is necessary here because a screenshot would not show both of the images in the stereo pair. However, the double image produced by stereo rendering is clearly visible in the photograph. A better view of the output can be seen in Color Plate 2.

Figure 9.8: Result of stereo rendering to a stereo display

Antialiasing

Aliasing is an artifact of *under-sampling* data. It is a term commonly used in signal processing fields. When aliasing occurs in an audio signal, it can be heard as a high-pitched whining or crunching sound. You may have noticed this in old video games, musical greeting cards, or children's toys that often include low-cost playback devices. Aliasing occurs when the rate at which a signal is sampled (the sampling rate) is too low for the content of that signal. The rate at which a sample must be sampled to preserve (most of) its content is known as the Nyquist rate, and is twice the frequency of the highest-frequency component present in the signal to be captured. In image terms, aliasing manifests as jagged edges wherever there is sharp contrast. These edges are sometimes referred to as *jaggies*.

There are two main approaches to deal with aliasing. The first is filtering, which removes high-frequency content from the signal before or during sampling. The second is increasing the sampling rate, which allows the higher-frequency content to be recorded. The additional samples captured can then be processed for storage or reproduction. Methods for reducing or eliminating aliasing are known as *antialiasing* techniques. OpenGL includes a number of ways to apply antialiasing to your scene. These include filtering geometry as it is rendered and various forms of over-sampling.

Antialiasing by Filtering

The first and simplest way to deal with the aliasing problem is to filter primitives as they are drawn. To do this, OpenGL calculates the *amount* of a pixel that is covered by a primitive (point, line, or triangle) and uses it to generate an alpha value for each fragment. This alpha value is multiplied by the alpha value of the fragment produced by your shader and so has an effect in blending when either blend factor includes the source alpha term. With this approach, as fragments are drawn to the screen, they are blended with its existing content using a function of the pixel coverage.

To turn on this form of antialiasing, we need to do two things. First, we need to enable blending and choose an appropriate blending function. Second, we need to enable GL_LINE_SMOOTH to apply antialiasing to lines and GL_POLYGON_SMOOTH to apply antialiasing to triangles. Figure 9.9 shows the result of doing this.

In the left image in Figure 9.9 we have drawn our spinning cube in line mode and zoomed in on a section of the image where a number of edges join together. In the inset, the aliasing artifacts are clearly visible—notice the jagged edges. In the image on the right in Figure 9.9, line smoothing and blending is enabled, but the scene is otherwise unchanged. Notice how the lines appear much smoother and the jagged edges are much reduced. Zooming into the inset, we see that the lines have been blurred slightly. This is the effect of filtering that is produced by calculating the coverage of the lines and using it to blend them with the background color. The code that sets up antialiasing and blending to render the image is shown in Listing 9.18.

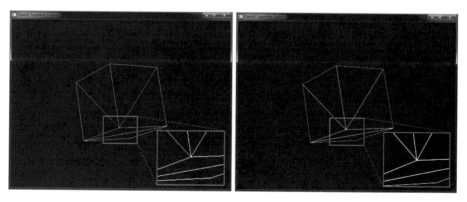

Figure 9.9: Antialiasing using line smoothing

```
glEnable(GL_BLEND);
glBlendFunc(GL_SRC_ALPHA, GL_ONE_MINUS_SRC_ALPHA);
glEnable(GL_LINE_SMOOTH);
```

Listing 9.18: Turning on line smoothing

Listing 9.18 seems pretty simple, doesn't it? Surely, if it's that simple, we should be able to turn this on for any geometry we like and everything will just look better. Well, no, that's not really true. This form of antialiasing works only in limited cases like the one shown in Figure 9.9. Take a look at the images in Figure 9.10.

The left image in Figure 9.10 shows our cube rendered in solid white. You can see that the jaggies in the middle where the individual triangles abut aren't visible, but on the edges of the cube you can see the aliasing effect quite clearly. In the image on the right in Figure 9.10, we have turned on polygon smoothing using code almost identical to that of Listing 9.18, only substituting GL_POLYGON_SMOOTH for GL_LINE_SMOOTH. Now, although the edges of the cube are smoothed and the jaggies are mostly gone, what happened to the interior edges? They have become visible!

Consider what happens when the edge between two adjoining triangles cuts exactly halfway through the middle of a pixel. First, our application clears the framebuffer to black, and then our first white triangle hits that pixel. OpenGL calculates that half the pixel is covered by the triangle, and uses an alpha value of 0.5 in the blending equation. This mixes half and half white and black, producing a mid-gray pixel. Next, our second, adjacent triangle comes along and covers the other half of the pixel. Again, OpenGL figures that half the pixel is covered by the new triangle

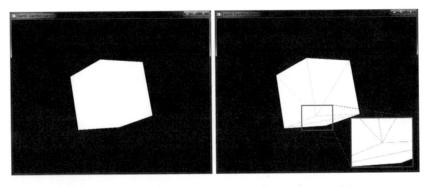

Figure 9.10: Antialiasing using polygon smoothing

and mixes the white of the triangle with the existing framebuffer content... except now the framebuffer is 50% gray! Mixing white and 50% gray produces 75% gray, which is the color we see in the lines between the triangles.

Ultimately, whenever a polygon edge cuts partway through a pixel and is written to the screen, OpenGL has no way of knowing which part is already covered and which part is not. This leads to artifacts like those seen in Figure 9.10. Another significant issue with this method is that there is only one depth value for each pixel, which means that if a triangle pokes into a not-yet-covered part of a pixel, it may still fail the depth test and not contribute at all if there's already a closer triangle covering a different part of that same pixel.

To circumvent these problems, we need more advanced antialiasing methods, all of which involve increasing the sample count.

Multi-Sample Antialiasing

To increase the sample rate of the image, OpenGL supports storing multiple samples for every pixel on the screen. This technique is known as multi-sample antialiasing (MSAA). Rather than sampling each primitive only once, OpenGL will sample the primitive at multiple locations within the pixel and, if any are hit, run your shader. Whatever color your shader produces is written into all of the hit samples. The actual location of the samples within each pixel might be different on different OpenGL implementations. Figure 9.11 shows an example arrangement of the sample positions for one-, two-, four-, and eight-sample arrangements.

Turning on MSAA for the default framebuffer is somewhat platform specific. In most cases, you need to specify a multi-sampled format for the default framebuffer when you set up your rendering window. In the

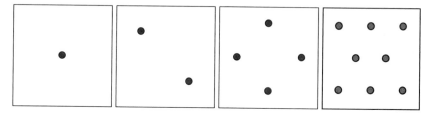

Figure 9.11: Antialiasing sample positions

sample programs included with this book, the application framework takes care of this for you. To enable multi-sampling with the sb7::application framework, simply override the sb7::application::init() function, call the base class method, and then set the samples member of the info structure to the desired sample count. Listing 9.19 shows an example of this.

```
virtual void init()
{
    sb7::application::init();

    info.samples = 8;
}
```

Listing 9.19: Choosing eight-sample antialiasing

After choosing eight-sample antialiasing and rendering our trusty spinning cube, we are presented with the images shown in Figure 9.12. In the leftmost image of Figure 9.12, no antialiasing is applied and we are given jaggies as usual. In the center image, we can see that antialiasing has been applied to the lines, but the result doesn't look that dissimilar to the image produced by enabling GL_LINE_SMOOTH, as shown in Figure 9.9. However, the real difference appears in the rightmost image of Figure 9.11. Here, we have good-quality antialiasing along the edges of our polygons, but the inner abutting edges of the triangles no longer show gray artifacts.

If you create a multi-sampled framebuffer, then multi-sampling is enabled by default. However, if you wish to render without multi-sampling even though the current framebuffer has a multi-sampled format, you can turn multi-sampling off by calling

```
glDisable(GL_MULTISAMPLE);
```

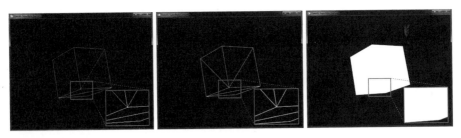

Figure 9.12: No antialising (left) and eight-sample antialiasing (center and right)

Of course, you can turn it back on again by calling

```
glEnable(GL_MULTISAMPLE);
```

When multi-sampling is disabled, OpenGL proceeds as if the framebuffer were a normal single-sample framebuffer and samples each fragment once. The only difference is that the shading results are written to every sample in the pixel.

Multi-Sample Textures

You have already learned how to render into off-screen textures using a framebuffer object, and you have just learned how to perform antialiasing using multi-sampling. However, the multi-sampled color buffer has been owned by the window system. It's possible to combine both of these features and create an off-screen, multi-sampled color buffer to render into. To do this, we can create a *multi-sampled texture* and attach it to a framebuffer object for rendering into.

To create a multi-sampled texture, create a texture name as usual with one of the multi-sampled texture targets such as GL_TEXTURE_2D_MULTISAMPLE or GL_TEXTURE_2D_MULTISAMPLE_ARRAY. Then, allocate storage for it using **glTextureStorage2DMultisample()** or **glTextureStorage3DMultisample()** (for array textures), whose prototypes are

```
void glTextureStorage2DMultisample(GLuint texture, GLsizei samples,
                                   GLenum internalformat, GLsizei width,
                                   GLsizei height,
                                   GLboolean fixedsamplelocations);

void glTextureStorage3DMultisample(GLuint texture, sizei GLsamples,
                                   GLenum internalformat, GLsizei width,
                                   GLsizei height, GLsizei depth,
                                   GLboolean fixedsamplelocations);
```

The **glTextureStorage2DMultisample()** and **glTextureStorage3DMultisample()** functions directly modify the texture you specify in texture. Alternatively, if you know that the texture you want to allocate storage for is already bound, you can call one of the following functions:

```
void glTexStorage2DMultisample(GLenum target,
                               GLsizei samples,
                               GLenum internalformat,
                               GLsizei width,
                               GLsizei height,
                               GLboolean fixedsamplelocations);
```

```
void glTexStorage3DMultisample(GLenum target,
                               GLsizei samples,
                               GLenum internalformat,
                               GLsizei width,
                               GLsizei height,
                               GLsizei depth,
                               GLboolean fixedsamplelocations);
```

These functions behave pretty much like **glTextureStorage2D()** and
glTextureStorage3D() (or **glTexStorage2D()** and **glTexStorage3D()**) but
have a few extra parameters. The first, samples, tells OpenGL how many
samples should be in the texture. The second, fixedsamplelocations, tells
OpenGL whether it should use standard sample locations for all texels in
the texture or whether it is allowed to vary sample locations spatially
within the texture. In general, allowing OpenGL to take the latter course
can improve image quality, but it may reduce consistency and even cause
artifacts if your application relies on the same object being rendered in
exactly the same way regardless of where it is in the framebuffer.

Once you have allocated storage for your texture, you can attach it to a
framebuffer with **glFramebufferTexture()** in the usual way. An example of
creating a depth and a color multi-sample texture is shown in Listing 9.20.

```
GLuint color_ms_tex;
GLuint depth_ms_tex;

glCreateTextures(GL_TEXTURE_2D_MULTISAMPLE, 1, &color_ms_tex);
glTextureStorage2DMultisample(color_ms_tex, 8,
                              GL_RGBA8, 1024, 1024, GL_TRUE);
glCreateTextures(GL_TEXTURE_2D_MULTISAMPLE, 1, &depth_ms_tex);
glTextureStorage2DMultisample(depth_ms_tex, 8,
                              GL_DEPTH_COMPONENT, 1024, 1024, GL_TRUE);

GLuint fbo;

glGenFramebuffers(1, &fbo);
glBindFramebuffer(GL_FRAMEBUFFER);
glFramebufferTexture(GL_FRAMEBUFFER, GL_COLOR_ATTACHMENT0,
                     color_ms_tex, 0);
glFramebufferTexture(GL_FRAMEBUFFER, GL_DEPTH_ATTACHMENT,
                     depth_ms_tex, 0);
```

Listing 9.20: Setting up a multi-sample framebuffer attachment

Multi-sample textures have several restrictions. First, there are no 1D or 3D
multi-sample textures. Second, multi-sample textures cannot have
mipmaps. The **glTexStorage3D()** Multisample and
glTextureStorage3DMultisample() functions are intended only for
allocating storage for 2D multi-sample array textures, and neither they nor
glTexStorage2DMultisample() and **glTextureStorage2DMultisample()**
accept a levels parameter. As a result, you may pass only 0 as the level

parameter to **glFramebufferTexture()**. Furthermore, you can't just use a multi-sample texture like any other texture, and such a texture doesn't support filtering. Rather, you must explicitly read texels from the multi-sample texture in your shader by declaring a special multi-sampled sampler type. The multi-sampled sampler types in GLSL are `sampler2DMS` and `sampler2DMSArray`, which represent 2D multi-sample and multi-sample array textures, respectively. Additionally, the `isampler2DMS` and `usampler2DMS` types represent signed and unsigned integer multi-sample textures, and `isampler2DMSArray` and `usampler2DMSArray` represent the array forms.

A typical use for sampling from multi-sample textures in a shader is to perform custom resolve operations. When you render into a window system–owned multi-sampled back buffer, you don't have a whole lot of control over how OpenGL combines the color values of the samples contributing to a pixel to produce its final color. However, if you render into a multi-sample texture and then draw a full-screen quad using a fragment shader that samples from that texture and combines its samples with code you supply, then you can implement any algorithm you wish. The example shown in Listing 9.21 demonstrates taking the brightest sample of those contained in each pixel.

```
#version 450 core

uniform sampler2DMS input_image;

out vec4 color;

void main(void)
{
    ivec2 coord = ivec2(gl_FragCoord.xy);
    vec4 result = vec4(0.0);
    int i;

    for (i = 0; i < 8; i++)
    {
        result = max(result, texelFetch(input_image, coord, i));
    }

    color = result;
}
```

Listing 9.21: Simple multi-sample "maximum" resolve

Sample Coverage

Coverage refers to how much of a pixel a fragment "covers." The coverage of a fragment is normally calculated by OpenGL as part of the rasterization process. However, you have some control over this behavior and can actually generate new coverage information in your fragment shader. There are three ways to do this.

First, you can have OpenGL convert the alpha value of a fragment directly to a coverage value to determine how many samples of the framebuffer will be updated by the fragment. To do so, pass the GL_SAMPLE_ALPHA_TO_COVERAGE parameter to **glEnable()**. The coverage value for a fragment is used to determine how many subsamples will be written. For instance, a fragment with an alpha value of 0.4 would generate a coverage value of 40%. When you use this method, OpenGL will first calculate the coverage for each of the samples in each pixel, producing a *sample mask*. It then calculates a second mask using the alpha value that your shader produces and logically ANDs it with the incoming sample mask. For example, if OpenGL determines that 66% of the pixel is originally covered by the primitive and then you produce an alpha value of 40%, it will produce an output sample mask of 40% × 66%, which is roughly 25%. Thus, for an eight-sample MSAA buffer, two of that pixel's samples would be written to.

Because the alpha value was already used to decide how many subsamples should be written, it wouldn't make sense to then blend those subsamples with the same alpha value. To help prevent these subpixels from also being blended when blending is enabled, you can force the alpha values for those samples to 1 by calling **glEnable()** (GL_SAMPLE_ALPHA_TO_ONE).

Using the alpha-to-coverage approach has several advantages over simple blending. When rendering to a multi-sampled buffer, the alpha blend would normally be applied equally to the entire pixel. With alpha-to-coverage, however, alpha-masked edges are antialiased, producing a much more natural and smooth result. This is particularly useful when drawing bushes, trees, or dense foliage where parts of the brush are alpha transparent.

OpenGL also allows you to set the sample coverage manually by calling **glSampleCoverage()**, whose prototype is

```
void glSampleCoverage(GLfloat value,
                      GLboolean invert);
```

Manually applying a coverage value for a pixel occurs after the mask for alpha-to-coverage is applied. For this step to take effect, sample coverage must be enabled by calling

```
glEnable(GL_SAMPLE_COVERAGE);
glSampleCoverage(value, invert);
```

The coverage value passed into the value parameter can be between 0 and 1. The invert parameter signals to OpenGL whether the resulting mask should be inverted. For instance, if you were drawing two overlapping trees, one with 60% coverage and the other with 40% coverage, you would want to invert one of the coverage values to make sure the same mask was not used for both draw calls.

```
glSampleCoverage(0.5, GL_FALSE);
// Draw first geometry set
. . .
glSampleCoverage(0.5, GL_TRUE);
// Draw second geometry set
. . .
```

Another way that you can generate coverage information is to explicitly set it right in your fragment shader. To facilitate this, you can use two built-in variables, gl_SampleMaskIn[] and gl_SampleMask[], that are available to fragment shaders. The first is an input variable and contains the coverage information generated by OpenGL during rasterization. The second variable is an output variable that you can write to in the shader to update coverage. Each bit of each element of the arrays corresponds to a single sample (starting from the least significant bit). If the OpenGL implementation supports more than 32 samples in a single framebuffer, then the first element of the array contains coverage information for the first 32 samples, the second element contains information about the next 32 samples, and so on.

The bits in gl_SampleMaskIn[] are set if OpenGL considered that particular sample covered. You can copy this array directly into gl_SampleMask[] and pass the information straight through without having any effect on coverage. If, however, you turn samples off during this process, they will effectively be discarded. While you can turn bits on in gl_SampleMask[] that weren't on in gl_SampleMaskIn[], this will have no effect, because OpenGL will just turn them off again for you. There's a simple work-around for this: Just disable multi-sampling by calling **glDisable()** and passing GL_MULTISAMPLE as described earlier. Now, when your shader runs, gl_SampleMaskIn[] will indicate that all samples are covered and you can turn bits off at your leisure.

Sample Rate Shading

Multi-sample antialiasing solves a number of issues related to under-sampling geometry. In particular, it captures fine geometric details and correctly handles partially covered pixels, overlapping primitives, and other sources of artifacts at the boundaries of lines and triangles. However, it cannot cope with whatever your shader throws at it elegantly. Remember, under normal circumstances, once OpenGL determines that a triangle hits a pixel, it will run your shader once and broadcast the resulting output to each sample that was covered by the triangle. This cannot accurately capture the result of a shader that itself produces high-frequency output. For example, consider the fragment shader shown in Listing 9.22.

```
#version 450 core

out vec4 color;

in VS_OUT
{
    vec2 tc;
} fs_in;

void main(void)
{
    float val = abs(fs_in.tc.x + fs_in.tc.y) * 20.0f;
    color = vec4(fract(val) >= 0.5 ? 1.0 : 0.25);
}
```

Listing 9.22: Fragment shader producing high-frequency output

This extremely simple shader produces stripes with hard edges (which produce a high-frequency signal). For any given invocation of the shader, the output will either be bright white or dark gray, depending on the incoming texture coordinates. If you look at the image on the left in Figure 9.13, you will see that the jaggies have returned. The outline of the cube is still nicely smoothed, but *inside* the triangles the stripes produced by our shader are jagged and badly aliased.

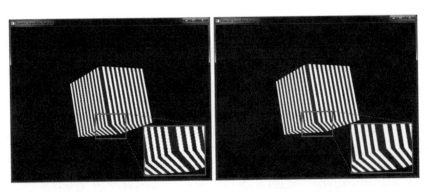

Figure 9.13: Antialiasing of high-frequency shader output

To produce the image on the right in Figure 9.13, we enabled *sample-rate shading*. In this mode, OpenGL will run your shader for each and every sample that a primitive hits. Be careful, though, as for eight-sample buffers, your shader will become eight times more expensive! To enable sample rate shading, call

```
glEnable(GL_SAMPLE_SHADING);
```

To disable sample rate shading, call

```
glDisable(GL_SAMPLE_SHADING);
```

Once you have enabled sample shading, you also need to let OpenGL know which portion of the samples it should run your shader for. By default, simply enabling sample shading won't do anything, and OpenGL will still run your shader once for each pixel. To tell OpenGL which fraction of the samples you want to shade independently, call **glMinSampleShading()**, whose prototype is

```
void glMinSampleShading(GLfloat value);
```

For example, if you want OpenGL to run your shader for at least half of the samples in the framebuffer, set the `value` parameter set to `0.5f`. To uniquely shade every sample hit by the geometry, set `value` to `1.0f`. As you can see from the right image in Figure 9.13, the jaggies on the interior of the cube have been eliminated. We set the minimum sampling fraction to 1.0 to create this image.

In addition to forcing a particular shader to run at sample rate by enabling `GL_SAMPLE_SHADING`, you can mark one or more inputs of your fragment shader as being evaluated per sample. This usually implies that the whole shader will run at sample rate so that OpenGL can give you a new value of that input for each sample in the framebuffer. To do this, we use the GLSL storage qualifier, `sample`. For example:

```
sample in vec2 tex_coord;
```

This declares the `tex_coord` input to our fragment shader as sample-rate shaded, which means we want a new value of `tex_coord` for each sample in the framebuffer. This implies that the shader must run at sample rate (or at least, OpenGL must make sure that the end result is as if it did).

Centroid Sampling

The `centroid` storage qualifier controls where in a pixel OpenGL interpolates the inputs to the fragment shader to. It applies only in situations where you're rendering into a multi-sampled framebuffer. You specify the `centroid` storage qualifier just like any other storage qualifier that is applied to an input or output variable. To create a varying that has the `centroid` storage qualifier, first, in the vertex, tessellation control, or geometry shader, declare the output with the `centroid` keyword:

```
centroid out vec2 tex_coord;
```

Then, in the fragment shader, declare the same input with the `centroid` keyword:

```
centroid in vec2 tex_coord;
```

You can also apply the `centroid` qualifier to an interface block to cause all of the members of the block to be interpolated to the fragment's centroid:

```
centroid out VS_OUT
{
    vec2 tex_coord;
} vs_out;
```

Now `tex_coord` (or `vs_out.tex_coord`) is defined to use the `centroid` storage qualifier. If you have a single-sampled draw buffer, this makes no difference, and the inputs that reach the fragment shader are interpolated to the pixel's center. Where centroid sampling becomes useful is when you are rendering to a multi-sampled draw buffer. According to the OpenGL specification, when centroid sampling is not specified (the default), fragment shader varyings will be interpolated to "the pixel's center, or anywhere within the pixel, or to one of the pixel's samples"—which basically means anywhere within the pixel. When you're in the middle of a large triangle, this doesn't really matter. Where it becomes important is when you're shading a pixel that lies right on the edge of the triangle—where an edge of the triangle cuts through the pixel. Figure 9.14 shows an example of how OpenGL might sample from a triangle.

Take a look at the left image in Figure 9.14. It shows the edge of a triangle passing through several pixels. The solid dots represent samples that are covered by the triangle, and the clear dots represent those that are not. OpenGL has chosen to interpolate the fragment shader inputs to the sample

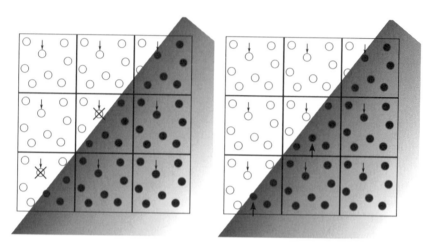

Figure 9.14: Partially covered multi-sampled pixels

closest to the pixel's center. Those samples are indicated by a small downward-pointing arrow.

For the pixels in the upper left, this is fine—they are entirely uncovered and the fragment shader will not run for those pixels. Likewise, the pixels in the lower right are fully covered. The fragment shader will run, but it doesn't really matter which sample it runs for. The pixels along the edge of the triangle, however, present a problem. Because OpenGL has chosen the sample closest to the pixel center as its interpolation point, your fragment shader inputs could actually be interpolated to a point that lies *outside* the triangle! Those samples are marked with an X. What would happen if you used the input, say, to sample from a texture? If the texture was aligned such that its edge was supposed to match the edge of the triangle, the texture coordinates would lie outside the texture. At best, you would get a slightly incorrect image. At worst, it would produce noticeable artifacts.

If we declare our inputs with the `centroid` storage qualifier, the OpenGL specification says, "The value must be interpolated to a point that lies in both the pixel and in the primitive being rendered, or to one of the pixel's samples that falls within the primitive." That means OpenGL chooses, for each pixel, a sample that is certainly within the triangle to which to interpolate all varyings. You are safe to use the inputs to the fragment shader for any purpose, and you know that they are valid and have not been interpolated to a point outside the triangle.

Now look at the right image in Figure 9.14. OpenGL has still chosen to interpolate the fragment shader inputs to the samples closest to the pixel centers for fully covered pixels. However, for those pixels that are partially covered, it has instead chosen another sample that lies within the triangle (marked with larger arrows). This means that the inputs presented to the fragment shader are valid and refer to points that are inside the triangle. You can use them for sampling from a texture or in a function whose result is defined only within a certain range and know that you will get meaningful results.

You may be wondering whether using the `centroid` storage qualifier guarantees that you're going to get valid results in your fragment shader and not using it may mean that the inputs are interpolated outside the primitive. So why not turn on centroid sampling all the time? Well, there are some drawbacks to using centroid sampling.

The most significant is that OpenGL can provide the gradients (or differentials) of inputs to the fragment shader. Implementations may differ, but most use discrete differentials, taking deltas between the values of the same inputs from adjacent pixels. This works well when the inputs are interpolated to the same position within each pixel. In this case, it doesn't matter which sample position is chosen; the samples will always be exactly one pixel apart. However, when centroid sampling is enabled for an input, the values for adjacent pixels may actually be interpolated to different positions within those pixels. As a consequence, the samples are not exactly one pixel apart, and the discrete differentials presented to the fragment shader could be inaccurate. If accurate gradients are required in the fragment shader, it is probably best not to use centroid sampling. Don't forget, the calculations that OpenGL performs during mipmapping depend on gradients of texture coordinates, so using a `centroid` qualified input as the source of texture coordinates to a mipmapped texture could lead to inaccurate results.

Using Centroid Sampling to Perform Edge Detection

An interesting use case for centroid sampling is hardware-accelerated edge detection. You just learned that using the `centroid` storage qualifier ensures that your inputs are interpolated to a point that definitely lies within the primitive being rendered. To do this, OpenGL chooses a sample that it knows lies inside the triangle at which to evaluate those inputs, and that sample may be different from the one that it would have chosen if the pixel was fully covered or the one that it would have selected if the centroid storage qualifier was not used. You can use this knowledge to your advantage.

To extract edge information, declare two inputs to your fragment shader, one with and one without the `centroid` storage qualifier, and assign the same value to each of them in the vertex shader. It doesn't matter what the values are, so long as they are different for each vertex. The x and y components of the transformed vertex position are probably a good choice because you know that they will be different for each vertex of any triangle that is actually visible.

```
out vec2 maybe_outside;
```

gives us our non-`centroid` input that may be interpolated to a point outside the triangle, and

```
centroid out vec2 certainly_inside;
```

gives us our `centroid` sampled input that we know is inside the triangle. Inside the fragment shader, we can compare the values of the two varyings. If the pixel is entirely covered by the triangle, OpenGL uses the same value for both inputs. However, if the pixel is only partially covered by the triangle, OpenGL uses its normal choice of sample for `maybe_outside` and picks a sample that is certain to be inside the triangle for `certainly_inside`. This could be a different sample than was chosen for `maybe_outside`, and that means that the two inputs may have different values. Now you can compare them to determine that you are on the edge of a primitive:

```
bool may_be_on_edge = any(notEqual(maybe_outside,
                                   certainly_inside));
```

This method is not foolproof. Even if a pixel is on the edge of a triangle, it is possible that it covers OpenGL's original sample of choice, and therefore you might still get the same values for `maybe_outside` and `certainly_inside`. However, this method marks most edge pixels.

To use this information, you can write the value to a texture attached to the framebuffer and subsequently use that texture for further processing later. Another option is to draw only to the stencil buffer. Set your stencil reference to 1, disable stencil testing, and set your stencil operation to GL_REPLACE. When you encounter an edge, let the fragment shader continue running. When you encounter a pixel that's not on an edge, use the `discard` keyword in your shader to prevent the pixel from being written to the stencil buffer. The result is that your stencil buffer contains 1s wherever there was an edge in the scene and 0s wherever there was no edge. Later, you can render a full-screen quad with an expensive fragment shader that runs only for pixels that represent the edges of geometry where a sample would have been chosen that was outside the triangle by enabling the stencil test, setting the stencil function to GL_EQUAL, and leaving the reference value at 1. The shader could implement an image processing operation at each pixel, for instance. Applying Gaussian blur using a convolution operation can smooth the edges of polygons in the scene, allowing the application to perform its own antialiasing.

Advanced Framebuffer Formats

Until now, you have been using either the window system–supplied framebuffer (i.e., the default framebuffer), or you have rendered into textures using your own framebuffer. However, the textures you attached to the framebuffer have been of the format GL_RGBA8, which is an 8-bit unsigned normalized format. This means that it can represent only values between 0.0 and 1.0, in 256 steps. However, the output of your fragment shaders has been declared as vec4—a vector of four floating-point elements. OpenGL can actually render into almost any format you can imagine and framebuffer attachments can have one, two, three, or four components, can be floating-point or integer formats, can store negative numbers, and can be wider than eight bits, providing much more definition.

In this section, we explore a few of the more advanced formats that can be used for framebuffer attachments and that allow you to capture more of the information that might be produced by your shaders.

Rendering with No Attachments

Just as you can attach multiple textures to a single framebuffer and render into all of them with a single shader, it's also possible to create a framebuffer and not attach any textures to it at all. This might seem like a strange thing to do. You might ask where your data goes. Well, any outputs declared in the fragment shader have no effect and data written to them will be discarded. However, fragment shaders can have a number of side effects besides writing to their outputs. For example, they can write into memory using the imageStore function, and they can increment and decrement atomic counters using the atomicCounterIncrement and atomicCounterDecrement functions.

Normally, when a framebuffer object has one or more attachments, it derives its maximum width and height, layer count, and sample count from those attachments. These properties define the size to which the viewport will be clamped and so on. When a framebuffer object has no attachments, limits imposed by the amount of memory available for textures, for example, are removed. However, the framebuffer must derive this information from another source. Each framebuffer object therefore has a set of parameters that are used in place of those derived from its attachments when no attachments are present. To modify these parameters, call **glFramebufferParameteri()**, whose prototype is

```
void glFramebufferParameteri(GLenum target,
                             GLenum pname,
                             GLint param);
```

target specifies the target where the framebuffer object is bound, and may be GL_DRAW_FRAMEBUFFER, GL_READ_FRAMEBUFFER, or simply GL_FRAMEBUFFER. If you specify GL_FRAMEBUFFER, then it is considered equivalent to GL_DRAW_FRAMEBUFFER and the framebuffer object bound to the GL_DRAW_FRAMEBUFFER binding point will be modified. pname specifies which parameter you want to modify and param is the value you want to change it to. pname can be one of the following:

- GL_FRAMEBUFFER_DEFAULT_WIDTH indicates that param contains the width of the framebuffer when it has no attachments.

- GL_FRAMEBUFFER_DEFAULT_HEIGHT indicates that param contains the height of the framebuffer when it has no attachments.

- GL_FRAMEBUFFER_DEFAULT_LAYERS indicates that param contains the layer count of the framebuffer when it has no attachments.

- GL_FRAMEBUFFER_DEFAULT_SAMPLES indicates that param contains the number of samples in the framebuffer when it has no attachments.

- GL_FRAMEBUFFER_DEFAULT_FIXED_SAMPLE_LOCATIONS indicates that param specifies whether the framebuffer uses the fixed default sample locations. If param is non-zero, then OpenGL's default sample pattern will be used; otherwise, OpenGL might choose a more advanced arrangement of samples for you.

The maximum dimensions of a framebuffer without any attachments can be extremely large because no real storage for the attachments is required.

Listing 9.23 demonstrates how to initialize a virtual framebuffer that is 10,000 pixels wide and 10,000 pixels high.

```
// Generate a framebuffer name and bind it
GLuint fbo;

glGenFramebuffers(1, &fbo);
glBindFramebuffer(GL_FRAMEBUFFER, fbo);

// Set the default width and height to 10000
glFramebufferParameteri(GL_FRAMEBUFFER_DEFAULT_WIDTH, 10000);
glFramebufferParameteri(GL_FRAMEBUFFER_DEFAULT_HEIGHT, 10000);
```

Listing 9.23: A 100-megapixel virtual framebuffer

If you render with the framebuffer object created in Listing 9.23 bound, you will be able to use **glViewport()** to set the viewport size to 10,000 pixels wide and high. Although there are no attachments on the framebuffer, OpenGL will rasterize primitives as if the framebuffer were really that size, and your fragment shader will run. The values of the x and y components of **gl_FragCoord** variable will range from 0 to 9999. You can use that how you wish—typically, you would want to make your fragment shader have a side effect such as writing to an image or incrementing atomic counters.

Floating-Point Framebuffers

One of the most useful framebuffer features is the ability to use attachments with floating-point formats. Although internally the OpenGL pipeline usually works with floating-point data, the sources (textures) and targets (framebuffer attachments) have often been fixed-point and of significantly less precision. As a result, many portions of the pipeline clamped all values between 0 and 1 so they could be stored in a fixed-point format in the end.

The data type passed into your vertex shader is up to you but is typically declared as **vec4**, or a vector of four floats. Similarly, you decide which outputs your vertex shader should write when you declare variables as **out** in a vertex shader. These outputs are then interpolated across your geometry and passed into your fragment shader. You have complete control over the type of data you will use for color throughout the whole pipeline, although it's most common to just use floats. You now have complete control over how and which format your data uses as it travels from vertex arrays all the way to the final output.

Now, instead of 256 values, you can color and shade using values from 1.18×10^{-38} to 3.4×10^{38}! You might wonder what happens if you are drawing to a window or monitor that supports only 8 bits per color. Unfortunately, the output is clamped to the range of 0 to 1 and then mapped to a fixed-point value. That's no fun! Until someone invents monitors or displays[6] that can understand and display floating-point data, you are still limited by the final output device.

That doesn't mean floating-point rendering isn't useful, though. Quite the contrary! You can still render to textures in full floating-point precision. Not only that, but you have complete control over how floating-point data gets mapped to a fixed output format. This can have a huge impact on the final result and is commonly referred to as having a high dynamic range (HDR).

Using Floating-Point Formats

Upgrading your applications to use floating-point buffers is easier than you may think. In fact, you don't even have to call any new functions. Instead, there are two new tokens you can use when creating buffers, GL_RGBA16F and GL_RGBA32F. They can be used when creating storage for textures:

```
glTextureStorage2D(texture, 1, GL_RGBA16F, width, height);
glTextureStorage2D(texture, 1, GL_RGBA32F, width, height);
```

In addition to the more traditional RGBA formats, Table 9.8 lists other formats allowed for creating floating-point textures. Having so many floating-point formats available allows applications to use the format that best suits the data that they will produce directly.

As you can see, there are 16- and 32-bit floating-point formats with one, two, three, and four channels. There is also a special format, GL_R11F_G11F_B10F, which contains two 11-bit floating-point components and one 10-bit component, packed together in a single 32-bit word. These are special, unsigned floating-point formats[7] with a 5-bit exponent and a 6-bit mantissa in the 11-bit components, and a 5-bit exponent and mantissa for the 10-bit component.

---

6. Some very high-end monitors are available today that can interpret 10 or even 12 bits of data in each channel. However, they're often prohibitively expensive and there aren't any displays that accept floating-point data outside of the lab.

7. Floating-point data is almost always signed, but it is possible to sacrifice the sign bit if only positive numbers will ever be stored.

Table 9.8: Floating-Point Texture Formats

Format	Content
GL_RGBA32F	Four 32-bit floating-point components
GL_RGBA16F	Four 16-bit floating-point components
GL_RGB32F	Three 32-bit floating-point components
GL_RGB16F	Three 16-bit floating-point components
GL_RG32F	Two 32-bit floating-point components
GL_RG16F	Two 16-bit floating-point components
GL_R32F	One 32-bit floating-point component
GL_R16F	One 16-bit floating-point component
GL_R11F_G11F_B10F	Two 11-bit floating-point components and one 10-bit floating-point component

In addition to using the formats shown in Table 9.8, you can create textures that have the GL_DEPTH_COMPONENT32F or GL_DEPTH_COMPONENT32F_STENCIL8 formats. The first is used to store depth information; such textures can be used as depth attachments on a framebuffer. The second represents both depth and stencil information stored in a single texture. This can be used for both the depth attachment and the stencil attachment of a frambuffer object.

High Dynamic Range

Many modern game applications use floating-point rendering to generate all of the great eye candy we now expect. The level of realism possible when generating lighting effects such as light bloom, lens flare, light reflections, light refractions, crepuscular rays, and the effects of participating media such as dust or clouds are often not possible without floating-point buffers. High dynamic range (HDR) rendering into floating-point buffers can make the bright areas of a scene really bright, keep shadow areas very dark, and still allow you to see detail in both. After all, the human eye has an incredible ability to perceive very high contrast levels well beyond the capabilities of today's displays.

Instead of drawing a complex scene with a lot of geometry and lighting in our sample programs to show how effective HDR can be, we use images already generated in HDR for simplicity. The first sample program, hdr_imaging, loads HDR (floating-point) images from .KTX files that store the original, floating-point data in its raw form. These images are generated by taking a series of aligned images of a scene with different exposures and combining them to produce an HDR result.

The low exposures capture detail in the bright areas of the scene, while the high exposures capture detail in the dark areas of the scene. Figure 9.15 shows four views of a scene of a tree lit by bright decorative lights (these images are also shown in Color Plate 3). The top-left image is rendered at a very low exposure and shows all of the details of the lights even though they are very bright. The top-right image increases the exposure such that you start to see details in the ribbon. On the bottom left, the exposure is increased to the level that you can see details in the pine cones. Finally, on the bottom right, the exposure has increased such that the branches in the foreground become very clear. The four images show the incredible amount of detail and range that are stored in a single image.

The only way to store so much detail in a single image is to use floating-point data. Any scene you render in OpenGL, especially if it has very bright or dark areas, can look more realistic when the true color output can be preserved instead of clamped between 0.0 and 1.0, and then divided into only 256 possible values.

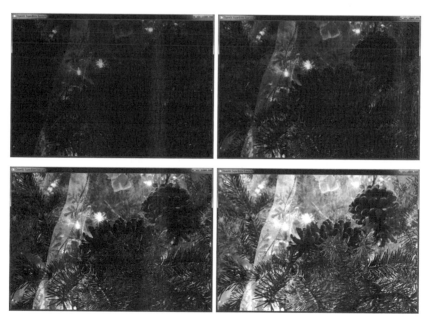

Figure 9.15: Different views of an HDR image

Tone Mapping

Now that you've seen some of the benefits of using floating-point rendering, how do you use that data to generate a dynamic image that still has to be displayed using values from 0 to 255? Tone mapping is the action of mapping color data from one set of colors to another or from one color space to another. Because we can't directly display floating-point data, it has to be tone-mapped into a color space that can be displayed.

The first sample program, hdrtonemap, uses three approaches to map the high-definition output to the low-definition screen. The first method, enabled by pressing the 1 key, is a simple and naïve direct texturing of the floating-point image to the screen. The histogram of the HDR image in Figure 9.15 is shown in Figure 9.16. From the graph, it is clear that while most of the image data has values between 0.0 and 1.0, many of the important highlights are well beyond 1.0. In fact, the highest luminance level for this image is almost 5.5!

If we send this image directly to our regular 8-bit normalized back buffer, the result is that the image is clamped and all of the bright areas look white. Additionally, because the majority of the data is in the first quater of the range, or between 0 and 63 when mapped directly to 8 bits, it all blends together to look black. Figure 9.17 shows the result: The bright areas such as the lamps are practically white, and the dark areas such as the pine cones are nearly black.

The second approach in the sample program is to vary the "exposure" of the image, similar to how a camera can vary exposure to the environment. Each exposure level provides a slightly different window into the texture

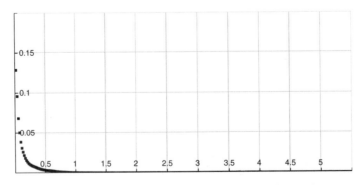

Figure 9.16: Histogram of levels for treelights.ktx

Figure 9.17: Naïve tone mapping by clamping

data. Low exposures show the detail in the very bright sections of the scene; high exposures allow you to see details in the dark areas but wash out the bright parts. This is similar to the images in Figure 9.15 with the low exposure on the upper left and the high exposure on the lower right. For our tone-mapping pass, the hdrtonemap sample program reads from a floating-point texture and writes to the default framebuffer with an 8-bit back buffer. This allows the conversion from HDR to LDR (low dynamic range) to occur on a pixel by pixel basis, which reduces artifacts that occur when a texel is interpolated between bright and dark areas. Once the LDR image has been generated, it can be displayed to the user. Listing 9.24 shows the simple exposure shader used in the example.

```
#version 450 core

layout (binding = 0) uniform sampler2D hdr_image;

uniform float exposure = 1.0;

out vec4 color;

void main(void)
{
    vec4 c = texelFetch(hdr_image, ivec2(gl_FragCoord.xy), 0);
    c.rgb = vec3(1.0) - exp(-c.rgb * exposure);
    color = c;
}
```

Listing 9.24: Applying a simple exposure coefficient to an HDR image

In the sample application, you can use the plus and minus keys on the numeric keypad to adjust the exposure. The range of exposures for this program goes from 0.01 to 20.0. Notice how the level of detail in different locations in the image changes with the exposure level. In fact, the images shown in Figure 9.15 were generated with this sample program by setting the exposure to different levels.

The last tone-mapping shader used in the first sample program performs dynamic adjustments to the exposure level based on the relative brightness of different portions of the scene. First, the shader needs to know the relative luminance of the area near the current texel being tone-mapped. The shader does this by sampling 25 texels centered on the current texel. All of the surrounding samples are converted to luminance values, which are then weighted and added together. The sample program uses a nonlinear function to convert the luminance to an exposure. In this example, the default curve is defined by the function

$$y = \sqrt{8.0(x + 0.25)}$$

The shape of the curve is shown in Figure 9.18.

The exposure is then used to convert the HDR texel to an LDR value using the same expression as in Listing 9.24. Listing 9.25 shows the adaptive HDR shader.

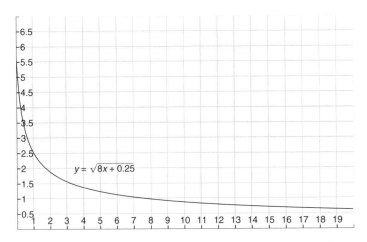

Figure 9.18: Transfer curve for adaptive tone mapping

```
#version 450 core
// hdr_adaptive.fs
//
//

in vec2 vTex;

layout (binding = 0) uniform sampler2D hdr_image;

out vec4 oColor;

void main(void)
{
    int i;
    float lum[25];
    vec2 tex_scale = vec2(1.0) / textureSize(hdr_image, 0);

    for (i = 0; i < 25; i++)
    {
        vec2 tc = (2.0 * gl_FragCoord.xy +
                   3.5 * vec2(i % 5 - 2, i / 5 - 2));
        vec3 col = texture(hdr_image, tc * tex_scale).rgb;
        lum[i] = dot(col, vec3(0.3, 0.59, 0.11));
    }

    // Calculate weighted color of region
    vec3 vColor = texelFetch(hdr_image,
                       2 * ivec2(gl_FragCoord.xy), 0).rgb;

    float kernelLuminance = (
        (1.0 * (lum[0] + lum[4] + lum[20] + lum[24])) +
        (4.0 * (lum[1] + lum[3] + lum[5] + lum[9] +
                lum[15] + lum[19] + lum[21] + lum[23])) +
        (7.0 * (lum[2] + lum[10] + lum[14] + lum[22])) +
        (16.0 * (lum[6] + lum[8] + lum[16] + lum[18])) +
        (26.0 * (lum[7] + lum[11] + lum[13] + lum[17])) +
        (41.0 * lum[12])
        ) / 273.0;

    // Compute the corresponding exposure
    float exposure = sqrt(8.0 / (kernelLuminance + 0.25));

    // Apply the exposure to this texel
    oColor.rgb = 1.0 - exp2(-vColor * exposure);
    oColor.a = 1.0f;
}
```

Listing 9.25: Adaptive HDR to LDR conversion fragment shader

When using one exposure for an image, you can adjust for the best results
by taking the range for the whole and using an average. Considerable
detail is still lost with this approach in the bright and dim areas. The
nonlinear transfer function used with the adaptive fragment shader brings
out the details in both the bright and dim areas of the image; take a look
at Figure 9.19 (also shown in Color Plate 4). The transfer function uses
a logarithmic-like scale to map luminance values to exposure levels. You
can change this function to increase or decrease the range of exposures
used and the resulting amount of detail in different dynamic ranges.

Figure 9.19: Result of adaptive tone-mapping program

Great, so now you know how to image process an HDR file, but what good is that in a typical OpenGL program? Lots! The HDR image is only a stand-in for any lit OpenGL scene. Many OpenGL games and applications now render HDR scenes and other content to floating-point framebuffer attachments and then display the result by doing a final pass using a technique such as the one discussed here. You can use the same methods you just learned to render in HDR, generating much more realistic lighting environments and showing the dynamic range and detail of each frame.

Making Your Scene Bloom

One of the effects that works very well with high dynamic range images is the bloom effect. Have you ever noticed how the sun or a bright light can sometimes engulf tree branches or other objects between you and the light source? That's called *light bloom*. Figure 9.20 shows how light bloom can affect an indoor scene.

Notice how you can see all the details in the lower exposure of the left image in Figure 9.20. The right image is a much higher exposure, and the grid in the stained glass is covered by the light bloom. Even the wooden post on the bottom right looks smaller as it gets covered by bloom. By adding bloom to a scene you can enhance the sense of brightness in certain areas.

Figure 9.20: The effect of light bloom on an image

You can simulate this bloom effect caused by bright light sources. Although you could also perform this effect using 8-bit precision buffers, it's much more effective when used with floating-point buffers on a high dynamic range scene.

The first step is to draw your scene with high dynamic range. For the hdrbloom sample program, a framebuffer is set up with two floating-point textures bound as color attachments. The scene is rendered in the usual way to the first bound texture. But the second bound texture gets only the bright areas of the field. The hdrbloom sample program fills both textures in one pass from one shader; see Listing 9.26. The output color is computed as usual and sent to the color0 output. Then, the luminance (brightness) value of the color is calculated and used to threshold the data. Only the brightest data is used to generate the bloom effect and is written to the second output, color1. The threshold levels used are adjustable via a pair of uniforms, bloom_thresh_min and bloom_thresh_max. To filter for the bright areas, we use the smoothstep function to smoothly force any fragments whose brightness is less than bloom_thresh_min to zero, and any fragments whose brightness is greater than bloom_thresh_max to four times the original color output.

```
#version 450 core

layout (location = 0) out vec4 color0;
layout (location = 1) out vec4 color1;

in VS_OUT
{
    vec3 N;
    vec3 L;
    vec3 V;
    flat int material_index;
} fs_in;

// Material properties
uniform float bloom_thresh_min = 0.8;
uniform float bloom_thresh_max = 1.2;

struct material_t
{
    vec3    diffuse_color;
    vec3    specular_color;
    float   specular_power;
    vec3    ambient_color;
};

layout (binding = 1, std140) uniform MATERIAL_BLOCK
{
    material_t material[32];
} materials;

void main(void)
{
    // Normalize the incoming N, L, and V vectors
    vec3 N = normalize(fs_in.N);
    vec3 L = normalize(fs_in.L);
    vec3 V = normalize(fs_in.V);

    // Calculate R locally
    vec3 R = reflect(-L, N);

    material_t m = materials.material[fs_in.material_index];

    // Compute the diffuse and specular components for each fragment
    vec3 diffuse = max(dot(N, L), 0.0) * m.diffuse_color;
    vec3 specular = pow(max(dot(R, V), 0.0), m.specular_power) * m.specular_color;
    vec3 ambient = m.ambient_color;

    // Add ambient, diffuse, and specular to find final color
    vec3 color = ambient + diffuse + specular;

    // Write final color to the framebuffer
    color0 = vec4(color, 1.0);

    // Calculate luminance
    float Y = dot(color, vec3(0.299, 0.587, 0.144));

    // Threshold color based on its luminance and write it to
    // the second output
    color = color * 4.0 * smoothstep(bloom_thresh_min, bloom_thresh_max, Y);
    color1 = vec4(color, 1.0);
}
```

Listing 9.26: Bloom fragment shader—output bright data to a separate buffer

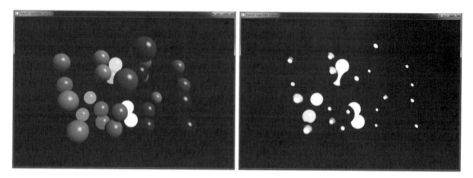

Figure 9.21: Original and thresholded output for bloom example

After the first shader has run, we obtain the two images shown in Figure 9.21. The scene we rendered is just a large collection of spheres with varying material properties. Some of them are configured to actually emit light, as they have properties that will produce values in the framebuffer greater than 1 no matter what the lighting effects are. The image on the left is the scene rendered with no bloom. Notice that it is sharp in all areas, regardless of brightness. The image on the right is the thresholded version of the image that will be used as input to the bloom filters.

After the scene has been rendered, there is still some work to do to finish the bright pass. The bright data must be blurred for the bloom effect to work. To implement this, we use a separable Gaussian filter. A separable filter is a filter that can be separated into two passes—generally one pass in the horizontal axis and one pass in the vertical axis. In this example, we use 25 taps in each dimension, sampling from the 25 samples around the center of the filter and multiplying each texel by a fixed set of weights. To apply a separable filter, we make two passes. In the first pass, we filter in the horizontal dimension. However, you might notice that we use gl_FragCoord.yx to determine the center of our filter kernel. This means that we will *transpose* the image during filtering. On the second pass, we apply the same filter again. This means that filtering in the horizontal axis is equivalent to filtering in the vertical axis of the original image, and the output image is transposed again, returning it to its original orientation. In effect, we have performed a 2D Gaussian filter with a diameter of 25 samples and a total sample count of 625. The shader that implements this operation is shown in Listing 9.27.

```
#version 450 core

layout (binding = 0) uniform sampler2D hdr_image;

out vec4 color;

const float weights[] = float[](0.0024499299678342,
                                0.0043538453346397,
                                0.0073599963704157,
                                0.0118349786570722,
                                0.0181026699707781,
                                0.0263392293891488,
                                0.0364543006660986,
                                0.0479932050577658,
                                0.0601029809166942,
                                0.0715974486241365,
                                0.0811305381519717,
                                0.0874493212267511,
                                0.0896631113333857,
                                0.0874493212267511,
                                0.0811305381519717,
                                0.0715974486241365,
                                0.0601029809166942,
                                0.0479932050577658,
                                0.0364543006660986,
                                0.0263392293891488,
                                0.0181026699707781,
                                0.0118349786570722,
                                0.0073599963704157,
                                0.0043538453346397,
                                0.0024499299678342);

void main(void)
{
    vec4 c = vec4(0.0);
    ivec2 P = ivec2(gl_FragCoord.yx) - ivec2(0, weights.length() >> 1);
    int i;

    for (i = 0; i < weights.length(); i++)
    {
        c += texelFetch(hdr_image, P + ivec2(0, i), 0) * weights[i];
    }

    color = c;
}
```

Listing 9.27: Blur fragment shader

The result of applying blur to the thresholded image on the right in
Figure 9.21 is shown in Figure 9.22.

After the blurring passes are complete, the blur results are combined with
the full color texture of the scene to produce the final results. In
Listing 9.28, notice that the final shader samples form two textures: the
original full color texture and the blurred version of the bright pass.
The original colors and and the blurred results are added together to form
the bloom effect, which is multiplied by a user-controlled uniform. The

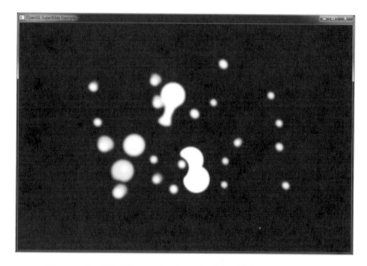

Figure 9.22: Blurred thresholded bloom colors

final HDR color result is then put through exposure calculations, which you should be familiar with from the last example program.

```
#version 450 core

layout (binding = 0) uniform sampler2D hdr_image;
layout (binding = 1) uniform sampler2D bloom_image;

uniform float exposure = 0.9;
uniform float bloom_factor = 1.0;
uniform float scene_factor = 1.0;

out vec4 color;

void main(void)
{
    vec4 c = vec4(0.0);

    c += texelFetch(hdr_image, ivec2(gl_FragCoord.xy), 0) * scene_factor;
    c += texelFetch(bloom_image, ivec2(gl_FragCoord.xy), 0) * bloom_factor;

    c.rgb = vec3(1.0) - exp(-c.rgb * exposure);
    color = c;
}
```

Listing 9.28: Adding a bloom effect to the scene

The exposure shader shown in Listing 9.28 is used to draw a screen-sized textured quad to the window. That's it! Dial the bloom effect up and down to your heart's content. Figure 9.23 shows the hdrbloom sample program with a high bloom level.

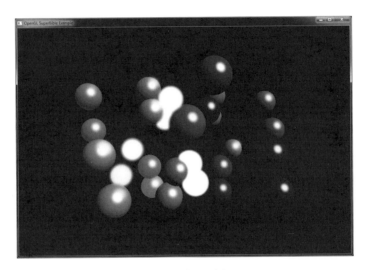

Figure 9.23: Result of the bloom program

A comparison of the output of this program with and without bloom is shown in Color Plate 5.

Integer Framebuffers

By default, the window system will provide your application with a *fixed-point* back buffer. When you declare a floating-point output from your fragment shader (such as a `vec4`), OpenGL will convert the data you write into it into a fixed-point representation suitable for storage in that framebuffer. In the previous section we covered floating-point framebuffer attachments, which provides the capability of storing an arbitrary floating-point value in the framebuffer. It's also possible to create an *integer* framebuffer attachment by creating a texture with an integer internal format and attaching it to a framebuffer object. When you do this, it becomes possible to use an output with an integer component type such as `ivec4` or `uvec4`. With an integer framebuffer attachment, the bit pattern contained in your output variables will be written verbatim into the texture. You don't need to worry about denormals, negative zero, infinities, or any other special bit patterns that might be a concern with floating-point buffers.

To create an integer framebuffer attachment, simply create a texture with an internal format made up of integer components and attach it to a framebuffer object. Internal formats that are made up of integers generally end in I or UI—for example, GL_RGBA32UI represents a format made up of four unsigned 32-bit integers per texel, and GL_R16I is a format made up of a single signed 16-bit component per texel. Code to create a framebuffer attachment with an internal format of GL_RGBA32UI is shown in Listing 9.29.

```
// Variables for the texture and FBO
GLuint tex;
GLuint fbo;

// Create the texture object
glCreateTextures(GL_TEXTURE_2D, 1, &tex);

// Allocate storage for it
glTextureStorage2D(tex, 1, GL_RGBA32UI, 1024, 1024);

// Now create an FBO and attach the texure as normal
glGenFrambuffers(1, &fbo);
glBindFramebuffer(GL_FRAMEBUFFER, fbo);

glFramebufferTexture(GL_FRAMEBFUFFER,
                     GL_COLOR_ATTACHMENT0,
                     tex,
                     0);
```

Listing 9.29: Creating integer framebuffer attachments

You can determine the component type of a framebuffer attachment by calling **glGetFramebufferAttachmentParameteriv()** with pname set to GL_FRAMEBUFFER_ATTACHMENT_COMPONENT_TYPE. The value returned in params will be GL_FLOAT, GL_INT, GL_UNSIGNED_INT, GL_SIGNED_NORMALIZED, or GL_UNSIGNED_NORMALIZED depending on the internal format of the color attachments. There is no requirement that the attachments to a framebuffer object all be of the same type. This means that you can have a combination of attachments, some of which use floating-point or fixed-point and others of which use integer formats.

When you render to an integer framebuffer attachment, the output declared in your fragment shader should match that of the attachment in the component type. For example, if your framebuffer attachment is an unsigned integer format such as GL_RGBA32UI, then your shader's output variable corresponding to that color attachment should be an unsigned integer format such as unsigned int, uvec2, uvec3, or uvec4. Likewise, for signed integer formats, your output should be int, ivec2, ivec3, or ivec4. Although the component formats should match, there is no requirement that the number of components match.

If the component width of the framebuffer attachment is less than 32 bits, then the additional most significant bits will be thrown away when you render to it. You can even write floating-point data directly into an integer color buffer by using the GLSL function `floatBitsToInt` (or `floatBitsToUint`) or packing functions such as `packUnorm2x16`.

While it might seem that integer framebuffer attachments offer some level of flexibility over traditional fixed- or floating-point framebuffers—especially in light of being able to write floating-point data into them—there are some trade-offs that must be considered. The first and most glaring issue is that blending is not available for integer framebuffers. A second issue is that having an integer internal format means that the resulting texture into which you rendered your image cannot be filtered.

The sRGB Color Space

Eons ago, computer users had large, clunky monitors made from glass vacuum bottles called cathode ray tubes (CRTs). These devices worked by shooting electrons at a fluorescent screen to make it glow. Unfortunately, the amount of light emitted by the screen was not linear in the voltage used to drive it. In fact, the relationship between light output and driving voltage was highly nonlinear. The amount of light output was a power function of the form:

$$L_{out} = V_{in}{}^{\gamma}$$

To make matters worse, γ didn't always take the same value. For NTSC systems (the television standard used in North America, much of South America, and parts of Asia), γ was about 2.2. However, SECAM and PAL systems (the standards used in Europe, Australia, Africa, and other parts of Asia) used a γ value of 2.8. That means that if you put a voltage of half the maximum into a CRT-based display, you'd get a little less than one-quarter of the maximum possible light output!

To compensate for this, in computer graphics we apply *gamma correction* (named after the γ term in the power function), by raising linear values by a small power, scaling the result, and offsetting it. The resulting color space is known as sRGB and the pseudocode to translate from a linear value to an sRGB value is as follows:

```
if (cl >= 1.0)
{
    cs = 1.0;
}
else if (cl <= 0.0)
{
    cs = 0.0;
}
```

```
else if (cl < 0.0031308)
{
    cs = 12.92 * cl;
}
else
{
    cs = 1.055 * pow(cl, 0.41666) - 0.055;
}
```

Further, to go from sRGB to linear color space, we apply the transformation illustrated by the following pseudocode:

```
if (cs >= 1.0)
{
    cl = 1.0;
}
else if (cs <= 0.0)
{
    cl = 0.0;
}
else if (cs <= 0.04045)
{
    cl = cs / 12.92;
}
else
{
    cl = pow((cs + 0.0555) / 1.055), 2.4)
}
```

In both cases, `cs` is the sRGB color space value and `cl` is the linear value. Notice that the transformation has a short linear section and a small bias. In practice, this is so close to raising our linear color values to the powers 2.2 (for sRGB to linear) and 0.454545, which is $\frac{1}{2.2}$ (for linear to sRGB), that some implementations will do this. Figure 9.24 shows the transfer functions of linear to sRGB and sRGB back to linear on the left, and a pair of simple power curves using the powers 2.2 and 0.45454 on the right. You should notice that the shapes of these curves are so close so as to be almost indistinguishable.

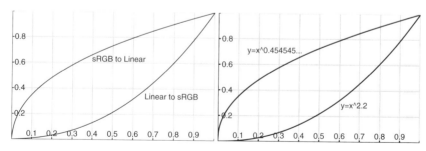

Figure 9.24: Gamma curves for sRGB and simple powers

To use the sRGB color space in OpenGL, we create textures with sRGB internal formats. For example, the GL_SRGB_ALPHA8 format represents the red, green, and blue components with an sRGB gamma ramp and the alpha component as a simple linear value. We can load data into the texture as usual. When you read from an sRGB texture in your shader, the sRGB format is converted to RGB when the texture is sampled but before it is filtered. That is, when bilinear filtering is turned on, the incoming texels are converted from sRGB to linear, and then the linear samples are blended together to form the final value returned to the shader. Also, only the RGB components are converted separately; the alpha component is left as is.

Framebuffers also support storage formats that are sRGB; specifically, the format GL_SRGB8_ALPHA8 must be supported. That means you can attach textures that have an internal sRGB format to a framebuffer object and then render to it. Because sRGB formats are not linear, you probably don't want your writes to sRGB framebuffer attachments to be linear, either; that would defeat the whole purpose! The good news is OpenGL can convert the linear color values your shader outputs into sRGB values automatically. However, this conversion isn't performed by default. To turn this feature on, you need to call **glEnable()** with the GL_FRAMEBUFFER_SRGB token. Remember, this works only for color attachments that contain an sRGB surface. You can call **glGetFramebufferAttachmentParameteriv()** with the value GL_FRAMEBUFFER_ATTACHMENT_COLOR_ENCODING to find out if the attached surface is sRGB. sRGB surfaces return GL_SRGB, while other surfaces return GL_LINEAR.

Point Sprites

The term *point sprites* is typically used to refer to textured points. OpenGL represents each point by a single vertex, so there is no opportunity to specify texture coordinates that can be interpolated as there is with the other primitive types. To get around this limitation, OpenGL will generate interpolated texture coordinates with which you can do anything you like. With point sprites, you can place a 2D textured image anywhere on the screen by drawing a single 3D point.

One of the most common applications of point sprites is for particle systems. A large number of particles moving on screen can be represented as points to produce a number of visual effects. However, representing these points as small overlapped 2D images can produce dramatic

Figure 9.25: A particle effect in the flurry screen saver

streaming animated filaments. For example, Figure 9.25 shows a well-known screen saver on the Macintosh powered by just such a particle effect.

Without point sprites, achieving this type of effect would be a matter of drawing a large number of textured quads (or triangle fans) on screen. This could be accomplished either by performing a costly rotation to each individual face to make sure that it faced the camera, or by drawing all particles in a 2D orthographic projection. Point sprites allow you to render a perfectly aligned textured 2D square by sending down a single 3D vertex. As they require only one-quarter the bandwidth of sending down four vertices for a quad and need no matrix math to keep the 3D quad aligned with the camera, point sprites are a potent and efficient feature of OpenGL.

Texturing Points

Point sprites are easy to use. On the application side, the only thing you have to do is simply bind a 2D texture and read from it in your fragment shader using a built-in variable called gl_PointCoord, which is a two-component vector that interpolates the texture coordinates across the point. Listing 9.30 shows the fragment shader for the PointSprites example program.

```
#version 450 core

out vec4 vFragColor;

in vec4 vStarColor;

layout (binding = 0) uniform sampler2D starImage;

void main(void)
{
    vFragColor = texture(starImage, gl_PointCoord) * vStarColor;
}
```

Listing 9.30: Texturing a point sprite in the fragment shader

Again, for a point sprite, you do not need to send down texture coordinates as an attribute because OpenGL will produce gl_PointCoord automatically. Since a point is a single vertex, you wouldn't have the ability to interpolate across the points surface any other way. Of course, there is nothing preventing you from providing a texture coordinate anyway or deriving your own customized interpolation scheme.

Rendering a Star Field

Let's now take a look at an example program that makes use of the point sprite features discussed so far. The starfield example program creates an animated star field that appears as if you were flying forward through it. This is accomplished by placing random points out in front of your field of view and then passing a time value into the vertex shader as a uniform. This time value is used to move the point positions so that over time they move closer to you and then recycle when they get to the near clipping plane by returning to the back of the frustum. In addition, we scale the sizes of the stars so that they start off very small but get larger as they get closer to your point of view. The result is a nice realistic effect... all we need is some planetarium or space movie music!

Figure 9.26 shows our star texture map that is applied to the points. It is simply a .KTX file that we load in the same manner as any other 2D texture. Points can also be mipmapped, and because they can range from very small to very large, it's probably a good idea to do so.

We won't cover all of the details of setting up the star field effect, as it's pretty routine. You can check the source yourself if you want to see how we pick random numbers. Of more importance is the actual rendering of code in the render function:

Figure 9.26: The star texture map

```
void render(double currentTime)
{
    static const GLfloat black[] = { 0.0f, 0.0f, 0.0f, 0.0f };
    static const GLfloat one[] = { 1.0f };
    float t = (float)currentTime;
    float aspect = (float)info.windowWidth /
                   (float)info.windowHeight;
    vmath::mat4 proj_matrix = vmath::perspective(50.0f,
                                                  aspect,
                                                  0.1f,
                                                  1000.0f);

    t *= 0.1f;
    t -= floor(t);

    glViewport(0, 0, info.windowWidth, info.windowHeight);
    glClearBufferfv(GL_COLOR, 0, black);
    glClearBufferfv(GL_DEPTH, 0, one);

    glEnable(GL_PROGRAM_POINT_SIZE);
    glUseProgram(render_prog);

    glUniform1f(uniforms.time, t);
    glUniformMatrix4fv(uniforms.proj_matrix, 1, GL_FALSE, proj_matrix);

    glEnable(GL_BLEND);
    glBlendFunc(GL_ONE, GL_ONE);

    glBindVertexArray(star_vao);

    glDrawArrays(GL_POINTS, 0, NUM_STARS);
}
```

We'll use additive blending to blend our stars with the background.
Because the dark area of our texture is black (0 in color space), we can get
away with just adding the colors together as we draw. Transparency with
alpha components would require that we depth-sort our stars, and that is
an expense we certainly can do without. After turning on point size

program mode, we bind our shader and set up the uniforms. Of interest here is that we use the current time, which drives what will end up being the z position of our stars; it recycles so that it just counts smoothly from 0 to 1. Listing 9.31 provides the source code to the vertex shader.

```
#version 450 core

layout (location = 0) in vec4 position;
layout (location = 1) in vec4 color;

uniform float time;
uniform mat4 proj_matrix;

flat out vec4 starColor;

void main(void)
{
    vec4 newVertex = position;

    newVertex.z += time;
    newVertex.z = fract(newVertex.z);

    float size = (20.0 * newVertex.z * newVertex.z);

    starColor = smoothstep(1.0, 7.0, size) * color;

    newVertex.z = (999.9 * newVertex.z) - 1000.0;
    gl_Position = proj_matrix * newVertex;
    gl_PointSize = size;
}
```

Listing 9.31: Vertex shader for the star field effect

The vertex z component is offset by the time uniform. This is what causes the animation where the stars move closer to you. We use only the fractional part of this sum so that the stars' positions loop back to the far clipping plane as they get closer to the viewer. At this point in the shader, vertices with a z coordinate of 0.0 are at the far plane and vertices with a z coordinate of 1.0 are at the near plane. We can use the square of the vertex's z coordinate to make the stars grow ever larger as they get nearer and set the final size in the gl_PointSize variable. If the star sizes are too small, you will sometimes get flickering, so we dim the color progressively using the smoothstep function so that any points with a size less than 1.0 will be black, fading to full intensity as they reach 7 pixels in size. This way, they fade into view instead of just popping up near the far clipping plane. The star color is passed to the fragment shader shown in Listing 9.32, which simply fetches from our star texture and multiplies the result by the computed star color.

Figure 9.27: Flying through space with point sprites

```
#version 450 core

layout (location = 0) out vec4 color;

uniform sampler2D tex_star;
flat in vec4 starColor;

void main(void)
{
    color = starColor * texture(tex_star, gl_PointCoord);
}
```

Listing 9.32: Fragment shader for the star field effect

The final output of the starfield program is shown in Figure 9.27.

Point Parameters

A few features of point sprites (and points in general) can be fine-tuned with the function **glPointParameteri()**. Figure 9.28 shows the two possible locations of the origin (0,0) of the texture applied to a point sprite. On the left, we see the origin on the upper left of the point sprite; on the right, we see the origin on the lower left.

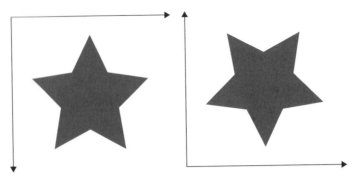

Figure 9.28: Two potential orientations of textures on a point sprite

The default orientation for point sprites is GL_UPPER_LEFT. Setting the GL_POINT_SPRITE_COORD_ORIGIN parameter to GL_LOWER_LEFT places the origin of the texture coordinate system at the lower-left corner of the point:

```
glPointParameteri(GL_POINT_SPRITE_COORD_ORIGIN, GL_LOWER_LEFT);
```

When the point sprite origin is set to its default of GL_UPPER_LEFT, gl_PointCoord will be 0.0, 0.0 at the top left of the point as it is viewed on the screen. However, in OpenGL, window coordinates are considered to start at the lower left of the window (the convention that gl_FragCoord adheres to, for example). Therefore, to get our point sprite coordinates to follow the window coordinate conventions and align with gl_FragCoord, we set the point sprite coordinate origin to GL_LOWER_LEFT.

Shaped Points

There is more you can do with point sprites besides apply a texture using gl_PointCoord for texture coordinates. You can use gl_PointCoord to derive a number of things other than just texture coordinates. For example, you can make non-square points by using the discard keyword in your fragment shader to throw away fragments that lie outside your desired point shape. The following fragment shader code produces round points:

```
vec2 p = gl_PointCoord * 2.0 - vec2(1.0);
if (dot(p, p) > 1.0)
    discard;
```

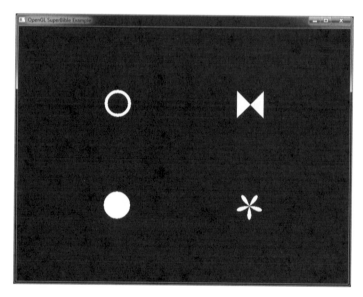

Figure 9.29: Analytically generated point sprite shapes

Or perhaps you might prefer an interesting flower shape:

```
vec2 temp = gl_PointCoord * 2.0 - vec2(1.0);
if (dot(temp, temp) > sin(atan(temp.y, temp.x) * 5.0))
    discard;
```

These simple code snippets allow arbitrary-shaped points to be rendered. Figure 9.29 shows a few more examples of interesting shapes that can be generated this way. To create Figure 9.29, we used the fragment shader shown in Listing 9.33.

```
#version 450 core

layout (location = 0) out vec4 color;

flat in int shape;

void main(void)
{
    color = vec4(1.0);
    vec2 p = gl_PointCoord * 2.0 - vec2(1.0);

    if (shape == 0)
    {
```

```
        // Simple disc shape
        if (dot(p, p) > 1.0)
            discard;
    }
    else if (shape == 1)
    {
        // Hollow circle
        if (abs(0.8 - dot(p, p)) > 0.2)
            discard;
    }
    else if (shape == 2)
    {
        // Flower shape
        if (dot(p, p) > sin(atan(p.y, p.x) * 5.0))
            discard;
    }
    else if (shape == 3)
    {
        // Bowtie
        if (abs(p.x) < abs(p.y))
            discard;
    }
}
```

Listing 9.33: Fragment shader for generating shaped points

The advantage of calculating the shape of your points analytically in the fragment shader rather than using a texture is that the shapes are exact and stand up well to scaling and rotation, as you will see in the next section.

Rotating Points

Because points in OpenGL are rendered as axis-aligned squares, rotating the point sprite must be done by modifying the texture coordinates used to read the sprite's texture or to analytically calculate its shape. To do this, you can simply create a 2D rotation matrix in the fragment shader and multiply it by gl_PointCoord to rotate it around the z axis. The angle of rotation could be passed from the vertex or geometry shader to the fragment shader as an interpolated variable. The value of the variable can, in turn, be calculated in the vertex or geometry shader or be supplied through a vertex attribute. Listing 9.34 shows a slightly more complex point sprite fragment shader that allows the point to be rotated around its center.

```
#version 450 core

uniform sampler2D sprite_texture;

in float angle;
```

```
out vec4 color;

void main(void)
{
    const float sin_theta = sin(angle);
    const float cos_theta = cos(angle);
    const mat2 rotation_matrix = mat2(cos_theta, sin_theta,
                                     -sin_theta, cos_theta);
    const vec2 pt = gl_PointCoord - vec2(0.5);
    color = texture(sprite_texture, rotation_matrix * pt + vec2(0.5));
}
```

Listing 9.34: Naïve rotated point sprite fragment shader

This example allows you to generate rotated point sprites. However, the
value of angle will not change from one fragment to another within the
point sprite. That means sin_theta and cos_theta will be constant and the
resulting rotation matrix constructed from them will be the same for every
fragment in the point. It is therefore much more efficient to calculate
sin_theta and cos_theta in the vertex shader and pass them as a pair of
variables into the fragment shader rather than calculating them at every
fragment. Here's an updated vertex and fragment shader that allows you to
draw rotated point sprites. First, the vertex shader is shown in Listing 9.35.

```
#version 450 core

uniform matrix mvp;

in vec4 position;
in float angle;

flat out float sin_theta;
flat out float cos_theta;

void main(void)
{
    sin_theta = sin(angle);
    cos_theta = cos(angle);

    gl_Position = mvp * position;
}
```

Listing 9.35: Rotated point sprite vertex shader

Next, the fragment shader is shown in Listing 9.36.

```
#version 450 core

uniform sampler2D sprite_texture;

flat in float sin_theta;
flat in float cos_theta;
```

```
out vec4 color;

void main(void)
{
    mat2 rotation_matrix = mat2(cos_theta, sin_theta,
                                -sin_theta, cos_theta);
    vec2 pt = gl_PointCoord - vec2(0.5);
    color = texture(sprite_texture, rotation_matrix * pt + vec2(0.5));
}
```

Listing 9.36: Rotated point sprite fragment shader

As you can see, the potentially expensive `sin` and `cos` functions have been moved out of the fragment shader and into the vertex shader. If the point size is large, this pair of shaders performs much better than the earlier, brute-force approach of calculating the rotation matrix in the fragment shader.

Even though you are rotating the coordinates you derived from `gl_PointCoord`, the point itself is still square. If your texture or analytic shape spills outside the unit diameter circle inside the point, you will need to make your point sprite larger and scale your texture coordinate down accordingly to get the shape to fit within the point under all angles of rotation. Of course, if your texture is essentially round, you don't need to worry about this at all.

Getting at Your Image

Once everything's rendered, your application will usually show the result to the user. The mechanism to do this is platform specific, so the book's application framework normally takes care of this for you. However, showing the result to the user might not always be what you want to do. There are many reasons why you might want to gain access to the rendered image directly from your application. For example, perhaps you want to print the image, save a screenshot, or even process it further with an offline process.

Reading from a Framebuffer

To allow you to read pixel data from the framebuffer, OpenGL includes the **glReadPixels()** function, whose prototype is

```
void glReadPixels(GLint x,
                  GLint y,
                  GLsizei width,
```

```
                    GLsizei height,
                    GLenum format,
                    GLenum type,
                    GLvoid * data);
```

The **glReadPixels()** function reads data from a region of the framebuffer currently bound to the GL_READ_FRAMEBUFFER target, or from the default framebuffer if no user-generated framebuffer object is bound, and writes it into your application's memory or into a buffer object. The x and y parameters specify the offset in window coordinates of the lower-left corner of the region, and width and height specify the width and height of the region to be read—remember, the origin of the window (which is at 0, 0) is the *lower-left* corner. The format and type parameters tell OpenGL the format in which you want the data to be read back in. These parameters work similarly to the format and type parameters that you might pass to **glTexSubImage2D()**, for example. For instance, format might be GL_RED or GL_RGBA and type might be GL_UNSIGNED_BYTE or GL_FLOAT. The resulting pixel data is written into the region specified by data.

If no buffer object is bound to the GL_PIXEL_PACK_BUFFER target, then data is interpreted as a raw pointer into your application's memory. However, if a buffer *is* bound to the GL_PIXEL_PACK_BUFFER target, then data is treated as an offset into that buffer's data store and the image data is written there. If you want to get at that data, you can then map the buffer for reading by calling **glMapBufferRange()** with the GL_MAP_READ_BIT set and access the data. Otherwise, you could use the buffer for any other purpose.

To specify where the color data comes from, you can call **glReadBuffer()**, passing GL_BACK or GL_COLOR_ATTACHMENT*i* where *i* indicates which color attachment you want to read from. The prototype of **glReadBuffer()** is

```
    void glReadBuffer(GLenum mode);
```

If you are using the default framebuffer rather than your own framebuffer object, then mode should be GL_BACK. This is the default, so if you never use framebuffer objects in your application (or if you only ever read from the default framebuffer), you can get away without calling **glReadBuffer()** at all. However, since user-supplied framebuffer objects can have multiple attachments, you need to specify which attachment you want to read from; thus you must call **glReadBuffer()** if you are using your own framebuffer object.

When you call **glReadPixels()** with the format parameter set to GL_DEPTH_COMPONENT, the data read will come from the depth buffer.

Likewise, if format is GL_STENCIL_INDEX, then the data comes from the stencil buffer. The special GL_DEPTH_STENCIL token allows you to read both the depth and stencil buffers at the same time. However, if you take this route, then the type parameter must be either GL_UNSIGNED_INT_24_8 or GL_FLOAT_32_UNSIGNED_INT_24_8_REV, which produces packed data that you would need to interpret to get at the depth and stencil information.

When OpenGL writes the data either into your application's memory or into the buffer object bound to the GL_PIXEL_PACK_BUFFER target (if there is one bound), it writes it from left to right in order of ascending y coordinate (recall that its origin is at the bottom of the window and it increases in an upward direction). By default, each row of the image starts at an offset from the previous row, which is a multiple of 4 bytes. If the product of the width of the region to be read and the number of bytes per pixel is a multiple of 4, then everything works out and the resulting data will be tightly packed. However, if things don't add up, then you could be left with gaps in the output. You can change this by calling **glPixelStorei()**, whose prototype is

```
void glPixelStorei(GLenum pname,
                   GLint param);
```

When you pass GL_PACK_ALIGNMENT in pname, the value you pass in param is used to round the distance in bytes between each row of the image. You can pass 1 in param to set the rounding to a single byte, effectively disabling the rounding. The other values you can pass are 2, 4, and 8.

Taking a Screenshot

Listing 9.37 demonstrates how to take a screenshot of a running application and save it as a .TGA file, which is a relatively simple image file format that is easy to generate.

```
int row_size = ((info.windowWidth * 3 + 3) & ~3);
int data_size = row_size * info.windowHeight;
unsigned char * data = new unsigned char [data_size];

#pragma pack (push, 1)
struct
{
    unsigned char identsize;      // Size of following ID field
    unsigned char cmaptype;       // Color map type 0 = none
    unsigned char imagetype;      // Image type 2 = rgb
```

```
    short cmapstart;                    // First entry in palette
    short cmapsize;                     // Number of entries in palette
    unsigned char cmapbpp;             // Number of bits per palette entry
    short xorigin;                      // X origin
    short yorigin;                      // Y origin
    short width;                        // Width in pixels
    short height;                       // Height in pixels
    unsigned char bpp;                  // Bits per pixel
    unsigned char descriptor;           // Descriptor bits
} tga_header;
#pragma pack (pop)

glReadPixels(0, 0,                                          // Origin
             info.windowWidth, info.windowHeight,          // Size
             GL_BGR, GL_UNSIGNED_BYTE,                      // Format, type
             data);                                        // Data

memset(&tga_header, 0, sizeof(tga_header));
tga_header.imagetype = 2;
tga_header.width = (short)info.windowWidth;
tga_header.height = (short)info.windowHeight;
tga_header.bpp = 24;

FILE * f_out = fopen("screenshot.tga", "wb");
fwrite(&tga_header, sizeof(tga_header), 1, f_out);
fwrite(data, data_size, 1, f_out);
fclose(f_out);

delete [] data;
```

Listing 9.37: Taking a screenshot with `glReadPixels()`

The `.TGA` file format simply consists of a header (which is defined by `tga_header`) followed by raw pixel data. The example of Listing 9.37 fills in the header and then writes the raw data into the file immediately following it.

Copying Data between Framebuffers

Rendering to these off-screen framebuffers is fine and dandy, but ultimately you have to do something useful with the result. Traditionally graphics APIs allowed an application to read pixel or buffer data back to system memory and also provided ways to draw it back to the screen. While these methods are functional, they require copying data from the GPU into CPU memory and then turning right around and copying it back. Very inefficient! We now have a way to quickly move pixel data from one spot to another using a blit command. *Blit* is a term that refers to direct, efficient bit-level data/memory copies. There are many theories of the origin of this term, but the most likely candidates are bit-level image transfer or block transfer. Whatever the etymology of blit

may be, the action is the same. Performing these copies is simple; the
function looks like this:

```
void glBlitFramebuffer(GLint srcX0, Glint srcY0,
                       GLint srcX1, Glint srcY1,
                       GLint dstX0, Glint dstY0,
                       GLint dstX1, Glint dstY1,
                       GLbitfield mask, GLenum filter);
```

Even though this function has "blit" in the name, it does much more than
a simple bitwise copy. In fact, it's more like an automated texturing
operation. The source of the copy is the read framebuffer's read buffer
specified by calling **glReadBuffer()**, and the area copied is the region
defined by the rectangle with corners at (srcX0, srcY0) and (srcX1, srcY1).
Likewise, the target of the copy is the current draw framebuffer's draw
buffer specified by calling **glDrawBuffer()**, and the area copied to is region
defined by the rectangle with corners at (dstX0, dstY0) and (dstX1, dstY1).
Because the rectangles for the source and destination do not have to be of
equal size, you can use this function to scale the pixels being copied. If
you have set the read and draw buffers to the same FBO and have bound
the same FBO to the GL_DRAW_FRAMEBUFFER and GL_READ_FRAMEBUFFER
bindings, you can even copy data from one portion of a framebuffer to
another (so long as you're careful that the regions don't overlap).

The mask argument can be any or all of GL_DEPTH_BUFFER_BIT,
GL_STENCIL_BUFFER_BIT, or GL_COLOR_BUFFER_BIT. The filter can be either
GL_LINEAR or GL_NEAREST, but must be GL_NEAREST if you are copying
depth or stencil data or color data with an integer format. These filters
behave in the same way as they would for texturing. In our example, we
are copying only non-integer color data and can use a linear filter.

```
GLint width = 800;
GLint height = 600;

GLenum fboBuffs[] = { GL_COLOR_ATTACHMENT0 };

glBindFramebuffer(GL_DRAW_FRAMEBUFFER, readFBO);
glBindFramebuffer(GL_READ_FRAMEBUFFER, drawFBO);

glDrawBuffers(1, fboBuffs);
glReadBuffer(GL_COLOR_ATTACHMENT0);
glBlitFramebuffer(0, 0, width, height,
                  (width *0.8), (height*0.8),
                  width, height,
                  GL_COLOR_BUFFER_BIT, GL_LINEAR );
```

Assume the width and height of the attachments of the FBO bound in the
preceding code are 800 and 600, respectively. This code creates a copy of
the whole of the first color attachment of readFBO, scales it down to 80%

of the total size, and places it in the upper-left corner of the first color attachment of drawFBO.

Copying Data into a Texture

As you read in the last section, you can read data from the framebuffer into your application's memory (or into a buffer object) by calling **glReadPixels()**, or from one framebuffer into another using **glBlitFramebuffer()**. If you intend to use this data as a texture, it may be more straightforward to simply copy the data directly from the framebuffer into the texture. The functions to do this are **glCopyTexSubImage2D()** and **glCopyTextureSubImage2D()**, which are similar to **glTextureStorageSubImage2D()**. However, rather than taking source data from application memory or a buffer object, they take their source data from the framebuffer. Their prototypes are

```
void glCopyTexSubImage2D(GLenum target,
                         GLint level,
                         GLint xoffset,
                         GLint yoffset,
                         GLint x,
                         GLint y,
                         GLsizei width,
                         GLsizei height);

void glCopyTextureSubImage2D(GLuint texture,
                             GLint level,
                             GLint xoffset, GLint yoffset,
                             GLint x, GLint y,
                             GLsizei width, GLsizei height);
```

The target parameter is the texture target to which the destination texture is bound. For regular 2D textures, this will be GL_TEXTURE_2D, but you can also copy from the framebuffer into one of the faces of a cubemap by specifying GL_TEXTURE_CUBE_MAP_POSITIVE_X, GL_TEXTURE_CUBE_MAP_NEGATIVE_X, GL_TEXTURE_CUBE_MAP_POSITIVE_Y, GL_TEXTURE_CUBE_MAP_NEGATIVE_Y, GL_TEXTURE_CUBE_MAP_POSITIVE_Z, or GL_TEXTURE_CUBE_MAP_NEGATIVE_Z. width and height represent the size of the region to be copied. x and y are the coordinates of the lower-left corner of the rectangle in the framebuffer, and xoffset and yoffset are the texel coordinates of the rectangle in the destination texture.

If your application renders directly into a texture (by attaching it to a framebuffer object), then this function might not be especially useful to you. However, if your application renders to the default framebuffer most of the time, you can use this function to move parts of the output into textures. In contrast, if you have data in a texture that you want to copy into *another* texture, you can achieve this by calling **glCopyImageSubData()**, which has a monsterous prototype:

```
void glCopyImageSubData(GLuint srcName,
                        GLenum srcTarget,
                        GLint srcLevel,
                        GLint srcX,
                        GLint srcY,
                        GLint srcZ,
                        GLuint dstName,
                        GLenum dstTarget,
                        GLint dstLevel,
                        GLint dstX,
                        GLint dstY,
                        GLint dstZ,
                        GLsizei srcWidth,
                        GLsizei srcHeight,
                        GLsizei srcDepth);
```

Unlike many of the other functions in OpenGL, this function operates *directly* on the texture objects you specify by name, rather than on objects bound to targets. srcName and srcTarget are the name and type of the source texture, and dstName and dstTarget are the name and type of the destination texture. You can pass pretty much any type of texture here, and so you have x, y, and z coordinates for the source and destination regions, and width, height, and depth for each as well. srcX, srcY, and srcZ are the coordinates of the source region, and dstX, dstY, and dstZ are the coordinates of the destination region. The width, height, and depth of the region to copy are specified in srcWidth, srcHeight, and srcDepth.

If the textures you're copying between don't have a particular dimension (for example, the z dimension doesn't exist for 2D textures), you should set the corresponding coordiate to 0 and the size to 1.

If your textures have mipmaps, you can set the source and destination mipmap levels in srcLevel and dstLevel, respectively. Otherwise, set these to 0. Note that there is no destination width, height, or depth—the destination region is the same size as the source region and no stretching or shrinking is possible. If you want to resize part of a texture and write the result into another texture, you'll need to attach both to framebuffer objects and use **glBlitFramebuffer()**.

Reading Back Texture Data

In addition to reading data from the framebuffer, you can read image data from a texture by calling one of the following functions:

```
void glGetTexImage(GLenum target,
                   GLint level,
                   GLenum format,
                   GLenum type,
                   GLvoid * img);

void glGetTextureImage(GLuint texture, GLint level,
                       GLenum format, GLenum type,
                       GLsizei bufSize,
                       void *pixels);
```

These functions work similarly to **glReadPixels()**, except that rather than reading data from a framebuffer, they read data directly from a texture. The **glGetTexImage()** function reads from the texture currently bound to target, whereas **glGetTextureImage()** reads from the texture whose name you give in texture. Note that **glGetTextureImage()** has an additional parameter—bufSize—which contains the size, in bytes, of the data buffer referred to by pixels. OpenGL will write only that much data to the buffer and will then stop. This is particularly important for applications that require bounds checking and robust[8] behavior.

The format and type parameters have the same meanings as in **glReadPixels()**, and the img parameter is equivalent to the data parameter to **glReadPixels()**, including its dual use as either a client memory pointer or an offset into the buffer bound to the GL_PIXEL_PACK_BUFFER target, if there is one. Although only being able to read a whole level of a texture back seems to be a disadvantage, **glGetTexImage()** does possess a couple of pluses. First, you have direct access to all of the mipmap levels of the texture. Second, if you need to read data from a texture object, you don't need to create a framebuffer object and attach the texture to it as you would with **glReadPixels()**.

Both **glGetTexImage()** and **glGetTextureImage()** read the entire texture level back into memory (either into application memory or into a buffer). If all you want is a small region of the texture, you can call

```
void glGetTextureSubImage(GLuint texture, GLint level,
                          GLint xoffset, GLint yoffset, GLint zoffset,
                          GLsizei width, GLsizei height, GLsizei depth,
                          GLenum format, GLenum type,
                          GLsizei bufSize, void *pixels);
```

As you can see, there are many more parameters to **glGetTextureSubImage()** than there are to either **glGetTexImage()** or **glGetTextureImage()**. **glGetTextureSubImage()** reads texture data from

---

8. More information about OpenGL's robustness features can be found in Chapter 15.

texture from the level specified in level, in the bounds that you specify using the xoffset, yoffset, zoffset, width, height, and depth parameters. Notice that **glGetTextureSubImage()** has only one form—one that takes a texture object directly and includes the bufSize parameter, both of which are facets of more recent OpenGL versions.

It might seem odd to read back data from a texture if you have put the data in the texture using a function such as **glTexSubImage2D()** in the first place. However, there are several ways to get data into a texture without putting it there explicitly or drawing into it with a framebuffer. For example, you can call **glGenerateMipmap()**, which will populate lower-resolution mips from the higher-resolution mip, or you can write directly to the image from a shader, as explained in the "Writing to Textures in Shaders" section in Chapter 5.

Summary

This chapter explained a lot about the back end of OpenGL. First, we covered fragment shaders, interoplation, and a number of the built-in variables that are available to fragment shaders. We also looked into the fixed-function testing operations that are performed using the depth and stencil buffers. Next, we proceeded to color output—color masking, blending, and logical operations—all of which affect how the data your fragment shader produces is written into the framebuffer.

Once we were done with the functions that you can apply to the default framebuffer, we proceeded to advanced framebuffer formats. The key advantages of user-specified framebuffers (or framebuffer objects) are that they can have multiple attachments and those attachments can be in advanced formats and color spaces such as floating-point numbers, sRGB, and pure integers. We also explored various ways to deal with resolution limits through antialiasing—antialiasing through blending, alpha-to-coverage, MSAA, and supersampling—and we covered the advantages and disadvantages of each.

Finally, we examined ways to get at the data you have rendered. Putting data into textures follows naturally from attaching textures to framebuffers and rendering directly to them. However, we also considered how you can copy data from a framebuffer into a texture, from one framebuffer to another framebuffer, from one texture to another texture, and from the framebuffer to your application's own memory or into buffer objects.

Chapter 10

Compute Shaders

WHAT YOU'LL LEARN IN THIS CHAPTER

- How to create, compile, and dispatch compute shaders.

- How to pass data between compute shader invocations.

- How to synchronize compute shaders and keep their work in order.

Compute shaders are a way to take advantage of the enormous computational power of graphics processors that implement OpenGL. Just like all shaders in OpenGL, they are written in GLSL and run in large parallel groups that simultaneously work on huge amounts of data. In addition to the facilities available to other shaders such as texturing, storage buffers, and atomic memory operations, compute shaders are able to synchronize with one another and share data among themselves to make general computation easier. They stand apart from the rest of the OpenGL pipeline and are designed to provide as much flexibility to the application developer as possible. In this chapter, we discuss compute shaders, examine their similarities and their differences to other shader types in OpenGL, and explain some of their unique properties and abilities.

Using Compute Shaders

Modern graphics processors are extremely powerful devices capable of performing a huge amount of numeric calculation. You were briefly introduced to the idea of using compute shaders for non-graphics work in Chapter 3, "Following the Pipeline," but there we really just skimmed the surface. In fact, the compute shader stage is effectively its own pipeline, somewhat disconnected from the rest of OpenGL. It has no fixed inputs or outputs, does not interface with any of the fixed-function pipeline stages, is very flexible, and has capabilities that other stages do not possess.

Having said this, a compute shader is just like any other shader from a programming point of view. It is written in GLSL, represented as a shader object, and linked into a program object. When you create a compute shader, you call **glCreateShader()** and pass the GL_COMPUTE_SHADER parameter as the shader type. You get back a new shader object from this call that you can use to load your shader code with **glShaderSource()**, compile with **glCompileShader()**, and attach to a program object with **glAttachShader()**. Then, you link the program object by calling **glLinkProgram()**, just as you would with any graphics program.

You can't mix and match compute shaders with shaders of other types. For example, you can't attach a compute shader to a program object that also has a vertex or fragment shader attached to it and then link the program object. If you attempt this, the link will fail. Thus, a linked program object can contain only compute shaders or only graphics shaders (vertex, tessellation, geometry, or fragment), but not a combination of the two. We will sometimes refer to a linked program object that contains compute shaders (and so only compute shaders) as a *compute program* (as opposed to a *graphics program*, which contains only graphics shaders).

Example code to compile and link our do-nothing compute shader (first introduced in Listing 3.13) is shown in Listing 10.1.

```
GLuint      compute_shader;
GLuint      compute_program;

static const GLchar * compute_source[] =
{
    "#version 450 core                                          \n"
    "                                                           \n"
    "layout (local_size_x = 32, local_size_y = 32) in;          \n"
    "                                                           \n"
    "void main(void)                                            \n"
```

```
        "{                                                    \n"
        "    // Do nothing                                     \n"
        "}                                                     \n"
};

// Create a shader, attach source, and compile.
compute_shader = glCreateShader(GL_COMPUTE_SHADER);
glShaderSource(compute_shader, 1, compute_source, NULL);
glCompileShader(compute_shader);

// Create a program, attach shader, link.
compute_program = glCreateProgram();
glAttachShader(compute_program, compute_shader);
glLinkProgram(compute_program);

// Delete shader because we're done with it.
glDeleteShader(compute_shader);
```

Listing 10.1: Creating and compiling a compute shader

Once you have run the code in Listing 10.1, you will have a ready-to-run compute program in compute_program. A compute program can use uniforms, uniform blocks, shader storage blocks, and so on, just as any other program does. You also make it current by calling **glUseProgram()**. Once it is the current program object, functions such as **glUniform*()** affect its state as normal.

Executing Compute Shaders

Once you have made a compute program current, and set up any resources that it might need access to, you need to actually execute it. To do this, we have a pair of functions:

```
void glDispatchCompute(GLuint num_groups_x,
                       GLuint num_groups_y,
                       GLuint num_groups_z);
```

and

```
void glDispatchComputeIndirect(GLintptr indirect);
```

The **glDispatchComputeIndirect()** function is to **glDispatchCompute()** as **glDrawArraysIndirect()** is to **glDrawArraysInstancedBaseInstance()**. That is, the indirect parameter is interpreted as an offset into a buffer object that contains a set of parameters that could be passed to **glDispatchCompute()**. In code, this structure would look like this:

```
typedef struct {
    GLuint num_groups_x;
    GLuint num_groups_y;
    GLuint num_groups_z;
} DispatchIndirectCommand;
```

However, we need to understand how these parameters are interpreted to use them effectively.

Global and Local Work Groups

Compute shaders execute in what are called *work groups*. A single call to **glDispatchCompute()** or **glDispatchComputeIndirect()** will cause a single *global work group*[1] to be sent to OpenGL for processing. That global work group will then be subdivided into a number of *local work groups*—the number of local work groups in each of the x, y, and z dimensions is set by the num_groups_x, num_groups_y, and num_groups_z parameters, respectively. A work group is fundamentally a 3D block of *work items*, where each work item is processed by an invocation of a compute shader running your code. The size of each local work group in the x, y, and z dimensions is set using an input layout qualifier in your shader source code. You can see an example of this in the simple compute shader that we introduced earlier:

```
layout (local_size_x = 4,
        local_size_y = 7,
        local_size_z = 10) in;
```

In this example, the local work group size would be $4 \times 7 \times 10$ work items or invocations, for a total of 280 work items per local work group. The maximum size of a work group can be found by querying the values of two parameters: GL_MAX_COMPUTE_WORK_GROUP_SIZE and GL_MAX_COMPUTE_WORK_GROUP_INVOCATIONS. For the first of these, you query it using the **glGetIntegeri_v()** function, passing it as the target parameter and 0, 1, or 2 as the index parameter to specify the x, y, or z dimension, respectively. The maximum size will be at least 1024 items in the x and y dimensions and 64 items in the z dimension. The value you get by querying the GL_MAX_COMPUTE_WORK_GROUP_INVOCATIONS constant is the maximum total number of invocations allowed in a single work group, which is the maximum allowed product of the x, y, and z dimensions, or the *volume* of the local work group. That value will be at least 1024 items.

It's possible to launch 1D or 2D work groups by simply setting either the y or z dimension (or both) to 1. In fact, the default size in all dimensions is 1. Thus, if you don't include them in your input layout qualifier, you will create a work group size of lower dimension than 3. For example,

```
layout (local_size_x = 512) in;
```

---

1. The OpenGL specification doesn't explicitly call the total work dispatched by a single command a *global work group*, but rather uses the unqualified term *work group* to mean *local work group* and never names the global work group.

will create a 1D local work group of 512 ($\times$ 1 $\times$ 1) items and

```
layout (local_size_x = 64,
        local_size_y = 64) in;
```

will create a 2D local work group of 64 $\times$ 64 ($\times$ 1) items. The local work group size is used when you link the program to determine the size and dimensions of the work groups executed by the program. You can find the local work group size of a program's compute shaders by calling **glGetProgramiv()** with pname set to GL_COMPUTE_WORK_GROUP_SIZE. It will return three integers giving the size of the work groups. For example, you could write

```
int size[3];

glGetProgramiv(program, GL_COMPUTE_WORK_GROUP_SIZE, size);

printf("Work group size is %d x %d x %d items.\n",
       size[0], size[1], size[2]);
```

Once you have defined a local work group size, you can dispatch a 3D block of workgroups to do work for you. The size of this block is specified by the num_groups_x, num_groups_y, and num_groups_z parameters to **glDispatchCompute()** or the equivalent members of the DispatchIndirectCommand structure stored in the buffer object bound to the GL_DISPATCH_INDIRECT_BUFFER target. This block of local work groups is known as the *global work group* and its dimension doesn't need to be the same as the dimension of the local work group. That is, you could dispatch a 3D global work group of 1D local work groups, a 2D global work group of 3D local work groups, and so on.

Compute Shader Inputs and Outputs

First and foremost, compute shaders *have no built-in outputs*. Yes, you read correctly—they have no built-in outputs at all, and you cannot declare any user-defined outputs as you are able to do in other shader stages. This is because the compute shader forms a kind of single-stage pipeline with nothing before it and nothing after it. However, like some of the graphics shaders, it does have a few built-in input variables that you can use to determine where you are in your local work group and within the greater global work group.

The first variable, gl_LocalInvocationID, is the index of the shader invocation within the local work group. It is implicitly declared as a uvec3 input to the shader and each element ranges in value from 0 to 1 less than the local work group size in the corresponding dimension (x, y, or z). The local work group size is stored in the gl_WorkGroupSize variable, which is also implicitly declared as a uvec3 type. Again, even if you declare your local work group size to be 1D or 2D, the work group will still essentially be 3D, but with the sizes of the unused dimensions set to 1. That is, gl_LocalInvocationID and gl_WorkGroupSize will still be implicitly declared as uvec3 variables, but the y and z components of gl_LocalInvocationID will be 0 and the corresponding components for gl_WorkGroupSize will be 1.

Just as gl_WorkGroupSize and gl_LocalInvocationID store the size of the local work group and the location of the current shader invocation within the work group, so gl_NumWorkGroups and gl_WorkGroupID contain the number of work groups and the index of the current work group within the global set, respectively. Again, both are implicitly declared as uvec3 variables. The value of gl_NumWorkGroups is set by the **glDispatchCompute()** or **glDispatchComputeIndirect()** commands and contains the values of num_groups_x, num_groups_y, and num_groups_z in its three elements. The elements of gl_WorkGroupID range in value from 0 to 1 less than the values of the corresponding elements of gl_NumWorkGroups.

These variables are illustrated in Figure 10.1. The diagram shows a global work group that contains three work groups in the x dimension, four work groups in the y dimension, and eight work groups in the z dimension. Each local work group is a 2D array of work items that contains six items in the x dimension and four items in the y dimension.

Between gl_WorkGroupID and gl_LocalInvocationID, you can tell where in the complete set of work items your current shader invocation is located. Likewise, between gl_NumWorkGroups and gl_WorkGroupSize, you can figure out the total number of invocations in the global set. However, OpenGL provides the global invocation index to you through the gl_GlobalInvocationID built-in variable. It is effectively calculated as

```
gl_GlobalInvocationID = gl_WorkGroupID * gl_WorkGroupSize +
                        gl_LocalInvocationID;
```

Finally, the gl_LocalInvocationIndex built-in variable contains a "flattened" form of gl_LocalInvocationID. That is, the 3D variable is converted to a 1D index using the following code:

```
gl_LocalInvocationIndex =
    gl_LocalInvocationID.z * gl_WorkGroupSize.x * gl_WorkGroupSize.y +
    gl_LocalInvocationID.y * gl_WorkGroupSize.x +
    gl_LocalInvocationID.x;
```

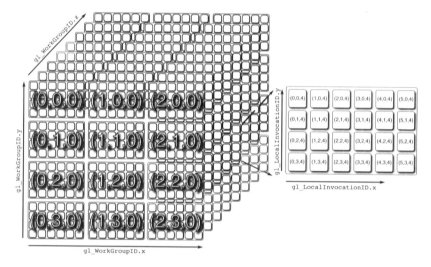

Figure 10.1: Global and local compute work group dimensions

The values stored in these variables allow your shader to know where it is in the local and global work groups and can be used as indices into arrays of data, texture coordinates, or random seeds, or for any other purpose.

Now we come to outputs. We started this section by stating that compute shaders have no outputs. That's true, but it doesn't mean that compute shaders can't output any data—it just means that there are no *fixed* outputs represented by built-in output variables, for example. Compute shaders can still produce data, but the data must be stored into memory explicitly by your shader code. For instance, in your compute shader you could write into a shader storage block, use image functions such as imageStore or atomics, or increment and decrement the values of atomic counters. These operations have *side effects*, which means that their operation can be detected because they update the contents of memory or otherwise have externally visible consequences.

Consider the shader shown in Listing 10.2, which reads from one image, logically inverts the data, and writes the data back out to another image.

```
#version 450 core

layout (local_size_x = 32,
        local_size_y = 32) in;

layout (binding = 0, rgba32f) uniform image2D img_input;
layout (binding = 1) uniform image2D img_output;
```

```
void main(void)
{
    vec4 texel;
    ivec2 p = ivec2(gl_GlobalInvocationID.xy);

    texel = imageLoad(img_input, p);
    texel = vec4(1.0) - texel;
    imageStore(img_output, p, texel);
}
```

Listing 10.2: Compute shader image inversion

To execute this shader, we would compile it and link it into a program object and then set up our images by binding a level of a texture object to each of the first two image units. As you can see from Listing 10.2, the local work group size is 32 invocations in x and y, so our images should ideally be integer multiples of 32 texels wide and high. Once the images are bound, we can call **glDispatchCompute()**, setting the num_groups_x and num_groups_y parameters to the width and height of the images divided by 32, respectively, and num_groups_z to 1. Code to do this is shown in Listing 10.3.

```
// Bind input image
glBindImageTexture(0, tex_input, 0, GL_FALSE,
                   0, GL_READ_ONLY, GL_RGBA32F);

// Bind output image
glBindImageTexture(1, tex_output, 0, GL_FALSE,
                   0, GL_WRITE_ONLY, GL_RGBA32F);

// Dispatch the compute shader
glDispatchCompute(IMAGE_WIDTH / 32, IMAGE_HEIGHT / 32, 1);
```

Listing 10.3: Dispatching the image copy compute shader

Compute Shader Communication

Compute shaders execute on work items in work groups much as tessellation control shaders execute on control points in patches[2]—both work groups and patches are created from groups of invocations. Within a single patch, tessellation control shaders can write to variables qualified with the **patch** storage qualifier and, if they are synchronized correctly,

---

2. This may also seem similar to the behavior of geometry shaders. However, there is an important difference—compute shaders and tessellation control shaders execute an invocation per work item or per control point, respectively. Geometry shaders, in contrast, execute an invocation for each primitive and each of those invocations has access to all of the input data for that primitive.

read the values that other invocations in the same patch wrote to them. As such, this allows a limited form of communication between the tessellation control shader invocations in a single patch. However, this comes with substantial limitations—for example, the amount of storage available for `patch` qualified variables is fairly limited, and the number of control points in a single patch is quite small.

Compute shaders provide a similar mechanism, but offer significantly more flexibility and power. Just as you can declare variables with the `patch` storage qualifier in a tessellation control shader, so you can declare variables with the `shared` storage qualifier, which allows them to be *shared* between compute shader invocations running in the *same local work group*. Variables declared with the `shared` storage qualifier are known as *shared variables*. Access to shared variables is generally much faster than access to main memory through images or storage blocks. Thus, if you expect multiple invocations of your compute shader to access the same data, it makes sense to copy the data from main memory into a shared variable (or an array of them), access the data from there, possibly updating it in place, and then write any results back to main memory when you're done.

Keep in mind, though, that you can use only a limited number of shared variables. A modern graphics board might have several gigabytes of main memory, whereas the amount of shared variable storage space might be limited to just a few kilobytes. The amount of shared memory available to a compute shader can be determined by calling `glGetIntegerv()` with pname set to GL_MAX_COMPUTE_SHARED_MEMORY_SIZE. The minimum amount of shared memory required to be supported in OpenGL is only 32 kilobytes, so while your implementation may have more than this, you shouldn't count on it being substantially larger.

Synchronizing Compute Shaders

The invocations in a work group will most likely run in parallel—this is where the vast computation power of graphics processors comes from. The processor will likely divide each local work group into a number of smaller[3] chunks, executing the invocations in a single chunk in lockstep. These chunks are then *time-sliced* onto the processor's computational resources and those timeslices may be assigned in any order. It may be that a chunk of invocations is completed before any other chunks from the same local work group begin, but more than likely there will be many "live" chunks present on the processor at any given time.

---

3. Chunk sizes of 16, 32, or 64 elements are common.

Because these chunks can effectively run out of order but are allowed to communicate, we need a way to ensure that messages received by a recipient are the most recent ones sent. Imagine if you were told to go to someone's office and perform the duty written on that individual's whiteboard. Each day, this person writes a new message on the whiteboard, but you don't know at what time that happens. When you go into the office, how do you know if the message on the whiteboard is what you're supposed to do, or if it's left over from the previous day? You'd be in a bit of trouble. Now suppose the owner of the office left the door locked until he or she had been there and written the message. If you showed up and the door was locked, you'd have to wait outside the office. This is known as a *barrier*. If the door is open, you can look at the message; if it's locked, you need to wait until the person arrives to open it.

A similar mechanism is available to compute shaders: the barrier() function, which executes a *flow control barrier*. When you call barrier() in your compute shader, it will be blocked until all other shader invocations in the same local work group have reached that point in the shader. We touched on this behavior in the "Communication between Shader Invocations" section in Chapter 8, where we described the behavior of the barrier() function in the context of tessellation control shaders. In a time-slicing architecture, executing the barrier() function means that your shader (along with the chunk it's in) will give up its timeslice so that another invocation can execute until it reaches the barrier. Once all the other invocations in the local work group reach the barrier (or if they have already gotten there before your invocation arrives) execution continues as usual.

Flow control barriers are important when shared memory is in use because they allow you to know when other shader invocations in the same local work group have reached the same point as the current invocation. If the current invocation has written to some shared memory variable, then you know that all the others must have written to theirs as well, so it's safe to read the data they wrote. Without a barrier, you would have no idea whether data that was supposed to have been written to shared variables actually has been. At best, you'd leave your application susceptible to *race conditions*; at worst, the application wouldn't work at all. Consider, for example, the shader in Listing 10.4.

```
#version 450 core

layout (local_size_x = 1024) in;

layout (binding = 0, r32ui) uniform uimageBuffer image_in;
```

```
layout (binding = 1) uniform uimageBuffer image_out;

shared uint temp_storage[1024];

void main(void)
{
    // Load from the input image
    uint n = imageLoad(image_in, gl_LocalInvocationID.x).x;

    // Store into shared storage
    temp_storage[gl_LocalInvocationID.x] = n;

    // Uncomment this to avoid the race condition
    // barrier();
    // memoryBarrierShared();

    // Read the data written by the invocation 'to the left'
    n = temp_storage[(gl_LocalInvocationID.x - 1) & 1023];

    // Write new data into the buffer
    imageStore(image_out, gl_LocalInvocationID.x, n);
}
```

Listing 10.4: Compute shader with race conditions

This shader loads data from a buffer image into a shared variable. Each invocation of the shader loads a single item from the buffer and writes it into its own "slot" in the shared variable array. Then, it reads from the slot owned by the invocation to its left and writes the data out to the buffer image. The result *should* be that the data in the buffer is *moved* along by one element. However, Figure 10.2 illustrates what actually happens.

As you can see in the figure, multiple shader invocations have been time-sliced onto a single computational resource. At t0, invocation A runs the first couple of lines of the shader and writes its value to temp_storage. At t1, invocation B runs a line and then at t2, invocation C takes over and runs the same first two lines of the shader. At time t3, A gets its timeslice back again and completes the shader. It's done at this point, but the other invocations haven't finished their work yet. At t4, invocation D finally gets a turn but is quickly interrupted by invocation C, which reads from temp_storage. Now we have a problem: Invocation C was expecting to read data from the shared storage that was written by invocation B, but invocation B hasn't reached that point in the shader yet! Execution continues blindly, and invocations D, C, and B all finish the shader, but the data stored by C will be garbage.

This is known as a *race condition*. The shader invocations race each other to the same point in the shader, and some invocations will read from the temp_storage shared variable before others have written their data into it. The result is that they pick up stale data, which then gets written into the output buffer image. Uncommenting the call to barrier() in Listing 10.4 produces an execution flow more like that shown in Figure 10.3.

Compare Figures 10.2 and 10.3. Both depict four shader invocations being time-sliced onto the same computational resource, except that Figure 10.3

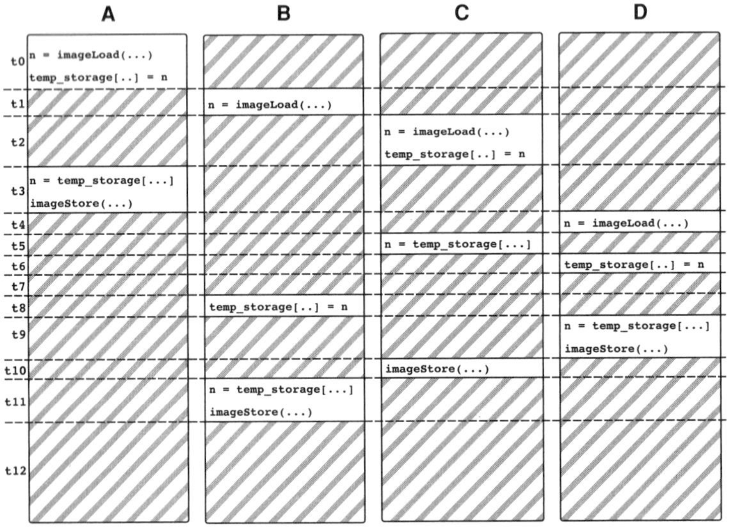

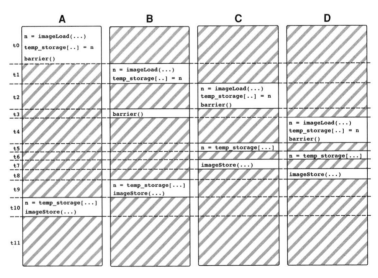

Figure 10.2: Effect of race conditions in a compute shader

Figure 10.3: Effect of barrier() on race conditions

does not exhibit the race condition. In Figure 10.3, we again start with shader invocation A executing the first couple of lines of the shader, but then it calls the `barrier()` function, which causes it to yield its timeslice. Next, invocation B executes the first couple of lines and then is preempted. Then, C executes the shader as far as the `barrier()` function and so yields. Invocation B executes its barrier but gets no further because D still has not reached the barrier function. Finally, invocation D gets a chance to run reads from the image buffer, writes its data into the shared storage area, and then calls `barrier()`. This signals all the other invocations that it is safe to continue running.

Immediately after invocation D executes the barrier, all other invocations are able to run again. Invocation C loads from the shared storage, then D, and C and D both store their results to the image. Finally invocations A and B read from the shared storage and write their results out to memory. As you can see, no invocation tried to read data that hasn't been written yet. The presence of the `barrier()` functions affected the scheduling of the invocations with respect to one another. Although these diagrams show only four invocations competing for a single resource, in real OpenGL implementations there are likely to be many hundreds of threads competing for perhaps a few tens of resources. As you might guess, the likelihood of data corruption due to race conditions is much higher in these scenarios.

Examples

This section contains several examples of the use of compute shaders. In our first example, the *parallel prefix sum*, we demonstrate how to implement an algorithm (which at first seems like a very serial process) in an efficient parallel manner. In our second example, an implementation of the classic *flocking* algorithm (also known as *boids*) is shown. In both examples, we make use of local and global work groups, synchronization using the `barrier()` command, and shared local variables—a feature unique to compute shaders.

Compute Shader Parallel Prefix Sum

A prefix sum operation is an algorithm that, given an array of input values, computes a new array where each element of the output array is the sum of all of the values of the input array up to (and optionally including) the current array element. A prefix sum operation that includes the current element is known as an *inclusive* prefix sum; one that does not is known as an *exclusive* prefix sum. For example, the code in Listing 10.5 is a simple C++ implementation of a prefix sum function that can be inclusive or exclusive.

```cpp
void prefix_sum(const float * in_array,
                float * out_array,
                int elements,
                bool inclusive)
{
    float f = 0.0f;
    int i;

    if (inclusive)
    {
        for (i = 0; i < elements; i++)
        {
            f += in_array[i];
            out_array[i] = f;
        }
    }
    else
    {
        for (i = 0; i < elements; i++)
        {
            out_array[i] = f;
            f += in_array[i];
        }
    }
}
```

Listing 10.5: Simple prefix sum implementation in C++

Notice that the only difference between the inclusive and exclusive prefix sum implementations is that the accumulation of the input array is performed before writing to the output array rather than afterward. The result of running this inclusive prefix sum on an array of values is illustrated in Figure 10.4.

You should appreciate that as the number of elements in the input and output arrays grows, the number of addition operations grows, too—and can become quite large. Also, given that the result written to each element

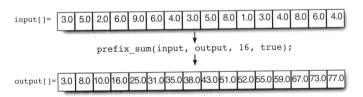

Figure 10.4: Sample input and output of a prefix sum operation

of the output array is the sum of all elements before it (and therefore dependent on all of them), it would seem at first glance that this type of algorithm does not lend itself well to parallelization. However, this is not the case: The prefix sum operation is highly parallizable. At is core, the prefix sum is nothing more than a huge number of additions of adjacent array elements. Take, for example, a prefix sum of four input elements, I_0 through I_3, producing an output array O_0 through O_3. The result is

$$O_0 = I_0$$
$$O_1 = I_0 + I_1$$
$$O_2 = I_0 + I_1 + I_2$$
$$O_3 = I_0 + I_1 + I_2 + I_3$$

The key to parallization is to break large tasks into groups of smaller, independent tasks that can be completed independently of one another. You can see that in the computation of O_2 and O_3, we use the sum of I_0 and I_1, which we also need to calculate O_1. So, if we break this operation into multiple steps, we see that we have in the first step

$$O_0 = I_0$$
$$O_1 = I_0 + I_1$$
$$O_2 = I_2$$
$$O_3 = I_2 + I_3$$

Then in a second step, we can compute

$$O_2 = O_2 + O_1$$
$$O_3 = O_3 + O_1$$

Now, the computations of O_1 and O_3 are independent of each other in the first step and therefore can be computed in parallel, as can the updates of the values of O_2 and O_3 in the second step. If you look closely, you will see that the first step simply takes a four-element prefix sum and breaks it into a pair of two-element prefix sums that are trivially computed. In the second step, we use the result of the previous step to update the results of the inner sums. In fact, we can break a prefix sum of any size into smaller and smaller chunks until we reach a point where we can compute the inner sum directly. This is shown pictorially in Figure 10.5.

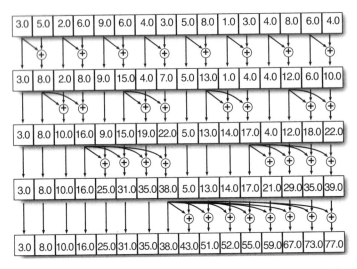

Figure 10.5: Breaking a prefix sum into smaller chunks

The recursive nature of this algorithm is apparent in Figure 10.5. The number of additions required by this method is actually more than the sequential algorithm for prefix sum calculation would require. In this example, we would require 15 additions to compute the prefix sum with a sequential algorithm, whereas here we require 8 additions per step and 4 steps for a total of 32 additions. However, because we can execute the 8 additions of each step in parallel, we are done in 4 steps instead of 15, making the algorithm amost 4 times faster than the sequential one.

As the number of elements in the input array grows, the potential speedup becomes greater. For example, if we expand the input array to 32 elements, we execute 5 steps of 16 additions each, rather than 31 sequential additions. Assuming we have enough computational resources to perform 16 additions at a time, we now take 5 steps instead of 31 and go around 6 times faster. Likewise, for an input array size of 64, we'd take 6 steps of 32 additions rather than 63 sequential additions, and go 10 times faster! Of course, we eventually hit a limit in the number of additions we can perform in parallel, the amount of memory bandwidth we consume when reading and writing the input and output arrays, or something else.

To implement this operation in a compute shader, we can load a chunk of input data into shared variables, compute the inner sums, synchronize with the other invocations, accumulate their results, and so on. An example compute shader that implements this algorithm is shown in Listing 10.6.

```
#version 450 core

layout (local_size_x = 1024) in;

layout (binding = 0) coherent buffer block1
{
    float input_data[gl_WorkGroupSize.x];
};

layout (binding = 1) coherent buffer block2
{
    float output_data[gl_WorkGroupSize.x];
};

shared float shared_data[gl_WorkGroupSize.x * 2];

void main(void)
{
    uint id = gl_LocalInvocationID.x;
    uint rd_id;
    uint wr_id;
    uint mask;

    // The number of steps is the log base 2 of the
    // work group size, which should be a power of 2
    const uint steps = uint(log2(gl_WorkGroupSize.x)) + 1;
    uint step = 0;

    // Each invocation is responsible for the content of
    // two elements of the output array
    shared_data[id * 2] = input_data[id * 2];
    shared_data[id * 2 + 1] = input_data[id * 2 + 1];

    // Synchronize to make sure that everyone has initialized
    // their elements of shared_data[] with data loaded from
    // the input arrays
    barrier();
    memoryBarrierShared();

    // For each step...
    for (step = 0; step < steps; step++)
    {
        // Calculate the read and write index in the
        // shared array
        mask = (1 << step) - 1;
        rd_id = ((id >> step) << (step + 1)) + mask;
        wr_id = rd_id + 1 + (id & mask);

        // Accumulate the read data into our element
        shared_data[wr_id] += shared_data[rd_id];

        // Synchronize again to make sure that everyone
        // has caught up with us
        barrier();
        memoryBarrierShared();
    }

    // Finally write our data back to the output image
    output_data[id * 2] = shared_data[id * 2];
    output_data[id * 2 + 1] = shared_data[id * 2 + 1];
}
```

Listing 10.6: Prefix sum implementation using a compute shader

The shader shown in Listing 10.6 has a local workgroup size of 1024, which means it will process arrays of 2048 elements, as each invocation computes two elements of the output array. The shared variable shared_data is used to store the data that is in flight. When execution starts, the shader loads two adjacent elements from the input arrays into the array. Next, it executes the barrier() function. This step ensures that all of the shader invocations have loaded their data into the shared array before the inner loop begins.

Each iteration of the inner loop performs one step of the algorithm. This loop executes $log_2(N)$ times, where N is the number of elements in the array. For each invocation, the shader calculates the index of the first and second elements to be added together and then computes the sum, writing the result back into the shared array. At the end of the loop, another call to barrier() ensures that the invocations are fully synchronized before the next iteration of the loop and ultimately when the loop exits. Finally, the shader writes the result to the output buffer.

Prefix sum algorithms can be applied in a *separable* manner to multidimensional data sets such as images and volumes. In Chapter 9, "Fragment Processing and the Framebuffer," you saw an example of a separable algorithm when we performed Gaussian filtering in our bloom example. To produce a prefix sum of an image, we first apply our prefix sum algorithm across each row of pixels in the image, producing a new image, and then apply another prefix sum on each of the columns of the result. The output of these two steps is a new 2D grid where each point represents the sum of all of the values contained in the *rectangle* whose corners are at the origin and at the point of interest. Figure 10.6 demonstrates the underlying principle.

As you can see, given the input in Figure 10.6(a), the first step simply computes a number of prefix sums over the rows of the image, producing

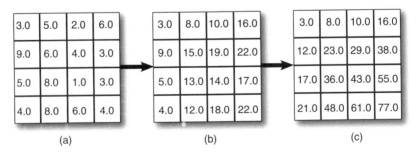

Figure 10.6: A 2D prefix sum

an output image that consists of the set of prefix sums shown in Figure 10.6(b). The second step performs prefix sum operations on the columns of the intermediate image, producing an output containing the 2D prefix sum of the original image, shown in Figure 10.6(c). Such an image, which is called a *summed area table*, is an extremely important data structure with many applications in computer graphics.

We can modify our shader of Listing 10.6 to compute the prefix sums of the rows of an image variable rather than a shader storage buffer. The modified shader is shown in Listing 10.7. As an optimization, the shader reads from the input image's rows but writes to the image's *columns*. This means that the output image will be transposed with respect to the input. However, we're going to apply this shader twice, and we know that transposing an image twice returns it to its original orientation; thus the final result will be correctly oriented with respect to the original input. If we wanted to avoid the transpose operation, the shader to process the rows would need to be different than the shader that processes the columns (or we would need to do extra work to figure out how to index the image). With this approach, the shader for both passes is identical.

```
#version 450 core

layout (local_size_x = 1024) in;

shared float shared_data[gl_WorkGroupSize.x * 2];

layout (binding = 0, r32f) readonly uniform image2D input_image;
layout (binding = 1, r32f) writeonly uniform image2D output_image;

void main(void)
{
    uint id = gl_LocalInvocationID.x;
    uint rd_id;
    uint wr_id;
    uint mask;
    ivec2 P = ivec2(id * 2, gl_WorkGroupID.x);

    const uint steps = uint(log2(gl_WorkGroupSize.x)) + 1;
    uint step = 0;

    shared_data[id * 2] = imageLoad(input_image, P).r;
    shared_data[id * 2 + 1] = imageLoad(input_image,
                                        P + ivec2(1, 0)).r;

    barrier();
    memoryBarrierShared();

    for (step = 0; step < steps; step++)
    {
        mask = (1 << step) - 1;
        rd_id = ((id >> step) << (step + 1)) + mask;
        wr_id = rd_id + 1 + (id & mask);
```

```
        shared_data[wr_id] += shared_data[rd_id];
        barrier();
        memoryBarrierShared();
    }

    imageStore(output_image, P.yx, vec4(shared_data[id * 2]));
    imageStore(output_image, P.yx + ivec2(0, 1),
               vec4(shared_data[id * 2 + 1]));
}
```

Listing 10.7: Compute shader to generate a 2D prefix sum

Each local work group of the shader in Listing 10.7 is still one dimensional. However, when we launch the shader for the first pass, we create a one-dimensional global work group containing as many local work groups as there are rows in the image. When we subsequently launch it for the second pass, we create as many local work groups as there are columns in the image (which are actually rows again at this point due to the transpose operation performed by the shader). Each local work group will therefore process the row or column of the image determined by the global workgroup index.

Given a summed area table for an image, we can actually compute the sum of the elements contained within an arbitrary rectangle of that image. To do this, we simply need four values from the table, each one giving the sum of the elements contained within the rectangle spanning from the origin to its coordinate. Given a rectangle of interest defined by upper-left and lower-right coordinates, we add the values from the summed area table at the upper-left and lower-right coordinates, and then *subtract* the values at its upper-right and lower-left coordinates. To see why this works, refer to Figure 10.7.

Now, the number of pixels contained in any given rectangle of the summed area table is simply the rectangle's area. Given this, we know that if we take the sum of all the elements contained with the rectangle and divide it through by the rectangle's area, we will be left with the *average* value of the elements inside the rectangle. Averaging a number of values together is a form of filtering known as a *box filter*. While it's pretty crude, it can be useful for certain applications. In particular, being able to take the average of an arbitrary number of pixels centered on an arbitrary point in an image allows us to create a variable-sized filter, where the dimensions of the filtered rectangle can be changed on a per-pixel basis.

As an example, Figure 10.8 shows an image that has a variable-sized filter applied to it. The image is least heavily filtered on the left and more

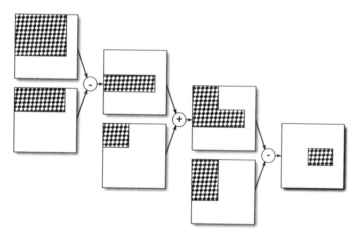

Figure 10.7: Computing the sum of a rectangle in a summed area table

Figure 10.8: Variable filtering applied to an image

heavily filtered on the right. As you can see, the right side of the image is substantially more blurry than the left side.

Simple filtering effects like this are great, but we can use the same technique to generate some much more interesting results. One such effect is *depth of field*. Cameras have two properties that are relevant to this effect—*focal distance* and *focal depth*. The focal distance refers to the distance from the camera at which an object must be placed to be perfectly in focus. The focal depth refers to the rate at which an object becomes out of focus as it moves away from this sweet spot. An example of this effect is seen in the photograph[4] shown in Figure 10.9. The glass closest to the camera is in sharp focus. However, as the row of glasses progresses from front to back, they become successively less well defined. The basket of oranges in the background is quite out of focus. The true blur of an image due to out-of-focus lenses is caused by a number of complex optical phenomena, but we can make a good approximation to the visual effect with our rudimentary box filter.

To simulate our depth of field effect, we'll first render our scene in the usual way, but save the depth of each fragment (which is approximately equal to its distance from the camera). When this depth value is equal to our simulated camera's focal distance, the image will be sharp and in focus, as it normally is with computer graphics. As the depth of a pixel strays from this perfect depth, the amount of blur we apply to the image should increase, too.

We have implemented this operation in the dof sample. In the program, we convert the rendered image into a summed area table using the

Figure 10.9: Depth of field in a photograph

---

4. Photograph courtesy of http://www.cookthestory.com.

compute shader shown in Listing 10.7, modified slightly to operate on
vec3 data rather than a single floating-point value per pixel. Also, as we
render the image, we store the per-pixel view-space depth in the fourth
alpha channel of the image so that our frament shader, shown in
Listing 10.8, will have access to it. The fragment shader then computes the
area of confusion (which is a fancy term for the size of the blurred region)
for the current pixel and uses it to build a filter width (m), reading data
from the summed area table to produce blurry pixels.

```glsl
#version 450 core

layout (binding = 0) uniform sampler2D input_image;

layout (location = 0) out vec4 color;

uniform float focal_distance = 50.0;
uniform float focal_depth = 30.0;

void main(void)
{
    // s will be used to scale our texture coordinates before
    // looking up data in our SAT image.
    vec2 s = 1.0 / textureSize(input_image, 0);
    // C is the center of the filter
    vec2 C = gl_FragCoord.xy;

    // First, retrieve the value of the SAT at the center
    // of the filter. The last channel of this value stores
    // the view-space depth of the pixel.
    vec4 v = texelFetch(input_image, ivec2(gl_FragCoord.xy), 0).rgba;

    // m will be the radius of our filter kernel
    float m;

    // For this application, we clear our depth image to zero
    // before rendering to it, so if it's still zero we haven't
    // rendered to the image here. Thus, we set our radius to
    // 0.5 (i.e., a diameter of 1.0) and move on.
    if (v.w == 0.0)
    {
        m = 0.5;
    }
    else
    {
        // Calculate a circle of confusion
        m = abs(v.w - focal_distance);

        // Simple smoothstep scale and bias. Minimum radius is
        // 0.5 (diameter 1.0), maximum is 8.0. Box filter kernels
        // greater than about 16 pixels don't look good at all.
        m = 0.5 + smoothstep(0.0, focal_depth, m) * 7.5;
    }

    // Calculate the positions of the four corners of our
    // area to sample from.
    vec2 P0 = vec2(C * 1.0) + vec2(-m, -m);
    vec2 P1 = vec2(C * 1.0) + vec2(-m, m);
    vec2 P2 = vec2(C * 1.0) + vec2(m, -m);
```

```
    vec2 P3 = vec2(C * 1.0) + vec2(m, m);

    // Scale our coordinates
    P0 *= s;
    P1 *= s;
    P2 *= s;
    P3 *= s;

    // Fetch the values of the SAT at the four corners
    vec3 a = textureLod(input_image, P0, 0).rgb;
    vec3 b = textureLod(input_image, P1, 0).rgb;
    vec3 c = textureLod(input_image, P2, 0).rgb;
    vec3 d = textureLod(input_image, P3, 0).rgb;

    // Calculate the sum of all pixels inside the kernel
    vec3 f = a - b - c + d;

    // Scale radius -> diameter
    m *= 2;

    // Divide through by area
    f /= float(m * m);

    // Output final color
    color = vec4(f, 1.0);
}
```

Listing 10.8: Depth of field using summed area tables

The shader in Listing 10.8 takes as input a texture containing the depth of each pixel and the summed area table of the image computed earlier, along with the parameters of the simulated camera. As the absolute value of the difference between the pixel's depth and the camera's focal distance increases, the shader uses this value to compute the size of the filtering rectangle (the area of confusion). It then reads the four values from the summed area table at the corners of the rectangle, computes the average value of its content, and writes this to the framebuffer. The result is that pixels that are "farther" from the ideal focal distance are blurred more, and pixels that are closer to it are blurred less. The result of this shader is shown in Figure 10.10. The same image is also shown in Color Plate 6.

As you can see in Figure 10.10, the depth of field effect has been applied to a row of dragons. In the image, the nearest dragon appears slightly blurred and out of focus, the second dragon is in focus, and the dragons beyond it become successively out of focus again. Figure 10.11 shows several more results from the same program. In the leftmost image in Figure 10.11, the closest dragon is in sharp focus and the farthest dragon is very blurry. In the middle image in Figure 10.11, the farthest dragon is the one in focus, whereas the closest is the most blurred. To achieve this affect, the depth of field of the simulated camera is quite shallow. By lengthening the camera's depth of field, we can obtain the image on the right in Figure 10.11, where

Figure 10.10: Applying depth of field to an image

Figure 10.11: Effects achievable with depth of field

the effect is far more subtle. However, all three images were produced in real time using the same program and varying only two parameters—the focal distance and the depth of field.

To simplify this example, we used 32-bit floating-point data for every component of every image. This allows us to not worry about precision issues. Because the precision of floating-point data gets lower as the magnitude of the data gets higher, summed area tables can suffer from precision loss. As the values of all of the pixels in the image are summed together, the values stored in the summed area tables can become very large. Then, as the output image is reconstructed, the difference between multiple (potentially large-valued) floating-point numbers is taken, which can lead to noise.

To improve our implementation of the algorithm, we could make the following changes:

- Render our initial image in 16-bit floating-point format rather than at full 32-bit precision.

- Store the depths of our fragments in a separate texture (or reconstruct them from the depth buffer), eliminating the need to store them in the intermediate image.

- Pre-bias our rendered image by −0.5, which keeps the summed area table values closer to zero even for larger images, thereby improving precision.

Compute Shader Flocking

The following example uses a compute shader to implement a flocking algorithm. Flocking algorithms show emergent behavior within a large group by updating the properties of individual members independently of all others. This kind of behavior is regularly seen in nature, and examples are swarms of bees, flocks of birds, and schools of fish apparently moving in unison even though the members of the group don't communicate globally. That is, the decisions made by an individual are based solely on its perception of the other nearby members of the group. However, no collaboration is made between members over the outcome of any particular decision: As far as we know, schools of fish don't have leaders. Because each member of the group is effectively independent, the new value of each of the properties can be calculated in parallel—ideal for a GPU implementation.

Here, we implement the flocking algorithm in a compute shader. We represent each member of the flock as a single element stored in a shader storage buffer. Each member has a position and a velocity that are updated by a compute shader, which reads the current values from one buffer and writes the result into another buffer. That buffer is then bound as a vertex buffer and used as an instanced input to the rendering vertex shader. Each member of the flock is an instance in the rendering draw. The vertex shader is responsible for transforming a mesh (in this case, a simple model of a paper airplane) into the position and orientation calculated in the first vertex shader. The algorithm then iterates, starting again with the compute shader, reusing the positions and velocities calculated in the previous pass. No data leaves the graphics card's memory, and the CPU is not involved in any calculations.

We use a pair of buffers to store the current positions of the members of the flock. We use a set of VAOs to represent the vertex array state for each pass so that we can render the resulting data. These VAOs also hold the the vertex data for the model we use to represent them. The flock positions and velocities need to be double-buffered because we don't want to partially update the position or velocity buffer while at the same time using them as a source for drawing commands. Figure 10.12 illustrates the passes that the algorithm makes.

In the top left image in Figure 10.12, we perform the update for an even frame. The first buffer containing position and velocity data is bound as a shader storage buffer that can be read by the compute shader, and the second buffer is bound such that it can be written by the compute shader. Next we render, in the top right image in Figure 10.12, using the same set of buffers as inputs as in the update pass. We use the same buffers as input in both the update and render passes so that the render pass has no dependency on the update pass. As a consequence, OpenGL may be able to start working on the render pass before the update pass has finished. The buffer containing the position and velocity data for the flock members is used to source instanced vertex attributes, and the additional geometry buffer is used to provide vertex position data.

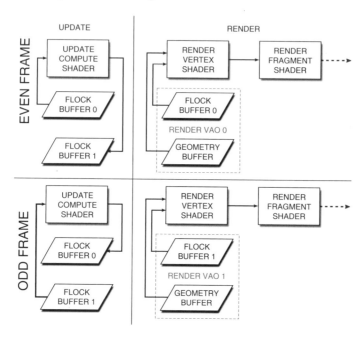

Figure 10.12: Stages in the iterative flocking algorithm

In the bottom left image in Figure 10.12, we move to the next frame. The buffers have been exchanged—the second buffer is now the input to the compute shader, and the first buffer is written by it. Finally, in the bottom right image in Figure 10.12, we render the odd frames. The second buffer is used as input to the vertex shader. Notice, though, that the flock_geometry buffer is a member of both rendering VAOs because the same data is used in both passes; consequently, we don't need two copies of it.

The code to set all that up is shown in Listing 10.9. It isn't particularly complex, but there is a fair amount of repetition, making it long. The listing contains the bulk of the initialization.

```
glGenBuffers(2, flock_buffer);
glBindBuffer(GL_SHADER_STORAGE_BUFFER, flock_buffer[0]);
glBufferData(GL_SHADER_STORAGE_BUFFER,
             FLOCK_SIZE * sizeof(flock_member),
             NULL,
             GL_DYNAMIC_COPY);
glBindBuffer(GL_SHADER_STORAGE_BUFFER, flock_buffer[1]);
glBufferData(GL_SHADER_STORAGE_BUFFER,
             FLOCK_SIZE * sizeof(flock_member),
             NULL,
             GL_DYNAMIC_COPY);

glGenBuffers(1, &geometry_buffer);
glBindBuffer(GL_ARRAY_BUFFER, geometry_buffer);
glBufferData(GL_ARRAY_BUFFER, sizeof(geometry), geometry, GL_STATIC_DRAW);

glGenVertexArrays(2, flock_render_vao);

for (i = 0; i < 2; i++)
{
    glBindVertexArray(flock_render_vao[i]);
    glBindBuffer(GL_ARRAY_BUFFER, geometry_buffer);
    glVertexAttribPointer(0, 3, GL_FLOAT, GL_FALSE,
                          0, NULL);
    glVertexAttribPointer(1, 3, GL_FLOAT, GL_FALSE,
                          0, (void *)(8 * sizeof(vmath::vec3)));

    glBindBuffer(GL_ARRAY_BUFFER, flock_buffer[i]);
    glVertexAttribPointer(2, 3, GL_FLOAT, GL_FALSE,
                          sizeof(flock_member), NULL);
    glVertexAttribPointer(3, 3, GL_FLOAT, GL_FALSE,
                          sizeof(flock_member),
                          (void *)sizeof(vmath::vec4));
    glVertexAttribDivisor(2, 1);
    glVertexAttribDivisor(3, 1);

    glEnableVertexAttribArray(0);
    glEnableVertexAttribArray(1);
    glEnableVertexAttribArray(2);
    glEnableVertexAttribArray(3);
}
```

Listing 10.9: Initializing shader storage buffers for flocking

In addition to running the code shown in Listing 10.9, we initialize our flock positions with some random vectors and set all of the velocities to zero.

Now we need a rendering loop to update our flock positions and draw the members of the flock. It's actually pretty simple now that our data is encapsulated in VAOs. The rendering loop is shown in Listing 10.10. You can clearly see the two passes that the loop makes. First, update_program is made current and used to update the positions and velocities of the flock members. The position of the goal is updated, the storage buffers are bound to the first and second GL_SHADER_STORAGE_BUFFER binding points for reading and writing, and then the compute shader is dispatched. Next, the window is cleared, the rendering program is activated, and we update our transform matrices, bind our VAO, and draw. The number of instances is the number of members of our simulated flock and the number of vertices is simply the amount of geometry we're using to represent our little paper airplane.

```
glUseProgram(flock_update_program);

vmath::vec3 goal = vmath::vec3(sinf(t * 0.34f),
                               cosf(t * 0.29f),
                               sinf(t * 0.12f) * cosf(t * 0.5f));

goal = goal * vmath::vec3(15.0f, 15.0f, 180.0f);

glUniform3fv(uniforms.update.goal, 1, goal);

glBindBufferBase(GL_SHADER_STORAGE_BUFFER, 0, flock_buffer[frame_index]);
glBindBufferBase(GL_SHADER_STORAGE_BUFFER, 1, flock_buffer[frame_index ^ 1]);

glDispatchCompute(NUM_WORKGROUPS, 1, 1);

glViewport(0, 0, info.windowWidth, info.windowHeight);
glClearBufferfv(GL_COLOR, 0, black);
glClearBufferfv(GL_DEPTH, 0, &one);

glUseProgram(flock_render_program);

vmath::mat4 mv_matrix =
    vmath::lookat(vmath::vec3(0.0f, 0.0f, -400.0f),
                  vmath::vec3(0.0f, 0.0f, 0.0f),
                  vmath::vec3(0.0f, 1.0f, 0.0f));
vmath::mat4 proj_matrix =
    vmath::perspective(60.0f,
                       (float)info.windowWidth / (float)info.windowHeight,
                       0.1f,
                       3000.0f);
vmath::mat4 mvp = proj_matrix * mv_matrix;

glUniformMatrix4fv(uniforms.render.mvp, 1, GL_FALSE, mvp);

glBindVertexArray(flock_render_vao[frame_index]);
```

```
glDrawArraysInstanced(GL_TRIANGLE_STRIP, 0, 8, FLOCK_SIZE);

frame_index ^= 1;
```

Listing 10.10: The rendering loop for the flocking example

That's pretty much the interesting part of the program side. Let's take a look at the shader side of things. The flocking algorithm works by applying a set of rules for each member of the flock to decide which direction to travel in. Each rule considers the current properties of the flock member and the properties of the other members of the flock as perceived by the individual being updated. Most of the rules require access to the other members' position and velocity data, so update_program uses a shader storage buffer containing that information. Listing 10.11 shows the beginning of the update compute shader. It lists the uniforms we'll use[5] during simulation, the declaration of the flock member, the two buffers used for input and output, and finally a shared array of members that will be used during the updates.

```
#version 450 core

layout (local_size_x = 256) in;

uniform float closest_allowed_dist2 = 50.0;
uniform float rule1_weight = 0.18;
uniform float rule2_weight = 0.05;
uniform float rule3_weight = 0.17;
uniform float rule4_weight = 0.02;
uniform vec3 goal = vec3(0.0);
uniform float timestep = 0.5;

struct flock_member
{
    vec3 position;
    vec3 velocity;
};

layout (std430, binding = 0) buffer members_in
{
    flock_member member[];
} input_data;

layout (std430, binding = 1) buffer members_out
{
    flock_member member[];
} output_data;

shared flock_member shared_member[gl_WorkGroupSize.x];
```

Listing 10.11: Compute shader for updates in flocking example

---

5. Most of these uniforms are not hooked up to the example program, but their default values can be changed by tweaking the shader.

Once we have declared all of the inputs to our shader, we have to define the rules that we'll use to update them. The rules we use in this example are as follows:

- Members try not to hit each other. They need to stay at least a short distance from each other at all times.

- Members try to fly in the same direction as those around them.

- Members of the flock try to reach a common goal.

- Members try to keep with the rest of the flock. They will fly toward the center of the flock.

The first two rules are the intra-member rules. That is, the effect of each of the members on the others is considered individually. Listing 10.12 contains the shader code for the first rule. If we're closer to another member than we're supposed to be, we simply move away from that member:

```
vec3 rule1(vec3 my_position,
           vec3 my_velocity,
           vec3 their_position,
           vec3 their_velocity)
{
    vec3 d = my_position - their_position;
    if (dot(d, d) < closest_allowed_dist2)
        return d;
    return vec3(0.0);
}
```

Listing 10.12: The first rule of flocking

The shader for the second rule is shown in Listing 10.13. It returns a change in velocity weighted by the inverse square of the distance from each member to the member. A small amount is added to the squared distance between the members to keep the denominator of the fraction from getting too small (and thus the acceleration too large), which keeps the simulation stable.

```
vec3 rule2(vec3 my_position,
           vec3 my_velocity,
           vec3 their_position,
           vec3 their_velocity)
{
    vec3 d = their_position - my_position;
    vec3 dv = their_velocity - my_velocity;
    return dv / (dot(d, d) + 10.0);
}
```

Listing 10.13: The second rule of flocking

The third rule (that flock members attempt to fly toward a common goal) is applied once per member. The fourth rule (that members attempt to get to the center of the flock) is also applied once per member, but requires the average position of all of the flock members (along with the total number of members in the flock) to calculate.

The main body of the program contains the meat of the algorithm. The flock is broken into groups and each group is represented as a single local work group (the size of which we have defined as 256 elements). Because every member of the flock needs to interact in some way with every other member of the flock, this algorithm is considered an $O(N^2)$ algorithm. This means that each of the N flock members will read all of the other N members' positions and velocities, and that each of the N members' positions and velocities will be read N times. Rather than read through the entirety of the input shader storage buffer for every flock member, we copy a local work group's worth of data into a shared storage buffer and use the local copy to update each of the members.

For each flock member (which is a single invocation of our compute shader), we loop over the number of work groups and copy a single flock member's data into the shared local copy (the shared_member array declared at the top of the shader in Listing 10.11). Each of the 256 local shader invocations copies one element into the shared array and then executes the barrier() function to ensure that all of the invocations are synchronized and have therefore copied *their* data into the shared array. Then, we loop over all of the data stored in the shared array, apply each of the intra-member rules in turn, sum up the resulting vector, and execute another call to barrier(). This again synchronizes the threads in the local work group and ensures that all of the other invocations have finished using the shared array before we restart the loop and write over it again. Code to do this is given in Listing 10.14.

```
void main(void)
{
    uint i, j;
    int global_id = int(gl_GlobalInvocationID.x);
    int local_id  = int(gl_LocalInvocationID.x);

    flock_member me = input_data.member[global_id];
    flock_member new_me;
    vec3 acceleration = vec3(0.0);
    vec3 flock_center = vec3(0.0);

    for (i = 0; i < gl_NumWorkGroups.x; i++)
    {
        flock_member them =
            input_data.member[i * gl_WorkGroupSize.x +
```

```
                             local_id];
shared_member[local_id] = them;
memoryBarrierShared();
barrier();
for (j = 0; j < gl_WorkGroupSize.x; j++)
{
    them = shared_member[j];
    flock_center += them.position;
    if (i * gl_WorkGroupSize.x + j != global_id)
    {
        acceleration += rule1(me.position,
                              me.velocity,
                              them.position,
                              them.velocity) * rule1_weight;
        acceleration += rule2(me.position,
                              me.velocity,
                              them.position,
                              them.velocity) * rule2_weight;
    }
}
barrier();
}

flock_center /= float(gl_NumWorkGroups.x * gl_WorkGroupSize.x);
new_me.position = me.position + me.velocity * timestep;
acceleration += normalize(goal - me.position) * rule3_weight;
acceleration += normalize(flock_center - me.position) * rule4_weight;
new_me.velocity = me.velocity + acceleration * timestep;
if (length(new_me.velocity) > 10.0)
    new_me.velocity = normalize(new_me.velocity) * 10.0;
new_me.velocity = mix(me.velocity, new_me.velocity, 0.4);
output_data.member[global_id] = new_me;
}
```

Listing 10.14: Main body of the flocking update compute shader

In addition to applying the first two rules on a per-member basis and then adjusting acceleration to try to get the members to fly toward the common goal and toward the center of the flock, we apply a few more rules to keep the simulation sane. First, if the velocity of the flock member gets too high, we clamp it to a maximum allowed value. Second, rather than output the new velocity verbatim, we calculate a weighted average between it and the old velocity. This forms a basic low-pass filter and stops the flock members from accelerating or decelerating too quickly or, more importantly, from changing direction too abruptly.

Putting all this together completes the update phase of the program. Now we need to produce the shaders that are responsible for rendering the flock. This program uses the position and velocity data calculated by the compute shader as instanced vertex arrays and transforms a fixed set of vertices into position based on the position and velocity of the individual member. Listing 10.15 shows the inputs to the shader.

```
#version 450 core

layout (location = 0) in vec3 position;
layout (location = 1) in vec3 normal;

layout (location = 2) in vec3 bird_position;
layout (location = 3) in vec3 bird_velocity;

out VS_OUT
{
    flat vec3 color;
} vs_out;

uniform mat4 mvp;
```

Listing 10.15: Inputs to the flock rendering vertex shader

In this shader, `position` and `normal` are regular inputs from our geometry
buffer, which in this example contains a simple model of a paper airplane.
The `bird_position` and `bird_vecocity` inputs will be the instanced
attributes that are provided by the compute shader and whose instance
divisor is set with the **glVertexAttribDivisor()** function. The body of our
shader (given in Listing 10.16) uses the velocity of the flock member to
construct a *lookat* matrix that can be used to orient the airplane model
such that it's always flying forward.

```
mat4 make_lookat(vec3 forward, vec3 up)
{
    vec3 side = cross(forward, up);
    vec3 u_frame = cross(side, forward);

    return mat4(vec4(side, 0.0),
                vec4(u_frame, 0.0),
                vec4(forward, 0.0),
                vec4(0.0, 0.0, 0.0, 1.0));
}

vec3 choose_color(float f)
{
    float R = sin(f * 6.2831853);
    float G = sin((f + 0.3333) * 6.2831853);
    float B = sin((f + 0.6666) * 6.2831853);

    return vec3(R, G, B) * 0.25 + vec3(0.75);
}

void main(void)
{
    mat4 lookat = make_lookat(normalize(bird_velocity),
                              vec3(0.0, 1.0, 0.0));
    vec4 obj_coord = lookat * vec4(position.xyz, 1.0);
    gl_Position = mvp * (obj_coord + vec4(bird_position, 0.0));

    vec3 N = mat3(lookat) * normal;
    vec3 C = choose_color(fract(float(gl_InstanceID / float(1237.0))));

    vs_out.color = mix(C * 0.2, C, smoothstep(0.0, 0.8, abs(N).z));
}
```

Listing 10.16: Flocking vertex shader body

Construction of the lookat matrix uses a method similar to that described in Chapter 4, "Math for 3D Graphics." Once we have oriented the mesh using this matrix, we add the flock member's position and transform the whole lot by the model–view-projection matrix. We also orient the object's normal by using the lookat matrix, which allows us to apply a very simple lighting calculation. We choose a color for the object based on the current instance ID (which is unique per mesh) and use it to compute the final output color, which we write into the vertex shader output. The fragment shader is a simple pass-through shader that writes this incoming color to the framebuffer. The result of rendering the flock is shown in Figure 10.13.

A possible enhancement that could be made to this program is to calculate the lookat matrix in the compute shader. Here, we calculate it in the vertex shader and therefore redundantly calculate it for every vertex. It doesn't matter so much in this example because our mesh is small, but if our instanced mesh were larger, generating it in the compute shader and passing it along with the other instanced vertex attributes would likely be faster. We could also apply more physical simulations rather than just ad hoc rules. For example, we could simulate gravity, making it easier to fly down than up, or we could allow the planes to crash into and bounce off of one another. However, for the purposes of this example, what we have here is sufficient.

Figure 10.13: Output of compute shader flocking program

Summary

In this chapter, we have taken an in-depth look at compute shaders—the "single-stage pipeline" that allows you to harness the computational power of modern graphics processors for more than just computer graphics. In our discussion of the execution model of compute shaders, you learned about work groups, synchronization, and intra-workgroup communication. We then covered some of the applications of compute shaders. First, we saw the applications of compute shaders in image processing, which is an obvious fit for computer graphics. Next, we explored how you might use compute shaders for physical simulation when we implemented the flocking algorithm. This should have allowed you to imagine some of the possibilities for the use of compute shaders in your own applications—for artificial intelligence, pre- and post-processing, or even audio applications!

Chapter 11

Advanced Data Management

WHAT YOU'LL LEARN IN THIS CHAPTER

- How write data into buffers and textures directly from your shaders.

- How to get OpenGL to interpret data in a flexible manner.

- How to directly share data between the CPU and the GPU.

So far in this book you have learned how to use buffers and textures to store data that your program can use. Buffers and textures can be bound to the OpenGL pipeline for writing in the form of transform feedback or framebuffers. In this chapter, we'll cover a few of the more advanced techniques involving data and data management. We'll dive into *texture views*, which allow you to apply more than one interpretation to data. We'll take a deeper look at texture compression and use a compute shader to compress texture data on the GPU. We'll also look at ways to share data directly between the CPU and the GPU, including how to arbitrate which processor owns the data at any particular time.

Eliminating Binding

Thus far, when we wanted to use a texture in a shader, we bound it to a texture unit, which we represented as a uniform variable of one of the sampler types (e.g., `sampler2D`, `samplerCube`). The sampler variable is associated with one of the texture units and that association forms an indirection to the underlying texture. This has two significant, related side effects:

- The number of textures that a single shader can access is limited to the number of texture units that the OpenGL driver supports. The minimum requirement in OpenGL 4.5 is 16 units per stage. Although some implementations support 32 units per stage or more, this is still a fairly small amount.

- Your application needs to spend time binding and unbinding textures between draws. This makes it difficult to combine draws that otherwise would be able to use the same state.

To get around these problems, we can use a feature known as *bindless textures*. This functionality will be available to your application if OpenGL reports that the `GL_ARB_bindless_texture` extension is supported. This extension allows you to get a *handle* for a texture and then use that handle directly in your shaders to refer to the underlying texture without having to bind it to a texture unit. Additionally, it allows you to control the list of textures that will be available to your shaders. In fact, it requires this because, as you are no longer using texture binding points, OpenGL has no way of knowing which textures might be used and therefore need to be in memory before running your shaders.

Once you have created a texture, you can get a handle for it by calling either of the following functions:

```
GLuint64 glGetTextureHandleARB(GLuint texture);
GLuint64 glGetTextureSamplerHandleARB(GLuint texture, GLuint sampler);
```

The first function produces a handle representing the texture named in the texture parameter, using its built-in sampler parameters. The second function returns a handle representing `texture` and the sampler given in `sampler` as if that pair had been bound to a texture unit. Notice that both **glGetTextureHandleARB()** and **glGetTextureSamplerHandleARB()** return a GLuint64 64-bit integer value. You will need to pass those values into your shaders to use them. The simplest way to do so is to put the value into a uniform block. That is, you declare one of GLSL's sampler types in a uniform block declaration and then place the 64-bit handle into a buffer and use it to back the uniform block. Listing 11.1 shows an example of making this type of declaration.

```
#version 450 core

#extension GL_ARB_bindless_texture : require

layout (binding = 0) uniform MYBLOCK
{
    sampler2D theSampler;
};

in vec2 uv;
out vec4 color;

void main(void)
{
    color = texture(theSampler, uv);
}
```

Listing 11.1: Declaring samplers inside uniform blocks

As you can see from Listing 11.1, once you have enabled the bindless texture exension and then declared samplers in your uniform blocks, using the samplers is identical to the ordinary non-bindless usage.

Before running any shaders that access bindless textures, you need to tell OpenGL which textures *might* be used. There is no specific upper limit to the number of textures that might be in use—you are limited only by the capabilities of the underlying OpenGL implementation and the resources available to it. When you bind textures to traditional texture units, OpenGL can determine from what's bound what might be used. However, once you eliminate binding points, you become responsible for making this notification yourself. To put a texture onto the "might be used" list, call

```
void glMakeTextureHandleResidentARB(GLuint64 handle);
```

To take a texture off the resident list, call

```
void glMakeTextureHandleNonResidentARB(GLuint64 handle);
```

In both cases, the handle parameter is the handle returned from a call to either **glGetTextureHandleARB()** or **glGetTextureSamplerHandleARB()**. The term *resident* refers to the underlying memory used to store the texture's data. You can think of the list of resident textures as a set of virtualized binding points that are not accessible to you, but which OpenGL uses to track what needs to be in memory at any given point in time.

With the simple example shown in Listing 11.1, which moves a single sampler declaration into a uniform block, this might not seem like a particularly useful feature, especially considering the additional steps required—create the texture, get its handle, make it resident, and so on. However, consider what happens if we put multiple textures inside a single uniform block, or even embed them inside a structure. Then textures become data just like regular constants. Now your material definitions can simply include textures, for example.

The `bindlesstex` example demonstrates the use of bindless textures. We adapted a shader to modulate the lighting of each pixel by a texture, the handle to which is stored in a uniform. Listing 11.2 shows the fragment shader from the example.

```
#version 450 core

// Enable bindless textures
#extension GL_ARB_bindless_texture : require

// Output
layout (location = 0) out vec4 color;

// Input from vertex shader
in VS_OUT
{
    vec3 N;
    vec3 L;
    vec3 V;
    vec2 tc;
    flat uint instance_index;
} fs_in;

// Material properties - these could also go in a uniform buffer
const vec3 ambient = vec3(0.1, 0.1, 0.1);
const vec3 diffuse_albedo = vec3(0.9, 0.9, 0.9);
const vec3 specular_albedo = vec3(0.7);
const float specular_power = 300.0;

// Texture block
layout (binding = 1, std140) uniform TEXTURE_BLOCK
{
    sampler2D    tex[384];
};

void main(void)
{
    // Normalize the incoming N, L, and V vectors
    vec3 N = normalize(fs_in.N);
    vec3 L = normalize(fs_in.L);
```

```
        vec3 V = normalize(fs_in.V);
        vec3 H = normalize(L + V);

        // Compute the diffuse and specular components for each fragment
        vec3 diffuse = max(dot(N, L), 0.0) * diffuse_albedo;
        // This is where we reference the bindless texture
        diffuse *= texture(tex[fs_in.instance_index], fs_in.tc * 2.0).rgb;
        vec3 specular = pow(max(dot(N, H), 0.0), specular_power) * specular_albedo;

        // Write final color to the framebuffer
        color = vec4(ambient + diffuse + specular, 1.0);
    }
```

Listing 11.2: Declaring samplers inside uniform blocks

As you can see in Listing 11.2, we declared a uniform block with 384
textures in it. This is significantly more than the number of traditional
texture binding points supported by the OpenGL implementation upon
which the sample was developed, and more than an order of magnitude
greater than the number of samplers supported in a single shader stage.

To actually *generate* 384 textures, we use a simple procedural algorithm
during application start-up to produce a pattern and then modify it
slightly for each texture. For each of the 384 textures, we create the
texture, upload a different set of data into it, get its handle, and make it
resident with a call to **glMakeTextureHandleResidentARB()**. We place the
handles into a buffer object that will be used as a uniform buffer by the
fragment shader. The code is shown in Listing 11.3.

```
glGenBuffers(1, &buffers.textureHandleBuffer);
glBindBuffer(GL_UNIFORM_BUFFER, buffers.textureHandleBuffer);

glBufferStorage(GL_UNIFORM_BUFFER,
                NUM_TEXTURES * sizeof(GLuint64) * 2,
                nullptr,
                GL_MAP_WRITE_BIT);

GLuint64* pHandles =
    (GLuint64*)glMapBufferRange(GL_UNIFORM_BUFFER,
                                0,
                                NUM_TEXTURES * sizeof(GLuint64) * 2,
                                GL_MAP_WRITE_BIT | GL_MAP_INVALIDATE_BUFFER_BIT);

for (i = 0; i < NUM_TEXTURES; i++)
{
    unsigned int r = (random_uint() & 0xFCFF3F) << (random_uint() % 12);
    glGenTextures(1, &textures[i].name);
    glBindTexture(GL_TEXTURE_2D, textures[i].name);
    glTexStorage2D(GL_TEXTURE_2D,
                   TEXTURE_LEVELS,
                   GL_RGBA8,
                   TEXTURE_SIZE, TEXTURE_SIZE);
    for (j = 0; j < 32 * 32; j++)
```

```
{
    mutated_data[j] = (((unsigned int *)tex_data)[j] & r) | 0x20202020;
}
glTexSubImage2D(GL_TEXTURE_2D,
                0,
                0, 0,
                TEXTURE_SIZE, TEXTURE_SIZE,
                GL_RGBA, GL_UNSIGNED_BYTE,
                mutated_data);
glGenerateMipmap(GL_TEXTURE_2D);
textures[i].handle = glGetTextureHandleARB(textures[i].name);
glMakeTextureHandleResidentARB(textures[i].handle);
pHandles[i * 2] = textures[i].handle;
}

glUnmapBuffer(GL_UNIFORM_BUFFER);
```

Listing 11.3: Making textures resident

To render all these textures on real objects, we created a simple test
wrapper that uses another uniform block to store an array of
transformation matrices; in the vertex shader, we then index into that
array using gl_InstanceID. We also pass the instance index to the
fragment shader of Listing 11.2, where it is used to index into the array of
texture handles. This allows us to render a single object with an instanced
drawing command. Each instance uses a different transformation matrix
and a different texture. The resulting output is shown in Figure 11.1.
This image is also shown in Color Plate 7.

Figure 11.1: Output of the bindlesstex example application

As you can see, each of the objects in Figure 11.1 has a different colored pattern on it. This pattern is created from the 384 unique textures. In an advanced application, each of these textures would originate from user-generated content and be unique rather than generated programmatically. Here, we have demonstrated that a single draw command can access hundreds of unique textures.

Sparsely Populated Textures

Texture data is probably the most expensive asset in a modern graphics application in terms of memory consumption. A single texture of 2048×2048 texels in GL_RGBA8 format consumes 16 megabytes of memory just for the base mipmap level. A third of this amount of memory is consumed by the mipmap chain, making the requirements reach over 21 megabytes. A typical graphically intensive application might have tens or hundreds of these chains in use at a time, pushing the total memory requirements for the application into the hundreds of megabytes and possibly well into the multiple gigabytes range. However, even in such an application, it is unlikely that all of that data will be needed at the same time. Rather, objects that would normally have a high-resolution texture applied to them might be seen only from a distance, meaning that only the lower-resolution mipmaps might be used. Another common use case is *atlas* textures—textures that are used to apply details to irregular objects where not all of the rectangular texture space is used for image data.

To accomodate these kinds of scenarios, you can use the GL_ARB_sparse_texture extension. This extension allows textures to be sparsely populated, separating the logical dimensions of the texture from the physical memory space required to store its texels. In a sparse texture, the texture itself is divided into a number of square or rectangular regions known as *pages*. Each page can either be committed or uncommitted. When a page is committed, you can use it like an ordinary texture. When a page is uncommitted, OpenGL will not use any memory to store data for it. Reading from it under this circumstance will not return useful data, and any data you write to such a region will just be discarded.

Before you can use sparse textures, you need to make sure that OpenGL supports the GL_ARB_sparse_texture extension. Once you have determined that the extension is supported, you can create sparse textures using the **glTextureStorage2D()** function. To create a sparse texture, you need to tell OpenGL about your intention *before* allocating storage for the

texture, by calling **glTextureParameteri()** with the
GL_TEXTURE_SPARSE_ARB parameter. This is demonstrated in Listing 11.4.

```
GLuint tex;

// Create a new texture
glCreateTexture(1, &tex);

// Tell OpenGL that we want this texture to be sparse
glTextureParameteri(tex, GL_TEXTURE_SPARSE_ARB, GL_TRUE);

// Now allocate storage for the texture
glTextureStorage2D(tex, 14, GL_RGBA8, 16384, 16384);
```

Listing 11.4: Creating a sparse texture

The code in Listing 11.4 creates a 16,384 × 16,384 texel texture with a
complete mipmap chain with an internal format of GL_RGBA8. Normally,
this texture would consume a gigabyte of memory. This is the largest size
of 2D texture that must be supported by OpenGL—larger textures may be
supported but this is not guaranteed. Because the texture is sparse,
however, the storage space is not consumed immediately. Only *virtual*
space is reserved for the texture and no physical memory is allocated. To
commit pages (that is, to allocate physical storage for them), we can call
glTexPageCommitmentARB(), whose prototype is

```
void glTexPageCommitmentARB(GLenum target,
                            GLint level,
                            GLint xoffset,
                            GLint yoffset,
                            GLint zoffset,
                            GLsizei width,
                            GLsizei height,
                            GLsizei depth,
                            GLboolean commit);
```

glTexturePageCommitmentEXT() can commit and decommit pages into the
sparse texture whose name is given in texture. The level parameter
specifies in which mipmap level the pages reside. The xoffset, yoffset,
and zoffset parameters give the offset, in texels, where the region to be
committed or decommitted begins, and the width, height, and depth
parameters specify the size of the region, again in texels. If the commit
parameter is GL_TRUE, the pages are committed; if it is GL_FALSE, they are
decommitted (freed).

All of the parameters—xoffset, yoffset, zoffset, width, height, and
depth—must be integer multiples of the page size for the texture. The page size
is determined by OpenGL based on the internal format of the texture. You can

determine the page size by calling **glGetInternalformativ()** and passing the tokens GL_VIRTUAL_PAGE_SIZE_X_ARB, GL_VIRTUAL_PAGE_SIZE_Y_ARB, and GL_VIRTUAL_PAGE_SIZE_Z_ARB to find the page size for the format in the x, y, and z dimensions, respectively. There may actually be more than one possible page size. **glGetInternalformativ()** can also be used to find out how many virtual page sizes are supported for a given format by passing the GL_NUM_VIRTUAL_PAGE_SIZES_ARB token. Listing 11.5 shows an example of determining the number of virtual page sizes and identifying what they are using **glGetInternalformativ()**.

```
GLuint num_page_Sizes;
GLuint page_sizes_x[10];
GLuint page_sizes_y[10];
GLuint page_sizes_z[10];

// Figure out how many page sizes are available for a 2D texture
// with internal format GL_RGBA8
glGetInternalformativ(GL_TEXTURE_2D,
                      GL_RGBA8,
                      GL_NUM_VIRTUAL_PAGE_SIZES_ARB,
                      sizeof(GLuint),
                      &num_page_sizes);

// We support up to 10 internal format sizes -- this is hard-coded
// in the arrays above. We could do this dynamically, but it's unlikely
// that an implementation supports more than this number, so it's not really
// worth it.
num_page_sizes = min(num_page_sizes, 10);

// One call for each dimension
glGetInternalformativ(GL_TEXTURE_2D,
                      GL_RGBA8,
                      GL_VIRTUAL_PAGE_SIZE_X_ARB,
                      num_page_sizes * sizeof(GLuint),
                      page_sizes_x);
glGetInternalformativ(GL_TEXTURE_2D,
                      GL_RGBA8,
                      GL_VIRTUAL_PAGE_SIZE_Y_ARB,
                      num_page_sizes * sizeof(GLuint),
                      page_sizes_y);
glGetInternalformativ(GL_TEXTURE_2D,
                      GL_RGBA8,
                      GL_VIRTUAL_PAGE_SIZE_Z_ARB,
                      num_page_sizes * sizeof(GLuint),
                      page_sizes_z);
```

Listing 11.5: Determining supported sparse texture page sizes

If the number of page sizes returned when retrieving GL_NUM_VIRTUAL_PAGE_SIZES_ARB is zero, your OpenGL implementation doesn't support sparse textures for the specified format and dimensionality of texture. If the number of page sizes is more than one, OpenGL will likely return the page sizes sorted into an order of its preference—probably based on memory allocation efficiency or performance under use. In that case, you're probably best off to pick the first one. Some combinations don't make a whole lot of sense. It is quite probable, for example, that all OpenGL implementations will return 1 for the page size in the z dimension when a format is used with a 2D texture, but they might return something else for a 3D texture. That is why the texture type is specified in the call to `glGetInternalformativ()`.

Not only do the regions of the texture need to be committed and decommitted in page-size blocks (which is why the parameters to `glTexturePageCommitmentEXT()` need to be multiples of the page size), but the texture itself also needs to be an integer multiple of the page size. This holds only for the base level of the mipmap. As each mipmap level is half the size of the previous level, eventually the size of a mipmap level becomes less than a single page. This so-called *mipmap tail* is the part of the texture where commitment cannot be managed at the page level. In fact, the whole tail is considered to be either committed or uncommitted as a single unit. Once you commit part of a mipmap tail, the whole tail becomes committed. Likewise, once any part of the mipmap tail is decommitted, the whole thing becomes decommitted. As a side effect of this constraint, you cannot make a sparse texture whose base mipmap level is smaller than a single page.

When pages of a texture are first committed with a call to `glTexPageCommitmentARB()`, their contents are initially undefined. However, once you have committed them, you can treat them like part of any ordinary texture. You can put data into them using `glTextureStorageSubImage2D()`, or attach them to a framebuffer object and render into them, for example.

The `sparsetexture` application shows a simple example of using sparse textures. In this example, we assume that the page size for the texture is a factor of 128 texels for GL_RGBA8 data (which works out to 64K). First, we allocate a large texture consisting of 16 pages × 16 pages (which works out to 2048 × 2048 texels for a 128 × 128 page size). Then, on each frame, we use the frame counter to generate an index by switching a few of its bits around and then making pages resident or nonresident at the computed location. For pages made newly resident, we upload new data from a small texture that we load on start-up.

For rendering, we draw a simple quad over the entire viewport. At each point, we sample from the texture. When pages are resident, we get the data stored in the texture. Where pages are not resident, we receive undefined data. In this application, that's not terribly important and we display whatever is read (even if it might be garbage). On the machine used to develop the sample application, the OpenGL implementation returns zero for unmapped regions of data. The implementation of the rendering loop is shown in Listing 11.6.

```
static int t = 0;
int r = (t & 0x100);
int tile = bit_reversal_table[(t & 0xFF)];

int x = (tile >> 0) & 0xF;
int y = (tile >> 4) & 0xF;

// If page is not resident...
if (r == 0)
{
    // Make it resident and upload data
    glTexPageCommitmentARB(GL_TEXTURE_2D,
                           0,
                           x * PAGE_SIZE, y * PAGE_SIZE, 0,
                           PAGE_SIZE, PAGE_SIZE, 1,
                           GL_TRUE);
    glTexSubImage2D(GL_TEXTURE_2D,
                    0,
                    x * PAGE_SIZE, y * PAGE_SIZE,
                    PAGE_SIZE, PAGE_SIZE,
                    GL_RGBA, GL_UNSIGNED_BYTE,
                    texture_data);
}
else
{
    // Otherwise make it nonresident
    glTexPageCommitmentARB(GL_TEXTURE_2D,
                           0,
                           x * PAGE_SIZE, y * PAGE_SIZE, 0,
                           PAGE_SIZE, PAGE_SIZE, 1,
                           GL_FALSE);
}

t += 17;
```

Listing 11.6: Simple texture commitment management

The output of the sparsetexture sample is shown in Figure 11.2. As you can see in the figure, there are missing data blocks in the texture and only parts of the texture are visible in the screenshot.

The example given in sparsetexture is very simple and serves only to demonstrate the feature. In a more advanced application, we may use multiple sparse textures and combine their results, or use secondary textures to store meta-data about the residency of our main texture. For example, a common use case for sparse textures is streaming texture data over time.

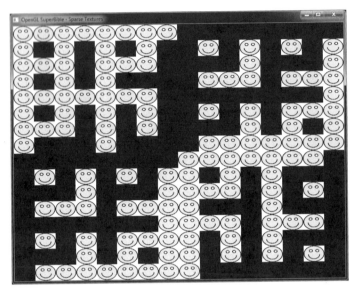

Figure 11.2: Output of the `sparsetexture` example application

Consider the scenario where you have a large level of a game that consumes hundreds of megabytes of texture data. When players first start the game, they are placed at a specific part of the map—most of the map will not be visible to them and many of the parts of the map will be far from them and therefore rendered at a low resolution. Making the players wait for all textures to be loaded (which could be a considerable amount of time if the textures are on a remote server across the Internet, or stored on slower media such as DVDs) would make for a poor user experience. However, delaying loading a texture until the first time the user sees an object can cause stuttering and in-game slowdowns, which also negatively affect the user's experience.

Using sparse textures can resolve the issue nicely. The idea is to allocate every texture as sparse and then populate only the lowest-resolution mipmap levels of *all of them* before the game starts. As the lowest mipmap levels consume exponentially less storage space than the texture base levels, the time taken to load them is substantially less than if all textures needed to be loaded ahead of time. When the user first sees part of the map, we can then guarantee that at least a low-resolution version of the texture is available in the smallest mipmap level. In many cases, this works very well because objects start far from the user and need only their lowest mipmap levels anyway. As the user gets closer and closer to an object, the higher-resolution mipmap levels for that object's textures can be loaded.

To properly sample from a texture, we need to *clamp* the level of detail that OpenGL will use to guarantee that we're going to pull from only committed texels. To do that, we need to know which pages are committed. This requires a second, level-of-detail texture, which we can sample from to find the lowest committed level-of-detail for a given texture coordinate. Listing 11.7 shows a snippet of shader code that samples from a sparse texture by calculating the required level-of-detail, fetching from the committed level-of-detail texture, and then clamping the result to the highest available level (the lowest-resolution level) before sampling from the actual sparse texture.

```
uniform sampler2D uCommittedLodTexture;
uniform sampler2D uSparseColorTexture;

vec4 sampleFromSparse(vec2 uv)
{
    // First, get the available levels of detail for each of the
    // four texels that make up our filtered sparse texel.
    vec4 availLod = textureGather(uCommitedLodTexture, uv);

    // Calculate the level-of-detail that OpenGL would like
    // to sample from.
    vec2 desiredLod = textureQueryLod(uSparseColorTexture, uv);

    // Find the maximum of the available and desired LoD.
    float maxAvailLod = max(max(availLod.x,
                                availLod.y),
                            max(availLod.z,
                                availLod.w));

    // Compute the actual LoD to be used for sampling.
    // Note that this is the maximum value of LoD, representing the
    // lowest-resolution mipmap -- our application fills the texture
    // from lowest to highest resolution (highest to lowest LoD).
    float finalLod = max(desiredLod.x, max(desiredLod.y, maxAvailLod));

    // Finally, sample from the sparse texture using the computed LoD.
    return textureLod(uSparseColorTexture, uv, lod);
}
```

Listing 11.7: Sampling a sparse texture with clamped level-of-detail (LoD)

By reusing some of the code in Listing 11.7, you can get the GPU to provide feedback to the application about which texture pages are needed. Bind an image as writable and, when the desired level-of-detail (the desiredLod variable in Listing 11.7) is lower (that is, higher resolution) than the available level-of-detail, write the desired level-of-detail into the image. Periodically, read the content of this image back into your application[1] and scan it. You can use this information to decide what to stream in next.

---

[1]. To avoid GPU stalls, remember to leave a good amount of time between updating the image containing the desired level-of-detail and reading it back.

Texture Compression

Compressed textures were briefly introduced in Chapter 5. However, we did not discuss how texture compression works or describe how to produce compressed texture data. In this section, we will cover one of the simpler texture compression formats supported by OpenGL in some detail and see how to write a compressor for such data.

The RGTC Compression Scheme

Most texture compression formats supported by OpenGL are *block based*. That is, they compress image data in small blocks, and each of those blocks is independent of all other blocks in the image. There is no global data, nor any dependency between blocks. Thus, while possibly suboptimal from a data compression standpoint, these formats are well suited to random access. When your shader reads texels from a compressed texture, the graphics hardware can very quickly determine which block the texel is in and then read that block into a fast local cache inside the GPU. As the block is read, it is decompressed. The blocks in these formats have fixed compression ratios, meaning that a fixed amount of compressed data always represents the same amount of uncompressed data.

The RGTC texture compression format is one of the simpler formats supported by OpenGL. It has been part of the core specification for a number of years and is designed to store one- and two-channel images. Like other similar formats, it is block based, and each compressed block of data represents a 4×4 texel region of the image. For simplicity, we will assume that source images are a multiple of 4 texels wide and high. Only two-dimensional images are supported by the RGTC format, although it should be possible to stack a number of 2D images into an array texture or even a 3D texture. It is not possible to render into a compressed texture by attaching it to a framebuffer object.

The RGTC specification includes signed and unsigned, one- and two-component formats:

- GL_COMPRESSED_RED_RGTC1 represents unsigned single-channel data.
- GL_COMPRESSED_SIGNED_RED_RGTC1 represeents signed single-channel data.
- GL_COMPRESSED_RG_RGTC2 represents unsigned two-channel data.
- GL_COMPRESSED_SIGNED_RG_RGTC2 represents signed two-channel data.

We will begin by discussing the GL_COMPRESSED_RED_RGTC1 format. This format represents each 4 × 4 block of texels using 64 bits of information. If each input texel is an 8-bit unsigned byte, then the input data comprises 128 bits, producing a compression ratio of 2:1. The principle of this compression format (like many others) is to take advantage of the limited range of values that are likely to appear inside a small region of image data. If we find the minimum and maximum values appearing inside a block, then we know that all texels within that block fall within that range. Therefore, all we need to do is determine *how far along that range* a given texel is, and then encode that information for each texel rather than the value of the texel itself. For images with smooth gradients, this works well. Even for images with hard edges, each texel might be at opposite ends of the range and still produce a reasonable approximation to the edge.

Figure 11.3 demonstrates this principle graphically. After finding the minimum and maximum values of the pixels in a small block, we encode them as the endpoints of a line. This is represented by the y axis in Figure 11.3. The line extends from the y coordinate of the highest value on the graph to the y coordinate of the graph. Then, we quantize the x axis into a number of small regions and encode the region into which each texel falls in our compressed image. Each of these regions is represented by a different hatching pattern on the graph. Each of the texel values (represented by the vertical bars) then falls into one of the four regions defined by subdividing the line. It is the index of this region that is encoded for each texel, along with the values of the endpoints of the line that are shared by the whole block.

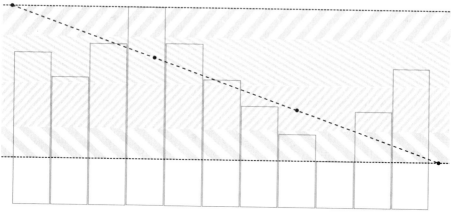

Figure 11.3: Representation of image data as endpoints of a line

Table 11.1: First RGTC Encoding for RED Images

Encoding	Resulting Value
0	R_{min}
1	R_{max}
2	$\frac{6}{7}R_{min} + \frac{1}{7}R_{max}$
3	$\frac{5}{7}R_{min} + \frac{2}{7}R_{max}$
4	$\frac{4}{7}R_{min} + \frac{3}{7}R_{max}$
5	$\frac{3}{7}R_{min} + \frac{4}{7}R_{max}$
6	$\frac{2}{7}R_{min} + \frac{5}{7}R_{max}$
7	$\frac{1}{7}R_{min} + \frac{6}{7}R_{max}$

Each 64-bit (8-byte) block begins with two bytes representing the values of the two endpoints of the line. This leaves 48 bits (64 − 16) in which to encode the values of the pixels. As there are 16 pixels in a 4 × 4 block, that leaves 3 bits for each texel. In the straightforward encoding, this divides our range into 8 pieces. Note that in the case where the minimum and maximum values of the texels in a block are within 8 gray levels of each other, this encoding scheme will produce lossless compression. The encoding is not quite direct, however. Table 11.1 shows how the value of each 3-bit field (values of 0 through 7) corresponds to the encoded texel value.

There is a special case that takes advantage of the fact that we can store additional information in the first 2 bytes of the block beyond only the endpoints of our line. If we store the mimimum value first, followed by the maximum value, then the usage for the 3 bits for each texel described previously holds. However, if we store the maximum value first, and then the minimum value, we can reverse the order of the regions, continuing to encode the same data, except we can now use this ordering to signal a slightly different encoding.

As you can see from Table 11.2, there are fewer regions that can be represented using this second encoding, but the values 0 and 1 can be exactly represented regardless of the values of the endpoints.[2] This allows us to use this encoding to better represent a solid black line against a lighter, textured background, for example.

2. Remember, this is a normalized texture, so 1 here represents a value of 255 when interpreted as an integer.

Table 11.2: Second RGTC Encoding for RED Images

Encoding	Resulting Value
0	R_{min}
1	R_{max}
2	$\frac{4}{5}R_{min} + \frac{1}{5}R_{max}$
3	$\frac{3}{5}R_{min} + \frac{2}{5}R_{max}$
4	$\frac{2}{5}R_{min} + \frac{3}{5}R_{max}$
5	$\frac{1}{5}R_{min} + \frac{4}{5}R_{max}$
6	0
7	1

In effect, the first two values in the block can be used to define an eight-entry palette. Upon reading the block, we compare the two endpoint values and generate the appropriate palette. Then, for each 3-bit field in the remaining 6 bytes of compressed data, we generate a single output texel by using it as an index into the palette we just generated.

Generating Compressed Data

The description of the RGTC compression scheme in the previous section should be sufficient to write a decompressor. However, decompression is not what we're after here—all modern graphics hardware can decompress RGTC data at a performance level likely exceeding that of sampling from uncompressed data due to the reduced bandwidth requirements. What we want to do here is compress our textures into this format.

To take advantage of the dual encodings supported by RGTC, we're going to write two variants of our compressor—one that produces data in the first encoding and one that produces data in the second encoding—and then decide, for each block, which of the two encodings to use based on the computed per-pixel error. We will look at the first encoding initially, and then see how we can modify it to produce the second encoding. The design is intended to produce an encoder that can execute in a compute shader. While we could try to compress a single block using many theads in parallel, the goal is not necessarily to encode a single block as quickly as possible, but rather to compress a large image quickly. As each block can be compressed independently of all others, it makes sense to write a compressor that runs inside a single thread, and then compress as many blocks as possible in parallel. This simplifies the encoder because compressing each block essentially becomes a single-threaded operation with no need to share data or synchronize with other work items.

First, our compressor loads a 4 × 4 block of texels into a local array. Because we are operating on single-channel data, we can use GLSL's textureGatherOffset function to read 4 texels from a 2 × 2 block in one function call. The texture coordinate passed to textureGatherOffset must lie in the center of the 2 × 2 region. Listing 11.8 shows the code that gathers 16 texels' worth of data in four calls to textureGatherOffset.

```
void fetchTexels(uvec2 blockCoord, out float texels[16])
{
    vec2 texSize = textureSize(input_image, 0);
    vec2 tl = (vec2(blockCoord * 4) + vec2(1.0)) / texSize;

    vec4 tx0 = textureGatherOffset(input_image, tl, ivec2(0, 0));
    vec4 tx1 = textureGatherOffset(input_image, tl, ivec2(2, 0));
    vec4 tx2 = textureGatherOffset(input_image, tl, ivec2(0, 2));
    vec4 tx3 = textureGatherOffset(input_image, tl, ivec2(2, 2));

    texels[0] = tx0.w;
    texels[1] = tx0.z;
    texels[2] = tx1.w;
    texels[3] = tx1.z;

    texels[4] = tx0.x;
    texels[5] = tx0.y;
    texels[6] = tx1.x;
    texels[7] = tx1.y;

    texels[8] = tx2.w;
    texels[9] = tx2.z;
    texels[10] = tx3.w;
    texels[11] = tx3.z;

    texels[12] = tx2.x;
    texels[13] = tx2.y;
    texels[14] = tx3.x;
    texels[15] = tx3.y;
}
```

Listing 11.8: Fetching a block of texels using textureGatherOffset

Once we have read the 16 texels of information from the source image, we can construct our palette. To do so, we will find the minimum and maximum values of the texels in the block, and then compute the resulting output color value for each of the eight possible encodings of data. Note that it's not necessary to *sort* the values of the texels—all we need to know is what the minimum and maximum values present are, not the order in which they occur. Listing 11.9 shows how we produce the palette for the first encoding. We will cover the second encoding shortly.

```
void buildPalette(float texels[16], out float palette[8])
{
    float minValue = 1.0;
    float maxValue = 0.0;
    int i;

    for (i = 0; i < 16; i++)
    {
        maxValue = max(texels[i], maxValue);
        minValue = min(texels[i], minValue);
    }

    palette[0] = minValue;
    palette[1] = maxValue;
    palette[2] = mix(minValue, maxValue, 1.0 / 7.0);
    palette[3] = mix(minValue, maxValue, 2.0 / 7.0);
    palette[4] = mix(minValue, maxValue, 3.0 / 7.0);
    palette[5] = mix(minValue, maxValue, 4.0 / 7.0);
    palette[6] = mix(minValue, maxValue, 5.0 / 7.0);
    palette[7] = mix(minValue, maxValue, 6.0 / 7.0);
}
```

Listing 11.9: Generating a palette for RGTC encoding

Once we have our palette, we need to map each of the texels in the block to one of the palette entries. To do this, we simply run through each palette entry and find the one with the closest absolute value to the texel under consideration. Listing 11.10 shows how this is done.

```
float palettizeTexels(float texels[16], float palette[8], out uint entries[16])
{
    uint i, j;
    float totalError = 0.0;

    for (i = 0; i < 16; i++)
    {
        uint bestEntryIndex = 0;
        float texel = texels[i];
        float bestError = abs(texel - palette[0]);
        for (j = 1; j < 8; j++)
        {
            float absError = abs(texel - palette[j]);
            if (absError < bestError)
            {
                bestError = absError;
                bestEntryIndex = j;
            }
        }
```

```
        entries[i] = bestEntryIndex;
        totalError += bestError;
    }

    return totalError;
}
```

Listing 11.10: Palettizing an RGTC block

Once we have palettized our block, we need to pack the resulting colors and indices into our output data structure. Remember, each compressed block starts with the two endpoint colors followed by 3 bits for each texel in the block. Three is not a convenient number when we're running on machines that operate natively on powers of 2. Also, GLSL has no 64-bit type, which means we'll need to use a uvec2 to hold our data. Worse yet, one of our 3-bit fields will need to straddle the boundary between the components of our uvec2. However, the resulting function still isn't overly complex and is shown in Listing 11.11.

```
void packRGTC(float palette0,
              float palette1,
              uint entries[16],
              out uvec2 block)
{
    uint t0 = 0x00000000;
    uint t1 = 0x00000000;

    t0 = (entries[0]  << 0u) +
         (entries[1]  << 3u) +
         (entries[2]  << 6u) +
         (entries[3]  << 9u) +
         (entries[4]  << 12) +
         (entries[5]  << 15) +
         (entries[6]  << 18) +
         (entries[7]  << 21);

    t1 = (entries[8]  << 0u) +
         (entries[9]  << 3u) +
         (entries[10] << 6u) +
         (entries[11] << 9u) +
         (entries[12] << 12u) +
         (entries[13] << 15u) +
         (entries[14] << 18u) +
         (entries[15] << 21u);

    block.x = (uint(palette0 * 255.0) << 0u) +
              (uint(palette1 * 255.0) << 8u) +
              (t0 << 16u);
    block.y = (t0 >> 16u) + (t1 << 8u);
}
```

Listing 11.11: Packing an RGTC block

Earlier, we mentioned that a second encoding for RGTC textures allows exact representation of 0 and 1 without making them one of the endpoints of the palette. Essentially, the only modification to our compressor is to produce a second palette, but rather than using the true maximum and minimum values from the block, we use the minimum and maxium values from the block that are *not either 0 or 1*. A modified version of our `buildPalette` function is shown in Listing 11.12.

```
void buildPalette2(float texels[16], out float palette[8])
{
    float minValue = 1.0;
    float maxValue = 0.0;
    int i;

    for (i = 0; i < 16; i++)
    {
        if (texels[i] != 1.0)
        {
            maxValue = max(texels[i], maxValue);
        }
        if (texels[i] != 0.0)
        {
            minValue = min(texels[i], minValue);
        }
    }

    palette[0] = maxValue;
    palette[1] = minValue;
    palette[2] = mix(maxValue, minValue, 1.0 / 5.0);
    palette[3] = mix(maxValue, minValue, 2.0 / 5.0);
    palette[4] = mix(maxValue, minValue, 3.0 / 5.0);
    palette[5] = mix(maxValue, minValue, 4.0 / 5.0);
    palette[6] = 0.0;
    palette[7] = 1.0;
}
```

Listing 11.12: Generating a palette for RGTC encoding

Did you notice how our `palettizeTexels` function returns a floating-point value? That value is the accumulated error across all texels in the block when converted from their true values to the values available from our palette. Once we have generated the second palette using the `buildPalette2` function from Listing 11.12, we palettize the block once with the first palette (using the first encoding scheme) and once with the second palette (using the second encoding scheme). Each function returns the error—we use the resulting palettized block from whichever function returns the smaller error metric.

After the `packRGTC` function shown in Listing 11.11 has run, the resulting `uvec2` holds the 64-bit compressed block distributed across its two components. All we need to do now is write the data out to a buffer. Unfortunately, there is no way to write the image data directly into a compressed texture that can be immediately used by OpenGL. Instead, we write the data into a buffer object. That buffer can then be mapped so that the data can be stored to disk, or it can be used as the source of data in a call to `glTexSubImage2D()`.

To store our image data, we'll use an `imageBuffer` uniform in our compute shader. The main entry point of our shader looks like Listing 11.13.

```
void main(void)
{
    float texels[16];
    float palette[8];
    uint entries[16];
    float palette2[8];
    uint entries2[16];
    uvec2 compressed_block;

    fetchTexels(gl_GlobalInvocationID.xy, texels);

    buildPalette(texels, palette);
    buildPalette2(texels, palette2);

    float error1 = palettizeTexels(texels, palette, entries);
    float error2 = palettizeTexels(texels, palette2, entries2);

    if (error1 < error2)
    {
        packRGTC(palette[0],
                 palette[1],
                 entries,
                 compressed_block);
    }
    else
    {
        packRGTC(palette2[0],
                 palette2[1],
                 entries2,
                 compressed_block);
    }

    imageStore(output_buffer,
               gl_GlobalInvocationID.y * uImageWidth + gl_GlobalInvocationID.x,
               compressed_block.xyxy);
}
```

Listing 11.13: Main function for RGTC compression

As noted, the RGTC compression scheme is ideally suited to images that have smooth regions. Figure 11.4 shows the result of applying this type of compression to the distance field texture from Subsection 13, along with magnified portions of the image. On the left is the original, uncompressed image. On the right is the compressed image. As you can tell, there is little or no visible difference between the two. In fact, the demo in Subsection 13 uses a texture compressed using RGTC.

Figure 11.4: Result of using RGTC texture compression on a distance field

Packed Data Formats

In most of the image and vertex specification commands you've encountered so far, we have been considering only natural data types—bytes, integers, floating-point values, and so on. For example, when passing a type parameter to **glVertexAttribFormat()**, you specified tokens such as GL_UNSIGNED_INT or GL_FLOAT. Along with a size parameter, that defines the layout of data in memory. In general, the types used in OpenGL correspond almost directly to the types used in C and other high-level languages. For example, GL_UNSIGNED_BYTE essentially represents an `unsigned char` type, and this is true for 16-bit (`short`) and 32-bit (`int`) data as well. For the floating-point types GL_FLOAT and GL_DOUBLE, the data in memory is represented as specified in the IEEE-754 standard for 32- and 64-bit precisions, respectively. This standard is almost universally implemented on modern CPUs, so the C data types `float` and `double` map to them. The OpenGL header files map GLfloat and GLdouble to these definitions in C.

However, OpenGL supports a few more data types that are not represented directly in C. They include the special data type GL_HALF_FLOAT and a number of *packed* data types. The first of these, GL_HALF_FLOAT, is a 16-bit representation of a floating-point number.

The 16-bit floating-point representation was introduced in the IEEE 754-2008 specification and has been widely supported in GPUs for a number of years. Modern CPUs do not generally support it, but this is slowly changing with specialized instructions appearing in newer models. The 32-bit floating-point format consists of a single sign bit, which is set when the number is negative; 8 exponent bits, which represent the remainder of the number to be raised to the exponent; and that remainder, which is known as the mantissa and is 23 bits long. In addition, there are several special encodings to represent things like infinity and undefined values (such as the result of division by zero). The 16-bit encoding is a simple extension of this scheme, in which the number of bits assigned to each component of the number is reduced. There is still a single sign bit, but there are only 5 exponent bits and 10 mantissa bits. Just as 32-bit floating-point numbers have a higher dynamic range than 32-bit integers, so 16-bit floating-point numbers have a higher dynamic range than 16-bit integers.

Regardless of the packing of bits within a 16-bit floating-point number, the raw bits of the number can still be manipulated, copied, and stored using other 16-bit types such as `unsigned short`. So, for example, if you have three channels of 16-bit floating-point data, you can extract any of the channels' data using a simple pointer dereference. The 16-bit type is still a natural length for computers that work with nice, round powers of 2. For the packed data formats, however, this is not true. Here, OpenGL stores multiple channels of data packed together into single, natural data types. For example, the `GL_UNSIGNED_SHORT_5_6_5` type stores three channels—two 5-bit channels and one 6-bit channel—packed togther into a single `unsigned short` quantity. The C language has no representation for this arrangement. To get at the individual components, you need to use bitfield operations, shifts, masks, or other techniques directly in your code (or helper functions to do it for you).

The OpenGL names for packed formats are broken into two parts. The first part consists of one of our familiar unsigned integer types—`GL_UNSIGNED_BYTE`, `GL_UNSIGNED_SHORT`, or `GL_UNSIGNED_INT`. It tells us the parent unit in which we should manipulate data. The second part of the name indicates how the data fields are laid out inside that unit. This is the `_5_6_5` part of `GL_UNSIGNED_SHORT_5_6_5`. The bits are laid out in most significant to least significant order, regardless of the endianness of the host machine, and appear in the order of the components as seen by OpenGL. So, for `GL_UNSIGNED_SHORT_5_6_5`, the 5 most significant bits are the first element of the vector, the next 6 bits are the second element, and the last 5 bits are the third element of the vector. Sometimes, however, the order of the vector elements can be reversed. In this case, `_REV` is appended to the type name. For example, the type `GL_UNSIGNED_SHORT_5_6_5_REV` uses the 5 most significant bits to represent the third channel of the

Table 11.3: Packed Data Formats Supported in OpenGL

Format	Bit Allocation (MSB:LSB)			
	R	G	B	A
GL_UNSIGNED_BYTE_3_3_2	7:5	4:2	1:0	—
GL_UNSIGNED_BYTE_2_3_3_REV	2:0	5:3	7:6	—
GL_UNSIGNED_SHORT_5_6_5	15:11	10:5	4:0	—
GL_UNSIGNED_SHORT_5_6_5_REV	4:0	10:5	15:11	—
GL_UNSIGNED_SHORT_4_4_4_4	15:12	11:8	7:4	3:0
GL_UNSIGNED_SHORT_4_4_4_4_REV	3:0	7:4	11:8	15:12
GL_UNSIGNED_SHORT_5_5_5_1	15:11	10:6	5:1	0
GL_UNSIGNED_SHORT_1_5_5_5_REV	4:0	9:5	14:10	15
GL_UNSIGNED_INT_8_8_8_8	31:24	23:16	15:8	7:0
GL_UNSIGNED_INT_8_8_8_8_REV	7:0	15:8	23:16	31:24
GL_UNSIGNED_INT_10_10_10_2	31:22	21:12	11:2	1:0
GL_UNSIGNED_INT_2_10_10_10_REV	9:0	19:10	29:20	31:30
GL_UNSIGNED_INT_24_8	31:8	7:0	—	—
GL_UNSIGNED_INT_10F_11F_11F_REV	10:0	21:11	31:22	—

vector, the next 6 bits to represent the second channel, and the final 5 least significant bits to represent the first channel of the result vector.

Table 11.3 shows the complete list of packed data formats supported by OpenGL. In addition to the formats listed in Table 11.3, the GL_FLOAT_32_UNSIGNED_INT_24_8_REV format interleaves a floating-point value in a first 32-bit word with an 8-bit quantitiy stored in the 8 least significant bits of a second 32-bit word. This format and GL_UNSIGNED_INT_24_8 are commonly used to store interleaved depth and stencil information. Further, the shared exponent format GL_UNSIGNED_INT_5_9_9_9_REV could be considered a packed data format, but is also a form of compression and is covered in "Shared Exponents."

High-Quality Texture Filtering

By now you should be quite familiar with the two texture filtering modes—*linear* and *nearest*. Nearest mode represents point sampling and simply chooses the texel whose center is closest to the texture coordinate

Figure 11.5: Linear interpolation under high magnification

you specify. By comparison, linear filtering mode mixes two or more texels together to produce a final color for your shader. The filtering method used in linear filtering is simple linear interpolation—hence the name. In many cases, this is of sufficiently high quality and has the advantage that it can be readily and efficiently implemented in hardware. However, under higher magnification factors, we can see artifacts. For example, take a look at the heavily zoomed-in portion of Figure 11.5.

In Figure 11.5 you can almost see the centers of the texels. In fact, the texel centers keep their original values from the underlying texture and the reproduced texel value given to your shader linearly moves from one texel to another. The jarring artifacts, appearing almost as lines running through the centers of the texels, is due to the discontinuity in the *gradient* of the intensity of the image. Between each texel center, the image intensity is interpolated in a straight line. As the texture coordinate passes through the center of a texel, that straight line suddenly changes direction. This change in direction is the artifact that you can see in the image. For clarification, take a look at Figure 11.6, which represents a one-dimensional texture in graph form.

The graph in Figure 11.6 illustrates the problem well. Imagine that this graph represents a one-dimensional texture. Each bar of the graph is a single texel, and the dotted line is the result of interpolating between them. We can clearly see the interpolated lines between the texel centers

Figure 11.6: Graph showing linear interpolation

and the abrupt change in direction that each new segment of the graph creates. Instead of using this linear interpolation scheme, it would be much better if we could move smoothly from one texel center to another, leveling off as we reach the texel center and avoiding the discontinuity at each.

As luck would have it, we do have a smooth interpolation function—smoothstep does exactly what we want. If we take the graph of Figure 11.6 and replace each of the linear sections with a smoothstep curve, we get a much nicer fit to the texel centers and, more importantly, no gradient discontinuities. We can see this result in Figure 11.7.

The question, then, is how to use this type of interpolation in our shaders. If you look closely at your linear interpolation function, OpenGL first takes your texture coordinate, which represents the extent of the texture in the range 0.0 to 1.0, and scales it to the size of the texture. The integer part of the resulting number is used to select a texel from the texture, and the

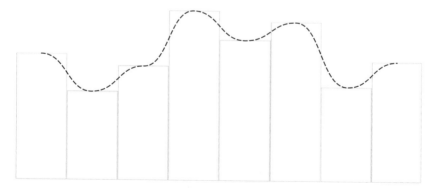

Figure 11.7: Graph showing smooth interpolation

fractional part of the number is used as a weight to linearly interpolate it with its neighbors. Given a fractional part f, the weights used to blend two adjacent texels are $(1 - f)$ and f (which sum to 1). What we'd like to do is replace f with another number—the result of the smoothstep function. Of course, we still need the weights for adjacent texels to sum to 1, and we'd like the number to start from 0 and reach 1 at the same time as f would have. Finally, we'd like the rate of change (the gradient) of this function to be 0 at its ends, which is also a property of the smoothstep function.

We can do all of this in our shader. All we need is a little arithmetic and a single, linear texture lookup (the same as we had before). We're going to modify the texture coordinates used for sampling from the texture to cause the graphics hardware to use our weights for interpolation rather than its own.

Listing 11.14 shows the GLSL code to do this math for us. As you can see, only a few lines of code are needed and the number of texture lookups is the same as it was before. In many OpenGL implementations, there should be almost no performance penalty for using this function instead of regular texture filtering.

```glsl
vec4 hqfilter(sampler2D samp, vec2 tc)
{
    // Get the size of the texture we'll be sampling from
    vec2 texSize = textureSize(tex, 0);

    // Scale our input texture coordinates up, move to center of texel
    vec2 uvScaled = tc * texSize + 0.5;

    // Find integer and fractional parts of texture coordinate
    vec2 uvInt = floor(uvScaled);
    vec2 uvFrac = fract(uvScaled);

    // Replace fractional part of texture coordinate
    uvFrac = smoothstep(0.0, 1.0, uvFrac);

    // Reassemble texture coordinate, remove bias, and
    // scale back to 0.0 to 1.0 range
    vec2 uv = (uvInt + uvFrac - 0.5) / texSize;

    // Regular texture lookup
    return texture(samp, uv);
}
```

Listing 11.14: High-quality texture filtering function

The result of sampling a texture using the function given in Listing 11.14 is given in Figure 11.8. As you can see, filtering the texture with this function produces a much smoother image. Texels are slightly more

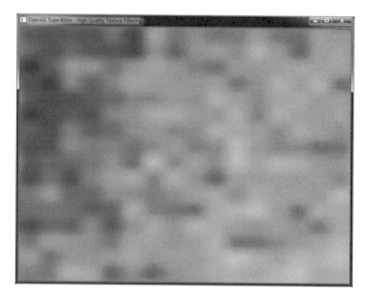

Figure 11.8: Result of smooth interpolation

visible, but they have smooth edges and there are no obvious discontinuities at texel centers.

Summary

In this chapter we have discussed a number of topics related to managing and using data efficiently. In particular, we covered *bindless* textures, which allow you to almost eliminate binding from your application and which provide simultanous access to a virtually unlimited number of textures from your shaders. We have looked at *sparse* textures, which allow you to manage how much memory is allocated to each of your texture objects. We also dug deeper into texture compression and wrote our own texture compressor for the RGTC texture format. Finally, we looked into the details of linear texture filtering and, using a little math in our shaders, greatly improved the image quality of textures under magnification.

Chapter 12

Controlling and Monitoring the Pipeline

WHAT YOU'LL LEARN IN THIS CHAPTER

- How to ask OpenGL about the progress of your commands down the graphics pipeline.

- How to measure the time taken for your commands to execute.

- How to synchronize your application with OpenGL and how to synchronize multiple OpenGL contexts with each other.

This chapter is about the OpenGL pipeline and how it executes your commands. As your application makes OpenGL function calls, work is placed in the OpenGL pipeline and makes its way down it one stage at a time. This takes time, and you can measure that span. This allows you to tune your application's complexity to match the performance of the graphics system and to measure and control latency, which is important for real-time applications. In this chapter, you'll also learn how to synchronize your application's execution to that of OpenGL commands you've issued and even how to synchronize multiple OpenGL contexts with each other.

Queries

Queries are a mechanism to ask OpenGL what's happening in the graphics pipeline. There's plenty of information that OpenGL can tell you; you just need to know what to ask—and how to ask the question.

Remember your early days in school? The teacher wanted you to raise your hand before asking a question. This was almost like reserving your place in line for asking the question—the teacher didn't know yet what your question was going to be, but she knew that you had something to ask. OpenGL is similar. Before we can ask a question, we have to reserve a spot so that OpenGL knows the question is coming. Questions in OpenGL are represented by query objects, and much like any other object in OpenGL, query objects must be reserved, or generated. To do this, call **glGenQueries()**, passing it the number of queries you want to reserve and the address of a variable (or array) where you would like the names of the query objects to be placed:

```
void glGenQueries(GLsizei n,
                  GLuint *ids);
```

The function reserves some query objects for you and gives you their names so that you can refer to them later. You can generate as many query objects you need in one go:

```
GLuint one_query;
GLuint ten_queries[10];
glGenQueries(1, &one_query);
glGenQueries(10, ten_queries);
```

In this example, the first call to **glGenQueries()** generates a single query object and returns its name in the variable one_query. The second call to **glGenQueries()** generates ten query objects and returns ten names in the array ten_queries. In total, 11 query objects have been created, and OpenGL has reserved 11 unique names to represent them. It is very unlikely, but still possible, that OpenGL will not be able to create a query for you; in this case it returns 0 as the name of the query. A well-written application always checks that **glGenQueries()** returns a non-zero value for the name of each requested query object. If there is a failure, OpenGL keeps track of the reason, and you can find that out by calling **glGetError()**.

Each query object reserves a small but measurable amount of resources from OpenGL. These resources must be returned to OpenGL because, if they are not, OpenGL may run out of space for queries and fail to generate more for the application later. To return the resources to OpenGL, call **glDeleteQueries()**:

```
void glDeleteQueries(GLsizei n,
                     const GLuint *ids);
```

This works similarly to **glGenQueries()**—it takes the number of query objects to delete and the address of a variable or array holding their names:

```
glDeleteQueries(10, ten_queries);
glDeleteQueries(1, &one_query);
```

After the queries are deleted, they are essentially gone for good. The names of the queries can't be used again unless they are given back to you by another call to **glGenQueries()**.

Occlusion Queries

Once you've reserved your spot using **glGenQueries()**, you can ask a question. OpenGL doesn't automatically keep track of the number of pixels it has drawn. It has to count, and it must be told when to start counting. To do this, use **glBeginQuery()**. The **glBeginQuery()** function takes two parameters—the question you'd like to ask, and the name of the query object that you reserved earlier:

```
glBeginQuery(GL_SAMPLES_PASSED, one_query);
```

GL_SAMPLES_PASSED represents the question you're asking, "How many samples passed the depth test?" Here, OpenGL counts samples because you might be rendering to a multi-sampled display format, and in that case, there could be more than one sample per pixel. In the case of a normal, single-sampled format, there is one sample per pixel and therefore a one-to-one mapping of samples to pixels. Every time a sample makes it past the depth test (meaning the sample hadn't previously been discarded by the fragment shader), OpenGL counts 1. It adds up all the samples from all the rendering it is doing and stores the answer in part of the space reserved for the query object. A query object that counts samples that might become visible (because they passed the depth test) is known as an *occlusion query*.

Now that OpenGL is counting samples, you can render as normal and OpenGL keeps track of all the samples generated as a result. Anything that you render is counted toward the total—even samples that have no contribution to the final image due to blending or being covered by later samples, for example. When you want OpenGL to add up everything rendered since you told it to start counting, you tell it to stop by calling **glEndQuery()**:

```
glEndQuery(GL_SAMPLES_PASSED);
```

This tells OpenGL to stop counting samples that have passed the depth test and made it through the fragment shader without being discarded. All the samples generated by all the drawing commands between the call to **glBeginQuery()** and **glEndQuery()** are added up.

Retrieving Query Results

Now that the pixels produced by your drawing commands have been counted, you need to retrieve them from OpenGL. This is accomplished by calling

```
glGetQueryObjectuiv(the_query, GL_QUERY_RESULT, &result);
```

Here, the_query is the name of the query object that's being used to count samples and result is the variable that you want OpenGL to write the result into (notice that we pass the *address* of this variable). This command instructs OpenGL to place the count associated with the query object into your variable. If no pixels were produced as a result of the drawing commands between the last call to **glBeginQuery()** and **glEndQuery()** for the query object, result will be 0. If anything actually made it to the end of the fragment shader without being discarded, result will contain the number of samples that got that far. By rendering an object between a call to **glBeginQuery()** and **glEndQuery()** and then checking if result is 0, you can determine whether the object is visible.

Because OpenGL operates as a pipeline, it may have many drawing commands queued up back-to-back waiting to be processed. It could be the case that not all of the drawing commands issued before the last call to **glEndQuery()** have finished producing pixels. In fact, some may not have even started to be executed. In that case, **glGetQueryObjectuiv()** causes OpenGL to wait until everything between **glBeginQuery()** and **glEndQuery()** has been rendered and it is ready to return an accurate count. If you're planning to use a query object as a performance optimization, this is certainly not what you want. All these short delays could add up and eventually slow down your application! The good news is that it's possible to ask OpenGL if it's finished rendering anything that might affect the result of the query and therefore has a result available for you. To do this, call

```
glGetQueryObjectuiv(the_query, GL_QUERY_RESULT_AVAILABLE, &result);
```

If the result of the query object is not immediately available and trying to retrieve it would cause your application to have to wait for OpenGL to finish what it is working on, result becomes GL_FALSE. If OpenGL is ready and has your answer, result becomes GL_TRUE. This tells you that retrieving the result from OpenGL will not cause any delays. Now you can do useful work while you wait for OpenGL to be ready to provide your pixel count, or you can make decisions based on whether the result is available. For example, if you would have skipped rendering something had result been 0, you could choose to just go ahead and render it anyway rather than waiting for the result of the query.

Using the Results of a Query

Now that you have this information, what will you do with it? A very common use for occlusion queries is to optimize an application's performance by avoiding unnecessary work. Consider an object that has a very detailed appearance. The object has many triangles and possibly a complex fragment shader with a lot of texture lookups and intensive math operations. Perhaps there are many vertex attributes and textures, and the application has a lot of work to do just to get ready to draw the object. The object is very expensive to render. It's also possible that the object may never end up being visible in the scene. Perhaps it's covered by something else. Perhaps it's off the screen altogether. It would be good to know this up front and just not draw the object at all if it's never going to be seen by the user anyway.

Occlusion queries are a good way to do this. Take your complex, expensive object and produce a much lower-fidelity version of it. Usually, a simple bounding box will do. Start an occlusion query, render the bounding box, and then end the occlusion query and retrieve the result. If no part of the object's bounding box produces any pixels, then the more detailed version of the object will not be visible, and it doesn't need to be sent to OpenGL.

Of course, you probably don't want the bounding box to be visible in the final scene. There are a number of ways you can make sure that OpenGL doesn't actually draw the bounding box. The easiest way is probably to use **glColorMask()** to turn off writes to the color buffer by passing GL_FALSE for all parameters. You could also call **glDrawBuffer()** to set the current draw buffer to GL_NONE. Whichever method you choose, don't forget to framebuffer writes back on again afterward!

Listing 12.1 shows a simple example of how to use **glGetQueryObjectuiv()** to get retrieve the result from a query object.

```
glBeginQuery(GL_SAMPLES_PASSED, the_query);
RenderSimplifiedObject(object);
glEndQuery(GL_SAMPLES_PASSED);
glGetQueryObjectuiv(the_query, GL_QUERY_RESULT, &the_result);
if (the_result != 0)
    RenderRealObject(object);
```

Listing 12.1: Getting the result from a query object

RenderSimplifiedObject is a function that renders the low-fidelity version of the object; RenderRealObject, in contrast, renders the object with all of its detail. RenderRealObject is called only if at least one pixel is produced by RenderSimplifiedObject. Remember that the call to **glGetQueryObjectuiv()** causes your application to wait if the result of the query is not ready yet. This situation is likely to occur if the rendering done by RenderSimplifiedObject is simple—which is the point of this example. If all you want to know is whether it's safe to skip rendering something, you can find out if the query result is available and render the more complex object if the result is unavailable (i.e., the object may be visible or hidden) or available and non-zero (i.e., the object is certainly visible). Listing 12.2 demonstrates how you might determine whether a query object result is ready before you ask for the actual count, allowing you to make decisions based on both the availability and the value of a query result.

```
GLuint the_result = 0;

glBeginQuery(GL_SAMPLES_PASSED, the_query);
RenderSimplifiedObject(object);
glEndQuery(GL_SAMPLES_PASSED);

glGetQueryObjectuiv(the_query, GL_QUERY_RESULT_AVAILABLE, &the_result);

if (the_result != 0)
    glGetQueryObjectuiv(the_query, GL_QUERY_RESULT, &the_result);
else
    the_result = 1;

if (the_result != 0)
    RenderRealObject(object);
```

Listing 12.2: Figuring out if occlusion query results are ready

In this new example, we determine whether the result is available and, if so, retrieve it from OpenGL. If it's not available, we put a count of 1 into the result so that the complex version of the object will be rendered.

It is possible to have multiple occlusion queries in the graphics pipeline at the same time so long as they don't overlap. Using multiple query objects is another way for the application to avoid having to wait for OpenGL. OpenGL can count and add up results into only one query object at a time, but it can manage several query objects and perform many queries back-to-back. We can expand our example to render multiple objects with multiple occlusion queries. If we had an array of ten objects to render, each with a simplified representation, we might rewrite the example as shown in Listing 12.3.

```
int n;

for (n = 0; n < 10; n++)
{
    glBeginQuery(GL_SAMPLES_PASSSED, ten_queries[n]);
    RenderSimplifiedObject(&object[n]);
    glEndQuery(GL_SAMPLES_PASSED);
}

for (n = 0; n < 10; n++)
{
    glGetQueryObjectuiv(ten_queries[n], GL_QUERY_RESULT, &the_result);
    if (the_result != 0)
        RenderRealObject(&object[n]);
}
```

Listing 12.3: Simple, application-side conditional rendering

As discussed earlier, OpenGL is modeled as a pipeline and can have many things going on at the same time. If you draw something simple such as a bounding box, it's likely that won't have reached the end of the pipeline by the time you need the result of your query. As a consequence, when you call **glGetQueryObjectuiv()**, your application may have to wait a while for OpenGL to finish working on your bounding box before it can give you the answer and you can act on it.

In our next example, we render ten bounding boxes before we ask for the result of the first query. This means that OpenGL's pipeline can be filled, and it can have a lot of work to do and is therefore much more likely to have finished working on the first bounding box before we ask for the result of the first query. In short, the more time you give OpenGL to finish working on what you've asked it for, the more likely it is that OpenGL will have the result of your query and the less likely it is that your application will have to wait for results. Some complex applications take this to the extreme and use the results of queries from the previous frame to make decisions about the new frame.

Finally, putting both techniques together into a single example, we have the code shown in Listing 12.4.

```
int n;

for (n = 0; n < 10; n++)
{
    glBeginQuery(GL_SAMPLES_PASSSED, ten_queries[n]);
    RenderSimplifiedObject(&object[n]);
    glEndQuery(GL_SAMPLES_PASSED);
}

for (n = 0; n < 10; n+)
{
    glGetQueryObjectuiv(ten_queries[n],
                        GL_QUERY_RESULT_AVAILABLE,
                        &the_result);
    if (the_result != 0)
        glGetQueryObjectuiv(ten_queries[n],
                        GL_QUERY_RESULT,
                        &the_result);
    else
        the_result = 1;
    if (the_result != 0)
        RenderRealObject(&object[n]);
}
```

Listing 12.4: Rendering when query results aren't available

Because the amount of work sent to OpenGL by `RenderRealObject` is much greater than that sent by `RenderSimplifiedObject`, by the time we ask for the result of the second, third, fourth, and additional query objects, more and more work has been sent into the OpenGL pipeline, and it becomes more likely that our query results will be ready. Within reason, the more complex our scene, and the more query objects we use, the more likely we are to see positive a performance impact.

Getting OpenGL to Make Decisions for You

The preceding examples show how you can ask OpenGL to count pixels and how to get the result back from OpenGL into your application so that it can make decisions about what to do next. However, in this application, we don't really care about the actual value of the result. We're just using it to decide whether to send more work to OpenGL or to make other changes to the way it might render things. The results have to be sent back from

OpenGL to the application, perhaps over a CPU bus or even a network connection when you're using a remote rendering system, just so the application can decide whether to send more commands to OpenGL. This causes latency and can hurt performance, sometimes outweighing any potential benefits from using the queries in the first place.

What would be much better is if we could send all the rendering commands to OpenGL and tell it to execute them only if the result of a query object says it should. This approach is called predication, and fortunately it is possible through a technique called *conditional rendering*. Conditional rendering allows you to wrap up a sequence of OpenGL drawing commands and send them to OpenGL along with a query object and a message that says, "Ignore all of this if the result stored in the query object is 0." To mark the start of this sequence of calls, use

```
glBeginConditionalRender(the_query, GL_QUERY_WAIT);
```

To mark the end of the sequence, use

```
glEndConditionalRender();
```

Any drawing command—including functions like **glDrawArrays()**, **glClearBufferfv()**, and **glDispatchCompute()**—that is called between **glBeginConditionalRender()** and **glEndConditionalRender()** is ignored if the result of the query object (the same value that you could have retrieved using **glGetQueryObjectuiv()**) is 0. In such a case, the actual result of the query doesn't have to be sent back to your application. The graphics hardware can make the decision as to whether to render for you. Keep in mind, though, that state changes such as binding textures, turning blending on or off, and so on are still executed by OpenGL—only rendering commands are discarded. To modify the previous example to use conditional rendering, we could use the code in Listing 12.5.

```
// Ask OpenGL to count the samples rendered between the start
// and end of the occlusion query
glBeginQuery(GL_SAMPLES_PASSED, the_query);
RenderSimplifiedObject(object);
glEndQuery(GL_SAMPLES_PASSED);

// Execute the next few commands only if the occlusion query says something
// was rendered
glBeginConditionalRender(the_query, GL_QUERY_WAIT);
RenderRealObject(object);
glEndConditionalRender();
```

Listing 12.5: Basic conditional rendering example

The two functions, RenderSimplifiedObject and RenderRealObject, are functions within our hypothetical example application that render simplified (perhaps just the bounding box, for example) and more complex versions of the object, respectively. Notice that we never call **glGetQueryObjectuiv()**, and we never read any information (such as the result of the query object) back from OpenGL.

The astute reader will have noticed the GL_QUERY_WAIT parameter passed to **glBeginConditionalRender()**. You may be wondering what its purpose is—after all, the application no longer has to wait for results to be ready. As mentioned earlier, OpenGL operates as a pipeline, which means that it may not have finished dealing with RenderSimplifiedObject before your call to **glBeginConditionalRender()** or the first drawing function called from RenderRealObject reaches the beginning of the pipeline. In this case, OpenGL can either wait for everything called from RenderSimplifiedObject to reach the end of the pipeline before deciding whether to execute the commands sent by the application, or it can go ahead and start working on RenderRealObject if the results aren't ready in time. To tell OpenGL not to wait and to just go ahead and start rendering if the results aren't available, call

```
glBeginConditionalRender(the_query, GL_QUERY_NO_WAIT);
```

This tells OpenGL, "If the results of the query aren't available yet, don't wait for them; just go ahead and render anyway." This technique is of greatest use when occlusion queries are being used to improve performance. Waiting for the results of occlusion queries can consume any time gained by using them in the first place. Thus, using the GL_QUERY_NO_WAIT flag essentially allows the occlusion query to be used as an optimization if the results are ready in time and to behave as if they aren't used at all if the results aren't ready. The use of GL_QUERY_NO_WAIT is similar to the use of GL_QUERY_RESULT_AVAILABLE in the preceding examples. Don't forget, though, that if you use GL_QUERY_NO_WAIT, the actual geometry rendered will depend on whether the commands contributing to the query object have finished executing. This could depend on the performance of the machine on which your application is running and can therefore vary from run to run. You should be sure that the result of your program is not dependent on the second set of geometry being rendered (unless this is what you want). If it is, your program might end up producing different output on a faster system than on a slower system.

Of course, it is also possible to use multiple query objects with conditional rendering. A final, combined example using all of the techniques in this section is given in Listing 12.6.

```
// Render simplified versions of 10 objects, each with its own occlusion
// query
int n;

for (n = 0; n < 10; n++)
{
    glBeginQuery(GL_SAMPLES_PASSSED, ten_queries[n]);
    RenderSimplifiedObject(&object[n]);
    glEndQuery(GL_SAMPLES_PASSED);
}

// Render the more complex versions of the objects, skipping them
// if the occlusion query results are available and 0
for (n = 0; n < 10; n++)
{
    glBeginConditionalRender(ten_queries[n], GL_QUERY_NO_WAIT);
    RenderRealObject(&object[n]);
    glEndConditionalRender();
}
```

Listing 12.6: A more complete conditional rendering example

In this example, simplified versions of ten objects are rendered first, each with its own occlusion query. Once the simplified versions of the objects have been rendered, the more complex versions of the objects are conditionally rendered based on the results of those occlusion queries. If the simplified versions of the objects are not visible, the more complex versions are skipped, potentially improving performance.

Advanced Occlusion Queries

The GL_SAMPLES_PASSED query target counts the exact number of samples that passed the depth test. Even if no significant rendering occurs, OpenGL must still effectively rasterize every primitive to determine the number of pixels it covers and the number that pass the depth and stencil tests. Even worse, if your fragment shader does something to affect the result (such as using a discard statement or modifying the fragment's depth value), then it must run your shader for every pixel as well. Sometimes, this really is what you want. However, very often, you will care only whether *any* sample passed the depth and stencil tests, or even whether any sample *might have* passed the depth and stencil tests.

To provide this kind of functionality, OpenGL provides two additional occlusion query targts: the GL_ANY_SAMPLES_PASSED and GL_ANY_SAMPLES_PASSED_CONSERVATIVE targets. They are known as *Boolean* occlusion queries.

The first of these targets, GL_ANY_SAMPLES_PASSED, will produce a result of 0 (or GL_FALSE) if no samples pass the depth and stencil tests, and 1 (the value of GL_TRUE) if any sample passes the depth test. In some circumstances, performance could be higher if the GL_ANY_SAMPLES_PASSED query target is used because OpenGL can stop counting samples as soon as any sample passes the depth and stencil tests. However, if no samples pass the depth and stencil tests, it is unlikely to provide any benefit.

The second Boolean occlusion query target, GL_ANY_SAMPLES_PASSED_CONSERVATIVE, is even more approximate. In particular, it will count as soon as a sample *might* pass the depth and stencil tests. Many implementations of OpenGL implement some form of hierarchical depth testing, where the nearest and furthest depth values for a particular region of the screen are stored; then as primitives are rasterized, the depth values for large blocks of them are tested against this hierarchical information to determine whether to continue to rasterize the interior of the region. A conservative occlusion query may simply count the number of these large regions and not run your shader at all, even if it discards fragments or modifies the final depth value.

In addition to executing drawing commands only if the result of query is non-zero, it's possible to *invert* the condition—that is, to execute the commands only if the query does have a zero result. For each query mode, there is a variant that ends in _INVERTED, which means to consider the inverse of the query codition. Not only does this mean that you can execute commands when the result of a query is 0, but because you can use the same query object more than once, you can execute simple if-else flow control inside rendering. Consider the example shown in Listing 12.7.

```
// Wrap an object in a query
glBeginQuery(GL_SAMPLES_PASSED, query);

// Draw the impostor geometry
glDrawElements(GL_TRIANGLES,
               impostor_count,
               GL_UNSIGNED_SHORT,
               impostor_indices);

glEndQuery(GL_SAMPLES_PASSED);

// If the query has at least one sample
glBeginConditionalRender(query, GL_QUERY_WAIT);

// Then draw geometry A
glDrawElements(GL_TRIANGLES,
               geometry_a_count,
               GL_UNSIGNED_SHORT,
               geometry_a_indices);

glEndConditionalRender();
```

```
// If the query DOES NOT have at least one sample
glBeginConditionalRender(query, GL_QUERY_WAIT_INVERTED);

// Then draw geometry B
glDrawElements(GL_TRIANGLES,
               geometry_b_count,
               GL_UNSIGNED_SHORT,
               geometry_b_indices);

glEndConditionalRender();
```

Listing 12.7: Simple control flow using queries

You should note that the sample shown in Listing 12.7 is rather simplified. Normally, you would try to perform the rendering that contributes to the query objects as early as possible in the frame and issue conditional rendering as late as possible in the frame. This allows OpenGL to do real work rather than waiting for the results of a query object. Also, unless the hypothetical "geometry A" and "geometry B" objects are very similar, there would very likely be more OpenGL calls made before the calls to **glDrawElements()**.

You should be careful when combining multiple uses of a query object with the _NO_WAIT modifiers. For example, imagine that you perform the query, then wrap the rendering of geometry A inside a query with mode set to GL_QUERY_NO_WAIT and the rendering of geometry B with mode set to GL_QUERY_NO_WAIT_INVERTED. Now think about what would happen if the result of the query was not available in time for the GL_QUERY_NO_WAIT conditional, but *becomes* available in time for the GL_QUERY_NO_WAIT_INVERTED conditional. It's possible that the result of the query indicates that no samples were visible. In that case, both geometry A and geometry B are drawn—the `if` *and* `else` parts of our control flow execute, which is almost certainly not what you wanted!

Timer Queries

One further query type that you can use to judge how long rendering is taking is the *timer query*. Timer queries are made by passing the GL_TIME_ELAPSED query type as the target parameter of **glBeginQuery()** and **glEndQuery()**. When you call **glGetQueryObjectuiv()** to get the result from the query object, the value is the number of nanoseconds that elapsed between when OpenGL executes your calls to **glBeginQuery()** and **glEndQuery()**. This is actually the amount of time it took OpenGL to process all the commands between the **glBeginQuery()** and **glEndQuery()**

commands. You can use this, for example, to identify the most expensive part of your scene. Consider the code shown in Listing 12.8.

```
// Declare our variables
GLuint queries[3];        // Three query objects that we'll use
GLuint world_time;        // Time taken to draw the world
GLuint objects_time;      // Time taken to draw objects in the world
GLuint HUD_time;          // Time to draw the HUD and other UI elements

// Create three query objects
glGenQueries(3, queries);

// Start the first query
glBeginQuery(GL_TIME_ELAPSED, queries[0]);

// Render the world
RenderWorld();

// Stop the first query and start the second...
// Note, we're not reading the value from the query yet
glEndQuery(GL_TIME_ELAPSED);
glBeginQuery(GL_TIME_ELAPSED, queries[1]);

// Render the objects in the world
RenderObjects();

// Stop the second query and start the third
glEndQuery(GL_TIME_ELAPSED);
glBeginQuery(GL_TIME_ELAPSED, queries[2]);

// Render the HUD
RenderHUD();

// Stop the last query
glEndQuery(GL_TIME_ELAPSED);

// Now we can retrieve the results from the three queries
glGetQueryObjectuiv(queries[0], GL_QUERY_RESULT, &world_time);
glGetQueryObjectuiv(queries[1], GL_QUERY_RESULT, &objects_time);
glGetQueryObjectuiv(queries[2], GL_QUERY_RESULT, &HUD_time);

// Done. world_time, objects_time, and hud_time contain the values we want.
// Clean up after ourselves.
glDeleteQueries(3, queries);
```

Listing 12.8: Timing operations using timer queries

After this code is executed, `world_time`, `objects_time`, and `HUD_time` will contain the number of nanoseconds it took to render the world, all the objects in the world, and the heads-up display (HUD), respectively. You can use this to determine what fraction of the graphics hardware's time is taken up rendering each of the elements of your scene. This is useful for profiling your code during development—you can figure out what the most expensive parts of your application are and determine where to spend your optimization effort. You can also use this technique during runtime to alter the behavior of your application and get the best possible performance out of the graphics subsystem. For example, you could increase or reduce the number of objects in the scene depending on the relative value of objects_time. You could also dynamically switch between more or less complex shaders for elements of the scene based on the power of the graphics hardware. If you just want to know how much time passes, according to OpenGL, between two actions that your program takes, you can use **glQueryCounter()**, whose prototype is

```
void glQueryCounter(GLuint id, GLenum target);
```

You need to set id to GL_TIMESTAMP and target to the name of a query object that you've created earlier. This function puts the query straight into the OpenGL pipeline, and when that query reaches the end of the pipeline, OpenGL records its view of the current time into the query object. The time 0 is not really defined—it just indicates some unspecified time in the past. To use this information effectively, your application needs to take deltas between multiple timestamps. To implement the previous example using **glQueryCounter()**, we could write code as shown in Listing 12.9.

```
// Declare our variables
GLuint queries[4];        // Now we need four query objects
GLuint start_time;        // The start time of the application
GLuint world_time;        // Time taken to draw the world
GLuint objects_time;      // Time taken to draw objects in the world
GLuint HUD_time;          // Time to draw the HUD and other UI elements

// Create four query objects
glGenQueries(4, queries);

// Get the start time
glQueryCounter(GL_TIMESTAMP, queries[0]);

// Render the world
RenderWorld();

// Get the time after RenderWorld is done
glQueryCounter(GL_TIMESTAMP, queries[1]);

// Render the objects in the world
RenderObjects();

// Get the time after RenderObjects is done
glQueryCounter(GL_TIMESTAMP, queries[2]);

// Render the HUD
RenderHUD();

// Get the time after everything is done
glQueryCounter(GL_TIMESTAMP, queries[3]);

// Get the result from the three queries, and subtract them to find deltas
glGetQueryObjectuiv(queries[0], GL_QUERY_RESULT, &start_time);
glGetQueryObjectuiv(queries[1], GL_QUERY_RESULT, &world_time);
```

```
glGetQueryObjectuiv(queries[2], GL_QUERY_RESULT, &objects_time);
glGetQueryObjectuiv(queries[3], GL_QUERY_RESULT, &HUD_time);
HUD_time -= objects_time;
objects_time -= world_time;
world_time -= start_time;

// Done. world_time, objects_time, and hud_time contain the values we want.
// Clean up after ourselves.
glDeleteQueries(4, queries);
```

Listing 12.9: Timing operations using `glQueryCounter()`

As you can see, the code in this example is not dramatically different from that in Listing 12.8. You need to create four query objects instead of three, and you need to subtract out the results at the end to find the time deltas. However, you don't need to call **glBeginQuery()** and **glEndQuery()** in pairs, which means that there are fewer calls to OpenGL in total. The results of the two samples aren't quite equivalent, however. When you issue a GL_TIMESTAMP query, the time is written when the query reaches the end of the OpenGL pipeline. However, when you issue a GL_TIME_ELAPSED query, internally OpenGL will take a timestamp when **glBeginQuery()** reaches the start of the pipeline and again when **glEndQuery()** reaches the end of the pipeline, and then subtract the two. Clearly, the results won't be quite the same. Nevertheless, so long as you are consistent in which method you use, your results should still be meaningful.

One important thing to note about the results of timer queries is that, because they are measured in nanoseconds, their values can get very large in a small amount of time. A single, unsigned 32-bit value can count as a little over 4 seconds' worth of nanoseconds. If you expect to time operations that take longer than this (ideally over the course of many frames!), you might want to consider retrieving the full 64-bit results that query objects keep internally. To do this, call

```
void glGetQueryObjectui64v(GLuint id,
                           GLenum pname,
                           GLuint64 * params);
```

Just as with **glGetQueryObjectuiv()**, id is the name of the query object whose value you want to retrieve and pname can be GL_QUERY_RESULT or GL_QUERY_RESULT_AVAILABLE to retrieve the result of the query or just an indication of whether it's available, respectively.

Finally, although not techically a query, you can get an instantaneous, synchronous timestamp from OpenGL by calling

```
GLint64 t;
void glGetInteger64v(GL_TIMESTAMP, &t);
```

After this code has executed, t will contain the current time as OpenGL sees it. If you take this timestamp and then immediately launch a timestamp query, you can retrieve the result of the timestamp query and subtract t from it; the result will be the amount of time that it took the query to reach the end of the pipeline. This is known as the *latency* of the pipeline and is approximately equal to the amount of time that will pass between your application issuing a command and OpenGL fully executing it.

Transform Feedback Queries

If you use transform feedback with a vertex shader but no geometry shader, the output from the vertex shader is recorded, and the number of vertices stored into the transform feedback is the same as the number of vertices sent to OpenGL unless the available space in any of the transform feedback buffers is exhausted. However, if a geometry shader is present, that shader may create or discard vertices, so the number of vertices written to the transform feedback buffer may be different than the number of vertices sent to OpenGL. Also, if tessellation is active, the amount of geometry produced will depend on the tessellation factors produced by the tessellation control shader. OpenGL can keep track of the number of vertices written to the transform feedback buffers through query objects. Your application can then use this information to draw the resulting data or to know how much to read back from the transform feedback buffer, should it want to keep the data.

Query objects were introduced earlier in this chapter in the context of occlusion queries. As noted then, many questions can be asked of OpenGL. Both the number of primitives generated and the number of primitives actually written to the transform feedback buffers are available as queries.

As before, to generate a query object, call

```
GLuint one_query;
glGenQueries(1, &one_query);
```

To generate a number of query objects, call

```
GLuint ten_queries[10];
glGenQueries(10, ten_queries);
```

Now that you have created your query objects, you can ask OpenGL to start counting primitives as it produces them by beginning a

GL_PRIMITIVES_GENERATED or
GL_TRANSFORM_FEEDBACK_PRIMITIVES_WRITTEN query of the appropriate
type. To start either query, call

```
glBeginQuery(GL_PRIMITIVES_GENERATED, one_query);
```

or

```
glBeginQuery(GL_TRANSFORM_FEEDBACK_PRIMITIVES_WRITTEN, one_query);
```

After a call to **glBeginQuery()** with either GL_PRIMITIVES_GENERATED or
GL_TRANSFORM_FEEDBACK_PRIMITIVES_WRITTEN, OpenGL keeps track of
how many primitives were produced by the front end, or how many were
actually written into the transform feedback buffers until the query is
ended using

```
glEndQuery(GL_PRIMITIVES_GENERATED);
```

or

```
glEndQuery(GL_TRANSFORM_FEEDBACK_PRIMITIVES_WRITTEN);
```

The results of the query can be read by calling **glGetQueryObjectuiv()**
with the GL_QUERY_RESULT parameter and the name of the query object.
As with other OpenGL queries, the result might not be available
immediately because of the pipelined nature of OpenGL. To find out
if the results are available, call **glGetQueryObjectuiv()** with the
GL_QUERY_RESULT_AVAILABLE parameter. See "Retrieving Query Results"
earlier in this chapter for more information about query objects.

There are a few subtle differences between the GL_PRIMITIVES_GENERATED
and GL_TRANSFORM_FEEDBACK_PRIMITIVES_WRITTEN queries. The
first is that the GL_PRIMITIVES_GENERATED query counts the
number of primitives emitted by the front end, but the
GL_TRANSFORM_FEEDBACK_PRIMITIVES_WRITTEN query counts only those
primitives that were successfully written into the transform feedback
buffers. The primitive count generated by the front end may be more or
less than the number of primitives sent to OpenGL, depending on
what it does. Normally, the results of these two queries would be the
same, but if not enough space is available in the transform feedback
buffers, GL_PRIMITIVES_GENERATED will keep counting, while
GL_TRANSFORM_FEEDBACK_PRIMITIVES_WRITTEN will stop.

You can check whether all of the primitives produced by your application were captured into the transform feedback buffer by running one of each query simultaneously and comparing the results. If they are equal, then all the primitives were successfully written. If they differ, the buffers you used for transform feedback were probably too small.

The second difference is that GL_TRANSFORM_FEEDBACK_PRIMITIVES_WRITTEN is meaningful only when transform feedback is active. That is why it has TRANSFORM_FEEDBACK in its name but GL_PRIMITIVES_GENERATED does not. If you run a GL_TRANSFORM_FEEDBACK_PRIMITIVES_WRITTEN query when transform feedback is not active, the result will be 0. However, the GL_PRIMITIVES_GENERATED query can be used at any time and will produce a meaningful count of the number of primitives produced by OpenGL. You can use this kind of query to find out how many vertices your geometry shader produced or discarded.

Indexed Queries

If you are using a single stream for storing vertices in transform feedback, then calling **glBeginQuery()** and **glEndQuery()** with the GL_PRIMITIVES_GENERATED or GL_TRANSFORM_FEEDBACK_PRIMITIVES_WRITTEN target works just fine. However, if your pipeline includes a geometry shader, then that shader could produce primitives on up to four output streams. In that case, OpenGL provides *indexed* query targets that you can use to count how much data is produced on each stream. The **glBeginQuery()** and **glEndQuery()** functions associate queries with the first stream—the one with index 0. To begin and end a query on a different stream, you can call **glBeginQueryIndexed()** and **glEndQueryIndexed()**, whose prototypes are

```
void glBeginQueryIndexed(GLenum target,
                         GLuint index,
                         GLuint id);

void glEndQueryIndexed(GLenum target,
                       GLuint index);
```

These two functions behave just like their non-indexed counterparts and the target and id parameters have the same meaning. In fact, calling **glBeginQuery()** is equivalent to calling **glBeginQueryIndexed()** with index set to 0. The same is true for **glEndQuery()** and **glEndQueryIndexed()**. When target is GL_PRIMITIVES_GENERATED, the query will count the primitives produced by the geometry shader on the

stream whose index is given in index. Likewise, when target is
GL_TRANSFORM_FEEDBACK_PRIMITIVES_WRITTEN, the query will count the
number of primitives actually written into the buffers associated with the
output stream of the geometry shader whose index is given in index. If no
geometry shader is present, you can still use these functions, but only
stream 0 will actually count anything.

You can actually use the indexed query functions with any query target
(such as GL_SAMPLES_PASSED or GL_TIME_ELAPSED), but the only value for
index that is valid for those targets is 0.

Using the Results of a Primitive Query

At this point, you have the results of the front end stored in a buffer. You
have also determined how much data is in that buffer by using a query
object. Now it's time to use those results in further rendering. Recall that
the results of the front end are placed into a buffer using transform
feedback—the only thing making the buffer a transform feedback buffer is
that it's bound to one of the GL_TRANSFORM_FEEDBACK_BUFFER binding
points. However, buffers in OpenGL are generic chunks of data and can be
used for other purposes.

Generally, after running a rendering pass that produces data into a
transform feedback buffer, you bind the buffer object to the
GL_ARRAY_BUFFER binding point so that it can be used as a vertex buffer. If
you are using a geometry shader that might produce an unknown amount
of data, you need to use a GL_TRANSFORM_FEEDBACK_PRIMITIVES_WRITTEN
query to figure out how many vertices to render on the second pass.
Listing 12.10 shows an example of what such code might look like.

```
// We have two buffers, buffer1 and buffer2. First, we'll bind buffer1 as the
// source of data for the draw operation (GL_ARRAY_BUFFER), and buffer2 as
// the destination for transform feedback (GL_TRANSFORM_FEEDBACK_BUFFER).
glBindBuffer(GL_ARRAY_BUFFER, buffer1);
glBindBuffer(GL_TRANSFORM_FEEDBACK_BUFFFER, buffer2);

// Now, we need to start a query to count how many vertices get written to
// the transform feedback buffer
glBeginQuery(GL_TRANSFORM_FEEDBACK_PRIMITIVES_WRITTEN, q);
// OK, start transform feedback...
glBeginTransformFeedback(GL_POINTS);

// Draw something to get data into the transform feedback buffer
DrawSomePoints();

// Done with transform feedback
glEndTransformFeedback();
```

```
// End the query and get the result back
glEndQuery(GL_TRANSFORM_FEEDBACK_PRIMITIVES_WRITTEN);
glGetQueryObjectuiv(q, GL_QUERY_RESULT, &vertices_to_render);

// Now we bind buffer2 (which has just been used as a transform
// feedback buffer) as a vertex buffer and render some more points
// from it.
glBindBuffer(GL_ARRAY_BUFFER, buffer2);
glDrawArrays(GL_POINTS, 0, vertices_to_render);
```

Listing 12.10: Drawing data written to a transform feedback buffer

Whenever you retrieve the results of a query from OpenGL, it has to finish
what it's doing so that it can provide an accurate count. This is true for
transform feedback queries just as it is for any other type of query. When
you execute the code shown in Listing 12.10, as soon as you call
glGetQueryObjectuiv(), the OpenGL pipeline will drain and the graphics
processor will idle. These steps ensure that the vertex count can make a
round trip from the GPU to your application and back again. To get
around this, OpenGL provides two things.

First is the *transform feedback object*, which represents the state of the
transform feedback stage. Up until now, you have been using the default
transform feedback object. However, you can create your own by calling
glGenTransformFeedbacks() followed by **glBindTransformFeedback()**:

```
void glGenTransformFeedbacks(GLsizei n,
                             GLuint * ids);

void glBindTransformFeedback(GLenum target,
                             GLuint  id);
```

For **glGenTransformFeedbacks()**, n is the number of object names to reserve
and ids is a pointer to an array into which the new names will be written.
Once you have a new name, you bind it using **glBindTransformFeedback()**,
whose first parameter, target, must be GL_TRANSFORM_FEEDBACK and
whose second parameter, id, is the name of the transform feedback object
to bind. You can delete transform feedback objects using
glDeleteTransformFeedbacks() and you can determine whether a given
value is the name of a transform feedback object by calling
glIsTransformFeedback():

```
void glDeleteTransformFeedbacks(GLsizei n,
                                const GLuint * ids);

GLboolean glIsTransformFeedback(GLuint id);
```

Once a transform feedback object is bound, all state related to transform feedback is kept in that object, including the transform feedback buffer bindings and the counts used to keep track of how much data has been written to each transform feedback stream. This is effectively the same data that would be returned in a transform feedback query, and we can use it to automatically draw the number of vertices captured using transform feedback. This is the second part of functionality that OpenGL provides for this purpose and it consists of four functions:

```
void glDrawTransformFeedback(GLenum mode,
                             GLuint id);

void glDrawTransformFeedbackInstanced(GLenum mode,
                                      GLuint id,
                                      GLsizei primcount);

void glDrawTransformFeedbackStream(GLenum mode,
                                   GLuint id,
                                   GLuint stream);

void glDrawTransformFeedbackStreamInstanced(GLenum mode,
                                            GLuint id,
                                            GLuint stream,
                                            GLsizei primcount);
```

For all four functions, mode is one of the primitive modes that can be used with other drawing functions such as **glDrawArrays()** and **glDrawElements()**, and id is the name of a transform feedback object that contains the counts.

- Calling **glDrawTransformFeedback()** is equivalent to calling **glDrawArrays()**, except that the number of vertices to process is taken from the first stream of the transform feedback object named in id.

- Calling **glDrawTransformFeedbackInstanced()** is equivalent to **glDrawArraysInstanced()**, with the vertex count again sourced from the first stream of the transform feedback object named in id and with the instance count specified in primcount.

- Calling **glDrawTransformFeedbackStream()** is equivalent to calling **glDrawTransformFeedback()**, except that the stream given in stream is used as the source of the count.

- Calling **glDrawTransformFeedbackStreamInstanced()** is equivalent to calling **glDrawTransformFeedbackInstanced()**, except that the stream given in stream is used as the source of the count.

When you use one of the functions that take a stream index, data must be recorded into the transform feedback buffers associated with streams other than zero using a geometry shader as discussed in the "Multiple Streams of Storage" section in Chapter 8.

Pipeline State Queries

In addition to the query types supported by the OpenGL core API, there are a large number of other queries that can be used to monitor the execution of your OpenGL programs and that are provided by the GL_ARB_pipeline_statistics_query extension. If your OpenGL drivers support this extension, then the following query types are available to you:

- GL_VERTICES_SUBMITTED_ARB tells you the number of vertices sent to OpenGL.

- GL_PRIMITIVES_SUBMITTED_ARB tells you the number of primitives sent to OpenGL.

- GL_VERTEX_SHADER_INVOCATIONS_ARB tells you the number of vertex shader invocations produced by the verices you sent, which might not be the same as the result of a GL_VERTICES_SUBMITTED_ARB query.

- GL_TESS_CONTROL_SHADER_PATCHES_ARB tells you the number of patches sent into the tessellation control shader.

- GL_TESS_EVALUATION_SHADER_INVOCATIONS_ARB tells you the number of evaluation shader invocations that the tessellator produced.

- GL_GEOMETRY_SHADER_INVOCATIONS tells you the number of times that the geometry shader executed.

- GL_GEOMETRY_SHADER_PRIMITIVES_EMITTED_ARB tells you the total number of primitives produced by the geometry shader.

- GL_FRAGMENT_SHADER_INVOCATIONS_ARB tells you the number of times the fragment shader was invoked.

- GL_COMPUTE_SHADER_INVOCATIONS_ARB tells you the number of times a compute shader was invoked.

- GL_CLIPPING_INPUT_PRIMITIVES_ARB tells you the number of primitives that were sent to the input of the clipper.

- GL_CLIPPING_OUTPUT_PRIMITIVES_ARB tells you the number of primitives that the clipper produced as a result.

You can pass any of the tokens in this list to the **glBeginQuery()** and **glEndQuery()** functions and OpenGL will count the relevant item for you. You should note that the results that they produce will not necessarily be what you expect them to be. For example, the GL_VERTICES_SUBMITTED_ARB query will produce the number of vertices that the OpenGL implementation submitted on your behalf; this number may not match the result of a GL_VERTEX_SHADER_INVOCATIONS_ARB query. A common optimization implemented in OpenGL drivers is that of *vertex reuse*. When this optimization is active, OpenGL can assume that when your element array buffer contains the same index more than once, then it can simply reuse the result of the previous vertex shader invocation rather than running it again. Therefore, when this optimization is active, the result of a GL_VERTEX_SHADER_INVOCATIONS_ARB query might be quite a bit lower than you expect.

Likewise, the result of a GL_FRAGMENT_SHADER_INVOCATIONS_ARB query could be quite a bit higher than you expect. This is because most graphics hardware renders fragments in *quad fragments*, which are little 2×2 blocks of pixels. By allowing the individual invocations to communicate in a limited way, differentials can be found across quads. On the edge of primitives, where only part of the quad fragment is covered, OpenGL might run the fragment shader for each of the four fragments anyway, killing their outputs before they have a chance to write to the window. In this case, you will see a GL_FRAGMENT_SHADER_INVOCATIONS_ARB query return a number higher than the actual number of fragments rendered. Conversely, if OpenGL is running an early depth test, then it might throw out whole quads and not run the fragment shader at all.

If you're interested in how close your application is driving a GPU to its limit, you can look up the peak theoretical performance for your particular GPU (vertices per second, pixels per second, and so on), and see if any of these counters is getting close to that limit. You can also check that the numbers are in line with what you expect to see for your application. As discussed earlier, they're likely to be a little off from what you expect, but if they're radically different there could be something wrong with your application.

Synchronization in OpenGL

In an advanced application, OpenGL's order of operation and the pipeline nature of the system may be important. Examples of such applications are those with multiple contexts and multiple threads, and those sharing data between OpenGL and other APIs such as OpenCL. In some cases, it may be necessary to determine whether commands sent to OpenGL have finished yet and whether the results of those commands are ready. In this section we discuss various methods of synchronizing various parts of the OpenGL pipeline.

Draining the Pipeline

OpenGL includes two commands to force it to start working on commands or to finish working on commands that have been issued so far. These are

```
glFlush();
```

and

```
glFinish();
```

There are subtle differences between these two commands. The first, **glFlush()**, ensures that any commands issued so far are at least placed into the start of the OpenGL pipeline and that they will eventually be executed. The problem is that **glFlush()** doesn't tell you anything about the execution status of the commands issued—only that they will eventually be executed. **glFinish()**, in contrast, actually ensures that all commands issued have been fully executed and that the OpenGL pipeline is empty. While **glFinish()** does ensure that all of your OpenGL commands have been processed, it will empty the OpenGL pipeline, causing a *bubble* and reducing performance, sometimes drastically. In general, it is recommended that you don't call **glFinish()** for any reason.

Synchronization and Fences

Sometimes it may be necessary to know whether OpenGL has finished executing commands up to some point without forcing an emptying of the pipeline. This is especially useful when you are sharing data between two contexts or between OpenGL and OpenCL, for example. This type of synchronization is managed by what are known as *sync objects*. Like any other OpenGL object, sync objects must be created before they are used and destroyed when they are no longer needed. Sync objects have two possible states: *signaled* and *unsignaled*. They start out in the unsignaled state, and when some particular event occurs, they move to the signaled state. The event that triggers their transition from unsignaled to signaled depends on their type. The type of sync object we are interested in is called a fence sync, which can be created by calling

```
GLsync glFenceSync(GL_SYNC_GPU_COMMANDS_COMPLETE, 0);
```

The first parameter is a token specifying the event we're going to wait for. In this case, GL_SYNC_GPU_COMMANDS_COMPLETE says that we want the GPU to have processed all commands in the pipeline before setting the state of the sync object to signaled. The second parameter is a flags field and is 0 here because no flags are relevant for this type of sync object. The **glFenceSync()** function returns a new GLsync object. As soon as the fence sync is created, it enters (in the unsignaled state) the OpenGL pipeline and is processed along with all the other commands without stalling OpenGL or consuming significant resources. When it reaches the end of the pipeline, it is "executed" like any other command, which sets its state to signaled. Because of the in-order nature of OpenGL, this tells us that any OpenGL commands issued before the call to **glFenceSync()** have completed, even though commands issued after the **glFenceSync()** may not have reached the end of the pipeline yet.

Once the sync object has been created (and has therefore entered the OpenGL pipeline), we can query its state to find out if it's reached the end of the pipeline, and we can ask OpenGL to wait for it to become signaled before returning to the application. To determine whether the sync object has become signaled yet, call

```
glGetSynciv(sync, GL_SYNC_STATUS, sizeof(GLint), NULL, &result);
```

When **glGetSynciv()** returns, result (which is a GLint) will contain GL_SIGNALED if the sync object was in the signaled state and GL_UNSIGNALED otherwise. This allows the application to poll the state of the sync object and use this information to potentially do some useful work while the GPU is busy with previous commands. For example, consider the code in Listing 12.11.

```
GLint result = GL_UNSIGNALED;
glGetSynciv(sync, GL_SYNC_STATUS, sizeof(GLint), NULL, &result);
while (result != GL_SIGNALED)
{
    DoSomeUsefulWork();
    glGetSynciv(sync, GL_SYNC_STATUS, sizeof(GLint), NULL, &result);
}
```

Listing 12.11: Working while waiting for a sync object

This code loops, doing a small amount of useful work on each iteration, until the sync object becomes signaled. If the application were to create a sync object at the start of each frame, the application could wait for the sync object from two frames ago and do a variable amount of work depending on how long it takes the GPU to process the commands for that frame. This allows an application to balance the amount of work done by the CPU (such as the number of sound effects to mix together or the number of iterations of a physics simulation to run, for example) with the speed of the GPU.

To actually cause OpenGL to wait for a sync object to become signaled (and, therefore, for the commands in the pipeline before the sync to complete), there are two functions that you can use:

```
glClientWaitSync(sync, GL_SYNC_FLUSH_COMMANDS_BIT, timeout);
```

or

```
glWaitSync(sync, 0, GL_TIMEOUT_IGNORED);
```

The first parameter to both functions is the name of the sync object that was returned by **glFenceSync()**. The second and third parameters to the two functions have the same names but must be set differently.

For **glClientWaitSync()**, the second parameter is a bitfield specifying additional behavior of the function. The GL_SYNC_FLUSH_COMMANDS_BIT tells **glClientWaitSync()** to ensure that the sync object has entered the OpenGL pipeline before beginning to wait for it to become signaled. Without this bit, there is a possibility that OpenGL could watch for a sync object that hasn't been sent down the pipeline yet, and the application could end up waiting forever and hang. The third parameter is a timeout value in nanoseconds to wait. If the sync object doesn't become signaled within this time, **glClientWaitSync()** returns a status code to indicate this fact. **glClientWaitSync()** won't return until either the sync object becomes signaled or a timeout occurs. There are four possible status codes that might be returned by **glClientWaitSync()**, as summarized in Table 12.1.

There are a couple of things to note about the timeout value. First, while the unit of measurement is nanoseconds, there is no accuracy requirement in OpenGL. If you specify that you want to wait for one nanosecond, OpenGL could round this up to the next millisecond or more. Second, if you specify a timeout value of 0, **glClientWaitSync()** will return GL_ALREADY_SIGNALED if the sync object was in a signaled state at the time of the call and GL_TIMEOUT_EXPIRED otherwise. It will never return GL_CONDITION_SATISFIED.

Table 12.1: Possible Return Values for **glClientWaitSync()**

Returned Status	Meaning
GL_ALREADY_SIGNALED	The sync object was already signaled when **glClientWaitSync()** was called, so the function returned immediately.
GL_TIMEOUT_EXPIRED	The timeout specified in the timeout parameter expired, meaning that the sync object never became signaled in the allowed time.
GL_CONDITION_SATISFIED	The sync object became signaled within the allowed timeout period (but was not already signaled when **glClientWaitSync()** was called).
GL_WAIT_FAILED	An error occurred (such as sync not being a valid sync object), and the user should check the result of **glGetError()** to get more information.

It's a good idea to set GL_SYNC_FLUSH_COMMANDS_BIT unless you have a really good reason not to. There are a couple of ways to avoid the flush implied by this bit:

- Explicitly call **glFlush()** after the corresponding **glFenceSync()**, which will ask OpenGL to submit the pending work to the GPU for you. This will give the GPU a head-start on the work, and means that you don't need to cause a flush by setting GL_SYNC_FLUSH_COMMANDS_BIT when calling **glClientWaitSync()**.

- Call **glClientWaitSync()** twice. The first time, set timeout to 0 and do not set GL_SYNC_FLUSH_COMMANDS_BIT. It will return either GL_ALREADY_SIGNALED if the fence is already signaled (in which case, we're done) or GL_TIMEOUT_EXPIRED if the sync was not signaled. In this case, we make the second call to **glClientWaitSync()** with the GL_SYNC_FLUSH_COMMANDS_BIT set and the real timeout value.

For **glWaitSync()**, the behavior is slightly different. The application won't actually wait for the sync object to become signaled; only the GPU will. Therefore, **glWaitSync()** will return to the application immediately. This makes the second and third parameters somewhat irrelevant. Because the application doesn't wait for the function to return, there is no danger of your application hanging; thus the GL_SYNC_FLUSH_COMMANDS_BIT is not needed and would actually cause an error if specified. Also, the timeout will actually be implementation dependent; the special timeout value GL_TIMEOUT_IGNORED is specified to make this clear. If you're interested, you can find the timeout value used by your implementation by calling **glGetInteger64()** with the GL_MAX_SERVER_WAIT_TIMEOUT parameter.

You might be wondering, "What is the point of asking the GPU to wait for a sync object to reach the end of the pipeline?" After all, the sync object will become signaled when it reaches the end of the pipeline. Thus, if you wait for it to reach the end of the pipeline, it will of course be signaled. Therefore, won't **glWaitSync()** just do nothing? This would be true if we considered just simple applications that use only a single OpenGL context and don't use other APIs. However, the power of sync objects is harnessed when using multiple OpenGL contexts. Sync objects can be shared between OpenGL contexts and between compatible APIs such as OpenCL. That is, a sync object created by a call to **glFenceSync()** on one context can be waited for by a call to **glWaitSync()** (or **glClientWaitSync()**) on another context.

Consider this: You can ask one OpenGL context to hold off rendering something until another context has finished doing something. This allows synchronization between two contexts. You can have an application with two threads and two contexts (or more, if you want). If you create a sync object in each context, and then in each context you wait for the sync objects from the other contexts using either **glClientWaitSync()** or **glWaitSync()**, you know that when all of the functions have returned, all of those contexts are synchronized with one another. Together with thread synchronization primitives provided by your OS (such as semaphores), you can keep rendering to multiple windows in sync.

An example of this type of usage is when a buffer is shared between two contexts. Suppose the first context is writing to the buffer using transform feedback, while the second context wants to draw the results of the transform feedback. The first context would draw using transform feedback mode. After calling **glEndTransformFeedback()**, it immediately calls **glFenceSync()**. Now, the application makes the second context current and calls **glWaitSync()** to wait for the sync object to become signaled. It can then issue more commands to OpenGL (on the new context), and those are queued up by the drivers, ready to execute. Only when the GPU has finished recording data into the transform feedback buffers with the first context does it start to work on the commands using that data in the second context.

There are also extensions and other functionality in APIs like OpenCL that allow asynchronous writes to buffers. You can use **glWaitSync()** to ask a GPU to wait until the data in a buffer is valid by creating a sync object on the context that generates the data and then waiting for that sync object to become signaled on the context that will consume the data.

Sync objects only ever go from the unsignaled to the signaled state. There is no mechanism to put a sync object back into the unsignaled state, even manually. This is because a manual flip of a sync object can cause a race condition and possibly hang the application. Consider the situation where a sync object is created, reaches the end of the pipeline, and becomes signaled, and then the application sets it back to unsignaled. If another thread tried to wait for that sync object but didn't start waiting until after the application had already set the sync object back to the unsignaled state, it would wait forever. Each sync object therefore represents a one-shot event, and every time a synchronization is required, a new sync object must be created by calling **glFenceSync()**. Although it is always important to clean up after yourself by deleting objects when you're done with them, this is particularly important with sync objects because you might be creating many new ones every frame. To delete a sync object, call

```
glDeleteSync(sync);
```

This command deletes the sync object. This may not occur immediately; any thread that is watching for the sync object to become signaled will still wait for its respective timeouts, and the object will actually be deleted when it is no longer being watched by anything. Thus, it is perfectly legal to call **glWaitSync()** followed by **glDeleteSync()** even though the sync object is still in the OpenGL pipeline.

Summary

This chapter discussed how to monitor the execution of your commands in the pipeline and get some feedback about their progress down it. You saw how to measure the time taken for your commands to complete, and have the tools necessary to measure the latency of the graphics pipeline. This, in turn, allows you to alter your application's complexity to suit the system it's running on and the performance targets you've set for it. We will use these tools for real-world performance tuning exercises in Chapter 14, "High Performance OpenGL." You also saw how it is possible to synchronize the execution of your application to the OpenGL context, and how to synchronize execution of multiple OpenGL contexts.

Part III

In Practice

Chapter 13

Rendering Techniques

WHAT YOU'LL LEARN IN THIS CHAPTER

- How to light the pixels in your scene.

- How to delay shading until the last possible moment.

- How to render an entire scene without a single triangle.

By this point in the book, you should have a good grasp of the fundamentals of OpenGL. You have been introduced to most of its features and should feel comfortable using it to implement graphics rendering algorithms. In this chapter, we take a look at a few of these algorithms—in particular those that might be interesting in a real-time rendering context. First, we will cover a few basic lighting techniques that allow you to apply interesting shading to the objects in your scene. Then, we will take a look at some approaches to rendering without the goal of photo-realism. Finally, we will discuss some algorithms that are really only applicable outside the traditional forward-rendering geometry pipeline, ultimately culminating with rendering an entire scene without a single vertex or triangle.

Lighting Models

Arguably, the job of any graphics rendering application is the simulation of light. Whether it be the simplest spinning cube or the most complex movie special effect ever invented, we are trying to convince users that they are seeing the real world, or an analog of it. To do this, we must model the way that light interacts with surfaces. Extremely advanced models exist that are as physically accurate as far as we understand the properties of light. However, most of these are impractical for real-time implementation, so we must assume approximations, or *models*, that produce plausible results even if they are not physically accurate. The following few sections show how a few of the lighting models that you might use in a real-time application can be implemented.

The Phong Lighting Model

One of the most common lighting models is the Phong lighting model. It works on a simple principle, which is that objects have three material properties: ambient, diffuse, and specular reflectivity. These properties are assigned color values, with brighter colors representing a higher amount of reflectivity. Light sources have these same three properties and are again assigned color values that represent the brightness of the light. The final calculated color value is then the sum of the lighting and material interactions of these three properties.

Ambient Light

Ambient light doesn't come from any particular direction. It has an original source somewhere, but the rays of light have bounced around the room or scene and become directionless. Objects illuminated by ambient light are evenly lit on all surfaces in all directions. You can think of ambient light as a global "brightening" factor applied per light source. This lighting component really approximates scattered light in the environment that originates from the light source.

To calculate the contribution an ambient light source makes to the final color, the ambient material property is scaled by the ambient light values (the two color values are just multiplied), which yields the ambient color contribution. In GLSL shader speak, we would write this like so:

```
uniform vec3 ambient = vec3(0.1, 0.1, 0.1);
```

Diffuse Light

Diffuse light is the directional component of a light source and was the subject of our previous example lighting shader. In the Phong lighting model, the diffuse material and lighting values are multiplied together, as is done with the ambient components. However, this value is then scaled by the dot product of the surface normal and light vector, which is the direction vector from the point being shaded to the light. Again, in shader speak, this might look something like this:

```
uniform vec3 vDiffuseMaterial;
uniform vec3 vDiffuseLight;
float fDotProduct = max(0.0, dot(vNormal, vLightDir));
vec3 vDiffuseColor = vDiffuseMaterial * vDiffuseLight * fDotProduct;
```

Note that we did not simply take the dot product of the two vectors, but also employed the GLSL function max. The dot product can also be a negative number, and we really can't have negative lighting or color values. Anything less than zero needs to just be zero.

Specular Highlight

Like diffuse light, specular light is a highly directional property, but it interacts more sharply with the surface and in a particular direction. A highly specular light (really a material property in the real world) tends to cause a bright spot on the surface it shines on, which is called the *specular highlight.* Because of its highly directional nature, it is even possible that, depending on a viewer's position, the specular highlight may not even be visible. A spotlight and the sun are good examples of sources that produce strong specular highlights, but of course they must be shining on an object that is "shiny."

The color contribution to the specular material and lighting colors is scaled by a value that requires a bit more computation than we've done so far. First we must find the vector that is reflected by the surface normal and the inverted light vector. The dot product of these two vectors is then raised to a "shininess" power. The higher the shininess number, the smaller the resulting specular highlight turns out to be. Some shader skeleton code that performs this calculation is shown here:

```
uniform vec3 vSpecularMaterial;
uniform vec3 vSpecularLight;
float shininess = 128.0;

vec3 vReflection = reflect(-vLightDir, vEyeNormal);
```

```
float EyeReflectionAngle = max(0.0, dot(vEyeNormal, vReflection);
fSpec = pow(EyeReflectionAngle, shininess);
vec3 vSpecularColor = vSpecularLight * vSpecularMaterial * fSpec;
```

The shininess parameter could easily be a uniform just like anything else. Traditionally (from the fixed-function pipeline days), the highest specular power is set to 128. Numbers greater than this tend to have a diminishingly small effect.

Now, we have formed a complete equation for modeling the effect of lighting on a surface. Given material with ambient term k_a, diffuse term k_d, specular term k_s, and shininess factor α, and a light with ambient term i_a, diffuse term i_d, and diffuse term i_s, the complete lighting formula is

$$I_p = k_a i_a + k_d(\vec{L} \cdot \vec{N})i_d + k_s(\vec{R} \cdot \vec{V})^\alpha i_s$$

This equation is a function of several vectors, $\vec{N}$, $\vec{L}$, $\vec{R}$, and $\vec{V}$, which represent the surface normal, the unit vector from the point being shaded to the light, the reflection of the *negative* of the light vector $\vec{L}$ in the plane defined by $\vec{N}$, and the vector to the viewer, $\vec{V}$, respectively. To understand why this works, consider the vectors shown in Figure 13.1.

In Figure 13.1, $-\vec{L}$ is shown pointing *away* from the light. If we then reflect that vector about the plane defined by the surface normal $\vec{N}$, it is obvious from the diagram that we end up with $\vec{R}$. This represents the reflection of the light source in the surface. When $\vec{R}$ points away from the

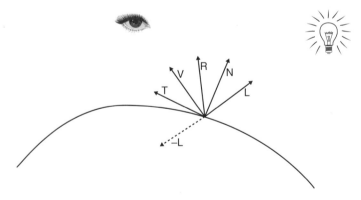

Figure 13.1: Vectors used in Phong lighting

viewer, the reflection will not be visible. However, when $\vec{R}$ points directly at the viewer, the reflection will appear brightest. At this point, the dot product (which is the cosine of the angle between two normalized vectors) will be greatest. This is the specular highlight, which is view dependent.

The effect of diffuse shading also becomes clearer when we examine Figure 13.1. When the light source shines directly on the surface, the vector $\vec{L}$ will be perpendicular to the surface and therefore be colinear with $\vec{N}$, where the dot product between $\vec{N}$ and $\vec{L}$ is greatest. When the light strikes the surface at a grazing angle, $\vec{L}$ and $\vec{N}$ will be almost perpendicular to each other and their dot product will be close to zero.

As you can see, the intensity of the light at point p (I_p) is calculated as the sum of a number of terms. The *reflection vector*, $\vec{R}$ (called R in the shader), is calculated by reflecting the light vector around the eye-space normal of the point being shaded.

The sample program phonglighting implements just such a shader. The sample implements a *Gouraud* technique known as *Gouraud shading*, where we compute the lighting values per vertex and then simply interpolate the resulting colors between vertices for the shading. This allows us to implement the entire lighting equation in the vertex shader. The complete code for the vertex shader is given in Listing 13.1.

```glsl
#version 420 core

// Per-vertex inputs
layout (location = 0) in vec4 position;
layout (location = 1) in vec3 normal;

// Matrices we'll need
layout (std140) uniform constants
{
    mat4 mv_matrix;
    mat4 view_matrix;
    mat4 proj_matrix;
};

// Light and material properties
uniform vec3 light_pos = vec3(100.0, 100.0, 100.0);
uniform vec3 diffuse_albedo = vec3(0.5, 0.2, 0.7);
uniform vec3 specular_albedo = vec3(0.7);
uniform float specular_power = 128.0;
uniform vec3 ambient = vec3(0.1, 0.1, 0.1);

// Outputs to the fragment shader
out VS_OUT
{
    vec3 color;
} vs_out;
```

```
void main(void)
{
    // Calculate view-space coordinate
    vec4 P = mv_matrix * position;

    // Calculate normal in view space
    vec3 N = mat3(mv_matrix) * normal;
    // Calculate view-space light vector
    vec3 L = light_pos - P.xyz;
    // Calculate view vector (simply the negative of the
    // view-space position)
    vec3 V = -P.xyz;

    // Normalize all three vectors
    N = normalize(N);
    L = normalize(L);
    V = normalize(V);

    // Calculate R by reflecting -L around the plane defined by N
    vec3 R = reflect(-L, N);

    // Calculate the diffuse and specular contributions
    vec3 diffuse = max(dot(N, L), 0.0) * diffuse_albedo;
    vec3 specular = pow(max(dot(R, V), 0.0), specular_power) *
                    specular_albedo;

    // Send the color output to the fragment shader
    vs_out.color = ambient + diffuse + specular;

    // Calculate the clip-space position of each vertex
    gl_Position = proj_matrix * P;
}
```

Listing 13.1: The Gouraud shading vertex shader

The fragment shader for Gouraud shading is very simple. As the final color
of each fragment is essentially calculated in the vertex shader and then
interpolated before being passed to the fragment shader, all we need to do
in our fragment shader is write the incoming color to the framebuffer. The
complete source code is shown in Listing 13.2.

```
#version 420 core

// Output
layout (location = 0) out vec4 color;

// Input from vertex shader
in VS_OUT
{
    vec3 color;
} fs_in;

void main(void)
{
    // Write incoming color to the framebuffer
    color = vec4(fs_in.color, 1.0);
}
```

Listing 13.2: The Gouraud shading fragment shader

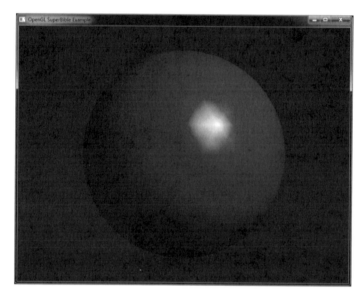

Figure 13.2: Per-vertex lighting (Gouraud shading)

Unless you use a very high level of tessellation, then for a given triangle, there are only three vertices and usually many more fragments that fill out the triangle. This makes per-vertex lighting and Gouraud shading very efficient, as all the computations are done only once per vertex.
Figure 13.2 shows the output of the phonglighting example program.

Phong Shading

One of the drawbacks to Gouraud shading is clearly apparent in Figure 13.2. Notice the starburst pattern of the specular highlight. On a still image, this might almost pass as an intentional artistic effect. The running sample program, however, rotates the sphere and shows a characteristic flashing that is a bit distracting and generally undesirable. This is caused by the discontinuity between triangles because the color values are being interpolated linearly through color space. The bright lines are actually the seams between individual triangles. One way to reduce this effect is to use more and more vertices in your geometry.

Another, and higher-quality, method is called *Phong shading*. Note that Phong shading and the Phong lighting model are separate things— although they were both invented by the same person at the same time. With Phong shading, instead of interpolating the color values between vertices, we interpolate the surface normals between vertices and then use

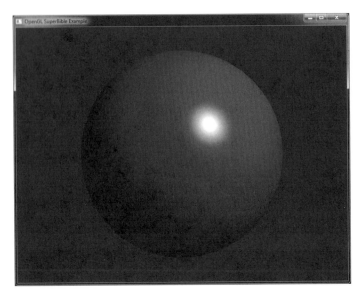

Figure 13.3: Per-fragment lighting (Phong shading)

the resulting normal to perform the entire lighting calculation for each pixel instead of per vertex. The phonglighting example program can be switched between evaluating the lighting equations per vertex (and therefore implementing Gouraud shading) and evaluating them per fragment (implementing Phong shading). Figure 13.3 shows the output from the phonglighting sample program performing shading per fragment.

The trade-off is, of course, that we are now doing significantly more work in the fragment shader, which will be executed significantly more times than the vertex shader. The basic code is the same as for the Gouraud shading example, but this time there is some significant rearranging of the shader code. Listing 13.3 shows the new vertex shader.

```
#version 420 core

// Per-vertex inputs
layout (location = 0) in vec4 position;
layout (location = 1) in vec3 normal;

// Matrices we'll need
layout (std140) uniform constants
{
    mat4 mv_matrix;
    mat4 view_matrix;
    mat4 proj_matrix;
};
```

```
// Inputs from vertex shader
out VS_OUT
{
    vec3 N;
    vec3 L;
    vec3 V;
} vs_out;

// Position of light
uniform vec3 light_pos = vec3(100.0, 100.0, 100.0);

void main(void)
{
    // Calculate view-space coordinate
    vec4 P = mv_matrix * position;

    // Calculate normal in view-space
    vs_out.N = mat3(mv_matrix) * normal;

    // Calculate light vector
    vs_out.L = light_pos - P.xyz;

    // Calculate view vector
    vs_out.V = -P.xyz;

    // Calculate the clip-space position of each vertex
    gl_Position = proj_matrix * P;
}
```

Listing 13.3: The Phong shading vertex shader

All the lighting computations depend on the surface normal, light direction, and view vector. Instead of passing a computed color value from each vertex, we pass these three vectors as the outputs vs_out.N, vs_out.L, and vs_out.V. Now the fragment shader has significantly more work to do than before, and it is shown in Listing 13.4.

```
#version 420 core

// Output
layout (location = 0) out vec4 color;

// Input from vertex shader
in VS_OUT
{
    vec3 N;
    vec3 L;
    vec3 V;
} fs_in;

// Material properties
uniform vec3 diffuse_albedo = vec3(0.5, 0.2, 0.7);
uniform vec3 specular_albedo = vec3(0.7);
uniform float specular_power = 128.0;

void main(void)
```

```
{
    // Normalize the incoming N, L, and V vectors
    vec3 N = normalize(fs_in.N);
    vec3 L = normalize(fs_in.L);
    vec3 V = normalize(fs_in.V);

    // Calculate R locally
    vec3 R = reflect(-L, N);

    // Compute the diffuse and specular components for each
    // fragment
    vec3 diffuse = max(dot(N, L), 0.0) * diffuse_albedo;
    vec3 specular = pow(max(dot(R, V), 0.0), specular_power) *
                    specular_albedo;

    // Write final color to the framebuffer
    color = vec4(diffuse + specular, 1.0);
}
```

Listing 13.4: The Phong shading fragment shader

On today's hardware, higher-quality rendering choices such as Phong shading are often practical. The visual quality is dramatic, and performance is often only marginally compromised. Still, on lower-powered hardware (such as an embedded device) or in a scene where many other already expensive choices have been made, Gouraud shading may be the best choice. A general shader performance optimization rule is to move as much processing out of the fragment shaders and into the vertex shader as possible. With this example, you can see why.

The main parameters that are passed to the Phong lighting equations (whether they are evaluated per vertex or per fragment) are the diffuse and specular *albedo* and the specular power. The first two are the colors of the diffuse and specular lighting effect produced by the material being modeled. Normally, either they are the same color or the diffuse albedo is the color of the material and the specular albedo is white. However, it's also possible to make the specular albedo a completely different color than the diffuse albedo. The specular power controls the sharpness of the specular highlight. Figure 13.4 shows the effect of varying the specular parameters of a material (this image is also shown in Color Plate 8). A single white point light is in the scene. From left to right, the specular albedo varies from almost black to pure white (essentially increasing the specular contribution) and from top to bottom, the specular power increases exponentially from 4.0 to 256.0, doubling in each row. As you can see, the sphere on the top left looks dull and evenly lit, whereas the sphere on the bottom right appears highly glossy.

Although the image in Figure 13.4 shows only the effect of a white light on the scene, colored lights are simulated by simply multiplying the

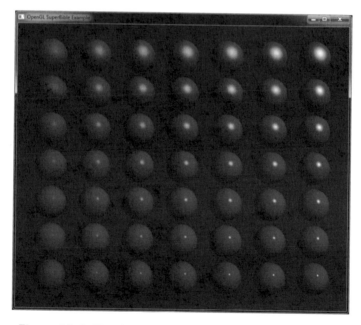

Figure 13.4: Varying specular parameters of a material

color of the light by the diffuse and specular components of each fragment's color.

Blinn-Phong Lighting

The Blinn-Phong lighting model could be considered an extension to or possibly an optimization of the Phong lighting model. Notice that in the Phong lighting model, we calculate $\vec{R} \cdot \vec{N}$ at each shaded point (either per vertex or per fragment). However, as an approximation, we can replace $\vec{R} \cdot \vec{N}$ with $\vec{N} \cdot \vec{H}$, where $\vec{H}$ is the halfway vector between the light vector $\vec{L}$ and the eye vector $\vec{E}$. This vector can be calculated as

$$\vec{H} = \frac{\vec{L} + \vec{E}}{\left| \vec{L} + \vec{E} \right|}$$

Technically, this calculation should also be applied wherever the Phong equations would have been applied, requiring a normalization at each step (the division by the vectors' magnitudes in the above equation). However, this comes in exchange for no longer needing to calculate the vector $\vec{R}$, avoiding the call to the reflect function. Modern graphics processors are generally powerful enough that the difference in cost between the vector normalization required to calculate $\vec{H}$ and the call to reflect is negligible. However, if the curvature of the underlying surface represented by a triangle is relatively small and if the triangle is small relative to the distance from the surface to the light and viewer, the value of $\vec{H}$ won't change much. In such a case, it's possible to calculate $\vec{H}$ in the vertex (or geometry or tessellation) shader and pass it to the fragment shader as a flat input. Even when the result is inaccurate, this can often be remedied by increasing the shininess (or specular) factor α. Listing 13.5 provides a fragment shader that implements Blinn-Phong lighting per fragment. This shader is included in the blinnphong example program.

```glsl
#version 450 core

// Output
layout (location = 0) out vec4 color;

// Input from vertex shader
in VS_OUT
{
    vec3 N;
    vec3 L;
    vec3 V;
} fs_in;

// Material properties
uniform vec3 diffuse_albedo = vec3(0.5, 0.2, 0.7);
uniform vec3 specular_albedo = vec3(0.7);
uniform float specular_power = 128.0;

void main(void)
{
    // Normalize the incoming N, L, and V vectors
    vec3 N = normalize(fs_in.N);
    vec3 L = normalize(fs_in.L);
    vec3 V = normalize(fs_in.V);

    // Calculate the half vector, H
    vec3 H = normalize(L + V);

    // Compute the diffuse and specular components for each fragment
    vec3 diffuse = max(dot(N, L), 0.0) * diffuse_albedo;

    // Replace the R.V calculation (as in Phong) with N.H
    vec3 specular = pow(max(dot(N, H), 0.0), specular_power) * specular_albedo;

    // Write final color to the framebuffer
    color = vec4(diffuse + specular, 1.0);
}
```

Listing 13.5: Blinn-Phong fragment shader

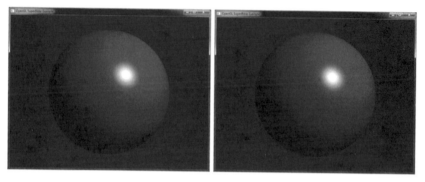

Figure 13.5: Phong lighting (left) versus Blinn-Phong lighting (right)

Figure 13.5 shows the result of using plain Phong shading (left) next to the result of using Blinn-Phong shading. In Figure 13.5, the specular exponent used for the Phong rendering is 128, whereas the the specular exponent used for the Blinn-Phong rendering is 200. As you can see, after adjustment of the specular powers, the results are very similar.

Rim Lighting

Rim lighting, which is also known as back-lighting, is an effect that simulates the bleeding of light "around" an object from sources that are behind it or otherwise have no effect on the shaded surfaces of the model. Rim lighting is so called because it produces a bright rim of light around the outline of the object being lit. In photography, this is attained by physically placing a light source behind the subject such that the object of interest sits between the camera and the light source. In computer graphics, we can simulate the effect by determining how closely the view direction comes to glancing off the surface.

To implement rim lighting, all we need is the surface normal and the view direction—two quantities we have at hand from any of the lighting models we have already described. When the view direction is face on to the surface, the view vector will be colinear to the surface normal; in this case, the effect of rim lighting will be least noticeable. When the view direction glances off the surface, the surface normal and view vector will be almost perpendicular to each other, so the rim light effect will be greatest.

You can see this in Figure 13.6. Near the edge of the object, the vectors $\vec{N_1}$ and $\vec{V_1}$ are almost perpendicular; this is where the most light from the lamp behind the object will leak around it. However, in the center of the

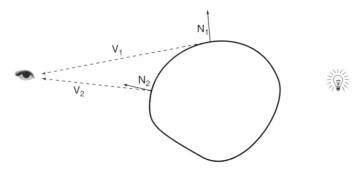

Figure 13.6: Rim lighting vectors

object, $\vec{N}_2$ and $\vec{V}_2$ point in almost the same direction. The lamp will be completly obscured by the object and the amount of light leaking through will be minimal.

A quantity that is easy to calculate and is proportional to the angle between two vectors is the dot product. When two vectors are colinear, the dot product between them will be 1. As the two vectors become closer to orthogonal, the dot product becomes closer to 0. Therefore, we can produce a rim light effect by taking the dot product between the view direction and the surface normal and making the rim light intensity inversely proportional to it. To provide further control over the rim light, we include a scalar brightness and an exponential sharpness factor. Thus, our rim lighting equation is

$$L_{rim} = C_{rim} \left(1.0 - \vec{N} \cdot \vec{V}\right)^{P_{rim}}$$

Here, $\vec{N}$ and $\vec{V}$ are our usual normal and view vectors, C_{rim} and P_{rim} are the color and power of the rim light, and L_{rim} is the resulting contribution of the rim light. The fragment shader to implement this is quite simple, and is shown in Listing 13.6.

```
// Uniforms controlling the rim light effect
uniform vec3 rim_color;
uniform float rim_power;

vec3 calculate_rim(vec3 N, vec3 V)
{
    // Calculate the rim factor
    float f = 1.0 - dot(N, V);

    // Constrain it to the range 0 to 1 using a smoothstep function
    f = smoothstep(0.0, 1.0, f);
```

```
    // Raise it to the rim exponent
    f = pow(f, rim_power);

    // Finally, multiply it by the rim color
    return f * rim_color;
}
```

Listing 13.6: Rim lighting shader function

Figure 13.7 shows a model illuminated with a Phong lighting model as described earlier in this chapter, but with a rim light effect applied. The code to produce this image is included in the `rimlight` example program. The top-left image has the rim light disabled for reference. The top-right image applies a medium-strength rim light with a moderate fall-off exponent. The bottom-left image increases both the exponent and the strength of the light. As a result, the rim is sharp and focused. The image on the bottom right in Figure 13.7 has the light intensity turned down but also has the rim exponent turned down. This causes the light to bleed further around the model, producing more of an ambient effect.

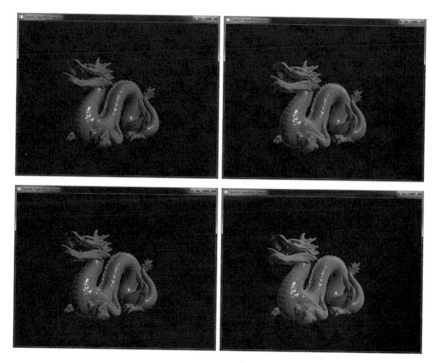

Figure 13.7: Result of rim lighting example

The images included in Figure 13.7 are also shown in Color Plate 9. For a given scene, the color of the rim light would normally be fixed or perhaps vary as a function of world space (otherwise, it would seem as though the different objects were lit by different lights, which might look odd). However, the power of the rim light is essentially an approximation of bleeding, which may vary by material. For example, soft materials such as hair or fur and translucent materials such as marble might bleed light quite a bit, whereas harder materials such as wood or rock might not bleed as much light.

Normal Mapping

In the examples shown so far, we have calculated the lighting contributions either at each vertex, in the case of Gouraud shading, or at each pixel but with vectors derived from per-vertex attributes that are then smoothly interpolated across each triangle, in the case of Phong shading. To really see surface features, that level of detail must be present in the original model. In most cases, this leads to an unreasonable amount of geometry that must be passed to OpenGL and to triangles that are so small that each one only covers a small number of pixels.

One method for increasing the perceived level of detail without actually adding more vertices to a model is *normal mapping*, which is sometimes called *bump mapping*. To implement normal mapping, we need a texture that stores a surface normal in each texel. This is then applied to our model and used in the fragment shader to calculate a local surface normal for each fragment. Our lighting model of choice is then applied in each invocation to calculate per-fragment lighting. An example of such a texture is shown in Figure 13.8.

The most common coordinate space used for normal maps is tangent space, which is a local coordinate system where the positive z axis is aligned with the surface normal. The other two vectors in this coordinate space are known as the *tangent* and *bitangent* vectors, and for best results, these vectors should line up with the direction of the u and v coordinates used in the texture. The tangent vector is usually encoded as part of the geometry data and passed as an input to the vertex shader. As an orthonormal basis, given two vectors in the frame, the third can be calculated using a simple cross product. Thus, given the normal and tangent vectors, we can calculate the bitangent vector using the cross product.

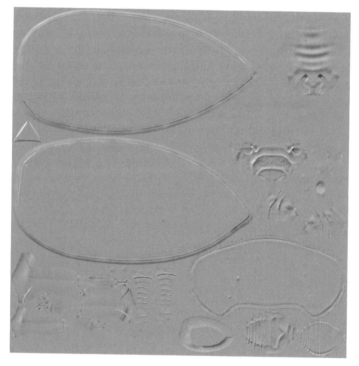

Figure 13.8: Example normal map

The normal, tangent, and bitangent vectors can be used to construct a rotation matrix that will transform a vector in the standard Cartesian frame into the frame represented by these three vectors. We simply insert the three vectors as the rows of this matrix. This gives us the following:

$$\vec{N} = \text{normal}$$
$$\vec{T} = \text{tangent}$$
$$\vec{B} = \vec{N} \times \vec{T}$$
$$TBN = \begin{bmatrix} \vec{T}.x & \vec{T}.y & \vec{T}.z \\ \vec{B}.x & \vec{B}.y & \vec{B}.z \\ \vec{N}.x & \vec{N}.y & \vec{N}.z \end{bmatrix}$$

The matrix produced here is often referred to as the TBN (tangent, bitangent, normal) matrix. Given the TBN matrix for a vertex, we can transform any vector expressed in Cartesian coordinates into the local frame at the vertex. This is important because the dot product operations we use in our lighting calculations are relative to pairs of vectors. As long as these two vectors are in the same frame, then the results will be correct. By transforming our view and light vectors into the local frame at each vertex and then interpolating them across each polygon as we would with normal Phong shading, we are presented with view and light vectors at each fragment that are in the same frame as the normals in our normal map. We can then simply read the local normal at each fragment and perform our lighting calculations in the usual manner.

A vertex shader that calculates the TBN matrix for a vertex, determines the light and view vectors, and then multiplies them by the TBN matrix before passing them to the fragment shader is shown in Listing 13.7. This shader, along with the rest of the code for this example, is included in the bumpmapping sample application.

```glsl
#version 450 core

layout (location = 0) in vec4 position;
layout (location = 1) in vec3 normal;
layout (location = 2) in vec3 tangent;
layout (location = 4) in vec2 texcoord;

out VS_OUT
{
    vec2 texcoord;
    vec3 eyeDir;
    vec3 lightDir;
} vs_out;

uniform mat4 mv_matrix;
uniform mat4 proj_matrix;
uniform vec3 light_pos = vec3(0.0, 0.0, 100.0);

void main(void)
{
    // Calculate vertex position in view space.
    vec4 P = mv_matrix * position;

    // Calculate normal (N) and tangent (T) vectors in view space from
    // incoming object space vectors.
    vec3 N = normalize(mat3(mv_matrix) * normal);
    vec3 T = normalize(mat3(mv_matrix) * tangent);
    // Calculate the bitangent vector (B) from the normal and tangent
    // vectors.
    vec3 B = cross(N, T);

    // The light vector (L) is the vector from the point of interest to
    // the light. Calculate that and multiply it by the TBN matrix.
    vec3 L = light_pos - P.xyz;
    vs_out.lightDir = normalize(vec3(dot(V, T), dot(V, B), dot(V, N)));

    // The view vector is the vector from the point of interest to the
    // viewer, which in view space is simply the negative of the position.
    // Calculate that and multiply it by the TBN matrix.
```

```
    vec3 V = -P.xyz;
    vs_out.eyeDir = normalize(vec3(dot(V, T), dot(V, B), dot(V, N)));

    // Pass the texture coordinate through unmodified so that the fragment
    // shader can fetch from the normal and color maps.
    vs_out.texcoord = texcoord;

    // Calculate clip coordinates by multiplying our view position by
    // the projection matrix.
    gl_Position = proj_matrix * P;
}
```

Listing 13.7: Vertex shader for normal mapping

The shader in Listing 13.7 calculates the view and light vectors expressed in the local frame of each vertex and passes them along with the vertex's texture coordinates to the fragment shader. In our fragment shader, which is shown in Listing 13.8, we simply fetch a per-fragment normal map and use it in our shading calculations.

```
#version 420 core

out vec4 color;

// Color and normal maps
layout (binding = 0) uniform sampler2D tex_color;
layout (binding = 1) uniform sampler2D tex_normal;

in VS_OUT
{
    vec2 texcoord;
    vec3 eyeDir;
    vec3 lightDir;
} fs_in;

void main(void)
{
    // Normalize our incomming view and light direction vectors
    vec3 V = normalize(fs_in.eyeDir);
    vec3 L = normalize(fs_in.lightDir);
    // Read the normal from the normal map and normalize it
    vec3 N = normalize(texture(tex_normal, fs_in.texcoord).rgb * 2.0 - vec3(1.0));
    // Calculate R ready for use in Phong lighting
    vec3 R = reflect(-L, N);

    // Fetch the diffuse albedo from the texture
    vec3 diffuse_albedo = texture(tex_color, fs_in.texcoord).rgb;
    // Calculate diffuse color with simple N dot L
    vec3 diffuse = max(dot(N, L), 0.0) * diffuse_albedo;
    // Uncomment this to turn off diffuse shading
    // diffuse = vec3(0.0);

    // Assume that specular albedo is white; it could also come from a texture
    vec3 specular_albedo = vec3(1.0);
    // Calculate Phong specular highlight
    vec3 specular = max(pow(dot(R, V), 5.0), 0.0) * specular_albedo;
    // Uncomment this to turn off specular highlights
    // specular = vec3(0.0);
```

```
// Final color is diffuse + specular
color = vec4(diffuse + specular, 1.0);
}
```

Listing 13.8: Fragment shader for normal mapping

Rendering a model with this shader clearly shows specular highlights on details that are present only in the normal map and do not have geometric representations in the model data. In Figure 13.9, the top-left image shows the diffuse shading result, the top-right image shows the specular shading results, and the bottom-left image shows the image produced by adding these two results together. For reference, the bottom-right image in Figure 13.9 shows the result of applying per-pixel Phong shading using only the normals that are interpolated by OpenGL and does not use the normal map. It should be clear from contrasting the bottom-left and bottom-right images that normal mapping can add substantial detail to an image. This image is also shown in Color Plate 10.

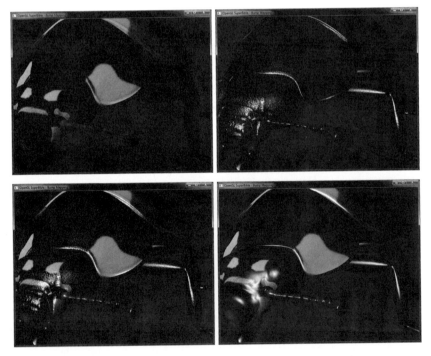

Figure 13.9: Result of normal mapping example

Environment Mapping

In the previous few subsections, you have learned how to compute the effect of lighting on the surface of objects. Lighting shaders can become extemely complex, but eventually they become so intensive that they start to affect performance. Also, it's virtually impossible to create an equation that can represent an arbitrary environment. This is where *environment maps* come in. A few types of environment maps are commonly used in real-time graphics applications: the spherical environment map, the equirectangular map, and the cubemap. The spherical environment map is represented as the image of a sphere illuminated by the simulated surroundings. As a sphere map can represent only a single hemisphere of the environment, an equirectangular map is a mapping of spherical coordinates onto a rectangle that allows a full 360° view of the environment to be represented. A cubemap, by comparison, is a special texture made up of six faces that essentially represent a box made of glass through which, if you were standing in its center, you would see your surroundings. We'll dig into these three methods of simulating an environment in the next few subsections.

Spherical Environment Maps

As noted, a spherical environment map is a texture map that represents the lighting produced by the simulated surroundings on a sphere made from the material being simulated. This works by taking the view direction and surface normal at the point being shaded and using these two vectors to compute a set of texture coordinates that can be used to look up into the texture to retrieve the lighting coefficients. In the simplest case, this is simply the color of the surface under these lighting conditions, although any number of parameters could be stored in such a texture map. A few examples[1] of environment maps are shown in Figure 13.10. These environment maps are also shown in Color Plate 12.

The first step in implementing spherical environment mapping is to transform the incoming normal into view space and to calculate the eye-space view direction. These will be used in our fragment shader to compute the texture coordinates to look up into the environment map. Such a vertex shader is shown in Listing 13.9.

---

1. The images shown in Figure 13.10 were produced by simply ray tracing a sphere using the popular POVRay ray tracer with different materials and lighting conditions.

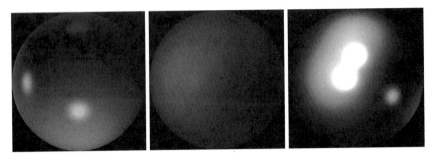

Figure 13.10: A selection of spherical environment maps

```
#version 420 core

uniform mat4 mv_matrix;
uniform mat4 proj_matrix;

layout (location = 0) in vec4 position;
layout (location = 1) in vec3 normal;

out VS_OUT
{
    vec3 normal;
    vec3 view;
} vs_out;

void main(void)
{
    vec4 pos_vs = mv_matrix * position;

    vs_out.normal = mat3(mv_matrix) * normal;
    vs_out.view = pos_vs.xyz;

    gl_Position = proj_matrix * pos_vs;
}
```

Listing 13.9: Spherical environment mapping vertex shader

Now, given the per-fragment normal and view direction, we can calculate the texture coordinates to look up into our environment map. First, we reflect the incoming view direction about the plane defined by the incoming normal. Then, by simply scaling and biasing the x and y components of this reflected vector, we can use them to fetch from the environment and shade our fragment. The corresponding fragment shader is given in Listing 13.10.

```
#version 420 core

layout (binding = 0) uniform sampler2D tex_envmap;
```

```
in VS_OUT
{
    vec3 normal;
    vec3 view;
} fs_in;

out vec4 color;

void main(void)
{
    // u will be our normalized view vector
    vec3 u = normalize(fs_in.view);

    // Reflect u about the plane defined by the normal at the fragment
    vec3 r = reflect(u, normalize(fs_in.normal));

    // Compute scale factor
    r.z += 1.0;
    float m = 0.5 * inversesqrt(dot(r, r));

    // Sample from scaled and biased texture coordinate
    color = texture(tex_envmap, r.xy * m + vec2(0.5));
}
```

Listing 13.10: Spherical environment mapping fragment shader

The result of rendering a model with the shader given in Listing 13.10 is shown in Figure 13.11. This image was produced by the envmapsphere example program, using the environment map in the rightmost image in Figure 13.10.

Figure 13.11: Result of rendering with spherical environment mapping

Equirectangular Environment Maps

The equirectangular environment map is similar to the spherical environment map except that it is less susceptible to the pinching effect sometimes seen when the poles of the sphere are sampled from. An example equirectangular environment texture is shown in Figure 13.12. Again, we use the view-space normal and view direction vectors, calculated in the vertex shader, interpolated, and passed to the fragment shader, and again the fragment shader reflects the incoming view direction about the plane defined by the local normal. Now, instead of directly using the scaled and biased x and y components of this reflected vector, we extract the y component and then project the vector onto the xz plane by setting the y component to zero and normalizing it again. From this normalized vector, we extract the x component, producing our second texture coordinate. These extracted x and y components effectively form the altitude and azimuth angles for looking up into our equirectangular texture.

A fragment shader implementing equirectangular environment mapping is included in the equirectangular example application and is shown in Listing 13.11. The result of rendering an object with this shader is shown in Figure 13.13.

```
#version 420 core

layout (binding = 0) uniform sampler2D tex_envmap;

in VS_OUT
{
    vec3 normal;
    vec3 view;
} fs_in;

out vec4 color;

void main(void)
{
    // u will be our normalized view vector
    vec3 u = normalize(fs_in.view);

    // Reflect u about the plane defined by the normal at the fragment
    vec3 r = reflect(u, normalize(fs_in.normal));

    // Compute texture coordinate from reflection vector
    vec2 tc;

    tc.y = r.y; r.y = 0.0;
    tc.x = normalize(r).x * 0.5;

    // Scale and bias texture coordinate based on direction
    // of reflection vector
    float s = sign(r.z) * 0.5;
```

```
    tc.s = 0.75 - s * (0.5 - tc.s);
    tc.t = 0.5 + 0.5 * tc.t;

    // Sample from scaled and biased texture coordinate
    color = texture(tex_envmap, tc);
}
```

Listing 13.11: Equirectangular environment mapping fragment shader

Figure 13.12: Example equirectangular environment map

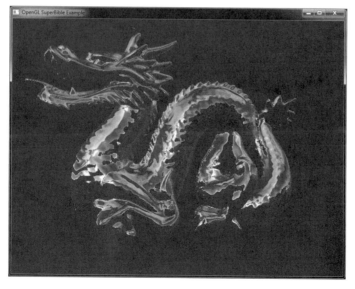

Figure 13.13: Rendering result of equirectangular environment map

Cubemaps

A cubemap is treated as a single texture object but it is made up of six square (yes, they must be square!) 2D images that make up the six sides of a cube. Applications of cubemaps range from 3D light maps, to reflections, to highly accurate environment maps. Figure 13.14 shows the layout of six square images composing a cubemap that we use[2] for the cubemap sample program. The images are arranged in a cross shape with their matching edges abutting. If you wanted to, you could cut and fold the image into a cube and the edges would align.

To load a cubemap texture, we create a texture object by binding a new name to the GL_TEXTURE_CUBE_MAP target, call **glTexStorage2D()** to specify the storage dimensions of the texture, and then load the cubemap data into the texture object by calling **glTexSubImage2D()** once for each face of the cubemap. The faces of the cubemap each have a special target named GL_TEXTURE_CUBE_MAP_POSITIVE_X, GL_TEXTURE_CUBE_MAP_NEGATIVE_X, GL_TEXTURE_CUBE_MAP_POSITIVE_Y, GL_TEXTURE_CUBE_MAP_NEGATIVE_Y, GL_TEXTURE_CUBE_MAP_POSITIVE_Z, and GL_TEXTURE_CUBE_MAP_NEGATIVE_Z. They are assigned numerical values in this order, so we can simply create a loop and update each face in turn. Example code to do this is shown in Listing 13.12.

```
GLuint texture;

glGenTextures(1, &texture);
glBindTexture(GL_TEXTURE_CUBE_MAP, texture);

glTexStorage2D(GL_TEXTURE_CUBE_MAP,
               levels, internalFormat,
               width, height);
for (face = 0; face < 6; face++)
{
    glTexSubImage2D(GL_TEXURE_CUBE_MAP_POSITIVE_X + face,
                    0,
                    0, 0,
                    width, height,
                    format, type,
                    data + face * face_size_in_bytes);
}
```

Listing 13.12: Loading a cubemap texture

Cubemaps also support mipmaps. Thus, if your cubemap has mipmap data, the code in Listing 13.12 would need to be modified to load the additional mipmap levels. The Khronos Texture File format has native

---

2. The six images used for the cubemap sample program were provided courtesy of The Game Creators, Ltd. (www.thegamecreators.com).

Figure 13.14: The layout of six cube faces in the cubemap sample program

support for cubemap textures, so the book's .KTX file loader is able to do this for you.

Texture coordinates for cubemaps have three dimensions, even though they are collections of 2D images. This seems a little odd at first glance. Unlike a true 3D texture, the S, T, and R texture coordinates represent a signed vector from the center of the texture map pointing outward. This vector will intersect one of the six sides of the cubemap. The texels around this intersection point are then sampled to create the filtered color value from the texture.

A very common use of cubemaps is to create an object that reflects its surroundings. The cubemap is applied to a sphere, creating the appearance of a mirrored surface. The same cubemap is also applied to the skybox, which creates the background being reflected.

A skybox is nothing more than a big box with a picture of the sky on it. Another way of looking at it is as a picture of the sky on a big box! Simple enough. An effective skybox contains six images that contain views from the center of your scene along the six directional axes. If this sounds just like a cubemap, congratulations, you're paying attention!

To render a cubemap, we could simply draw a large cube around the viewer and apply the cubemap texture to it. However, there's an even easier way to do it. Any part of the virtual cube that is outside the viewport will be clipped away, but what we need is for the entire viewport to be covered. We can do this by rendering a full-screen quad. All we need to do then is to compute the texture coordinates at each of the four corners of the viewport and we'll be able to use them to render our cubemap.

Now, if the cubemap texture were mapped directly to our virtual cube, the cube's vertex positions would be our texture coordinates. We would take the cube's vertex positions, multiply their x, y, and z components by the rotational part of our view matrix (which is the upper-left 3×3 sub-matrix) to orient them in the right direction, and render the cube in world space. In world space, the only face we'd see is the one we are looking directly at. Therefore, we can render a full-screen quad, and transform its corners by the view matrix to orient it correctly. All this occurs in the vertex shader shown in Listing 13.13.

```
#version 420 core

out VS_OUT
{
    vec3    tc;
} vs_out;

uniform mat4 view_matrix;

void main(void)
{
    vec3[4] vertices = vec3[4](vec3(-1.0, -1.0, 1.0),
                               vec3( 1.0, -1.0, 1.0),
                               vec3(-1.0,  1.0, 1.0),
                               vec3( 1.0,  1.0, 1.0));

    vs_out.tc = mat3(view_matrix) * vertices[gl_VertexID];

    gl_Position = vec4(vertices[gl_VertexID], 1.0);
}
```

Listing 13.13: Vertex shader for skybox rendering

Notice that because the vertex coordinates *and* the resulting texture coordinates are hard-coded into the vertex shader, we don't need any vertex attributes, and therefore don't need any buffers to store them. If we wished, we could scale the field of view by scaling the z component of the vertex data—the larger the z component becomes, the smaller the x and y components become after normalization, and so the smaller the field of view. The fragment shader for rendering the cubemap is also equally simple and is shown in its entirety in Listing 13.14.

```
#version 420 core

layout (binding = 0) uniform samplerCube tex_cubemap;

in VS_OUT
{
    vec3    tc;
} fs_in;

layout (location = 0) out vec4 color;

void main(void)
{
    color = texture(tex_cubemap, fs_in.tc);
}
```

Listing 13.14: Fragment shader for skybox rendering

Once we've rendered our skybox, we need to render something into the scene that reflects the skybox. The texture coordinates used to fetch from a cubemap texture are interpreted as a vector pointing from the origin outward toward the cube. OpenGL will determine which face this vector eventually hits as well as the coordinate within the face that it hits, and then retrieve data from this location. What we need to do is calculate this vector for each fragment. Again, we need the incoming view direction and the normal at each fragment.

These items are produced in the vertex shader as before and passed to the fragment shader and normalized. Again, we reflect the incoming view direction about the plane defined by the surface normal at the fragment to compute an outgoing reflection vector. Under the assumption that the scenery shown in the skybox is sufficiently far away, this reflection vector can be considered to emanate from the origin and so can be used as the texture coordinate for our skybox. The vertex and fragment shaders are shown in Listings 13.15 and 13.16.

```
#version 420 core

uniform mat4 mv_matrix;
uniform mat4 proj_matrix;
```

```
layout (location = 0) in vec4 position;
layout (location = 1) in vec3 normal;

out VS_OUT
{
    vec3 normal;
    vec3 view;
} vs_out;

void main(void)
{
    vec4 pos_vs = mv_matrix * position;

    vs_out.normal = mat3(mv_matrix) * normal;
    vs_out.view = pos_vs.xyz;

    gl_Position = proj_matrix * pos_vs;
}
```

Listing 13.15: Vertex shader for cubemap environment rendering

```
#version 420 core

layout (binding = 0) uniform samplerCube tex_cubemap;

in VS_OUT
{
    vec3 normal;
    vec3 view;
} fs_in;

out vec4 color;

void main(void)
{
    // Reflect view vector about the plane defined by the normal
    // at the fragment
    vec3 r = reflect(fs_in.view, normalize(fs_in.normal));

    // Sample from scaled using reflection vector
    color = texture(tex_cubemap, r);
}
```

Listing 13.16: Fragment shader for cubemap environment rendering

The result of rendering an object surrounded by a skybox using the shaders shown in Listings 13.13 through 13.16 is shown in Figure 13.15. This image was produced by the cubemapenv example program.

Of course, there is no reason that the final color of the fragment must be taken directly from the environment map. For example, you could multiply it by the base color of the object you're rendering to tint the

Figure 13.15: Cubemap environment rendering with a skybox

environment it reflects. Color Plate 13 shows a golden version of the dragon being rendered.

Material Properties

In the examples presented so far in this chapter, we have used a single material for the entire model. This means that our dragons are uniformly shiny, and our ladybug looks somewhat plastic. However, there is no reason that every part of our models has to be made from the same material. In fact, we can assign material properties per surface, per triangle, or even per pixel by storing information about the surface in a texture. For example, the specular exponent can be stored in a texture and applied to a model when rendering. This allows some parts of the model to be more reflective than others.

Another technique that allows a sense of roughness to be applied to a model is to pre-blur an environment map and then use a gloss factor (also stored in a texture) to gradually fade between sharp and blurred versions of the map. In this example, we will again use a simple spherical environment map. Figure 13.16 shows two environment maps, and a shininess map used to blend between them. The left image shows a fully sharp environment map, whereas the image in the center contains a

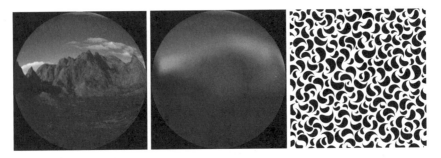

Figure 13.16: Pre-filtered environment maps and gloss map

pre-blurred version of the same environment. The rightmost image is our gloss map, which will be used to filter between the sharp and blurry versions of the environment map. Where the gloss map is brightest, the sharper environment map will be used. Where it is darkest, we will use the blurrier environment map.

We can combine the two environment textures together into a single, 3D texture that is only 2 texels deep. Then, we can sample from our gloss texture and use the fetched texel value as the third component of the texture coordinate used to fetch from the environment map (with the first two components being calculated as usual). With the sharp image as the first layer of the 3D environment texture and the blurry image as the second layer of the 3D environment, OpenGL will smoothly interpolate between the sharp and the blurry environment maps for you.

Listing 13.17 shows the fragment shader that reads the material property texture to determine per-pixel gloss and then reads the environment map texture using the result.

```
#version 420 core

layout (binding = 0) uniform sampler3D tex_envmap;
layout (binding = 1) uniform sampler2D tex_glossmap;

in VS_OUT
{
    vec3 normal;
    vec3 view;
    vec2 tc;
} fs_in;

out vec4 color;

void main(void)
{
    // u will be our normalized view vector
    vec3 u = normalize(fs_in.view);
```

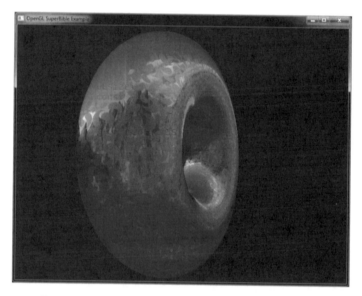

Figure 13.17: Result of per-pixel gloss example

```
    // Reflect u about the plane defined by the normal at the fragment
    vec3 r = reflect(u, normalize(fs_in.normal));

    // Compute scale factor
    r.z += 1.0;
    float m = 0.5 * inversesqrt(dot(r, r));

    // Sample gloss factor from glossmap texture
    float gloss = texture(tex_glossmap, fs_in.tc * vec2(3.0, 1.0) * 2.0).r;

    // Sample from scaled and biased texture coordinate
    vec3 env_coord = vec3(r.xy * m + vec2(0.5), gloss);

    // Sample from two-level environment map
    color = texture(tex_envmap, env_coord);
}
```

Listing 13.17: Fragment shader for per-fragment shininess

Figure 13.17 was produced by the `perpixelgloss` example and shows the result of rendering a torus with the map applied.

Casting Shadows

The shading algorithms presented so far have all assumed that each light will contribute to the final color of each fragment. However, in a complex scene with lots of objects, this is not the case. Objects will cast shadows on each other and upon themselves. If these shadows are omitted from the rendered scene, a great deal of realism can be lost. This section outlines some techniques for simulating the effects of shadowing on objects.

Shadow Mapping

The most basic operation of any shadow calculation must be to determine whether the point being considered has any light hitting it. In effect, we must determine whether there is line of sight from the point being shaded to a light and, therefore, from the light to the point being shaded. This turns out to be a visibility calculation. As luck might have it, we have extremely fast hardware to determine whether a piece of geometry is visible from a given vantage point—the depth buffer.

Shadow mapping is a technique that produces visibility information for a scene by rendering it from the point of view of a light source. Only the depth information is needed, so to do this, we can use a framebuffer object with only a depth attachment. After rendering the scene into a depth buffer from the light's perspective, we will be left with a per-pixel distance of the nearest point to the light in the scene. When we render our geometry in a forward pass, we can calculate, for each point, what the distance to the light is and compare that to the distance stored in the depth buffer. To do so, we project our point from view space (where it is being rendered) into the coordinate system of the light.

Once we have this coordinate, we simply read from the depth texture we rendered earlier, compare our calculated depth value against the one stored in the texture, and if we are not the closest point to the light for that particular texture, we know we are in shadow. In fact, this is such a common operation in graphics that OpenGL even has a special sampler type that does the comparison for us, called the *shadow sampler*. In GLSL, it is declared as a variable with a `sampler2DShadow` type for 2D textures, which we'll be using in this example. You can also create shadow samplers for 1D textures (`sampler1DShadow`), cubemaps (`samplerCubeShadow`), and rectangle textures (`samplerRectShadow`) as well as for arrays of these types (except, of course, rectangle textures).

Listing 13.18 shows how to set up a framebuffer object with only a depth attachment ready for rendering the shadow map into.

```
GLuint shadow_buffer;
GLuint shadow_tex;

glGenFramebuffers(1, &shadow_buffer);
glBindFramebuffer(GL_FRAMEBUFFER, shadow_buffer);
```

```
glGenTextures(1, &shadow_tex);
glBindTexture(GL_TEXTURE_2D, shadow_tex);
glTexStorage2D(GL_TEXTURE_2D, 1, GL_DEPTH_COMPONENT32,
               DEPTH_TEX_WIDTH, DEPTH_TEX_HEIGHT);
glTexParameteri(GL_TEXTURE_2D, GL_TEXTURE_MIN_FILTER, GL_LINEAR);
glTexParameteri(GL_TEXTURE_2D, GL_TEXTURE_MAG_FILTER, GL_LINEAR);
glTexParameteri(GL_TEXTURE_2D, GL_TEXTURE_COMPARE_MODE,
               GL_COMPARE_REF_TO_TEXTURE);
glTexParameteri(GL_TEXTURE_2D, GL_TEXTURE_COMPARE_FUNC, GL_LEQUAL);

glFramebufferTexture(GL_FRAMEBUFFER, GL_DEPTH_ATTACHMENT,
                     shadow_tex, 0);

glBindFramebuffer(GL_FRAMEBUFFER, 0);
```

Listing 13.18: Getting ready for shadow mapping

In Listing 13.18, notice the two calls to **glTexParameteri()** with the
parameters GL_TEXTURE_COMPARE_MODE and GL_TEXTURE_COMPARE_FUNC.
The first of these calls turns on texture comparison and the second sets the
function that should be used. Once we have created our FBO for rendering
depth, we can render the scene from the point of view of the light. Given
a light position, light_pos, which is pointing at the origin, we can
construct a matrix that represents the model–view-projection matrix for
the light. This is shown in Listing 13.19.

```
vmath::mat4 model_matrix = vmath::rotate(currentTime, 0.0f, 1.0f, 0.0f);
vmath::mat4 light_view_matrix =
    vmath::lookat(light_pos,
                  vmath::vec3(0.0f),
                  vmath::vec3(0.0f, 1.0f, 0.0f);
vmath::mat4 light_proj_matrix =
    vmath::frustum(-1.0f, 1.0f, -1.0f, 1.0f,
                   1.0f, 1000.0f);
vmath::mat4 light_mvp_matrix = light_projection_matrix *
                               light_view_matrix *
                               model_matrix;
```

Listing 13.19: Setting up matrices for shadow mapping

Rendering the scene from the light's position results in a depth buffer that
contains the distance from the light to each pixel in the framebuffer. This
can be visualized as a grayscale image with black being the closest possible
depth value (zero) and white being the farthest possible depth value (one).
Figure 13.18 shows the depth buffer of a simple scene rendered with this
technique.

To make use of this stored depth information to generate shadows, we
need to make a few modifications to our rendering shader. First, of course,

Figure 13.18: Depth as seen from a light

we need to declare our shadow sampler and read from it. The interesting part is how we determine the coordinates at which to read from the depth texture. In fact, this step turns out to be quite simple. In our vertex shader, we normally calculate the output position in clip coordinates, which is a projection of the vertex's world-space coordinate into the view space of our virtual camera and then into the camera's frustum. At the same time, we need to perform the same operations using the light's view and frustum matrices. As the resulting coordinate is interpolated and passed to the fragment shader, that shader then has the coordinate of each fragment in the light's clip space.

In addition to the coordinate space transforms, we must scale and bias the resulting clip coordinates. Remember, OpenGL's normal clip coordinate frame ranges from -1.0 to 1.0 in the x, y, and z axes. The matrix that transforms vertices from object space into the light's clip space is known as the *shadow matrix* and the code to calculate it is shown in Listing 13.20.

```
const vmath::mat4 scale_bias_matrix =
    vmath::mat4(vmath::vec4(0.5f, 0.0f, 0.0f, 0.0f),
                vmath::vec4(0.0f, 0.5f, 0.0f, 0.0f),
                vmath::vec4(0.0f, 0.0f, 0.5f, 0.0f),
                vmath::vec4(0.5f, 0.5f, 0.5f, 1.0f));
```

```
vmath::mat4 shadow_matrix = scale_bias_matrix *
                            light_proj_matrix *
                            light_view_matrix *
                            model_matrix;
```

Listing 13.20: Setting up a shadow matrix

The shadow matrix can be passed as a single uniform to the original vertex shader. A simplified version of the shader is shown in Listing 13.21.

```
#version 420 core

uniform mat4 mv_matrix;
uniform mat4 proj_matrix;
uniform mat4 shadow_matrix;

layout (location = 0) in vec4 position;

out VS_OUT
{
    vec4 shadow_coord;
} vs_out;

void main(void)
{
    gl_Position = proj_matrix * mv_matrix * position;
    vs_out.shadow_coord = shadow_matrix * position;
}
```

Listing 13.21: Simplified vertex shader for shadow mapping

The shadow_coord output is sent from the vertex shader, interpolated, and passed into the fragment shader. This coordinate must be *projected* into normalized device coordinates to use them to look up into the shadow map we made earlier. This would normally mean dividing the whole vector through by its own w component. However, because projecting a coordinate in this way is such a common operation, there is a version of the overloaded texture function that will do this for us called textureProj. When we use textureProj with a shadow sampler, it first divides the x, y, and z components of the texture coordinate by its own w component and then uses the resulting x and y components to fetch a value from the texture. Next it compares the returned value against the computed z component using the chosen comparison function, producing a value of 1.0 or 0.0 depending on whether the test passed or failed, respectively.

If the selected texture filtering mode for the texture is GL_LINEAR or would otherwise require multiple samples, then OpenGL applies the test to each of the samples individually before averaging them together. The result of the `textureProj` function is therefore a value between 0.0 and 1.0 based on which and how many of the samples passed the comparison. All we need to do, then, is to call `textureProj` with our shadow sampler containing our depth buffer using the interpolated shadow texture coordinate, and the result will be a value that we can use to determine whether the point is in shadow. A highly simplified shadow mapping fragment shader is shown in Listing 13.22.

```
#version 420 core

layout (location = 0) out vec4 color;

layout (binding = 0) uniform sampler2DShadow shadow_tex;

in VS_OUT
{
    vec4 shadow_coord;
} fs_in;

void main(void)
{
    color = textureProj(shadow_tex, fs_in.shadow_coord) * vec4(1.0);
}
```

Listing 13.22: Simplified fragment shader for shadow mapping

Of course, the result of rendering a scene with the shader shown in Listing 13.22 is that no real lighting is applied and everything is drawn in black and white. However, as you can see in the shader code, we have simply multiplied the value `vec4(1.0)` by the result of the shadow map sample. In a more complex shader, we would apply our normal shading and texturing and multiply the result of *those* calculations by the result of the shadow map sample. Figure 13.19 shows a simple scene rendered as just shadow information on the left and with full lighting calculations on the right. This image was produced by the `shadowmapping` example.

Shadow maps have both advantages and disadvantages. They can be very memory intensive, because each light requires its own shadow map. Each light also requires a pass over the scene, which carries a performance cost. This can quickly add up and slow your application down. The shadow maps must be of a very high resolution, given that what might have mapped to a single texel in the shadow map may cover several pixels in screen space, which is effectively where the lighting calculations are performed. Finally, effects of self-occlusion may be visible in the output as stripes or a "sparkling" image in shadowed regions. It is possible to mitigate this to some degree using *polygon offset*. This small offset can be

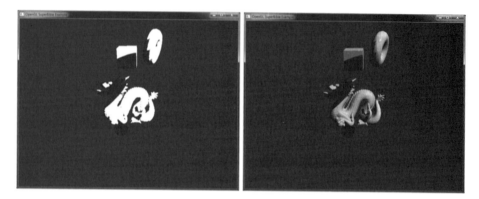

Figure 13.19: Results of rendering with shadow maps

applied automatically by OpenGL to all polygons (triangles) to push them toward or away from the viewer. To set the polygon offset, call

```
void glPolygonOffset(GLfloat factor,
                     GLfloat units);
```

The first parameter, `factor`, is a scale factor that is multiplied by the change in depth of the polygon relative to its screen area. The second parameter, `units`, is an implementation-defined scaling value that is internally multiplied by the smallest change guaranteed to produce a different value in the depth buffer. If this sounds a bit handwavy, it can be. You need to play with these two values until the depth-fighting effects go away. Once you've set up your polygon offset scaling factors, you can enable the effect by calling **glEnable()** with the GL_POLYGON_OFFSET_FILL parameter, and disable it again by passing the same parameter to **glDisable()**.

Atmospheric Effects

In general, rendering in computer graphics is the modeling of light as it interacts with the world around us. Most of the rendering we've done so far has not taken into consideration the medium in which the light travels. Usually, this is air. The air around us isn't perfectly transparent, however: It contains particles, vapor, and gases that absorb and scatter light as it travels. We use this scattering and absorption to gauge depth and infer distance as we look out into the world. Modeling it, even approximately, can add quite a bit of realism to our scenes.

Fog

We are all familiar with fog. On a foggy day, it might be impossible to see more than a few feet in front of us and dense fog can present a danger. However, even when fog is not heavy, it's still there—you may just need to look farther to see it. Fog is caused by water vapor hanging in the air or by other gases or particles such as smoke or pollution. As light travels through the air, two things happen: Some of the light is absorbed by the particles and some bounces off the particles (or is possibly re-emitted by those particles). When light is absorbed by fog, this condition is known as *extinction* because eventually all of the light will be absorbed and none will be left. However, light will generally find a way to get out of the fog by bouncing around and being absorbed and re-emitted by the fog particles. We call this condition *inscattering*. We can build a simple model of both extinction and inscattering to produce a simple yet effective simulation of fog.

For this example, we will return to the tessellated landscape example of Chapter 8, "Primitive Processing." If you refer back to Figure 8.12, you will notice that we left the sky black and used only a simple texture with shading information baked into it to render the landscape. It is quite difficult to infer depth from the rendered result, so we will adapt the sample to apply fog.

To add fog effects to the sample, we modify our tessellation evaluation shader to send both the world-space and eye-space coordinates of each point to the fragment shader. The modified tessellation evaluation shader is shown in Listing 13.23.

```
#version 420 core

layout (quads, fractional_odd_spacing) in;

uniform sampler2D tex_displacement;

uniform mat4 mv_matrix;
uniform mat4 proj_matrix;
uniform float dmap_depth;

out vec2 tc;

in TCS_OUT
{
    vec2 tc;
} tes_in[];

out TES_OUT
```

```
{
    vec2 tc;
    vec3 world_coord;
    vec3 eye_coord;
} tes_out;

void main(void)
{
    vec2 tc1 = mix(tes_in[0].tc, tes_in[1].tc, gl_TessCoord.x);
    vec2 tc2 = mix(tes_in[2].tc, tes_in[3].tc, gl_TessCoord.x);
    vec2 tc = mix(tc2, tc1, gl_TessCoord.y);

    vec4 p1 = mix(gl_in[0].gl_Position,
                  gl_in[1].gl_Position, gl_TessCoord.x);
    vec4 p2 = mix(gl_in[2].gl_Position,
                  gl_in[3].gl_Position, gl_TessCoord.x);
    vec4 p = mix(p2, p1, gl_TessCoord.y);
    p.y += texture(tex_displacement, tc).r * dmap_depth;

    vec4 P_eye = mv_matrix * p;

    tes_out.tc = tc;
    tes_out.world_coord = p.xyz;
    tes_out.eye_coord = P_eye.xyz;

    gl_Position = proj_matrix * P_eye;
}
```

Listing 13.23: Displacement map tessellation evaluation shader

In the fragment shader, we fetch from our landscape texture in the usual way, but then apply our simple fog model to the resulting color. We use the length of the eye-space coordinate to determine the distance from the viewer to the point being rendered. This tells us how far through the atmosphere light from the point of interest must travel to reach our eyes, which is the input term to the fog equations. We will apply exponential fog to our scene. The extinction and inscattering terms will be

$$f_e = e^{-zd_e}$$
$$f_i = e^{-zd_i}$$

Here, f_e is the extinction factor and f_i is the inscattering factor. Likewise, d_e and d_i are the extinction and inscattering coefficients that we can use to control our fog effect. z is the distance from the eye to the point being shaded. As z approaches 0, the exponential term tends toward 1. As z increases (i.e., the point being shaded gets farther from the viewer), the exponential term gets smaller and smaller, tending toward 0. These curves are illustrated by the graph in Figure 13.20.

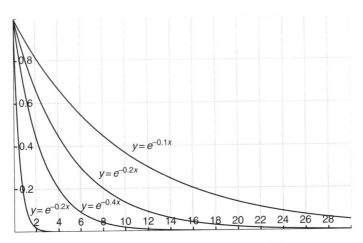

Figure 13.20: Graphs of exponential decay

The modified fragment shader that applies fog is shown in Listing 13.24.

```
#version 420 core

out vec4 color;

layout (binding = 1) uniform sampler2D tex_color;

uniform bool enable_fog = true;
uniform vec4 fog_color = vec4(0.7, 0.8, 0.9, 0.0);

in TES_OUT
{
    vec2 tc;
    vec3 world_coord;
    vec3 eye_coord;
} fs_in;

vec4 fog(vec4 c)
{
    float z = length(fs_in.eye_coord);

    float de = 0.025 * smoothstep(0.0, 6.0,
                                  10.0 - fs_in.world_coord.y);
    float di = 0.045 * smoothstep(0.0, 40.0,
                                  20.0 - fs_in.world_coord.y);

    float extinction   = exp(-z * de);
    float inscattering = exp(-z * di);

    return c * extinction + fog_color * (1.0 - inscattering);
}

void main(void)
```

```
{
    vec4 landscape = texture(tex_color, fs_in.tc);

    if (enable_fog)
    {
        color = fog(landscape);
    }
    else
    {
        color = landscape;
    }
}
```

Listing 13.24: Application of fog in a fragment shader

In our fragment shader, the fog function applies fog to the incoming fragment color. It first calculates the fog factor for the extinction and inscattering components of the fog. It then multiplies the original fragment color by the extinction term. As the extinction term approaches 0, so this term approaches black. It then multiplies the fog color by 1 minus the inscattering term. As the distance from the viewer increases, so the inscattering term approaches 0 (just like the extinction term). Taking 1 minus this value causes the inscattering term to approach 1 as the distance to the viewer increases, meaning that as the scene gets farther from the viewer, its color approaches the color of the fog.

The result of rendering the tessellated landscape scene with this shader is shown in Figure 13.21. The left image shows the original scene without fog, and the right image shows the scene with fog applied. You should be able to see that the sense of depth is greatly improved in the image on the right.

Figure 13.21: Applying fog to a tessellated landscape

Non-Photo-Realistic Rendering

Normally, the goal of rendering and generating computer graphics is to produce an image that appears as realistic as possible. However, for some applications or artistic reasons, it may be desirable to render an image that isn't realistic at all. For example, perhaps we want to render using a pencil-sketch effect or in a completely abstract manner. This is known as non-photo-realistic rendering (NPR).

Cell Shading: Texels as Light

Many of our examples of texture mapping in the last few chapters have used 2D textures. Two-dimensional textures are typically the simplest and easiest to understand. Most people can quickly get the intuitive feel for putting a 2D picture on the side of a piece of 2D or 3D geometry. Let's take a look now at a one-dimensional texture mapping example that is commonly used in computer games to render geometry that appears on screen like a cartoon. Toon shading, which is often referred to as cell shading, uses a one-dimensional texture map as a lookup table to fill geometry with a solid color (using GL_NEAREST) from the texture map.

The basic idea is to use the diffuse lighting intensity (the dot product between the eye-space surface normal and light directional vector) as the texture coordinate into a one-dimensional texture that contains a gradually brightening color table. Figure 13.22 shows one such texture, with four increasingly bright red texels (defined as RGB unsigned byte color components).

Recall that the diffuse lighting dot product varies from 0.0 at no intensity to 1.0 at full intensity. Conveniently, this maps nicely to a one-dimensional texture coordinate range. Loading this one-dimensional texture is relatively straightforward:

```
static const GLubyte toon_tex_data[] =
{
    0x44, 0x00, 0x00, 0x00,
    0x88, 0x00, 0x00, 0x00,
```

Figure 13.22: A one-dimensional color lookup table

```
    0xCC, 0x00, 0x00, 0x00,
    0xFF, 0x00, 0x00, 0x00
};

glGenTextures(1, &tex_toon);
glBindTexture(GL_TEXTURE_1D, tex_toon);
glTexStorage1D(GL_TEXTURE_1D, 1, GL_RGB8, sizeof(toon_tex_data) / 4);
glTexSubImage1D(GL_TEXTURE_1D, 0,
                0, sizeof(toon_tex_data) / 4,
                GL_RGBA, GL_UNSIGNED_BYTE,
                toon_tex_data);
glTexParameteri(GL_TEXTURE_1D, GL_TEXTURE_MAG_FILTER, GL_NEAREST);
glTexParameteri(GL_TEXTURE_1D, GL_TEXTURE_MIN_FILTER, GL_NEAREST);
glTexParameteri(GL_TEXTURE_1D, GL_TEXTURE_WRAP_S, GL_CLAMP_TO_EDGE);
```

This code is from the example program toonshading, which renders a
spinning torus with the toon shading effect applied. Although the torus
model file, which we use to create the torus, supplies a set of
two-dimensional texture coordinates, we ignore them in our vertex shader,
which is shown in Listing 13.25, and use only the incoming position and
normal.

```
#version 420 core

uniform mat4 mv_matrix;
uniform mat4 proj_matrix;

layout (location = 0) in vec4 position;
layout (location = 1) in vec3 normal;

out VS_OUT
{
    vec3 normal;
    vec3 view;
} vs_out;

void main(void)
{
    vec4 pos_vs = mv_matrix * position;

    // Calculate eye-space normal and position
    vs_out.normal = mat3(mv_matrix) * normal;
    vs_out.view = pos_vs.xyz;

    // Send clip-space position to primitive assembly
    gl_Position = proj_matrix * pos_vs;
}
```

Listing 13.25: The toon vertex shader

Other than the transformed geometry position, the outputs of this shader
are an interpolated eye-space normal and position that are passed to the
fragment shader, which is shown in Listing 13.26. The computation of the

diffuse lighting component is virtually identical to that performed in the earlier diffuse lighting examples.

```
#version 420 core

layout (binding = 0) uniform sampler1D tex_toon;

uniform vec3 light_pos = vec3(30.0, 30.0, 100.0);

in VS_OUT
{
    vec3 normal;
    vec3 view;
} fs_in;

out vec4 color;

void main(void)
{
    // Calculate per-pixel normal and light vector
    vec3 N = normalize(fs_in.normal);
    vec3 L = normalize(light_pos - fs_in.view);

    // Simple N dot L diffuse lighting
    float tc = pow(max(0.0, dot(N, L)), 5.0);

    // Sample from cell shading texture
    color = texture(tex_toon, tc) * (tc * 0.8 + 0.2);
}
```

Listing 13.26: The toon fragment shader

The fragment shader for our toon shader calculates the diffuse lighting coefficient in the usual way, but rather than applying it directly, it uses this coefficient to look up into a texture containing our four cell colors. In a traditional toon shader, the diffuse coefficient would be used unmodified as a texture coordinate and the resulting color would be sent directly to the output of the fragment shader. However, here we raise the diffuse coeffient to a small power and then scale that color returned from the ramp texture by the diffuse lighting coefficient before outputting the result. This makes the toon highlights slightly sharper and leaves the image with some depth rather than the plain flat shading that would be achieved with the content of the toon ramp texture only.

The resulting output is shown in Figure 13.23, where the banding and highlighting due to the toon shader are clearly visible. Both the red color ramp texture and the toon-shaded torus are also shown together in Color Plate 15.

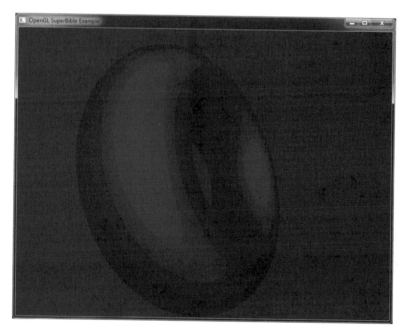

Figure 13.23: A toon-shaded torus

Alternative Rendering Methods

Traditional forward rendering executes the complete graphics pipeline, starting with a vertex shader and following through with any number of subsequent stages, most likely terminating with a fragment shader. That fragment shader is responsible for calculating the final color of the fragment,[3] and after each drawing command, the content the framebuffer becomes more and more complete. However, it doesn't have to be this way. As you will see in this section, it's quite possible to partially calculate some of the shading information and finish the scene after all of the objects have been rendered, or even to forego traditional vertex-based geometry representations and do all of your geometry processing in the *fragment shader*.

Deferred Shading

In almost all of the examples you've seen so far, the fragment shader is used to calculate the final color of the fragment that it's rendering. Now, consider what happens when you render an object that ends up covering

---

3. Post-processing not withstanding.

something that's already been drawn to the screen. This is known as *overdraw*. In this case, the result of the previous calculation is replaced with the new rendering, essentially throwing away all of the work that the first fragment shader did. If the fragment shader is expensive, or if there is a lot of overdraw, this can add up to a large drain on performance. To get around this, we can use a technique called *deferred shading*, which is a method to delay the heavy processing that might be performed by a fragment shader until the last moment.

To do this, we first render the scene using a very simple fragment shader that outputs into the framebuffer any parameters of each fragment that we might need for shading it later. In most cases, multiple framebuffer attachments will be required. If you refer to the earlier sections on lighting, you will see that the types of information you might need for lighting the scene would be the diffuse color of the fragment, its surface normal, and its position in world space. The last piece of information can usually be reconstructed from screen space and the depth buffer, but it can be convenient to simply store the world space coordinate of each fragment in a framebuffer attachment. The framebuffer used for storing this intermediate information is often referred to as a *G-buffer*. Here, G stands for "geometry," as the buffer stores information about the geometry at that point rather than image properties.

Once the G-buffer has been generated, it is possible to shade each and every point on the screen using a single full-screen quad. This final pass will use the full complexity of the final lighting algorithms, but rather than being applied to each pixel of each triangle, it is applied to each pixel in the framebuffer exactly once. This can substantially reduce the cost of shading fragments, especially if many lights or a complex shading algorithm is in use.

Generating the G-Buffer

The first stage of a deferred renderer is to create the G-buffer, which is implemented using a framebuffer object with several attachments. OpenGL can support framebuffers with up to eight attachments and each attachment can have up to four 32-bit channels (using the GL_RGBA32F internal format, for example). However, each channel of each attachment consumes some *memory bandwidth*. If we don't pay attention to the amount of data we write to the framebuffer, the savings from deferring the shading may be outweighed by the added cost of the memory bandwidth required to save all of this information.

In general, 16-bit floating-point values are more than enough to store colors[4] and normals. Usually, 32-bit floating-point values are preferred to store the world-space coordinates to preserve accuracy. Additional components that might be stored for the purposes of shading might be derived from the material. For example, we may store the specular exponent (or shininess factor) at each pixel. Given all of the data, the varying precision requirements, and the consideration of efficiency of memory bandwidth, it's a good idea to attempt to pack the data together into otherwise unrelated components of wider framebuffer formats.

In our example, we'll use three 16-bit components to store the normal at each fragment, three 16-bit components to store the fragment's albedo (flat color), three 32-bit floating-point components to store[5] the world-space coordinate of the fragment, a 32-bit integer component to store a per-pixel object or material index, and a 32-bit component to store the per-pixel specular power factor.

The sum total of these bits is six 16-bit components and five 32-bit components. How on earth will we represent this with a single framebuffer? Actually, it's fairly simple. For the six 16-bit components, we can pack them into the first three 32-bit components of a GL_RGBA32UI format framebuffer. This leaves a fourth component that we can use to store our 32-bit object identifier. Now, we have four more 32-bit components to store—the three components of our world-space coordinate and the specular power. These can simply be packed into a GL_RGBA32F format framebuffer attachment. The code to create our G-buffer framebuffer is shown in Listing 13.27.

```
GLuint gbuffer;
GLuint gbuffer_tex[3];

glGenFramebuffers(1, &gbuffer);
glBindFramebuffer(GL_FRAMEBUFFER, gbuffer);

glGenTextures(3, gbuffer_tex);
glBindTexture(GL_TEXTURE_2D, gbuffer_tex[0]);
glTexStorage2D(GL_TEXTURE_2D, 1, GL_RGBA32UI,
               MAX_DISPLAY_WIDTH, MAX_DISPLAY_HEIGHT);
glTexParameteri(GL_TEXTURE_2D, GL_TEXTURE_MIN_FILTER, GL_NEAREST);
glTexParameteri(GL_TEXTURE_2D, GL_TEXTURE_MAG_FILTER, GL_NEAREST);

glBindTexture(GL_TEXTURE_2D, gbuffer_tex[1]);
glTexStorage2D(GL_TEXTURE_2D, 1, GL_RGBA32F,
               MAX_DISPLAY_WIDTH, MAX_DISPLAY_HEIGHT);
```

---

4. Even when rendering in HDR, the color content of a G-buffer can be stored as 8-bit values so long as the final passes operate at higher precision.

5. Several methods exist to reconstruct the world-space coordinates of a fragment from its screen space coordinates, but for this example, we'll store them directly in the framebuffer.

```
glTexParameteri(GL_TEXTURE_2D, GL_TEXTURE_MIN_FILTER, GL_NEAREST);
glTexParameteri(GL_TEXTURE_2D, GL_TEXTURE_MAG_FILTER, GL_NEAREST);

glBindTexture(GL_TEXTURE_2D, gbuffer_tex[2]);
glTexStorage2D(GL_TEXTURE_2D, 1, GL_DEPTH_COMPONENT32F,
               MAX_DISPLAY_WIDTH, MAX_DISPLAY_HEIGHT);

glFramebufferTexture(GL_FRAMEBUFFER, GL_COLOR_ATTACHMENT0,
                     gbuffer_tex[0], 0);
glFramebufferTexture(GL_FRAMEBUFFER, GL_COLOR_ATTACHMENT1,
                     gbuffer_tex[1], 0);
glFramebufferTexture(GL_FRAMEBUFFER, GL_DEPTH_ATTACHMENT,
                     gbuffer_tex[2], 0);

glBindFramebuffer(GL_FRAMEBUFFER, 0);
```

Listing 13.27: Initializing a G-buffer

Now that we have a framebuffer to represent our G-buffer, it's time to start
rendering into it. We mentioned packing multiple 16-bit components into
half as many 32-bit components. This can be achieved using the GLSL
function packHalf2x16. Assuming our fragment shader has all of the
necessary input information, it can export all of the data it needs into two
color outputs, as seen in Listing 13.28.

```
#version 420 core

layout (location = 0) out uvec4 color0;
layout (location = 1) out vec4 color1;

in VS_OUT
{
    vec3      ws_coords;
    vec3      normal;
    vec3      tangent;
    vec2      texcoord0;
    flat uint     material_id;
} fs_in;

layout (binding = 0) uniform sampler2D tex_diffuse;

void main(void)
{
    uvec4 outvec0 = uvec4(0);
    vec4 outvec1 = vec4(0);

    vec3 color = texture(tex_diffuse, fs_in.texcoord0).rgb;

    outvec0.x = packHalf2x16(color.xy);
    outvec0.y = packHalf2x16(vec2(color.z, fs_in.normal.x));
    outvec0.z = packHalf2x16(fs_in.normal.yz);
    outvec0.w = fs_in.material_id;

    outvec1.xyz = fs_in.ws_coords;
    outvec1.w = 60.0;

    color0 = outvec0;
    color1 = outvec1;
}
```

Listing 13.28: Writing to a G-buffer

As you can see from Listing 13.28, we have made extensive use of the
`packHalf2x16` and `floatBitsToUint` functions. Although this seems like
quite a bit of code, it is generally "free" relative to the memory bandwidth
cost of storing all of this data. Once you have rendered your scene to the
G-buffer, it's time to calculate the final color of all of the pixels in the
framebuffer.

Consuming the G-Buffer

Given a G-buffer with diffuse colors, normals, specular powers,
world-space coordinates, and other information, we need to read from it
and reconstruct the original data that we packed in Listing 13.28.
Essentially, we employ the inverse operations to our packing code and
make use of the `unpackHalf2x16` and `uintBitsToFloat` functions to
convert the integer data stored in our textures into the floating-point data
we need. The unpacking code is shown in Listing 13.29.

```
layout (binding = 0) uniform usampler2D gbuf0;
layout (binding = 1) uniform sampler2D gbuf1;

struct fragment_info_t
{
    vec3 color;
    vec3 normal;
    float specular_power;
    vec3 ws_coord;
    uint material_id;
};

void unpackGBuffer(ivec2 coord,
                   out fragment_info_t fragment)
{
    uvec4 data0 = texelFetch(gbuf_tex0, ivec2(coord), 0);
    vec4 data1 = texelFetch(gbuf_tex1, ivec2(coord), 0);
    vec2 temp;

    temp = unpackHalf2x16(data0.y);
    fragment.color = vec3(unpackHalf2x16(data0.x), temp.x);
    fragment.normal = normalize(vec3(temp.y, unpackHalf2x16(data0.z)));
    fragment.material_id = data0.w;

    fragment.ws_coord = data1.xyz;
    fragment.specular_power = data1.w;
}
```

Listing 13.29: Unpacking data from a G-buffer

We can visualize the contents of our G-buffer using a simple fragment
shader that reads from the resulting textures that are attached to it,
unpacks the data into its original form, and then outputs the desired parts
to the normal color framebuffer. Rendering a simple scene into the
G-buffer and visualizing it gives the result shown in Figure 13.24.

Figure 13.24: Visualizing components of a G-buffer

The upper-left quadrant of Figure 13.24 shows the diffuse albedo, the upper-right quadrant shows the surface normals, the lower-left quadrant shows the world-space coordinates, and the lower-right quadrant shows the material ID at each pixel, represented as different levels of gray.

Once we have unpacked the contents of the G-buffer into our shader, we have everything we need to calculate the final color of the fragment. We can use any of the techniques covered in the earlier part of this chapter. In this example, we use standard Phong shading. After unpacking the fragment_info_t structure in Listing 13.29, we can pass it directly to a lighting function that will calculate the final color of the fragment from the lighting information. Such a function is shown in Listing 13.30.

```
vec4 light_fragment(fragment_info_t fragment)
{
    int i;
    vec4 result = vec4(0.0, 0.0, 0.0, 1.0);

    if (fragment.material_id != 0)
```

```
{
    for (i = 0; i < num_lights; i++)
    {
        vec3 L = fragment.ws_coord - light[i].position;
        float dist = length(L);
        L = normalize(L);
        vec3 N = normalize(fragment.normal);
        vec3 R = reflect(-L, N);
        float NdotR = max(0.0, dot(N, R));
        float NdotL = max(0.0, dot(N, L));
        float attenuation = 50.0 / (pow(dist, 2.0) + 1.0);

        vec3 diffuse_color = light[i].color * fragment.color *
                             NdotL * attenuation;
        vec3 specular_color = light[i].color *
                              pow(NdotR, fragment.specular_power)
                              * attenuation;

        result += vec4(diffuse_color + specular_color, 0.0);
    }
}

return result;
}
```

Listing 13.30: Lighting a fragment using data from a G-buffer

The final result of lighting a scene using deferred shading is shown in Figure 13.25. In the scene, more than 200 copies of an object are rendered using instancing. Each pixel in the frame has some overdraw. The final pass over the scene calculates the contribution of 64 lights. Increasing and decreasing the number of lights in the scene has little effect on performance. In fact, the most expensive part of rendering the scene is generating the G-buffer in the first place and then reading and unpacking it in the lighting shader, which is performed once in this example, regardless of the number of lights in the scene. In this example, we have used a relatively inefficient G-buffer representation for the sake of clarity. This consumes quite a bit of memory bandwidth, and the performance of the program could probably be increased somewhat by reducing the storage requirements of the buffer.

Normal Mapping and Deferred Shading

In the "Normal Mapping" section earlier in this chapter, you read about normal mapping, which is a technique to store local surface normals in a texture and then use them to add detail to rendered models. To achieve this, most normal mapping algorithms (including the one described in the "Normal Mapping" section) use *tangent space normals* and perform all lighting calculations in that coordinate space. This involves calculating the light and view vectors, $\vec{L}$ and $\vec{V}$, in the vertex shader, transforming them into tangent space using the TBN matrix, and passing them to the

Figure 13.25: Final rendering using deferred shading

fragment shader where lighting calculations are performed. However, in deferred renderers, the normals that you store in the G-buffer are generally in world or view space.

To generate view-space normals[6] that can be stored into a G-buffer for deferred shading, we need to take the tangent-space normals read from the normal map and transform them into view space during G-buffer generation. This requires minor modifications to the normal mapping algorithm.

First, we do not calculate $\vec{V}$ or $\vec{L}$ in the vertex shader, nor do we construct the TBN matrix there. Instead, we calculate the view-space normal and tangent vectors $\vec{N}$ and $\vec{T}$ and pass them to the fragment shader. In the fragment shader, we renormalize $\vec{N}$ and $\vec{T}$ and take their cross product to produce the bitangent vector $\vec{B}$. This is used in the fragment shader to construct the TBN matrix local to the fragment being shaded. We read the tangent-space normal from the normal map as usual, but transform it through the inverse of the TBN matrix (which is simply its transpose,

6. View space is generally preferred for lighting calculations over world space, as the former has consistent accuracy independent of the viewer's position. When the viewer is placed at a large distance from the origin, world-space precision breaks down near the viewer, which can affect the accuracy of lighting calculations.

assuming it encodes only rotation). This moves the normal vector from tangent space into view space. The normal is then stored in the G-buffer. The remainder of the shading algorithm that performs lighting calculations is unchanged from that described earlier.

The vertex shader used to generate the G-buffer with normal mapping applied is almost unmodified from the version that does not apply normal mapping. However, the updated fragment shader is shown in Listing 13.31.

```glsl
#version 420 core

layout (location = 0) out uvec4 color0;
layout (location = 1) out vec4 color1;

in VS_OUT
{
    vec3        ws_coords;
    vec3        normal;
    vec3        tangent;
    vec2        texcoord0;
    flat uint   material_id;
} fs_in;

layout (binding = 0) uniform sampler2D tex_diffuse;
layout (binding = 1) uniform sampler2D tex_normal_map;

void main(void)
{
    vec3 N = normalize(fs_in.normal);
    vec3 T = normalize(fs_in.tangent);
    vec3 B = cross(N, T);
    mat3 TBN = mat3(T, B, N);

    vec3 nm = texture(tex_normal_map, fs_in.texcoord0).xyz * 2.0 - vec3(1.0);
    nm = TBN * normalize(nm);

    uvec4 outvec0 = uvec4(0);
    vec4 outvec1 = vec4(0);

    vec3 color = texture(tex_diffuse, fs_in.texcoord0).rgb;

    outvec0.x = packHalf2x16(color.xy);
    outvec0.y = packHalf2x16(vec2(color.z, nm.x));
    outvec0.z = packHalf2x16(nm.yz);
    outvec0.w = fs_in.material_id;

    outvec1.xyz = floatBitsToUint(fs_in.ws_coords);
    outvec1.w = 60.0;

    color0 = outvec0;
    color1 = outvec1;
}
```

Listing 13.31: Deferred shading with normal mapping (fragment shader)

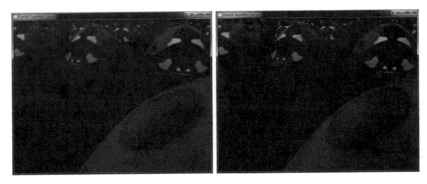

Figure 13.26: Deferred shading with (left) and without (right) normal maps

Finally, Figure 13.26 shows the difference between applying normal maps to the scene (left) and using the interpolated per-vertex normal (right). As you can see, substantially more detail is visible in the left image that has normal maps applied. All of this code is contained in the deferredshading example, which generated these images.

Deferred Shading: Downsides

While deferred shading can reduce the impact of complex lighting or shading calculations on the performance of your application, it won't solve all of your problems. Besides being very bandwidth heavy and requiring a lot of memory for all of the textures you attach to your G-buffer, there are a number of other downsides to deferred shading. With a bit of effort, you might be able to work around some of them, but before you launch into writing a shiny new deferred renderer, you should consider the following issues.

First, the bandwidth considerations of a deferred shading implementation should be considered carefully. In our example, we used 256 bits of information for each pixel in the G-buffer, but we didn't make particularly efficient use of them. We packed our world-space coordinates directly in the G-buffer, consuming 96 bits of space (remember, we used three 32-bit floating-point entries for this). However, we have the screen-space coordinates of each pixel when we render our final pass, which we can retrieve from the x and y components of gl_FragCoord and from the content of the depth buffer. To obtain world-space coordinates, we need to undo the viewport transform (which is simply a scale and bias) and then move the resulting coordinates from clip space into world space by applying the inverse of the projection and view matrices (which normally transforms coordinates from world space to view space). As the view matrix usually encodes only translation and rotation, it is generally easy to invert. However, the projection matrix and subsequent homogenous division are more difficult to reverse.

We also used 48 bits to encode our surface normals in the G-buffer by using three 16-bit floating-point numbers per normal. We could instead store only the x and y components of the normal and reconstruct the z coordinate using the knowledge that the normal should be a unit-length vector and, therefore, $z = \sqrt{x^2 + y^2}$. We must also deduce the sign of z. In general, the safest way to do this is to use one additional bit (possibly coming at the expense of an LSB of one of x or y) to encode the sign. We reconstruct the z component as if it were positive, and then negate it based on the value of this bit. There are other, more advanced encodings for packing normals into G-buffers, but they are beyond the scope of this chapter.

Finally, the specular power and material ID components were stored using full 32-bit quantities. It is likely that you won't have more than 60,000 unique materials in your scene and can therefore use 16 bits for a material ID. Also, it is reasonable to store specular powers as logarithms and raise 2 to the power of the shininess factor in your lighting shader. This will require substantially fewer bits to store the specular power factor in the G-buffer.

Another downside of deferred shading algorithms is that they generally don't play well with antialiasing. Normally, when OpenGL *resolves* a multi-sample buffer, it will take a (possibly weighted) average of the samples in the pixel. Averaging depth values, normals, and in particular meta-data such as material IDs just doesn't work. So, if you want to implement antialiasing, you'll need to use multi-sampled textures for all of the off-screen buffers attached to your G-buffer. What's worse, because the final pass consists of a single large polygon (or possibly two) that covers the entire scene, none of the interior pixels will be considered edge pixels, breaking traditional multi-sample antialiasing. For the resolve pass, you will need to either write a special custom resolve shader or run the whole thing at sample rate, which will substantially increase the cost of lighting your scene.

Finally, most deferred shading algorithms can't deal with transparency. This is because at each pixel in the G-buffer, we store only the information for a single fragment. To properly implement transparency, we would need to know all of the information for every fragment starting closest to the viewer until an opaque fragment is hit. There are algorithms that do this, and they are often used to implement order-independent transparency, for example. Another approach is simply to render all non-transparent surfaces using deferred shading and then to render transparent materials in a second pass through the scene. This requires your renderer either to keep a list of transparent surfaces that it skipped as it traversed the scene or to traverse your scene twice. Either option can be pretty expensive.

In summary, deferred shading can bring substantial performance improvements to your application if you keep in mind the limitations of the techniques and restrict yourself to algorithms that it handles well.

Screen-Space Techniques

Most of the rendering techniques described in this book so far have been implemented per primitive. However, in the "Deferred Shading" section, we discussed deferred shading, which suggested that at least some of the rendering procedures can be implemented in screen space. In this subsection, we discuss a few more algorithms that push shading into screen space. In some cases, this is the only way to implement certain techniques. In other cases, we can achieve a significant performance advantage by delaying processing until all geometry has already been rendered.

Ambient Occlusion

Ambient occlusion is a technique for simulating one component of *global illumination*. Global illumination is the observed effect of light bouncing from object to object in a scene such that surfaces are lit indirectly by the light reflected from nearby surfaces. Ambient light is an approximation to this scattered light and is a small, fixed amount added to lighting calculations. However, in deep creases or gaps between objects, less light will illuminate them due to the nearby surfaces *occluding* the light sources—hence the term *ambient occlusion*. Real-time global illumination is a topic of current research, and while some fairly impressive work has been presented, this is an unsolved problem. However, we can produce some reasonably good results with ad hoc methods and gross approximations. One such approximation is *screen-space ambient occlusion* (SSAO), which we will discuss here.

To explain the technique, we will start in two dimensions. Ambient light could be considered to be the amount of light that would hit a point on a surface if it were surrounded by an arbitrarily large number of small point lights. On a perfectly flat surface, any point is visible to all of the lights above that surface. However, on a bumpy surface, not all of the lights will

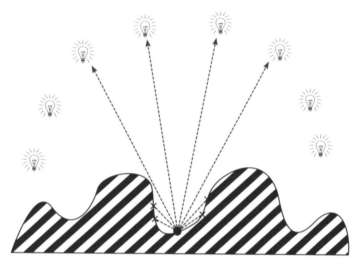

Figure 13.27: Bumpy surface occluding points

be visible from all points on that surface—the bumpier the surface, the fewer lights that will be visible from any given point. This is illustrated in Figure 13.27.

In the diagram, you can see that we have eight point lights distributed roughly equally around a surface. For the point under consideration, we draw a line from that point to each of the eight lights. You can see that a point at the bottoms of a valley in the surface can see only a small number of the lights. A point at the top of a peak, however, should be able to see most, if not all, of the lights. The bumps in the surface occlude the lights from points at the bottoms of valleys, so they will receive ambient light. In a full global illumination simulation, we would literally trace lines (or rays) from each point being shaded in hundreds, perhaps thousands, of directions and determine what was hit. That's far too expensive for a real-time solution; instead, we use a method that allows us to calculate the occlusion of a point directly in screen space.

To implement this technique, we are going to march rays from each position in screen space along a random direction and determine the amount of occlusion at each point along that ray. First, we render our scene into depth and color buffers attached to an FBO. Along with this, we render the normal at each fragment and its linear depth[7] in view space

---

7. We could reconstruct a linear view-space depth from the content of the depth buffer produced in the first pass by inverting the mapping of eye-space z into the 0.0 to 1.0 range stored in the depth buffer. However, for simplicity, we'll use the extra channel on our framebuffer attachment.

into a second color attachment on the same FBO. In a second pass, we use this information to compute the level of occlusion at each pixel. In this pass, we render a full-screen quad with our ambient occlusion shader. The shader reads the depth value that we render in our first pass, selects a random direction to walk in, and takes several steps along that direction. At each point along the walk, it tests whether the value in the depth buffer is less than the depth value computed along the ray. If it is, then we consider the point to be occluded.

To select a random direction, we pre-initialize a uniform buffer with a large number of random vectors in a unit radius sphere. Although our random vectors may point in any direction, we really want to consider only vectors that point *away* from the surface. That is, we consider just vectors lying in the hemisphere oriented around the surface normal at the point. To produce a random direction oriented in this hemisphere, we take the dot product of the surface normal (which we rendered into our color buffer earlier) and the selected random direction. If the result is negative, then the selected direction vector points into the surface and we negate it to point it back into the correctly oriented hemisphere. Figure 13.28 demonstrates the technique.

In Figure 13.28, you can see that vectors V_0, V_1, and V_4 already lie in the hemisphere that is aligned with the normal vector, N. This means that the dot product of any of these three vectors and N will be positive. However, V_2 and V_3 lie outside the desired hemisphere and it should be clear that the dot product of either of these two vectors and N will be negative. In this case, we simply negate V_2 and V_3, reorienting them into the correct hemisphere.

Once we have our random set of vectors, it's time to walk along them. To do this, we start at the point on the surface and step a small distance along our chosen distance vector. This produces a new point, complete with x, y,

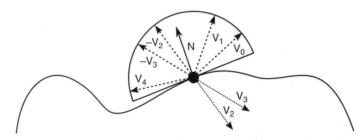

Figure 13.28: Selection of random vector in an oriented hemisphere

and z coordinates. We use the x and y components to read from the linear depth buffer that we rendered earlier and look up the value stored there. We compare this depth to that of the interpolated position vector and if it is closer (i.e., smaller) than the interpolated value, then our interpolated point is obscured from view in the image, and thus we consider the original point to be occluded for the purposes of the algorithm. While this is clearly far from accurate, *statistically* it works out. The number of random directions to choose, the number of steps along each direction, and the size of each step are all parameters that we can choose to control the output image quality. The more directions we choose, the farther we step, and the more steps we take in each direction, the better the output image quality will be. Figure 13.29 shows the effect of adding more sample directions on the result of the ambient occlusion algorithm.

In Figure 13.29, directions are added from left to right, top to bottom, starting with a single direction in the top left image, with 4 in the top right image, 16 in the bottom left image, and 64 in the bottom right image. As you can see, it is not until we have 64 directions that the image becomes smooth. With fewer directions, severe banding is seen in the image. There are many approaches to reduce this, but one

Figure 13.29: Effect of increasing direction count on ambient occlusion

Figure 13.30: Effect of introducing noise in ambient occlusion

of the most effective is to *randomize* the distance along each of the occlusion rays we take for each sample. This introduces noise into the image, but also smoothes the result, improving overall quality. Figure 13.30 shows the result of introducing this randomness into the image.

As you can see in Figure 13.30, the introduction of randomness in the step rate along the occlusion rays improves image quality substantially. Again, from left to right, top to bottom, we have taken 1, 4, 16, and 64 directions, respectively. With random ray step rates, the image produced by considering only a single ray direction has gone from looking quite corrupted to looking noisy, but correct. Even the 4-direction result (shown in the top right image in Figure 13.30) has acceptable quality, whereas the equivalent image in Figure 13.29 still exhibits considerable banding. The 16-sample image in the bottom right of Figure 13.30 is almost as good as the 64-sample image in Figure 13.29, and the 64-sample image in Figure 13.30 does not show much improvement over it. It is even

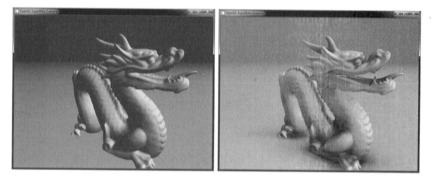

Figure 13.31: Ambient occlusion applied to a rendered scene

possible to compensate for the noise introduced by this method, but that is beyond the scope of this example.

Once we have our ambient occlusion term, we need to apply it to our rendered image. Ambient occlusion is simply the amount by which ambient light is occluded. Therefore, all we need to do is multiply the ambient lighting term in our shading equation by the occlusion term, which causes the creases of our model to have less ambient lighting applied to them. Figure 13.31 shows the effect of applying the screen-space ambient occlusion algorithm to a rendered scene.

In Figure 13.31, the image on the left is the diffuse and specular terms of the lighting model only. The dragon is suspended just over a plane, although depth is very hard to judge in the image. The image on the right has screen-space ambient occlusion applied. As you can see, not only is the definition of some of the dragon's details more apparent, but the dragon also casts a soft shadow on the ground below it, increasing the sense of depth.

In our first pass, we simply render the diffuse and specular terms into one color attachment as usual, and then we render the surface normal and linear eye-space depth into a second color attachment. The shader to do this is relatively straightforward and is similar to many of the shaders presented thus far in the book. The second pass of the algorithm is the interesting part—this is where we apply the ambient occlusion effect. It is shown in its entirety in Listing 13.32, which is part of the ssao sample application.

```glsl
#version 450 core

// Samplers for prerendered color, normal, and depth
layout (binding = 0) uniform sampler2D sColor;
layout (binding = 1) uniform sampler2D sNormalDepth;

// Final output
layout (location = 0) out vec4 color;

// Various uniforms controlling SSAO effect
uniform float ssao_level = 1.0;
uniform float object_level = 1.0;
uniform float ssao_radius = 5.0;
uniform bool weight_by_angle = true;
uniform uint point_count = 8;
uniform bool randomize_points = true;

// Uniform block containing up to 256 random directions (x,y,z,0)
// and 256 more completely random vectors
layout (binding = 0, std140) uniform SAMPLE_POINTS
{
    vec4 pos[256];
    vec4 random_vectors[256];
} points;

void main(void)
{
    // Get texture position from gl_FragCoord
    vec2 P = gl_FragCoord.xy / textureSize(sNormalDepth, 0);
    // ND = normal and depth
    vec4 ND = textureLod(sNormalDepth, P, 0);
    // Extract normal and depth
    vec3 N = ND.xyz;
    float my_depth = ND.w;

    // Local temporary variables
    int i;
    int j;
    int n;

    float occ = 0.0;
    float total = 0.0;

    // n is a pseudo-random number generated from fragment coordinate
    // and depth
    n = (int(gl_FragCoord.x * 7123.2315 + 125.232) *
         int(gl_FragCoord.y * 3137.1519 + 234.8)) ^
         int(my_depth);
    // Pull one of the random vectors
    vec4 v = points.random_vectors[n & 255];

    // r is our 'radius randomizer'
    float r = (v.r + 3.0) * 0.1;
    if (!randomize_points)
        r = 0.5;

    // For each random point (or direction)...
    for (i = 0; i < point_count; i++)
    {
        // Get direction
        vec3 dir = points.pos[i].xyz;
```

```
                // Put it into the correct hemisphere
                if (dot(N, dir) < 0.0)
                    dir = -dir;

                // f is the distance we've stepped in this direction
                // z is the interpolated depth
                float f = 0.0;
                float z = my_depth;

                // We're going to take 4 steps; we could make this
                // configurable
                total += 4.0;

                for (j = 0; j < 4; j++)
                {
                    // Step in the right direction
                    f += r;
                    // Step _towards_ viewer reduces z
                    z -= dir.z * f;

                    // Read depth from current fragment
                    float their_depth =
                        textureLod(sNormalDepth,
                                    (P + dir.xy * f * ssao_radius), 0).w;

                    // Calculate a weighting (d) for this fragment's
                    // contribution to occlusion
                    float d = abs(their_depth - my_depth);
                    d *= d;

                    // If we're obscured, accumulate occlusion
                    if ((z - their_depth) > 0.0)
                    {
                        occ += 4.0 / (1.0 + d);
                    }
                }
            }

        // Calculate occlusion amount
        float ao_amount = vec4(1.0 - occ / total);

        // Get object color from color texture
        vec4 object_color =  textureLod(sColor, P, 0);

        // Mix in ambient color scaled by SSAO level
        color = object_level * object_color +
                mix(vec4(0.2), vec4(ao_amount), ssao_level);
    }
```

Listing 13.32: Ambient occlusion fragment shader

Rendering without Triangles

In the previous section, we covered techniques that can be applied in
screen space, all of which are implemented by drawing a full-screen quad
over geometry that's already been rendered. In this section we take it one
step further and demonstrate how to render entire scenes with a single
full-screen quad.

Rendering Julia Fractals

In this next example, we render a *Julia set*, creating image data from nothing but the texture coordinates. Julia sets are related to the *Mandelbrot set*—the iconic bulblike fractal. The Mandelbrot image is generated by iterating the formula

$$Z_n = Z_{n-1}^2 + C$$

until the magnitude of Z exceeds a threshold and calculating the number of iterations. If the magnitude of Z never exceeds the threshold within the allowed number of iterations, that point is determined to be inside the Mandelbrot set and is colored with some default color. If the magnitude of Z exceeds the threshold within the allowed number of iterations, then the point is outside the set. A common visualization of the Mandelbrot set colors the point using a function of the iteration count at the time the point was determined to be outside the set. The primary difference between the Mandelbrot set and the Julia set is the initial conditions for Z and C.

When rendering the Mandelbrot set, Z is set to $(0 + 0i)$, and C is set to the coordinate of the point at which the iterations are to be performed. When rendering the Julia set, however, Z is set to the coordinate of the point at which iterations are performed, and C is set to an application-specified constant. Thus, while there is only one Mandelbrot set, there are infinitely many Julia sets—one for every possible value of C. Because of this, the Julia set can be controlled parametrically and even animated. Just as in some of the previous examples, we invoke this shader at every fragment by drawing a full-screen quad. However, rather than consuming and postprocessing data that might already be in the framebuffer, we generate the final image directly.

Let's set up the fragment shader with an input block containing just the texture coordinates. We also need a uniform to hold the value of C. To apply interesting colors to the resulting Julia image, we use a one-dimensional texture with a color gradient in it. When we've iterated a point that escapes from the set, we color the output fragment by indexing into this texture using the iteration count. Finally, we define a uniform containing the maximum number of iterations we want to perform. This allows the application to balance performance against the level of detail in the resulting image. Listing 13.33 shows the setup for our Julia renderer's fragment shader.

```
#version 450 core

in Fragment
{
    vec2 tex_coord;
} fragment;

// Here's our value of c
uniform vec2 c;

// This is the color gradient texture
uniform sampler1D tex_gradient;

// This is the maximum iterations we'll perform before we consider
// the point to be outside the set
uniform int max_iterations;

// The output color for this fragment
out vec4 output_color;
```

Listing 13.33: Setting up the Julia set renderer

Now that we have the inputs to our shader, we are ready to start rendering the Julia set. The value of C is taken from the uniform supplied by the application. The initial value of Z is taken from the incoming texture coordinates supplied by the vertex shader. Our iteration loop is shown in Listing 13.34.

```
int iterations = 0;
vec2 z = fragment.tex_coords;
const float threshold_squared = 4.0;

// While there are iterations left and we haven't escaped from
// the set yet...
while (iterations < max_iterations &&
       dot(z, z) < threshold_squared)
{
    // Iterate the value of Z as Z^2 + C
    vec2 z_squared;
    z_squared.x = z.x * z.x - z.y * z.y;
    z_squared.y = 2.0 * z.x * z.y;
    z = z_squared + c;
    iterations++;
}
```

Listing 13.34: Inner loop of the Julia renderer

The loop terminates under one of two conditions: Either we reach the maximum number of iterations allowed (iterations == max_iterations) or the magnitude of Z passes our threshold. Note that in this shader, we compare the squared magnitude of Z (found using the dot function) to the square of the threshold (the threshold_squared uniform). The two operations are equivalent, but this approach avoids a square root in the shader, improving performance. If, at the end of the loop, iterations is equal to max_iterations, we know that we ran out of iterations and the point is inside the set, so we color it black. Otherwise, our point left the set *before* we ran out of iterations, and we can color the point accordingly. To do this, we can just figure out which fraction of the total allowed iterations we used up and use that information to look up into the gradient texture. Listing 13.35 shows what the code looks like.

```
if (iterations == max_iterations)
{
    output_color = vec4(0.0, 0.0, 0.0, 0.0);
}
else
{
    output_color = texture(tex_gradient,
                           float(iterations) / float(max_iterations));
}
```

Listing 13.35: Using a gradient texture to color the Julia set

Now all that's left is to supply the gradient texture and set an appropriate value of c. For our application, we update c on each frame as a function of the currentTime parameter passed to our render function. By doing this, we can animate the fractal. Figure 13.32 shows a few frames of the Julia animation produced by the julia example program. (See Color Plate 16 in the color insert for another example.)

Ray Tracing in a Fragment Shader

OpenGL usually works by using rasterization to generate fragments for primitives such as lines, triangles, and points. This should be obvious to you by now. We send geometry into the OpenGL pipeline and for each triangle, OpenGL figures out which pixels it covers, and then runs your shader to figure out what color it should be. Ray tracing effectively inverts the problem. We throw a bunch of pixels into the pipeline (actually represented by rays) and then for each one, we figure out which pieces of geometry cover that pixel (which means our per-pixel ray hits the geometry). The biggest disadvantage of this approach when compared to traditional rasterization is that OpenGL doesn't include direct support for it, which means we have to do all of the work in our own shaders. However, this provides us with a number of advantages—in particular, we

Figure 13.32: A few frames from the Julia set animation

aren't limited[8] to just points, lines, and triangles, *and* we can figure out what happens to a ray after it hits an object. Using the same techniques as we use for figuring out what's visible from the camera, we can render reflections, shadows, and even refraction with little additional code.

In this subsection, we discuss the construction of a simple recursive ray tracer using a fragment shader. The ray tracer we produce here will be capable of rendering images consisting of simple spheres and infinite planes—enough to produce the classic "glossy spheres in a box" image. Certainly, substantially more advanced implementations exist, but this should be sufficient to convey the basic techniques. Figure 13.33 shows a simplified, 2D illustration of the basics of a simple ray tracer.

In Figure 13.33, we see the eye position that forms the origin of a ray, O, shot toward the image plane (which is our display) and intersecting it at point P. This ray is known as the primary ray and is denoted here by $R_{primary}$. The ray intersects a first sphere at the intersection point I_0. At

---

8. In fact, points, lines, and triangles are among the more complex shapes to render in a ray tracer.

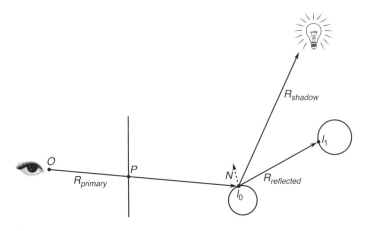

Figure 13.33: Simplified 2D illustration of ray tracing

this point, we create two additional rays. The first is directed toward the light source and is denoted by R_{shadow}. If this ray intersects anything along its way to the light source, then point I_0 is in shadow; otherwise, it is lit by the point. In addition to the shadow ray, we shoot a second ray, $R_{reflected}$, by reflecting the incoming ray $R_{primary}$ around the surface normal at I_0, N.

Shading for ray tracing isn't all that different from the types of shading and lighting algorithms we've looked at already in this book. We can still calculate diffuse and specular terms, apply normal maps and other textures, and so on. However, we also consider the contribution of the rays that we shoot in other directions. So, for I_0, we'll shade it using $R_{primary}$ as our view vector, N as our normal, R_{shadow} as our light vector, and so on. Next, we'll shoot a ray off toward I_1 ($R_{reflected}$), shade the surface *there*, and then add that contribution (scaled by the reflectivity of the surface at I_0) back to the color accumulated at P. The result is crisp, clean reflections.

Now, given the origin (O), which is usually at the origin in view space and point P, we calculate the direction of ray $R_{primary}$ and begin the ray tracing process. This involves calculating the intersection of a line (our ray) and an object in the scene (each sphere). The intersection of a ray with a sphere works as follows.

Given a ray R with origin O and direction $\vec{D}$, then at time t, a point on that ray is $O + t\vec{D}$. Also, given a sphere at center C with radius r, any point on its surface is at distance r from C; moreover, the squared distance between C and any point on the sphere's surface is r^2. This is convenient because the dot product of a vector with itself is its squared length. Thus, we can say that for a point P at $O + t\vec{D}$,

$$(P - C) \cdot (P - C) = r^2$$

Substituting for P, we have

$$(O + t\vec{D} - C) \cdot (O + t\vec{D} - C) = r^2$$

Expanding this gives us a quadratic equation in t:

$$(\vec{D} \cdot \vec{D})t^2 + 2(O - C) \cdot \vec{D}t + (O - C) \cdot (O - C) - r^2 = 0$$

Writing this in the more familiar form of $At^2 + Bt + C = 0$, we have

$$A = \vec{D} \cdot \vec{D}$$
$$B = 2(O - C) \cdot \vec{D}$$
$$C = (O - C) \cdot (O - C) - r^2$$

As a simple quadratic equation, we can solve for t, knowing that there are either zero, one, or two solutions.

$$t = \frac{-B \pm \sqrt{B^2 - 4AC}}{2A}$$

Given that we know that our direction vector $\vec{D}$ is normalized, then its length is 1, and, therefore, A is 1 as well. This simplifies things a little, and we can simply say that our solution for t is

$$t = \frac{-B \pm \sqrt{B^2 - 4C}}{2}$$

If $4C$ is greater than B^2, then the term under the square root is negative and there is no solution for t, which means that there is no intersection between the ray and the sphere. If B^2 is equal to $4C$, then there is only one solution, meaning that the ray just grazes the sphere. If that solution is positive, then this occurs in front of the viewer and we have found our intersection point. If the single solution for t is negative, then the intersection point is behind the viewer. Finally, if there are two solutions to the equation, we take the smallest non-negative solution for t as our intersection point. We simply plug this value back into $P = O + t\vec{D}$ and retrieve the coordinates of the intersection point in 3D space.

Shader code to perform this intersection test is shown in Listing 13.36.

```
struct ray
{
    vec3 origin;
    vec3 direction;
};

struct sphere
{
    vec3 center;
    float radius;
};

float intersect_ray_sphere(ray R,
                           sphere S,
                           out vec3 hitpos,
                           out vec3 normal)
{
    vec3 v = R.origin - S.center;
    float B = 2.0 * dot(R.direction, v);
    float C = dot(v, v) - S.radius * S.radius;
    float B2 = B * B;

    float f = B2 - 4.0 * C;

    if (f < 0.0)
        return 0.0;

    float t0 = -B + sqrt(f);
    float t1 = -B - sqrt(f);
    float t = min(max(t0, 0.0), max(t1, 0.0)) * 0.5;

    if (t == 0.0)
        return 0.0;

    hitpos = R.origin + t * R.direction;
    normal = normalize(hitpos - S.center);

    return t;
}
```

Listing 13.36: Ray–sphere interesection test

Given the structures ray and sphere, the function intersect_ray_sphere in Listing 13.36 returns 0.0 if the ray does not hit the sphere and the value of t if it does. If an intersection is found, the position of that intersection is returned in the output parameter hitpos and the normal of the surface at the intersection point is returned in the output parameter normal. We use the returned value of t to determine the closest intersection point along each ray by initializing a temporary variable to the longest allowed ray length, and taking the minimum between it and the distance returned by intersect_ray_sphere for each sphere in the scene. The code to do this is shown in Listing 13.37.

```
// Declare a uniform block with our spheres in it
layout (std140, binding = 1) uniform SPHERES
{
    sphere      S[128];
};

// Textures with the ray origin and direction in them
layout (binding = 0) uniform sampler2D tex_origin;
layout (binding = 1) uniform sampler2D tex_direction;

// Construct a ray using the two textures
ray R;

R.origin = texelFetch(tex_origin, ivec2(gl_FragCoord.xy), 0).xyz;
R.direction = normalize(texelFetch(tex_direction, ivec2(gl_FragCoord.xy), 0).xyz);

float min_t = 1000000.0f;
float t;

// For each sphere...
for (i = 0; i < num_spheres; i++)
{
    // Find the intersection point
    t = intersect_ray_sphere(R, S[i], hitpos, normal);

    // If there is an intersection
    if (t != 0.0)
    {
        // And that intersection is less than our current best
        if (t < min_t)
        {
            // Record it
            min_t = t;
            hit_position = hitpos;
            hit_normal = normal;
            sphere_index = i;
        }
    }
}
```

Listing 13.37: Determining closest intersection point

If all we do at each point is write white wherever we hit something, and then trace rays into a scene containing a single sphere, we produce the image shown in Figure 13.34.

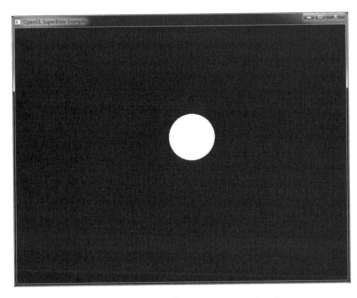

Figure 13.34: Our first ray-traced sphere

However, this isn't particularly interesting—we'll need to light the point. The surface normal is important for lighting calculations (as you have read already in this chapter), and this is returned by our intersection function. We perform lighting calculations in the usual way in the ray tracer—taking the surface normal, the view-space coordinate (calculated during the intersection test), and material parameters and shading the point. By applying the lighting equations you've already learned about, we can retrieve the image shown in Figure 13.35.

Although the normal is used in lighting calculations, it is also very important for the next few steps in the ray tracer. For each light in the scene, we calculate its contribution to the surface's shading and accumulate all of these contributions to produce the final color. This is where the first real advantage of ray tracing comes in. Given a surface point P and a light coordinate L, we form a new ray, setting its origin O to P and its direction $\vec{D}$ to the normalized vector from P to L, $\frac{L-P}{|L-P|}$. This is known as a *shadow ray* (pictured as R_{shadow} in Figure 13.33). We can then test the objects in the scene to see if the light is visible from that point. If the ray doesn't hit anything, then there is line-of-sight from the point being shaded to the light; otherwise, it is occluded and therefore in shadow. As you can imagine, shadows are something that ray tracers do very well.

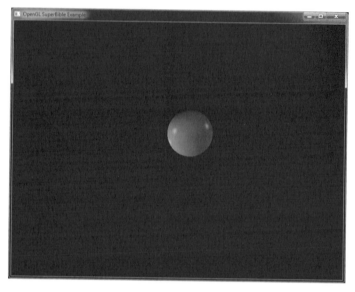

Figure 13.35: Our first lit ray-traced sphere

However, it doesn't end there. Just as we constructed a new ray starting from our intersection and pointing in the direction of our light source, so we can construct a ray pointing in any direction. For example, given that we know the surface normal at the ray's intersection with the sphere, we can use GLSL's reflect to reflect the incoming ray direction around the plane defined by this normal and shoot a new ray away from the plane in this direction. This ray is simply sent as input to our ray tracing algorithm, the intersection point it generates is shaded, and the resulting color is added into the the scene.

You may have noticed in Listing 13.37 that at each pixel, we read an origin and a direction from a texture. Ray tracing is a recursive algorithm; that is, you trace the ray, shade the point, create a new ray, trace it, and continue. GLSL doesn't allow recursion, so instead we implement this operation using a stack maintained in an array of textures.

To maintain all the data that we'll need for our ray tracer, we create an array of framebuffer objects, and to each we attach four textures as color attachments. These hold, for each pixel in the framebuffer, the final composite color, the origin of a ray, the current direction of the ray, and the accumulated reflected color of the ray. In our application, we allow each ray to take up to five bounces; thus we need five framebuffer objects, each with four textures attached to it. The first (the composite color) is

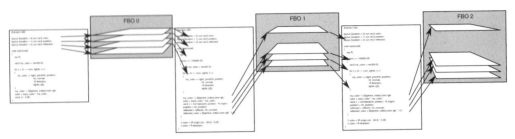

Figure 13.36: Implementing a stack using framebuffer objects

common to all framebuffer objects, but the other three are unique to each framebuffer. During each pass, we read from one set of textures and write into the next set via the framebuffer object. This is illustrated in Figure 13.36.

To initialize our ray tracer, we run a shader that writes the starting origin and ray direction into the first origin and direction textures. We also initialize our accumulation texture to 0s, and our reflection color texture to all 1s. Next, we run our actual ray tracing shader by drawing a full-screen quad once for each bounce of the rays we want to trace. On each pass, we bind the origin, direction, and reflected color textures from the previous pass. We also bind a framebuffer that has the outgoing origin, direction, and reflection textures attached to it as color attachments—these textures will be used in the next pass. Then, for each pixel, the shader forms a ray using the origin and direction stored in the first two textures, traces it into the scene, lights the intersection point, multiplies the result by the value stored in the reflected color texture, and sends it to its first output.

To enable composition into the final output texture, we attach it to the first color attachment of each framebuffer object and enable blending for that attachment with the blending function set to GL_ONE for both the source and destination factors. This causes the output to be added to the existing content of that attachment. To the other outputs, we write the intersection position, the reflected ray direction, and the reflectivity coeffient of the material that we use for shading the ray's intersection point.

If we add a few more spheres to the scene, we can have them reflect one another by applying this technique. Figure 13.37 shows the scene with a few more spheres thrown in with an increasing number of bounces of each ray.

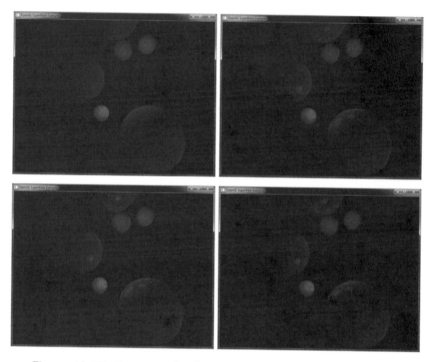

Figure 13.37: Ray-traced spheres with increasing ray bounces

As you can see in Figure 13.37, the top left image (which includes no secondary rays) is pretty dull. As soon as we introduce the first bounce in the top right image, we begin to see reflections of the spheres. Adding a second bounce in the bottom left image, we can see reflections of spheres in the reflections of the spheres. In the third bounce on the second right, the effect is more subtle, but if you look very closely, there are reflections of spheres in spheres in spheres.

Of course, a scene made entirely of spheres really isn't very exciting. What we need to do is add more object types. Although in theory any object could be ray traced, another form that is relatively easy to perform intersection tests with is the plane. One representation of a plane is a normal (which is constant for a plane) and a distance from the origin of the point on the plane that lies along that normal. The normal is a three-dimensional vector and the distance is a scalar value. As such, we can describe a plane with a single four-component vector. We pack the normal into the x, y, and z components of the vector and the distance from the origin into the w component. In fact, given a plane normal N

and distance from the origin d, the implicit equation of a plane can be represented as

$$P \cdot N + d = 0$$

where P is a point in the plane. Given that we have P, a point on our ray defined as

$$P = O + t\vec{D}$$

we can simply substitute this value of P into the implicit equation to retrieve

$$(O + t\vec{D}) \cdot N + d = 0$$

Solving for t, we arrive at

$$O \cdot N + t\vec{D} \cdot N + d = 0$$
$$t\vec{D} \cdot N = -(O \cdot N + d)$$
$$t = \frac{-(O \cdot N + d)}{\vec{D} \cdot N}$$

As you can see from the equation, if $\vec{D} \cdot N$ is zero, then the denominator of the fraction is zero and there is no solution for t. This occurs when the ray direction is parallel to the plane (thus it is perpendicular to the plane's normal and their dot product is zero), and so never intersects it. Otherwise, we can find a real value for t. Again, once we know the value of t, we can substitute it back into our ray equation, $P = O + t\vec{D}$, to retrieve our intersection point. If t is less than zero, we know that the ray intersects the plane *behind* the viewer, which we consider here to be a miss. Code to perform this intersection test is shown in Listing 13.38.

```
float intersect_ray_plane(ray R,
                          vec4 P,
                          out vec3 hitpos,
                          out vec3 normal)
```

```
{
    vec3 O = R.origin;
    vec3 D = R.direction;
    vec3 N = P.xyz;
    float d = P.w;

    float denom = dot(N, D);

    if (denom == 0.0)
        return 0.0;

    float t = -(d + dot(O, N)) / denom;

    if (t < 0.0)
        return 0.0;

    hitpos = O + t * D;
    normal = N;

    return t;
}
```

Listing 13.38: Ray–plane interesection test

Adding a plane to our scene behind our spheres produces the image shown on the left of Figure 13.38. Although this adds some depth to our scene, it doesn't show the full effect of the ray tracer. By adding a couple of bounces, we can clearly see the reflections of the spheres in the plane, and of the plane in the spheres.

Now, if we add a few more planes, we can enclose our scene in a box. The resulting image is shown in the top left image in Figure 13.39. However, when we bounce the rays further, the effect of reflection becomes more and more apparent. You can see the result of adding more bounces as

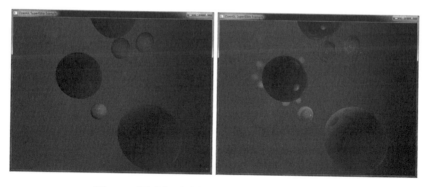

Figure 13.38: Adding a ray-traced plane

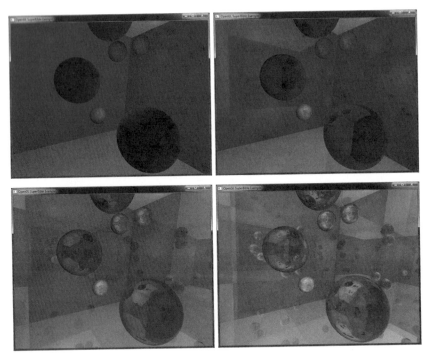

Figure 13.39: Ray-traced spheres in a box

we progress from left to right, top to bottom in Figure 13.39, with no bounces, and then one, two, and three bounces, respectively. A higher-resolution image using four bounces is shown in Color Plate 17.

The ray tracing implementation presented here and in the raytracer example application is a *brute-force* approach that simply intersects every ray against every object. As your objects get more complex and the number of objects in the scene grows, you may wish to implement *acceleration structures*. An acceleration structure is a data structure constructed in memory that allows you to quickly determine which objects *might* be hit by a ray given an origin and a direction. As you have seen from this example, ray tracing is actually pretty easy so long as you have an intersection algorithm for your primitive of choice. Shadows, reflections, and even refraction come for free with ray tracing. However, ray tracing is certainly not cheap, and without dedicated hardware support it leaves a lot of work for you to do in your shaders. Using an acceleration structure is vital if you really want to use ray-traced scenes containing more than a handful of spheres and a bunch of planes in real time. Current research in ray tracing is almost entirely focused on efficient acceleration structures, including how to generate them, store them, and traverse them.

Two-Dimensional Graphics

While a good portion of this book has been dedicated to rendering, there are cases where two-dimensional rendering is important and OpenGL is reasonably well prepared to get images onto the screen. Examples of places where you might want to render two-dimensional graphics are user interfaces and text. In this section, we'll cover a couple of techniques to get text and other elements onto the screen. There are, of course, other APIs and advanced libraries that will render user interfaces for you. However, these techniques should mix reasonably well with your existing applications without the need to learn or link to more external code.

Distance Field Textures

One important element of two-dimensional rendering is that of smooth curves, straight lines, and sharp edges. This is common in logos, decals, text, and so on. The straightforward approach is simply to use a texture containing the two-dimensional elements and call it a day. However, to achieve good-quality rendering can require a very high-resolution input texture. For example, Figure 13.40 shows a zoomed-in region of the OpenGL logo. The input source texture is 512×512 texels in size[9] and, as you can see, there are significant artifacts visible in the edges.

If we were to apply the logo shown in Figure 13.40 to an object that is to be viewed up close, the edges would become either jagged or blurry, depending on the texture filtering mode we choose. To make the edges appear sharp and clear requires a much higher-resolution image. Figure 13.41 shows the same logo, rendered at a much higher resolution of 8192×8192 texels. This is really quite large and consumes more than 64 megabytes of memory.

The effect of extreme magnification is most apparent for sharp edges such as those in the logo. To render cleanly, we can represent the image as a *distance field* rather than a binary image. In a distance field texture, we

---

9. The logo in Figure 13.40 has an incorrect aspect ratio because it will be used as a texture and its size corrected at rendering time.

Figure 13.40: Low-resolution texture used for a logo

store at each texel not a color but rather the *distance* to the edge. We use the sign of the distance to determine whether we're inside or outside the edge. Negative numbers mean that we're on the outside (clear or white part) of the logo, and positive numbers mean that we're on the inside (solid or black) part of the logo. A value of zero represents the exact edge of the logo. To render the image, we then apply a simple threshold to the values sampled from the texture. Figure 13.42 shows the distance field generated from the OpenGL logo.

In Figure 13.42, we've biased the values in the distance field—we can't very well print negative values! Black therefore represents values outside the logo, white represents values inside the logo, and mid-gray is the value on the very edge of the logo.

To understand why this works, consider what happens if we generate a distance field for a point and a line. Figure 13.43 shows the distance fields for a line.

Figure 13.41: High-resolution texture used for a logo

At every point the distance from the transition from black to white is encoded as a texel (again, we've biased the image to be able to print it). As we travel in the positive x direction, we get closer and closer to the line, so the value in the texture approaches zero. Even when we are partway between two texels, our distance to the line will be the average distance from the centers of those two texels—and this is exactly what linear texture filtering gives us. As a consequence, we can use standard OpenGL texture filtering and arbitrarily interpolate our texture while keeping a sharp edge. In fact, the distance field of our OpenGL logo is also only 512×512 pixels, but it was generated by using the original 8192-pixel-wide image and downsampling the resulting distance field.

Figure 13.44 shows the output of our test application rendering the OpenGL logo from the distance field shown in Figure 13.42.

The inset in Figure 13.44 shows a zoomed-in portion of the resulting output. Notice that the edges of the logo are not jagged and pixelated as you might expect from a simple threshold. That is because we can use the

Figure 13.42: Distance field of the OpenGL logo

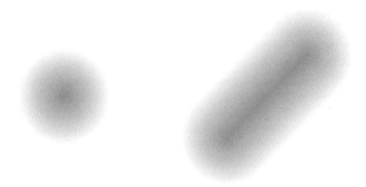

Figure 13.43: Distance fields for a line

Figure 13.44: Output of distance field rendering application

information about how far we are from the edge of the logo to determine an approximate coverage value for our current pixel. We use GLSL's smoothstep function to soften our threshold. The fragment shader used to produce Figure 13.44 is shown in Listing 13.39.

```
#version 450 core

layout (location = 0) out vec4 color;

layout (binding = 0) uniform sampler2D sdf_texture;

in vec2 uv;

void main(void)
{
    const vec4 c1 = vec4(0.1, 0.1, 0.2, 1.0);
    const vec4 c2 = vec4(0.8, 0.9, 1.0, 1.0);
    float val = texture(sdf_texture, uv).x;

    color = mix(c1, c2, smoothstep(0.52, 0.48, val));
}
```

Listing 13.39: Fragment shader for distance field rendering

Because filtering works so well with distance fields, a much lower-resolution distance field can be used to render a given image than would be required if the image was stored as a plain texture. The distance field used in our example application shown in Figure 13.44 is only 512×512 texels. This makes distance fields an appropriate method of storing more than just logos.

Rendering Fonts with Distance Fields

Something that is particularly well suited to rendering with distance fields is text. Figure 13.45 shows the distance field for a few letters of the English alphabet. However, the English alphabet is relatively small and it's not a big sacrifice to encode the whole ASCII character set as raw images. Encoding of the 256 ASCII characters as a 64×64 texture at 1 byte per texel still consumes only a megabyte of memory.

Now, consider the set of Chinese characters. It is unknown exactly how many characters there are in the traditional Chinese "alphabet." Estimates have been placed at anywhere from 60,000 to 80,000. Of these, about 3500 are in use in everyday newspapers and magazines. Of course, Chinese characters can also be much more detailed than Western characters, so the resolution requirements to encode them as bitmaps might be much higher than with Western alphabets. In fact, 3500 characters at 256×256 pixels works out to require a minimum of 220 megabytes! Figure 13.46 shows the distance field for the Chinese character for *sharp* rendered as a distance field.

The distance field shown in Figure 13.46 was generated by rendering the original character at 2048×2048 pixels, creating the distance field, and then downsampling that to 64×64 texels. The image on the left shows the original, high-resolution character and the image on the right shows the much lower-resolution distance field. We can do this for a number of

Figure 13.45: Distance field for English characters

Figure 13.46: Distance field of a Chinese character

characters and use the results to render high-quality text. Figure 13.47 shows a sample of Chinese text output using this method.

The demos shown in this section so far have simply used the distance field data sampled by our shader to blend between two colors—a background color and a foreground color. However, the GPU has blending hardware that we can use to do this for us. In fact, if we output a constant color

Figure 13.47: Chinese text rendered using distance fields

from our shader but feed the distance information into the *alpha* component of the output, then with the appropriate blending modes we can have OpenGL blend our text over an existing background.

Colored Rendering with Distance Fields

In the examples presented so far, we have rendered single-colored images by simply thresholding our distance field. However, it's possible to use distance fields to produce colored output. In Listing 13.39 we used the GLSL function `mix` to interpolate between two colors based on the value stored in the distance field. In that example, the colors we used were constants defined in the shader—but they don't have to be. You could interpolate them (use inputs to the fragment shader), generate the values procedurally, or even load them from other textures. Also, we can use more than one distance field to control rendering of several, overlapping layers.

In our first example, we use a distance field to blend between two textures. Using one texture containing tiling gravel and another containing a grass texture, we can use a third to store a set of paths through fields. In Figure 13.48, we see the gravel and grass textures. Notice that these are relatively low resolution—only 1024×1024 texels each. Because these textures tile, they can be repeated over a large surface. However, the repeating pattern becomes obvious if it is used over a wide area.

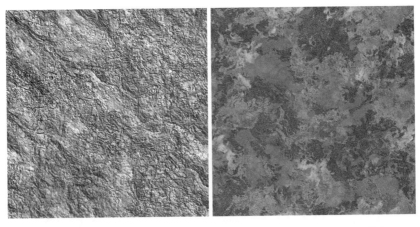

Figure 13.48: Two textures to be mixed using a distance field

Figure 13.49: Landscape map texture and distance field

To mix the two textures shown in Figure 13.48, we use a third texture representing paths, roads, or other terrain features. This texture is shown in Figure 13.49 along with its corresponding distance field texture.

The result of combining the textures in Figure 13.48 using the distance field in Figure 13.49 is shown in Figure 13.50. As you can see, when zoomed in closely (as shown on the left), the boundary between the grass and the rocks remains well defined. However, when the image is zoomed out (as shown on the right), the repeating pattern of the grass and rocks textures is broken up by the hand-drawn landscape pattern. All three textures are 1024 × 1024 texels in size. However, the grass and rocks textures are repeated at a frequency 12 times higher than the map texture.

Figure 13.50: Result of landscape texturing with distance fields

Bitmap Fonts

In many applications, you may just want to get text onto the screen. Whether it's an integral part of your application, such as the user interface, or simply a debugging aid, text output is an important part of an application. In this section, we'll demonstrate a simple and effective way to use a bitmap font to get text onto the screen with a couple of textures and a single program object. We will not be digging into complex vector font rendering, glyph caches, hinting, or anything like that—just brute-force text rendering. It's not going to be print-ready, but it'll get information onto the screen and maybe even some ASCII art. We're really going for that retro feel!

A long time ago, computers had only a simple text mode output. Before there were textures and shaders, vertex buffers, and atomic operations, there was very simple display hardware. The display memory was essentially divided into two parts—the character ROM, which held a copy of a font, and the screen buffer, which held the map of characters on the screen and perhaps some attributes such as color (if you were lucky), bold, or blinking attributes. We're going to emulate this using a simple shader.

First, we'll need a texture that'll act as our character ROM. The font we'll use is a reproduction of the codepage 437 character set from a PC VGA BIOS. Each character is 9×16 pixels in size, and the codepage consists of 256 characters. We have encoded this texture as a 256-layer array texture where the dimensions of the layer are 9×16.

Next, we'll need a texture to represent our screen buffer. For this, we'll use a 256×256 texel image with format GL_R8UI—one 8-bit unsigned integer per character, which is 64K of data (trivial for a modern graphics card). We'll also keep a system memory copy of the screen buffer. To render text, we'll draw into the system memory copy of the screen buffer and mark it as dirty. Once each frame, if the buffer is dirty, we'll use it to update the OpenGL's texture. The code to set all this up is shown in Listing 13.40.

```
// Compile the text rendering shaders
glShaderSource(vs, 1, vs_source, nullptr);
glCompileShader(vs);

glShaderSource(fs, 1, fs_source, nullptr);
glCompileShader(fs);

// Create our text rendering program
text_program = glCreateProgram();
glAttachShader(text_program, vs);
glAttachShader(text_program, fs);
glLinkProgram(text_program);
```

```
// Done with the shaders, delete them - keep the program
glDeleteShader(fs);
glDeleteShader(vs);

// Create an empty VAO
glCreateVertexArrays(1, &vao);

// Create the texture storing character map
glCreateTextures(GL_TEXTURE_2D, 1, &text_buffer);
glTextureStorage2D(text_buffer, 1, GL_R8UI, width, height);

// Load the font texture from disk
font_texture = sb6::ktx::file::load(font);

// Allocate system memory for the framebuffer
screen_buffer = new char[width * height];
memset(screen_buffer, 0, width * height);
```

Listing 13.40: Getting ready for bitmap fonts

After we have rendered whatever else the application is doing, the final screen buffer is rendered by compositing it over everything using a single fragment shader. To invoke the shader, we draw our full-screen quad, rendered as a triangle fan and a hard-coded vertex shader as we have done many times before.

As the fragment shader runs, it determines the fragment coordinate using the gl_FragCoord variable and the size of the characters in the font texture using the textureSize function. By dividing the integer fragment coordinate by the font texture size (remember, integer division in GLSL rounds toward zero), the shader determines where in the screen buffer it needs to look to find out which character to read from the font texture.

The screen buffer is bound as an isampler2D texture and texelFetch is used to pull a texel from it. This texel is the character code for the position on the screen that we're currently rendering. The *remainder* of the division (found using the modulo operator) is the texel coordinate within the selected character. We use a texture array for the font data, so we form a 3D vector from the texel coordinate and use texelFetch again to read from the font data. Texels that have non-zero return values are rendered in white, while texels that return zero are discarded. Listing 13.41 shows the main body of the shader.

```
#version 440 core

// Set origin to top-left; we want left-to-right, top-to-bottom
layout (origin_upper_left) in vec4 gl_FragCoord;

// Output a single color
layout (location = 0) out vec4 o_color;
```

```
// Character map
layout (binding = 0) uniform isampler2D text_buffer;

// Font
layout (binding = 1) uniform isampler2DArray font_texture;

void main(void)
{
    // Get integer fragment coordinate
    ivec2 frag_coord = ivec2(gl_FragCoord.xy);

    // Get size of font
    ivec2 char_size = textureSize(font_texture, 0).xy;

    // Find location in text buffer
    ivec2 char_location = frag_coord / char_size;

    // Find texel within character
    ivec2 texel_coord = frag_coord % char_size;

    // Fetch character index
    int character = texelFetch(text_buffer, char_location, 0).x;

    // Write character data out
    o_color = texelFetch(font_texture, ivec3(texel_coord, character), 0).xxxx;
}
```

Listing 13.41: Bitmap font rendering shader

At any time during rendering of our frame, we can modify the contents of screen_buffer. Before the end of our frame, simply update the contents of the screen buffer texture to reflect the content of the application memory copy with a call to **glTextureStorageSubImage2D()** to draw the full-screen quad. The code to do this is shown in Listing 13.42.

```
// If the system memory copy has changed...
if (dirty)
{
    // Update the underlying texture and clear the dirty flag
    glTextureSubImage2D(text_buffer,
                        0,
                        0, 0,
                        buffer_width, buffer_height,
                        GL_RED_INTEGER, GL_UNSIGNED_BYTE,
                        screen_buffer);
    dirty = false;
}
// Bind the text buffer and font textures
glBindTextureUnit(0, text_buffer);
glBindTextureUnit(1, font_texture);

// Bind our program and VAO, and draw a triangle strip over the display
glUseProgram(text_program);
glBindVertexArray(vao);
glDrawArrays(GL_TRIANGLE_STRIP, 0, 4);
```

Listing 13.42: Bitmap font rendering shader

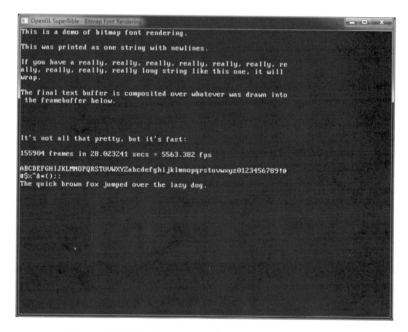

Figure 13.51: Output of font rendering demo

The result is that simple bitmap text is rendered over whatever was on the display before. The output of the demo is shown in Figure 13.51.

The font rendering code described here is wrapped up into a class included with the sb7 application framework and is used by some of the examples to display messages and other text over the rendered output. In Figure 13.51, we used a large, 9×16 texel font. If when initializing the text overlay class, you get to choose your own font, it must be a 256-layer array texture stored in a .KTX file. A few alternatively sized (though less complete) font textures are included in the distribution for you to experiment with.

Summary

In this chapter, we have applied the fundamentals that you have learned throughout the book to a number of rendering techniques. At first, we focused heavily on lighting models, considering how to shade the objects that you're drawing. In particular, we discussed the Phong lighting model, the Blinn-Phong model, and rim lighting. We also looked at ways to produce higher-frequency lighting effects than are representable by your geometry by using normal maps, environment maps, and other textures. We showed how you can cast shadows and simulate basic atmospheric effects. We also discussed some techniques that have no basis in reality.

In the final section, we stepped away from shading at the same time as rendering our geometry and examined some techniques that can be applied in screen space. Deferred shading allows expensive shading calculations to be decoupled from the initial pass that renders our geometry. By storing positions, normals, colors, and other surface attributes in framebuffer attachments, we are able to implement arbitrarily complex shading algorithms without worrying about wasting work. At first, we used this approach to apply standard lighting techniques only to pixels we knew would be visible. However, with screen-space ambient occlusion, we demonstrated a technique that relies on having data from neighboring pixels available. Ultimately, we introduced the topic of ray tracing, and in our implementation, we rendered an entire scene without a single triangle.

Chapter 14

High-Performance OpenGL

WHAT YOU'LL LEARN IN THIS CHAPTER

- How to optimize your applications for performance.
- Techniques for reducing the CPU overhead of your programs.
- How to use tools to analyze the behavior of your GPU.

Optimizing CPU Performance

In this section, we'll cover a number of techniques that you can use either to lower the CPU overhead of your applications or to better utilize the CPU of your machine. If your application's performance is limited by CPU overhead, then these techniques can make your application go faster. If not, then they still give you more CPU cycles to spend on other things—physics, audio, artificial intelligence, networking, and so on. Even if you don't need all those spare cycles, the system may be able to shut down the CPU when it's idle, saving power and increasing battery life in mobile applications.

Multi-Threading in OpenGL

The OpenGL API was designed more than 22 years ago. At the time, machines with multiple CPUs were rare and extremely expensive. Graphics hardware acceleration was nascent, and even when available, wasn't faster than software rendering by such a huge margin as it is today. Modern GPUs are orders of magnitude faster and more efficient at rendering graphics than a CPU would be if you were to implement the same things in software. Unfortunately, a side effect of the legacy of OpenGL is that it simply *isn't very good* at multi-threading. It's possible to use multiple threads in an OpenGL application by creating multiple contexts and sharing objects between them. However, this can be quite inefficient and might not work as well as you might expect. That's not to say, though, that you can't use multi-threading to make your OpenGL applications go faster.

The key to getting high performance out of multiple threads in OpenGL is to find a way that *only one thread* calls OpenGL functions, but that is *the only thing* that the one thread does. There are two complementary ways to offload the OpenGL thread by moving work to other threads:

- Use multiple threads to generate data that will be consumed by OpenGL by mapping a buffer and sharing the pointer between several threads. Have the other threads write their data directly into the mapped buffer, synchronizing only so that the OpenGL thread can call OpenGL commands.
- Use multiple threads to create *commands* for OpenGL by packing their parameters into a buffer and signaling the main OpenGL threads to turn them into real OpenGL commands.

We will explore both of these techniques in the next few sections.

Using Threads to Generate Data

In our first example of parallelism using threads, we're going to use all available cores of our host CPU to execute a particle simulation. The OpenGL side of the program is actually pretty simple. In fact, in our inner loop, all we're doing is clearing the framebuffer and doing a single draw. All of the hard work is done by the CPU in this example.

Rather than use a hand-coded thread, we're going to use OpenMP (Open Multi-Processing), which is an API and set of language extensions that enables advanced compilers to automatically parallelize workloads based on your guidance. With OpenMP, we can tell the compiler that iterations of a loop are to be run in parallel and to invoke the OpenMP runtime to schedule the work to threads that it creates for each core in the system.

During initialization of our ompparticles application, we tell OpenMP how many threads we'd like to run. In this case, we'd like it to use all available CPU resources. To do this, we add the following code to our startup() function:

```cpp
int maxThreads = omp_get_max_threads();
omp_set_num_threads(maxThreads);
```

Now we're ready to write our simple particle simulation. We declare a data stucture that contains the position and velocity of each particle:

```cpp
struct PARTICLE
{
    vmath::vec3 position;
    vmath::vec3 velocity;
};
```

In our application, we create two buffers in application memory, each big enough to store all of the particles in the system. On each frame of animation, we'll read from one of these buffers and write updated positions and velocities into the other. On the subsequent frame, we'll go the other way. Each particle in the system is considered to have a small mass and, therefore, to be attracted to all other particles through gravitational attraction. The force asserted on the object affects its velocity, which at each step is added to its position. The inner loop of the particle simulation is shown in Listing 14.1.

```cpp
void ompparticles_app::update_particles_omp(float deltaTime)
{
    // Double-buffer source and destination
    const PARTICLE* const __restrict src = particles[frame_index & 1];
    PARTICLE* const __restrict dst = particles[(frame_index + 1) & 1];

    // For each particle in the system
#pragma omp parallel for schedule (dynamic, 16)
    for (int i = 0; i < PARTICLE_COUNT; i++)
    {
        // Get my own data
        const PARTICLE& me = src[i];
        vmath::vec3 delta_v(0.0f);

        // For all the other particles
        for (int j = 0; j < PARTICLE_COUNT; j++)
```

```
            {
                if (i != j) // ... not me!
                {
                    //  Get the vector to the other particle
                    vmath::vec3 delta_pos = src[j].position - me.position;
                    float distance = vmath::length(delta_pos);
                    // Normalize
                    vmath::vec3 delta_dir = delta_pos / distance;
                    // This clamp stops the system from blowing up if
                    // particles get too close...
                    distance = distance < 0.005f ? 0.005f : distance;
                    // Update velocity
                    delta_v += (delta_dir / (distance * distance));
                }
            }
            // Add my current velocity to my position
            dst[i].position = me.position + me.velocity;
            // Produce new velocity from my current velocity plus
            // the calculated delta
            dst[i].velocity = me.velocity + delta_v * deltaTime * 0.01f;
            // Write to mapped buffer
            mapped_buffer[i].position = dst[i].position;
        }

        // Count frames so we can double-buffer next frame
        frame_index++;
    }
```

Listing 14.1: OpenMP particle updater

As you can see, the code in Listing 14.1 looks like regular C++ code with variables and loops right where you would expect them to be. However, before the body of the outer `for` loop, you'll see the line starting `#pragma` omp ..., which tells the compiler that we want to execute this loop in parallel. This particular declaration tells the compiler to schedule work dynamically in blocks of 16 iterations of the loop. It will create as many threads as there are CPU cores in the system and then allocate blocks of 16 particles to each thread in turn until all particles have been processed.

This is a very crude particle system whose only purpose is to demonstrate basic use of OpenMP to take advantage of multiple CPU cores in a system. However, you should notice that the inner loop writes to mapped_buffer after updating the position of the particles in system memory. This is the *actual data store* of the buffer object we'll be drawing from. In effect, the particle system is sending its output directly to OpenGL.

The mapped_buffer variable points to a buffer we mapped earlier in the application. During start-up, we created a buffer object and mapped it with a *persistent* map, which means we can leave it mapped and render directly from it. The code to create the buffer is shown in Listing 14.2.

```
// Create GPU buffer
glGenBuffers(1, &particle_buffer);
glBindBuffer(GL_ARRAY_BUFFER, particle_buffer);
glBufferStorage(GL_ARRAY_BUFFER,
                PARTICLE_COUNT * sizeof(PARTICLE),
                nullptr,
                GL_MAP_WRITE_BIT | GL_MAP_PERSISTENT_BIT);
mapped_buffer = (PARTICLE*)glMapBufferRange(
    GL_ARRAY_BUFFER,
    0,
    PARTICLE_COUNT * sizeof(PARTICLE),
    GL_MAP_WRITE_BIT | GL_MAP_PERSISTENT_BIT | GL_MAP_FLUSH_EXPLICIT_BIT);
```

Listing 14.2: Setting up a persistent mapped buffer

When we map the buffer in Listing 14.2, we specify the GL_MAP_WRITE_BIT, GL_MAP_PERSISTENT_BIT, and GL_MAP_FLUSH_EXPLICIT_BIT flags. The first tells OpenGL that we're going to write to the mapped buffer, the second tells OpenGL that we want to leave the buffer mapped for an extended period of time and render from it while it's mapped, and the third tells OpenGL that we'll let it know when we're done changing data in the buffer. We store the returned pointer in mapped_buffer for the lifetime of the application.

Our main rendering loop is very simple. All it does is compute a time delta, update the particles, clear the viewport, and execute a single drawing command. The complete code is shown in Listing 14.3.

```
void ompparticles_app::render(double currentTime)
{
    static const GLfloat black[] = { 0.0f, 0.0f, 0.0f, 0.0f };
    static double previousTime = 0.0;

    // Calculate delta time
    float deltaTime = (float)(currentTime - previousTime);
    previousTime = currentTime;

    // Update particle positions using OpenMP... or not
    if (use_omp)
    {
        update_particles_omp(deltaTime * 0.001f);
    }
    else
    {
        update_particles(deltaTime * 0.001f);
    }

    // Clear
    glViewport(0, 0, info.windowWidth, info.windowHeight);
    glClearBufferfv(GL_COLOR, 0, black);

    // Bind our vertex arrays
    glBindVertexArray(vao);
```

```
    // Let OpenGL know we've changed the contents of the buffer
    glFlushMappedBufferRange(GL_ARRAY_BUFFER, 0,
                             PARTICLE_COUNT * sizeof(PARTICLE));

    // Draw!
    glUseProgram(draw_program);
    glDrawArrays(GL_POINTS, 0, PARTICLE_COUNT);
}
```

Listing 14.3: OpenMP particle rendering loop

As you can see, before calling **glDrawArrays()** in Listing 14.3, we call
glFlushMappedBufferRange(). This tells OpenGL that the data in the
mapped buffer has changed and that it should invalidate any caches that
might be holding data from the buffer or otherwise prepare to use the new
data that has been written to the shared memory.

Notice that we do not call any other OpenGL functions to actually transfer
data around. There are no calls to **glBufferSubData()**, **glMapBufferRange()**
(except for the one in start-up), or other similar functions in the inner
rendering loop.

Also notice that this program does not include any synchronization. That
is, we don't wait for OpenGL to finish drawing from the buffer before
overwriting it with the next frame's data. In this case, such an approach
works well because the worst that will happen is that a particle will be
drawn with the next frame's position rather than the current frame's. If
there were more sensitivity to data correctness, you'd want to double- or
triple-buffer the GPU data, too.

The result of running this application is shown in Figure 14.1. In this
screenshot, we bumped the point size up to 3.0 to make the particles a
little easier to see.

The ompparticles application contains two versions of the particle update
function. They are identical to each other except that one uses OpenMP
and the other does not. On the author's machine, which is fitted with a
six-core processor, the application runs almost exactly six times faster with
OpenMP enabled than it does with OpenMP disabled. Figure 14.2 shows
the CPU utilization with OpenMP enabled.

As you can see in Figure 14.2, the ompparticles application fully utilizes
all CPU cores in the system. It is using 99% of the available CPU time. The
observant reader may notice that the application has actually created

Figure 14.1: Output of the OpenMP particle simulator

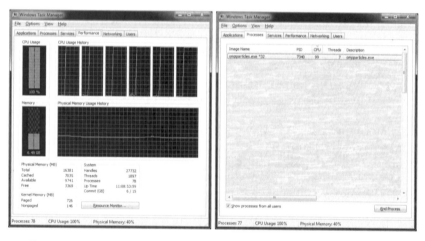

Figure 14.2: CPU utilization of the `ompparticles` application

seven threads, even though the host CPU contains only six cores. Most OpenGL drivers are themselves multi-threaded and create at least one worker thread for internal use. When OpenGL is idle (because it is waiting for the application to create work for it), the internal driver thread goes idle. In this case, it is the six application threads that are using all of the CPU time, not the driver.

Packet Buffers

In the previous section we demonstrated how it is possible, by sharing the pointer to a mapped buffer with other threads, to make use of the multiple processor cores provided by today's CPUs. However, we're still stuck with the issue of how to generate OpenGL *commands* from multiple threads. Normally, we would have a single context for each thread. We can create more than one context, but that can be a pretty heavy burden for the application and drivers—OpenGL needs to manage multiple complete copies of all state for you, and must assume that you're going to share any object across any number of threads at any time. In theory, you could even create a new context while you're already rendering with another context and start sharing its objects. This makes for a pretty inefficient system.

When we think about what an OpenGL implementation does, we realize that it's really translating the OpenGL commands and parameters that you pass it into something that the underlying graphics card can understand. It packages up lists of commands and then fires them off as they become ready for the GPU to execute them. These blocks of commands are commonly known as *command buffers*. Command buffer generation can be quite an involved process but, in theory, assuming the only thing your application does is call OpenGL functions, one thread should be enough to drive a modern GPU efficiently. In practice, in a complex application, it's hard to *only* call OpenGL. You need to at least figure out *what* to render and rendering code generally ends up interspersed with logic, data access, and other mundane tasks that your application performs.

Building Packet Buffers

The strategy presented in this section is to try to separate the logic that decides what to do from the calls that end up in OpenGL. Ideally, we'll be able to work in parallel while deciding what to draw from the intricacies of calling OpenGL and the pitfalls associated with trying to render from multiple threads. We're basically going to create our own command buffers—we'll call them *packet buffers*. The packet buffers are what our rendering code will generate; when they're ready, a single, tightly optimized loop will fire them off to OpenGL as quickly as possible.

In code, each packet represents one or more commands for OpenGL. As we produce the packets, though, rather than calling OpenGL directly, we store the parameters away in a data structure that we append to a list. This is a really low-overhead operation and we can build multiple lists in parallel on multiple threads. An example data structure from the `packetbuffer` sample is shown in Listing 14.4, along with its base class.

```
// Forward declare base packet structure so we can use
// it in a function declaration
struct base;

// Define the base execution function pointer
typedef void (APIENTRYP PFN_EXECUTE)(const base* __restrict pParams);

// Base packet only includes pointer to execution function
struct base
{
    PFN_EXECUTE      pfnExecute;
};

// This packet represents a call to glDrawElementsBaseVertexBaseInstance
struct DRAW_ELEMENTS : public base
{
    // All the OpenGL parameters go here.
    GLenum mode;
    GLsizei count;
    GLenum type;
    GLvoid *indices;
    GLsizei primcount;
    GLint basevertex;
    GLuint baseinstance;

    // This is the execution function
    static void APIENTRY execute(const DRAW_ELEMENTS* __restrict pParams)
    {
        // Simply send all the parameters to OpenGL
        glDrawElementsInstancedBaseVertexBaseInstance(
            pParams->mode,
            pParams->count,
            pParams->type,
            pParams->indices,
            pParams->primcount,
            pParams->basevertex,
            pParams->baseinstance);
    }
};
```

Listing 14.4: Example packet data structure

In the example packet shown in Listing 14.4, the DRAW_ELEMENTS packet derives from the base packet called base (don't worry about the generic names—this is all wrapped up in a namespace) from which all of our packets are derived. The base class consists solely of a pointer to a function with a prototype that matches PFN_EXECUTE. In the derived packet, we store all the parameters needed to make a call to OpenGL.

Further, there is a class that maintains a list of these packets. In the most basic form, we form a union of all known packet types and then use an array of these unions to store the packets appended during rendering. The start of this union is shown in Listing 14.5.

```
union ALL_PACKETS
{
public:
    PFN_EXECUTE           execute;
private:
    base                  Base;
    BIND_PROGRAM          BindProgram;
    BIND_VERTEX_ARRAY     BindVertexArray;
    DRAW_ELEMENTS         DrawElements;
    DRAW_ARRAYS           DrawArrays;
    // More packet types go here...
};
```

Listing 14.5: Union of all packets

In the union shown in Listing 14.5, the first member is the function pointer, execute, which matches the function pointer stored in base, which, because all other packets derive from it, appears in the same location in memory in all packets. As we fill in packets in our packet buffer, we point this function at the appropriate execution function for that packet. Appending a packet therefore becomes a simple operation of getting a pointer to the next packet in the buffer, filling in its parameters, and pointing the execution function at the right place. An example is shown in Listing 14.6.

```
void packet_stream::DrawElements(
    GLenum mode,
    GLsizei count,
    GLenum type,
    GLuint start,
    GLsizei instancecount,
    GLint basevertex,
    GLuint baseinstance)
{
    packet::DRAW_ELEMENTS* __restrict pPacket =
        NextPacket<packet::DRAW_ELEMENTS>();

    pPacket->pfnExecute = packet::PFN_EXECUTE(packet::DRAW_ELEMENTS::execute);
    pPacket->mode = mode;
    pPacket->count = count;
    pPacket->indices = (GLvoid*)start;
    pPacket->primcount = instancecount;
    pPacket->basevertex = basevertex;
    pPacket->baseinstance = baseinstance;
}
```

Listing 14.6: Appending a packet to a packet buffer

Notice that the `packet_stream::DrawElements` function does almost no work. The `NextPacket<>` function simply returns a pointer to a packet of the right type and increments the internal packet pointer. We can replace the implementation of `NextPacket<>` at any time (using a linked list, resizing array, or some other mechanism) and this code will keep working. This is the code that's executed from your rendering code, *not* the actual call into OpenGL. You can have as many instances of the `packet_stream` class as you like—you can build multiple packet buffers in parallel, you can rebuild them and fire them off once, or you can keep some of them around for many frames. For example, if part of your scene never changes, build a packet buffer that represents it and keep it. Dynamic parts of the scene, meanwhile, would be rebuilt more frequently.

When it comes time to render the packet buffers, we simply execute their contents. This is accomplished by calling the `packet_stream::execute` function, whose body is shown in Listing 14.7.

```
void packet_stream::execute(void)
{
    const packet::ALL_PACKETS* __restrict pPacket;

    // Quick check for empty buffers
    if (!num_packets)
        return;

    // Go until you get a packet that's got a null execution function
    for (pPacket = m_packets; pPacket->execute != nullptr; pPacket++)
    {
        // Call the packet's execution function
        pPacket->execute((packet::base*)pPacket);
    }
}
```

Listing 14.7: Executing a packet buffer

The code shown in Listing 14.7 is the only code here that actually talks to OpenGL (via the packet execution functions). The loop is extremely tight and consumes very little CPU overhead relative to the OpenGL implementation underneath. Just to demonstrate, the disassembly[1] of the inner loop of `packet_stream::execute` is shown in Listing 14.8. Don't worry if you don't understand assembly—this example is provided just to illustrate how tight the final loop ends up being.

---

1. As generated by Visual Studio 2013 for 32-bit X86 in release mode.

```
loop:
    push   esi               ; Push pointer to packet on stack
    call   eax               ; Call execute function
    mov    eax, [esi+20h]    ; Get next packet's execute function
    add    esi, 20h          ; Move to next packet
    test   eax, eax          ; If its execute function is not NULL...
    jnz    short loop        ; Go around again
```

Listing 14.8: Disassembly of `packet_stream::execute`

Tiny chunks of code like that of Listing 14.8, along with the packet execution functions (which tend to be just as small), also have an excellent chance of remaining in an instruction cache relative to generalized rendering code, which tends to be spread out across a large executable.

Optimizing Packet Buffers

In an application, we can create one or more instances of our `packet_stream` class and fill them from any threads we like. Once they're built, we can submit them from our main rendering thread without worrying about the current context or calling OpenGL from multiple threads. The compiling of OpenGL commands in this way also provides opportunities beyond simply allowing effective multi-threaded access to OpenGL.

One such opportunity arises when we *optimize* our command stream. An example optimization is the elimination of *redundant state* setting commands. By recording a small amount of state in each packet stream, we can do two things:

- Ignore attempts to set one of OpenGL's states to the value it's already set to. This includes binding the same programs, textures, or buffers; enabling or disabling things that are already enabled or disabled; or otherwise sending the same value to OpenGL more than once.

- Send only the states that will be used by draws. For example, if the application disables a state and then enables it again without drawing anything in between, then we can safely ignore the request to disable that state, and possibly the request to re-enable it (assuming it becomes redundant once we eliminate the disablement).

As an example, take a look at Listing 14.9, which shows the implementation of `packet_stream::EnableDisable`. Here you will see that we have added the `state` member structure that tracks a small amount of OpenGL's state as the packet buffer sees it. If the incoming state change matches what the state tracker believes it is already, then it returns early and does not append to the packet buffer. If the state is different, then the tracked state is updated and the command appended to the buffer. Also, if the state is not one we're tracking (or not one we recognize at all), then we let it through to the buffer.

```
void packet_stream::EnableDisable(GLenum cap, GLboolean enable)
{
    switch (cap)
    {
        case GL_CULL_FACE:
            if (state.valid.cull_face == 1 &&
                state.enables.cull_face == enable)
                return;
            state.enables.cull_face = enable;
            state.valid.cull_face = 1;
            break;
        case GL_RASTERIZER_DISCARD:
            if (state.valid.rasterizer_discard == 1 &&
                state.enables.rasterizer_discard == enable)
                return;
            state.enables.rasterizer_discard = enable;
            state.valid.rasterizer_discard = 1;
            break;
        case GL_DEPTH_TEST:
            if (state.valid.depth_test == 1 &&
                state.enables.depth_test == enable)
                return;
            state.enables.depth_test = enable;
            state.valid.depth_test = 1;
            break;
        case GL_STENCIL_TEST:
            if (state.valid.stencil_test == 1 &&
                state.enables.stencil_test == enable)
                return;
            state.enables.stencil_test = enable;
            state.valid.stencil_test = 1;
            break;
        case GL_DEPTH_CLAMP:
            if (state.valid.depth_clamp == 1 &&
                state.enables.depth_clamp == enable)
                return;
            state.enables.depth_clamp = enable;
            state.valid.depth_clamp = 1;
            break;
        default:
            break;
    }

    packet::ENABLE_DISABLE* __restrict pPacket =
        NextPacket<packet::ENABLE_DISABLE>();

    if (enable)
    {
        pPacket->pfnExecute =
            packet::PFN_EXECUTE(packet::ENABLE_DISABLE::execute_enable);
    }
```

```
        else
        {
            pPacket->pfnExecute =
                packet::PFN_EXECUTE(packet::ENABLE_DISABLE::execute_disable);
        }
    }
```

Listing 14.9: Implementation of packet_stream::EnableDisable

The other thing you'll notice about Listing 14.9 is that we've changed the API slightly. Rather than having separate Enable and Disable functions as OpenGL usually does, we have only a single EnableDisable function that takes, as inputs, both the setting to change and what to change it to. With this strategy, we can track state with a single switch statement and employ a more data-driven approach to state settings: The calling code doesn't need to look at state to know which functions to call, but rather just passes the state through to our API to change it.

After packet_stream::EnableDisable determines that the state is indeed not redundant, it sets the execution function to one of two values—execute_enable to enable the state and execute_disable to disable it. Both of these values are members of the ENABLE_DISABLE packet and call through to **glEnable()** and **glDisable()**, respectively. As far as OpenGL is concerned, your application is just calling **glEnable()** and **glDisable()** directly without any extra fuss.

In Listing 14.9, you'll see that we have also associated a valid bit with each of the states we're tracking. For state tracking to work correctly, it's important to know that your idea of state is actually what's current in OpenGL. For that reason, we need to allow the packet buffer to reset state to some known defaults. We provide the packet_stream::reset function that can reset the packet buffer in one of three modes:

- Reset all states to known defaults, including sending the state to OpenGL.

- Inherit the state from another packet_stream object, assuming it will be executed immediately before this one.

- Inherit the state from an unknown source, marking all tracked state as invalid.

For the first mode, in a naïve implementation, we could simply mark all tracked state as invalid, and then call our own functions to reset the state to the defaults. However, this could potentially burn quite a bit of packet space in the buffer and be quite inefficient to execute because each individual state would be set by a separate packet. Alternatively, we can create a special packet that means "copy all tracked state to OpenGL" and calls a whole bunch of OpenGL functions to get its state to match ours. Now all we need to do is set all state to the desired defaults, mark it valid, and then insert this packet.

For the second mode, we simply copy all state and valid bits from another packet_stream instance. Assuming the new packet_stream instance is executed immediately after the one from which it inherits its state, then we can continue sending state changes to OpenGL uninterrupted with no incoherence between our state mirror and OpenGL.

For the final mode, we just take all current state as is. Marking all state as invalid just means that the next request to change state will be honored no matter what that state is.

Finally, we include a packet_stream::sync() function that synchronizes the OpenGL state with our shadow. By default, it sends only state that is not marked valid to OpenGL (and then marks it valid). By setting the force parameter to true, we can force the packet stream to send *all* state to OpenGL, including those state items that it believes to already be valid.

Using these mechanisms—resetting to defaults, inheriting from another stream, and invalidating everything—we can efficiently move between states and chain packet buffers together.

- Creating a new packet stream and immediately resetting it with RESET_TO_DEFAULT mode gives us a stream that we can use to get OpenGL state to some known defaults.

- Inheriting state from a default stream, changing a few states, and then syncing produces a stream that updates all state to a specified set of defaults.

- Inheriting state from a longer stream and then issuing a reset to the default values produces a stream that will move state from the tail of one stream to the defaults. Other streams subsequently executed may safely assume that state is in its default.

Packet Buffer Specialization

Another optimization is to recognize certain patterns of commands or parameters as very commonly executed and to provide more optimal execution functions. For example, suppose that the most common primitive mode in your application is GL_TRIANGLES, and that you normally don't use instancing (that is, instanceCount is usually 1). We can provide the slightly optimized modified versions of packet_stream::DrawElements shown in Listing 14.10 and DRAW_ELEMENTS::execute shown in Listing 14.11.

```
void packet_stream::DrawElements(
    GLenum mode,
    GLsizei count,
    GLenum type,
    GLuint start,
    GLsizei instancecount,
    GLint basevertex,
    GLuint baseinstance)
{
    packet::DRAW_ELEMENTS* __restrict pPacket =
        NextPacket<packet::DRAW_ELEMENTS>();

    // If parameters match some very commonly used defaults...
    if (mode == GL_TRIANGLES &&
        instancecount == 1 &&
        baseinstance == 0)
    {
        // Use a more optimal execution function
        pPacket->pfnExecute =
            packet::PFN_EXECUTE(
                packet::DRAW_ELEMENTS::execute_tris_noinstance);
    }
    else
    {
        // Otherwise, use a more generic execution function
        pPacket->pfnExecute =
            packet::PFN_EXECUTE(packet::DRAW_ELEMENTS::execute);
    }
    // Either way, record the parameters as normal
    pPacket->mode = mode;
    pPacket->count = count;
    pPacket->indices = (GLvoid*)start;
    pPacket->primcount = instancecount;
    pPacket->basevertex = basevertex;
    pPacket->baseinstance = baseinstance;
}
```

Listing 14.10: Optimized packet insertion

As you can see in Listing 14.10, we check for our expected defaults (mode is GL_TRIANGLES, instancecount is 1, and baseinstance is 0). If we see a match, we simply point the execution function at the slightly more optimal version shown in Listing 14.11.

```
void APIENTRY DRAW_ELEMENTS::execute_tris_noinstance(
    const DRAW_ELEMENTS* __restrict pParams)
{
    // Simply send a subset of the parameters to OpenGL
    glDrawElementsBaseVertex(
        // Hard-code GL_TRIANGLES instead of reading pParams->mode
        GL_TRIANGLES,
        pParams->count,
        pParams->type,
        pParams->indices,
        pParams->basevertex);
    // pParams->primcount, pParams->basevertex, and
    // pParams->baseinstance are ignored
}
```

Listing 14.11: Optimized packet execution

When using the code in Listings 14.10 and 14.11 there will be slightly more overhead when recording the packet buffer, but there will be lower overhead when executing it. Overall, this can be a performance boost for a number of reasons. First, the idea is to record multiple packet buffers in parallel across many threads, so we have more CPU cycles to spend during recording than playback. Second, if the parameters being checked are passed as constant literals, the compiler may be able to eliminate the additional `if` check, eliminating the expense on both ends. Finally, because the packet buffers can be built once and submitted many times, we get to pay the cost once but reap the benefits many times.

Low-Overhead OpenGL

In the previous section we covered some techniques to make better use of CPU cycles to drive OpenGL. By buffering work and reusing it, and by moving work to other CPU cores, you can get the same work done in less time (or more work done in the same time). However, we haven't fundamentally reduced the *amount* of work your application does. In fact, the overhead of buffering and spreading the work across many execution threads actually means that your application does *more* work, even though it may do it in less time.

In this section, we cover some techniques designed to reduce the overhead of OpenGL. Some of them have become known as the *AZDO* (Approaching Zero Driver Overhead) techniques, after a talk given by the author and some of his colleagues at a developer conference that subsequently became quite popular.

Indirect Rendering

In Chapter 7, "Vertex Processing and Drawing Commands," we introduced the idea of *indirect draws*, which are drawing commands where the parameters are passed in buffer objects rather than directly through your code. We also introduced `glMultiDrawArraysIndirect()` and `glMultiDrawElementsIndirect()`, which allow a large number of drawing commands to be batched and sent to OpenGL in a single call. The asteroid rendering program presented in Chapter 7, for example, is able to produce tens of millions of independent draws each second. However, in that example, the list of draws is fixed—it is generated on the CPU ahead of time and the number of draws is known. Also, the transformation matrix for each object is calculated directly in the vertex shader, and so although performance is great, flexibility is very limited.

In this section, we'll cover a few methods to increase the scope of what can be done with indirect rendering, and show how to generate indirect rendering lists on the GPU.

Flexible Indirect Rendering

One of the significant drawbacks of indirect rendering is that during a long sequence of draws produced by `glMultiDrawArraysIndirect()` or `glMultiDrawElementsIndirect()`, no states can change. All objects must use the same program, same vertex buffers, same set of textures, and so on. On the surface, it would seem that this limits what we can do with these commands. However, it's possible with some creative arrangement of our shaders and data to get around some of these limitatons. Remember, we're not trying to cram an entire frame of rendering into a single call to `glMultiDrawElementsIndirect()`; rather, we're trying to batch enough work that the GPU becomes busy and we free up CPU cycles to go do something else in the meantime.

The first technique available to us is to make use of the `baseInstance` member of the indirect draw command structures. Again, for reference, the structures consumed by `glMultiDrawArraysIndirect()` and `glMultiDrawElementsIndirect()` are, respectively,

```
typedef struct {
    GLuint vertexCount;
    GLuint instanceCount;
    GLuint firstVertex;
    GLuint baseInstance;
} DrawArraysIndirectCommand;
```

```
typedef struct {
    GLuint vertexCount;
    GLuint instanceCount;
    GLuint firstIndex;
    GLint  baseVertex;
    GLuint baseInstance;
} DrawElementsIndirectCommand;
```

Note that each has a baseInstance member into which we can place
whatever we like. The data fetched for any instanced vertex attributes will
be fetched from their respective vertex buffers at a location offset by this
member's value. We can also get at the values found in this structure
(and passed directly to any other drawing command) using the
GL_ARB_shader_draw_parameters extension, which introduces three new
built-in variables to GLSL that become available to the vertex shader

- gl_BaseVertexARB contains the value passed in the baseVertex
  parameter.

- gl_BaseInstanceARB contains the value passed in the baseInstance
  parameter.

- gl_DrawIDARB contains the index of the draw.

The first two of these are self-explanatory; they each contain the value of
the similarly named parameter to the draw function. gl_BaseVertexARB
contains the value of baseVertex passed to **glDrawElementsBaseVertex()**
or any of the other functions that accepts this parameter. For functions
that don't have a baseVertex parameter, its value is still available in the
shader, but will be zero. Likewise, gl_BaseInstanceARB contains the value
passed to **glDrawArraysInstancedBaseInstance()** or similar functions; as
with gl_BaseVertexARB, if the function has no baseInstance parameter, it
will be zero. Both of these inputs also work when the parameters are
sourced from memory by one of the indirect drawing commands.

We could use gl_BaseInstanceARB to do some of the work needed in the
example presented earlier—rather than filling a buffer with an identity
mapping as we did in the asteroids sample, we could just use the value of
gl_BaseInstanceARB directly. This means less data to fetch, but still uses
the baseInstance field in a way that it wasn't strictly designed for and is
therefore incompatible with many instancing techniques. Instead, we use
the last of these parameters, gl_DrawIIDARB, which contains the raw index
of the draw.

In the `indirectmaterial` application, we put together a simple example to demonstrate how you might be able to batch a lot of draws into a single buffer while still allowing each object to have different material properties. We have reused the asteroid models from Chapter 7 and the lighting shader from the `blinnphong` example from Chapter 13. When given a shiny, colorful material, the asteroids look like gemstones. There are 100 unique objects in the asteroids model file, and each is drawn using a separate element of the draw indirect buffer.

To combine the many draws into one, first we make a large uniform block with the object transforms in it, declared in our vertex shader. Next we use a second uniform block to store per-frame data. These blocks' declarations are shown in Listing 14.12.

```
layout (std140, binding = 0) uniform FRAME_DATA
{
    mat4 view_matrix;
    mat4 proj_matrix;
    mat4 viewproj_matrix;
};

layout (std430, binding = 0) readonly buffer OBJECT_TRANSFORMS
{
    mat4 model_matrix[];
};
```

Listing 14.12: Uniform block declarations for indirect materials

The per-frame data (stored in the `FRAME_DATA` block) is bound to uniform block binding 0. The per-object transform data (`OBJECT_TRANSFORMS`) is bound at shader storage buffer binding 0. Note that the number of objects we can batch together is limited by the size of the shader storage block used to store their transforms. As each matrix is 16 floating-point values, for a total of 64 bytes each, the maximum number of matrices we can put into a single shader storage block is more than 2 million! If we were to use a uniform block for the transforms, then we'd be limited to 16K.[2]

In our vertex shader, we read positions and normals using regular vertex attributes, and do our vertex transformations as we did in the `blinnphong` sample from Chapter 13. However, rather than using a single model–view matrix, we use a separate model matrix for each mesh, indexed by `gl_DrawIDARB`, and form the model–view matrix locally in the shader. In

---

2. All implementations of OpenGL must be able to support uniform blocks of at least 16K, but some implementations may support much larger blocks.

addition to outputting the normal, light, and view vectors, we output the material index, which we derive from gl_BaseInstanceARB. This makes the shaders incompatible with instanced vertex attributes. However, that might not be an issue, as we can turn small batches of instances into multiple draws of a single instance. The main body of this shader is shown in Listing 14.13.

```
out VS_OUT
{
    smooth vec3 N;
    smooth vec3 L;
    smooth vec3 V;
    flat int material_id;
} vs_out;

void main(void)
{
    vec4 position = vec4(position_3, 1.0);
    mat4 mv_matrix = view_matrix * model_matrix[gl_DrawIDARB];

    // Calculate view-space coordinate
    vec4 P = mv_matrix * position;

    // Calculate normal in view space
    vs_out.N = mat3(mv_matrix) * normal;

    // Calculate light vector
    vs_out.L = light_pos - P.xyz;

    // Calculate view vector
    vs_out.V = -P.xyz;

    vs_out.material_id = gl_BaseInstanceARB;
    gl_Position = proj_matrix * P;
}
```

Listing 14.13: Passing material index through a vertex shader

When the data stored in the VS_OUT block arrives in the fragment shader, we apply our shading computations using the parameters stored in yet another uniform block. We put the parameters for our Blinn-Phong shading model into a structure and create a uniform block with a large array of these structures in it. This block is associated with binding 2 in our shader, and its definition is shown in Listing 14.14.

```
struct MaterialProperties
{
    vec4        ambient;
    vec4        diffuse;
    vec3        specular;
    float       specular_power;
};
```

```
layout (binding = 2) uniform MATERIALS
{
    MaterialProperties material[100];
};
```

Listing 14.14: Declaration of material properties

The main body of our shader is basically the same as it was in the
blinnphong example, except that rather than using values directly from
our uniform block, we use values taken from the array, indexed by the
value given to us by the vertex shader. The main body of the fragment
shader is shown in Listing 14.15.

```
void main(void)
{
    vec3 ambient = material[fs_in.material_id].ambient.rgb;
    vec3 specular_albedo = material[fs_in.material_id].specular.rgb;
    vec3 diffuse_albedo = material[fs_in.material_id].diffuse.rgb;
    float specular_power = material[fs_in.material_id].specular_power;

    // Normalize the incoming N, L, and V vectors
    vec3 N = normalize(fs_in.N);
    vec3 L = normalize(fs_in.L);
    vec3 V = normalize(fs_in.V);
    vec3 H = normalize(L + V);

    // Compute the diffuse and specular components for each fragment
    vec3 diffuse = max(dot(N, L), 0.0) * diffuse_albedo;
    vec3 specular = pow(max(dot(N, H), 0.0), specular_power * 1.0) * specular_albedo;

    o_color = vec4(ambient + specular + diffuse, 1.0);
}
```

Listing 14.15: Passing material index through a vertex shader

As you can see from Listing 14.15, each material has a unique ambient,
specular, and diffuse color, and its own specular power factor. The shading
function here is relatively simple. Of course, our material structure could
contain texture handles to *bindless textures*, like those introduced in
Chapter 11. Which material to use in the fragment shader is specified
entirely in the baseInstance field of the indirect draw parameters
structure. The output of this program is shown in Figure 14.3.

Every object shown in Figure 14.3 is effectively a separate object. Each has
its own set of vertices and can use a different material—so long as all of the
objects use the same shader. As you can see from the frame capture, this
image is generated in roughly 2.5 ms on a modern GPU that is by no
means a top-of-the-line model. In fact, as we reduce the number of objects
in the frame, we see that the frame time does not go down, suggesting that

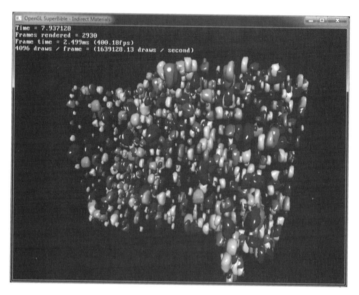

Figure 14.3: Indirect material parameters

even with thousands of draws every frame, we're limited by the speed of the CPU in this demo. If we use a larger uniform block to store our transforms, we could easily throw more draws at the GPU. In fact, it's very unlikely that you can render a complex scene with a single shader. However, it's reasonable to expect that an advanced rendering application could break its content into a handful of fairly generic shaders and batch draws by shader. Each batch would be represented by one section of the indirect draw buffer and rendered with a single call to `glMultiDrawArraysIndirect()`.

GPU Work Generation

In the previous section (and in the original `asteroids` sample), we skimmed over a few minor limitations of stock OpenGL. The most problematic of these constraints is that the draws sent to the GPU are all fixed, and the list of draws is of a known length. As the draw indirect buffer is just a regular OpenGL buffer object, we can generate it on the GPU using image stores, transform feedback, or even `glReadPixels()` if we wish. However, that leaves us with one problem: How do we know how many draws were produced? If we want to pass the list back to `glMultiDrawArraysIndirect()`, then we need to read back the draw count so that we can pass it straight back to OpenGL.

In this section, we'll demonstrate how to dynamically generate the list of draws and dispatch a list of commands, the length of which is never known to your application. To implement this, we'll use the GL_ARB_indirect_parameters extension, which introduces the following two functions:

```
void glMultiDrawArraysIndirectCountARB(GLenum mode,
                                       const void *indirect,
                                       GLintptr drawcount,
                                       GLsizei maxdrawcount,
                                       GLsizei stride);

void glMultiDrawElementsIndirectCountARB(GLenum mode,
                                         GLenum type,
                                         const void *indirect,
                                         GLintptr drawcount,
                                         GLsizei maxdrawcount,
                                         GLsizei stride);
```

glMultiDrawArraysIndirectCountARB() and **glMultiDrawElementsIndirectCountARB()** behave similarly to **glMultiDrawArraysIndirect()** and **glMultiDrawElementsIndirect()**, respectively, except that the drawcount parameter now specifies an offset into a buffer where the actual count is stored. This can be any old buffer but it is bound to a new target, GL_PARAMETER_BUFFER_ARB.

To demonstrate the use of these two functions, we'll adapt the previous example to perform culling using a compute shader, produce a new indirect draw buffer by appending draws into a shader storage buffer using an atomic counter, resolve the atomic counter into a buffer, and then use that buffer to source the draw count for a call to **glMultiDrawArraysIndirectCountARB()**.

The first complication is that because we are removing draws from the list, there is no longer a one-to-one relationship between gl_DrawID and the array of model matrices presented to our vertex shader. Therefore, in addition to producing a new list of draws, we'll need to produce a new list of model matrices, or otherwise communicate the original matrix to the vertex shader via some kind of indirection. We'll choose the latter approach here because it's simpler, as we have less data to forward from the compute shader into our graphics shaders.

In the cullindirect sample, we'll use the compute shader to cull entire objects that won't be seen by the viewer. The compute shader we'll implement will process a list of draws, determine the visibility for each of them, and then copy the parameters for those draws that may contribute to the scene into an output buffer. The number of draws copied is stored in an atomic counter. The resulting output buffer and count are referenced by a call to **glMultiDrawArraysIndirectCountARB()** to actually draw the visible geometry.

We define a structure, CandidateDraw, which contains the center (in object coordinates) and radius of a sphere that completely surrounds the object, and the parameters that can be used to draw the object. We place an unsized array of these parameter structures in an SSBO declared in our compute shader. Its definition is shown in Listing 14.16.

```
struct CandidateDraw
{
    vec3 sphereCenter;
    float sphereRadius;
    uint firstVertex;
    uint vertexCount;
    uint pad0;
    uint pad1;
};

layout (binding = 0, std430) buffer CandidateDraws
{
    CandidateDraw draw[];
};
```

Listing 14.16: Candidate draws used for culling

In addition to the candidate draws, the compute shader has access to the model, view, and projection matrices that will be used by the vertex shader to draw the resulting geometry, along with a precomputed view-projection matrix. These matrices are declared and placed in a pair of uniform blocks as shown in Listing 14.17.

```
layout (binding = 0, std140) uniform MODEL_MATRIX_BLOCK
{
    mat4    model_matrix[1024];
};

layout (binding = 1, std140) uniform TRANSFORM_BLOCK
{
    mat4    view_matrix;
    mat4    proj_matrix;
    mat4    view_proj_matrix;
};
```

Listing 14.17: Matrix data used for compute shader culling

As you can see in Listing 14.17, we have separated the model matrices from the view, projection, and view-projection product matrices. This allows us to have as many model matrices as will fit into a single uniform block. The shader uses its global invocation index to look up the incoming model matrix from the MODEL_MATRIX_BLOCK uniform block, uses that matrix along with the view_proj_matrix to transform the center of the sphere defined for the candidate draw into clip space, and then determines whether anything within that sphere could potentially be visible. Of course, we could implement a more advanced culling mechanism—we could use a tighter bounding volume than a sphere, or multiple volumes per object, for example—but this serves to demonstrate the principle.

We expand the culling distance to allow for the radius of the sphere. The definition of clip space tells us that if the projection of the sphere intersects the region from $-w$ to w in the x and y dimensions (we're not worrying about z in this example), then the object may be visible. Therefore, we can make this comparison in our compute shader to perform culling. The main body of our compute shader is shown in Listing 14.18.

```
struct DrawArraysIndirectCommand
{
    uint vertexCount;
    uint instanceCount;
    uint firstVertex;
    uint baseInstance;
};

layout (binding = 1, std430) writeonly buffer OutputDraws
{
    DrawArraysIndirectCommand command[];
};

layout (binding = 0, offset = 0) uniform atomic_uint commandCounter;

void main(void)
{
    const CandidateDraw thisDraw = draw[gl_GlobalInvocationID.x];
    const mat4 thisModelMatrix = model_matrix[gl_GlobalInvocationID.x];

    vec4 position = view_proj_matrix *
                    thisModelMatrix *
                    vec4(thisDraw.sphereCenter, 1.0);

    if ((abs(position.x) - thisDraw.sphereRadius) < (position.w * 1.0) &&
        (abs(position.y) - thisDraw.sphereRadius) < (position.w * 1.0))
    {
        uint outDrawIndex = atomicCounterIncrement(commandCounter);

        command[outDrawIndex].vertexCount = thisDraw.vertexCount;
        command[outDrawIndex].instanceCount = 1;
        command[outDrawIndex].firstVertex = thisDraw.firstVertex;
        command[outDrawIndex].baseInstance = uint(gl_GlobalInvocationID.x);
    }
}
```

Listing 14.18: Object culling in a compute shader

As you can see in Listing 14.18, we declared an SSBO called `OutputDraws` into which we're writing the resulting draw commands. We've also declared our atomic counter, `commandCounter`, which stores the count of the number of draws produced. We're using the `baseInstance` member of the output command to record the original invocation index that produced it. We can use this information later in our vertex shader, through the `gl_BaseInstanceARB` built-in variable, to look up the appropriate model matrix to transform the real geometry into world coordinates.

The code to drive all this from the application might seem a little complex at first, but it is not really all that advanced. First, we bind our atomic counter buffer and clear it with a call to **glClearBufferSubData()**, which resets the counter to zero. Next, we bind the model matrix uniform buffer, map it, and update all the model matrices for the objects in the scene. We do this again for the view, projection, and view-projection product matrices. In a more advanced application, we could do this work ahead of time, or through a persistent mapping. Next, we dispatch our culling compute shader.

After the compute shader has run, the `commandCounter` atomic counter contains the number of draws written to the `OutputDraws` SSBO. Because we're about to use this buffer as the source of commands for an indirect drawing command, we need to issue a memory barrier. To do so, we call **glMemoryBarrier()** with the GL_COMMAND_BARRIER_BIT flag set. This ensures that all the commands written to the buffer by the compute shader will be seen by the subsequent indirect draw command. The buffer bound to the GL_ATOMIC_COUNTER_BUFFER binding that backs commandCounter is then bound to the GL_PARAMETER_BUFFER_ARB binding. Next, we call **glMultiDrawArraysIndirectCountARB()**, passing a zero offset for both the base of the commands and the offset of the count parameter.

glMultiDrawArraysIndirectCountARB() also takes a maximum number of draws to process. We set this parameter to the total number of objects in our scene, as we know that we can never render more objects than this limit. The final code is shown in Listing 14.19.

```
void cullindirect_app::render(double currentTime)
{
    static const GLfloat farplane[] = { 1.0f };
    static float lastTime = 0.0f;
    static int frames = 0;
    float nowTime = float(currentTime);
    int i;
```

```
// Set viewport and clear
glViewport(0, 0, info.windowWidth, info.windowHeight);
glClearBufferfv(GL_COLOR, 0, sb7::color::Black);
glClearBufferfv(GL_DEPTH, 0, farplane);

// Bind and clear atomic counter
glBindBufferBase(GL_ATOMIC_COUNTER_BUFFER, 0, buffers.parameters);
glClearBufferSubData(GL_ATOMIC_COUNTER_BUFFER, GL_R32UI,
                     0, sizeof(GLuint),
                     GL_RED_INTEGER, GL_UNSIGNED_INT, nullptr);

// Bind shader storage buffers
glBindBufferBase(GL_SHADER_STORAGE_BUFFER, 0, buffers.drawCandidates);
glBindBufferBase(GL_SHADER_STORAGE_BUFFER, 1, buffers.drawCommands);

// Bind model matrix UBO and fill with data
glBindBufferBase(GL_UNIFORM_BUFFER, 0, buffers.modelMatrices);
vmath::mat4* pModelMatrix =
    (vmath::mat4*)glMapBufferRange(GL_UNIFORM_BUFFER,
                                   0, 1024 * sizeof(vmath::mat4),
                                   GL_MAP_WRITE_BIT |
                                   GL_MAP_INVALIDATE_BUFFER_BIT);

for (i = 0; i < 1024; i++)
{
    float f = float(i) / 127.0f + nowTime * 0.025f;
    float g = float(i) / 127.0f;
    const vmath::mat4 model_matrix =
        vmath::translate(70.0f * vmath::vec3(sinf(f * 3.0f),
                                             cosf(f * 5.0f),
                                             cosf(f * 9.0f))) *
        vmath::rotate(nowTime * 140.0f,
            vmath::normalize(vmath::vec3(sinf(g * 35.0f),
                                         cosf(g * 75.0f),
                                         cosf(g * 39.0f))));
    pModelMatrix[i] = model_matrix;
}

glUnmapBuffer(GL_UNIFORM_BUFFER);

// Bind view + projection matrix UBO and fill
glBindBufferBase(GL_UNIFORM_BUFFER, 1, buffers.transforms);
TransformBuffer* pTransforms =
    (TransformBuffer*)glMapBufferRange(GL_UNIFORM_BUFFER,
                                       0, sizeof(TransformBuffer),
                                       GL_MAP_WRITE_BIT |
                                       GL_MAP_INVALIDATE_BUFFER_BIT);

float t = nowTime * 0.1f;

const vmath::mat4 view_matrix =
    vmath::lookat(vmath::vec3(150.0f * cosf(t), 0.0f, 150.0f * sinf(t)),
                  vmath::vec3(0.0f, 0.0f, 0.0f),
                  vmath::vec3(0.0f, 1.0f, 0.0f));
const vmath::mat4 proj_matrix =
    vmath::perspective(50.0f,
                       (float)info.windowWidth / (float)info.windowHeight,
                       1.0f,
                       2000.0f);

pTransforms->view_matrix = view_matrix;
pTransforms->proj_matrix = proj_matrix;
pTransforms->view_proj_matrix = proj_matrix * view_matrix;
```

```
glUnmapBuffer(GL_UNIFORM_BUFFER);

// Bind the culling compute shader and dispatch it
glUseProgram(programs.cull);
glDispatchCompute(CANDIDATE_COUNT / 16, 1, 1);

// Barrier
glMemoryBarrier(GL_COMMAND_BARRIER_BIT);

// Get ready to render
glEnable(GL_DEPTH_TEST);
glEnable(GL_CULL_FACE);

glBindVertexArray(object.get_vao());

glActiveTexture(GL_TEXTURE0);
glBindTexture(GL_TEXTURE_2D, texture);

// Bind indirect command buffer and parameter buffer
glBindBuffer(GL_DRAW_INDIRECT_BUFFER, buffers.drawCommands);
glBindBuffer(GL_PARAMETER_BUFFER_ARB, buffers.parameters);

glUseProgram(programs.draw);

// Draw
glMultiDrawArraysIndirectCountARB(GL_TRIANGLES, 0, 0,
                                  CANDIDATE_COUNT, 0);

// Update overlay
if (nowTime > (lastTime + 0.25f))
{
    fps = float(frames) / (nowTime - lastTime);
    frames = 0;
    lastTime = nowTime;
}

glDisable(GL_CULL_FACE);
updateOverlay();

frames++;
}
```

Listing 14.19: Driving compute culling shaders

The astute reader might have noticed $* 1.0$ sitting in the middle of our culling shader in Listing 14.18:

```
if ((abs(position.x) - thisDraw.sphereRadius) < (position.w * 1.0) &&
    (abs(position.y) - thisDraw.sphereRadius) < (position.w * 1.0))
{
    // Produce output draw...
```

Of course, as this shader simply culls items that would not be visible to you anyway, the program's output doesn't differ from the output that would be produced if the culling did not happen. However, by reducing the value in the shader from 1.0, we effectively reduce the visible area of clip space.

Changing it to 0.5, for example, reduces clip space by half, and we start to see objects being culled as they approach halfway from the center of the viewport to the edge. The output of the program is shown in Figure 14.4.

The top image in Figure 14.4 is the full-frame output of the application. Again, we've used our asteroid pack to demonstrate the technique. The bottom image in Figure 14.4 is the same application but with the culling region reduced by half. As you can see, the asteroids have been reduced to fit within a window half the width and height of the viewport.

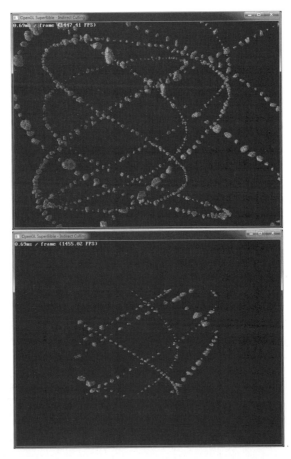

Figure 14.4: Output of the `cullindirect` application

Zero Copy

By now you should be very familiar with functions like **glMapBufferRange()** and **glTextureStorageSubImage2D()**, which allow you to get a pointer to a buffer object's data store and place texture data into memory, respectively. Sometimes, these functions will make a *copy* of your data, transferring it from your application's memory into OpenGL's own memory, usually located on the graphics card or otherwise managed by OpenGL. If your application uses the data only once or twice, this copy can be a significant amount of work done by OpenGL on your behalf. By managing shared memory yourself with the help of *persistent* maps, we can avoid that overhead.

We mentioned persistent maps earlier in this chapter and briefly introduced them when we first discussed the flags that you can pass to **glMapNamedBufferRange()** and **glNamedBufferStorage()**. In this section we cover a few methods you can use to synchronize access to shared memory, to use it to upload texture data, and to update the contents of buffers synchronously without stalling OpenGL.

Persistent Mapping

A persistent map is so called because the mapping—getting a pointer valid for the application—sticks around until you release it. If a mapping is not marked as persistent, then you are responsible for releasing it before you draw anything that might access the buffer. OpenGL will do its best to find buffers that are mapped when you call one of the drawing commands and generate a GL_INVALID_OPERATION error, but it's not required to find every last case. In practice, this means that drawing from a mapped buffer produces undefined behavior. We can make that behavior well defined by telling OpenGL that this is really what we want to do.

There are two steps to making a persistent mapped buffer. First, you need to declare, when you allocate storage for the buffer, that you want to be able to map it persistently. This doesn't make the persistent map, but it does give OpenGL the opportunity to allocate storage for the buffer object in a region of memory that can be seen by both the GPU and the CPU in the system. Next, we need to actually map the buffer using **glMapNamedBufferRange()** and tell OpenGL that this is the mapping we want to keep around. At this point, you are presented with a pointer that you can use to access the same memory that OpenGL is using to draw from.

An example of creating this kind of mapping can be found in Listing 14.2 earlier in this chapter. Here, we specify the GL_MAP_PERSISTENT_BIT flag both when we call **glNamedBufferStorage()** *and* when we call **glMapNamedBufferRange()**. Once we have a persistent mapped buffer, we are responsible for synchronization of any access to it.

Synchronizing Access to Buffers

When the GPU and the CPU can both access the same memory at the same time, we need to make sure that the two parts of our process are in sync. If we start overwriting chunks of data that are in use by the GPU, we will get inconsistent results. This might have no ill effect in our application, but more than likely it will result in parts of a frame being rendered with old information and other parts being rendered with new information. Readers familiar with multi-threaded programming will recognize this as a *race condition*. The visible side effect might be objects being out of place, pieces of geometry missing, or corrupted textures or other elements. In the worst case, it could be catastrophic.

In the example presented earlier in this chapter, we decided that we didn't care if the frame was partially updated. However, that will not always be the case, especially in more complex applications. There are several mechanisms for dealing with synchronization, presented here from most naïve to most advanced:

- Just call **glFinish()** before starting any frame. This ensures that the GPU has completely finished rendering everything from the previous frame and is done with any shared data.

- Use a fence object associated with the resource, ask OpenGL to signal it with a call to **glFenceSync()** after it's done consuming the shared data on the GPU side, and then wait on the resulting fence with a call to **glClientWaitSync()** before overwriting that data on the CPU side.

- Partition the shared data into multiple regions and then use several fences, one for each region, to allow the CPU to move ahead of the GPU without waiting.

We have implemented the pmbstreaming application to demonstrate all three methods, along with the "I don't care" strategy of not waiting at all. The example application renders a spinning object with a simple lighting model and a texture applied to it. On the author's machine, the application runs at several thousand frames per second regardless of synchronization settings. When fences are in use, the application also tests the fences to see if it will be stalled by waiting on them.

The application creates a buffer and uses it as a uniform buffer that contains the matrices used by the program. We use a persistent map to share the uniform buffer between the CPU and the GPU, and we update the values of the uniforms in the buffer by simply writing new values into memory. The application never unmaps the buffer.

If we just let the application run with no synchronization, we see a frame time of 0.36 milliseconds per frame. The rendered output looks good in this application because the frame is very simple and we're updating only a few uniform block members—there is little chance for partial updates and incoherent data to slip in. When we introduce synchronization using the first strategy (just call `glFinish()`), we can assume that the application will stall. After all, we just asked OpenGL to do a lot of work for us and then immediately asked it to do everything. In this scenario, the frame time increases to 0.64 milliseconds per frame—almost *double* the time associated with not waiting at all.

Next, we move to the strategy of using a single fence to marshal access to the shared buffer. Fences in OpenGL are single-use objects. That is, calling `glFenceSync()` creates a new fence in the unsignaled state. When the GPU executes the fence, it moves to the signaled state. We can check the state later with `glGetSynciv()` and we can wait for it to become signaled by calling `glClientWaitSync()`. Once a fence becomes signaled, it can never become unsignaled again; all we can do with it is delete it. Therefore, after issuing the drawing command that uses the data in the shared buffer, we call `glFenceSync()` and store the result. Before updating the mapped buffer, we call `glClientWaitSync()`. This causes the application to wait before writing into the buffer. We then delete the sync object using `glDeleteSync()` and start the procedure again in the next frame.

When we run this strategy inside the `pmbstreaming` application, we see that when we begin waiting for the sync object, it is not yet signaled and therefore we know that the application will stall. Indeed, we see the frame time remain at roughly 0.60 milliseconds. We haven't done much better than our brute-force method of calling `glFinish()` at the start of every frame.

Now we get to the last method, which involves keeping multiple copies of our shared data and associating a fence with each one. Here, we make our buffer big enough to hold four complete copies of our uniforms. We also create an array of four sync objects to represent our fences. Each copy of our uniform data is associated with one of the fences. Each time we need to send a new copy of the uniforms to our shader, we wait for the fence associated with the next available slot in the buffer to become signaled. Then we delete that fence, update the uniforms, send the drawing command to OpenGL, and create a new fence object to represent that draw. On each frame, we move to the next slot in the buffer and its associated fence. Every four frames, we wrap around and reuse the old slots.

The slot is communicated to the shader by using the `baseInstance` parameter to the drawing command and is picked up in the shader using the `gl_BaseInstanceARB` built-in variable, which is part of the `GL_ARB_shader_draw_parameters` extension. Of course, you can use any other mechanism to communicate the slot index to the shader—vertex attributes work quite well for this. With this synchronization mechanism, the application reports that it is never stalled and the frame time decreases to 0.37 milliseconds per frame, which is almost exactly the same as the no-synchronization version.

Figure 14.5 shows the output of the application. In the upper left of each image is the frame time (and the corresponding frame rate), the mode that the application is in, and the stall marker.

As you can see in Figure 14.5, the unsynchronized update method is fastest, but it is technically incorrect. This is shown in the upper-left image. Calling `glFinish()` (as seen in the upper-right image) synchronizes access in a brute-force manner. While correct, it's certainly sub-optimal, with a frame time almost double that of the unsynchronized method. On the lower left, we see the "single fence" method. Again, this is correct, but the frame time is really no better than with the full `glFinish()` method. Finally, on the lower right, we see the result of the "ringed fence" method, which subdivides a large buffer into several small parts and arbitrates access to each part individually with its own fence. This method is both correct and fast, with a frame time approximately equal to that of the unsynchronized method, and no detected stalls.

Unmappable Resources

In the last few sections, we've discussed directly sharing data between the GPU and the CPU by using *persistent mapped* buffers. With this technique, you map a buffer and then keep it mapped even while you're drawing.

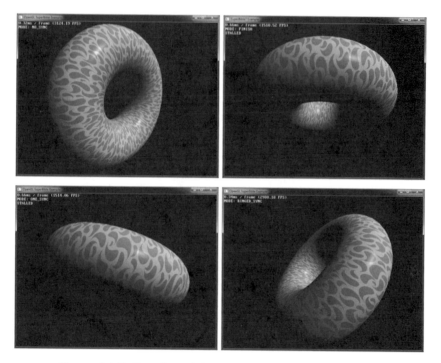

Figure 14.5: Synchronizing access to a mapped buffer

With careful organization of your data and some thought devoted to synchronization, you can remove any calls to upload or copy data from your application into OpenGL's memory, and instead use the data in place. In some cases, though, it's not possible to do this. There are a couple things that you can't map, as the following examples highlight:

- It's currently not possible to map a texture. If you want to give OpenGL data that it can use as a texture, you still need to move the data into a texture object before you can bind it into your shaders.

- If you have very large buffers—on the order of hundreds of megabytes—it's very likely that OpenGL will not be able to map them because memory that can be shared between application and GPU is limited.

Even so, we can employ certain techniques to take advantage of persistent mapped buffers while still being able to use these kinds of resources.

For textures, we can copy the data from a persistent mapped buffer into a texture using calls to **glTextureStorageSubImage2D()** (or the appropriate version for different dimensionalities of texture). Compare this approach to calling **glTextureStorageSubImage2D()** using client memory. When you do this, OpenGL must make a copy of your texture data before returning control to your application because you're allowed to overwrite that data right away. By using a persistent mapped buffer, you can still write data directly to memory as you can with client data, but OpenGL can delay uploading data from there into the texture, probably avoiding at least one copy.

For buffers, we can copy from our persistent mapped buffer into the target buffer using **glCopyNamedBufferSubData()**. Again, there is a copy here, so this is not technically zero-copy. However, as with textures, if the source of the data is memory that is not otherwise accessible to the GPU, then OpenGL may need to make a first copy to get the data ready for upload and then a second copy to get the data into its final location. Further, unless you mark the target buffer as dynamic (using the GL_DYNAMIC_STORAGE_BIT flag when you call **glBufferStorage()**), then you can't directly load data into it from application memory—uploading from another buffer is your only choice, so you may as well make that staging buffer a persistent mapped buffer.

In the pmbfractal example, we demonstrate the use of a persistent mapped buffer to update a texture. To create this example, we ported[3] the Julia fractal example shown in Listing 13.34 from the GPU back to the CPU. The resulting fractal generation loop is shown in Listing 14.20.

```
void pmbfractal_app::update_fractal()
{
    const vmath::vec2 C = fractparams.C; // (0.03f, -0.2f);
    const float thresh_squared = 256.0f;
    const float zoom = fractparams.zoom;
    const vmath::vec2 offset = fractparams.offset;

#pragma omp parallel for schedule (dynamic, 16)
    for (int y = 0; y < FRACTAL_HEIGHT; y++)
    {
        for (int x = 0; x < FRACTAL_WIDTH; x++)
        {
            vmath::vec2 Z;
            Z[0] = zoom * (float(x) / float(FRACTAL_WIDTH) - 0.5) + offset[0];
            Z[1] = zoom * (float(y) / float(FRACTAL_WIDTH) - 0.5) + offset[1];
            unsigned char * ptr = mapped_buffer + y * FRACTAL_WIDTH + x;
```

---

3. Clearly, the best place for this code to run is the GPU, but this example is provided for illustration purposes.

```
        int it;
        for (it = 0; it < 256; it++)
        {
            vmath::vec2 Z_squared;

            Z_squared[0] = Z[0] * Z[0] - Z[1] * Z[1];
            Z_squared[1] = 2.0f * Z[0] * Z[1];
            Z = Z_squared + C;

            if ((Z[0] * Z[0] + Z[1] * Z[1]) > thresh_squared)
                break;
        }
        *ptr = it;
    }
}
}
```

Listing 14.20: Julia fractals on the CPU

As you can see from Listing 14.20, we have again used OpenMP to accelerate our fractal rendering function. The mapped_buffer variable is a pointer to our persistent mapped buffer, which we create and map during application start-up.

In the inner rendering loop, which is shown in Listing 14.21, we bind the persistent mapped buffer to the GL_PIXEL_UNPACK_BUFFER target and call **glTexSubImage2D()** to update the contents of the texture. This causes OpenGL to copy the texture data that we just generated into our texture. We then immediately draw the texture to the screen using a simple full-screen quad program.

```
void pmbfractal_app::render(double currentTime)
{
    static float lastTime = 0.0f;
    static int frames = 0;
    float nowTime = float(currentTime);

    fractparams.C = vmath::vec2(1.5f - cosf(nowTime * 0.4f) * 0.5f,
                                1.5f + cosf(nowTime * 0.5f) * 0.5f) * 0.3f;
    fractparams.offset = vmath::vec2(cosf(nowTime * 0.14f),
                                     cosf(nowTime * 0.25f)) * 0.25f;
    fractparams.zoom = (sinf(nowTime) + 1.3f) * 0.7f;

    update_fractal();

    glViewport(0, 0, info.windowWidth, info.windowHeight);

    glUseProgram(program);
    glActiveTexture(GL_TEXTURE0);
    glBindTexture(GL_TEXTURE_2D, texture);

    glBindBuffer(GL_PIXEL_UNPACK_BUFFER, buffer);
    glTexSubImage2D(GL_TEXTURE_2D, 0,
                    0, 0,
                    FRACTAL_WIDTH, FRACTAL_HEIGHT,
```

```
                   GL_RED, GL_UNSIGNED_BYTE,
                   nullptr);
    glBindBuffer(GL_PIXEL_UNPACK_BUFFER, 0);

    glBindVertexArray(vao);
    glDrawArrays(GL_TRIANGLE_STRIP, 0, 4);

    if (nowTime > (lastTime + 0.25f))
    {
        fps = float(frames) / (nowTime - lastTime);
        frames = 0;
        lastTime = nowTime;
    }

    updateOverlay();

    frames++;
}
```

Listing 14.21: Persistent mapped fractal rendering

The resulting output is shown in Figure 14.6. As you can see, we have been able to render a moderately detailed fractal in roughly 13 milliseconds. In this application, we use six threads to render the fractal into memory shared with the GPU. There is a single-step copy from that buffer into a texture that is immediately usable by our shader.

Rendering Julia fractals is perhaps not the greatest use for our CPU—after all, we already saw that the GPU is very well suited to this kind of highly

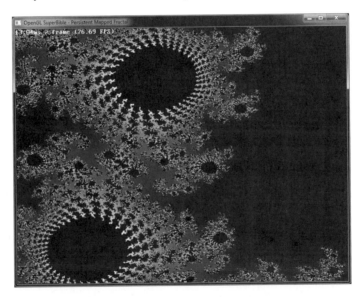

Figure 14.6: Persistent mapped Julia fractal

parallel workload. However, the data written here could be anything. For example, it could be the output of a video codec in a video streaming application, or data produced by a third-party library that doesn't interface natively with OpenGL. In this case, we can map the buffer and hand the pointer to the library as if it's normal application memory, and the library will know no different.

A word of caution is warranted, however, when sharing pointers to mapped buffers with software that's not expecting this kind of use case. Mapped buffers are very often uncached and *write combined*. This means that write performance is very good, and writing to those buffers does not pollute caches that might hold other, more useful data. However, read performance of these kinds of mappings can be extremely slow. In fact, unless you map the buffer with the GL_MAP_READ_BIT flag set, it's not even legal to read from the resulting memory. You should ensure that whatever software you use (especially third-party software that you didn't write), it doesn't try to read from a write-only buffer or write to a read-only buffer.

Performance Analysis Tools

In this section we'll cover some of the performance analysis tools that are freely available and don't rely on any non-free tools. That is, you can download and install them right now! The first of these tools is GPUView, which is part of the Windows Performance Toolkit offered by Microsoft. The second is AMD's GPU PerfStudio. Both of these tools are available for download from their respective vendors' Web sites.

Windows Performance Toolkit and GPUView

Microsoft's Windows Performance Toolkit (WPT) is a suite of tools for measuring the performance of various parts of the Windows operating system. It can measure CPU usage and events, memory and disk accesses, network activity, and a multitude of other things. What we are most interested in here is measuring GPU activity.

Modern graphics processors operate by processing *command buffers*, which are sequences of commands encoded in some form of byte code and sent from the application (or in this case, the OpenGL driver) to the graphics card. Sending a command buffer to the graphics card is sometimes known as submission. The GPU picks up the command buffers, interprets their contents, and acts on the instructions they contain. Command buffers are stored in one or more queues. When the driver first submits a command buffer for execution, the operating system (or some component of it) manages that queue and holds the command buffer in a ring waiting to send it to the hardware; this queue is referred to as the *software queue* or *CPU queue*. Once the hardware is ready to execute a new command buffer, a low-level component of the graphics driver signals the GPU to pick up the command buffer at the front of the queue and execute it. The GPU can usually get one or more command buffers lined up and ready to execute while it is still working on previously enqueued buffers. The command buffers that have been sent to the hardware but are still waiting to execute are held in a *hardware queue.*

GPUView is a tool included in the WPT that allows you to visualize command buffer submission and the activity in the hardware and software queues. It can track all of the submissions that the application makes (through the OpenGL driver) into the operating system queues, tell you which types of submissions are being made, and show how they are batched, sent to the hardware, and executed. You can see how long each command buffer spent waiting in the software queue before being sent to the hardware, how long each spent in the hardware queue, and how long it spent being executed. An annotated screenshot of GPUView is shown in Figure 14.7.

The application under analysis in Figure 14.7 is the asteroid field example from Chapter 7, a screenshot of which is shown in Figure 7.9. This particular application uses almost all of the available GPU time. The

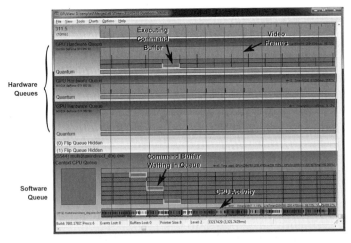

Figure 14.7: GPUView in action

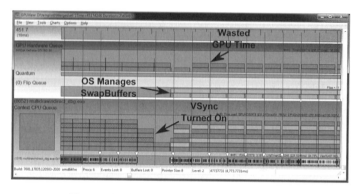

Figure 14.8: Vsync seen in GPUView

system used to capture this trace contained an AMD Phenom X6 1050T processor with six CPU cores and an NVIDIA GeForce GTX 560 SE graphics card with two displays attached to it. The application was running in full screen on one of the displays while the other display was used for development tools. The top hardware queue is clearly executing the application under test. The small submissions on the second queue are related to Windows' Desktop Window Manager (DWM) performing composition on the second display. The vertical lines running through the trace are the vertical refresh events that are associated with the display. In this application, synchronization to vertical refresh (also known as vsync) is off. Now take a look at Figure 14.8.

In Figure 14.8, we start running the application in full-screen mode with vsync turned off (which is the default). Then, during the run, we turn on vsync. This point is clearly visible in the GPUView image. When vsync is turned on, the software and hardware queues drain, and the operating system takes over presentation of the rendered frames. When vsync is off, OpenGL tells the graphics hardware to finish its rendering and show the result to the user as soon as possible. When it's on, the operating system holds back the graphics hardware and tells it to wait for a vertical refresh event before showing the frame to the user. This causes the GPU to idle for short periods of time between each frame, which shows up as gaps in the hardware queue. This is effectively wasted time. Here, we have wasted time on purpose to prevent the application from getting too far ahead of the display (and to show what this looks like in the tool). However, anything that causes the GPU to wait will waste GPU time.

When you install the WPT, its program directory will contain a `gpuview` folder, which is where the GPUView tool is located. In that same directory is the file `log.cmd`, which is a script for starting and stopping recording of logging events into ETL files—event trace logs. These files contain the raw data that is interpreted by the GPUView tool. ETL files can be extremely large. To start recording data, run log.cmd from a command prompt with administrative privileges; to stop it, run log.cmd again. Even running a simple application for a minute or so can generate gigabytes of data, so it's best to keep recording times short and sweet. Other suggestions include minimizing the number of other applications running (especially those with graphical output) and disabling the Aero user interface (which turns off DWM composition). Also, you can implement a pause feature in your application such that it can be made to stop rendering. Then, pause the application, start logging, allow the application to render for a few seconds, pause it again, and stop logging. When logging is active, a number of ETL files are written into the directory from which logging is started. One file is created for each of several of the major Windows subsystems. When logging is terminated, they are all merged together into a single file called Merged.etl, which is what is loaded into GPUView.

In addition to regular command buffer submissions (referred to by GPUView as *standard queue packets* in the CPU queue and *standard DMA packets* once they reach the hardware), the tool can show you a number of other events that might be inserted into the graphics pipeline. For example, *present packets* are events that instruct the operating system to display the results of rendering (triggered by the **SwapBuffers()** command) with a cross-hatch pattern in GPUView. Clicking on a packet brings up a dialog similar to the one shown in Figure 14.9.

You can see a number of useful pieces of information in the dialog shown in Figure 14.9. First, we see several timestamps; the first is the packet creation time, which is the time that the command buffer was allocated (which is when the OpenGL would start filling it in). Next, we see the SubmittedToHardwareQueueTime, which is when the packet was sent to the hardware for processing. It is then picked up by the hardware at the time noted by GpuStartProcessingTime. When the GPU is done processing the packet, it triggers an interrupt, which is handled by an interrupt service routine (ISR)—the time at which this interrupt is serviced by the ISR is shown in CompletedByISRTime. Next, the graphics subsystem processes the packet using a deferred procedure call (DPC); the time at which this completes is shown as CompletedByDPCTime. The total time between when the command buffer is submitted to the hardware (SubmittedToHardwareQueueTime) and when the command buffer is completed and signals the ISR (CompletedByISRTime) is given by Time in HW queue. This is effectively the amount of time it took the GPU

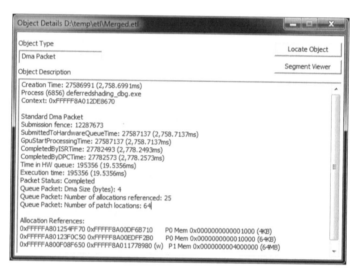

Figure 14.9: A packet dialog in GPUView

to execute the command buffer. The sum of these packets for a given frame places the upper limit on the frame rate of your application.

GPUView can show you quite a bit more information about your application's use of the graphics processor. As your applications become more and more complex, they will start to exhibit behavior that only a tool such as GPUView can illustrate. The goal of performance tuning is twofold:

- Ensure that the GPU does as much work as possible by feeding it efficiently and not causing it to stall.

- Ensure that the work the GPU does contributes to the final scene and don't ask it to do more than necessary.

In the remainder of this chapter, we'll use GPUView to analyze our applications and show the effects of the tuning advice we'll give.

GPU PerfStudio

GPU PerfStudio is a free tool provided by AMD that's designed for the analysis of graphics applications written using OpenGL and other graphics

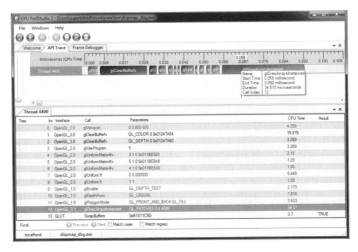

Figure 14.10: GPU PerfStudio running an example application

APIs. GPU PerfStudio supports three major modes of operation: an API
trace tool, a frame debugger, and a frame profiler. The frame profiler
requires AMD hardware to be present, but the API trace and the frame
debugger work well on hardware from any vendor. Figure 14.10 shows a
screenshot of GPU PerfStudio's API trace window running the
displacement example from Chapter 8, "Primitive Processing."

As you can see, GPU PerfStudio has captured all of the OpenGL calls made
by the application and has produced a timeline of the application making
those calls. Along with each OpenGL command, the amount of CPU time
taken to execute the call is shown in both the timeline and the function
call list. The function call list also logs the parameters sent to each
command. The frame debugger window of GPU PerfStudio is shown in
Figure 14.11.

In the GPU PerfStudio frame debugger in Figure 14.11, you can see the
OpenGL pipeline with the vertex array object (VAO), vertex shader (VS),
tessellation control and evaluation shaders (TCS and TES), fragment shader
(FS), and framebuffer (FB) active. We also see that this particular drawing
command is not using the geometry or compute shader stages (GS and
CS). The fragment shader stage is selected, and in the main window we see
the source code of the current fragment shader along with the texture
that's bound for rendering.

Finally, in addition to being able to display information about the timing
of drawing commands, the resources bound, and the code used for

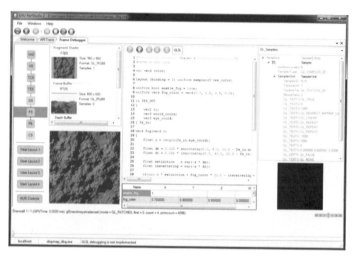

Figure 14.11: GPU PerfStudio frame debugger

shaders, GPU PerfStudio is able to overlay data *in your application*. Clicking on the "HUD Controls" button in the frame debugger displays the window shown in Figure 14.12.

By using the HUD control window shown in Figure 14.12, we can select certain textures for viewing inside the application whenever the application is paused. A screenshot of the landscape example from

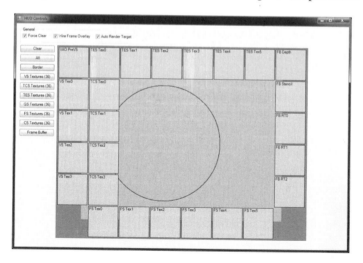

Figure 14.12: GPU PerfStudio HUD control window

Figure 14.13: GPU PerfStudio overlaying information

Chapter 8 with the in-use textures is shown in Figure 14.13. In the top left, the height map used by the tessellation evaluation shader is visible. On the top right of the screenshot is the depth buffer (pure white because it's been cleared to 1.0) and the content of the framebuffer. At the bottom left is the texture used by the fragment shader for shading the terrain.

If you happen to have access to AMD hardware, GPU PerfStudio can read a number of hardware *performance counters* from OpenGL to measure the impact of the drawing commands that your application executes. This includes measurements of things like primitives processed, the amount of texture data read, the amount of information written to the framebuffer, and so on. This feature is called the Frame Profiler, and a screenshot of GPU PerfStudio in this mode is shown in Figure 14.14.

Because this mode isn't universally available, we will leave it as an exercise for AMD users to explore this feature on their own. GPU PerfStudio comes with some excellent help documentation and more is available online.

Tuning Your Application for Speed

In this section, we discuss a number of things that you can do to make sure that your application runs more efficiently, minimize the amount of

Figure 14.14: GPU PerfStudio showing AMD performance counters

work that the OpenGL driver needs to do, and maximize the amount of work you can get from a GPU.

Reading State or Data from OpenGL

In general, reading state or data back from OpenGL into your application is not a great idea. If we can offer one piece of advice, it's to not do anything that might stall the OpenGL pipeline. This includes reading the framebuffer using `glReadPixels()`; reading the results[4] of occlusion queries, transform feedback queries, or other objects whose results depend on rendering; or performing a wait on a fence that is unlikely to have completed. In particular, it should never be necessary to call `glFinish()`.

Furthermore, cases that might be less obvious can be avoided. For example, functions such as `glGetError()`, `glGetIntegerv()`, `glGetUniformLocation()`, and so on may not stall the GPU, but could well stall a multi-threaded driver and damage application performance. It's best to stay away from functions that have the words "get" or "is" in their names. Also, while it should be common sense to not allocate and destroy objects frequently during the normal operation of your application, try to avoid generating names through the various "gen" functions.

---

4. As noted in the "Getting OpenGL to Make Decisions for You" section in Chapter 12, you can use conditional rendering to avoid reading the result of occlusion queries.

When reading data from OpenGL back into client memory, there are ways to achieve this without stalling—most of which involve allowing the GPU to lag far enough behind your application that it's almost certainly done gathering the information you need before you read it.

The first case we cover here is reading data from the framebuffer using **glReadPixels()**. If the intent is to use the resulting data for some other purpose in OpenGL, simply bind a buffer to the GL_PIXEL_PACK_BUFFER target, read pixel data into it, bind the buffer to whichever target you want to use it with, and continue rendering. There is no reason for the pixel data to ever leave the graphics card's memory or for the CPU to ever see it. If, however, you really must have the data in application memory, you can get at it in a number of ways.

First and simplest, you can call **glReadPixels()** and pass the address of a region of your application's memory into which OpenGL should place the data. In almost all cases, this will cause a bubble to form in the OpenGL pipeline. You can see the effect in Figure 14.15.

In Figure 14.15, the application starts by not calling **glReadPixels()** at all. As you can see on the left side of the screenshot, the GPU is nicely utilized, is not stalling, and always has at least one frame queued up ready to render. As soon as the application starts calling **glReadPixels()**, the CPU and GPU synchronize and we can clearly see that the GPU is starving for work to do, with big gaps in its execution queue. Of course, we can bind a buffer to the GL_PIXEL_PACK_BUFFER target before calling **glReadPixels()** to retrieve data into a pixel pack buffer, which is what we're doing toward the end of the trace in Figure 14.15. However, although there seems to be a significant change in activity, there are still gaps in the queue, which is not what we want.

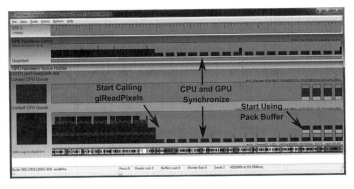

Figure 14.15: GPUView showing the effect of **glReadPixels()** into system memory

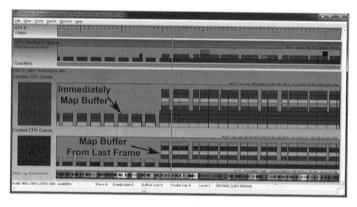

Figure 14.16: GPUView showing the effect of **glReadPixels()** into a buffer

What's happening here is that we're still calling **glReadPixels()**, but with a buffer bound to the GL_PIXEL_PACK_BUFFER target. This allows the GPU to complete rendering and then copy the resulting data into the buffer object without interruption. However, we then *read the data back* into the application by calling **glMapBufferRange()**. As a consequence, our application has to wait for OpenGL to copy the data from the framebuffer into the buffer object before it can continue. This is even worse! Not only do we stall the GPU, but it actually does *more* work between each stall.

Now take a look at Figure 14.16. In this new trace, something interesting is going on. At first, we continue to call **glReadPixels()** to get the data into the buffer object and then immediately map it to get the data into our application. This is causing stalls and inefficient use of the GPU. However, partway through Figure 14.16, we change our strategy: We still call **glReadPixels()** to transfer data from the framebuffer into a buffer object, but then map the buffer from the *previous frame*. We create multiple buffer objects, but because we map only buffers that haven't been written to in at least one frame time, the GPU has more time to keep up with us. Although quite a bit of work is going on, the GPU remains fully utilized and the performance of our application is not significantly impacted.

Effective Buffer Mapping

Once you have a buffer object whose data store has been allocated using a call to **glBufferData()**, you can map the entire buffer into the application's memory by calling **glMapBuffer()**. However, several caveats apply to the use of this function. First, if you just overwrite some part of the buffer, the rest of the buffer remains intact, meaning that OpenGL has to keep that data alive. Second, the buffer itself could be quite large and OpenGL could fail to find enough available address space to provide you with a single pointer to one contiguous region of memory representing the buffer. Finally, if you want to write into the buffer, either OpenGL has to wait until the GPU is done reading from it before giving you the pointer, or it must keep multiple copies of the data around, giving you a pointer to one of the copies that is not currently being used by the GPU.

To address these issues, we can call the **glMapBufferRange()** function, which allows you to map only *part* of the buffer into your application, and which provides several more flags that can be used to control how the data is mapped and how synchronization is performed with the rest of the OpenGL pipeline. The prototype of **glMapBufferRange()** is

```
void *glMapBufferRange(GLenum target,
                       GLintptr offset,
                       GLsizeiptr length,
                       GLbitfield access);
```

The target parameter is the buffer target to which the buffer you wish to map is bound, just as in the other buffer functions such as **glMapBuffer()** and **glBindBuffer()**. The offset and length parameters specify the range of the buffer that you want to map. Their units are bytes, with offset 0 being the first byte in the buffer and length being the size of the mapped range, in bytes. Besides being able to map a small part of the buffer, the additional power of **glMapBufferRange()** comes from the last parameter, access, which is used to specify a number of flags that control how the mapping is performed. Table 14.1 shows the possible bitfield values that can be passed in access.

Table 14.1: Map Buffer Access Types

Access Flags (GL_MAP_*)	Usage
READ_BIT	Returned pointer may be used for reading the buffer.
WRITE_BIT	Returned pointer may be used for modifying the buffer.
INVALIDATE_RANGE_BIT	Signals that OpenGL can throw away the previous contents of the mapped range. Data in the range is undefined unless updated by the application.

continued

Table 14.1: *Continued*

Access Flags (GL_MAP_*)	Usage
INVALIDATE_BUFFER_BIT	Signals that OpenGL can throw away the previous contents of the entire buffer. Data in the buffer is undefined unless updated by the application.
FLUSH_EXPLICIT_BIT	Using this bit with GL_MAP_WRITE_BIT requires an application to explicitly flush each range updated by calling **glFlushMappedBufferRange()**. If this bit is not specified, the entire mapped range will be flushed when **glUnmapBuffer()** is called.
UNSYNCHRONIZED_BIT	Tells OpenGL to avoid trying to synchronize any pending GPU writes to this buffer before mapping.

As you can see, **glMapBufferRange()** gives you quite a bit of control over how OpenGL performs the requested mapping operation. The GL_MAP_READ_BIT and GL_MAP_WRITE_BIT flags are self-explanatory. Setting the read bit indicates that you wish to read from the buffer and setting the write bit indicates that you want to write to it. Those preferences are more strictly enforced with **glMapBufferRange()** than the equivalent GL_READ_ONLY and GL_WRITE_ONLY parameters to **glMapBuffer()**, though. Incorrect use can cause your application to crash, so get them right! Of course, you can specify both the GL_MAP_READ_BIT and GL_MAP_WRITE_BIT flags at the same time by simply ORing them together.

The GL_MAP_INVALIDATE_RANGE_BIT and GL_MAP_INVALIDATE_BUFFER_BIT flags tell OpenGL that you no longer care about the data in the buffer and that it can throw that data out if it wishes. If you don't need the old contents of the buffer after the mapping operation, it's important to set one of these bits[5]; otherwise, OpenGL has to make sure that whatever you don't write in the buffer has valid data after you unmap it. Setting the GL_MAP_INVALIDATE_RANGE_BIT flag tells OpenGL to discard the data in the range being mapped, whereas setting GL_MAP_INVALIDATE_BUFFER_BIT tells it to discard everything in the buffer—even parts outside the mapped range.

---

5. You could set both, but GL_MAP_INVALIDATE_BUFFER_BIT is clearly a superset of GL_MAP_INVALIDATE_RANGE_BIT.

If you map the whole range of the buffer by setting offset to 0 and length to the size of the buffer object, then these two bits become equivalent.

You use the GL_MAP_FLUSH_EXPLICIT_BIT flag if you want to overwrite only part of the buffer, but you don't know which part when you call **glMapBufferRange()**. This flag tells OpenGL that you might overwrite the whole range, or just a single byte of it, and that when you know what was overwritten, you will tell it. To do that, call **glFlushMappedBufferRange()**, whose prototype is

```
GLvoid glFlushMappedBufferRange(GLenum target,
                                GLintptr offset,
                                GLsizeiptr length);
```

You can also use this function if you want to update multiple independent regions of the buffer but don't want to make multiple calls to **glMapBufferRange()**. A second possible benefit of calling **glFlushMappedBufferRange()** is that if you map a very large buffer and then update different ranges of it over time, you can use **glFlushMappedBufferRange()** to tell OpenGL that you're done with updating parts of it as you go. This might allow OpenGL to overlap work such as moving data to the GPU's memory with any additional work that your application might be doing, such as reading data from a file. You should be careful with GL_MAP_FLUSH_EXPLICIT_BIT, however: Setting it and then not calling **glFlushMappedBufferRange()** correctly will likely result in your new data not being used.

Finally, GL_MAP_UNSYNCHRONIZED_BIT tells OpenGL not to wait until it has finished using the data in a buffer before giving you a pointer to the buffer's memory. If you don't set this flag and OpenGL is planning to provide a pointer to the same memory that's about to be used by a previously issued command, it will wait for that command to finish executing before returning, which can slow your application down. However, if you know that you won't overwrite any data that hasn't already been used, you can set this bit to turn off the synchronization. If you do this, though, you're on your own. There are a number of mechanisms to provide your own synchronization, from calling **glFinish()** (which is a bit like a sledgehammer—don't call this function) to fences, which were covered in the "Synchronization and Fences" section in Chapter 12.

Finally, it should be clear that calling **glMapBufferRange()** with offset set to 0, length set to the size of the buffer object being mapped, and the GL_MAP_READ_BIT and GL_MAP_WRITE_BIT flags set appropriately is essentially equivalent to calling **glMapBuffer()**. However, `glMapBufferRange()` gives you so much additional flexibility that it's recommended that you always prefer `glMapBufferRange()` over `glMapBuffer()`, making sure to set the read, write, invalidation, and synchronization flags appropriately.

Use the Features OpenGL Gives You

OpenGL is a large and feature-packed programming interface. Some parts of it are more advanced than others, while other things aren't quite optimal. One advantage of OpenGL's expansive nature is that it is relatively easy to just get something simple working quickly. The disadvantage, of course, is that you need to know an awful lot to make a OpenGL program that truly makes use of all of the advanced features of the API.

Notably, OpenGL has quite a few *container objects*. These objects represent blocks of state; examples are vertex array objects, framebuffer objects, and transform feedback objects. In general, you should prefer to use a container object rather than modifying lots of state. For example, a vertex array object contains the state for all of the vertex arrays associated with the front end of OpenGL. This includes the bound buffer stores, the vertex attribute formats, strides and offsets within those stores, and which attributes are enabled and disabled. You can very quickly switch between complete sets of information using a single call to `glBindVertexArray()`. The sb7::object object wrapper internally uses a vertex array object to represent all of its vertex array state. When you call sb7::object::render, it simply binds the vertex array object and calls the appropriate drawing command, giving it extremely low software overhead.

Likewise, for framebuffer state, framebuffer objects wrap up all of the parameters describing the color, depth, and stencil attachments of the current framebuffer. It is far more efficient to create a framebuffer once at initialization time and then bind it before rendering than it is to explicitly reconfigure the current attachments on a single framebuffer object right before rendering.

Finally, transform feedback objects wrap up all of the state required to represent the transform feedback stage of OpenGL. Not only is it required to use a transform feedback object if you want to make use of `glDrawTransformFeedback()` or any of its variants, but it is substantially more efficient to make a single call to `glBindTransformFeedback()` than it is to reconfigure all of the transform feedback-related state directly before use.

Performance Analysis Tools   **713**

Use Only the Data You Need

Just because the inputs to your vertex shader are floating-point numbers, or the return value from the GLSL texture function is a floating-point number, it doesn't mean that you need to store the data in memory as floating-point data. In many cases, smaller data formats are sufficient to represent the data you'll actually be using. Using more data than you need can have two effects:

- Your application will use more memory than is really necessary, meaning that OpenGL may not be able to fit all your data in the most optimal areas of memory—or worse, it may fail to allocate data for your objects at all.

- The more data OpenGL must read from your buffers, the more pressure will be put on resources such as caches, memory controllers, and so on. This can reduce absolute performance. Also, the buses that connect the GPU to memory are big power consumers, so generating more memory accesses can increase the power consumption of a device and drain batteries faster.

For example, for position data (which is normally stored in object space), there is almost no requirement for full floating-point precision. In a preprocessing step, try normalizing your object-space data such that it lies in the region −1.0 to 1.0. This will allow you to store coordinates using signed normalized data—for example, by passing GL_SHORT to `glVertexAttribPointer()` and setting the normalized parameter to GL_TRUE. You can then include a scale factor in any model matrices to return the object to its original scale, for free. This allows you to use only 16 bits per component rather than the 32 bits that would be needed for full-precision floating-point data, and at the same time provides for more precision than would be afforded by 16-bit half-precision floating-point data.

Furthermore, for object-space coordinate data, the w component is virtually always 1.0. Therefore, there's really no reason to store it—you may as well store only three components and assume that the fourth is 1.0. Similar tactics can be used for object normals and tangents. Many OpenGL implementations will internally require that each vertex's data be aligned on a 4-byte boundary, even if it's not a multiple of 4 bytes. Three 16-bit components is 6 bytes or 48 bits and is not a multiple of 4. Therefore, when you want to use 16-bit components and store only three of them, it's best to try to fill the fourth component with something useful rather than leave it out.

In object files, normals (and tangents) are usually stored in object space. When you want to perform normal mapping, bump mapping, or any other technique that might rely on tangents and normals (see the "Normal Mapping" section in Chapter 13), you use the tangent and normal to construct the binormal by taking their cross product, and then use the tangent, binormal, and normal to construct the TBN matrix. The precision required for the normal and tangent vectors is usually not that high. In fact, 10 bits is generally enough, so you could consider using packed data for them. To do this, pass GL_INT_2_10_10_10_REV as the type parameter to **glVertexAttribPointer()**. Again, this uses signed normalized data (the normalized parameter is set to GL_TRUE) and provides a similar level of precision as 16-bit half-precision floating-point data in the range −1.0 to 1.0.

When it comes to storing normals in textures, you can take this one step further by making the assumption that because normals are in tangent space and they all point *away* from the surface, their z components are always positive. Now, also considering that the normals stored in your normal map are always unit length (that is, they are normalized), we know that

$$x^2 + y^2 + z^2 = 1.0$$
$$z^2 = 1.0 - x^2 - y^2$$
$$z = \sqrt{1.0 - x^2 - y^2}$$

Given this, we can store only the x and y components of our tangent-space normals in our normal maps and then reconstruct the z component in our fragment shader. This is known as trading texture performance for arithmetic and logic unit (ALU) performance. Graphics processors generally have substantially more performance available for performing general math operations than memory transactions. It can often turn out to be a net win to do more math in your shader if that approach can avoid consumption of memory bandwidth. A reasonable format for normal maps is a 2-component, 8-bit signed normalized format. Here, x and y are stored with 7 bits of precision (plus the sign bit) and the z component is reconstructed from the x and y components on use.

Applying texture compression to normal maps doesn't turn out well unless the compression format is chosen well and a good-quality compressor is used to compress the data. Some texture compression formats are designed to be able to cope with normal data (some of the BPTC formats, for example), but all too often discontinuities in normals are seen. However, for other data such as diffuse and specular albedos, compressed textures can work well. You should always consider whether a compressed texture can adequately represent your data.

The preceding advice focuses on data that might be read by OpenGL, but it also holds for data *written* by OpenGL. For example, if you are rendering to an off-screen texture using an FBO and want to use HDR, it might be tempting to make all of your framebuffer attachments use the GL_RGBA32F internal format and be done with it. However, this consumes very large amounts of memory both for storage and in bandwidth terms. If you don't need the rendered textures to hold an alpha channel, don't allocate one! Rather, use GL_RGB32F. Better yet, if you don't need a full 32 bits of precision, consider using GL_RGBA16F.

Similar advice applies for operations such as writing into images from a shader or using transform feedback, although you should be aware that the number of formats that are writable with these methods may not be as great as those that are writable through framebuffer operations or readable by the front end. Even so, in many of these cases, it's quite possible to use GLSL's packing functions to construct the data in your shader and then write it into integer images or buffers.

Shader Compilation Performance

Not only does OpenGL do graphics well, but it also includes a complete compiler environment! Of course, you've been using this throughout this book and by now you should have realized that GLSL is pretty complex. GLSL compilers have to do quite a bit of work to make sure that your shaders are compiled correctly and efficiently to run on the underlying graphics hardware. While you might not think that shader compilation performance can affect the running time of your application (after all, you don't compile shaders in the middle of rendering... do you?), it actually does impact the user's experience when running your application.

First, and most obviously, the start-up time of your application will be affected by how quickly you can get all the shaders ready for running. Some OpenGL implementations may use additional CPU threads to compile your shaders and may even be able to compile multiple shaders in parallel. However, just as you should consider the OpenGL pipeline as something that shouldn't be stalled, so you can consider OpenGL drivers and implementations as pipelines—even before the GPU gets involved. So, if you compile a shader using **glCompileShader()** and then immediately call **glGetShaderiv()** to get the compilation status or the shader's information log, you will stall the implementation because it must complete compilation of your shader to provide your answer. Rather than simply running through all the shaders your application needs, compiling them one at a time, and then querying their compilation results, you can do the following:

- Run through the list of shaders that you'll need to compile, create their shader objects, and call **glCompileShader()** on each one, but don't query the compilation result.

- In *debug* or *development* builds of your application, either query the compilation results and the information log after all of the shaders have been compiled, or simply rely on debug output to send the log to you. Make sure you have a way to turn this off, though. Presumably, once your shaders are debugged and your application is ready to ship, you won't need the compilation status—you can assume that it's always successful.

- Likewise, run through a list of all of the program objects your application needs, attach shaders to them, and call **glLinkProgram()**, but don't query the link result. Again, this step can be deferred or included only in debug builds of your application.

In large applications, you will undoubtedly have a very large number of shaders, and possibly a huge number of combinations of shaders that need to be linked into program objects. A naïve way to manage this is to simply create a set of shader objects for each combination, recompile each shader as it's referenced, and attach it to the resulting program objects in a one-to-one relationship. However, given that you can attach a shader to multiple program objects, it's reasonable to load all of the shaders you might need, compile them each once, and then attach the compiled shaders as needed to program objects and link them. This allows the OpenGL implementation to cache compiled shader data inside the shader objects and not have to regenerate it multiple times.

There may be some GPU-side performance advantages to using large, monolithic program objects, but more often than not, well-written shaders don't see much gain from this approach. Therefore, if you have a large number of shaders, you might want to consider compiling and linking them into *separable program objects*. You might want to have a program object for each combination of front-end shaders that you're likely to use and a program object with just a fragment shader in it for the back end. This technique might allow the OpenGL implementation to, for example, optimize tessellation control and evaluation shaders together, or vertex and geometry shaders, while leaving the interface from the front end and the back end as separable.

When you do use separate shader objects and link your program in separable mode, you attach them to another container object, the *program pipeline object*. This object can store validated information about the stages in the current pipeline, and it will be more efficient to switch between multiple program pipeline objects than to reconfigure a single program pipeline object when you want to switch shaders. While creating a program pipeline object for each combination of shaders your application is going to use might land you with the same combinatorial explosion of pipeline objects, it may be worthwhile maintaining a list of 100 or so objects and then using them as a cache. If the pipeline object you need is still in the cache, pull it out and use it. If not, either add a new object to the cache or pull an object from the cache and reconfigure it for your use. This allows you to rapidly switch between combinations of program stages without necessarily maintaining a pipeline object for each combination of states.

Once you have done your best to get your application's shader management in good shape, it might be worthwhile to take a look at the complexity of your shaders themselves. Shader compilation consists of many parts. First, the preprocessor is run, which expands macros, removes comments, and so on. Next, the shader is tokenized, checked for syntax, and finally compiled into an internal format, at which point optimization and code generation takes place. Often, a code optimizer will operate by making a pass over a section of code, performing local optimizations if it can, and then saving the result. It will then make subsequent passes, repeating the process until no more optimizations can be made or some maximum number of passes is performed. When the optimizer stops running, one of two things will have happened:

- If the optimizer stops because it cannot find any more transformations to make on your code, the resulting executable is probably as efficient as possible, but the optimizer may have taken many passes over the shader to reach this point, increasing optimization time.

- If the optimizer stops because it has run out of available passes, it's quite possible that the code is not as optimal as it could be.

In addition, the optimizer has burned all of the time that it has allotted to it.

To cope with this, it is in your best interest as a developer to help the shader compiler to do the best job that it can. First, and most obviously, try to write efficient shader code. However, you can do a number of other things to improve the runtime performance of OpenGL shader compilers. First, you can run your compiler through a preprocessor offline, ahead of shipping your application. This allows you to use macros, preprocessor definitions, and other features of the preprocessor, but doesn't place a burden on the shader compiler to produce the final shader for you.

If you want take things further, you can *pre-optimize* your shaders. This effectively involves running them through an offline shader compiler that preprocesses, parses, and compiles your shader code into an intermediate representation and then performs many common optimizations on it (such as dead code elimination, constant folding and propagation, common subexpression elimination, and so forth) before spitting the optimized code back out as GLSL. When the runtime GLSL compiler takes this shader and tries to optimize it, it should find that there's not much to do and finish quickly.

Finally, recall that we covered *program binaries* in Chapter 6, "Shaders and Programs." Program binaries offer you a way to compile your shaders and link them into program objects once, and then save the results into files. When you need the program again, rather than compiling it from source code, you can simply load up the program binary and hand it to OpenGL to use. OpenGL can almost certainly skip most, if not all, of the compilation procedures by caching information in the binaries it gives you. With program binaries, you may be able to eliminate shader compilation, or at least greatly reduce the time it takes.

Making Use of Multiple GPUs

Some users choose to install multiple graphics cards in a single machine and produce what is known as a *multi-GPU* system. AMD calls this *CrossFire*, while NVIDIA calls it *SLI*. Whatever the name, the technique to improve performance by using multiple graphics cards usually involves what is known as *alternate frame rendering* (AFR) mode, where one GPU renders a frame, the next GPU renders the next frame, and so on for as many GPUs as there are in the system. Most such systems have two GPUs in them, but some may have three, four, or even more GPUs present. Also,

AFR isn't the only way to achieve scaling using multiple GPUs, although it is certainly the most common.

One piece of advice is commonly given when optimizing for AFR systems: Avoid producing data on one GPU and then using that data on another GPU. There are two reasons for this. First, this approach requires that the two GPUs be synchronized—because one relies on the output of the other, the GPUs can't run in parallel and the performance advantages of having two or more GPUs in a single system are lost. Second, the cost of actually moving the data from one GPU to another is high because the data must generally cross a bus (such as PCI-express), which has much lower throughput than the memory on the graphics card.

While this advice might seem obvious, it's not obvious at first which types of operations might trigger OpenGL to have to transfer data from one GPU to another. Here is a list of behaviors that might trigger a copy operation from one GPU to another:

- Rendering into a texture and then using it in the next frame. This is perhaps the most obvious reason to need to transfer a texture between GPUs. For example, if you write an application that produces a dynamic environment map and try to optimize it by only updating the environment every other frame, you might find that this operation does indeed go faster on single-GPU systems. However, on a multi-GPU system, that environment must cross the bus after being rendered into, which will cause a GPU synchronization. It may be better to generate a new environment map every frame in this case, and avoid the copy. If you must reuse resources, try to reuse the resource from *two* frames ago if there is a chance you're running on a dual-GPU system.

- Rendering into a texture without clearing it first. This was a common trick used in the late 1990s to avoid the memory bandwidth costs of clearing the framebuffer when application developers knew that they would overwrite the whole thing by the end of the frame anyway. This is almost universally a bad idea on modern graphics hardware. First, any hardware designed in the last decade likely implements some form of compression for framebuffers, which can *very* quickly clear the framebuffer. Not clearing the framebuffer will likely turn off compression and make your application run more slowly, even on single-GPU systems. On multi-GPU systems, the issue is more severe. If you don't clear the framebuffer, then OpenGL doesn't know that when you start drawing into it again, you're going to overwrite everything. In this situation, before it can execute the first drawing command, OpenGL must wait for the previous frame to complete (on the other GPU), and then transfer the result to the new GPU so that any part of it that's not overwritten contains valid data.

- Writing into buffer objects in one frame and then using the result in another frame. This practice can cause synchronization and transfers. For example, if you implement one of the physics simulation algorithms described earlier in the book, you may find that the application doesn't scale because each step of the algorithm relies on data produced in the previous frame. If your application has some awareness that it's running on two GPUs, you may want to effectively run two copies of the physics simulation in parallel, with the second a half-step ahead of the first, and occasionally synchronize them.

- Using conditional rendering with the result of an occlusion query generated by one GPU being used to determine execution of commands on the other. Again, this behavior will cause synchronization of the GPUs. While the amount of data transferred to convey the result of the occlusion query probably isn't large, the synchronization may have a devastating effect on performance. If you can, either issue the occlusion queries very early in the frame and then use their results very late in the frame, or use two sets of occlusion queries so that you can use the result of queries issued two frames earlier. Don't forget—you'll need to make this delay longer if there are more GPUs present.

Unfortunately, there is no standard way of determining whether your application is running on a multi-GPU system or how many GPUs are present. Although some extensions exist for this purpose, other extensions allow you to create contexts that render explicitly to one of the GPUs in a multi-GPU set. If these extensions are available, and you're willing to go that far, you might want to see if you can scale the performance of your application by rendering different parts of your scene on different GPUs and explicitly merging the results.

Using Multiple Threads

OpenGL is fully multi-threaded and has a well-defined threading model. Each thread owns a "current context" and changing contexts for a thread is performed by calling **wglMakeCurrent()**, **glXMakeCurrent()**, or the equivalent for your platform from that thread. Once contexts are current for a thread, the thread can create objects, compile shaders, load textures, and even render into windows at the same time. This is in addition to any multi-threading that OpenGL drivers may implement internally on your behalf. In fact, if you look at your application running inside a debugger or other profiling tool, you may well see multiple threads that have their starting procedure inside the OpenGL driver for your graphics card.

Although OpenGL does have a well-supported multi-threading system and a well-defined object sharing model that allows multiple contexts that are current in different threads to use the same set of objects, this may not be what you want. For example, it's very tempting to simply decide that you'll create two contexts, make one current in each of two threads, and then use one for loading textures and compiling shaders while the other does the rendering. If you do this, though, you might find that you don't get the performance scaling that you want. Ultimately, there is one GPU and one command buffer, and OpenGL guarantees that everything is rendered in a well-defined order. That means that most access to OpenGL will be serialized, and the overhead of synchronizing and coordinating access to OpenGL from multiple threads may well outweigh any benefits of having multiple CPUs work on your application.

To avoid the serialization issues, it's also tempting to create two or more contexts and just switch between them using **wglMakeCurrent()** (or your platform's equivalent) in a single thread. While this does help you isolate state changes from one context to another, switching contexts can be an expensive operation. In particular, most window system bindings specify that switching contexts comes with an implicit flush.

Having said that, there are many ways to use multiple threads in an OpenGL application. First, most complex applications will have non-graphics tasks (such as artificial intelligence, sound effects, object management, input and network handling, physics simulation, and so on) going on that can be offloaded to other threads. If you create a single OpenGL context and make it current in your main "rendering" thread, this thread will be the only one that actually talks to OpenGL—it will be the arbiter of all things graphics.

Next, suppose you want to upload some texture data from a file into a texture object. Here, your main OpenGL thread will create a buffer object, bind it to the GL_PIXEL_UNPACK_BUFFER target, and then map it for writing into. It will then signal a worker thread that the buffer is ready for writing and send it a pointer to write to. The worker thread will then read the texture data from the file and into the buffer object via the pointer it received from the main thread, signaling back to the main thread when it has finished loading the texture. At this point, the main thread can call `glTexSubImage2D()` to copy the now loaded data from the buffer into the target texture object.

This same technique can be applied to any data that's stored in buffer objects, including vertex and index data, shader constants stored in uniform blocks, image data for textures and images, and even parameters to drawing commands via the `GL_DRAW_INDIRECT_BUFFER` target. You can use this to your advantage and essentially make your rendering engine *data driven*. In your rendering thread, create two sets of all the buffers that might be buffers updated dynamically by your application. Before rendering a frame, map all of the buffers for *the next frame*. You can, of course, bind new buffers for rendering while the buffers for the next frame are mapped. Now, in one or more worker threads, prepare all of the data for the next frame—perform CPU culling, implement dynamic vertex generation, update constants, and set up drawing parameters. Each batch of drawing should have its constants placed at a new offset within any uniform buffers. You can allocate space in these buffers in a thread-safe manner using atomic additions on the CPU.

While your worker threads are busy getting ready for the next frame, the OpenGL thread is rendering the current frame. This thread walks through a list of draws generated by the worker threads, binding objects needed by each draw—for example, textures, buffers (or ranges of them), and so on—and then issuing drawing commands. If you can merge textures together into texture arrays and store the offsets within the arrays in uniform blocks, even that data preparation can be offloaded to other threads. The upshot is that while scene traversal, culling, data preparation, and so on are fully offloaded to worker threads and should scale nicely across multiple CPU cores (keeping in mind, of course, that some CPU time should be preserved for sound, AI, physics, communication, and so on), only the main OpenGL thread actually calls any OpenGL commands. However, the workload of the main thread is really light, as it performs only buffer maps and unmaps, basic state changes, and draws, and does not do any work in between. Between this and the efficient multi-threading implemented in most OpenGL drivers, good scaling across multiple CPU cores should be achievable in most scenarios.

Throw Out What You Don't Need

Graphics applications can use a tremendous amount of memory. Textures, framebuffer attachments, and the buffers you use for vertices and other data can all consume a lot of resources. In the previous subsections, we recommended that you always clear a framebuffer before you start rendering to it. This is partly so that optimizations such as framebuffer compression can be effective. It's also a signal to OpenGL that you're done with the contents of the framebuffer and that it is free to reuse that memory for something else. After all, it's pretty easy for OpenGL to recreate the cleared framebuffer attachments if it needs to.

This is fine, but it's not ideal to rely on hints and suggestions for optimization. In fact, OpenGL allows you to tell it much more explicitly which resources it should keep around and which ones it's free to throw out. First, for textures, we have two functions—**glInvalidateTexImage()** and **glInvalidateTexSubImage()**. Their prototypes are

```
void glInvalidateTexImage(GLuint texture,
                          GLint level);

void glInvalidateTexSubImage(GLuint texture,
                             GLint level,
                             GLint xoffset,
                             GLint yoffset,
                             GLint zoffset,
                             GLsizei width,
                             GLsizei height,
                             GLsizei depth);
```

The first function, **glInvalidateTexImage()**, tells OpenGL that you're done with an entire mipmap level of a texture. The name of the texture object should be given in texture and the mipmap level given in level. When you call this function, OpenGL knows that it's free to throw out the data in the image (although the texture itself remains allocated). At this point, the contents of the texture's mipmap level become undefined. In a multi-GPU setup, for example, OpenGL would then know that it doesn't need to copy data from one GPU to another to keep the texture in sync across the system. The second function, **glInvalidateTexSubImage()**, is slightly more gentle in that it invalidates only the region you specify in the xoffset, yoffset, zoffset, width, height, and depth parameters. The first three are the origin of the region and the last three are its size—these parameters have the same meanings as they do in **glTexSubImage3D()**.

Next, we have similar functions for buffer objects: **glInvalidateBufferData()** and **glInvalidateBufferSubData()**. Their prototypes are

```
void glInvalidateBufferData(GLuint buffer);

void glInvalidateBufferSubData(GLuint buffer,
                               GLintptr offset,
                               GLsizeiptr length);
```

Like **glInvalidateTexImage()**, **glInvalidateBufferData()** throws out any data contained in the buffer object whose name you pass in buffer. After you call this function, the entire contents of the buffer become undefined, but are still allocated and owned by OpenGL. You might call this function, for example, if you store data into an intermediate buffer using transform feedback and then immediately draw from the buffer by calling **glDrawTransformFeedback()**. After calling **glDrawTransformFeedback()**, you can call **glInvalidateBufferData()** to tell OpenGL that you're done with the data and that it's free to reuse the buffer for another pass if necessary. The second function, **glInvalidateBufferSubData()**, is the finer version and throws out only the contents of the buffer defined by the offset and length parameters.

The final two functions essentially perform the same operations on framebuffer attachments; they are **glInvalidateFramebuffer()** and **glInvalidateSubFramebuffer()**. Their prototypes are

```
void glInvalidateFramebuffer(GLenum target,
                             GLsizei numAttachments,
                             const GLenum * attachments);

void glInvalidateSubFramebuffer(GLenum target,
                                GLsizei numAttachments,
                                const GLenum * attachments,
                                GLint x,
                                GLint y,
                                GLint width,
                                GLint height);
```

For both functions, target is the target of the operation and can be GL_FRAMEBUFFER, GL_DRAW_FRAMEBUFFER, or GL_READ_FRAMEBUFFER (where GL_FRAMEBUFFER is treated as equivalent to GL_DRAW_FRAMEBUFFER). The numAttachments parameter is the number of elements in the array pointed to by attachments, which is a list of attachments to invalidate. The elements of the array should be values such as GL_COLOR_ATTACHMENT0, GL_DEPTH_ATTACHMENT, or GL_STENCIL_ATTACHMENT.

If you want to invalidate the contents of a framebuffer that's not currently bound, then you can call either **glInvalidateNamedFramebufferData()** or **glInvalidateNamedFramebufferSubData()**, whose prototypes are

```
void glInvalidateNamedFramebufferData(GLuint framebuffer,
                                      GLsizei numAttachments,
                                      const GLenum *attachments);

void glInvalidateNamedFramebufferSubData(GLuint framebuffer,
                                         GLsizei numAttachments,
                                         const GLenum *attachments,
```

```
GLint x,
GLint y,
GLsizei width,
GLsizei height);
```

These two functions work exactly like the variants that take a target parameter, except that they directly affect the framebuffer object you give them in the framebuffer parameter rather than indirectly affecting it through a binding point.

glInvalidateFramebuffer() and glInvalidateNamedFramebufferData() throw out the contents of each of the attachments in the attachments array. However, the glInvalidateSubFramebuffer() and glInvalidateNamedFramebufferSubData() functions are again a little gentler and allow you to throw away only a region of the framebuffer attachments. This region is specified by the x, y, width, and height parameters.

Invalidating resources allows OpenGL to do a number of things that otherwise might have adverse effects. For example:

- OpenGL may be able to reclaim memory for buffers or textures that have been invalidated and are no longer in use.

- It can avoid copying data from resource to resource, especially in multi-GPU systems.

- It can return framebuffer attachments to a compressed state without necessarily making their contents valid.

In general, you should call one of the invalidation functions when you're done with the contents of a resource but may reuse it for something else later. At worst, OpenGL will ignore you and do nothing. At best, you can avoid expensive copies, clears, paging operations, or memory starvation that may otherwise occur.

Summary

In this chapter, you have seen a number of techniques that you can use to improve the performance of your OpenGL programs. We took a look at multi-threading in OpenGL—that is, the use of multiple threads to feed data to OpenGL by sharing a pointer to a mapped buffer between many threads, and by decoupling logic that decides what to render from the code that calls OpenGL functions. We also saw how to move more work from the CPU to the GPU in the form of indirect rendering, and how to have the GPU feed itself work with very little interaction from your program. In addition, we considered how to avoid calling expensive OpenGL functions such as `glMapBufferRange()`, which could otherwise lead to stalls or copies between CPU and GPU memory.

We have discussed several methods to analyze the performance of your application and to figure out how to make it go faster and use the graphics processing resources as efficiently as possible. With this knowledge, you should be able to make best use of OpenGL and produce high-performance programs.

Chapter 15

Debugging and Stability

WHAT YOU'LL LEARN IN THIS CHAPTER

- How to figure out what's wrong when your application isn't doing what you want it to.

- How to achieve the highest possible performance.

- How to enhance your application's security and robustness.

By now, you've learned a lot about OpenGL. You have probably started writing some pretty complex programs of your own, but chances are they won't work the first time—and even when you get them working, they won't go as fast as you'd like them to. In this chapter we take a look at two important skill sets: debugging and performance tuning. The first helps you to get your application running *correctly*. The second helps you to get it running *fast*. Both are important for production-quality applications that must run on the widest range of hardware possible.

Debugging Your Applications

It is an all too common scenario that you'll invent a nifty new algorithm for rendering something; set up all your textures, vertices, framebuffers, and other data that you'll need; start calling drawing commands; and then either see nothing or see something other than what you wanted. In this section we'll cover two very powerful assets that are available to assist in the debugging of your application. The first is the *debug context*, which is a mode of OpenGL that provides thorough error checking and feedback about your use of the OpenGL API. The second is the tools that are freely available to help you debug your application. Running your application inside one of these tools can provide you with great insight about its behavior and use of OpenGL. Some tools can even provide advice about how you might change your application to make it run faster.

Debug Contexts

When you create an OpenGL context, you have the option of creating it in one of several modes. One of these modes is the *debug context*. When you create a debug context, OpenGL installs additional layers between your application and the normal paths it will take into the drivers and ultimately to the GPU. These additional layers perform strict error checking, analysis of your parameters, recording of errors, and a number of other things that would normally be too expensive to apply to a production-ready, debugged application. The method with which you create a debug context is platform specific and so is handled by the book's application framwork. Therefore, we can use the sb7 application class to create a debug context for us. To explicitly create a debug context, override the sb7::application::init() function and set the debug flag in the application info structure as shown in Listing 15.1.

```
void my_application::init()
{
    sb7::application::init();

    info.flags.debug = 1;
}
```

Listing 15.1: Creating a debug context with the sb7 framework

In debug builds, the sb7 base class automatically sets this bit; if debug contexts are available, it will create one. In this case, you don't need to do anything. If you want to create a debug context in release builds of your application (or if you want to force a non-debug context in a debug build), you'll need to override the init() function as shown in Listing 15.1.

Once you have created a debug context, you need to give it a way to notify your application when something goes wrong. To do this, OpenGL uses a *callback function*, which is specified using a function pointer. The definition of the callback function pointer type is

```
typedef void (APIENTRY * GLDEBUGPROC)(GLenum source,
                                      GLenum type,
                                      GLuint id,
                                      GLenum severity,
                                      GLsizei length,
                                      const GLchar* message,
                                      void* userParam);
```

The function is defined to have the same calling conventions as OpenGL API functions—this is the purpose of the APIENTRY macro, which is defined by the OpenGL header files correctly for the platform for which the code is being compiled. To implement the debug callback, create a function with the appropriate signature, and then call **glDebugMessageCallback()**, whose prototype is

```
void glDebugMessageCallback(GLDEBUGPROC callback,
                            void * userParam);
```

Here, callback is a pointer to your debug output callback function, and the userParam parameter is simply stored by OpenGL and passed back to your callback function in its userParam parameter. An example of this is shown in Listing 15.2.

```
static void APIENTRY simple_print_callback(GLenum source,
                                           GLenum type,
                                           GLuint id,
                                           GLenum severity,
                                           GLsizei length,
                                           const GLchar* message,
                                           void* userParam)
{
    printf("Debug message with source 0x%04X, type 0x%04X, "
           "id %u, severity 0x%0X, '%s'\n",
           source, type, id, severity, message);
}

void initialize_debug_output()
{
    glDebugMessageCallback(&simple_print_callback, NULL);
}
```

Listing 15.2: Setting the debug callback function

Once you have set up a debug callback function, OpenGL will call it whenever it needs to report information to your application. You should be careful not to call any OpenGL functions from inside the callback function. This is not legal, and should your OpenGL code cause an error (which might end up calling your callback function again), it could easily create an infinite loop and crash your program. In the simple example of Listing 15.2, we just print the message along with the raw values of several of the parameters using the C function printf. As noted earlier, in debug builds, the sb7 application framework installs a default debug callback function that simply prints the received message. If you want more advanced control over the formatting of your messages, or if you're not using the sb7 application framework, you can use the parameters of the callback function to your advantage.

In the callback function, the source parameter indicates which part of OpenGL the message originated from. It may be one of the following values:

- GL_DEBUG_SOURCE_API indicates that the message was generated by the use of the OpenGL API—perhaps you passed an incorrect value for a parameter, for example. The message will tell you which parameter is the source of the problem, why the value was incorrect, and what the range of acceptable values is.

- GL_DEBUG_SOURCE_SHADER_COMPILER is normally used by OpenGL to send compilation errors and warning messages to your application. Very often, this will be the same information that is stored in the shader and program information logs.

- GL_DEBUG_SOURCE_WINDOW_SYSTEM indicates that the issue was raised by some interaction with the window system or perhaps the operating system.

- GL_DEBUG_SOURCE_THIRD_PARTY suggests that the message came from a tool, utility library, or other source outside the OpenGL driver.

- GL_DEBUG_SOURCE_APPLICATION says that the message came from *your application*. That's right—you can insert messages into the log, which we will get to in a moment.

- GL_DEBUG_SOURCE_OTHER is a catch-all category for anything that doesn't fit anywhere else.

The type parameter gives you further information about what the message is for. It can take one of the following values:

- GL_DEBUG_TYPE_ERROR means that an error has occurred. For example, if the source is the OpenGL API, **glGetError()** will probably return an error code. If the source is the shader compiler, then it probably means that one of your shaders failed to compile.

- GL_DEBUG_TYPE_DEPRECATED_BEHAVIOR means that you've attempted to use features that are marked for deprecation (which means that they will be removed from future versions of OpenGL).

- GL_DEBUG_TYPE_UNDEFINED_BEHAVIOR indicates that something your application is trying to do will produce undefined behavior, and that even if it might work on *this particular* OpenGL implementation, this is not standard and and might break if you run it on another computer.

- GL_DEBUG_TYPE_PERFORMANCE messages are generated by OpenGL to warn you that something you're doing isn't likely to perform well. The message may even include information about what you could consider doing instead.

- GL_DEBUG_TYPE_PORTABILITY suggests that you are using OpenGL in a way that is well defined, but possibly only on your implementation of OpenGL. This means that your code might not be portable.

- GL_DEBUG_TYPE_MARKER is used to insert events into the OpenGL command stream that can be picked up by tools and other debugging aids.

- GL_DEBUG_TYPE_PUSH_GROUP and GL_DEBUG_TYPE_POP_GROUP messages are generated when you use the **glPushDebugGroup()** and **glPopDebugGroup()** functions, which are explained later in this section.

- GL_DEBUG_TYPE_OTHER is used for any messages that don't fit neatly into any of the preceding categories.

The severity argument may be one of GL_DEBUG_SEVERITY_LOW, GL_DEBUG_SEVERITY_MEDIUM, or GL_DEBUG_SEVERITY_HIGH to indicate that the message is of low, medium, or high severity, respectively. It could also be GL_DEBUG_SEVERITY_NOTIFICATION if the message is for informational purposes and has no negative connotations.

In addition to the source, type, and severity properties, each message is assigned a unique identifier, which is passed to your callback function in the id parameter. Its actual value is implementation defined, but it can be used to refer to a specific message. The other parameters to the debug callback function are the length of the message string (in length), a pointer to the string itself (in message), and the userParam parameter that you passed to **glDebugMessageCallback()**. You can use this for whatever you want. For example, you could put a pointer to an instance of a class in it, a file handle, or any other type of object that can be represented as a pointer.

You can tell OpenGL which types of messages you want to receive by calling the **glDebugMessageControl()** function. Its prototype is

```
void glDebugMessageControl(GLenum source,
                           GLenum type,
                           GLenum severity,
                           GLsizei count,
                           const GLuint * ids,
                           GLboolean enabled);
```

The source, type, and severity parameters together form a filter that is used to select the group of debugging messages that the function will affect. Each of the parameters can have one of the values that are passed in the similarly named parameters to the debug message callback function described earlier. Additionally, any combination of these parameters can be set to GL_DONT_CARE. If one of the parameters is GL_DONT_CARE, then it is effectively ignored for the purposes of filtering; otherwise, any message whose source, type, or severity matches the value passed will be included in the filter. Furthermore, if ids is not NULL, then it is considered to be a pointer to an array of count message identifiers. Any message whose identifier is in this list will be considered part of the filter.

Once the filter has been formed, the reporting of the resulting group of messages is enabled if enabled is GL_TRUE and disabled if it is GL_FALSE. Using **glDebugMessageControl()**, you can effectively turn on or off reporting of particular classes of messages. For example, to turn on all high-severity messages but turn off any message produced by the shader compiler, you could call

```
// Enable all messages with high severity
glDebugMessageControl(GL_DONT_CARE,                 // Source
                      GL_DONT_CARE,                 // Type
                      GL_DEBUG_SEVERITY_HIGH,       // Severity
                      0, NULL,                      // Count, ids
                      GL_TRUE);                     // Enable

// Disable messages from the shader compiler
glDebugMessageControl(GL_DEBUG_SOURCE_SHADER_COMPILER,
                      GL_DONT_CARE,
                      GL_DONT_CARE,
                      0, NULL,
                      GL_FALSE);
```

In addition to debug messages that might be produced by the OpenGL implementation, you can insert your own messages into the debug output stream. When you do this, your debug callback function will be called. You can record these messages using the same logging mechanisms you might implement for regular debugging messages. To inject your own message into the debug output log, call

```
void glDebugMessageInsert(GLenum source,
                          GLenum type,
                          GLuint id,
                          GLenum severity,
                          GLsizei length,
                          const char * message);
```

Again, the source, type, id, and severity parameters have the same meanings as they do in the debug callback function. In fact, you can even pass sources such as GL_DEBUG_SOURCE_SHADER_COMPILER in these parameters, although the GL_DEBUG_SOURCE_APPLICATION token is actually reserved for application use and GL_DEBUG_SOURCE_THIRD_PARTY is designed for tools and utility libraries. OpenGL will not generate messages with these sources. As most of the debug messages are intended to warn you of bad behavior, GL_DEBUG_TYPE_MARKER is reserved for informational messages. Tools may intercept this message stream and treat it in a special manner. The length parameter contains the length of the string pointed to by message. If length is 0, then message is considered to be a nul-terminated string.

You can group messages together into hierarchical sets called *debug groups*. Tools that capture debug output may, for instance, indent groups of messages or color them differently in a log viewer. When OpenGL starts up, it will use the default group. Additional groups can be created by pushing them onto the debug group stack. To do this, call

```
void glPushDebugGroup(GLenum source,
                      GLuint id,
                      GLsizei length,
                      const char * message);
```

When you call this function, a copy of the current debug state will be made and copied to the top location of the debug stack. At the same time, a debug message will be generated and sent to your callback function. It will have its type set to GL_DEBUG_TYPE_PUSH_GROUP and its severity set to GL_DEBUG_SEVERITY_NOTIFICATION. It will have the source and the identifier specified in the source and id parameters, respectively. As with **glDebugMessageInsert()**, message and length specify the address of the message string and its length, respectively. If `length` is 0, then `message` is considered to point to a nul-terminated string.

When you want to leave a debug group, call

```
void glPopDebugGroup(void);
```

Again, **glPopDebugGroup()** will produce another debug message, this time with the `type` parameter set to GL_DEBUG_TYPE_POP_GROUP but with all the other parameters set to the same thing as the corresponding message from when the group was pushed.

When OpenGL produces debug messages, it will usually refer to objects such as textures, buffers, framebuffers, and so on by their number (the name you pass to OpenGL functions). This might be a bit confusing if you need to trawl through hundreds of lines of log entries looking for usage of a specific texture. To make this a little easier, you can assign human-readable names to objects by calling **glObjectLabel()** or **glObjectPtrLabel()**, whose prototypes are

```
void glObjectLabel(GLenum identifier,
                   GLuint name,
                   GLsizei length,
                   const char * label);
void glObjectPtrLabel(void * ptr,
                      GLsizei length,
                      const char * label);
```

When you call **glObjectLabel()**, you should pass in `identifier` the type of object referred to by name, which is the name of the object. `identifier` may be one of the following:

- GL_BUFFER if name is the name of a buffer object.

- GL_FRAMEBUFFER if name is the name of a framebuffer object.

- GL_PROGRAM_PIPELINE if name is the name of a program pipeline object.

- GL_PROGRAM if name is the name of a program object.

- GL_QUERY if name is the name of a query object.

- GL_RENDERBUFFER if name is the name of a renderbuffer object.

- GL_SAMPLER if name is the name of a sampler object.

- GL_SHADER if name is the name of a shader object.

- GL_TEXTURE if name is the name of a texture object.

- GL_TRANSFORM_FEEDBACK if name is the name of a transform feedback object.

- GL_VERTEX_ARRAY if name is the name of a vertex array object.

For `glObjectPtrLabel()`, the object is identified by a pointer type. This function is used for objects that have pointer types in OpenGL, which are currently only sync objects.

For both functions, the `label` and `length` parameters specify the name of the object and the length of the name, respectively. Again, if `length` is 0, then `label` is considered to point to a nul-terminated string. Once you've given an object a name, OpenGL will use the text name rather than the raw number in debug messages. For example, you could set the debug object label of texture objects to the name of the file from which they were loaded.

Security and Robustness

In recent times, running *untrusted* content has become more of a factor in OpenGL programming. With the advent of WebGL, Web browsers routinely run shaders loaded from arbitrary Web sites, and execute OpenGL programs written in JavaScript in the context of a Web page. In this environment, it has become important to provide a level of security to browsers and other applications that might otherwise expose OpenGL to alien invasion from evil third parties. To address this concern, OpenGL has a number of security features that help prevent inadvertent abuse and catch programming errors.

Graphics Reset

Modern CPUs and operating systems are really very good at executing many different tasks at the same time. Most newer CPUs have multiple cores, and operating systems handle threads and processes so well that you could quite literally have hundreds of applications running all apparently at the same time without any one of them noticing a significant hitch. Of course, if absolute performance is what you're looking for, a big, beefy

CPU is hard to beat and the operating system will dedicate as much of its resources as it can to getting your application going fast.

To run multiple applications at the same time—more applications than there are CPUs in your computer—the operating system will divide CPU time between the processes and threads that need it, making sure everyone gets its fair share. CPUs have relatively little state, and support features such as interrupts and multiple privilege modes to make sure that you can always shut down an errant task and that no process can adversely affect another application or the system as a whole. While current CPUs and operating systems are far from perfect in this regard, it is an unfortunate fact that current GPUs and graphics drivers are still far from perfect.

About the best that can be done when a single process hogs all of the GPU time is to kick everyone off the graphics processor, reset everything, and try to get the system started again. In fact, if you run the very simple vertex shader shown in Listing 15.3, depending on your operating system and GPU, you may see the screen flicker, other applications stop working, or your whole machine lock up. Run this shader at your own risk (and remember to save your work first)!

```
#version 450 core

void main(void)
{
    for (;;)
    {
        /* Spin forever */
    }
}
```

Listing 15.3: Shader with an infinite loop

The shader shown in Listing 15.3 is a trivial example—obviously it will never complete. The problem is that most GPUs don't deal with this situation elegantly and will stop working if you execute this kind of code. Such a condition is known as a *hang*. Web browsers, for example, try to detect this kind of "never-ending" shader and stop malicious (or simply erroneous) programs from ruining your GPU's day. However, they're not perfect either, and need a little help from OpenGL.

If you run this shader inside one of your programs, it will affect other applications running on your computer. Likewise, if another application runs a shader like this, it will affect *you*. What will happen is that your context will be *lost*—all of your state will be thrown out, your textures will be gone, and any rendering that was happening will be stopped. In this situation, you will need to stop your context, delete it, and start over. To find out if this is the case, you can call

```
GLenum glGetGraphicsResetStatus();
```

The **glGetGraphicsResetStatus()** function returns one of four error codes that indicate the status of your context with respect to a graphics hang condition.

- GL_NO_ERROR: This is our familiar, *all is good* error code and is what you would expect to receive if everything is running as normal.

- GL_GUILTY_CONTEXT_RESET: Your context has been lost because the GPU was reset due to a hang, and it was your fault! Whatever you were doing last very likely caused the problem and you should probably stop it.

- GL_INNOCENT_CONTEXT_RESET: Your context was reset, but it wasn't your fault. Something else caused a serious error condition, but assuming that application has stopped, you should be safe to reinitialize everything and try to get back to what you were doing.

- GL_UNKNOWN_CONTEXT_RESET: Your context was reset, but OpenGL can't tell if you caused the problem. You can try to set up everything again and restart your application, but if the hang keeps happening, the source of the problem probably *is* you—and you should stop and attempt to exit as cleanly as you can.

It's really not necessary to check this status too often. If all is going well, **glGetGraphicsResetStatus()** will keep returning GL_NO_ERROR, so you're not helping safe, trusted applications by calling this function very frequently. It might be a good idea to call it once per frame. It usually takes a few seconds or longer for OpenGL or the operating system it's running on to realize that the GPU has become hung, and that can mean hundreds of frames in a high-performance application. Calling **glGetGraphicsResetStatus()** is probably sufficient to make sure that everything's on track.

Elegantly detecting a hang condition in a GPU is pretty tricky for OpenGL drivers, and in some cases it's just too hard to do it in an efficient manner. In some cases, you need to "opt in" to this robustness behavior when you create your context. This is done in a platform-dependent manner.

Depending on the GPU, operating system, driver version, and application behavior at start-up, GPU resets may or may not be detected fully. To determine the behavior of the implementation you're running on, call **glGetIntegerv()** and pass GL_RESET_NOTIFICATION_STRATEGY as the parameter to retrieve. This will return one of two things:

- GL_NO_RESET_NOTIFICATION means that OpenGL will never tell you about GPU resets. **glGetGraphicsResetStatus()** will always return GL_NO_ERROR. This might be because the OpenGL context is incapable of detecting whether the GPU has been reset, or it might be because the GPU is hang-proof. The former is more likely.

- GL_LOSE_CONTEXT_ON_RESET means that if a GPU reset is detected, you will lose your context as described earlier.

These are the only two defined values for GL_RESET_NOTIFICATION_STRATEGY at this time. However, it's possible that new strategies may be defined in the future—perhaps it will be possible to stop a single draw without resetting an entire context, for example.

After a GPU reset has occurred, the content of the context is undefined and all you can do is delete it and start over. Any attempt to keep using the context will generate a GL_CONTEXT_LOST error. Technically, it's not legal to keep calling OpenGL functions on a context that's been reset. The only exceptions are that **glGetError()** and **glGetGraphicsResetStatus()** still return the correct values (so that you can tell this has happened), and that functions that would otherwise have waited for the GPU, such as **glClientWaitSync()**, will return immediately so that your application doesn't stop dead.

Range-Checked Reads

In OpenGL, a handful of functions are available that read data back into your application's memory to create a pointer, but OpenGL computes the size for you. Examples are functions like **glReadPixels()** and **glGetTexImage()**. For these two functions, the total amount of data returned by OpenGL (that is, written into your application's memory) is a function of the current state of the context and of the format passed to the function. This information includes things like the pixel pack row height and stride. In theory, if you knew all of that state, you could calculate the total amount of data that would be returned. In many cases, however, that's simply not possible. For example, `glGetCompressedTexImage()` returns a compressed texture—but what happens if the compression scheme produces a variable-length encoding that depends on *what's* been compressed? What happens if someone turns on a feature from an extension you didn't know about that magically doubles the length of all readbacks? Pain ensues.

As these scenarios suggest, it's very easy to create a buffer-overrun issue where OpenGL walks right past the end of your buffer and stomps on other, possibly important data.

For these cases, OpenGL provides a number of functions in which you can specify the maximum amount of data that you're willing to accept. You can compute the amount of data you're expecting, round up a little, and then pass the size of your buffer to OpenGL. In turn, OpenGL promises to not overrun the end of your buffer. Rather, it will generate an error and return without doing anything if your buffer is too small.

As a range-checked replacement for **glReadPixels()**, we can call

```
void glReadnPixels(GLint x, GLint y,
                   GLsizei width, GLsizei height,
                   GLenum format, GLenum type,
                   GLsizei bufSize, void *data);
```

Notice that **glReadnPixels()** has a new parameter, bufSize. This is the size of the buffer you passed in data. No matter what, OpenGL will not write more than bufSize bytes of data into data, regardless of the state of your context.

For reading textures back, OpenGL provides two functions—one for compressed textures and one for uncompressed textures:

```
void glGetnCompressedTexImage(GLenum target, GLint lod,
                              GLsizei bufSize, void *img);

void glGetnTexImage(GLenum target, GLint level,
                    GLenum format, GLenum type,
                    GLsizei bufSize, void *img);
```

Again, notice that both **glGetnCompressedTexImage()** and **glGetnTexImage()** include the additional bufSize parameter.

In all three cases (**glReadnPixels()**, **glGetnTexImage()**, and **glGetnCompressedTexImage()**), OpenGL will generate a GL_INVALID_OPERATION error if bufSize is too small to store the resulting data. There are many more `glGet` functions in OpenGL, but they all either return a fixed amount of data, already take a specific data size to return, have trivially calculable output buffer sizes, or have a specific upper bound on the amount of data they could return. In these cases, a specialized function is not required.

It's your decision as to whether to use these functions in preference to their non-sized counterparts. However, **glReadnPixels()**, **glGetnTexImage()**, and **glGetnCompressedTexImage()** are not expected to be performance-critical parts of your code and they are objectively safer than their non-ranged versions. For these reasons, using them might be a good habit to develop.

Summary

This chapter introduced a number of debugging techniques, including the use of debug contexts in your application and some of the tools available to help you solve problems. We also discussed methods to make sure that your program is more robust by giving OpenGL the information it needs to avoid buffer overruns and other such errors. You will then be able to tell if something has gone horribly wrong (through your fault or otherwise).

By ensuring that your program doesn't generate any errors, doesn't produce any warnings when running on a debug context, performs as well as it possibly can, and is resilient to failure of the GPU, you increase the range of hardware that can run it and end up with a larger potential user base.

Appendix A

The SuperBible Tools

This book's source code not only includes most of the examples from the book in compilable form for many platforms, it also includes a number of tools that were used to create the .SBM and .KTX files used by those examples. You can use these tools to create and manipulate .SBM and .KTX files to use in your own applications.

The ktxtool Utility

The ktxtool program is a utility for processing .KTX files. Its usage is as follows:

```
ktxtool -i <inputfile> [-i <inputfile>*] [-o output file] {options}
```

Input files are sent to ktxtool by specifying them with the -i option. More than one input file can be specified by including multiple -i options.

The --info option prints information about the input files as they are read. For example, taking a look at the aliens.ktx texture file that contains the array texture full of little monsters used in the "Alien Rain" example in Chapter 5, we see the following:

```
$ ktxtool.exe -i aliens.ktx --info
endianness              = 0x04030201
gltype                  = 0x00001401 (GL_UNSIGNED_BYTE)
gltypesize              = 0x00000001
glformat                = 0x000080E1 (GL_BGRA)
glinternalformat        = 0x00008058 (GL_RGBA8)
glbaseinternalformat    = 0x000080E1 (GL_BGRA)
pixelwidth              = 0x00000100
pixelheight             = 0x00000100
pixeldepth              = 0x00000000
```

```
arrayelements        = 0x00000040
faces                = 0x00000000
miplevels            = 0x00000001
keypairbytes         = 0x00000000
```

As we can see from the output of ktxtool, the aliens.ktx file is an array texture containing GL_BGRA data stored in unsigned bytes. It is 0x100 × 0x100 (256 × 256) texels in size, and there are 0x40 (64) slices in the array. The texture does not include mipmaps and has no additional data stored in key-pairs.

The --fromraw option allows you to create a .KTX file from raw data by specifying all of the parameters that are to be included in the file header, which is prepended to the raw data you specify. First, the raw data in all of the input files is loaded and appended together to make one large blob. Next, the following arguments are used to assign properties to the output file:

- --width specifies the width of the output texture, in texels.

- --height specifies the height of the output texture, in texels.

- --depth specifies the depth of the output texture, in texels.

- --slices specifies the number of slices in an output array texture.

- --glformat specifies the OpenGL format and is placed in the glformat field of the header.

- --gltype specifies the OpenGL type and is placed in the gltype field of the header.

- --glinternalformat specifies the OpenGL format and is placed in the glinternalformat field of the header.

As an example, the following command converts the raw file data.raw into a 256 × 256 2D array texure with 32 slices and the data format GL_R32F, and then saves it into the array.ktx output file:

```
$ ktxtool.exe -i data.raw --fromraw -o array.ktx --width 256 --height 256 \
--slices 32 --glformat GL_RED --gltype GL_FLOAT --glinternalformat GL_R32F
```

ktxtool will automatically figure out the base internal format and the required size of the data. Note that ktxtool doesn't do any data processing or validation of your arguments—it simply puts into the header whatever you tell it to. This can result in invalid .KTX files.

The --toraw option will take data the other way—that is, by stripping the .KTX header from the file and writing the raw data into the output.

Next, we come to the --makearray, --make3d, and --makecube options, which allow you to construct array textures, 3D textures, and cubemaps from separate .KTX files. To use these options, the input textures must be compatible with one another and with the resulting outputs.

First, --makearray will take a sequence of 1D or 1D array textures and create a new 1D array texture from it, or take a sequence of 2D or 2D array textures and create a new 2D array texture from it. For 1D textures, the widths of all of the textures must be the same; for 2D textures, the widths and heights of all of the textures must be the same. All of the input textures must have the same data format. The texture data from the inputs is concatenated in the order that the inputs were specified. If array textures are encountered in the inputs, then their slices are simply concatenated to the end of the resulting array texture. For example, the following command will take the slice1.ktx, slice2.ktx, and slice3.ktx files and create a three-slice array texture from them in array.ktx:

```
$ ktxtool.exe -i slice1.ktx -i slice2.ktx -i slice3.ktx -o array.ktx --makearray
```

Again, ktxtool does no format conversion. If the files' data formats don't match, ktxtool will simply refuse to create the output file. The --make3d option works similarly to the --makearray option, except that it creates a 3D texture rather than an array texture. Only 2D or 3D input textures are accepted, and each must have the same width, height, and data format. All of the slices of the input textures are stacked in the order that the inputs are encountered.

The dds2ktx Utility

The dds2ktx utility is a tool for converting .DDS format files to .KTX files. .DDS is a file format used in many content creation tools for storing textures for use in DirectX applications. "DDS" stands for DirectDraw Surface. Although DirectDraw, the API, is long deprecated, the format lives on and is capable of representing almost any texture format that can be consumed by Direct3D. Virtually every Direct3D texture type and format is also supported by OpenGL and can be represented as a .KTX file.

dds2ktx takes two parameters—the input file name and the output file name. It attempts to do a blind conversion of the .DDS file to a .KTX file. It decodes the .DDS file header, translates the parameters to a .KTX file header, and then dumps the data from the .DDS file into the .KTX file. It does very little error checking or sanity checking. However, it does support use of common content creation tools, including several texture compressors, to produce .DDS files that can then be converted to .KTX files for use with this book's .KTX loader.

The sb6mtool Utility

The sb6mtool utility is a general-purpose tool for dealing with the .SBM model files used in this book. The command-line parameters and syntax are similar to those employed with the ktxtool utility. One or more input files are specified with the --input or -i parameters, each followed by a file name.

The --info parameter instructs sb6mtool to dump information about the object. For example, to dump the information about the asteroids.sbm object file that was used for the asteroid field example in Chapter 7, we can issue the following command:

```
$ sb6mtool --input asteroids.sbm --info
FILE: asteroids.sbm
Raw data size: 888100 bytes
No indices
Vertex count = 44352, data offset = 0x00000424
Attribute count: 2
    Attribute 0:
        name        = position
        size        = 3
        format      = 0x1406 (GL_FLOAT)
        stride      = 0
        flags       = 0x00000000
        data_offset = 0x00000000
    Attribute 1:
        name        = normal
        size        = 4
        format      = 0x140B (GL_HALF_FLOAT)
        stride      = 0
        flags       = 0x00000000
        data_offset = 0x00081F00
Number of sub-objects: 100
    Sub-object 0: first 0, count 432
    Sub-object 1: first 432, count 576
```

```
Sub-object 2: first 1008, count 576
Sub-object 3: first 1584, count 576
Sub-object 4: first 2160, count 432
Sub-object 5: first 2592, count 504
Sub-object 6: first 3096, count 432
Sub-object 7: first 3528, count 576
Sub-object 8: first 4104, count 432
Sub-object 9: first 4536, count 576
<...>
Sub-object 89: first 39528, count 504
Sub-object 90: first 40032, count 576
Sub-object 91: first 40608, count 288
Sub-object 92: first 40896, count 432
Sub-object 93: first 41328, count 288
Sub-object 94: first 41616, count 504
Sub-object 95: first 42120, count 432
Sub-object 96: first 42552, count 432
Sub-object 97: first 42984, count 504
Sub-object 98: first 43488, count 288
Sub-object 99: first 43776, count 576
```

As we can see, the `asteroids.sbm` file contains roughly 850 kilobytes of raw data. There are two vertex attributes named `position` and `normal`, the data does not have indices, and the file contains 100 sub-objects. The start vertex and the vertex count for each of the sub-objects are listed. Each of the sub-objects in this particular file is one of the unique asteroids from the sample application.

To do more than just print the information from the input file(s), we need to specify an output file. To do this, we use the `--output` command-line option, followed by a file name. It is possible to convert the format of one or more of the model's attributes by using the `--convertattrib` command-line option. This option takes the attribute name followed by one of the OpenGL format enumerants. For example, to convert the `position` attribute to GL_RGB16F (three components of half-precision 16-bit floating-point data) and write the output to an output file called `asteroids2.sbm`, we can issue this command:

```
$ sb6mtool --input asteroids.sbm --output asteroids2.sbm \
        --convertattrib position GL_RGB16F
```

If you just want to nuke an attribute altogether, you can instead use the `--deleteattrib` command-line option. This simply takes the name of the attribute to delete. To delete the `normal` attribute, for instance, we can issue this command:

```
$ sb6mtool --input asteroids.sbm --output asteroids2.sbm \
        --deleteattrib normal
```

The `sb6mtool` utility can also stitch objects together into sub-objects of the same file. To do this, all of the input files must have the same number, layout, and type of attributes. Simply specify all of the input files on the command line, each with its own `--input` argument; set the output file; and then use the `--makesubobj` command. For example, to stitch a bunch of rock models together to make an asteroid field, issue the following command:

```
$ sb6mtool --input rock1.sbm \
           --input rock2.sbm \
           --input rock3.sbm \
           --input rock4.sbm \
           --input rock5.sbm \
           --input rock6.sbm \
           --input rock7.sbm \
           --output asteroids.sbm --makesubobj
```

The tool will take all of the sub-objects in each of the files, in the order that they're specified, and stuff them into one big output file. You can even keep reading and outputting to the same file to append more and more data onto the end of it. This is exactly how we made the `asteroids.sbm` file that accompanies the asteroid field example.

Appendix B

The SBM File Format

The SBM model file format is a simple geometry data file format devised specifically for this book. The format is chunk-based and extensible, with several chunk types defined for use in the book's examples. This appendix documents the file format. SBM files begin with a file header, followed by a number of chunks, each started with a header, followed by raw data that may be referenced by chunks. Multi-byte fields in structures are defined to follow little-endian byte ordering. All structures are tightly packed.

File Header

All SBM files start with a header of the following form:

```
typedef struct SB6M_HEADER_t
{
    union
    {
        unsigned int    magic;
        char            magic_name[4];
    };
    unsigned int        size;
    unsigned int        num_chunks;
    unsigned int        flags;
} SB6M_HEADER;
```

The magic and magic_name fields are contained in a union and, therefore, occupy the same 4 bytes of the file header. SBM files start with the magic number 0x4d364253, which when encoded as a little-endian 32-bit word causes the magic_name field to contain the characters

{'S', 'B', '6', 'M'} (SuperBible 6 Model—the format was designed for the sixth edition of this book and hasn't changed significantly). If this file is being loaded on a big-endian system, then the field will contain {'M', '6', 'B', 'S'}.

The following field, size, encodes the size of the file header, in bytes. This represents the offset in bytes from the beginning of the file header to the beginning of the first chunk header, described in the next section. The size of the SB6_HEADER structure as defined is 16 bytes, so size will normally be 0x10. However, it is legal to store data between the header and the first chunk. As such, loaders should add the value of size to the location of the file header to find the first chunk.

The num_chunks field stores the number of chunks contained in the SBM file. It is legal for loaders to skip chunks that are not recognized. Thus you must know the num_chunks field when the chunk list is fully parsed and be confident that the chunk ID is not just garbage following the last valid chunk.

The final field, flags, is a bitfield that encodes a series of flags further defining the SB6M file. At this time, no flags are defined and this field should be set to zero.

Chunk Headers

Following the file header is a list of chunks. Each chunk starts with a chunk header of the following form:

```
typedef struct SB6M_CHUNK_HEADER_t
{
    union
    {
        unsigned int    chunk_type;
        char            chunk_name[4];
    };
    unsigned int        size;
} SB6M_CHUNK_HEADER;
```

Again, the chunk_type and chunk_name fields are members of a union and, therefore, share storage space in memory. The chunk_type field encodes the type of the chunk and is unique per chunk type; it is documented in the following section and its subsections. The chunk_name field is part of the structure definition for debugging purposes. The size field stores the number of bytes contained in the chunk, *including the header*. The next chunk in the file begins size bytes beyond the start of the current chunk's header. Loaders may skip unrecognized chunks by simply adding size bytes to the current file pointer, although this may result in loading or rendering errors. Additionally, size should always be a multiple of 4, ensuring that chunks always start at 4-byte aligned offsets from the beginning of the file.

Defined Chunks

This section documents the chunks that have been defined at this time.

Data Chunk

The data chunk stores raw data. All model files should have at least one data chunk. It is expected that a model loader will load the data from the file into a buffer object from which it can be rendered. The structure of the data chunk is as follows:

```
typedef struct SB6M_DATA_CHUNK_t
{
    SB6M_CHUNK_HEADER          header;
    unsigned int               encoding;
    unsigned int               data_offset;
    unsigned int               data_length;
} SB6M_DATA_CHUNK;
```

The first member of the chunk (as with all chunks) is the chunk header. The chunk_type field of the header is 0x41544144, so the chunk_name field will contain {'D', 'A', 'T', 'A'}. The data_offset field gives the offset, in bytes, from the beginning of the chunk. Normally, this field will contain 20. However, this allows the data chunk header to expand in future versions of the format without needing a new chunk ID. The data_length field is the final length of the data. This will likely be different from the size field in the chunk's header—the chunk header's size field is the number of bytes from the beginning of the data chunk to the beginning of the next chunk, whereas the data_length field is the length of the stored data.

The encoding field contains the data encoding token. It must be one of the following token values:

```
typedef enum SB6M_DATA_ENCODING_t
{
    SB6M_DATA_ENCODING_RAW            = 0
} SB6M_DATA_ENCODING;
```

Currently, only the SB6M_DATA_ENCODING_RAW token is defined. It indicates that the data is stored verbatim in the file and should be loaded directly into a buffer object. Additional tokens could be assigned for compressed data, for example. If a compressed encoding scheme were defined, then all information required to decode the file should be stored within the data block, with the data_length field still representing the final, *uncompressed* size of the data.

Index Data Chunk

The index data chunk encodes a reference to index data stored in the file's data chunk.[1] Its structure is as follows:

```
typedef struct SB6M_CHUNK_INDEX_DATA_t
{
    SB6M_CHUNK_HEADER    header;
    unsigned int         index_type;
    unsigned int         index_count;
    unsigned int         index_data_offset;
} SB6M_CHUNK_INDEX_DATA;
```

The chunk_type field of the index data chunk's header is 0x58444e49 and its chunk_name field will contain {'I', 'N', 'D', 'X'}. The normal size of the index data chunk is 20 bytes, so the header's size field is expected to be 0x14, although it is legal to store arbitrary data between the chunks.

The following fields describe the index data. The index_type field encodes the value of an OpenGL token that determines the types. Legal values for the index type are 0x1401 (GL_UNSIGNED_BYTE), 0x1403 (GL_UNSIGNED_SHORT), and 0x1405 (GL_UNSIGNED_INT). While other values could be encoded in this field, these values would be considered unsupported and proprietary. Loaders will generally fail to load the SBM

---

1. In earlier versions of the SBM file format, the data chunk was not defined and offsets to data were interpreted as offsets into the file itself. Backward-compatible loaders may interpret offsets in this manner if a data chunk is not found, but all newly created files should include at least one data chunk.

file, or pass the value unaltered to OpenGL, resulting in failure to render correctly on unextended implementations.

The index_count field stores the number of indices that are contained in the file. To determine the total size of the index data, the element size of an index must be determined from the index_type field and multiplied by the index_count field. The index_data_offset field stores the offset, in bytes, from the beginning of the first data chunk where the index data starts.

If an SBM file has no index data chunk, then the resulting vertex data is assumed to not need indices and can be drawn with a call to **glDrawArrays()**, for example. Otherwise, the index data defined by the index chunk is passed to a call to **glDrawElements()** or another similar function to index into the vertex arrays.

Vertex Data Chunk

Raw vertex data is stored in SBM files and is then referenced by vertex data chunks, whose structure is as follows:

```
typedef struct SB6M_CHUNK_VERTEX_DATA_t
{
    SB6M_CHUNK_HEADER    header;
    unsigned int         data_size;
    unsigned int         data_offset;
    unsigned int         total_vertices;
} SB6M_CHUNK_VERTEX_DATA;
```

The header of a vertex data chunk has the chunk_type 0x58545256, which corresponds to a chunk_name of { 'V', 'R', 'T', 'X' }. The size of a vertex data chunk is expected to be 20 (0x14) bytes. The data_size member contains the raw size, in bytes, of the vertex data, and the data_offset field contains the offset, in bytes, from the beginning of the first data chunk of the vertex data. The total number of vertices encoded in the vertex data chunk is stored in total_vertices.

Vertex Attribute Chunk

The vertex attribute chunk stores the definitions of vertex attributes. It is made up of a header followed by a *variable-sized* array of vertex attribute declarations. Its structure is as follows:

```
typedef struct SB6M_VERTEX_ATTRIB_CHUNK_t
{
    SB6M_CHUNK_HEADER           header;
    unsigned int                attrib_count;
    SB6M_VERTEX_ATTRIB_DECL     attrib_data[1];
} SB6M_VERTEX_ATTRIB_CHUNK;
```

The chunk_type field for vertex attributes is 0x42525441, corresponding to
a chunk_name of {'A', 'T', 'R', 'B'}. The size of the vertex attribute
chunk is variable and will depend on the number of vertex attributes
contained in the chunk, which is stored in its attrib_count field. The
attrib_data field is declared here as an array of size 1, but is in fact a
variable-length array with attrib_count elements. At least one vertex
attribute is assumed to be contained in the file—hence the minimal size
declaration.

The attrib_data field is an array of SB6M_VERTEX_ATTRIB_DECL structures,
whose definition is

```
typedef struct SB6M_VERTEX_ATTRIB_DECL_t
{
    char                name[64];
    unsigned int        size;
    unsigned int        type;
    unsigned int        stride;
    unsigned int        flags;
    unsigned int        data_offset;
} SB6M_VERTEX_ATTRIB_DECL;
```

Each attribute is given a name that may be up to 64 characters long,
including the terminating NUL character, and is stored in the name field.
The size field identifies the number of elements per vertex encoded by the
attribute, and the type contains the value of an OpenGL token that defines
the data type of the attribute. Examples are 0x1406 (GL_FLOAT), 0x1400
(GL_BYTE), and 0x140B (GL_HALF_FLOAT), although any legal OpenGL type
token may be used here. It is expected that loaders will cast this field to a
GLenum token and pass it to OpenGL unmodified. The stride field encodes
the number of bytes between the starting points of the elements. As in
OpenGL, a stride value of zero indicates that the data is tightly packed.
Again, this value can be directly passed to OpenGL unmodified.

The flags field is a bitfield encoding information about the vertex
attribute. Currently, the defined flags are

```
#define SB6M_VERTEX_ATTRIB_FLAG_NORMALIZED      0x00000001
#define SB6M_VERTEX_ATTRIB_FLAG_INTEGER         0x00000002
```

If flags contains SB6M_VERTEX_ATTRIB_FLAG_NORMALIZED, then the attribute is assumed to be normalized integer data and this information will be conveyed to OpenGL—for example, by setting the normalized parameter to GL_TRUE in a call to **glVertexAttribPointer()**. If flags contains SB6M_VERTEX_ATTRIB_FLAG_INTEGER, then the vertex attribute is assumed to be an integer attribute. In this case, loaders should use a function such as **glVertexAttribIPointer()** to intialize vertex attributes in preference to **glVertexAttribPointer()**, for example.

Finally, the data_offset field encodes the offset, in bytes, of the beginning of the vertex attribute data from the beginning of the first data chunk in the file. The absolute position of an attribute's data in the file (assuming a data chunk with encoding set to SB6M_DATA_ENCODING_RAW) is

```
(uintptr_t)data_chunk           // Address of data chunk
        + data_chunk->data_offset   // plus offset of data in chunk
        + attribute->data_offset;   // plus relative offset of attribute
```

Comment Chunk

The comment chunk is provided to allow arbitrary data to be stored inside the SBM file. There is no requirement to parse the comment chunk, although it is guaranteed to never be used for any purpose that will affect rendering of a model.

```
typedef struct SB6M_CHUNK_COMMENT_t
{
    SB6M_CHUNK_HEADER           header;
    char                        comment[4];
} SB6M_CHUNK_COMMENT;
```

The header field of the comment chunk has a chunk_type field of 0x544E4D43, which corresponds to a chunk_name of {'C','M','N','T'}. Parsers are expected to skip comment chunks, although it is possible to embed text, meta-data, or even rendering information in a proprietary chunk. Note that the total size of the comment chunk should be a multiple of 4, even if the data stored in its comment field is not a multiple of 4. In such a case, the chunk should be padded to correctly align the next chunk.

Object List Chunk

Object list chunks represent sub-objects within a single SBM file. Each SBM file may contain many sub-objects. Sub-objects share a single vertex declaration, and their vertex and index data is contained within the same buffer or buffers.

```
typedef struct SB6M_CHUNK_SUB_OBJECT_LIST_t
{
    SB6M_CHUNK_HEADER           header;
    unsigned int                count;
    SB6M_SUB_OBJECT_DECL        sub_object[1];
} SB6M_CHUNK_SUB_OBJECT_LIST;
```

The header field of the sub-object list chunk has a chunk_type field of 0x54534C4F, which corresponds to a chunk_name of {'O','L','S','T'}. The count field specifies how many sub-objects are contained in the SBM file. Following the count field is an array of one or more SB6M_SUB_OBJECT_DECL structures, whose definition is

```
typedef struct SB6M_SUB_OBJECT_DECL_t
{
    unsigned int                first;
    unsigned int                count;
} SB6M_SUB_OBJECT_DECL;
```

Each sub-object consists of a first vertex and a count of the number of vertices in the object, stored in the first and count fields, respectively. If the object data is indexed, then the first and count fields specify the first index and the number of indices, respectively, in the sub-object. If the object has no index data, then first and count specify the first vertex and the number of vertices in the sub-object.

Example

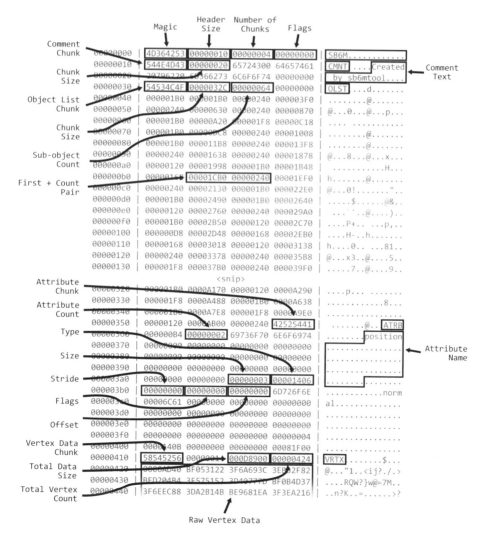

Figure B.1: Dump of example SBM file

Example   **757**

Appendix C

OpenGL Features and Versions

For more than two decades, OpenGL has been updated and enhanced, with each revision adding more features and functionality to the core specification. Although this book is about version 4.5 of OpenGL, many of the examples and topics covered here are applicable to earlier versions of the standard. When designing an OpenGL application that is intended to run on a broad range of hardware, it's important to pick a baseline—a version of OpenGL that's *absolutely required* for your application to run correctly. You can then choose additional functionality (perhaps from extensions or newer versions of OpenGL) that will enhance your application's performance or features, but that aren't strictly required.

The tables in this appendix provide a guide to the versions of OpenGL in which specific functions, features, and tokens were introduced. It also includes a list of extensions and the features that they introduced, and a list of OpenGL versions and the features and functions that they introduced. We cover only OpenGL version 4.0 and later, which serves as a reasonable baseline—we do not recommend targeting versions of OpenGL earlier than 4.0 in new applications.

List of OpenGL Functions

Table C.1: OpenGL Functions

Function	Available in Version								
	3.2	3.3	4.0	4.1	4.2	4.3	4.4	4.5
glActiveShaderProgram()	—	—	—	✓	✓	✓	✓	✓
glActiveTexture()	✓	✓	✓	✓	✓	✓	✓	✓
glAttachShader()	✓	✓	✓	✓	✓	✓	✓	✓
glBeginConditionalRender()	✓	✓	✓	✓	✓	✓	✓	✓
glBeginQuery()	✓	✓	✓	✓	✓	✓	✓	✓
glBeginQueryIndexed()	—	—	✓	✓	✓	✓	✓	✓
glBeginTransformFeedback()	✓	✓	✓	✓	✓	✓	✓	✓
glBindAttribLocation()	✓	✓	✓	✓	✓	✓	✓	✓
glBindBuffer()	✓	✓	✓	✓	✓	✓	✓	✓
glBindBufferBase()	✓	✓	✓	✓	✓	✓	✓	✓
glBindBufferRange()	✓	✓	✓	✓	✓	✓	✓	✓
glBindBuffersBase()	—	—	—	—	—	—	✓	✓
glBindBuffersRange()	—	—	—	—	—	—	✓	✓
glBindFragDataLocation()	✓	✓	✓	✓	✓	✓	✓	✓
glBindFragDataLocationIndexed()	✓	✓	✓	✓	✓	✓	✓	✓
glBindFramebuffer()	✓	✓	✓	✓	✓	✓	✓	✓
glBindImageTexture()	—	—	—	—	✓	✓	✓	✓
glBindImageTextures()	—	—	—	—	—	—	✓	✓

Continued

Table C.1: *Continued*

Function	Available in Version							
	3.2	3.3	4.0	4.1	4.2	4.3	4.4	4.5
glBindProgramPipeline()	—	—	—	✓	✓	✓	✓	✓
glBindRenderbuffer()	✓	✓	✓	✓	✓	✓	✓	✓
glBindSampler()	—	✓	✓	✓	✓	✓	✓	✓
glBindSamplers()	—	—	—	—	—	—	✓	✓
glBindTexture()	✓	✓	✓	✓	✓	✓	✓	✓
glBindTextures()	—	—	—	—	—	—	✓	✓
glBindTextureUnit()	—	—	—	—	—	—	—	✓
glBindTransformFeedback()	—	—	✓	✓	✓	✓	✓	✓
glBindVertexArray()	✓	✓	✓	✓	✓	✓	✓	✓
glBindVertexBuffer()	—	—	—	—	—	✓	✓	✓
glBindVertexBuffers()	—	—	—	—	—	—	✓	✓
glBlendColor()	✓	✓	✓	✓	✓	✓	✓	✓
glBlendEquation()	✓	✓	✓	✓	✓	✓	✓	✓
glBlendEquationi()	—	—	✓	✓	✓	✓	✓	✓
glBlendEquationSeparate()	✓	✓	✓	✓	✓	✓	✓	✓
glBlendEquationSeparatei()	—	—	✓	✓	✓	✓	✓	✓
glBlendFunc()	✓	✓	✓	✓	✓	✓	✓	✓
glBlendFunci()	—	—	✓	✓	✓	✓	✓	✓
glBlendFuncSeparate()	✓	✓	✓	✓	✓	✓	✓	✓
glBlendFuncSeparatei()	—	—	✓	✓	✓	✓	✓	✓

Continued

Table C.1: *Continued*

Function	Available in Version							
	3.2	3.3	4.0	4.1	4.2	4.3	4.4	4.5
glBLitFramebuffer()	✓	✓	✓	✓	✓	✓	✓	✓
glBlitNamedFramebuffer()	—	—	—	—	—	—	—	✓
glBufferData()	✓	✓	✓	✓	✓	✓	✓	✓
glBufferStorage()	—	—	—	—	—	—	✓	✓
glBufferSubData()	✓	✓	✓	✓	✓	✓	✓	✓
glCheckFramebufferStatus()	✓	✓	✓	✓	✓	✓	✓	✓
glCheckNamedFramebufferStatus()	—	—	—	—	—	—	—	✓
glClampColor()	✓	✓	✓	✓	✓	✓	✓	✓
glClear()	✓	✓	✓	✓	✓	✓	✓	✓
glClearBuffer*()	✓	✓	✓	✓	✓	✓	✓	✓
glClearBufferData()	—	—	—	—	—	✓	✓	✓
glClearBufferSubData()	—	—	—	—	—	✓	✓	✓
glClearColor()	✓	✓	✓	✓	✓	✓	✓	✓
glClearDepth()	✓	✓	✓	✓	✓	✓	✓	✓
glClearStencil()	✓	✓	✓	✓	✓	✓	✓	✓
glClearTexImage()	—	—	—	—	—	—	✓	✓
glClearTexSubImage()	—	—	—	—	—	—	✓	✓
glClientWaitSync()	✓	✓	✓	✓	✓	✓	✓	✓
glColorMask()	✓	✓	✓	✓	✓	✓	✓	✓
glCompileShader()	✓	✓	✓	✓	✓	✓	✓	✓

Continued

Table C.1: *Continued*

Function	Available in Version							
	3.2	3.3	4.0	4.1	4.2	4.3	4.4	4.5
`glCompressedTexImage1D()`	✓	✓	✓	✓	✓	✓	✓	✓
`glCompressedTexImage2D()`	✓	✓	✓	✓	✓	✓	✓	✓
`glCompressedTexImage3D()`	✓	✓	✓	✓	✓	✓	✓	✓
`glCompressedTexSubImage1D()`	✓	✓	✓	✓	✓	✓	✓	✓
`glCompressedTexSubImage2D()`	✓	✓	✓	✓	✓	✓	✓	✓
`glCompressedTexSubImage3D()`	✓	✓	✓	✓	✓	✓	✓	✓
`glCopyBufferSubData()`	✓	✓	✓	✓	✓	✓	✓	✓
`glCopyImageSubData()`	—	—	—	—	—	✓	✓	✓
`glCopyTexImage1D()`	✓	✓	✓	✓	✓	✓	✓	✓
`glCopyTexImage2D()`	✓	✓	✓	✓	✓	✓	✓	✓
`glCopyTexSubImage1D()`	✓	✓	✓	✓	✓	✓	✓	✓
`glCopyTexSubImage2D()`	✓	✓	✓	✓	✓	✓	✓	✓
`glCopyTexSubImage3D()`	✓	✓	✓	✓	✓	✓	✓	✓
`glCreateProgram()`	✓	✓	✓	✓	✓	✓	✓	✓
`glCreateShader()`	✓	✓	✓	✓	✓	✓	✓	✓
`glCreateShaderProgram()`	—	—	—	✓	✓	✓	✓	✓
`glCullFace()`	✓	✓	✓	✓	✓	✓	✓	✓
`glDebugMessageCallback()`	—	—	—	—	—	✓	✓	✓
`glDebugMessageControl()`	—	—	—	—	—	✓	✓	✓
`glDebugMessageInsert()`	—	—	—	—	—	✓	✓	✓

Continued

Table C.1: *Continued*

Function	Available in Version							
	3.2	3.3	4.0	4.1	4.2	4.3	4.4	4.5
glDeleteBuffers()	✓	✓	✓	✓	✓	✓	✓	✓
glDeleteFramebuffers()	✓	✓	✓	✓	✓	✓	✓	✓
glDeleteProgram()	✓	✓	✓	✓	✓	✓	✓	✓
glDeleteProgramPipelines()	—	—	—	✓	✓	✓	✓	✓
glDeleteQueries()	✓	✓	✓	✓	✓	✓	✓	✓
glDeleteRenderbuffers()	✓	✓	✓	✓	✓	✓	✓	✓
glDeleteSamplers()	✓	✓	✓	✓	✓	✓	✓	✓
glDeleteShader()	✓	✓	✓	✓	✓	✓	✓	✓
glDeleteSync()	✓	✓	✓	✓	✓	✓	✓	✓
glDeleteTextures()	✓	✓	✓	✓	✓	✓	✓	✓
glDeleteTransformFeedbacks()	✓	✓	✓	✓	✓	✓	✓	✓
glDeleteVertexArrays()	—	—	—	✓	✓	✓	✓	✓
glDepthFunc()	✓	✓	✓	✓	✓	✓	✓	✓
glDepthMask()	✓	✓	✓	✓	✓	✓	✓	✓
glDepthRange()	✓	✓	✓	✓	✓	✓	✓	✓
glDepthRangeArray()	—	—	—	✓	✓	✓	✓	✓
glDepthRangef()	—	—	—	✓	✓	✓	✓	✓
glDepthRangeIndexed()	—	—	—	✓	✓	✓	✓	✓
glDetachShader()	✓	✓	✓	✓	✓	✓	✓	✓
glDisable()	✓	✓	✓	✓	✓	✓	✓	✓

Continued

Table C.1: *Continued*

Function	Available in Version							
	3.2	3.3	4.0	4.1	4.2	4.3	4.4	4.5
glDisableVertexArrayAttrib()	—	—	—	—	—	—	—	✓
glDisableVertexAttribArray()	✓	✓	✓	✓	✓	✓	✓	✓
glDispatchCompute()	—	—	—	—	—	✓	✓	✓
glDispatchComputeIndirect()	—	—	—	—	—	✓	✓	✓
glDrawArrays()	✓	✓	✓	✓	✓	✓	✓	✓
glDrawArraysIndirect()	—	—	✓	✓	✓	✓	✓	✓
glDrawArraysInstanced()	✓	✓	✓	✓	✓	✓	✓	✓
glDrawArraysInstancedBaseInstance()	—	—	—	—	✓	✓	✓	✓
glDrawBuffer()	✓	✓	✓	✓	✓	✓	✓	✓
glDrawBuffers()	✓	✓	✓	✓	✓	✓	✓	✓
glDrawElements()	✓	✓	✓	✓	✓	✓	✓	✓
glDrawElementsBaseVertex()	✓	✓	✓	✓	✓	✓	✓	✓
glDrawElementsIndirect()	—	—	✓	✓	✓	✓	✓	✓
glDrawElementsInstanced()	✓	✓	✓	✓	✓	✓	✓	✓
glDrawElementsInstancedBaseInstance()	—	—	—	—	✓	✓	✓	✓
glDrawElementsInstancedBaseVertex()	✓	✓	✓	✓	✓	✓	✓	✓
glDrawElementsInstancedBaseVertexBaseInstance()	—	—	—	—	✓	✓	✓	✓
glDrawRangeElements()	✓	✓	✓	✓	✓	✓	✓	✓
glDrawRangeElementsBaseVertex()	✓	✓	✓	✓	✓	✓	✓	✓
glDrawTransformFeedback()	—	—	✓	✓	✓	✓	✓	✓

Continued

Table C.1: *Continued*

| Function | \multicolumn{8}{c}{Available in Version} |
	3.2	3.3	4.0	4.1	4.2	4.3	4.4	4.5
glDrawTransformFeedbackInstanced()					✓	✓	✓	✓
glDrawTransformFeedbackStream()			✓	✓	✓	✓	✓	✓
glDrawTransformFeedbackStreamInstanced()					✓	✓	✓	✓
glEnable()	✓	✓	✓	✓	✓	✓	✓	✓
glEnableVertexArrayAttrib()								✓
glEnableVertexAttribArray()	✓	✓	✓	✓	✓	✓	✓	✓
glEndQuery()	✓	✓	✓	✓	✓	✓	✓	✓
glEndQueryIndexed()					✓	✓	✓	✓
glEndTransformFeedback()	✓	✓	✓	✓	✓	✓	✓	✓
glFenceSync()	✓	✓	✓	✓	✓	✓	✓	✓
glFinish()	✓	✓	✓	✓	✓	✓	✓	✓
glFlush()	✓	✓	✓	✓	✓	✓	✓	✓
glFlushMappedBufferRange()	✓	✓	✓	✓	✓	✓	✓	✓
glFlushMappedNamedBufferRange()								✓
glFramebufferParameteri()						✓	✓	✓
glFramebufferRenderbuffer()	✓	✓	✓	✓	✓	✓	✓	✓
glFramebufferTexture()	✓	✓	✓	✓	✓	✓	✓	✓
glFramebufferTextureLayer()	✓	✓	✓	✓	✓	✓	✓	✓
glFrontFace()	✓	✓	✓	✓	✓	✓	✓	✓
glGenBuffers()	✓	✓	✓	✓	✓	✓	✓	✓

Continued

Table C.1: *Continued*

Function	Available in Version							
	3.2	3.3	4.0	4.1	4.2	4.3	4.4	4.5
`glGenerateMipmap()`	✓	✓	✓	✓	✓	✓	✓	✓
`glGenerateTextureMipmap()`	—	—	—	—	—	—	—	✓
`glGenFramebuffers()`	✓	✓	✓	✓	✓	✓	✓	✓
`glGenProgramPipelines()`	—	—	—	✓	✓	✓	✓	✓
`glGenQueries()`	✓	✓	✓	✓	✓	✓	✓	✓
`glGenRenderbuffers()`	✓	✓	✓	✓	✓	✓	✓	✓
`glGenSamplers()`	—	✓	✓	✓	✓	✓	✓	✓
`glGenTextures()`	✓	✓	✓	✓	✓	✓	✓	✓
`glGenTransformFeedbacks()`	—	—	✓	✓	✓	✓	✓	✓
`glGenVertexArrays()`	✓	✓	✓	✓	✓	✓	✓	✓
`glGet*()`	✓	✓	✓	✓	✓	✓	✓	✓
`glGetActiveAtomicCounterBufferiv()`	—	—	—	—	✓	✓	✓	✓
`glGetActiveAttrib()`	✓	✓	✓	✓	✓	✓	✓	✓
`glGetActiveSubroutineName()`	—	—	✓	✓	✓	✓	✓	✓
`glGetActiveSubroutineUniform()`	—	—	✓	✓	✓	✓	✓	✓
`glGetActiveSubroutineUniformName()`	—	—	✓	✓	✓	✓	✓	✓
`glGetActiveUniform()`	✓	✓	✓	✓	✓	✓	✓	✓
`glGetActiveUniformBlock()`	✓	✓	✓	✓	✓	✓	✓	✓
`glGetActiveUniformBlockName()`	✓	✓	✓	✓	✓	✓	✓	✓
`glGetActiveUniformName()`	✓	✓	✓	✓	✓	✓	✓	✓

Continued

Table C.1: *Continued*

Function	Available in Version							
	3.2	3.3	4.0	4.1	4.2	4.3	4.4	4.5
glGetActiveUniformsiv()	✓	✓	✓	✓	✓	✓	✓	✓
glGetAttachedShaders()	✓	✓	✓	✓	✓	✓	✓	✓
glGetAttribLocation()	✓	✓	✓	✓	✓	✓	✓	✓
glGetBufferParameter()	✓	✓	✓	✓	✓	✓	✓	✓
glGetBufferPointerv()	✓	✓	✓	✓	✓	✓	✓	✓
glGetBufferSubData()	✓	✓	✓	✓	✓	✓	✓	✓
glGetCompressedTexImage()	✓	✓	✓	✓	✓	✓	✓	✓
glGetCompressedTextureImage()	—	—	—	—	—	—	—	✓
glGetDebugMessageLog()	—	—	—	—	—	✓	✓	✓
glGetError()	✓	✓	✓	✓	✓	✓	✓	✓
glGetFragDataIndex()	—	✓	✓	✓	✓	✓	✓	✓
glGetFragDataLocation()	✓	✓	✓	✓	✓	✓	✓	✓
glGetFramebufferAttachmentParameter()	✓	✓	✓	✓	✓	✓	✓	✓
glGetFramebufferParameter()	—	—	—	—	—	✓	✓	✓
glGetInternalformativ()	—	—	—	—	✓	✓	✓	✓
glGetInternalformati64v()	—	—	—	—	—	✓	✓	✓
glGetMultisamplefv()	✓	✓	✓	✓	✓	✓	✓	✓
glGetNamedBufferParameter()	—	—	—	—	—	—	—	✓
glGetNamedBufferPointer()	—	—	—	—	—	—	—	✓
glGetNamedBufferSubData()	—	—	—	—	—	—	—	✓

Continued

Function	\multicolumn{8}{c}{Available in Version}							
	3.2	3.3	4.0	4.1	4.2	4.3	4.4	4.5
glGetNamedRenderbufferParameter()	—	—	—	—	—	—	—	✓
glGetnCompressedTexImage()	—	—	—	—	—	—	—	✓
glGetnTexImage()	—	—	—	—	—	—	—	✓
glGetnUniform()	—	—	—	—	—	—	—	✓
glGetObjectLabel()	—	—	—	—	—	✓	✓	✓
glGetObjectPtrLabel()	—	—	—	—	—	✓	✓	✓
glGetProgram()	✓	✓	✓	✓	✓	✓	✓	✓
glGetProgramBinary()	—	—	—	✓	✓	✓	✓	✓
glGetProgramInfoLog()	✓	✓	✓	✓	✓	✓	✓	✓
glGetProgramInterface()	—	—	—	—	—	✓	✓	✓
glGetProgramPipeline()	—	—	—	✓	✓	✓	✓	✓
glGetProgramPipelineInfoLog()	—	—	—	✓	✓	✓	✓	✓
glGetProgramResource()	—	—	—	—	—	✓	✓	✓
glGetProgramResourceIndex()	—	—	—	—	—	✓	✓	✓
glGetProgramResourceLocation()	—	—	—	—	—	✓	✓	✓
glGetProgramResourceLocationIndex()	—	—	—	—	—	✓	✓	✓
glGetProgramResourceName()	—	—	—	—	—	✓	✓	✓
glGetProgramStage()	—	—	✓	✓	✓	✓	✓	✓
glGetQueryIndexediv()	—	—	✓	✓	✓	✓	✓	✓
glGetQueryObject()	✓	✓	✓	✓	✓	✓	✓	✓

Continued

Table C.1: *Continued*

Function	Available in Version							
	3.2	3.3	4.0	4.1	4.2	4.3	4.4	4.5
glGetQueryiv()	✓	✓	✓	✓	✓	✓	✓	✓
glGetRenderbufferParameter()	✓	✓	✓	✓	✓	✓	✓	✓
glGetSamplerParameter*()	—	✓	✓	✓	✓	✓	✓	✓
glGetShader()	✓	✓	✓	✓	✓	✓	✓	✓
glGetShaderInfoLog()	✓	✓	✓	✓	✓	✓	✓	✓
glGetShaderPrecisionFormat()	—	—	—	✓	✓	✓	✓	✓
glGetShaderSource()	✓	✓	✓	✓	✓	✓	✓	✓
glGetString()	✓	✓	✓	✓	✓	✓	✓	✓
glGetSubroutineIndex()	—	—	✓	✓	✓	✓	✓	✓
glGetSubroutineUniformLocation()	—	—	✓	✓	✓	✓	✓	✓
glGetSync()	✓	✓	✓	✓	✓	✓	✓	✓
glGetTexImage()	✓	✓	✓	✓	✓	✓	✓	✓
glGetTexLevelParameter*()	✓	✓	✓	✓	✓	✓	✓	✓
glGetTexParameter*()	✓	✓	✓	✓	✓	✓	✓	✓
glGetTransformFeedback()	—	—	—	—	—	—	—	✓
glGetTransformFeedbackVarying()	✓	✓	✓	✓	✓	✓	✓	✓
glGetUniform*()	✓	✓	✓	✓	✓	✓	✓	✓
glGetUniformBlockIndex()	✓	✓	✓	✓	✓	✓	✓	✓
glGetUniformIndices()	✓	✓	✓	✓	✓	✓	✓	✓
glGetUniformLocation()	✓	✓	✓	✓	✓	✓	✓	✓

Continued

Table C.1: *Continued*

Function	Available in Version							
	3.2	3.3	4.0	4.1	4.2	4.3	4.4	4.5
glGetUniformSubroutine*()	—	—	✓	✓	✓	✓	✓	✓
glGetVertexAttrib()	✓	✓	✓	✓	✓	✓	✓	✓
glGetVertexAttribPointerv()	✓	✓	✓	✓	✓	✓	✓	✓
glHint()	✓	✓	✓	✓	✓	✓	✓	✓
glInvalidateBufferData()	—	—	—	—	—	✓	✓	✓
glInvalidateBufferSubData()	—	—	—	—	—	✓	✓	✓
glInvalidateFramebuffer()	—	—	—	—	—	✓	✓	✓
glInvalidateSubFramebuffer()	—	—	—	—	—	✓	✓	✓
glInvalidateTexImage()	—	—	—	—	—	✓	✓	✓
glInvalidateTexSubImage()	—	—	—	—	—	✓	✓	✓
glIsBuffer()	✓	✓	✓	✓	✓	✓	✓	✓
glIsEnabled()	✓	✓	✓	✓	✓	✓	✓	✓
glIsFramebuffer()	✓	✓	✓	✓	✓	✓	✓	✓
glIsProgram()	✓	✓	✓	✓	✓	✓	✓	✓
glIsProgramPipeline()	—	—	—	✓	✓	✓	✓	✓
glIsQuery()	✓	✓	✓	✓	✓	✓	✓	✓
glIsRenderbuffer()	✓	✓	✓	✓	✓	✓	✓	✓
glIsSampler()	—	✓	✓	✓	✓	✓	✓	✓
glIsShader()	✓	✓	✓	✓	✓	✓	✓	✓
glIsSync()	✓	✓	✓	✓	✓	✓	✓	✓

Continued

Table C.1: *Continued*

Function	| 3.2	3.3	4.0	4.1	4.2	4.3	4.4	4.5
				Available in Version				
glIsTexture()	✓	✓	✓	✓	✓	✓	✓	✓
glIsTransformFeedback()	—	—	✓	✓	✓	✓	✓	✓
glIsVertexArray()	✓	✓	✓	✓	✓	✓	✓	✓
glLineWidth()	✓	✓	✓	✓	✓	✓	✓	✓
glLinkProgram()	✓	✓	✓	✓	✓	✓	✓	✓
glLogicOp()	✓	✓	✓	✓	✓	✓	✓	✓
glMapBuffer()	✓	✓	✓	✓	✓	✓	✓	✓
glMapBufferRange()	✓	✓	✓	✓	✓	✓	✓	✓
glMemoryBarrier()	—	—	—	—	✓	✓	✓	✓
glMinSampleShading()	✓	✓	✓	✓	✓	✓	✓	✓
glMultiDrawArrays()	✓	✓	✓	✓	✓	✓	✓	✓
glMultiDrawArraysIndirect()	—	—	—	—	—	✓	✓	✓
glMultiDrawElements()	✓	✓	✓	✓	✓	✓	✓	✓
glMultiDrawElementsBaseVertex()	✓	✓	✓	✓	✓	✓	✓	✓
glMultiDrawElementsIndirect()	—	—	—	—	—	✓	✓	✓
glObjectLabel()	—	—	—	—	—	✓	✓	✓
glObjectPtrLabel()	—	—	—	—	—	✓	✓	✓
glPatchParameter()	—	—	✓	✓	✓	✓	✓	✓
glPauseTransformFeedback()	—	—	✓	✓	✓	✓	✓	✓
glPixelStore()	✓	✓	✓	✓	✓	✓	✓	✓

Continued

Table C.1: *Continued*

Function	Available in Version							
	3.2	3.3	4.0	4.1	4.2	4.3	4.4	4.5
glPointParameter()	✓	✓	✓	✓	✓	✓	✓	✓
glPointSize()	✓	✓	✓	✓	✓	✓	✓	✓
glPolygonMode()	✓	✓	✓	✓	✓	✓	✓	✓
glPolygonOffset()	✓	✓	✓	✓	✓	✓	✓	✓
glPopDebugGroup()						✓	✓	✓
glPrimitiveRestartIndex()	✓	✓	✓	✓	✓	✓	✓	✓
glProgramBinary()				✓	✓	✓	✓	✓
glProgramParameter()				✓	✓	✓	✓	✓
glProgramUniform*()				✓	✓	✓	✓	✓
glProvokingVertex()	✓	✓	✓	✓	✓	✓	✓	✓
glPushDebugGroup()						✓	✓	✓
glQueryCounter()		✓	✓	✓	✓	✓	✓	✓
glReadBuffer()	✓	✓	✓	✓	✓	✓	✓	✓
glReadPixels()	✓	✓	✓	✓	✓	✓	✓	✓
glReleaseShaderCompiler()				✓	✓	✓	✓	✓
glRenderbufferStorage()	✓	✓	✓	✓	✓	✓	✓	✓
glRenderbufferStorageMultisample()	✓	✓	✓	✓	✓	✓	✓	✓
glResumeTransformFeedback()			✓	✓	✓	✓	✓	✓
glSampleCoverage()	✓	✓	✓	✓	✓	✓	✓	✓
glSampleMaski()	✓	✓	✓	✓	✓	✓	✓	✓

Continued

Table C.1: *Continued*

Function	Available in Version							
	3.2	3.3	4.0	4.1	4.2	4.3	4.4	4.5
glSamplerParameter*()	✓	✓	✓	✓	✓	✓	✓	✓
glScissor()	✓	✓	✓	✓	✓	✓	✓	✓
glScissorArray()	—	—	—	✓	✓	✓	✓	✓
glScissorIndexed()	—	—	—	✓	✓	✓	✓	✓
glShaderBinary()	—	—	—	✓	✓	✓	✓	✓
glShaderSource()	✓	✓	✓	✓	✓	✓	✓	✓
glShaderStorageBlockBinding()	—	—	—	—	—	✓	✓	✓
glStencilFunc()	✓	✓	✓	✓	✓	✓	✓	✓
glStencilFuncSeparate()	✓	✓	✓	✓	✓	✓	✓	✓
glStencilMask()	✓	✓	✓	✓	✓	✓	✓	✓
glStencilMaskSeparate()	✓	✓	✓	✓	✓	✓	✓	✓
glStencilOp()	✓	✓	✓	✓	✓	✓	✓	✓
glStencilOpSeparate()	✓	✓	✓	✓	✓	✓	✓	✓
glTexBuffer()	✓	✓	✓	✓	✓	✓	✓	✓
glTexBufferRange()	—	—	—	—	—	✓	✓	✓
glTexImage1D()	✓	✓	✓	✓	✓	✓	✓	✓
glTexImage2D()	✓	✓	✓	✓	✓	✓	✓	✓
glTexImage2DMultisample()	✓	✓	✓	✓	✓	✓	✓	✓
glTexImage3D()	✓	✓	✓	✓	✓	✓	✓	✓
glTexImage3DMultisample()	✓	✓	✓	✓	✓	✓	✓	✓

Continued

Function	Available in Version							
	3.2	3.3	4.0	4.1	4.2	4.3	4.4	4.5
glTexParameter*()	✓	✓	✓	✓	✓	✓	✓	✓
glTexStorage1D()	—	—	—	—	✓	✓	✓	✓
glTexStorage2D()	—	—	—	—	✓	✓	✓	✓
glTexStorage2DMultisample()	—	—	—	—	—	✓	✓	✓
glTexStorage3D()	—	—	—	—	✓	✓	✓	✓
glTexStorage3DMultisample()	—	—	—	—	—	✓	✓	✓
glTexSubImage1D()	✓	✓	✓	✓	✓	✓	✓	✓
glTexSubImage2D()	✓	✓	✓	✓	✓	✓	✓	✓
glTexSubImage3D()	✓	✓	✓	✓	✓	✓	✓	✓
glTextureView()	—	—	—	—	—	✓	✓	✓
glTransformFeedbackVaryings()	✓	✓	✓	✓	✓	✓	—	✓
glUniform*()	✓	✓	✓	✓	✓	✓	✓	✓
glUniformBlockBinding()	✓	✓	✓	✓	✓	✓	✓	✓
glUniformSubroutines()	—	—	✓	✓	✓	✓	✓	✓
glUseProgram()	✓	✓	✓	✓	✓	✓	✓	✓
glUseProgramStages()	—	—	—	✓	✓	✓	✓	✓
glValidateProgram()	✓	✓	✓	✓	✓	✓	✓	✓
glValidateProgramPipeline()	—	—	—	✓	✓	✓	✓	✓
glVertexAttrib*()	✓	✓	✓	✓	✓	✓	✓	✓
glVertexAttribBinding()	✓	✓	✓	✓	✓	✓	✓	✓

Continued

Table C.1: *Continued*

Function	Available in Version							
	3.2	3.3	4.0	4.1	4.2	4.3	4.4	4.5
`glVertexAttribDivisor()`	✓	✓	✓	✓	✓	✓	✓	✓
`glVertexAttribFormat()`	✓	✓	✓	✓	✓	✓	✓	✓
`glVertexAttribPointer()`	✓	✓	✓	✓	✓	✓	✓	✓
`glVertexBindingDivisor()`	—	—	—	—	—	✓	✓	✓
`glViewport()`	✓	✓	✓	✓	✓	✓	✓	✓
`glViewportArray()`	—	—	✓	✓	✓	✓	✓	✓
`glViewportIndexed()`	—	—	✓	✓	✓	✓	✓	✓
`glWaitSync()`	✓	✓	✓	✓	✓	✓	✓	✓

Functions Introduced by OpenGL Extensions

Table C.2: OpenGL Extensions (Core)

Extension	Core Version	Description

GL_ARB_base_instance	4.2	Allows offset of instance index for instanced draws. Introduces the following functions:
		`glDrawArraysInstancedBaseInstance()`
		`glDrawElementsInstancedBaseInstance()`
		`glDrawElementsInstancedBaseVertexBaseInstance()`

GL_ARB_blend_func_extended	3.3	Adds dual-source blending to OpenGL. Introduces the following functions:
		`glBindFragDataLocationIndexed()`
		`glGetFragDataIndex()`

GL_ARB_buffer_storage	4.4	Provides finer-grained control over buffer memory allocation. Introduces immutable buffer storage. Adds the following function: `glBufferStorage()`
GL_ARB_clear_buffer_object	4.3	Allows portions of buffer objects to be directly cleared. Introduces the following functions:

Continued

Table C.2: *Continued*

Extension	Core Version	Description
GL_ARB_clear_texture	4.4	Allows portions of textures to be cleared without attaching to a framebuffer object. Adds the following functions: **glClearTexImage()** **glClearTexSubImage()**
GL_ARB_clip_control	4.5	Provides control over how clip space is mapped to window space. Adds the following function: **glClipControl()**
GL_ARB_conditional_render_inverted	4.5	Allows inversion of the predicate used for conditional rendering. Does not add new functions.
GL_KHR_context_flush_control	4.5	Provides control over how flushing is performed when switching between OpenGL contexs. Needs to be accompanied by a corresponding window system extension.

*(The description column also includes at top: **glClearBufferData()** **glClearBufferSubData()**)*

Continued

Table C.2: *Continued*

Extension	Core Version	Description
GL_ARB_compressed_texture_pixel_storage	4.2	Provides a mechanism to allow applications to set the packing and alignment of compressed images during transfer.
GL_ARB_compute_shader	4.3	Adds compute shaders to OpenGL. Adds the following functions: **glDispatchCompute()** **glDispatchComputeIndirect()**
GL_ARB_cull_distance	4.5	Allows primitives to be culled rather than clipped based on vertex clip distances. Adds gl_CullDistance to GLSL.
GL_ARB_debug_output	4.3	Provides an application-supplied callback function for receiving plain-text diagnosis messages that the OpenGL implementation can use to report errors and other information. Adds the following functions: **glDebugMessageControl()** **glDebugMessageInsert()**

Continued

Table C.2: *Continued*

Extension	Core Version	Description
		glDebugMessageCallback() **glGetDebugMessageLog()**
GL_ARB_depth_clamp	3.2	Allows fragments that would otherwise have been clipped against the near or far depth planes to instead be clamped to it.
GL_ARB_derivative_control	4.5	Provides specialized functions to provide coarse or fine derivative calculations to be performed in shaders. *Shading language only.*
GL_ARB_direct_state_access	4.5	Allows OpenGL objects to be manipulated without them being bound to a context. Adds *many new functions to OpenGL.*
GL_ARB_draw_buffers_blend	4.0	Allows each attachment of a framebuffer object to have its own blend factors and equations. Adds the following functions: **glBlendEquationi()** **glBlendEquationSeparatei()**

Continued

Table C.2: *Continued*

Extension	Core Version	Description

GL_ARB_draw_elements_base_vertex	3.2	Allows the vertex index consumed by indexed drawing commands to be offset by a draw-specified amount. Adds the following functions:
		
		`glDrawElementsBaseVertex()`
		`glDrawRangeElementsBaseVertex()`
		`glDrawElementsInstancedBaseVertex()`
		`glMultiDrawElementsBaseVertex()`

GL_ARB_ES2_compatibility	4.1	Adds functionality that is part of OpenGL ES 2.0 and that would otherwise not be part of desktop OpenGL. Adds the following functions:
		
		`glReleaseShaderCompiler()`
		`glShaderBinary()`
		`glGetShaderPrecisionFormat()`
		`glDepthRangef()`
		`glClearDepthf()`

Continued

Table C.2: *Continued*

Extension	Core Version	Description
GL_ARB_ES3_1_compatibility	4.5	Adds functionality that is part of OpenGL ES 3.1 and that would otherwise not be part of desktop OpenGL. Adds the following function: **glMemoryBarrierByRegion()**
GL_ARB_explicit_uniform_location	4.3	Allows the location of uniforms to be specified in shader text rather than being assigned by OpenGL. *Shading language only.*
GL_ARB_fragment_coord_conventions	3.2	Allows a fragment shader to specify the conventions for gl_FragCoord.
GL_ARB_fragment_layer_viewport	4.3	Provides as an input to the fragment shader the current layer and viewport index being rendered to. *Shading language only.*
GL_ARB_framebuffer_no_attachments	4.3	Allows rendering into a framebuffer with no attachments and provides functions to specify the framebuffer's virtual dimensions. Adds the following functions:

Continued

Table C.2: *Continued*

Extension	Core Version	Description
		`glFramebufferParameteri()` `glGetFramebufferParameteriv()`
GL_ARB_geometry_shader4	3.2	Adds geometry shaders to OpenGL. Adds the following functions: `glProgramParameteri()` `glFramebufferTexture()` `glFramebufferTextureLayer()` `glFramebufferTextureFace()`
GL_ARB_get_program_binary	4.1	Provides a means to retrieve binary representations of program objects from an OpenGL implementation. Provides the following functions: `glGetProgramBinary()` `glProgramBinary()` `glProgramParameteri()`
GL_ARB_get_texture_sub_image	4.5	Allows applications to read back sub-regions of textures. Adds the following functions:

Continued

Table C.2: *Continued*

Extension	Core Version	Description
		`glGetTextureSubImage()` `glGetCompressedTextureSubImage()`
GL_ARB_gpu_shader5	4.0	Adds a number of new features and built-in functions to the GLSL shading language.
GL_ARB_gpu_shader_fp64	4.0	Introduces double-precision floating-point support to GLSL. Adds *double-precision variants* of `glUniform*()`.
GL_ARB_instanced_arrays	3.3	Allows different versions of vertex attributes to be consumed by different instances in an instanced draw. Adds the following function: `glVertexAttribDivisor()`
GL_ARB_internalformat_query	4.2	Allows applications to retrieve information about the properties of texture formats. Adds the following function: `glGetInternalformativ()`

Continued

Table C.2: *Continued*

Extension	Core Version	Description

GL_ARB_invalidate_subdata	4.3	Provides facilities to instruct OpenGL that it may discard data. Adds the following functions:
		
		`glInvalidateTexSubImage()`
		`glInvalidateTexImage()`
		`glInvalidateBufferSubData()`
		`glInvalidateBufferData()`
		`glInvalidateFramebuffer()`
		`glInvalidateSubFramebuffer()`

GL_ARB_multi_bind	4.4	Adds functions to bind multiple buffers, textures, or images in one call. Adds the following functions:
		
		`glBindBuffersBase()`
		`glBindBuffersRange()`
		`glBindTextures()`
		`glBindSamplers()`
		`glBindImageTextures()`
		`glBindVertexBuffers()`

GL_ARB_multi_draw_indirect	4.3	Allows multiple draws to be produced using data in memory. Adds the following functions:

Continued

Table C.2: *Continued*

Extension	Core Version	Description
		glMultiDrawArraysIndirect() **glMultiDrawElementsIndirect()**
GL_ARB_occlusion_query2	3.3	Adds Boolean occlusion queries (GL_ANY_SAMPLES_PASSED).
GL_ARB_program_interface_query	4.3	Provides a reflection API for querying information from programs. Adds the following functions: **glGetProgramInterfaceiv()** **glGetProgramResourceIndex()** **glGetProgramResourceName()** **glGetProgramResourceiv()** **glGetProgramResourceLocation()** **glGetProgramResourceLocationIndex()**
GL_ARB_provoking_vertex	3.2	Provides control over which vertex provokes a new primitive. Adds the following function: **glProvokingVertex()**

Continued

Table C.2: *Continued*

Extension	Core Version	Description
GL_KHR_robustness	4.5	Allows an application to determine whether OpenGL has crashed as a result of its behavior and provides range-checked data access functions. Adds the following functions: **glGetGraphicsResetStatus()** **glReadnPixels()** **glGetnUniformiv()** **glGetnUniformfv()** **glGetnUniformuiv()**
GL_ARB_sampler_objects	3.3	Separates sampling parameters into a new object that may be reused. Adds the following functions: **glGenSamplers()** **glDeleteSamplers()** **glIsSampler()** **glBindSampler()** **glSamplerParameter*()** **glGetSamplerParameter*()**

Continued

Table C.2: *Continued*

Extension	Core Version	Description
GL_ARB_sample_shading	4.0	Allows fragment shaders to run at sample rate. Adds the following function: **glMinSampleShading()**
GL_ARB_seamless_cube_map	3.2	Adds support for linear sampling across faces of cubemaps.
GL_ARB_separate_shader_objects	4.1	Allows different shader stages to be linked and exchanged without relinking entire program objects. Adds the following functions: **glUseProgramStages()** **glActiveShaderProgram()** **glCreateShaderProgramv()** **glBindProgramPipeline()** **glDeleteProgramPipelines()** **glGenProgramPipelines()** **glIsProgramPipeline()** **glGetProgramPipelineiv()** **glProgramUniform*()** **glProgramUniformMatrix*()**

Continued

Table C.2: *Continued*

Extension	Core Version	Description
GL_ARB_shader_atomic_counters	4.2	Adds atomic counters to GLSL and atomic counter buffers to OpenGL. Adds the following function: `glGetActiveAtomicCounterBufferiv()`
GL_ARB_shader_bit_encoding	3.3	Adds reinterpret casts between integers and floating-point numbers to GLSL. *Shading language only.*
GL_ARB_shader_image_load_store	4.2	Allows textures to be written by shaders. Adds the following functions: `glBindImageTexture()` `glMemoryBarrier()`
GL_ARB_shader_precision	4.1	Tightly defines floating-point precision in shaders. *Shading language only.*
GL_ARB_shader_subroutine	4.0	Adds shader subroutines to GLSL. Adds the following functions:

Continued

Note: The first row's description reads:
`glValidateProgramPipeline()`
`glGetProgramPipelineInfoLog()`

Table C.2: *Continued*

Extension	Core Version	Description

GL_ARB_shader_storage_buffer_object	4.3	`glGetSubroutineUniformLocation()`
		`glGetSubroutineIndex()`
		`glGetActiveSubroutineUniformiv()`
		`glGetActiveSubroutineUniformName()`
		`glGetActiveSubroutineName()`
		`glUniformSubroutinesuiv()`
		`glGetProgramStageiv()`
		
		Introduces the ability to read, write, and perform atomic operations on buffers directly from shaders. Adds the following function:
		`glShaderStorageBlockBinding()`

GL_ARB_shader_texture_image_samples	4.5	Allows the number of samples in a multisample texture to be determined by GLSL shaders. *Shading language only.*
GL_ARB_stencil_texturing	4.3	Provides access to the stencil component of depth–stencil interleaved textures.

Continued

Table C.2: *Continued*

Extension	Core Version	Description

GL_ARB_sync	3.2	Adds synchronization primitives to OpenGL. Adds the following functions:
		`glFenceSync()`
		`glIsSync()`
		`glDeleteSync()`
		`glClientWaitSync()`
		`glWaitSync()`
		`glGetInteger64()` v
		`glGetSynciv()`

GL_ARB_tessellation_shader	4.0	Introduces tessellation to OpenGL. Adds the following function: `glPatchParameter()`
GL_ARB_texture_barrier	4.5	Provides a memory barrier that operates on texture objects. Adds the following function: `glTextureBarrier()`
GL_ARB_texture_buffer_object_rgb32	4.0	Allows texture buffers to be accessed in 96-bit formats.

Continued

Table C.2: Continued

Extension	Core Version	Description
GL_ARB_texture_buffer_range	4.3	Allows a sub-range of a buffer object to be bound to a buffer texture. Adds the following function: `glTexBufferRange()`
GL_ARB_texture_cube_map_array	4.0	Adds cubemap array textures to OpenGL.
GL_ARB_texture_gather	4.0	Adds `textureGather` to GLSL.
GL_ARB_texture_multisample	3.2	Adds multisample textures and framebuffer attachments. Adds the following functions: `glTexImage2DMultisample()` `glTexImage3DMultisample()` `glGetMultisamplefv()` `glSampleMaski()`
GL_ARB_texture_query_lod	4.0	Adds the `textureQueryLOD` GLSL functions. *Shading language only.*
GL_ARB_texture_rgb10_a2ui	3.3	Adds the GL_RGB10_A2UI texture format.

Continued

Table C.2: *Continued*

Extension	Core Version	Description
GL_ARB_texture_storage	4.2	Provides finer control over the allocation of texture memory. Adds the following functions: **glTexStorage1D()** **glTexStorage2D()** **glTexStorage3D()**
GL_ARB_texture_storage_multisample	4.3	Extends GL_ARB_texture_storage to include multisample textures. Ads the following functions: **glTexStorage2DMultisample()** **glTexStorage3DMultisample()**
GL_ARB_texture_swizzle	3.3	Allows texture data to be swapped between channels before being presented to shaders.
GL_ARB_texture_view	4.3	Adds texture views to OpenGL. Adds the following function: **glTextureView()**
GL_ARB_timer_query	3.3	Adds mechanisms to allow time to be queried from the perspective of OpenGL. Adds the following functions:

Continued

Table C.2: *Continued*

Extension	Core Version	Description
		glQueryCounter() glGetInteger64v() glGetQueryObjectui64v()
GL_ARB_transform_feedback2	4.0	Adds transform feedback objects and allows their contents to be automatically drawn. glBindTransformFeedback() glDeleteTransformFeedbacks() glGenTransformFeedbacks() glIsTransformFeedback() glPauseTransformFeedback() glResumeTransformFeedback() glDrawTransformFeedback()
GL_ARB_transform_feedback3	4.0	Exposes multiple streams of transform feedback as produced by geometry shaders. Adds the following functions: glDrawTransformFeedbackStream() glBeginQueryIndexed() glEndQueryIndexed() glGetQueryIndexediv()

Continued

Table C.2: *Continued*

Extension	Core Version	Description
GL_ARB_transform_feedback_instanced	4.2	Adds instancing functionality to transform feedback. Adds the following functions: **glDrawTransformFeedbackInstanced()** **glDrawTransformFeedbackStreamInstanced()**
GL_ARB_vertex_array_bgra	3.2	Allows for four-channel vertex attributes in BGRA order using GL_BGRA for size.
GL_ARB_vertex_attrib_64bit	4.1	Adds 64-bit vertex attribute support to OpenGL. Adds the following functions: **glVertexAttribL*()** **glVertexAttribLPointer()** **glGetVertexAttribLdv()**
GL_ARB_vertex_attrib_binding	4.3	Separates vertex buffer bindings from vertex formats. Adds the following functions: **glBindVertexBuffer()** **glVertexAttribIFormat()** **glVertexAttribLFormat()** **glVertexAttribBinding()** **glVertexBindingDivisor()**

Continued

Table C.2: *Continued*

Extension	Core Version	Description
GL_ARB_vertex_type_2_10_10_10_rev	3.3	Adds packed vertex attributes. Adds the following function: `glVertexAttribP*()`

GL_ARB_viewport_array	4.1	Adds indexed viewport and scissor rectangles. Adds the following functions:
		
		`glViewportArrayv()`
		`glViewportIndexedf()`
		`glViewportIndexedfv()`
		`glScissorArrayv()`
		`glScissorIndexed()`
		`glScissorIndexedv()`
		`glDepthRangeArrayv()`
		`glDepthRangeIndexed()`
		`glGetFloati_v()`
		`glGetDoublei_v()`

Glossary

Aliasing Technically, the loss of signal information in an image reproduced at some finite resolution. It is most often characterized by the appearance of sharp jagged edges along points, lines, or polygons due to the nature of having a limited number of fixed-sized pixels.

Alpha A fourth color value added to provide a degree of transparency to the color of an object. An alpha value of 0.0 means complete transparency; a value of 1.0 denotes no transparency (opaque).

Ambient light Light in a scene that doesn't come from any specific point source or direction. Ambient light illuminates all surfaces evenly and on all sides.

Antialiasing A rendering method used to smooth lines and curves and polygon edges. This technique averages the color of pixels adjacent to the line. It has the visual effect of softening the transition from the pixels on the line to the pixels adjacent to the line, thereby providing a smoother appearance.

ARB Architecture Review Board. The committee body consisting of three-dimensional graphics hardware vendors, previously charged with maintaining the OpenGL specification. This function has since been assumed by the Khronos Group.

Aspect ratio The ratio of the width of a window to the height of the window. Specifically, the width of the window in pixels divided by the height of the window in pixels.

Associativity A sequence of operations is said to be associative if changing the order of the operations (but not the order of the arguments) does not affect the result. For example, addition is associative because $a + (b + c) = (a + b) + c$.

Atomic operation A sequence of operations that must be indivisible for correct operation. Usually refers to a read–modify–write sequence on a single memory location.

Barrier A point in a computer program that serves as a marker across which operations may not be reordered. Between barriers, certain operations may be exchanged if their movement does not logically change the operation of the program.

Bézier curve A curve whose shape is defined by control points near the curve rather than by the precise set of points that define the curve itself.

Bitplane An array of bits mapped directly to screen pixels.

Branch prediction An optimization strategy used in processor design whereby the processor tries to guess (or predict) the outcome of some conditional code and start executing the more likely branch before it is certain that it is required. If it's right, it gets ahead by a few instructions. If it's wrong, it needs to throw away the work and start again with the other branch.

Buffer An area of memory used to store image information. This can be color, depth, or blending information. The red, green, blue, and alpha buffers are often collectively referred to as the color buffers.

Cartesian A coordinate system based on three directional axes placed at a 90° orientation to one another. These coordinates are labeled x, y, and z.

Clip coordinates The two-dimensional geometric coordinates that result from the model–view and projection transformation.

Clipping The elimination of a portion of a single primitive or group of primitives. The points that would be rendered outside the clipping region or volume are not drawn. The clipping volume is generally specified by the projection matrix. Clipped primitives are reconstructed such that the edges of the primitive do not lie outside the clipping region.

Commutative An operation is said to be commutative if changing the order of its operands does not change its result. For example, addition is commutative, whereas subtraction is not.

Compute shader A shader that executes a work item per invocation as part of a local work group, a number of which may be grouped together into a global work group.

Concave A reference to the shape of a polygon. A polygon is said to be concave if a straight line can be drawn through it that will enter and subsequently exit the polygon more than once.

Contention The condition in which two or more threads of execution attempt to use a single shared resource.

Convex A reference to the shape of a polygon. A convex polygon has no indentations, and no straight line can be drawn through the polygon that intersects it more than twice (once entering, once leaving).

Culling The elimination of graphics primitives that would not be seen if rendered. Back-face culling eliminates the front or back face of a primitive so that the face isn't drawn. Frustum culling eliminates whole objects that would fall outside the viewing frustum.

Destination color The stored color at a particular location in the color buffer. This terminology is used when describing blending operations to distinguish between the color already present in the color buffer and the color coming into the color buffer (source color).

Dispatch A command that begins the execution of compute shaders.

Dithering A method used to simulate a wider range of color depth by placing different-colored pixels together in patterns that give the illusion of shading between the two colors.

Double buffering A drawing technique used by OpenGL. The image to be displayed is assembled in memory and then placed on the screen in a single update operation, rather than being built primitive by primitive on the screen. Double buffering is a much faster and smoother update operation and can produce animations.

Extrusion The process of taking a two-dimensional image or shape and adding a third dimension uniformly across the surface. This process can transform two-dimensional fonts into three-dimensional lettering.

Eye coordinates The coordinate system based on the position of the viewer. The viewer's position is placed along the positive z axis, looking down the negative z axis.

FMA Fused multiply add; an operation commonly implemented in a single piece of hardware multiplies two numbers together and adds a third, with the intermediate result generally being computed at higher precision than a stand-alone multiplication or addition operation.

Fragment A single piece of data that may eventually contribute to the color of a pixel in an image.

Fragment shader A shader that executes once per fragment and generally computes the final color of that fragment.

Frustum A pyramid-shaped viewing volume that creates a perspective view. (Near objects are large; far objects are small.)

Garbage Uninitialized data that is read and consumed by a computer program, often resulting in corruption, crashes, or other undesired behavior.

Geometry shader A shader that executes once per primitive, having access to all vertices making up that primitive.

Gimbal lock A state where a sequence of rotations essentially becomes stuck on a single axis. This occurs when one of the rotations early in the sequence rotates from one Cartesian axis onto another. After this, rotation around either of the axes results in the same rotation, making it impossible to escape from the locked position.

GLSL OpenGL Shading Language; a high-level C-like shading language.

GPU Graphics processing unit; a specialized processor that does most of the heavy lifting for OpenGL.

Hazard In reference to memory operations, a situation in which an undefined order of transactions in memory may lead to undefined or undesired results. Typical examples include read-after-write (RAW) hazards, write-after-write (WAW) hazards, and write-after-read (WAR) hazards.

Implementation A software- or hardware-based device that performs OpenGL rendering operations.

Invocation A single execution of a shader. Most commonly used to describe compute shaders, but applicable to any shader stage.

Khronos Group The industry consortium that manages the maintenance and promotion of the OpenGL specification.

Literal A value, not a variable name. A specific string or numeric constant embedded directly in source code.

Matrix A two-dimensional array of numbers. Matrices can be operated on mathematically and are used to perform coordinate transformations.

Mipmapping A technique that uses multiple levels of detail for a texture. This technique selects from among the different sizes of an image available, or possibly combines the two nearest-sized matches to produce the final fragments used for texturing.

Model–view matrix The OpenGL matrix that transforms position vectors from model (or object) space to view (or eye) space.

Normal A directional vector that points perpendicularly to a plane or surface. When used, normals must be specified for each vertex in a primitive.

Normalize The reduction of a normal to a unit normal. A unit normal is a vector that has a length of exactly 1.0.

Occlusion query A graphics operation whereby hidden (or, more accurately, visible) pixels are counted and the count returned to the application.

Orthographic A drawing mode in which no perspective or foreshortening takes place; also called parallel projection. The lengths and dimensions of all primitives are undistorted regardless of orientation or distance from the viewer.

Out-of-order execution The ability of a processor to determine inter-instruction dependencies and start executing those instructions whose inputs are ready *before* other instructions that may have preceded them in program order.

Overloading In computer languages, the practice of creating two or more functions that share the same name but differ in their function signatures.

Perspective A drawing mode in which objects farther from the viewer appear smaller than nearby objects.

Pixel Condensed from the words "picture element"; the smallest visual division available on the computer screen. Pixels are arranged in rows and columns and are individually set to the appropriate color to render any given image.

Pixmap A two-dimensional array of color values that make up a color image. Pixmaps are so called because each picture element corresponds to a pixel on the screen.

Polygon A two-dimensional shape drawn with any number of sides (must be at least three sides).

Primitive A group of one or more vertices formed by OpenGL into a geometric shape such as a line, point, or triangle. All objects and scenes are composed of various combinations of primitives.

Projection The transformation of lines, points, and polygons from eye coordinates to clipping coordinates on the screen.

Quadrilateral A polygon with exactly four sides.

Race condition A state encountered when multiple parallel processes such as threads in a program or invocations of a shader attempt to communicate or otherwise depend on each other in some way, but where no assurance of ordering is performed.

Rasterization The process of converting projected primitives and bitmaps into pixel fragments in the framebuffer.

Render The conversion of primitives in object coordinates to an image in the framebuffer. The rendering pipeline is the process by which OpenGL commands and statements become pixels on the screen.

Scintillation A sparkling or flashing effect produced on objects when a non-mipmapped texture map is applied to a polygon that is significantly smaller than the size of the texture being applied.

Scissor A fragment ownership test that rejects fragments that lie outside a window-aligned rectangle.

Shader A small program that is executed by the graphics hardware, often in parallel, to operate on individual vertices or pixels.

Source color The color of the incoming fragment, as opposed to the color already present in the color buffer (destination color). This terminology is used when describing how the source and destination colors are combined during a blending operation.

Specification The design document that specifies OpenGL operation and fully describes how an implementation must work.

Spline A general term used to describe any curve created by placing control points near the curve, which have a pulling effect on the curve's shape. This is similar to the reaction of a piece of flexible material when pressure is applied at various points along its length.

Stipple A binary bit pattern used to mask out pixel generation in the framebuffer. This is similar to a monochrome bitmap, but one-dimensional patterns are used for lines and two-dimensional patterns are used for polygons.

Super scalar A processor architecture that is capable of executing two or more independent instructions at the same time on multiple processor pipelines, which may or may not have the same capabilities.

Tessellation The process of breaking down a complex polygon or analytic surface into a mesh of convex polygons. This process can also be applied to separate a complex curve into a series of less complex lines.

Tessellation control shader A shader that runs before fixed-function tessellation occurs. It executes once per control point in a patch primitive and produces tessellation factors and a new set of control points as an output primitive.

Tessellation evaluation shader A shader that runs after fixed-function tessellation occurs. It executes once per vertex generated by the tessellator.

Tessellation shader Either a tessellation control shader or a tessellation evaluation shader.

Texel A texture element. A texel represents a color from a texture that is applied to a pixel fragment in the framebuffer.

Texture An image pattern of colors applied to the surface of a primitive.

Texture mapping The process of applying a texture image to a surface. The surface does not have to be planar (flat). Texture mapping is often used to wrap an image around a curved object or to produce patterned surfaces such as wood or marble.

Token A constant value used by OpenGL to represent parameters. Examples are GL_RGBA and GL_COMPILE_STATUS.

Transformation The manipulation of a coordinate system. This can include rotation, translation, scaling (both uniform and non-uniform), and perspective division.

Translucence The degree of transparency of an object. In OpenGL, this is represented by an alpha value ranging from 1.0 (opaque) to 0.0 (transparent).

Vector A directional quantity usually represented by x, y, and z components.

Vertex A single point in space. Except when used for point and line primitives, it also defines the point at which two edges of a polygon meet.

Vertex shader A shader that executes once per incoming vertex.

Viewing volume The area in three-dimensional space that can be viewed in the window. Objects and points outside the viewing volume are clipped (cannot be seen).

Viewport The area within a window that is used to display an OpenGL image. Usually, this encompasses the entire client area. Stretched viewports can produce enlarged or shrunken output within the physical window.

Wireframe The representation of a solid object by a mesh of lines rather than solid shaded polygons. Wireframe models are usually rendered faster and can be used to view both the front and the back of an object at the same time.

Index